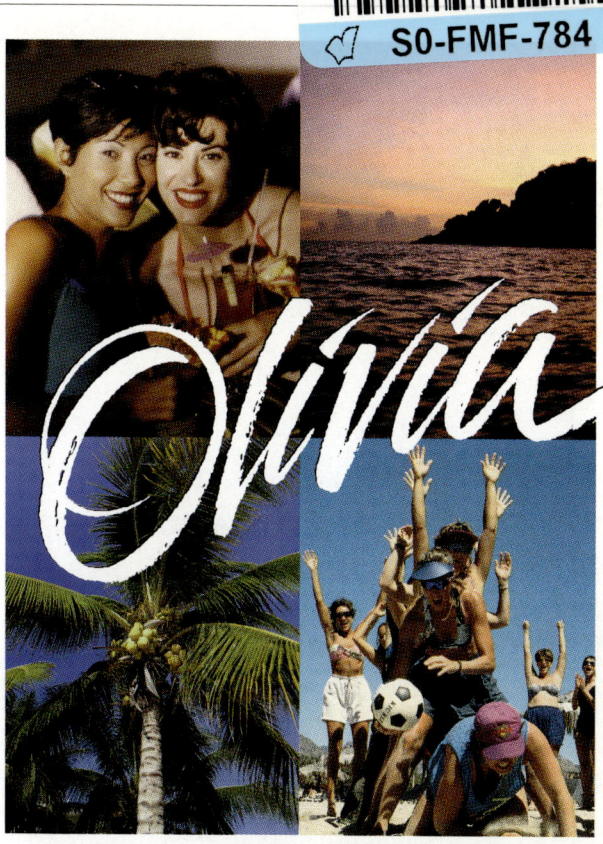

Olivia Cruises & Resorts *Vacations for Women*
Call 800-631-6277 Today!

1998
Costa Rica Windstar Cruise, February
Eastern Caribbean Cruise, April
Alaska Cruise, August
Mexico Resort, October
Southern Caribbean, November

1999
Bali/Singapore Windstar Cruise, February
Deep Southern Caribbean Cruise, April

Call for our free catalog!

4400 Market, Oakland, CA 94608
Phone: 510-655-0364
Fax: 510-655-4334
email: info@oliviatravel.com
Web: http://www.oliviatravel.com

CST31009281-40/CT#1009273-40

AmericanAirlines Official Airline of Olivia Cruises and 800-433-1790 · Star Refernce #S9900

New on Maui

Alohalani's Guest House

Lesbian owned and operated

- ▲ *Private, quiet*
- ▲ *Spacious cottage and lanai*
- ▲ *Across from State beach park*
- ▲ *Full Ocean View*
- ▲ *Private pool, clothing optional*
- ▲ *Reasonably priced*

The perfect place to renew romance and revitalize your soul.

800-511-3121
808-249-0395
www.remotepo.com/cottage.html

- Hawaiian Wedding Specialists
- Complete Individual Travel Packages to Hawaii
- Group Tours for Women

800-511-3121

Remote Possibilities
122 Central Avenue
Wailuku, Maui, HI 96793
808-249-0395
Fax: 808-249-0396
remotepo@maui.net
www.remotepo.com

IGLTA

AFRICA

KENYA	43
NAMIBIA	43
NIGERIA	43
SOUTH AFRICA	43
ZIMBABWE	46

ASIA

BANGLADESH	50
CAMBODIA	52
CHINA	46
INDIA	50
INDONESIA	52
JAPAN	46
KOREA, SOUTH	49
MALAYSIA	52
NEPAL	51
PAKISTAN	51
PHILIPPINES	52
SINGAPORE	53
SRI LANKA	51
TAIWAN	50
THAILAND	53

EUROPE

ALBANIA	54
AUSTRIA	54
BELGIUM	56
BULGARIA	59
CROATIA	60
CZECH REPUBLIC	60
DENMARK	61
ESTONIA	63
FINLAND	63
FRANCE	65
GERMANY	77
GREECE	93
HUNGARY	97
ICELAND	97
IRELAND	98
ITALY	101
LATVIA	107
LITHUANIA	107
LUXEMBOURG	107
NETHERLANDS	108
NORWAY	115
POLAND	115
PORTUGAL	116
RUSSIA	118
SLOVAKIA	119
SLOVENIA	119
SPAIN	119
SWEDEN	126
SWITZERLAND	130
TURKEY	133
UK (ENGLAND)	134
UK (N. IRELAND)	155
UK (SCOTLAND)	155
UK (WALES)	158
UKRAINE	160

MIDDLE EAST

ISRAEL	160
LEBANON	161

PACIFIC REGION

AUSTRALIA	161
NEW ZEALAND	177
COOK ISLANDS	182
FIJI ISLANDS	182
FRENCH POLYNESIA	182
GUAM	182

CANADA

ALBERTA	183
BRITISH COLUMBIA	184
MANITOBA	189
NEW BRUNSWICK	190
NEWFOUNDLAND	190
NOVA SCOTIA	191
ONTARIO	191
QUEBEC	197
SASKATCHEWAN	201
YUKON	201

CARIBBEAN & ATLANTIC ISLANDS

CUBA	202
DOMINICAN REPUBLIC	202
DUTCH WEST INDIES	202
FRENCH WEST INDIES	203
PUERTO RICO	203
VIRGIN ISLANDS	205
WEST INDIES	207

LATIN AMERICA

ARGENTINA	208
BOLIVIA	210
BRAZIL	210
CHILE	213
COLOMBIA	214
COSTA RICA	214
EL SALVADOR	217
GUATEMALA	217
HONDURAS	217
MEXICO	218
NICARAGUA	225
PANAMA	225
PARAGUAY	225
PERU	225
URUGUAY	226
VENEZUELA	226

USA

ALABAMA	227
ALASKA	228
ARIZONA	229
ARKANSAS	236
CALIFORNIA	237
COLORADO	269
CONNECTICUT	274
DELAWARE	275
DISTRICT OF COLUMBIA	277
FLORIDA	280
GEORGIA	298
HAWAII	302
IDAHO	310
ILLINOIS	311
INDIANA	316
IOWA	318
KANSAS	320
KENTUCKY	320
LOUISIANA	321
MAINE	326
MARYLAND	331
MASSACHUSETTS	333
MICHIGAN	354
MINNESOTA	360
MISSISSIPPI	362
MISSOURI	362
MONTANA	366
NEBRASKA	367
NEVADA	368
NEW HAMPSHIRE	369
NEW JERSEY	371
NEW MEXICO	373
NEW YORK	378
NORTH CAROLINA	389
NORTH DAKOTA	395
OHIO	395
OKLAHOMA	399
OREGON	400
PENNSYLVANIA	405
RHODE ISLAND	410
SOUTH CAROLINA	412
SOUTH DAKOTA	414
TENNESSEE	414
TEXAS	416
UTAH	422
VERMONT	424
VIRGINIA	427
WASHINGTON	430
WEST VIRGINIA	437
WISCONSIN	438
WYOMING	442

_3_

CONTENTS

FERRARI GUIDES' WOMEN'S TRAVEL IN YOUR POCKET™

18th Edition

- Table of Contents 3
- Index by Country 4
- Key to Symbols
    - English 5
    - Multi-Lingual 6
- How to Use this Book 8
- Tour Operators Directory 9
- Trip/Events Calendar 21
- Women's Mail Order 443

On the Cover

Cover photograph
by Tim Orden

Remote Possibilities is the lesbian company noted for their annual lesbian event Wahine Week on Maui. Now you can visit Maui with Remote Possibilities anytime during the year, staying at their own Alohalani's Guesthouse or at one of the lesbian or lesbian-friendly accommodations on Maui that they recommend. They will give you the benefit of their inside knowledge of the island – which condos have the best views, which resort is most luxurious, or has the best deal, which activities or excursions are most lesbian-friendly.

Those not Hawaii bound this year can cruise through France on a luxury hotel barge with Remote Possibilities between September 26-October 2, 1998.

*For more information about Remote Possibilities,
see color section in front of book.*

Ferrari Guides' Women's Travel In Your Pocket™
18th edition

Published by

> Ferrari International Publishing, Inc.
> PO Box 37887
> Phoenix, AZ 85069 USA
> (602) 863-2408 Fax: (602) 439-3952
> Email: ferrari@q-net.com
> Web: http://www.q-net.com

Published
> June, 1998

Ferrari, Marianne
> Ferrari Guides' Women's Travel In Your Pocket
>
> Includes Index
> ISBN 0-942586-66-2

Copyright © 1998
by Ferrari International Publishing, Inc.

All rights reserved. No part of this book may be reproduced in any form, or by any means, electronic or mechanical, including photocopying, recording, or by any information storage and retrieval system, without the express written permission of the publisher.

Listing of a group, organization or business in *Ferrari Guides' Women's Travel In Your Pocket*™ does not indicate that the sexual orientation of owners or operators is homosexual, nor that the sexual orientation of any given member of that group or client of that business is homosexual, nor that the organization or business specifically encourages membership or patronage of homosexuals as a group. This book is sold without warranties or guarantees of any kind, expressed or implied, and the authors and publisher disclaim any liability for loss, damage or injury in connection with it.

FERRARI GUIDES™

Women's Travel
In Your Pocket™

Accommodations, Nightlife, Tours & Outdoor Adventure - USA & Worldwide

18th Edition

PUBLISHED ANNUALLY SINCE 1981
Formerly Ferrari For Women
(original title was Places of Interest to Women)

Ferrari International Publishing, Inc.
PO Box 37887
Phoenix, AZ 85069 USA
(602) 863-2408 Fax: (602) 439-3952
Email: ferrari@q-net.com
Web: http://www.q-net.com

PUBLISHER
Marianne Ferrari

ISBN 0-942586-66-2 · Printed in USA

Clip art image sources: Corel Corporation,
Aldus Corporation, Microsoft Corporation and Weka Publishing Inc.

Australian Gay & Lesbian Travel Assn. &
International Gay & Lesbian Travel Assn. Member

KEY TO SYMBOLS

	Mostly women		Female or male "go go" dancers or strippers
	Mostly men		Female impersonator shows
	Both women & men, well-mixed (50/50 or 60/40)		Live entertainment
	A non-gay place (gay-friendly, if noted)		Both liquor & beer available (only exceptions noted for bars)
	Mature clientele 30's, 40's (NO longer "wrinkle room")		Beer, or beer & wine, only
	Black and white clientele		Bring your own "booze" (BYOB)
	Neighborhood-style bar		Alcohol-free environment
樂	Asian clientele		Snacks and/or sandwiches served
Ñ	Latin clientele		Nudity permitted (for ex. when swimming)
	Professional clientele		Swimming (lake, ocean, pool, etc)
	Leather		
U	Country & Western bar	★	Popular place
	Dancing (disco only if under Dance Bar category)		Wheelchair accessibility

KEY TO SYMBOLS
DEUTSCH · FRANCAIS · ESPAÑOL · ITALIANO

 Frauen, femmes
mujeres, donne

 Männer, hommes
hombres, uomini

 Frauen und Männer,
femmes/hommes, mujeres
y hombres, donne e uomini

 Hetero, plutôt hétérosexuelle
clientela heterosexual,
clientela mista

 für Ältere, plutôt agées
personas mayores, non
troppo giovane

 Schwarze/Weisse, noirs et
blancs, negros y blancos,
bianchi e neri

 Stammbar, bar du quartier
bar de vecinidad, bar del
quartiere

 Asiaten, Asiatique,
asiaticos, asiatici

 Mexikanisch, latins
hispánicos, latinoamericani

 Geschäftsmann/frau,
hommes/femmes d'affairs
profesionales, uomini/donne
d'affari

 Leder, cuir
cuero, leather

 Country & Western, western
tipo oeste, tipo Far West

 Tanzen, danse
bailar, ballare

 go go, go go
bailarines exoticos, ballerini
esotici

 Transvestitenshow
spectacles travestis
imitar a las estrellas
spettacoli di travestiti

 live Unterhaltung
spectacles, espectáculos
spettacoli

 Cocktailbar, alcool
cocteles, liquori

 nur Bier und Wein
bière et vin
cerveza y vino
solo birra e vino

 alkoholische Getränke
dürfen mitgebracht
werden
apporter boissons
traer bebidas alcoholicas
portare tutto da bere

 Getränke verboten
pas d'alcool
no se permite alcohol
divieto di bere alcool

 Imbiss, collation
comidas
colazione/tramezzini

 Nacktheit erlaubt
nudisme permis
se permite desnudo
permesso andare

 nudoSchwimmen, piscine/mer
piscina/mar, piscina/mare

 sehr beliebten Ort
endroit branché
recomendado
popular de ambiente

KEY TO SYMBOLS
CHINESE

♀ 女同志佔多

♂ 男同志佔多

♀♂ 男女同志比率相約 (50/50或60/40)

🚫 非同志場所 (如有記號, 對同志友善)

成熟型30至40(非年老同志)

👥 黑人和白人同志

本地式酒吧

樂 華人同志

Ñ 西班牙人同志

青少年同志

事業型同志

U 牛仔吧

👣 的士高 (如在跳舞目錄下只作的士高)

有男或女「Go Go」舞蹈員 或脫衣舞

👠 人妖表演

🎵 現場表演

🍸 提供酒類或其它飲品(如非在酒吧欄內有特別記號)

🍺 只提供酒類飲品

可自攜飲品

不提供任何酒精飲品

🍴 只提供小食或三文治

 准許裸體

 游泳(湖, 海灘, 泳池...其它)

★ 受歡迎場所

HOW TO USE THIS BOOK

Who to Call

Tours Section

Women's and gay/lesbian tour and cruise operators are described in a special tours section in the front of the book. See page 9.

When to Go

A calendar of trip departures and women's and gay/lesbian events follows the tours section. See page 21.

Where to Go

Accommodations, Nightlife and Shopping Worldwide are listed. The world is divided into logical regions, such as "Europe" or "Caribbean." Within regions, listings are in order by country, by state or province (in US, Canada and Australia only), by city, by category and then alphabetically by name. See page 4 for an index by region and country.

What Entries Contain

Name, address, telephone, 800 number (if available) fax, e-mail (sometimes), and brief description. A star, or asterisk, after the name means a popular place. Pictorial "international symbols" are also used to describe what goes on in a given location. See pages 5 - 7 for keys to these symbols in English, French, Spanish and Italian.

Tour Companies

⚥ ABOVE & BEYOND TOURS
230 N Via las Palmas, Palm Springs, CA, USA 92262, (760) 325-0702, (800) 397-2681, Fax: (760) 325-1702. Email: info@abovebeyondtours.com. Web: www.abovebeyondtours.com.

Specializing in Australia, New Zealand, Fiji, Sydney Gay Mardi Gras, Sleaze Ball and European destinations. Thanksgiving in Amsterdam or Fiji, New Years 1999 in Paris, Sydney, Fiji or Rio. Exclusively gay and lesbian. Both independent itineraries and scheduled group tours.
IGLTA aglta

♀ ADVENTURE ASSOCIATES
PO Box 16304, Seattle, WA, USA 98116, (206) 932-8352, (888) 532-8352. Fax: (206) 938-2654, E-mail: AdvntrAssc@aol.com.

Worldwide outdoor adventures for women in destinations like Africa, NW US, Greece and the Pacific. Activities include hiking, kayaking, climbing, skiing, backpacking, safaris, cultural tours, personally-designed itineraries. No experience needed. Lesbian-owned and -operated.

♀ ADVENTURES FOR WOMEN
PO Box 515, Montvale, NJ, USA 07645, Tel/Fax: (201) 930-0557.

A variety of short (one-, two-, three- or four-day) outdoor excursions for women who want to get or stay in shape, as well as make new friends. Getting in Shape for the Outdoors are weekday hikes. They also offer longer wilderness challenges, hiking, skiing, canoeing, contemplation weekends, and valuable breathing workshops led by an expert. Locations are mostly in NY, New Jersey, Pennsylvania, the Adirondacks, also South Carolina and the Austrian Alps.

⚥ ALOHA LAMBDA WEDDINGS HAWAII
2979 Kalakaua Ave #304, Honolulu, HI, USA 96815, (808) 922-5176, (800) 982-5176. Email: gayweddings@global-

ADVENTURE ASSOCIATES

WOMEN TRAVELLERS LIVE YOUR DREAMS IN '98

Since 1987, hundreds of women have travelled with us to the most exotic and spectacular corners of the world! You don't have to be an experienced traveller or an athlete. Enjoy excellent women guides, small groups (8-12), relaxed pace, great fun! **International trips**...Safari Africa, Sail Turkey, Greece, Trek Nepal, Kayak Baja, Adventure New Zealand and more! **Pacific NW Summer trips**... Seakayak San Juans, fly fish Yellowstone, hike Tetons, lodge-hikes North Cascades, Snorkel Kauai, hike High Sierras and so much more!

Call us now for your free brochure!!!

206-932-8352 • PO 16304 SEATTLE WA 98116

10 WHO TO CALL

aloha.com. Web: http://global-aloha.com/gayweddings.

Complete same-sex wedding coordination on any of the Hawaiian Islands. they handle everything — ministers, flowers, photographers, videographers, limo service, receptions, accommodations. Complete ceremony packages start at $260.

♀♂ ALYSON ADVENTURES

PO Box 180179, Boston, MA, USA 02118, (617) 542-1177, (800) 825-9766, E-mail: info@alysonadventures.com. Web: www.alysonadventures.com.

Fun & excitement outdoors, for gays & lesbians, hiking in switzerland, cycling the Natchez Trace, diving in the Caribbean. **IGLTA**

♀♂ AMSTERDAM HOUSE & SAIL

Amsterdam, Netherlands (31 36) 53 49 309, Fax: (31 36) 53 49 309. Email: sante@xs4all.nl. Web: http://www.xs4all.nl/~sante.

Lodging on a Dutch barge during the Gay Games and sailing on the barges through the Netherlands during the week preceding the Games. Barges will be moored conveniently near the Central Station during the Games. One barge for men, one for women. Breakfast during the week. Full board during sailing.

♀♂ ARIZONA TERRITORIAL TOURS

PO Box 4271, Prescott, AZ, USA 86302, (520) 778-0659, Fax: (520) 717-1013. Email: atttours@primenet.com.

Seven-day tours in Arizona which include two custom-fitted, authentic 1880's western outfits that are yours to wear and keep. Meals include pit barbecue, traditional Mexican comidas and fine dining at The Palace on historic Whiskey Row in Prescott. You take a scenic railroad to the Grand Canyon and particpate in re-enactments of scenes from famous western movies. Gay and lesbian.

♀ ARTEMIS WILDERNESS TOURS

(512) 708-0756.

Under new manageent and now based in Austin, Texas, this established company still offers whitewater adventures for women, including float trips and sea kayaking, canoeing, boating and rafting in New Mexico, Texas and Colorado.

♀♂ ATLANTIS EVENTS

9060 Santa Monica Blvd #310, West Hollywood, CA, USA 90069, (310) 281-5450, (800) 628-5268, Fax: (310) 281-5455.

Exclusively gay/lesbian company specializing in all-gay resorts and cruises in exotic locations, such as Mexico, the Caribbean. Annyal Sydney Mardi Gras programs. **IGLTA**

♀ BAR H RANCH

Box 297, Driggs, ID, USA 83422, (208) 354-2906, (888) 216-6025.

Wilderness trail riding trips and backcountry horse pack trips for women in Wyoming and Idaho. Or stay in deluxe accommodations at the ranch and get riding, roping, ranching experience.

♀♂ BCN TURÍSTIC

Carrer Nou de La Rambla, 85, Barcelona, Spain 08001, (34) 93442 4076, Fax: (34) 93442 0270. Email: BCNTUR@santandersupernet.com. Web: http://www.webshow.com/Barcelona/BCNTUR.

Hotel and apartment finding service for Barcelona, Sitges and other nearby Spanish coastal resorts. They also conduct guided walking tours of Barcelona's old city. They also arrange guided tours, restaurants, entertainment, etc. They speak English, German, French, Spanish and Catalan. For gays and lesbians.

♀ BEST OF BOTH WORLDS

PO Box 763, Bridgeton, NC, USA 28519, (919) 322-5804.

An experienced woman captain teaches women to sail and how to handle an oceangoing sailing sloop off the coast of North Carolina. Day sailing trips and overnights, deepsea fishing, shelling, golf, uncrowded beaches. Teaching packages take you from basic sailing to handling the boat yourself.

♀♂ BLUE MOON EXPLORATIONS

PO Box 2568, Bellingham, WA, USA 98227, Tel/Fax: (360) 856-5622 (tel/fax), (800) 966-8806.

Hiking, kayaking and whale watching in Alaska, British Columbia, and the San Juan Islands of WA. Snorkel with dolphins, hike active volcanoes. Scheduled and custom trips, both co-od and women-only trips. Reasonable prices. Accommodation available for before and after the trips.

♀♂ BRENDITA'S LATIN TOUR
San Francisco, CA, USA (415) 921-0625.

Walk San Francisco's Mission District and learn about latin foods, art, music and culture. Visit tortilla factories, latin music stores, buy obscure varieties of chile peppers at a famous latino grocery store, and more.

♀♂ BRITISH AIRWAYS HOLIDAYS
(800) 359-8722.

British Airways offers its entire schedule of holidays to gay and lesbian travelers. They verify every suppliers as gay-friendly. Packages are available to destinations in the UK, Euroep and Africa.

IGLTA

♀ BUSHWISE WOMEN
PO Box 28010, Christchurch, New Zealand Tel/Fax: (64 3) 332 4952 (tel/fax). Email: bushwise@bushwise.co.nz. Web: www.bushwise.co.nz.

Women's wilderness adventures, New Zealand's unspoilt wilderness, explore rainforest, mountains, lakes, learn bushcraft skills, canoeing, kayaking, goldpanning, maximum of 8 women, any age.

♀♂ CAMP CAMP
21 Palmer Square East, Princeton, NJ, USA 08542, (609) 924-6504, (888) 924-8380, Fax: (609) 683-1745. Email: billcole@worldnet.att.net. Web: www.campcamp.com.

A very special summer camp in Maine for gay, lesbian, bisexual and transgender adults. Remember summer camp? Singing around the campfire, etc? If you were a camper and loved it, Camp Camp may be fore you.

♀ CAMP LLAMA WOMEN'S LLAMA TREKS
PO Box 116, Lockwood, CA, USA 93932, (408) 385-6755 (tel/fax).

Women's llama treks in the Los Padres National Forest's Ventana Wilderness. Enjoy day treks, returning to Camp Llama for an after-trek barbecue and hot tub, then camping on the 20-acre property. Limited B&B accommodation also available.

♀ CANYON CALLING TOURS
215 Disney Lane, Sedona, AZ, USA 86336, (520) 282-0916, (800) 664-8922, Fax: (520) 282-3586.

Women's outdoor adventures in Arizona, Colorado, Utah, the Canadian Rockies and New Zealand. Trips combine various activities like rafting, horseback riding, hiking, biking, to enhance one's experience of each scenic locale.

♀♂ CASTLEMAIN YACHT CHARTERS
Suite 308 2550 Eisenhower Blvd, Ft. Lauderdale, FL, USA 33316, (954) 760-4730, (888) 760-4730, Fax: (954) 760-4737. info@castlemain-yachts.com. Web: www.castlemain-yachts.com.

Gay and lesbian yacht charter company. They maintain a charter database with every qualified yacht and crew worldwide. The staff travels all over the world checking on yachts and keeping track of news and reputations in the yachting world.

♀ CLOUD CANYON BACKPACKING
PO Box 41359, Santa Barbara, CA, USA 93140, (805) 969-0982, E-mail: areitz@silcom.com.

Women's hiking adventures, lighthearted & easygoing, women of all skills welcome, groups of 6-8 women of all ages, Utah, Alaska, New Zealand, backpacking, spiritual quests.

♀ CLUB LE BON
PO Box 444, Woodbridge, NJ, USA 07095, (908) 826-1577, (800) 836-8687, Fax: (908) 826-1577. E-mail: clublebon@aol.com, Web: www.provincetown.com/clublebon.

Lesbian tropical resort vacations, all-inclusive prices, no crowds - 30-100 lesbians, Barbados & Mexico locations, swim with dolphins, white sand beaches.

♀ CLUB SKIRTS WOMEN'S EVENTS
584 Castro St #206, San Francisco, CA, USA 94114, (415) 337-4962, (888) 44-DINAH for Dinah Shore event or (888) 5-SKIRTS for Gay Day event. Fax: (415)

431-7832. Email: info@clubskirts.com. Web: www.clubskirts.com.

This company, already known for its Dinah Shore events, has now organized the first all-women's party to be held as part of Gay Day at Disney. Particpants can book the party along with an entire Gay Day package. Club Skirts also organizes a Labor Day in Monterey Women's Weekend.

♀ COMMON EARTH ADVENTURES

PO Box 1191, Fairfax, CA, USA 94978, (415) 455-0646, Fax: (415) 454-3967.

Women's adventure travel, backpacking, kayaking, x-country skiing, snow camping, ropes course

Arizona, California & Alaska, sliding fee scale.

♀♂ CRUISIN' THE CASTRO

375 Lexington St, San Francisco, CA, USA 94110, (415) 550-8110, E-mail: trvrhailey@aol.com.

Fascinating San Fran Castro walking tours Learn gay history. Tours last 3 1/2 hr tours and include brunch. Available Tues-Sat & holidays. Guided by Trevor Hailey. **IGLTA**

♀♂ DIFFERENT ROADS TRAVEL

119 W. 40th St #1400, New York, NY, USA 10018, (212) 944-2121, (888) 762-3755, Fax: (2128) 405-220. Email: robw@tzell.com. Web: www.different roads.com.

The gay arm of a very large mass-market travel agency is directed by a gay professional. Their goal: To provide gays and lesbians unique travel experiences at competitive prices. Offerings range from middle to high and luxury itineraries, with more focus at the higher end. **IGLTA**

♀♂ DOIN' IT RIGHT/TRANSFORMATIONAL JOURNEYS

1010 University Ave #C-113-741, San Diego, CA, USA 92103, (619) 297-3646, (800) 936-3646, Fax: (619) 297-3642. Email: GayPVR@aol.com.

This specialist in gay travel packages to Puerto Vallarta has over 175 villas, condos and gay-friendly hotels at price levels from moderate to luxury. Their local land operator in PV will greet you at the airport and has a variety of private tours and local excursions for you to choose from. **IGLTA**

♀ EARTHING SPIRIT

18 Summerwood Rd, West Simsbury, CT, USA 06092, (860) 658-1326, Fax: (860) 658-0568. Email: awmason@snet.net.

Vision quests for women will be held on a Montana ranch and on farmland in northern Vermont. The goal is to increase one's spiritual awareness. Quests are recommended for women entering a time of transition in their lives. Directors Dorothy Mason and Dianne Timberlake are experienced psychotherapists. Lesbians are most welcome at these all-woman events.

♀♂ EAT QUICHE TOUR & TRAVEL

42 ave des Pins ouest #2, Montreal, QC, Canada H2W 1R1, (514) 845-4188, (800) 575-6955, Fax: (800) 575-6855, E-mail:EQuiche@aol.com.

These experts on gay Canada offer gay packages to major Canadian cities, including air, accommodations and car rentals. Their Canadian Rockies vacation packages include rail/motorcoach transportation, accommodation and excursions.they also offer whalewatching in Quebec. **IGLTA**

♀ EQUINOX WILDERNESS EXPEDITIONS

618 West 14th Ave, Anchorage, AK, USA 99501, (907) 274-9087 (to fax, call first). Email: equinox@alaska.net. Web: www.alaska.net/~equinox.

Truly adventurous trips for women in Alaska's most spectacular wilderness areas (They've never had an accident). Director Karen Jettmar is author of two books, The Nature of Southeast Alaska and Alaska's Glacier Bay: A Traveler's Guide.

♀♂ FAMILY ABROAD

40 W 57th St, #430, New York, NY 10019-4001, (212) 459-1800, (800) 999-5500, Fax: (212) 581-3756.

Global touring for gay men and women in a gay-friendly environment. Europe, Asia, Australia, Africa and Egypt. Stay in first-class hotels. Talented guides escort each tour. The Orient Explorer Cruise visits Hong Kong, Vietnam, Thailand, Brunei, Malaysia and Singapore. Full liability coverage for client funds. Gay-owned and -operated.

Bookings: Call travel agent or direct. *Est:* 1993. *TAC:* 10. *License #:* 13-3743313. *Pymt:* Checks, Visa, MC, Amex, Discover. *Member:* ASTA

♀ FAWCETT MILL FIELDS

Gaisgill, Tebay, Penrith, Cumbria, England CA10 3UB, (44 15396) 24408.

Year-round women's and lesbian programs at a women's retreat in rural England. Activities include walking, massage, meditation, circle dancing, theatre workshops, a bonfire weekend. Also bed & breakfast stays in the main house and in a detached cottage.

♀ FRAUEN UNTERWEGS

Potsdamerstr 139, Berlin, Germany 1028, (49 30) 215 1022, Fax: (49 30) 216 9852.

An important German women's tour company offering a gigantic, year-round array of tours worldwide, both outdoor adventure and sightseeing tours with a focus on women's history and culture. Tours are for German-speakers only.

♀♂ GAY HAWAIIAN EXCURSIONS

256 Front St, Lahaina, HI, USA 96753, (808) 667-5902, (800) 311-4460, Fax: (808) 667-5401. Email: gaytours@maui.net. Web: www.gayexcursions.com.

All arrangements for gays and lesbians going to Hawaii: Air, car rental and room reservations in Hawaii. Hawaiian luaus, sunset sailing, dinner cruises, catamaran snorkeling, wild dolphin adventure, helicopter sightseeing, biking a volcano, horseback riding, surfing, kayhaking, commitment ceremonies. IGLTA

♀ GIRLS OWN ADVENTURES/AUST PAC TRAVEL

PO Box 81, Annandale, NSW, Australia 2038, (61-2) 9660 3199, (800) 151 051, Fax: (61-2) 9660 8662. Email: a0021943@tiasnet.com.au.

This Australian tour operator organizes one or two trips a year especially designed for professional women who want their vacation to be completely different from their day-to-day activities. For 1998, a soft adventure in Southern Africa with heavy concentration on Zimbabwe and a new South American adventure. a∃lta

♀♂ GL TOURS

Centro Comercial Plaza América,, Loc A-24, S.M. 4, Cancun, Quintana Roo, México 77500, (52-98) 87 63 21, (52-98) 87 57 75, Fax: (52-98) 87 67 78, E-mail: gltours@sybcom.com.

A Cancun, Mexico-based tour operator with a bilingual, mostly-gay staff. They provide individual and group tour itineraries for Cuba, Mexico's Playa del Carmen, Cancun, Cozumel and Isla Mujeres, and other Latin American destinations. They are working to promote Cancun as an important gay vacation destination, and are co-sponsors of a fall, 1998 gay week in Cancun. Special offers monthly. IGLTA

♀♂ GOOD TIME GAY PRODUCTIONS

450 W 62nd St, Miami Beach, FL, USA 33140, (305) 864-9431, (888) 429-3527, Fax: (305) 866-6955, E-mail: gayfla@aol.com, Web: www.goodtimegaytravel.com.

Everything in Florida, from hotel accommodations to complete travel packages for individuals and groups. Hosted gay groups on major cruise lines — about fifteen per year. The longest-running tour operator providing packages for Gay Day at Disney. Ask for the Official Good Time Package. IGLTA

♀ GRAND CANYON FIELD INSTITUTE

PO Box 399, Grand Canyon, AZ, USA 86023, (520) 638-2485, Fax: (520) 638-2484. Email: gcfi@thecanyon.com.

Women's backpacking trips around the Grand Canyon in Arizona. Schedule includes trips for beginners to advanced backpackers, with all ages welcome. These are mainstream women's trips, but the organizers response each year is that lesbians are most welcome.

♀♂ GRUPO CACASA

Parian Plaza Local 3.2, Zona Hotelera, Cancun, Mexico 77500, (5298) 83 3294, Fax: (5298) 83 0900. Email: cancuntours@sybcom.com. Web: http://www.cancun-net.com/.

Continued next page

Company based in Cancun and specializing in travel to Mexico. Packages include transfers, apartment or hotel accommodations and can include a choice of excursions. Available excursions include a Booze Cruise, Grupo Cacasa's own Jungle Paradise Club tour for gays and lesbians, Chichen Itza, Tulum/Xelha, Xcaret, an Isla Mujeres day cruise, jungle tour, among many others.

♀ HAWK, I'M YOUR SISTER

PO Box 9109-F, Santa Fe, NM, USA 87504-9109, (505) 984-2268.

Specializing in women's river trips, retreats and international journeys to provide non-competitive opportunities for women to live in the wilderness, learn outdoor skills and participate in adventure travel.

♀♂ HIMALAYAN HIGH TREKS

241 Dolores St, San Francisco, CA, USA 94103-2211, (415) 551-1005, (800) 455-8735, Fax: (415) 861-2391. Email: effie@himalayanhightreks.com. Web: www.himalayanhightreks.com.

Trekking in the Himalayas, hike with views of the hIghest mountains, visit local monasteries and homes, experience indigenous Buddhist and Hindu cultures, from walking tours to strenuous ski tours, departures throughout the year.

♀♂ IDEM TOURS

1307, rue Ste-Catherine est, Montreal, QC, Canada H2L 5B1, (514) 524-0046, (888) 273-4336, Fax: (514) 524-3302. Email: idem@mlink.net. www.mlink.net/~idem.

Tours to destinations popular with gay travelers, using gay and gay-friendly hotels and suppliers. Gay packages to major cities and major gay vacation destinations like Puerto Vallarta, Amsterdam, London, Moscow, Toronto, Montreal, Key West, Provincetown, South Beach, Mykonos. Scheduled trips year-round. IGLTA

♀ INTERNATIONAL WOMEN'S STUDIES INSTITUTE

PO Box 1067, Palo Alto, CA, 94302, (650) 323-2013. Email: bonepart@bigisland.com or lillian33@juno.com.

A crosscultural travel study program in women's studies, sponsored by Educational Beginnings, Inc., a non-profit corporation. Current programs are taking place in Greece and Hawaii. Topics vary. The next program is Women Across the Millennia, a travel-study tour to Greece, celebrating 5000 years of women's culture, in June, 1999. A large number of lesbian women have participated over the years.

♀ IT'S OUR NATURE

929 Bay Esplanade, Clearwater, FL, USA 33767, (813) 441-2599 (tel/fax). E-mail: itsrnature@aol.com, Web: www.itsournature.com.

Tai Chi on the beach. Women's nature hikes and kayaking in the Tampa Bay area of Florida. Move quietly thru slash pine forest as natural history is told in storybook fashion. Visit virgin forests, bird sanctuaries, beach habitats with a lifelong naturalist guide. Reconnecting with nauture enhances creativity, she says.

♀ IZARRA CRUISES

2442 NW Market St #467, Seattle, WA, USA 98107, (206) 789-2175.

Women's Sailing Adventures in the northwestern US and British Columbian waters usually cruising amongst the San Juan Islands between May 30 and October 1, annually. The Izarra holds up to 5 women plus Coast Guard-licensed skipper. Learn sail trimming, helmswomanship, navigation, etc. In 1998, you can come aboard for any period of time you are interested in.

♀♂ JORNADA

Level 1 263 Liverpool St, PO Box 604, Darlinghurst, NSW, Australia 2010, (61 2) 9360 9611, Toll-free: (800) 672 120, Fax: (61 2) 9326 0199. Email: justask@jornada.com.au. Web: www.jornada.com.au.

Gay-owned and -operated Australian tour operator offering inbound and outbound independent travel arrangements for gays and lesbians. Both land-only, or with airfare included. Their comprehensive brochure includes both gay and gay-friendly destinations and establishments in Australia, Asia, Europe, South America and the USA. Also — a special event packages for Sydney Mardi Gras

WHO TO CALL 15

parade and party. New in 1998: A second office in Cologne, Germany. IGLTA aglta

♀♂ JORNADA (GERMANY OFFICE)
Ellsenstrasse 4-10, Koln, Germany 50667, (49-221) 258 48 04, Fax: (49-221) 258 48 05. Email: jornada@t-online.de. Web: www.jornada.com.au.

Gay-owned and -operated tour operator offering inbound and outbound independent travel arrangements for gays and lesbians. Both land-only, or with airfare included. Their comprehensive brochure includes both gay and gay-friendly destinations and establishments in Australia, Asia, Europe, South America and the USA. Also — a special event packages for Sydney Mardi Gras parade and party. New in 1998: Their Pacific office is in Sydney, Australia. IGLTA

♀ KATHMANDU VALLEY TOURS
PO Box 873, Bolinas, CA, 94924, (415) 868-0285, Fax: (415) 868-9766.

Tours for people who are interested in exploring Buddhism, Hinduism, Shamanism and the relevance of the Goddess in those religions. Mainly women participate, but the trips are open to both women and men. On this cultural tour, you'll visit the Goddesses of Mewari and Tibetan religion and culture, meet female shamans who channel the Goddess, attend pujas and festivals, and more.

♀♂ KAYAK HISTORICAL DISCOVERY TOURS
87-3187 Honu Moe Road, Captain Cook, HI, USA 96704, (808) 328-8911. Email: gokayak@kona.net. Web: www.21stcenturyhawaii.com/kayakhawaii.

Kayak off Hawaii's Big Island on half-day, full-day, two-day or five-day camping trips. Camp and kayak beautiful bays like Kealakekua or Keauhou. Snorkel, see dolphins and whales. Enjoy grilled fish on the beach on the camping trips. Equipment and guide is provided.

♀♂ LODESTAR ADVENTURES
Box 84, Procter, BC, Canada V0G 1V0, (250) 229-5354, E-mail: mgrove@netidea.com. Web: http://www.netidea.com/~lodestar.

Gay/lesbian llama treks, llama-assisted backpacking, mountain bike tours, multi-activiity, small-group adventure excursions in British Columbia, Canada. "Wir schicken Ihnen gerne Information in deutsch."

♀♂ L'ARC EN CIEL VOYAGES
PO Box 234, Wayne, PA, USA 19087-0234, (610) 964-7888, (800) 965-LARC (5272), Fax: (610) 964-8220. E-mail: larc@galaxytours.com.

Highly respected tour operator offering a full range of gay and lesbian travel options. They will custom design gay/lesbian adventures for any group. Excellent individual packages can be tailor-made to the needs of specific travelers. Thirty-six years experience in over 60 countries. They also have a full schedule of creatively conceived gay and lesbian group tours each year. They go far more than the extra mile to please their clients. IGLTA

♀♂ MARIAH WILDERNESS EXPEDITIONS
PO Box 248, Point Richmond, CA, USA 94807, (510) 233-2303, (800) 462-7424, Fax: (510) 233-0956, E-mail: rafting@mariahwe.com, Web: www.mariahwe.com.

California's only women-owned whitewater rafting company, a pioneer of women's whitewater rafting trips, high-quality adventure travel, Costa Rica and Baja Mexico rafting, kayaking and beaches, rafting on California, Idaho, Oregon and Utah rivers.

♀ MCNAMARA RANCH
4620 County Rd 100, Florissant, CO, USA 80816, (719) 748-3466.

Stay on a working women's ranch, ride horses above timberline, rides are tailored to your stamina, camp overnight or return to ranch house for good food, shear sheep, move sheep from pasture to pasture, feed newborn lambs, go trout fishing, relax in hot tub under the stars, nearby rodeos, gambling town.

♀♂ MIX TRAVEL
Maipu 971 5-C, Buenos Aires, Argentina 1006, (54 1) 312 3410, Fax: (54 1) 313 4432. Email: davos@mail.interserver.com.ar. Web: www.davostours.com.

Haunt the Tango bars of Buenos Aires or live the gaucho life on a great colonial estancia. Trek on horseback into the

16 WHO TO CALL

Andes or in rugged Patagonia. Hike the Conquistadores' trails. Take a look at rare and exotic wildlife at Iguazu Falls, or at the crystal lakes and glaciers of the south. Mix Travel offers unusual, unique experiences in a gay-friendly environment, specialty: individual travel, groups on request. Mix reports that, in 1997, one very satisfied gay American client recommended them to 20 friends who also used their service. **IGLTA**

♀ OCEANWOMYN KAYAKING

USA (206) 325-3970.

The first women's company to offer all-womyn's sea kayaking adventures, Baja Mexico, British Columbia, San Juan Islands, Alaska, great for beginners, no experience necessary, expert lesbian guides/instructors, vegetarian cuisine and great coffee on the beach.

♀ OCTOPUS REEF DIVE TRAINING & TOURS

Maui, HI, (808) 572-4774. E-mail: octopus@maui.net. Web: www.divemaui.com.

Women's SCUBA diving in Maui with experienced female guides who are veterans of over 6,000 dives. Minimal training allows you to explore reefs underwater, entering the water right from the shore. They offer all training, from beginners through certification to advanced instruction. Day and night dives, boat dives, shore dives and check-out dives are conducted.

♀ OLIVIA CRUISES & RESORTS

4400 Market St, Oakland, CA, USA 94608, (510) 655-0364, (800) 631-6277, Fax: (510) 655-4334. E-mail: info@oliviatravel.com. Web:www.oliviatravel.com. Travel Agents, use this web: www.olivia.agents.com.

Largest US women's travel company, has taken more than 15,000 women on vacations, destinations like the Caribbean, Alaska, Greece, the Riviera, the Galapagos, Canada, the Bahamas, Mexico, Costa Rica and the Panama Canal. **IGLTA**

♀♂ PADDLING SOUTH & SADDLING SOUTH

4510 Silverado Tr, Calistoga, CA, USA 94515, (707) 942-4550, (800) 398-6200. Web: www.tourbaja.earthlink.net.

Sea kayaking and horse packing adventures, Baja, Mexico, mostly mixed, two women-only trips per year and private trips for as few as 3-4 people.

♀ PROFESSIONAL MARINE SERVICES

16293 Orchard Creek Hwy, Ocqueoc, MI, USA 49757, (517) 733-8569 (winter), (906) 847-6580 (summer), (888) 847 6580. Email: dehartec@svr1.pace.k12.mi.us. Web: http://www.mackinac.com/services/ProMarine.html.

Lesbian weddings on board a power boat off Mackinac Island, sightseeing trips, dinner cruises. Although lesbian weddings are not yet legal in Michigan, we can still "tie the knot" for you and your life partner, and will issue a certificate.

♀♂ PUFFIN FAMILY CHARTERS

Box 90743, Anchorage, AK, USA 99509, (907) 278-3346, (800) 978-3346.

Gay and lesbian company providing sightseeing and fishing charters for gays and lesbians, on a 30-foot charter boat, in Alaska's Resurrection Bay and the Kenai Fjord. See whales, seals, otters, porpoises, puffins and magnificent views of glaciers and mountains. There are abundant halibut, salmon, black bass, red snapper. The boat is fully electronic and has a heated cabin. Experienced woman captain.

♀ RAINBOW ADVENTURES

15033 Kelly Canyon Rd, Bozeman, MT, USA 59715, (406) 587-3883, (800) 804-8686, Fax: (406) 587-9449.

Worldwide outdoor adventure vacations, for women over 30, gay women are welcome, but most particpants are married women, NO lesbian-only trips.

♀♂ RAINBOW ADVENTURES INC. & RAINBOW'S INN

PO Box 983, Pahoa, HI, 96778, (808) 965-9011 (tel/fax). Email: RainbwAdv@aol.com.

A lesbian-owned company providing a variety of excursions on the Big Island of Hawaii. Tours include kayak tours, twilight lava flow tours, 4X4 tours to the top of Mauna Kea to view the universe by telescope, secluded jungle tours, secluded black- and green-sand beaches,

WHO TO CALL

swims in volcanically-heated ponds and a few hot moments inside rejuvenating steam vents. Scuba and snorkeling are also available.

♀♂ RAINBOW RESORTS
2000 Rockledge Rd, Atlanta, GA, USA 30324, (404) 876-1695, Fax: (404) 876-1499. Email: rainbowrst.aol.com. In Mexico: (52 98) 780 174, Fax: (52 98) 876 504. Email: mexlnc@acnet.net.

All-inclusive gay resort vacation packages in Cancun, Mexico, using a new, exclusively gay and lesbian resort with secluded white-sand beach, just 15 minutes from downtown Cancun. Two-level, air conditioned villa-style accommodations with color TV and phone. See article on the Cancun pages for details of the many amenities included in the packages. This company deals exclusively with IGLTA agents. To open in May, 1998. **IGLTA**

♀ REMOTE POSSIBILITIES
122 Central Ave, Wailuku, Maui, HI, USA 96793, (808) 249-0395, (800) 511-3121, Fax: (808) 249-0396. E-mail: remotepo@maui.net. Web: www.remotepo.com.

Lesbian tour company specializing in Hawaii itineraries for women. These experts on lesbian-friendly locations and activities can help you plan your individual vacation year-round. They are the organizers of the annual Wahine Week, a luxury lesbian resort week on Maui. Tours in 1998: A luxury barge cruise in France featuring winetasting and a women's cruise to Alaska. They also conduct gay and lesbian weddings in Hawaii. **IGLTA**

♀ ROBIN TYLER'S WOMEN'S TOURS, CRUISES & EVENTS
15842 Chase St, North Hills, CA, USA 91343, (818) 893-4075, (800) 936-8514, Fax: (818) 893-1593, E-mail: RobinTyler@aol.com.

Women's tours and cruises to worldwide destinations.

♀♂ ROYAL HAWAIIAN WEDDINGS
PO Box 424, Puunene, Maui, HI, USA 96784, (808) 875-8569, (800) 659-1866, Fax: (808) 875-0623. E-mail: jrenner@maui.net. Web: www.hawaiigaywed.com.

This company was the first on the planet to offer gay and lesbian wedding and commitment ceremonies. Choose from one of their plans or customize your own ceremony. They offer romantic, secluded beach locations, tropical garden locations or private beachfront home settings. A tremendous variety of amenities are available to choose from. **IGLTA**

♀♂ RSVP TRAVEL PRODUCTIONS/CLUB RSVP
2800 University Ave SE, Minneapolis, MN, USA 55414, (612) 379-4697, (800) 328-7787, Fax: (612) 379-0484, Web: www.rsvp.net.

Gay and lesbian tour company offering three kinds of vacations, cruises, Club RSVP resort vacations, PLAANET RSVP hotel and air packages, group or independent travel, air provided by American Airlines, RSVP always reserves an entire ship or resort. **IGLTA**

♀ SACRED JOURNEYS FOR WOMEN
PO Box 893, Occidental, CA, USA 95465, (707) 874-9040, Fax: (707) 824-8176. Email: alaura@wco.com. Web: http://www.wco.com/~sacredjourneys/.

Journeys for women to sacred sites around the world, looking at history from a feminine perspective, getting back to the roots of prehistory, discovering hidden history. "It's not coincidental that Christian sites are built over older pagan sites." Both directors are extremely knowledgeable and interesting to listen to. In 1998: England Aug 22-Sept 3 and Ireland September 14-25.

♀♂ SAN FRANCISCO GAY TOURS
(415) 826-9001. Email: tours@sfgaytours.com.

Individualized, customized tours of San Francisco can include a driver/guide for gay restaurants, theatre and night clubbing. Group tours are arranged for big gay San Francisco events, such as Gay parade, Folsom and Castro Street Fairs, Halloween. Most tours are in the evening hours, but this company is NOT an escort service. They also conduct full-service gay weddings.

WHO TO CALL

♀ SEA SENSE
PO Box 1961, St Petersburg, FL, USA 33731, (813) 865-1404, (800) 332-1404, Fax: (813) 865-1450. Email: seasense@aol.com.

Women's sailing and power boating school with summer and winter locations. Locations are chosen to provide a variety of sailing challenges and include New London (Connecticut), Miami, the Florida Keys, the Caribbean and Florida's Gulf Coast. The woman captains have over 50 yrs experience.

♀♂ SEDONA RAINBOW ADVENTURE TOURS
PO Box 10147, Sedona, AZ, USA 86339, (520) 204-9967, (888) 282-9967, Fax: (520) 204-1399. Email: rainbowranger@sedona.net

Gay and lesbian half-day and full-day tours of Sedona, the red rocks, Oak Creek Canyon, the energy vortexes, the Grand Canyon, and more, by the Rainbow Rangers. Both 4X4 and helicoptor tours, or a combination of the two. Helicoptor to a mesa top and shoot a real colt .45s and other unusual guns. Also art gallery tours. Customized tours are available.

♀ SILKE'S TRAVEL
263 Oxford St, Darlinghurst, NSW, Australia 2010, (61-2) 9380 6244, Fax: (61-2) 9361 3729. E-mail: silba@magna.com.au, Web: www.magna.com.au/~silba.

An Australian tour company "devoted to women's travel." Accredited Sydney Mardi Gras tour operator whose packages include Mardi Gras tickets. "Cairns for Women" program includes Great Barrier Reef and women's accommodations. Worldwide tours for 1998include The Inca Trail in Peru and Aspen Gay Ski Week in the United States. **IGLTA** aglta

♀♂ SIRIUS ADVENTURES
PO Box 1130, Kununurra, WA, Australia 6743, (61-8) 9168 2110 (tel/fax). Email: sirius2@ozemail.com.au. Web: www.ozemail.com.au/-sirius2.

Customized lesbian and gay bushwalks in Western Australia and Northern Territory. Lesbian guide plans itinerary to fit interests and skill levels of participants. See the Kimberley, one of the world's last wilderness areas, where you can still drink water from streams. Also visits famous Kakadu Nat'l Park.

♀ SKADI WOMEN'S WALKING HOLIDAYS
High Grassrigg Barn, Killington, Sedbergh, Cumbria, England LA10 5EW, (44-15396) 211 88

Women's walking holidays in rural England. Choose from gentle, energetic, and strenuous tours.

♀♂ SOPHISTICATED TRAVELER, THE
(404) 843-1646, (800) 522-8093. Web: www.sophtraveler.com/lambda.htm.

Gay and lesbian tour company operating exclusive luxury tours to destinations worldwide, such as London, Costa Rica, Austria, Ireland, Zimbabwe, Scotland.
IGLTA

♀ SOUNDS & FURIES
PO Box 21510, 1850 Commercial Dr, Vancouver, BC, Canada V5N 4A0, (604) 253-7189, Fax: (604) 253-2191. Email: path@lynx.bc.ca.

A women's mystical journey into Ireland visits ancient stone circles, pagan sites and burial mounds. Stay in a Georgian mansion near Cork, walk green meadows and misty woods to Blarney, touch history with your own hands, discover different perspectives. Attend a large festival for women, which will take place in Cork during the tour.

♀♂ TEN THOUSAND WAVES
PO Box 7924, Missoula, MT, USA 59807, (406) 549-6670, (800) 537-8315. Email: theowwl@aol.com. Web: www.10000waves.com.

Rafting and kayaking in western Montana. Departures daily between April 15 and October 15 annually. Paddle rafting, kayaking in sit-on-top kayaks and instructin using standard kayaks. They also operate ghost town tours/day hikes near the Bob Marshall Wilderness.

♀♂ TRAVEL LOFT SPAIN
5100 State Rd, Drexel Hill, PA, USA 19026, (610) 626-6331, Fax: (610) 626-4467. Email: TravelLoft@aol.com.

Travel packages, using Iberia Airlines, to resorts on Spain's Costa del Sol for individuals or groups. Gay-friendly.

♀ TROPICAL TUNE-UPS

PO Box 4488, Waikolua, HI, USA 96738, (808) 882-7355 (tel/fax), E-mail: retreats@tropicaltuneups.com. Web: http://tropicaltuneups.com.

Hawaiian retreats for women on the sunny Kona Coast at a secluded beachfront home on Waialea Bay on the Big Island. Week-long retreats feature massage, yoga, meditation, snorkeling, kayaking, hiking, massage, vegetarian meals and more. Customized retreats are also available.

♀ VAARSCHOOL GRIETJE

Prinsengracht t/o 187, Amsterdam, The Netherlands 1015 AZ, (31 20) 625 91 05 (tel/fax).

Sail the canals of Holland, Belgium and France on a women's barge. Get a different view of these countries from the water. Summer, 1998: Sail Belgian canals, through Brussels and Bergen, up the French river Sambre, on to Reims, France. At Petit-Saonne, close to the Swiss border, it's north again and through Dutch canals, back to Amsterdam. Handle the ship, maneuver through locks or relax. The ship accommodates four women with rustic amenities.

♀♂ VICTORIAN HOME WALK

2226 15th St, San Francisco, CA, USA 94114, (415) 252-9485, Fax: (415) 863-7577, E-mail: jay@victorianwalk.com, Web: www.victorianwalk.com.

San Francisco walking tours of Victorian homes. Walking is low-impact, and at an easy pace. See spectacular views of the bay, visit Mrs. Doubtfire's Victorian and learn about Victorian styles. Small groups depart daily at 11:00 a.m. year-round. The tour lasts 2 1/2 hours. Cost: $20.00 pp. **IGLTA**

♀ WANDERWOMEN

PO Box 68 058, Newton, Auckland, New Zealand (64 9) 360 7330, Fax: (64 9) 360 7332. Mobile: (64 25) 333 360. Email: lizzie@wanderwomen.co.nz. Web: http://www.wanderwomen.co.nz/.

Women's outdoor adventure company based in Auckland, New Zealand. A variety of adventures from day trips to multi-day trips. Climbing, hiking, caving, snorkeling, kayaking, sailing, confidence courses and more. Most trips are one-day events, making it easier for visitors to participate.

♀ WHELK WOMEN

PO Box 1006, Boca Grande, FL, USA 33921, (941) 964-2027.

Sailing for women among barrier islands off Florida's west coast. Watch dolphins and many birds. Eagles, osprey, pelicans and others. Fish and collect shells, swim, sun. Stay in rustic cabin or tent. Bring food, bedding, towels. Camping gear supplied.

♀♂ WILD IRIS FISHING & SIGHTSEEING ADVENTURES

(907) 389-2725. Cellphone: (907) 255-8917. Fax: (907) 451-9506. In Valdez: (907) 835-IRIS (4747).

Sightseeing and fishing cruises aboard the Wild Iris, a 28-foot Bayliner Super Classic Cruiser that sleeps 4 people plus crew. Luxury cabin areas, full bathroom, kitchen. Half-day and full-day fishing and sightseeing trips or overnighters including anchoring in a cove and barbecuing, while eagles look on. Equipped with electric reels for the differently-abled. Gay-friendly.

♀ WILD WOMEN EXPEDITIONS

PO Box 145, Station B, Sudbury, ON, Canada P3E 4N5, (705) 866-1260, (888) 993-1222. Email: beth@vianet.on.ca. Web: www.wildwomenexp.com.

Women's 3- to 7-day canoe trips in Ontario's wilderness. By car: 5 hours from Toronto, 3 hrs from Michigan's border. Spectacular wilderness abounds. Less demanding 3- to 7-day vacations are at the riverside base camp with cozy cabins. Gourmet meals and massage therapist on-site.

♀♂ WINDMILLS TRAVEL & TOURISM

PO Box 154, Mykonos, Greece 84600, (30 289) 23877/26555/26556/26557, Fax: (30 289) 22066. E-mail: windmills@travelling.gr.

For individual travelers looking for the right hotel. For travel agents seeking professional assistance with reservations for valued clients. Your personal contact

20   WHO TO CALL

on Mykonos is Pam Taylor. She is an accommodations, transportation, and excursions expert for Mykonos, the Cycladic Islands, and Greece. Windmills is Official Tour Operator for the Nine Muses Party, a gay and lesbian event. **IGLTA**

♀ WINTERMOON
3388 Petrell, Brimson, MN, USA 55602, (218) 848-2442.

Alaskan Huskies love to run and pull a sled. Learn dogsledding 50 miles north of Duluth. Kathleen Anderson has mushed for 12 years. She bred and trained her 28 dogs. Stay in a rustic log cabin, with sauna, wood heater, solar power, hand pump for well water, outhouse. All trips include lodging, meals, instruction.

♀ WITCHENCROFT 4WD & BUSHWALKING TOURS
PO Box 685, Atherton, QLD, Australia 4883, (61-740) 912 683 (tel/fax). E-mail: jj@bushnet.qld.edu.au.

Four-wheel-drive tours and bushwalking for women in rural Queensland, Australia. Your guide is a 4th-generation North Queenslander. Accommodations are at Witchencroft, Australia's oldest women's guest house. The climate in this area virtually guarantees fine weather, thanks to the diversity of the landscape within an hour of Witchencroft's location. **aglta**

♀ WOMANTOURS
PO Box 68, Coleman Falls, VA, USA 84536, (804) 384-7328, (800) 247-1444

Bicycling for women to such destinations as Natchez Trace, Utah, Canadian Rockies, Yellowstone.

♀ WOMEN IN MOTION
PO Box 4533, Oceanside, CA, USA 92052-4533, (760) 754-6747, (888) GO-WOMEN (469-6636), Fax: (760) 754-8066. E-mail: eventsrus@aol.com, Web: http://gowomen.com.

Active vacations for women, with women, by women. You choose the vacation. You set the pace. Rafting, kayaking, golfing, packages to women's festivals, cycling, rock climbing. Mostly gay women participants.

♀ WOMEN IN THE WILDERNESS
566 Ottawa Ave, St Paul, MN, USA 55107, (612) 227-2284, Fax: (612) 227-4028

Teaches women skills to really enjoy the wilderness. Canoeing, kayaking, dog sledding, snowshoeing. Learn to be at home in the wilds. Worldwide destinations, like Finland's Lapland, Peru's Macchu Picchu and Amazon rainforest, Utah's canyons, Minnesota's northwoods and waterways. Nearly 20 years experience guiding women's adventure trips.

♀ WOMEN SAIL ALASKA
PO Box 20348, Juneau, AK, USA 99802, (907) 463-3372, (888) 272-4525. Email: sailak@alaska.net.

Sailing excursions for women, around Juneau, Alaska, sheltered anchorages among barrier islands, abundant wildlife, hiking, beachcombing, fishing, hot springs, icebergs, catch halibut or salmon for dinner, view pods of whales, sea lions, bears. Groups of up to 4 women.

♀ WOMEN'S WEEK AT KOKSETNA LODGE
All year: , (800) 391-8651. Winter phone: (916) 458-7446.

A special women-only week of fishing, hiking, relaxing in thet Alaska wilderness. The lodge provides modern comfort in a wilderness setting that gives you the feel of the vastness that is Alaska. A maximum of six women at a time. Scheduled for June 21-26, 1998, but women's weeks can be arranged anytime there are six women who wish to come.

♀ WOODSWOMEN
25 W Diamond Lake Rd, Minneapolis, MN, USA 55419, (612) 822-3809, (800) 279-0555, Fax: (612) 822-3814. Email: woodswomen@juno.com. Web: www.woodswomen.mn.org.

The oldest, largest women's outdoor adventure travel company operates trips for women of all ages, skill and fitness levels. Flexible pace, easy group interaction. Canoeing, bicycling, backpacking, hiking, kayaking, climbing, etc., in exotic destinations worldwide.

TRIP/EVENTS CALENDAR 21

July 98

TBA	♀	**Fairbanks Alaska Women's Fest,** Held over the July 4th weekend, this event begins with potluck-type gatherings at private homes, then blossoms into camping &/or enjoying the outdoors. We host name entertainers, as well as some of our own impromptu local talent. Vendors sell food, drink & T-shirts, and massage therapists are on hand. Contact: www.geocities.com/wellesley/8170; Tracy at Tracwa@webtv.net; Doris at fbxhotl.alaska.net; Louise at (907) 479-0618.
TBA	♀	**Fat Women's Gatherings,** These are gatherings, for women only, of large-sized women. Workshops, parties, swimming and a representation of vendors specializing in products for large-sized women, especially clothing, are included. This is not a lesbian organization, per se, but all fat women are most welcome. Location: Northern New Jersey. For all meetings, contact Carole Campbell, PO Box 1154, New York, NY 10023 (212) 721-8259.
TBA	♀♂	**Pink Monday at the Tilburg Fair,** This annual gay Monday held in July each year is the gay portion of a larger fair dating back 425 years. Approximately 25,000 gays & lesbians attend festivities at local gay establishments and other programmes. Location: Tilburg, The Netherlands. Contact: De GAY Krant, PO Box 10, NL-Best, The Netherlands, (31) 499 391 000, Fax: (31) 499 372 638, E-mail: gaykrant@pop3.worldaccess.nl.
TBA	♀♂	**Summer Sports Festival,** Held on the 4th of July Weekend. Events in 27 different sports, such as softball, volleyball, swimming, diving, sailing & crew, marathons, bowling, croquet & darts, will be held. Special events surrounding the athletics include parties & the annyal Orca Boat Cruise. Location: Seattle, WA. Contact: Team Seattle, 1202 E. Pike St #515, Seattle, WA 98112, (206) 322-7769.
TBA	♀♂	**Trekking in Pakistan's Northern Areas,** see Himalayan High Treks
TBA	♀	**Whitewater Canoeing, Missinaibi River, Ontario,** see Women in the Wilderness
TBA	♀♂	**Fouth of July in Vancouver, Canada,** see New England Vacation Tours
01 - 14	♀♂	**London Gay Pride Vacation,** see Idem Tours
01 - 15	♀♂	**Toronto Gay Pride Vacation Pkg,** see Idem Tours
01 - 31	♀♂	**Trekking in India's Himalayas— Zanskar & Ladakh,** see Himalayan High Treks
02 - 07	♀♂	**England, Germnay, Netherlands Cruise,** see Pied Piper Travel
02 - 08	♀	**Colorado & Women's Rodeo,** see Canyon Calling Tours
03 - 05	♀	**July 4th Kick-Back,** Join us for 4 days of playful adventure. Cool off in Towanda Lake with water games, contests, and a luau & live performances on July 6. All other days will be spent in hammocks, lying on the beach, volleyball games & kick-back activities of your choice. No athletic ability is necessary. Camping and cabins are on site. Prizes will be awarded. Location: Ferncliff, VA. Contact: InTouch, Rte 2, Box 1096, Kent's Store, VA 23084, (804) 589-6542, E-mail: intouch@aol.com.
03 - 10	♀	**Alaska Exploration,** see Women in Motion
03 - 10	♀	**Cuzco & Macchu Picchu Expedition,** see South American Expeditions
04	♀♂	**London Gay Pride Pkg,** see Connections Tours
04	♀♂	**Pride (London),** London ,England. Contact local businesses for details or (44-171) 737 6903, E-mail: info@pride.org.uk.
04	♀	**Waitakere Tramp,** see Wanderwomen
04 - 10	♀	**Glacier Bay Adventure Cruise,** see Equinox Wilderness Expeditions
04 - 10	♀	**Sea Kayaking in Glacier Bay Alaska,** see Equinox Wilderness Expeditions
04 - 11	♀	**Amazon & Shamans Expedition,** see South American Expeditions
04 - 11	♀♂	**Costa Rica Tour,** see Holbrook Travel
04 - 11	♀	**Discovering Newfoundland,** see Woodswomen
05 - 09	♀	**San Juan Islands Whale Watch Kayak,** see Blue Moon Explorations
05 - 11	♀	**Alaska Cruise,** see Remote Possibilities
05 - 11	♀	**BWCA Northern Lakes Canoeing,** see Woodswomen
05 - 11	♀	**Cruise Dutch, Belian Canals, Rivers Weert to Mons,** see Vaarschool Grietje
09 - 12	♀	**Mt Baker, Wa Snow & GLacier School,** see Adventure Associates
09 - 12	♀♂	**Spa Retreat in California's Sonoma Valley,** see Progressive Travels
09 - 15	♀	**Basecamp Day Hiking, Denali Wilderness, Alaska,** see Equinox Wilderness Expeditions
09 - 15	♀	**Denali Alpine Wilderness Trek, Alaska,** see Equinox Wilderness Expeditions
10 - 12	♀	**Kayak Retreat in the San Juan Islands,** see Adventure Associates

INTOUCH
JULY 4TH KICK-BACK
July 3-5
1998

22 WHEN TO GO

10 - 12	♀♂	**Mountain Biking in Lake Tahoe**, *see* Outside Sports
10 - 12	♀♂	**North Star Regional Rodeo**, St. Paul, MN. Call: NSGRA, (612) 641-0069.
10 - 12	♀	**Sea Kayaking**, *see* Women in Motion
10 - 16	♀	**Mountaineering & Glacier Travel**, *see* Woodswomen
10 - 18	♀	**Sea Kayaking in Tonga**, *see* Bushwise Women
11	♀	**Begining Rock Climbing**, *see* Woodswomen
11	♀	**Rock Climbing Day Trip 1**, *see* Wanderwomen
11 - 12	♀	**Kayaking in Northern California**, *see* Outside Sports
11 - 13	♀♂	**San Juan Islands Whale Watch Kayak**, *see* Blue Moon Explorations
11 - 18	♀♂	**Copper River Rafting to Pr. William Sound, Alaska**, *see* Equinox Wilderness Expeditions
11 - 24	♀♂	**Italy's Campania Region**, *see* Stay & Visit Italy
11 - 25	♀	**Amazon & Shamans Expedition**, *see* South American Expeditions
11 - 25	♀	**Biological Stations in Bolivia's Rainforest**, *see* South American Expeditions
11 - 26	♀♂	**European Panorama**, *see* Family Abroad
12	♀	**Movement on the Rocks — Climbing**, *see* Woodswomen
12 - 17	♀♂	**Humpback Whales by Kayak — Alaska**, *see* Equinox Wilderness Expeditions
12 - 18	♀	**Cruise Belgian & French Canals Mons to Landrecis**, *see* Vaarschool Grietje
12 - 19	♀♂	**Gay/Lesbian Family Vacation in Costa Rica**, *see* Toto Tours
14 - 26	♀♂	**Spain Tour**, *see* Family Abroad
15 - 19	♀	**Colorado Horseback, Hike, Raft & B&B**, *see* Spiritual Adventures Unlimited
15 - 20	♀	**Sea Kayak Washington's San Juan Islands**, *see* Oceanwomyn Kayaking
15 - AG 09	♀♂	**Christopher Street Day—Zurich, Switzerland**, *see* L'Arc en Ciel Voyages
16 - 18	♀♂	**San Juan Islands Whale Watch Kayak**, *see* Blue Moon Explorations
16 - 30	♀♂	**Stockholm Europride Vacation Pkg**, *see* Idem Tours
17 - 18	♀	**Camping Adventure**, *see* Woodswomen
17 - 19	♀	**Contemplation Weekends**, *see* Adventures for Women
17 - 19	♀	**Hiking Retreat at Mt. Ranier, WA**, *see* Adventure Associates
17 - 19	♀	**Int'l Ms. Leather Contest**, A leather contest for SM women, with a welcome beer bust, play parties and other events. Location: Atlanta, GA. Contact: Int'l Ms. Leather, Inc., 2215-R Market St, San Francisco, CA 94114, (402) 451-7987.
17 - 19	♀	**Int'l Ms. Leather Contest**, A leather contest for SM women, with a welcome beer bust, play parties and other events. Location: Atlanta, GA. Contact: Int'l Ms. Leather, Inc., 2215-R Market St, San Francisco, CA 94114, (402) 451-7987.
17 - 19	♀♂	**Rocky Mtn. Regional Rodeo**, Denver, CO. Call: IGRA, (303) 839-8810.
18	♀♂	**Kayaking in Northern California**, *see* Outside Sports
18 - 19	♀♂	**Gay/Lesbian Rafting-South Fork of the American**, *see* Mariah Wilderness Expeditions
18 - 21	♀	**Women's Rafting on the Rogue River**, *see* Mariah Wilderness Expeditions
18 - 24	♀	**Canyon Lands of Utah**, *see* Canyon Calling Tours
18 - 25	♀♂	**Butch Cassidy Days—Rafting, Balooning the Rockies**, *see* Alyson Adventures
18 - 26	♀♂	**Alaska Adventure River Float, Camping Near Glacier**, *see* Out West Adventures
18 - 26	♀♂	**EuroPride '98**, This annual event, a celebration of gay life in Europe, takes place in a different European country each year. Activities include parties, art exhibits and photography. Various festivals, such as singing, dance and film are highlighted. The event culminates in a large parade. Location: Stockholm, Sweden. Contact: Stockholm Europride '98, Box 3444, 103 69 Stockholm, Sweden, Tel: (46-8) 335 955, Fax: (46-8) 304 730, E-mail: travel@europride98.se.
19 - 23	♀	**Paddling the Adirondack Lake Country**, *see* Adventures for Women
19 - 23	♀	**Women's Photography Workshop & Llama Trek**, *see* Lodestar Adventures
19 - 24	♀♂	**Hike, Raft the Grant Tetons, WY**, *see* Adventure Associates
19 - 24	♀	**Hiking in Washington's North Cascades**, *see* Adventure Associates
19 - 25	♀	**BWCA Lakes, Rivers, Pictographs Canoeing**, *see* Woodswomen
19 - 25	♀	**Cruise French Canals Landrecis to Reims**, *see* Vaarschool Grietje
20 - 24	♀	**Mothers & Daughters Gathering with Jenifer Louden**, *see* Hawk, I'm Your Sister
20 - 25	♀	**Walking & Well-Being Holiday in England**, *see* Fawcett Mill Fields
24 - 25	♀	**All Wonen's Rafting-Middle Fork of the American**, *see* Mariah Wilderness Expeditions
24 - 26	♀♂	**Pride (San Diego)**, San Diego, CA. Contact local businesses for details.
24 - 27	♀	**Apstle Islands Voyage**, *see* Woodswomen
24 - AG 01	♀♂	**Normandy, Brittany, Chateaux Country**, *see* Family Abroad

TRIP/EVENTS CALENDAR

25	♀	**Canoeing Day Trips on Delaware River at Water Gap,** see Adventures for Women
25	♀	**Rock Climbing Day Trip 2,** see Wanderwomen
25 - 27	♀♂	**San Diego Gay Pride Pkg,** see Men on Vacation
25 - 30	♀	**Biking Idaho and the Grand Tetons,** see Womantours
25 - 30	♀	**Kenai Fjords Kayaking, Alaska,** see Equinox Wilderness Expeditions
25 - 30	♀	**Kenai Fjords Sea Kayak,** see Woodswomen
25 - AG 04	♀♂	**England, Scotland & Wales,** see Family Abroad
26		**Mountain Biking Day Trip,** see Wanderwomen
26	♀♂	**Up-Your-Alley Fair (Dore Alley Fair),** San Francisco's Leather Block Party is held at Dore Alley on Folsom between 9th and 10th, from 11am-6pm. Contact: (415) 861-FAIR, Fax: (415) 861-2312.
26 - 31	♀	**Seakayaking in the San Juan Islands, Washington,** see Adventure Associates
26 - 31	♀	**Women's Motorcycle Festival,** An Adventure in the Catskills is the theme of this year's festival, taking place in the heart of the Catskill Mtns. The cost of $297 includes hotel, breakfast, dinners, gorup rides, workshops, Vendo expo, Dice Run, parade, Hudson River boat ride with dinner on the boat, BBQ, and nightly entertainment. For more information call: (914) 657-6227, or e-mail: The2Rays@aol.com.
26 - AG 01		**BWCA Northern Lakes Canoeing,** see Woodswomen
26 - AG 01	♀	**Cruise French Canals Reims to Chaumont,** see Vaarschool Grietje
26 - AG 01	♀	**Olympic National Park Backpacking,** see Woodswomen
26 - AG 01	♀	**Sea Kayak West Vancouver Island, BC,** see Oceanwomyn Kayaking
27 - 31	♀	**Inside Passage Whale Watch Kayak BC Canada,** see Blue Moon Explorations
27 - AG 02	♀♂	**Backcountry Bliss—Backpacking in Montana,** see Out West Adventures
28 - AG 04	♀♂	**Alaska Cruise,** see RSVP Travel Productions/Club RSVP
29 - AG 02	♀♂	**I.G.R.A. Annual Convention,** Baltimore, MD. Call: IGRA (303) 832-4472.
29 - AG 08		**Walking in the Swiss Alps,** see Woodswomen
30 - 31	♀♂	**Gay/Lesbian Family Rafting Trip,** see Mariah Wilderness Expeditions
30 - AG 09	♀	**Women's Sacred Circle,** see Women in Motion
31 - AG 01	♀♂	**G/L Rafting-Middle/South Fork of the American,** see Mariah Wilderness Expeditions
31 - AG 02	♀	**Kings Canyon Nat'l Park Beginning Backpack,** see Alpenglow Adventure Tours
31 - AG 06	♀♂	**Alaska Inside Passage Cruise,** see Ocean Voyager
31 - AG 08	♀	**Vision Quest for Women at a Montana Ranch,** see Earthing Spirit
31 - AG 09	♀♂	**Gay Games Amsterdam,** see Above & Beyond Tours
31 - AG 09	♀♂	**Gay Games in Amsterdam,** see L'Arc en Ciel Voyages
31 - AG 09	♀	**Women's Tour to Amsterdam Gay Games,** see Robin Tyler's Women's Tours, Cruises & Events

August 98

TBA	♀	**Elderflower Womenspirit Festival (10th annual),** Workshops, rituals, movement, crafts, drumming, music, discussions, and fun in the woods for women and girls. A part of the camp is a Clean and Sober area. Tent and cabin camping. Relaxed atmosphere, reasonably rates. Location: Near Mendocino, CA. Contact: Elderflower, PO Box 460790, San Francisco, CA 94146-0790, (916) 658-0697 or (415) 263-5119.
TBA	♀♂	**Gay & Lesbian Softball World Series '98,** Fifty gay & lesbian softball leagues from the USA & Canada send teams to participate in the softball world series. Twenty-two fields are reserved and 2,500 athletes are expected to attend. Location: Minneapolis, MN. Contact: Emerald City Softball Assoc., 1202 E Pike #1177, Seattle, WA 98112, (206) 322-7769.
TBA	♀♂	**Gay Games 98 Party Package,** see Rainbowworld Custom Tours
TBA	♀♂	**Gay Games Amsterdam Pkgs,** see Beyond the Blue
TBA	♀	**Hiking & B&B in Wisconsin,** see Spiritual Adventures Unlimited
TBA	♀♂	**Hotlanta River Expo (20th annual),** A welcome party and the Miss Hotlanta Contest kicks off the weekend, then there is the Mr. Hotlanta National Finals with contestants from Australia and Canada included. Rafting the Chattahoochee River on Saturday is the main event, with a contest fo the Best Theme Raft '97. A Saturday night party is scheduled afterward. Location: Atlanta, GA. Contact: Hotlanta, PO Box 8375, Atlanta, GA 31106, (404) 874-3976.
TBA	♀	**Maine-ly for You Spring Fling & Autumn Fests,** June and August each year on the premises of a campground with 1800 feet of waterfront, a dock and swimming float. Activities nearby include climbing, canoeing, hiking, water sports. The festivals include women's music,

24 WHEN TO GO

		workshops, dancing, crafts, sports. Contact: Maine-ly For You, RR 2 Box 745, Waterford, ME 04088. Oct-May contact: 114 Bennett Ave, Auburn, ME 04210. Tel: (207) 583-6980.
TBA	♀♂	**Northalsted Market Days,** A giant 2-day street fair on Halsted St, Chicago's gayest street. Contact any local gay & lesbian business for information. Location: Chicago, IL.
TBA	♀♂	**Pride (Amsterdam),** Amsterdam, Netherlands. Contact local businesses for details.
TBA	♀	**Taos Conference on Feminine Spirituality,** A weekend festival with workshops, crafts & food. This conference investigates the emerging Goddess as alternative spirituality. Speakers have included Z Budapest, Ruth Barrett & Julia Cameron. Rituals will be performed. Both men & women are welcome, but participation is 85% women. Location: Taos, NM. Contact: The Corn Maiden, 127 Bent St, Taos, NM 87571, (505) 751-3739.
TBA	♀♂	**Twist IV,** Bad Boy Club of Montreal (BBCM) celebrates Montreal Pride Weekend (Divers/Cit, 98) with this mid-summer white event party. Dress code: white with a twist. Location: Montreal, Canada. Contact: (514) 875-7026, Fax: (514) 875-9323, E-mail: information@bbcm.org.
01	♀	**Waitakere Tramp,** see Wanderwomen
01 - 07	♀	**Hiking in Denali Park, Alaska,** see Woodswomen
01 - 08	♀	**Amazon & Shamans Expedition,** see South American Expeditions
01 - 08	♀♂	**Gay Games Amsterdam Package,** see Stonewall Connection Travel & Tours
01 - 08	♀♂	**Gay Games V,** Gay Games V will have the theme of Friendship Through Culture & Sports. Also featured is a cultural festival including artists, theater, film, sculpture, history, architecture, literature, performance art and photography. Location: Amsterdam, Netherlands. Contact: Federation of Gay & Lesbian Games Amsterdam, PO Box 2837, 1000 CV Amsterdam, Netherlands, (31-20) 620 1998, Fax: (31-20) 626 1998. E-mail: info@gaygames.nl.
02 - 07	♀♂	**Multi-Adventure on the Olympic Peninsula,** see Progressive Travels
02 - 08	♀♂	**Cruise French Canals & Rivers Chaumont to Corre,** see Vaarschool Grietje
02 - 15	♀♂	**Scandinavia & St Petersburg,** see Family Abroad
02 - 16	♀	**Cycling in Ireland,** see Woodswomen
03 - 07	♀	**Inside Passage Whale Watch—BC,** see Blue Moon Explorations
03 - 09	♀	**Mt. Rainier Backpack,** see Woodswomen
03 - 09	♀	**Women's Week Backpacking in Montana,** see Out West Adventures
04 - 09	♀	**Kings Canyon Nat'l Park Women's Backpack,** see Alpenglow Adventure Tours
04 - 10	♀	**Southeast Alaska Sailing Safari,** see Equinox Wilderness Expeditions
04 - 11	♀	**Hidden Valleys of the Arctic Trek—Alaska,** see Equinox Wilderness Expeditions
04 - 15	♀	**Backpacking in Alaska,** see Cloud Canyon Backpacking
04 - 25	♀♂	**Trekking in India's Markha Valley (Little Tibet),** see Himalayan High Treks
05 - 11	♀♂	**Montana by Rail,** see Out West Adventures
06 - 10	♀	**Trail Riding in the Tetons-North Leigh,** see Bar H Ranch
06 - 13	♀	**John River Canoeing in Alaska,** see Equinox Wilderness Expeditions
07 - 09	♀♂	**Greater Motown Int'l Rodeo,** Detroit, MI. Call: MIGRA, (313) 438-1305, ext 3..
07 - 09	♀	**Kayak Retreat in the San Juan Islands, WA,** see Adventure Associates
07 - 09	♀	**Mt. Ruapehu Climb - New Zealand,** see Wanderwomen
07 - 09	♀	**Rodeo Wichita,** Wichita, KS. Call: IGRA (303) 832-4472.
07 - 14	♀♂	**Cuzco & Macchu Picchu Expedition,** see South American Expeditions
07 - JY 24	♀	**Sailing the Greek Islands,** see Adventure Associates
08 - 09	♀♂	**Sea Kayaking in Northern California,** see Outside Sports
08 - 14	♀	**Canadian Rockies,** see Canyon Calling Tours
08 - 14	♀	**Multi-Adventure in the Norh Cascades (WA),** see Adventure Associates
08 - 15	♀	**Cuzco & Macchu Picchu,** see South American Expeditions
08 - 21	♀♂	**Imperial Capitals of Europe,** see Family Abroad
08 - 23	♀♂	**Hungary, Austria, Czech Republic,** see David's Trips and Tours
08 - 31	♀♂	**Austria-Prague-Budapest (wheelchair-accessible),** see Crown Tours
09 - 13	♀	**Inside Passage Whale Watch, Kayak, BC Canada,** see Blue Moon Explorations
09 - 13	♀	**Walking Adirondack Lake Country,** see Adventures for Women
09 - 14	♀	**Kenai Fjords Kayaking—Alaska,** see Blue Moon Explorations
09 - 15	♀♂	**Cruise French Canals, Rivers Corre to Toul,** see Vaarschool Grietje
09 - 15	♀	**Hiking in Denali Park, Alaska,** see Woodswomen
09 - 16	♀♂	**Cycle Holland,** see Above & Beyond Tours
09 - 16	♀♂	**Hot Spanish Nights,** see Above & Beyond Tours

TRIP/EVENTS CALENDAR 25

10 - 13	♀	**Women's Rafting on the Green River,** *see* Mariah Wilderness Expeditions
10 - 16	♀♂	**Gay Games Recovery Extentions,** *see* Rainboworld Custom Tours
11 - 16	♀	**Michigan Womyn's Music Festival 1998,** A 6-day, all-womyn, camping event on 650 acres near Hart, in a beautifully wooded area of northwest Michigan. This is the oldest and largest of the U.S. womyn's music festivals. Activities include 40 performances on 3 stages, 300 workshops and 140 craftswomyn. It is a magical week in a village of womyn's culture, with music, dance, theater, arts, sports and lots of networking. Services for childcare, over-50's camping, differently-abled resources and ASL. 6000-7000 womyn from the US, Canada and many other countries throughout the world will attend. Contact: WWTMC, PO Box 22, Walhalla, MI 49458, (616) 757-4766.
11 - 18	♀	**Jungle Lodge in Manu National Park, Peru,** *see* South American Expeditions
12 - 16	♀	**Trail Riding Grand Tetons - North Leigh,** *see* Bar H Ranch
13 - 20	♀	**Alaska Caribou Migration Photography & Hiking,** *see* Equinox Wilderness Expeditions
14 - 16	♀	**Women's Rafting on the Tuolumne River,** *see* Mariah Wilderness Expeditions
14 - 17	♀	**Horseback Riding in Wisconsin,** *see* Woodswomen
14 - 23	♀♂	**Canoeing Odyssey Gates of the Arctic, Alaska,** *see* Equinox Wilderness Expeditions
15	♀♂	**Kayaking in Northern California,** *see* Outside Sports
15 - 21	♀♂	**Backcountry Bliss— Backpacking in Montana,** *see* Out West Adventures
15 - 29	♀	**Amazon & Shamans Expedition,** *see* South American Expeditions
16 - 20	♀	**Adirondack Hiking Sampler,** *see* Adventures for Women
16 - 21	♀♂	**Multi-Adventure on the Olympic Peninsula,** *see* Progressive Travels
16 - 21	♀	**Natural History, Hiking on the Olympic Peninsula,** *see* Adventure Associates
16 - 21	♀	**Seakayaking in the San Juan Islands, Washington,** *see* Adventure Associates
16 - 22	♀	**Biking Vermont,** *see* Womantours
16 - 22	♀	**Cruise French Canals & Rivers Toul to Revin,** *see* Vaarschool Grietje
16 - 22	♀	**Isle Royale Backpack,** *see* Woodswomen
16 - 23	♀	**Women's Resort Vacation Week on Pacific Island,** *see* Silke's Travel
17 - 22	♀	**Summer Walking Magic for Women in England,** *see* Fawcett Mill Fields
17 - 24	♀♂	**Russia Discovery Tour,** *see* Idem Tours
18 - 22	♀	**Trail Riding Grand Tetons - North Leigh,** *see* Bar H Ranch
18 - 23	♀	**Fly Fishing School in West Yellowstone, MT,** *see* Adventure Associates
18 - 25	♀	**Alaska Cruise,** *see* Olivia Cruises & Resorts
20 - 23	♀♂	**Multi-Sport Tour in Lake Tahoe Area,** *see* Outside Sports
21 - 23	♀	**Whitewater Rafting,** *see* Women in Motion
22 - 26	♀	**Lesbian Identity, Lesbian Lives — A Course,** *see* Fawcett Mill Fields
22 - 28	♀♂	**Dover - Lisbon - Venice Cruise,** *see* Pied Piper Travel
22 - SE 02	♀♂	**Scandinavia & Russia Cruise,** *see* Ocean Voyager
22 - SE 03	♀	**Austria, Hiking Vorarlberg Alps,** *see* Adventures for Women
22 - SE 13	♀♂	**Trekking in India — Exploring the Tibetan Plateau,** *see* Himalayan High Treks
23 - 28	♀	**Biking the Canadian Rockies — Banff, Jasper,** *see* Womantours
23 - 28	♀	**Hike, Bike, Kayak, Camp in the San Juan Islands,** *see* Adventure Associates
23 - 29	♀♂	**Camp Camp — A Summer Camp for Gays & Lesbians,** *see* Camp Camp
23 - 29	♀	**Cruise French, Dutch Canals Revin to Weert,** *see* Vaarschool Grietje
23 - 29	♀♂	**Outwestern Trails Gay/Lesbian Ranch Vacations,** *see* Out West Adventures

CAMP CAMP

A Summer Camp in Maine for Gay & Lesbian Adults

August 23-August 29 and August 31-September 6

Toll Free: 1-888-924-8380

www.campcamp.com

26   WHEN TO GO

23 - SE 06	♀♂	**montreal Int'l Film Festival Pkg,** *see* Idem Tours
24 - 28	♀	**Trail Riding in the Tetons - North Leigh,** *see* Bar H Ranch
25 - 29	♀	**Kenai Alpine Lakes Retreat—Alaska,** *see* Equinox Wilderness Expeditions
25 - 29	♀	**W Vancouver Island & Clayquot Sound Kayak,** *see* Blue Moon Explorations
25 - SE 03	♀♂	**River rafting in Alaska's Arctic,** *see* Equinox Wilderness Expeditions
25 - SE 05	♀♂	**Canoeing & Rafting, Russia's Far East,** *see* Hawk, I'm Your Sister
25 - SE 05	♀	**Classical Greece & Turkey,** *see* Family Abroad
26 - SE 01	♀	**Women's Playback Theatre Workshop,** *see* Fawcett Mill Fields
27 - 30	♀	**Int'l Goddess Festival,** A biannual festival, held during a full moon in spring, in a beautiful redwood forest camp in La Honda, CA. A celebration of the returning Goddess culture, music, spirit, body. Lodging in wood cabins or camping, swimming pool and ocean, goddess singers, musicians, actresses, workshops. Contact: Women's Spirituality Forum, PO Box 11363, Piedmont, CA 94611, tel/fax: (510) 444-7724.
27 - 31	♀♂	**Manchester UK European Mardi Gras Pkg,** *see* Connections Tours
28 - 30	♀	**Mt Ruapehu Climb,** *see* Wanderwomen
28 - 30	♀♂	**Windy City Gay Rodeo,** Chicago, IL. Call: ILGRA, (773) 477-5793.
28 - 30	♀	**Women Celebrating Our Diversity,** A multicultural gathering highlighting creative expression with workshops, networking, drumming, camping, movement, sweat and mud pits, volleyball, entertainment and talent shows, dances, dye painting, sharing, writing, drawing, swimming, outdoor gallery. Location: Twin Oaks Community, Louisa, VA. Contact: Twin Oaks Community Women's Gathering, 138 Twin Oak Rd, Box 169, Louisa, VA 23093, (540) 894-5126.
28 - 31	♀♂	**Mardi Gras Manchester,** *see* Teddy Travel
28 - SE 03	♀♂	**British Columbia - Alaska Cruise,** *see* Pied Piper Travel
28 - SE 07	♀♂	**England's Rose and the Jewel of Europe,** *see* Sophisticated Traveler, The
28 - SE 10	♀♂	**Pilgrimage to the Mystic Andes—Peru,** *see* Spirit Journeys
29 - SE 04	♀♂	**Arizona Spectacular,** *see* Canyon Calling Tours
29 - SE 04	♀	**Backpack the Olympic Coast, Washington,** *see* Adventure Associates
29 - SE 05	♀	**Hiking, Horsepacking in California's High Sierras,** *see* Adventure Associates
30 - SE 05	♀	**Cruise Dutch Canals Weert to Amsterdam,** *see* Vaarschool Grietje
30 - SE 06	♀♂	**Montana Big Sky Adventure in Yellowstone Park,** *see* Out West Adventures
31 - SE 06	♀♂	**Camp Camp — A Summer Camp for Gays and Lesbians,** *see* Camp Camp
31 - SE 08	♀	**Biking the Canadian Rockies — Hot Springs, Lakes,** *see* Womantours
31 - SE 09	♀♂	**Liguria Regional Tour — Italy,** *see* Stay & Visit Italy

September 98

TBA	♀♂	**Dive the Red Sea,** *see* Undersea Expeditions, Inc.
TBA	♀♂	**Nat'l Conference of Gay & Lesbian Catholics,** Over 100 lesbian & gay Catholics and religious & lay ministers gather from across the USA. Discussed are common goals of welcoming gays & lesbians, offering spiritual support, helping reconcile past hurts & providing educational opportunities for parents, clergy & the faith community at large. Location: Long Beach, CA. Contact: NACDLGM, 433 Jefferson St, Oakland, CA 94607, (510) 465-9344, Fax: (510) 451-6998, E-mail: nacdlgm@aol.com.
TBA	♀	**Ohio Lesbian Festival,** An all-day event from 11am to midnight, with crafts, workshops, performances, volleyball, picnic and play area, market area and cafe. Contact: LBA (Lesbian Business Assn), PO Box 82086, Columbus, OH 43202, (614) 267-3953.
TBA	♀	**Sappho Lesbian Witch Camp,** A gathering of lesbian witches will take place in mid-September, 1998. Site still being selected at press time. Call for information: (604) 253-7189.
TBA	♀♂	**Twelve Gods Party on Mykonos,** *see* Men on Vacation
TBA	♀	**Women's Weekend II,** A smaller gathering than the women's weekend in May, this event marks the end of the summer season in Russian River, CA. It usually takes place towards the end of September. Contact: We the People newspaper, (707) 573-8896.
01 - 05	♀	**W Vancouver Island & Clayquot Sound Kayak,** *see* Blue Moon Explorations
02 - 06	♀♂	**Twelve Gods Party in Mykonos,** *see* Above & Beyond Tours
03 - 06	♀♂	**Southern Decadence in New Orleans — Gay Package,** *see* Destination Management
03 - 06	♀	**Trail Riding - Progressive Horse Pack Trip-Tetons,** *see* Bar H Ranch
04 - 06	♀	**Club Skirts Labor Bay in Monteray Women's Weekend,** *see* Club Skirts Women's Events
04 - 06	♀♂	**MGRA Show Me State Rodeo,** Kansas City, MO. Call: (816) 697-3269 (8am-8pm) or IGRA (303) 832-4472.

TRIP/EVENTS CALENDAR 27

04 - 06	♀♂	**Zia Regional Rodeo,** Albuquerque, NM. Call: NMGRA, (505) 255-5045.
04 - 07	♀♂	**Labor Day Weekend in Montreal,** *see* New England Vacation Tours
04 - 07	♀♂	**RIP'D '98,** Austin, Texas rolls out its second party of the summer over Labor Day Weekend. There are five different events throughout the weekend including the RIP'D 98 dance party Saturday Night with DJs Julian Marsh & Brian Norwood (Philadelphia) & "Last Splash" on Sunday at Lake Travis. Contact: (514) 478-1210, E-mail: benpar@10.com.
04 - 07	♀♂	**Southern Decadence (25th Anniversary),** A 3-day (Labor Day Wknd) gay Mardi Gras with parties, river cuises, drag queen parade (Sunday) & more. Events take place at or near the French Quarter gay bars. Contact: French Quarter Reservation Service, (504) 523-1246, Fax: (504) 527-6327, Email: fqrs@accesscom.net. http://www.southerndecadence.com
04 - 11	♀	**Cuzco & Macchu Picchu Expedition,** *see* South American Expeditions
04 - 17	♀♂	**Italian Holiday,** *see* Family Abroad
04 - AP 12	♀♂	**Windstar French & Italian Riviera Cruise,** *see* Family Abroad
05 - 06	♀♂	**Gay/Lesbian Rafting Middle Fork of the American,** *see* Mariah Wilderness Expeditions
05 - 12	♀	**Amazon & Shamans Expedition,** *see* South American Expeditions
05 - 15	♀♂	**England, Scotland & Wales,** *see* Family Abroad
05 - 19	♀	**Amazon & Shamans Expedition,** *see* South American Expeditions
05 - 22	♀	**Women's Trek on the Inca Trail—Peru,** *see* Silke's Travel
06 - 10	♀	**Women Over 40 — Photography Workshop & Llama Trek,** *see* Lodestar Adventures
06 - 12	♀	**BWCA Autumn Canoe Trip,** *see* Woodswomen
07 - 12	♀♂	**Nine Muses Party on Island of Mykonos, Greece,** *see* Windmills Travel & Tourism
07 - 13	♀	**Women's Week in Key West Pkg,** *see* Connections Tours
08 - 12	♀	**W Vancouver Island & Clayquot Sound Kayak,** *see* Blue Moon Explorations
08 - 20	♀♂	**Italy's Tuscany and Umbria Regions,** *see* Stay & Visit Italy
08 - OC 07	♀♂	**Around the World Voyager,** *see* Crown Tours
09 - 15	♀	**Womenfest '98,** Women take over Key West during this women's week featuring sunset cruises, glass bottom boat rides, a tennis tournament, water & sand volleyball, scuba diving, a film festival, and trolley tours of Key West. There will be a fair with vendors carrying women-oriented products, as well as women's art, live entertainment, food & drink. Location: Key West, FL. Contact: Jacqueline Harrington, director, Womenfest '98, 201 Coppitt Rd #106A, Key West, FL 33040, Hdq: (800) 374-2784, (305) 296-4238, KWF Bus. Guild (800) 535-7797. E-mail: women@key-west.com.
10 - 13	♀	**Trail Riding - Progressive Horse Pack Trip-Tetons,** *see* Bar H Ranch
10 - 17	♀♂	**Arizona Autumn Quest,** *see* Spirit Journeys
11 - 13	♀	**Sea Kayaking,** *see* Women in Motion
11 - 19	♀	**Vision Quest for Women in Northern Vermont,** *see* Earthing Spirit
12	♀♂	**Amazon Party in Rio de Janeiro Pkg,** *see* Connections Tours
12	♀	**New Hampshire Women's Music Festival,** This 5th annual festival will take place rain OR shine. Featuring children's activities, collaborative weaving, vendors, food. Net proceeds benefit NH Breast Cancer Coalition. Location: Ragged Mtn. Ski area, 30 miles NW of Concord. Call NH Feminist Connection at (603) 225-3501 for details.
12	♀♂	**Swim for Life in Provincetown,** A 1.4-mile swimathon held in Provincetown Harbor at one of the most famous gay and lesbian resort destinations. Weekend activities include a Mermaid Brunch after the swim. Both leisurely swimmers and real competitors participate in this AIDS benefit. Location: Provincetown, MA. Contact: Provincetown Swim For Life, PO Box 819, Provincetown, MA 02657, (508) 487-3684, E-mail: reroot@tiac.net.
12 - 13	♀♂	**Sea Kayaking in Northern California,** *see* Outside Sports
12 - 14	♀	**Garden of Delight Circle Dancing in England,** *see* Fawcett Mill Fields
12 - 17	♀♂	**Big Loire, Little Loir—Bike France's Heartland,** *see* Alyson Adventures
12 - 19	♀♂	**Int'l Gay Summer Meeting,** An international gathering of gays to be held in Paestum - Campagnia, Italy, about 80 km from Naples. Contact: Zipper Travel in Rome, (39-6) 488 2730, Fax: (39-6) 488 2729, E-mail: zippertravel@flashnet.it.
12 - 19	♀♂	**Int'l Gay Summer Party (near Naples),** *see* Zipper Travel Association
12 - 20	♀♂	**Heidi's Alpine Hiking—Davos, Switzerland,** *see* L'Arc en Ciel Voyages
12 - 26	♀	**Biological Stations in Bolivia's Rainforest,** *see* South American Expeditions
13	♀	**Joy Paddles near Pine Barrens, NJ,** *see* Adventures for Women
13 - 19	♀♂	**Cabin-to-Cabin Llama Trek,** *see* Lodestar Adventures
13 - 19	♀♂	**Outwestern Trails Gay/Lesbian Ranch Vacations,** *see* Out West Adventures
13 - 21	♀♂	**Club Med Gay Week in Italy (Otranto),** *see* Idem Tours
15 - 27	♀♂	**Italy, Greece, Turkey, Russia Cruise,** *see* Pied Piper Travel

28 WHEN TO GO

Dates		Event
16 - 26	♀♂	**Burgundy Barge Cruise & Paris,** *see* Family Abroad
16 - OC 18	♀♂	**Around the World Voyager,** *see* Crown Tours
17 - 20	♀	**North Shore Hike,** *see* Woodswomen
18 - 20	♀	**Fire Island's Sixth Annual Women's Weekend,** A full weekend of round-the-clock lesbian activities, entertainment, workshops, vendors and more. Location: Fire Island, NY. Contact any Fire Island Business or (212) 337-3519 or (516) 597-6600.
18 - 20	♀♂	**Pikes Peak United Rodeo,** Colorado Springs, CO. Call: CGRA, (719) 576-2472.
18 - 20	♀♂	**Rock Climbing in Bear Valley, CA,** *see* Outside Sports
18 - 20	♀	**Wild Western Women's Weekend,** Learn and show off your two steppin', line dancing, clogging and square dancing. Dance all day and night! What a weekend with live bands playing country & western music all evening! Also Crazy Feats rodeo, contests and a hay ride. Location: At Intouch. Contact Intouch, Rte 2, Box 1096, Kent's Store, VA 23084, (804) 589-6542, E-mail: intouch@aol.com.
18 - 25	♀♂	**Valley of the Kings—Bike Chateau Country,** *see* Alyson Adventures
18 - 26	♀♂	**Cruising & Hiking Turkey's Turquoise Coast,** *see* Progressive Travels
19	♀♂	**Fall Heat Party in Miami Beach - Pkg,** *see* Connections Tours
19	♀♂	**Kayaking in Northern California,** *see* Outside Sports
19 - 26	♀	**Biking Bryce, Escalante & Capitol Reef Parks,** *see* Womantours
19 - OC 02	♀♂	**Imperial Capitals of Europe,** *see* Family Abroad
19 - OC 02	♀♂	**Italy's Campania Region,** *see* Stay & Visit Italy
19 - OC 03	♀♂	**Mykonos Vacation Package,** *see* Idem Tours
20 - 26	♀	**Grand Canyon Backpack,** *see* Woodswomen
21 - 27	♀♂	**Walking Adventure in France,** *see* Progressive Travels
21 - 29	♀	**Backpacking in Utah—Going Deeper,** *see* Cloud Canyon Backpacking
23 - 27	♀	**Horseback, Hiking & B&B in Colorado,** *see* Spiritual Adventures Unlimited
23 - 30	♀♂	**Biking on Cephalonia — Greece,** *see* Family Abroad
24 - 26	♀♂	**Folsom Street Fair,** A street fair with live bands, dancing, entertainment and booths with leather items for sale. The fair is just one of the many events surrounding the Mr. Drummer Contest Finals, which take place the same weekend. Location: San Francisco, CA. Contact: Drummer Magazine, (415) 252-1195 or SMMILE, (415) 861-FAIR, Fax: (415) 861-2312, Web: http://www.folsomstfair.com.
25 - 27	♀♂	**Greater San Diego Rodeo,** San Diego, CA. Call: GSGRA (San Diego Chapter), (619) 298-4708.
25 - 27	♀♂	**Mountain Biking in Lake Tahoe,** *see* Outside Sports
25 - OC 03	♀	**Amsterdam Germany Tour,** *see* Women in Motion
26	♀♂	**Mr. Drummer Contest,** These are the finals for winners of numerous regional Mr. Drummer contests throughout the world. Each contestant will perform a fantasy skit. Location: San Francisco, CA. Contact: Mr. Drummer Contest, PO Box 410390, San Francisco, CA 94141-0390, (415) 252-1195.
26	♀♂	**Sleaze Ball,** An annual theme ball in which participants dress in sleezy costumes. About 17,000 participate annually in the ball. Location: R.A.S. Showgrounds in Sydney, Australia. Contact: Box 1064, Darlinghurst 2010, NSW Australia or call: (61-2) 9557 4332
26 - OC 01	♀♂	**Mad About Kids Gay/Lesbian Family Vacation in Bali,** *see* Silke's Travel
26 - OC 02	♀♂	**Bicycling in Tuscany, Italy,** *see* Progressive Travels
26 - OC 02	♀	**French Wine Tasting Cruise in Burgundy,** *see* Remote Possibilities
27		**Getting in Shape for the Outdoors,** *see* Adventures for Women
27 - 30	♀	**Mountain Biking in Utah,** *see* Woodswomen
27 - OC 03	♀	**Hike and Kayak, Kauai, Hawaii,** *see* Adventure Associates
27 - OC 04	♀♂	**Proven‡al—Bike in Southern France,** *see* Alyson Adventures
28		**Getting in Shape for the Outdoors,** *see* Adventures for Women
28 - OC 04	♀♂	**Bicycling in France,** *see* Progressive Travels
29 - OC 06	♀♂	**SleazeBall in Sydney, Australia,** *see* Men on Vacation
30 - OC 05	♀♂	**Sydney Sleaze Ball,** *see* Above & Beyond Tours
30 - OC 09	♀♂	**Hawaii Transpacific Cruise,** *see* Ocean Voyager

INTOUCH Wild Western Women's Weekend

Sept 18-20, 1998

TRIP/EVENTS CALENDAR 29

October 98

TBA	♀♂	**Fantasy Fest in Key West,** Held on Halloween weekend, this is an island-wide Halloween party, with dances, shows, crowds in the streets, non-stop revelry for men and women. Location: Key West, FL. Contact any gay business in the Key West listings for information, or call: (305) 296-1817, Web: http://www.gaykeywestfl.com
TBA	♀♂	**Hellball '98,** Held over Halloween, Hellball is San Francisco's largest costume/dance party extravaganza. Large cash prizes for the costume contest draw participants from all over the USA. Benefits Continuum and Halloween San Francisco. Contact: Hellball info line (415) 674-1214.
TBA	♀	**Hiking & B&B in Wisconsin,** see Spiritual Adventures Unlimited
TBA	♀♂	**Int'l Gay & Lesbian Aquatics Competition,** Swimming, diving, synchronized swimming and water polo are among the events featured at this international competiton which takes place on the Columbus Day weekend. Location: San Diego, CA.
TBA	♀	**Ladies Only Spa Adventure in Iceland,** see L'Arc en Ciel Voyages
TBA	♀	**Lesbenwoche (Lesbian Week in Berlin, Germany),** Held in late Oct. during Lesbian Week in Berlin, the lesbian presence is felt throughout the city. This year's program incudes women's music performances, films, slide shows, poetry readings and thousands of lesbians. Workshops will feature lesbian sexuality, safer sex, lesbian prostitution, lesbians of color, immigreps and exiles and lesbians with AIDS. Accommodation can be arranged. Contact: Berliner Lesbenwoche, c/o Rat und Tat, Schillerpromenade 1, 1000 Berlin 44, Germany (49) (30) 621 47 53.
TBA		**Nepal, Himalayas,** see Club Le Bon
TBA	♀	**Sistahfest,** An annual retreat for Black lesbians sponsored by United Lesbians of African Heritage. Location: Camp JCA (Camp Shalom), Malibu, CA. Contact: ULOAH, 1626 S Wilcox Ave #190, Los Angeles, CA 90028, (213) 960-5051.
TBA	♀♂	**Sydney Sleaze Ball,** see Beyond the Blue
TBA	♀	**Wise Festival,** Held in October in Western Australia around the full moon. A 4-day full-moon camping festival with workshops, arts, crafts, spirituality & entertainment. Participatory - bring your own music, too. Contact RMB, 335 Forest Grove 6286, WA, Australia, (61-97) 577 578.
TBA	♀	**Hawaii Women's Week,** see Remote Possibilities
01 - 04	♀♂	**Group Tour to Barcelona,** see Teddy Travel
01 - 04	♀♂	**Sierra Fall Foliage/Hotspring Tour - Mammoth Lakes,** see Alpenglow Adventure Tours
01 - 10	♀♂	**Sicily Regional Tour,** see Stay & Visit Italy
01 - 17	♀♂	**Trekking in Bhutan — In-Depth Cultural Tour,** see Himalayan High Treks
01 - 18	♀♂	**Trekking Nepal — Essential Everest — Best Views,** see Himalayan High Treks
02 - 04	♀♂	**Atlantic Stampede Rodeo,** Washington, DC. Call: ASGRA, (202) 298-0928.
02 - 04	♀♂	**To the Next Level— Journey Into Ourselves,** see Spirit Journeys
02 - 05	♀♂	**San Diego Gay Rodeo Pkg,** see Men on Vacation
02 - 09	♀	**Cuzco & Macchu Picchu Expedition,** see South American Expeditions
02 - 11	♀♂	**Turkey,** see Family Abroad
03 - 08	♀	**Biking in Kentucky,** see Womantours
03 - 09	♀	**Arizona Spectacular,** see Canyon Calling Tours
03 - 10	♀	**Amazon & Shamans Expedition,** see South American Expeditions
03 - 16	♀♂	**Italy's Campania Region,** see Stay & Visit Italy
03 - 16	♀	**Whitewater Kayaking, Rafting in Bolivia,** see South American Expeditions
03 - 17	♀	**Lesbian Lesbos Discovery Tour,** see Idem Tours
03 - 19	♀♂	**Gay & Lesbian Trip to South Africa,** see Teddy Travel
04	♀	**Getting in Shape for the Outdoors,** see Adventures for Women
04 - 10	♀♂	**Walking in Tuscany, Italy,** see Progressive Travels
05	♀	**Getting in Shape for the Outdoors,** see Adventures for Women
05 - 10	♀♂	**Tropical Daze Bali,** see Above & Beyond Tours
05 - 12	♂	**Mistral-Biking for Gay Men in Southern France,** see Alyson Adventures
06 - 17	♀♂	**Classical Greece & Turkey,** see Family Abroad
06 - 18	♀♂	**Spain Tour,** see Family Abroad
07 - 18	♀♂	**Moonstruck: Italan Romance,** see Sophisticated Traveler, The
08 - 11	♀♂	**Montreal Black and Blue Party Pkg,** see Idem Tours
08 - 14	♀	**Quebed to New York Cruise,** see Pied Piper Travel
08 - 24	♀	**Sail the Kingdom of Tonga & Fiji,** see Izarra Cruises
09 - 11	♀♂	**Awakening Your Spiritual Heart,** see Spirit Journeys

30 WHEN TO GO

Dates		Event
09 - 11	♀♂	**Living in Leather XIII, Nat'l Conference,** A conference celebrating the diversity of the pan-sexual leather, SM, fetish community, with panel discussions, seminars, workshops, craftspeople, erotic equipment and literature. Location: Dallas, TX. Contact: NLA International, 3439 N.E. Sandy Blvd. #155, Portland, OR 97232, (619) 899-4406, Web: http://www.nla-i.com.
09 - 12	♀♂	**Early Fall Fiest in Cancun, Mexico,** see Arco Iris Services
09 - 12	♀♂	**Int'l Cancun Gay Festival,** Meet men & women from all over the world at one of the planet's most beautiful beach areas. A full weekend of activities includes a welcome party, Caribbean cruise, sightseeing, bar hopping and beach BBQ. Contact: Arco Iris Travel (800) 795-5549 or www.freeyellow.com/members/arco/page1.html.
09 - 12	♀♂	**Int'l Gay & Lesbian Weekend in Cancun,** see Connections Tours
09 - 13	♀♂	**Gay & Lesbian Weekend in Cancun Pkg,** see GL Tours
09 - 18	♀♂	**Liguria Regional Tour — Italy,** see Stay & Visit Italy
09 - 22	♀	**Cuzco, Macchu Picchu & Tambopata Reserve,** see South American Expeditions
10 - 10	♀♂	**Pride (Erie),** Erie, PA will celebrate its very first Pride Rally from noon to 4pm in Perry Square. Contact: Erie Gay News, 1115 W 7th St, Erie, PA 16502-1105, (814) 456-9833, Fax: (814) 452-1392. E-mail: egcn@ncinter.net.
10 - 11	♀♂	**Sea Kayaking in Northern California,** see Outside Sports
10 - 17	♀	**Mexico Resort Vacation in Sonora Bay,** see Olivia Cruises & Resorts
10 - 17	♀♂	**Quebec Fall Foliage Package,** see Idem Tours
10 - 18	♀	**Biking the Natchez Trace,** see Womantours
10 - 22	♀♂	**Southern Italy & Sicily,** see Family Abroad
12 - 18	♀	**Women's Week in Provincetown (13th annual),** The world's finest lesbian resort goes all out for this week-long, town-wide extravaganza. Special gallery exhibitions, workshops & seminars, the biggest and brightest names in women's entertainment, community dinner and, of course, the formal prom are why thousands of women make this so much fun! Sponsored by the Women Innkeepers of Provincetown. Make reservations early. Location: Provincetown, MA. Contact: Box 573, Provincetown, MA 02657 FMI.
12 - 19	♀♂	**Israel Discovery Tour,** see Idem Tours
14 - 18	♀	**Women's Week in Provincetown,** see Idem Tours
14 - NO 01	♀	**Trekking in the Himalayas,** see Woodswomen
15	♀	**Rock Climbing - Indoor,** see Wanderwomen
15 - 18	♀	**Yosemite Hiking, Sightseeing,** see Women in Motion
15 - 31	♀♂	**Sacred India,** see Spirit Journeys
16 - 18	♀	**Cycling/Wine in the Alexander Valley,** see Women in Motion
16 - 18	♀♂	**Road Biking in N. California Wine Country,** see Outside Sports
16 - 26	♀	**Ancient Egypt,** see Family Abroad
16 - 29	♀♂	**Italian Holiday,** see Family Abroad
17	♀	**Mountain Biking Day Trip,** see Wanderwomen
17 - 24	♀♂	**Club Atlantis in Costa Rica,** see Atlantis Events
17 - 29	♀♂	**Italy's Tuscany and Umbria Regions,** see Stay & Visit Italy
18	♀	**Getting in Shape for the Outdoors,** see Adventures for Women
18 - NO 15	♀♂	**Trekking in Nepal — Annapurna Circuit,** see Himalayan High Treks
19	♀	**Getting in Shape for the Outdoors,** see Adventures for Women
19 - 24	♀	**Biking in California,** see Womantours
19 - 27	♀♂	**Western Europe / Holland Cruise,** see Ocean Voyager
19 - NO 04	♀♂	**Orient Explorer Cruise,** see Family Abroad
19 - NO 08	♀	**Kilimanjaro & the Serengeti,** see Woodswomen
22 - 25	♀♂	**I.G.R.A. 1998 Finals Rodeo,** Phoenix, AZ. Call: AGRA, (602) 265-8166 or IGRA (303) 832-4472.
23 - 26	♀♂	**Lake Tarawera Sea Kayak & Tramp,** see Wanderwomen
23 - 30	♀	**Yoga Workshops in Peru,** see South American Expeditions
23 - NO 14	♀♂	**Trekking in Nepal — Peaks & Tigers,** see Himalayan High Treks
24	♀	**Introductory Abseiling,** see Wanderwomen
24	♀♂	**Kayaking in Northern California,** see Outside Sports
24 - 26	♀	**Meditation & Shiatsu for Women,** see Fawcett Mill Fields
24 - 31	♀♂	**Club RSVP Resort in Sonora Bay, Mexico,** see RSVP Travel Productions/Club RSVP
24 - NO 02	♀♂	**Cruise the Panama Canal, Acapulco, San Juan,** see Anywhere Travel - Cruise Brothers
25	♀	**High Ropes Confidence Course,** see Wanderwomen
26 - 31	♀	**Biking in California,** see Womantours

TRIP/EVENTS CALENDAR 31

28 - NO 02	♀♂	**New Orleans for Halloween Parties,** *see* David's Trips and Tours
28 - NO 17	♀♂	**Capetown to Victoria Falls,** *see* Crown Tours
29	♀	**Rock Climbing at a Quarry,** *see* Wanderwomen
29 - NO 01	♀♂	**Mid-Atlantic Writers Conference '98,** Conference for gay, lesbian, bisexual & transgender writers. Location: Wahington, DC. Contact: Lambda Book Report, PO Box 73910, Washington, DC 20056-3910, (202) 462-7924, Fax: (202) 462-5264, E-mail: LBREeditor@aol.com.
30 - NO 01	♀♂	**Halloween in New Orleans 2-Night Package,** *see* Destination Management
30 - NO 02	♀♂	**Key West/Bahamas/Fantasyfest Cruise,** *see* Ocean Voyager
31	♀	**Waitakere Tramp,** *see* Wanderwomen
31 - NO 02	♀♂	**Halloween in New Orleans,** *see* Men on Vacation
31 - NO 02	♀	**Lesbian Bonfire Weekend,** *see* Fawcett Mill Fields

November 98

TBA	♀♂	**Dive Reefs of Belize,** *see* Undersea Expeditions, Inc.
TBA	♀♂	**Texas Gay Rodeo (15th annual),** Houston, TX. Call: TGRA (Houston chapter), (713) 777-1444.
01 - 08	♀♂	**Cancun Gay Festival,** *see* Idem Tours
01 - 29	♀♂	**Trekking Nepal — Everest Classic Adventure,** *see* Himalayan High Treks
05 - 14	♀	**Costa Rica Whitewater, Sea Kayaking, Rainforests,** *see* Mariah Wilderness Expeditions
06 - 08	♀♂	**Exploring A Partnered Relationship Couples Worshop,** *see* Spirit Journeys
06 - 13	♀	**Cuzco & Macchu Picchu Expedition,** *see* South American Expeditions
06 - 16	♀♂	**Legacy of the Incas — Bolivia, Peru,** *see* Family Abroad
07 - 14	♀♂	**Club Atlantis in Puerto Vallarta, Mexico,** *see* Atlantis Events
07 - 14	♀♂	**Costa Rica Tour,** *see* Holbrook Travel
07 - 14	♀♂	**Prague and Vienna,** *see* Family Abroad
07 - 15	♀♂	**An American Jungle Book: Costa Rica,** *see* Sophisticated Traveler, The
08	♀	**Waitakere Tramp,** *see* Wanderwomen
08 - 15	♀	**Women's Wellness Vacation on Maui,** *see* Destination Discovery
08 - 17	♀♂	**Cruise the Nile River in Egypt,** *see* Progressive Travels
09 - 14	♀	**Baja California, Mexico,** *see* Women in Motion
12	♀	**Rock Climbing at a Quarry,** *see* Wanderwomen
12 - 15	♀♂	**Spa Retreat in California's Sonoma Valley,** *see* Progressive Travels
13 - 15	♀♂	**Journey Into Ourselves,** *see* Spirit Journeys
13 - 15	♀	**Motutapu Island Adventure Weekend,** *see* Wanderwomen
13 - 26	♀	**Cuzco, Macchu Picchu & Tambopata Reserve,** *see* South American Expeditions
14 - 29	♀♂	**Kenya & Tanzania Safari,** *see* Family Abroad
15 - DE 01	♀♂	**Trekking Sikkim — A Tibetan Buddhist Renaissance,** *see* Himalayan High Treks
18 - 27	♀♂	**Panama Canal & Costa Rica Cruise,** *see* Ocean Voyager
19 - 28	♀♂	**Thanksgiving in Fiji,** *see* Above & Beyond Tours
20 - 28	♀♂	**Russia Discovery Tour,** *see* Idem Tours
20 - 30	♀♂	**Ancient Egypt,** *see* Family Abroad
21	♀	**Rock Climbing Day Trip,** *see* Wanderwomen
21	♀	**Sea Kayaking Introduction,** *see* Wanderwomen
21 - 25	♀	**Golf in Arizona,** *see* Women in Motion
21 - 27	♀♂	**Southern Caribbean Cruise,** *see* Ocean Voyager
21 - 27	♀♂	**West Caribbean Cruise,** *see* Ocean Voyager
21 - 28	♀♂	**Tall Ship Caribbean Sailing at Thanksgiving,** *see* Men on Vacation
22 - 29	♀♂	**London and Paris,** *see* Family Abroad
22 - 29	♀	**Southern Caribbean Cruise,** *see* Olivia Cruises & Resorts
25 - 30	♀♂	**White Party in Miami Beach Pkg,** *see* Connections Tours
25 - DE 02	♀♂	**Paris & Amsterdam,** *see* Family Abroad
26 - 30	♀♂	**Thanksgiving in Amsterdam,** *see* Above & Beyond Tours
27 - 09	♀♂	**Acapulco, Panama Canal, Puerto Rico Cruise,** *see* Pied Piper Travel
27 - 29	♀	**Motutapu Island Adventure Weekend,** *see* Wanderwomen
27 - DE 06	♀♂	**Mexico City Plus Cuernavaca,** *see* Idem Tours

December 98

TBA	♀	**Summer Program at Bushline Lodge — New Zealand,** see Bushwise Women
02 - 06	♀♂	**Christmas Shopping,** see Teddy Travel
04	♀	**Okahu Bay Moonlight Paddle,** see Wanderwomen
04 - 05	♀	**Snorkeling Introduction,** see Wanderwomen
05 - 11	♀♂	**Christmas Shopping in London (other dates avail),** see L'Arc en Ciel Voyages
05 - 12	♀♂	**Windstar Costa Rica Cruise,** see Family Abroad
06	♀	**Introductory Abseiling,** see Wanderwomen
10 - 25	♀♂	**Bicycling Saigon to Hanoi,** see VeloAsia Cycling Adventures
11 - 13	♀	**Kaimai Tramping Weekend,** see Wanderwomen
11 - 24	♀	**Cuzco, Macchu Picchu & Tambopata Reserve,** see South American Expeditions
12	♀	**Rock Climbing Day Trip,** see Wanderwomen
18 - 25	♀	**Cuzco & Macchu Picchu Expedition,** see South American Expeditions
18 - 28	♀♂	**Ancient Egypt,** see Family Abroad
19 - JA 02	♀	**Amazon & Shamans Expedition,** see South American Expeditions
20 - JA 02	♀♂	**Christmas DownUnder,** see Above & Beyond Tours
20 - JA 03	♀♂	**Mexico City + Cuernavaca, Acapulco, Cancun or PV,** see Idem Tours
21 - 28	♀♂	**An Austrian White Christmas,** see Sophisticated Traveler, The
22 - 27	♀	**Women's Christmas House Party,** see Fawcett Mill Fields
26 - JA 02	♀	**Amazon & Shamans Expedition,** see South American Expeditions
26 - JA 02	♀♂	**Costa Rica Tour,** see Holbrook Travel
26 - JA 02	♀♂	**New Year's Even in Puerto Vallarta, Mexico,** see Arco Iris Services
27 - JA 02	♀♂	**Camp it Up,** Family camp for gays, lesbians & their children. Contact: Kalani Eco-Resort, RR2 Box 4500, Kehena Beach, HI 96778, (808) 965-7828, for reservations only: (800) 800-6886.
27 - JA 02	♀♂	**Eastern Caribbean Cruise,** see Ocean Voyager
28 - JA 01	♀	**Dogsledding in the Northland,** see Woodswomen
28 - JA 01	♀♂	**New Year's Eve at the Top of the World—Iceland,** see L'Arc en Ciel Voyages
29 - JA 02	♀	**Lake Waikaremoana Sea Kayaking,** see Wanderwomen
30 - JA 03	♀♂	**New Years in Montreal,** see Idem Tours
30 - JA 04	♀♂	**New Years in Paris,** see Above & Beyond Tours
31 - JA 03	♀	**San Francisco New Years,** see Women in Motion

January 99

TBA	♀♂	**Aspen Gay Ski Week,** A full week of skiing and varied activities for gay men and lesbians in Usually held the last week of January in Aspen, Colorado, it includes the "Coors Light World Famous Mountain Bump Your Buns Downhill Costume Party." Over 6000 participants attend. For information on travel, lodging and events, contact: The Aspen Gay & Lesbian Community (AGLC) PO Box 3486, Aspen, CO 81612, (970) 925-4123, Email: aspengay@rof.net.
TBA	♀♂	**Aspen Gay Ski Week Tour,** see Out West Adventures
TBA	♀♂	**Dive the Cocos Islands, Costa Rica,** see Undersea Expeditions, Inc.
TBA	♀	**Galapagos and Ecuador Cruise,** see Adventure Associates
TBA	♀♂	**Gay Games VI (Sydney),** The Gay Games of 2002 will be held in Sydney, Australia. For information see their website at http://www.sydney2002.org.au/gaygames.html.
TBA	♀♂	**Midsumma Festival,** Melbourne, Australia's outrageous and incredible summer bash with parties, theater, bus trips, art exhibits, fetish events, drag workshops and forums, AIDS forums, to mention a few. Don't forget, summer "down under" is winter in the northern hemisphere. Contact: Midsumma, 5th floor, 258 Flinders Lane, Melbourne, VIC 3000, Australia, (61-3) 650 6080.
TBA	♀	**Nat'l Women & Motorcycling Foundation Conference,** Workshops, informational activities and entertainment. Location: Westerville, OH. Contact: Women's Motorcyclist Foundation, 7 Lent Ave, LeRoy, NY 14482, (716) 768-6054.
TBA	♀♂	**P-FLAG Conferences,** The next major national conference will be held in 2000. For information see the various regional conferences held throughout the country, contact: P-FLAG, 1101 14th St NW #1030, Washington, DC 20005, Tel: (202) 638-4200, Fax: (202) 638-0243, E-mail: info@pflag.org.
TBA	♀♂	**Road Runner Regional Rodeo,** Phoenix, AZ. Call: AGRA (602) 237-3302; rodeo hotline: (602) 265-0618.

TRIP/EVENTS CALENDAR 33

01 - 14	♀	**Cuzco, Macchu Picchu & Tambopata Reserve,** see South American Expeditions
02 - 23	♀♂	**Southern Africa,** see Crown Tours
03 - 17	♀♂	**Mexico City Plus Cuernavaca,** see Idem Tours
05 - 12	♀	**Jungle Lodge in Manu National Park, Peru,** see South American Expeditions
15 - 22	♀♂	**Key West Getaway,** see Idem Tours
15 - 23	♀♂	**European Gay Ski Week,** see Idem Tours
17 - 18	♀	**Integrated Leadership,** see Woodswomen
17 - 31	♀♂	**Mexico City Plus Acapulco,** see Idem Tours
21 - 25	♀	**Bay of Islands Sea Kayaking,** see Wanderwomen
23 - 30	♀	**Women's Vacation Pkg to Aspen Gay Ski Week,** see Silke's Travel
24 - FE 08	♀♂	**India & Nepal,** see Family Abroad
28 - 31	♀	**Jackson Hole 1999 Women's Ski Camp,** Open to skiers of intermediate skills or better who want to improve their skiing and enjoy the camaraderie of other women. Top female instructors. Location: Jackson Hole, WY. Contact: Jackson Hole 1999 Women's Ski Camp, PO Box 290, Teton Village, WY 83025, (307) 739-2686.
28 - FE 01	♀	**Dogsledding in the Northland,** see Woodswomen
29 - FE 01	♀♂	**Philadelphia Blue Ball Package,** see Idem Tours
30 - FE 06	♀	**Crosscountry Skiing in Yellowstone, WY,** see Adventure Associates
31 - FE 07	♀♂	**World's Largest Gay Cruise!,** see Atlantis Events
31 - FE 14	♀♂	**Mexico City Plus Cancun,** see Idem Tours

February 99

TBA	♀	**Alpine Meadows Women's Ski Week,** see Women in Motion
TBA	♀♂	**Altitude 99 - Whistler Gay Ski Week,** (tentative date: Jan 31-Feb 7, 1999) A one-week ski and party event combination for gays and lesbians. Over 2000 participants and 30 eventes. Packages include seven nights lodging, ski pass, admission to parties and events. Location: Whistler, BC, Canada. Contact: Out on the Slopes Productions, P.O. Box 1370, Whistler, BC Canada V0N 1B0, (604) 688-5079, Fax: (604) 688-5033, (888) 258-4883, E-mail: altitude@outontheslopes.com.
TBA	♀♂	**American Tea Dance in Sydney,** see Men on Vacation
TBA	♀♂	**Atlantis Events Sydney Mardi Gras,** see Atlantis Events
TBA	♀♂	**Big Sky Gay Ski Tours,** see Out West Adventures
TBA	♀♂	**Carnaval in Veracruz, Mexico,** see Arco Iris Services
TBA	♀♂	**Carnival in Rio,** see Sundance Travel
TBA	♀	**Forest Footing — Bushline Lodge, New Zealand,** see Bushwise Women
TBA	♀♂	**Gay Ski East '99,** This gay ski event highlights ski competitions (Alpine & cross-country), bobsledding & luge, ice skating, as well as cocktail parties, an awards dinner and admission to the Olympic Museum. Location: Lake Placid, NY. Contact: (813) 734-1111, E-mail:gayskiest@compuserve.com.
TBA	♀	**Girls in the Snow,** Women's ski and winter sports weekend in Colorado. Contact: Circles Magazine, (303) 417-1385, Fax: (303) 417-1453.
TBA	♀	**Hawaii Kayak and Hike Kona Island,** see Blue Moon Explorations
TBA	♀♂	**Hero Festival,** The 2-week festival includes a series of parties, gay art exhibits, entertainment, a short-course swim meet, beach parties, nightclub shows, gay church services, and the Gay Day Party on Wahiki Island, including the Mr. Gay New Zealand Competition, all preceding the Hero Parade & Party, New Zealand's biggest bash of the year. Location: Auckland, New Zealand. Contact: Hero Project Office, 492 Karangahape Rd, Auckland, NZ.
TBA	♀♂	**Igloo Weekend in Stowe, Vermont,** A weekend of gay skiing, parties, snowshoeing hikes, ski lessons, and cross-country ski hikes. This event is usually held in late February or early March. Call for details. Location: Stowe, VT. Contact: Buccaneer Country Lodge (802) 253-4772.
TBA	♀♂	**Nat'l Black Gay & Lesbian Leadership Forum,** One of the largest gatherings of black lesbians and gay men, this event focuses on issues, challenges and the direction of the Black lesbian & gay community. Each year, it attracts hundreds of national & international presenters and attendees. It is always held on President's Day weekend, and is organized by the Black Gay & Lesbian Leadership Forum. Contact: BGLLF, 1436 U St NW #200, Washington, DC 20009, (202) 483-6786.
TBA	♀♂	**New Orleans Mardi Gras Gay Package,** see Destination Management
TBA	♀♂	**Outwrite '99,** Over 2000 writers, editors, publishers, critics & agents meet for this 2-1/2 day conference to discuss the latest trends in lesbian & gay publishing. Event includes panel

34   WHEN TO GO

TBA		discussions, keynote speakers & entertainment. Location: Boston, MA. Contact: Outwrite '99, 29 Stanhope St, Boston, MA 02116, (617) 262-6969, Fax: (617) 267-0852.
TBA	♀♂	**Pantheon of Leather,** Annual service awards to men, women and businesses of the leather community. Events include cocktail parties, the award presentation and the Mr. and Ms Olympus Leather 1999 Contest. Sunday Night is the "Black Hearts Ball" a costume party and contest where the top vote getters are crowned King and Queen of the ball. Location: New Orleans, LA. Contact: The Leather Journal, 7985 Santa Monica Blvd #109-368, West Hollywood, CA 90046, (213) 656-5073, Fax: (213) 656-3120, Email: tljandcuir@aol.com
TBA	♀♂	**Pride (Adelaide),** Adelaide, Australia. Contact local gay businesses for details.
TBA	♀♂	**Pride (Melbourne),** Melbourne, Australia. Contact local gay businesses for details.
TBA	♀	**Sea Kayak Baja Mexico,** see Oceanwomyn Kayaking
TBA	♀	**Sea Kayaking in New Zealand,** see Bushwise Women
TBA	♀♂	**Sydney Gay & Lesbian Mardi Gras,** A month-long festival of gay and lesbian cultural events, including theatre, cabaret, film festivals, sporting events, exhibitions, parties, dances on the biggest dance floor in the world, harbor cruises, a parade and major entertainment productions. Many gay and lesbian travel agents offer travel packages including this event. Location: Sydney, Australia. Contact: (61-2) 9360 9755, Fax: (61-2) 9320 9169.
TBA	♀♂	**Sydney Gay & Lesbian Mardi Gras Dance Party,** A month-long festival of gay and lesbian cultural events which culminates in the dance party of a lifetime. More that 25,000 participants are entertained by top-name performers and dance on the biggest dance floor in the world at a party that lasts beyond sunrise. Many gay and lesbian travel agents offer travel packages including this event. Location: Sydney, Australia. Contact: (61-2) 9360 9755, Fax: (61-2) 9320 9169.
TBA	♀♂	**Sydney Gay Mardi Gras Package,** see Jornada
TBA	♀♂	**Sydney Mardi Gras Pkgs,** see Atlantis Travel
TBA	♀♂	**Ultimate New Zealand Adventure,** see Men on Vacation
TBA	♀♂	**Winter Gayla '99,** Over Valentine's & President's Day weekend & up to 10 days prior, join Ft. Lauderdale, FL in its celebration of gay pride. Events include a Saturday beach party and evening open-air dance. Sunday features the Winter Pride Parade & Festival. Monday morning enjoy the party aboard double decker boats that wind through the "Venice of America." Contact: AAR Productions, Inc., PO. Box 2467, Ft. Lauderdale, FL 33303-2467, (954) 525-4567, Email: aarinc@earthlink.net
TBA	♀♂	**Winter Gayla '99,** Over Valentine's & President's Day weekend & up to 10 days prior, join Ft. Lauderdale, FL in its celebration of gay pride. Events include a Saturday beach party and evening open-air dance. Sunday features the Winter Pride Parade & Festival. Monday morning enjoy the party aboard double decker boats that wind through the "Venice of America." Contact: AAR Productions, Inc., PO. Box 2467, Ft. Lauderdale, FL 33303-2467, (954) 525-4567, Email: aarinc@earthlink.net
TBA	♀♂	**Yellowstone Winter Adventure,** see Out West Adventures
04 - 08	♀♂	**Bicycling in Cambodia,** see VeloAsia Cycling Adventures
04 - 08	♀	**Dogsledding in the Northland,** see Woodswomen
05 - 20	♀	**New Zealand Adventure,** see Canyon Calling Tours
06 - 19	♀	**Peru—MacchuPicchu, Nazca Lines, Lake Titicaca,** see Hawk, I'm Your Sister
07 - 12	♀♂	**Gay Ski Week at Mt. Snow, Vermont,** see New England Vacation Tours
10 - 25	♀♂	**Bicycling in Vietnam During Tet Lunar New Year,** see VeloAsia Cycling Adventures
10 - MR 06	♀♂	**Best of the South Pacific,** see Above & Beyond Tours
12 - 13	♀♂	**Hot Lava,** A new entry on the party circuit in 1998, this 3-day event includes cocktail party, beach beer bash and the Hot Lava dance party. Location: Honolulu, HI. Contact: (800) 538-1786, E-mail: sdenevents@aol.com.
12 - 14	♀♂	**Hearts Party (BOHT),** 12th anniversary gala weekend celebration in Chicago, IL, which includes a variety of events that benefit the TPA Network. Events include: Friday night: auction and entertainment & the King of Hearts Ball; Saturday night: 1999 Hearts Party dance; Sunday: Tea dance. Contact: Test Postive Aware Network (TPA), 1258 W. Belmont, Chicago, IL 60657 (773) 404-8726; Party hotline: (773) 404-3784, (888) 473-4327, E-mail: info@heartsparty.com.
12 - 22	♀♂	**Ancient Egypt,** see Family Abroad
12 - 25	♀	**Cuzco, Macchu Picchu & Tambopata Reserve,** see South American Expeditions
13 - 18	♀♂	**Caribbean Cruise,** see RSVP Travel Productions/Club RSVP
13 - 19	♀♂	**New Zealand Adventure,** see Above & Beyond Tours
14 - 21	♀♂	**Carnival in Las Palmas,** see Family Abroad
14 - 21	♀♂	**London and Paris,** see Family Abroad
17 - 24	♀♂	**Paris & Amsterdam,** see Family Abroad

TRIP/EVENTS CALENDAR 35

17 - 27	♀♂	**Australia & Great Barrier Reef Cruise,** see Ocean Voyager
18 - 27	♀♂	**Caribbean Cruise - Costa Rica, Panama Canal,** see RSVP Travel Productions/Club RSVP
18 - MR 05	♀♂	**Boomerang,** see Alyson Adventures
19 - MR 01	♀♂	**HERO Party & Sydney Mardi Gras,** see Above & Beyond Tours
20 - 27	♀♂	**Gay Ski Week in Austria,** see Atlantis Travel
21 - 27	♀♂	**Indonesia Cruise,** see Ocean Voyager
21 - MR 01	♀♂	**Sydney Gay and Lesbian Mardi Gras,** see Above & Beyond Tours
21 - MR 01	♀♂	**Sydney Gay Mardi Gras,** see Family Abroad
21 - MR 03	♀	**Singapore to Bali, Indonesia Cruise,** see Olivia Cruises & Resorts
27 - MR 01	♀	**Lesbian Massage Weekend,** see Fawcett Mill Fields
27 - MR 08	♀♂	**Bicycling in the Tonkinese Alps,** see VeloAsia Cycling Adventures
27 - MR 13	♀♂	**Australia Tour & Great Barrier Reef,** see Family Abroad
27 - MR 14	♀♂	**Ultra-Luxurious South Africa Tour,** see David's Trips and Tours

March 99

TBA	♀♂	**Barrier Reef Recovery,** see Men on Vacation
TBA	♀♂	**Bighorn Rodeo,** Las Vegas, NV. Call: NGRA, (702) 593-3193.
TBA	♀♂	**Canadian Rockies Ski Tour,** see Out West Adventures
TBA	♀	**Canyons of the Escalante Backpacking,** see Equinox Wilderness Expeditions
TBA	♀♂	**Chill Out in Daylesford,** Australia's only gay & lesbian country festival day. Lots of fun & games, including high-heel skipping races, gumboot tossing, sack races, horse-shoe pitching, etc. Held at the Showgrounds, there are also food & wine stalls, arts & crafts, massage & more. Location: Daylesford, VIC, Australia. Contact: Springs Connection Gay & Lesbian Network, PO Box 424, Daylesford, VIC 3460, Australia, (61-3) 5345 8386, E-mail: springhil@cbl.com.au.
TBA	♀	**Club Skirts/Girl Bar/ Dinah Shore Weekend,** In addition to the many other activities associated with Dinah Shore Weekend, Club Skirts & Girl Bar host one of the largest parties for women on the planet. Top-notch DJs are featured and the crowd swells to over 6,000 women. Location: Palm Springs, CA. Contact: (888) 44 DINAH.
TBA	♀	**Dinah Shore Tournament Week Womens' Events,** It is estimated that 8,000 women come to Palm Springs for the multitude of women's parties and events taking place during the week of the Dinah Shore Golf Tournament. Dances, pool parties, breakfasts, lunches, cocktail parties and other events take place. Contact any gay or lesbian business listed in the Palm Springs section of this book for details.
TBA	♀	**Galapagos/Ecuador Cruise,** see Adventure Associates
TBA	♀	**Hawaii Kayak & Hike Konalsland,** see Blue Moon Explorations
TBA	♀♂	**Int'l Gay Ski Week (SWING) 1999,** This event is held in the Swiss Alps each year, attended by skiiers from Europe and the USA. Events include hiking by torchlight, skating, cinema, concerts, disco & a costume ball. The decision on which city and country is never made until after this book goes to press. Contact the organization for the 1998 schedule. Contact: SWING, Lindenstr. 4, 8152 Glattbrugg, Switzerland. Tel: (41-1) 810 4441.
TBA	♀	**Kayak Sea of Cortez, Baja, Mexico,** see Blue Moon Explorations
TBA	♀	**Lesbian Pride Weekend (Denver),** A series of lesbian parties and events, sponsored by Out Front newspaper. Location: Denver, CO. Contact: Out Front, 244 Washington St, Denver, CO 80203, (303) 778-7900.
TBA	♀	**Marlborough Wine & Bike Trail,** see Bushwise Women
TBA	♀♂	**Park City Ski Daze (4th annual),** The resort area of Park City/Deer Valley is the site of this 4-day ski event, featuring ski races & competitions, special events, parties and "fun runs". Location: Park City, UT. Call: (213) 464-5388.
TBA	♀♂	**Park City Ski Daze (5th annual),** The resort area of Park City/Deer Valley is the site of this 4-day ski event, featuring ski races & competitions, special events, parties and "fun runs". Location: Park City, UT. Call: (213) 464-5388.
TBA	♀♂	**Saguaro Regional Rodeo,** Tucson, AZ. Call: AGRA (Tucson Chapter), (520) 323-0805.
TBA	♀	**Sea Kakak Baja Mexico,** see Oceanwomyn Kayaking
TBA	♀	**Sea Kayaking in New Zealand,** see Bushwise Women
TBA	♀	**Sea of Cortez Baja Mexico Sea Kayaking,** see Mariah Wilderness Expeditions
TBA	♀	**Whales of Magdalena Bay Kayaking,** see Blue Moon Explorations
TBA	♀♂	**Winterfest '99,** Sponsored by Ski Connections, this gay & lesbian event in Innsbruck, Austria, includes ski racing, a costume party, photo contest, gay nightclub crawl and sightseeing. Contact any IGLTA travel agent or call (800) SKI-1888.

36　WHEN TO GO

TBA	♀♂	**Winterfest Lake Tahoe,** A gay & lesbian winter festival featuring live entertainment, parties, as well as activities such as skiing, sleighrides, snowmobiling & snowboarding. Location: Lake Tahoe, CA. Contact any IGTA travel agent for details.
TBA	♀	**Women's Havasu Canyhon Backpack,** see Grand Canyon Field Institute
01 - 05	♀	**Lake Tahoe Downhill Tour,** see Alpenglow Adventure Tours
01 - 06	♀♂	**Tropical Daze Queensland,** see Above & Beyond Tours
05 - 14	♀♂	**Gay Winterfest Ski Vacation in Europe,** see Ski Connections
05 - 22	♀♂	**Wild Kiwi,** see Alyson Adventures
06 - 13	♀	**Sea Kayaking in Baja, California, Mexico,** see Adventure Associates
06 - 14	♀♂	**Ultra-Luxurious Imperial Cities Tour,** see David's Trips and Tours
07 - 14	♀♂	**Barcelona and Madrid,** see Family Abroad
12 - 21	♀♂	**Irish Lullaby: St Patrick's Day in Ireland,** see Sophisticated Traveler, The
13 - 19	♀♂	**Eastern Caribbean Cruise,** see Ocean Voyager
13 - 20	♀♂	**Far East Cruise,** see RSVP Travel Productions/Club RSVP
16 - 31	♀♂	**Backpacking in New Zealand,** see Cloud Canyon Backpacking
19 - 29	♀♂	**Ancient Egypt,** see Family Abroad
20 - AP 02		**Amazon, Cuzco, Macchu Picchu,** see South American Expeditions
21 - 27	♀♂	**Cruise the Mexican Riviera from Los Angeles,** see Anywhere Travel - Cruise Brothers
23 - 28	♀	**Lake Tahoe Downhill Tour,** see Alpenglow Adventure Tours
25 - 28	♀	**Club Skirts & Girl Bar Dinah Shore Weekend,** see Club Skirts Women's Events
25 - 29	♀	**Dinah Shore Classic Women's Pkg,** see Women in Motion

April 99

TBA	♀♂	**American Brotherhood Weekend,** Includes three contests: American Leatherman, American Leatherwoman, and American Leatherboy. Host hotel is the Howard Johnson Hotel & Suites and host bar is the Club Improv, both located in the heart of gay businesses in Washington, DC. Contact: ABLE Productions, Inc. P.O. Box 5130, Utica, NY 13505-5130, Email: ABLEprod@aol.com
TBA	♀	**Canoeing Utah's Green River,** see Hawk, I'm Your Sister
TBA	♀	**Gulf Coast Women's Festival (11th annual),** Held on Easter weekend, '99. Get ready for a laid-back good time! Workshops, women musicians in a jam tent, a nightly dance, campfires, affinity spaces, and craftswomen displaying a variety of unique gifts. Location: North of New Orleans, LA. Contact: GCWF, Camp Sisterspirit, PO Box 12, Ovett, MS 39464, (601) 344-1411, tel/fax (601) 344-2005, E-mail: sisterspir@aol.com.
TBA	♀	**Int'l Lesbian Volleyball Tournament,** 56 teams from around Europe gather to compete in this annual event held in a different city each year. Contact: (49-30) 215 9000, E-mail: seitenwechsel.berlin@gaysport.org.
TBA	♀♂	**Jazz Fest in New Orleans— Gay Package,** see Destination Management
TBA	♀	**Kayak Sea of Cortez, Baja, Mexico,** see Blue Moon Explorations
TBA	♀♂	**L.A. Rodeo '99,** Los Angeles, CA. Call: GSGRA (LA Chapter), (310) 498-1675.
TBA	♀♂	**Pride (Phoenix),** Contact Arizona Central Pride, PO Box 16847, Phoenix, AZ 33407, (602) 279-1771, Fax: (602) 487-8641, E-mail: info@azpride.org.
TBA	♀♂	**Queens Day in Amsterdam,** see Men on Vacation
TBA	♀♂	**Rodeo in the Rock,** Little Rock, AR. Call: DSRA, (501) 562-4466.
TBA	♀	**Sailing New Zealand's Fjords,** see Bushwise Women
TBA	♀	**Slickrock Journey in Utah,** see Cloud Canyon Backpacking
TBA	♀♂	**Slide for Pride,** Athletes from Europe, Canada & USA will participate in this men's & women's winter sports festival. Events include Alpine skiing, snowboard giant slalom, Nordic races, ice hockey & figure skating. Location: Seattle. WA. Contact: Team Seattle, 1202 E Pike St #515, Seattle, WA 98112, (206) 322-7769.
TBA	♀♂	**Utah Red Rock Adventure,** see Out West Adventures
TBA	♀♂	**We're Funny That Way,** Comedians from all over the world are expected to perform in this 4-day festival to be held at Buddies in Bad Times Theatre in the gay district of downtown Toronto, Canada. Last year's event sold out early, so it's best to get tickets early. Hosted & produced by queer comic Maggie Cassella. Contact: Buddies in Bad Times Theatre, (416) 975-8555.
TBA	♀	**Women's Beginning Backpacking: Colorado R.,** see Grand Canyon Field Institute
TBA	♀	**Women's Clear Creek Backpack,** see Grand Canyon Field Institute
01 - 20	♀♂	**Leatherfest,** A thousand people from around the world are expected for this event, which

TRIP/EVENTS CALENDAR 37

includes a weekend of education and entertainment, receptions, workshops, awards banquet, LeatherTip Square Dance. Location: San Diego, CA. Contact: NLA, San Diego Chapter, PO Box 3092, San Diego, CA 92163, (800) 598-1859, email: Lasher@connectnet.com

03 - 10	♀	**Amazon Adventure,** *see* Women in Motion
03 - 10	♀	**Deep Caribbean Cruise,** *see* Olivia Cruises & Resorts
04 - 10	♀♂	**Eastern Caribbean Cruise,** *see* Ocean Voyager
04 - 11	♀	**Western Caribbean Cruise,** *see* Olivia Cruises & Resorts
16 - 18	♀	**Canoe, Camp on the California & Arizona Border,** *see* Women in Motion
17 - 23	♀	**Tour to Paris, France,** *see* Women in Motion
22 - MA 06	♀	**Women's Sacred Journey to Ireland,** *see* Sounds & Furies
23 - 27		**New Orleans Jazz Festival,** *see* Women in Motion
27 - MA 04		**Jungle Lodge in Manu National Park, Peru,** *see* South American Expeditions
30	♀♂	**Queen's Day in Amsterdam,** A huge gay and lesbian street party in Amsterdam held on April 30 every year. The gay and lesbian community joins in this enormous national celebration as over a million people, both straight and gay, converge on Amsterdam for street fairs, theatre, musical entertainment and partying.

May 99

TBA	♀♂	**Canadian GALA Choruses: Festival '99,** Canadian gay & lesbian choruses invite singers from across Canada & around the world to Edmonton, Alberta for this event. Featured are performances by gay & lesbian choruses, workshops, and performances by singers, dancers & visual artists. Contact: Edmonton Vocal Minority, P.O. Box 12091, Main Post Office, Edmonton, Alberta, Canada T5J 3L2, (403) 988-4620, Fax: (403) 425-8543, Email: evm@freenet.edmonton.ab.ca
TBA	♀	**Canoeing in Montana,** *see* Hawk, I'm Your Sister
TBA	♀♂	**Dixieland Regional Rodeo,** Atlanta, GA. Call: SEGRA, (770) 662-9510.
TBA	♀♂	**Gay & Lesbian Run in Berlin (9th annual),** All lesbians and gays are invited to participate as athletes and to join us in cultural exchange and celebration. High achievement is not the most important goal of this event, rather it is the centerpiece of a broad spectrum of sporting and fun activities. A wide variety of tourist, cultural and culinary programs will also be available. In the 10,000-meter run, the men and women will start together, but all other events will be separated by gender. Wheelchair participation is encouraged. Location: Berlin, Germany. Contact: Gay & Lesbian Run Berlin, PO Box 420 703, 12067 Berlin, Germany. Call: (49-30) 8418 5315, E-mail: erdmann@zib.de.
TBA	♀♂	**Gay and Lesbian Golf in Scotland,** *see* Club Hommes/Worldguest
TBA	♀♂	**Gay Week in Bogota, Colombia,** The second annual party event takes place May, 1999 and will include conferences, workshops, a film festival and party events. Travel packages are available through Antinoo VIP Travel in Bogota. (57-1) 530 0260 or 530 0261, Fax: (57-1) 245 6035, Email: antinoo_co@hotmail.com. Web: http://www.angelfire.com/biz/antinoogaytravel/index.html.
TBA	♀♂	**Gay Week in Bogota, Colombia — Packages,** *see* Antinoo VIP Travelers
TBA	♀♂	**Great Plains Regional Rodeo,** Oklahoma City, OK. Call: OGRA, (405) 842-0849.
TBA	♀	**Hawaii Exotic Adventure,** "Play the Hawaiian way" at this lesbian spirit gathering. Contact: Kalani Eco-Resort, RR2 Box 4500, Kehena Beach, HI 96778, (808) 965-7828, for reservations only: (800) 800-6886.
TBA	♀♂	**Int'l Mr. Leather Contest 1997 (IML),** Leather men and women from all over the world will descend on Chicago on Memorial Day Weekend for a celebration of the leather, SM and fetish lifestyle. The weekend includes non-stop parties at Chicago's infamous leather bars, a leather market, a meet-the-contestants cocktail reception, the legendary Black-and-Blue Ball and the contest, itself. Location: Chicago, IL. Contact: International Mr. Leather, 5015 N Clark St, Chicago, IL 60640, (312) 878-6360, (800) 545-6753.
TBA	♀	**Into the Womb of Pele, Hawaii,** A spiritual adventure women's retreat. Contact: Kalani Eco-Resort, RR2 Box 4500, Kehena Beach, HI 96778, (808) 965-7828, for reservations only: (800) 800-6886.
TBA	♀	**Ladies' Gay Day in May,** A 3-day, 4-night shindig for women during the long Memorial Day weekend featuring theme parks, feasting & dancing. Special entertainment activities include Disney, SeaWorld, Universal Studios, The Hard Rock Cafe and the Celebrate Sisterhood dinner & dance banquet. Contact: Company of Women, PO Box 522344, Longwood, FL 32752. E-mail: event@companyofwomen.com.
TBA	♀	**Lesbian Liberation Rally,** A day of fun and celebration that is free to all lesbians. Lesbians gather together and play, talk politics. The event includes an afternoon stage with featured musicians, poets, comedians and speakers. There are craftswimmin and food vendors. Location: Northampton, MA. Contact: Lesbians for Lesbians, PO Box 1062, Greenfield, MA 01302.

38 WHEN TO GO

TBA ♀ **Lesbies Doe-Front Lesbian Day,** Among the many events are a special lesbian theater, authors, workshops, films and photo & art exhibits. Over 800 lesbians are expected to attend. The final event is a huge dance party. Location: Belgium. Contact: Lesbies Doe-Front, Postbus 621, 9000 Gent, Belgium, (32-9) 223 69 29.

TBA ♀♂ **Magical England & Scotland,** *see* Spirit Journeys

TBA ♀ **Maryland Womyn's Gathering,** Over 160 acres of waterfront, wetlands & woods set the tone for this year's gathering. Events include opening & closing circles, sharing stage, fire circles, drum council, crafts & dancing. Rustic cabins, newly renovated bath houses, camping welcome. Vegetarian meals. Childcare available (boys under 5 years only). Location: Southern Maryland. Contact: In Gaia's Lap, PO Box 39, Maryland Line, MD 21105, (410) 435-3111.

TBA ♀♂ **Meltdown '99,** Celebrated over Memorial Day weekend in Austin, Texas, Meltdown includes 5 events. The main event is Meltdown '99 on Saturday night followed by the Captain Morgan's Rum Run (a flotilla of party boats on Lake Travis) on Sunday. Benefits: Helping Hands for Life, Inc. Contact: (512) 478-1210, (512) 419-4763, E-mail: benpar@10.com.

TBA ♀♂ **Pensacola Beach Maneuvers 6,** On Memorial Day Weekend, Pensacola, Florida (otherwise known as the Gay Riveria) is flooded with over 50,000 gay men and women for the annual "Beach Maneuvers" festivities. Benefits: White Heat Foundation. Contact: (888) 777-8886.

TBA ♀♂ **Pride (Brussels),** Brussels, Belgium. Contact local businesses for details.

TBA ♀♂ **PrideFest '99 (Philadelphia),** Philadelphia, PA. Contact: PrideFest Philadelphia, 200 South Broad St #200, Philadelphia, PA 19102, (800) 990 -FEST, (215) 732-FEST, E-mail: info@pridefest.org

TBA ♀ **Texas Lesbian Conference (12th annual),** Over 400 women are expected to attend. Featured are keynote speakers, workshop presenters & a comedy performance. Location: San Antonio, TX. Contact: TLC '98, PO Box 12327, San Antonio, TX 78212, E-mail: txlescon98@aol.com.

TBA ♀♂ **Tokyo Int'l Lesbian & Gay Film & Video Festival,** The Tokyo festival is expected to attract 4,000 attendees. From Tokyo, the film festival will travel to Kyoto and Osaka. Location: Tokyo, Japan. Contact: Tokyo Int'l Gay & Lesbian Film & Video Office, Tel/Fax: (81-3) 5380 5760, http://www.wax.or.jp/L-GFF/. For specific information in English, call (81-3) 3316 1029.

TBA ♀ **Veranstaltungen Lesbenfruhlingstreffen,** (Lesbian Spring Gathering). Workshops, seminars, sporting events, social activities, crafts, books, music. Contact last year's organizers: Lesbenfrnhlingstreffen, c/o Frauen in Bewegung, Schwarzwaldstrasse 107, D-W-7800 Freiburg, Germany, tel: 49-761-33339 Tues 8-10p.m.

TBA ♀ **Virginia Women's Music Festival,** Join us for our 11th annual festival held at Intouch for 106 acres of music, workshops, games and fun! Swim, boat & go fishing in 7-acre Towanda Lake. Drumfest prior to festival. Location: 20 miles east of Charlottesville, VA. Contact: Intouch, Rte 2, Box 1096, Kent's Store, VA 23084, (804) 589-6542.

TBA ♀ **Wiminfest '99,** Usually held over Memorial Day weekend. Open mike, fun in the sun, dances, arts and crafts. Reserved seating for performances. Festival passes sell out every year, so reservations are a MUST! There is space ONLY for the number of tickets issued. Single concert tickets may be available at door, call for availability. Memorial Day Weekend. Location: Albuquerque, NM. Contact W.I.M.I.N., PO Box 80204, Albuquerque, NM 87198-0204, (505) 899-3627, (800) 499-5688.

TBA ♀ **Women's Weekend,** A large gathering of thousands of women from around the USA, this event takes place annually in Russian River, CA during the first week of May. Contact: We the People newspaper, (707) 573-8896.

Virginia Women's Music Festival
MAY 1999
INTOUCH

06 - 08 ♀ **Russian River Women's Weekend,** *see* Women in Motion
07 - 09 ♀ **Las Vegas Social,** *see* Women in Motion
15 - 22 ♀ **Women's Bahamas Resort Vacation on Eleuthra,** *see* Olivia Cruises & Resorts
19 - 23 ♀ **Sierra Spring Sampler Ski Tour,** *see* Alpenglow Adventure Tours

June 99

TBA ♀♂ **Bay Area Regional Rodeo,** San Francisco, CA. Call: GSGRA, (415) 985-5200.

TBA ♀ **Camp SCWU,** A weekend of assorted activities and seminars, sponsored by Southern California Women for Understanding. Location: Pilgrim Pines, CA, in the San Bernadino Mountains. Contact: Southern California Women for Understanding, 7985 Santa Monica Blvd #207,

TRIP/EVENTS CALENDAR 39

Los Angeles, CA 90046, (213) 654-SCWU, fax: (213) 654-7268.

TBA ♀ **Campfest,** Five days of magic in a scenic, private camp near Oxford, PA. Workshops, day and evening live entertainment, crafts area, activities for singles, vegetarian and non-vegetarian meals, choice of cabin space or tenting, hot water and flush toilets, dining hall, olympic pool, sports, lake fishing, tennis and more. Held on Memorial Day weekend. Contact: Campfest, PO Box 559, Franklinville, NJ 08322, (609) 694-2037, e-mail: campfest@aol.com.

TBA ♀♂ **Canadian Rockies Int'l Rodeo,** Calgary, AB, Canada. Call: ARGRA, (403) 541-8140.

TBA ♀ **Club Skirts Harem Gala,** This women's party is held during Gay Day at Disney. Produced by MT productions & included in all travel packages from Good Time Gay Productions. Call: (888) 429-3527, (888) 539-7429, E-mail: gaydays@bridge.net or gayfla@bridge.net.

TBA ♀ **Euro Fun Cup '99,** Held in conjunction with Oslo's gay pride week, this tournament is open to all lesbians who play handball. Both teams and singles participate. In addition to lots of sport, there are many social activities and a final Great Cup party planned. Location: Oslo, Norway. Contact: S. Kvalheim, Orknoygt. 4, 0658 Oslo, Norway, (47) 2219 4080.

TBA ♀ **Femo Prideweek,** The Danish women's FemOcamp, in Maribo, is the setting for an international lesbian week. The themes of this year's event include how to maintain love & intimacy, sex without borders & limits, & being a lesbian in your own country. In addition to workshops, there is plenty of opportunity to participate in sports, sunbathe & relax. During this week English will be the main language. Contact: Forenningen Femo, Kvindehuset, Gothersgade 37, 1123 Copenhagen, Denmark.

TBA ♀ **Galapagos/Ecuador Cruise,** *see* Adventure Associates

TBA ♀ **Golden Threads Celebration,** A celebration for lesbians over 50 and their friends from the US, Canada, and other countries, held in Provincetown, MA. There is no age restriction and membership in Golden Threads is not required to participate. Events include workshops, a banquet, dance and live entertainment. Contact: Golden Threads, PO Box 60475, Northampton, MA 01060-0475. Web: http://members.aol.com/goldentred/index.htm

TBA ♀♂ **Heartland Regional Rodeo,** Omaha, NE. Call: HGRA, (800) 561-6918.

TBA ♀ **Hopland Women's Festival,** This annual women's festival takes place in a rural California area & features comedy, music and arts & crafts. There is camping available. Location: Hopland, CA. Contact: HWF, PO Box 416, Hopland, CA 95449.

TBA ♀♂ **Int'l Gay & Lesbian Badminton Tournament,** Europe's largest badminton tournament with various levels of competition, singles, doubles and a championship. Events also include a party and a farewell brunch. Location: Hamburg, Germany. Contact: Schwul/Lesbischer Sportverein Hamburg, Kleinerpulverteich 1721, 20099 Hamburg, Germany, (49-30) 215 9000, E-Mail: seitenwechsel.berlin@gaysport.org.

TBA ♀ **Nat'l Women's Music Festival (15th annual),** The '99 event was held in Muncie, Indiana, 1 hour NE of Bloomington, on the campus of Ball State University. Evening concerts, writer's and spirituality conferences, a full complement of intensive workshops, an older & young women's series, a performers' series, health, fitness, sexuality and sports series and a video series. Contact: National Women's Music Festival, PO Box 1427, Indianapolis, IN 46206-1427, (317) 927-9355, Fax: (317) 923-4995, E-mail: wia@indy.net.

TBA ♀♂ **Pride (Atlanta),** Contact Atlanta Pride Committee, 828 W Peachtree #206, Atlanta, GA 30308, (404) 876-3700.

TBA ♀♂ **Pride (Berlin),** Berlin, Germany. Contact local businesses for details.

TBA ♀♂ **Pride (Boise),** Boise, ID. Contact local gay businesses or e-mail: hrair@earthlink.net.

TBA ♀♂ **Pride (Boston),** Boston, MA. Contact local businesses for details.

TBA ♀♂ **Pride (Chicago),** Chicago, IL. Contact local businesses for details.

TBA ♀♂ **Pride (Copenhagen),** Gay pride festivities in Copenhagen, Denmark. Contact: Mermaid Pride, Borgmester Jensens Alle 23 C, Copenhagen 1666, Demark, (45) 35 43 73 70, Fax: (45) 33 32 03 00.

TBA ♀♂ **Pride (Denver),** Denver, CO. Contact local businesses for details.

TBA ♀♂ **Pride (Ft Lauderdale),** Events taking place in February & June. Contact local businesses for details or Pride South Florida, PO Box 24804, Ft Lauderdale, FL, (954) 561-2020.

TBA ♀♂ **Pride (Hartford),** Hartford, CT. Contact local businesses for details.

TBA ♀♂ **Pride (Houston),** Houston, TX. Contact local businesses for details. E-mail: info@pridehouston.org/.

TBA ♀♂ **Pride (Kansas City),** Kansas City, MO. Contact local businesses for details.

TBA ♀♂ **Pride (Key West),** Key West, FL. Contact: (305) 293-0494

TBA ♀♂ **Pride (Los Angeles),** Los Angeles, CA. Contact: (213) 860-0701, Email: Lapride@aol.com

TBA ♀♂ **Pride (Minneapolis),** Minneapolis, MN. Contact local businesses for details.

40 WHEN TO GO

TBA	♀♂	**Pride (New York City),** Gay pride festivities in New York City & Manhattan. Contact local gay businesses or e-mail: nycpride@aol.com.
TBA	♀♂	**Pride (Oslo),** Oslo, Norway. Contact local businesses for details.
TBA	♀♂	**Pride (San Francisco),** San Francisco, CA. Contact local businesses for details.
TBA	♀♂	**Pride (Seattle),** Seattle, WA. Contact local businesses for details.
TBA	♀♂	**Pride (Vienna),** Vienna, Austria. Contact local gay businesses or CSD Vienna, Berggasse 7, Vienna, Austria 1090, (43-1) 317 4031. E-mail: rainbow@via.at
TBA	♀♂	**Pride (Washington, DC),** Contact local businesses for details.
TBA	♀♂	**Queen's Birthday Weekend in Sydney,** A weekend of gay and lesbian parties are held annually in Sydney to commemorate the queen's birthday. Location: Sydney, Australia. Contact: Sydney Gay & Lesbian Mardi Gras, PO Box 1064, Darlinghurst, 2010, NSW, Australia.
TBA	♀	**Sappho Lesbian Witch Camp,** Join 35-40 women at a private campsite on Loon Lake, 40 miles east of Vancouver, BC Canada. This residential, week-long gathering of lesbians & lesbian-positive women features workshops, rituals, singing, drumming, an artisan's marketplace, great food (mostly vegetarian), and the opportunity to deepen our knowledge of women's spirituality. Contact: Sappho, PO Box 21510, 1850 Commercial Dr, Vancouver, BC V5N 4A0, Canada. Include 2 self-addressed envelopes (+ US $2 if outside Canada).
TBA	♀	**Women's Travel-Study Program in Greece,** see International Women's Studies Institute
TBA	♀	**Womongathering,** A warm and friendly festival for womyn only at a scenic, private camp. We feature local and nationally-recognized womyn spiritual leaders presenting intensive, experiential workshops reflecting the diversity of beliefs known as Womyn's Spirituality. The crafts area features womyn-made items, such as crystals, also readers, body workers and herbalists. Rain will not disturb your enjoyment, because our dining and workshop areas are covered. Location: In the Pocono Mts. Contact: Womongathering, Box 559, Franklinville, NJ 08322, (609) 694-2037, e-mail: womongathr@aol.com.
03 - 09	♀♂	**Bahamas Cruise,** see Ocean Voyager
11 - 13	♀	**Sea Kayaking,** see Women in Motion
15 - 22	♀	**Jungle Lodge in Manu National Park, Peru,** see South American Expeditions
18 - 20	♀	**Sea Kayaking,** see Women in Motion
30 - JY 11	♀♂	**Scandinavia & Russia Cruise,** see Ocean Voyager

July 99

TBA	♀	**Canoeing the Reisa River in Norway,** see Hawk, I'm Your Sister
TBA	♀	**Fairbanks Alaska Women's Fest,** Held over the July 4th weekend, this event begins with potluck-type gatherings at private homes, then blossoms into camping &/or enjoying the outdoors. We host name entertainers, as well as some of our own impromptu local talent. Vendors sell food, drink & T-shirts, and massage therapists are on hand. Contact: www.geocities.com/wellesley/8170; Tracy at Tracwa@webtv.net; Doris at fbxhotl.alaska.net; Louise at (907) 479-0618.
TBA	♀	**Fat Women's Gatherings,** These are gatherings, for women only, of large-sized women. Workshops, parties, swimming and a representation of vendors specializing in products for large-sized women, especially clothing, are included. This is not a lesbian organization, per se, but all fat women are most welcome. Location: Northern New Jersey. For all meetings, contact Carole Campbell, PO Box 1154, New York, NY 10023 (212) 721-8259.
TBA	♀♂	**I.G.R.A. Annual Convention,** Call IGRA, (303) 832-4472.
TBA	♀♂	**North Star Regional Rodeo,** St. Paul, MN. Call: NSGRA, (612) 641-0069.
TBA	♀♂	**Pink Monday at the Tilburg Fair,** This annual gay Monday held in July each year is the gay portion of a larger fair dating back 425 years. Approximately 25,000 gays & lesbians attend festivities at local gay establishments and other programmes. Location: Tilburg, The Netherlands. Contact: De GAY Krant, PO Box 10, NL-Best, The Netherlands, (31) 499 391 000, Fax: (31) 499 372 638, E-mail: gaykrant@pop3.worldaccess.nl.
TBA	♀♂	**Pride (London),** London ,England. Contact local businesses for details or (44-171) 737 6903, E-mail: info@pride.org.uk.
TBA	♀♂	**Pride (San Diego),** San Diego, CA. Contact local businesses for details.
TBA	♀♂	**Rocky Mtn. Regional Rodeo,** Denver, CO. Call: IGRA, (303) 839-8810.
10 - 25	♀♂	**Budapest, Prague, Salzburg, Vienna,** see David's Trips and Tours
10 - 25	♀♂	**Fantasy Tour of South Africa,** see David's Trips and Tours
24 - 31	♀	**Cruise to Greece & Turkey on the club Med II,** see Olivia Cruises & Resorts
24 - AG 05	♀♂	**Alaska by Rail Cruise & Tour,** see Ocean Voyager
28 - AG 03	♀	**Jungle Lodge in Manu National Park, Peru,** see South American Expeditions

TRIP/EVENTS CALENDAR 41

August 99

TBA	♀♂	**Greater Motown Int'l Rodeo,** Detroit, MI. Call: MIGRA, (313) 438-1305, ext 3.
TBA	♀	**Midwest Womyn's Autumnfest (5th annual),** Labor Day weekend. A one-day outdoor womyn's music & cultural festival held in a meadow, with workshops, craftswomyn, theater & performing arts. Work exchange available. Approximately 1,500 womyn are expected to attend this 3rd annual event. Electricity & flush toilets on site. Location: Dekalb, IL. Contact: Athena Productions, 217 S 2nd St #193, Dekalb, IL 60115, (815) 748-5359, e-mail: Autumnfest@aol.com.
TBA	♀♂	**Pride (Amsterdam),** Amsterdam, Netherlands. Contact local businesses for details.
TBA	♀♂	**Rodeo Wichita,** Wichita, KS. Call: IGRA (303) 832-4472.
TBA	♀♂	**Windy City Gay Rodeo,** Chicago, IL. Call: ILGRA, (773) 477-5793.
TBA	♀♂	**Zia Regional Rodeo,** Albuquerque, NM. Call: NMGRA, (505) 255-5045.
01 - 13	♀	**Women's Grand Canyon Trip,** see Mariah Wilderness Expeditions
05 - 13	♀♂	**Solar Eclipse, Greece, Turkey, Black Sea Cruise,** see Ocean Voyager
06	♀	**Midwest Womyn's Autumnfest (4th annual),** A one-day outdoor womyn's music & cultural festival held in a meadow, with workshops, craftswomyn, theater & performing arts. Work exchange available. Approximately 1,500 womyn are expected to attend this 3rd annual event. Electricity & flush toilets on site. Location: Dekalb, IL. Contact: Athena Productions, 217 S 2nd St #193, Dekalb, IL 60115, (815) 748-5359, e-mail: Autumnfest@aol.com.
07 - 22	♀♂	**Luxury Tour of Budapest, Prague, Salzburg, Vienna,** see David's Trips and Tours
20 - 22	♀	**Whitewater Rafting,** see Women in Motion
20 - 26	♀♂	**EuroGames,** The European gay & lesbian sports championships featuring events such as basketball, soccer, bowling, handball, swimming, table-tennis, chess & ballroom dancing. 4,000 people expected to attend. Location: Manchester, England. Contact: eurogames99@gaysport.org, http://www.gaysport.org.
24 - 31	♀	**Jungle Lodge in Manu National Park, Peru,** see South American Expeditions
30 - SE 06	♀♂	**Classic Greek Cruise With Crete, Mykonos,** see RSVP Travel Productions/Club RSVP

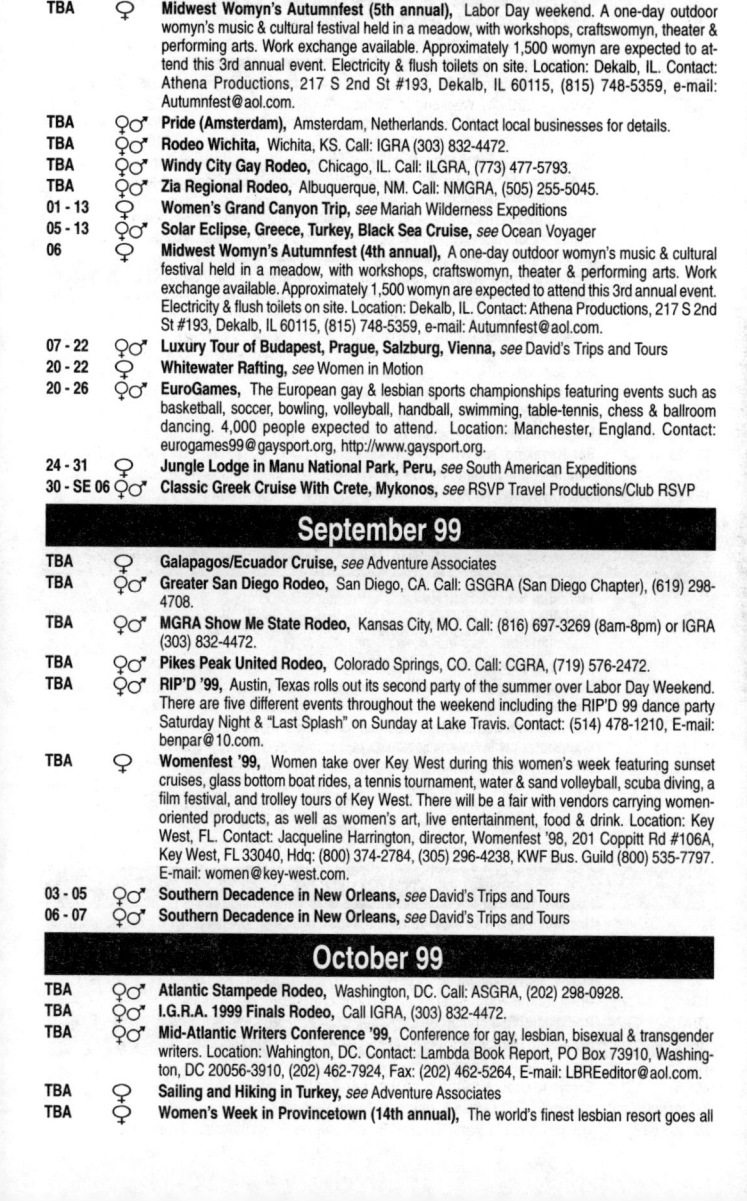

September 99

TBA	♀	**Galapagos/Ecuador Cruise,** see Adventure Associates
TBA	♀♂	**Greater San Diego Rodeo,** San Diego, CA. Call: GSGRA (San Diego Chapter), (619) 298-4708.
TBA	♀♂	**MGRA Show Me State Rodeo,** Kansas City, MO. Call: (816) 697-3269 (8am-8pm) or IGRA (303) 832-4472.
TBA	♀♂	**Pikes Peak United Rodeo,** Colorado Springs, CO. Call: CGRA, (719) 576-2472.
TBA	♀♂	**RIP'D '99,** Austin, Texas rolls out its second party of the summer over Labor Day Weekend. There are five different events throughout the weekend including the RIP'D 99 dance party Saturday Night & "Last Splash" on Sunday at Lake Travis. Contact: (514) 478-1210, E-mail: benpar@10.com.
TBA	♀	**Womenfest '99,** Women take over Key West during this women's week featuring sunset cruises, glass bottom boat rides, a tennis tournament, water & sand volleyball, scuba diving, a film festival, and trolley tours of Key West. There will be a fair with vendors carrying women-oriented products, as well as women's art, live entertainment, food & drink. Location: Key West, FL. Contact: Jacqueline Harrington, director, Womenfest '98, 201 Coppitt Rd #106A, Key West, FL 33040, Hdq: (800) 374-2784, (305) 296-4238, KWF Bus. Guild (800) 535-7797. E-mail: women@key-west.com.
03 - 05	♀♂	**Southern Decadence in New Orleans,** see David's Trips and Tours
06 - 07	♀♂	**Southern Decadence in New Orleans,** see David's Trips and Tours

October 99

TBA	♀♂	**Atlantic Stampede Rodeo,** Washington, DC. Call: ASGRA, (202) 298-0928.
TBA	♀♂	**I.G.R.A. 1999 Finals Rodeo,** Call IGRA, (303) 832-4472.
TBA	♀♂	**Mid-Atlantic Writers Conference '99,** Conference for gay, lesbian, bisexual & transgender writers. Location: Wahington, DC. Contact: Lambda Book Report, PO Box 73910, Washington, DC 20056-3910, (202) 462-7924, Fax: (202) 462-5264, E-mail: LBREditor@aol.com.
TBA	♀	**Sailing and Hiking in Turkey,** see Adventure Associates
TBA	♀	**Women's Week in Provincetown (14th annual),** The world's finest lesbian resort goes all

42 WHEN TO GO

out for this week-long, town-wide extravaganza. Special gallery exhibitions, workshops & seminars, the biggest and brightest names in women's entertainment, community dinner and, of course, the formal prom are why thousands of women make this so much fun! Sponsored by the Women Innkeepers of Provincetown. Make reservations early. Location: Provincetown, MA. Contact: Box 573, Provincetown, MA 02657 FMI.

| 21 - 31 | ♀♂ | **New England Fall Foliage Cruise,** *see* Ocean Voyager |

November 99

TBA	♀♂	**Texas Gay Rodeo (16th annual),** Houston, TX. Call: TGRA (Houston chapter), (713) 777-1444.
06 - 14	♀♂	**Ultra-Luxurious Morocco, Casablanca and More,** *see* David's Trips and Tours
06 - 21	♀♂	**Ultra-Luxurious South Africa Tour,** *see* David's Trips and Tours
08 - 13	♀	**Baja California, Mexico,** *see* Women in Motion
18 - 21	♀	**Baja, California Mexico,** *see* Women in Motion
20 - 26	♀♂	**Project Eagle Thanksgiving East Caribbean Cruise,** *see* Ocean Voyager

December 99

TBA	♀♂	**A Dickens Xmas in London & 1999 New Years in Paris,** *see* Going Your Way Tours
TBA	♀♂	**Colossus V (Dallas),** Cheer Dallas presents its smashing, 5th annual New Year's Eve party that attracts nearly 5,000 people from all over the world. For tickets & location information call: (214) 521-9111.
TBA	♀♂	**Exclusive 21st Century Time Travel Adventure,** *see* L'Arc en Ciel Voyages
TBA	♀♂	**Holly Folly (3rd annual),** Holiday festivities taking place all weekend include: a Snow Ball Dance, His & Hers Santas, caroling, a Reindeer Run and open houses at some of Provincetown's cozy & warm B&Bs. Location: Provincetown, MA. Contact: Women Innkeepers of P'town, PO Box 573, Provincetown, MA, (800) 933-1963.
TBA	♀♂	**Millennium New Years in Oaxaca, Mexico,** *see* Spirit Journeys
TBA	♀♂	**New Years Millennium Caribbean Cruise,** *see* Ocean Voyager
TBA	♀♂	**Pied Piper Millenium Cruises,** *see* Pied Piper Travel
19 - JA 02	♀	**Peru and Macchupicchu for New Year's 1999,** *see* Mariah Wilderness Expeditions
25 - JA 02	♀♂	**Millenium New Years in Morocco,** *see* David's Trips and Tours
26 - JA 02	♀	**Millenium New Years in Hawaii,** *see* Women in Motion
26 - JA 02	♀	**Millennium New Year's in Cuzco, Macchu Picchu,** *see* South American Expeditions
26 - JA 04	♀♂	**Millenium New Years in Rio,** *see* Sundance Travel
26 - JA 06	♀	**Sea Kayak Baja for New Year's 1999,** *see* Mariah Wilderness Expeditions
26 - JA 09	♀♂	**Millenium New Years in South Africa,** *see* David's Trips and Tours
26 - JA 09	♀♂	**New Years 1999 in South African Summer with Luxury,** *see* David's Trips and Tours
29 - JA 02	♀♂	**Millenium New Years in New Orleans,** *see* David's Trips and Tours
29 - JA 02	♀♂	**New Years 1999 in Vienna or New Orleans,** *see* David's Trips and Tours
30 - JA 02	♀	**Millennium New Years in San Francisco,** *see* Women in Motion
31	♀♂	**Miami Millenium,** A party Incorporating all 4 halls of the Miami Beach Convention Center, there will be over 200,000 square feet of dancing & 4 different themes: Carnival in Rio, Gay Paris, Sydney Mardi Gras & New York's Times Square. Location: Miami Beach, FL.

April 2000

| 30 | ♀♂ | **Millennium March on Washington,** The fourth March on Washington, DC, aims to articulate the concerns of the gay/lesbian/bi/transgendered community and focus our nation's attention on our quest for equality in all aspects of life. Contact: March On Washington, (818) 891-1748, Email: MMOW2000@aol.com, or Human Rights Campaign, (202) 628-4160, Fax: (202) 347-5323. |

December 2000

| TBA | ♀♂ | **Year 2000 Millenium in Sydney, Fiji, Rio or Paris,** *see* Above & Beyond Tours |

AFRICA

KENYA

COUNTRY CODE: (254)

NAIROBI

Retail & Bookstores
BINTI LEGACY, THE, Write: PO Box 68077, Nairobi., Women's bookstore.

NAMIBIA

COUNTRY CODE: (264),

WINDHOEK

Information
NAMIBIAN GAY & LESBIAN ADVICE BUREAU, 644 007 20, answers 19:00-22:00.

RAINBOW PROJECT, Write: PO Box 26122, Windhoek, Fax: (061) 236 371, gay & lesbian organization.

NIGERIA

COUNTRY CODE: (234),

CALABAR

Information
GIRLS' POWER INITIATIVE, Write: GPI, PO Box 3663, Unical Post Office, Calabar, Group promoting the rights, education, protection & advancement of girls in Nigeria.

SOUTH AFRICA

COUNTRY CODE: (27),

BLOEMFONTEIN

Bars
BLOEMFONTEIN CLUB, (051) 228 720. Party held by the Gay Association of Bloemfontein, Sat till 03:00.

CAPE TOWN

Information
AIDS INFO, (021) 215 420, 24hrs.
HELPLINE, (021) 222 500.

Women's Accommodations
OWL AND THE PUSSYCAT, THE, 56 Jefferson Rd, Milkwood Park, Noordhoek, Cape Town, 7975, (27-21) 785 2454 (Tel/Fax)." Lesbian-owned & -operated women-only B&B guesthouse with bar. Breathtaking beaches, mountain walks, scenic drived, 5 min from ocean & 30 min drive from Cape Town nightlife.

Bars
ANGELS, 27 Somerset Rd, Greenpoint, (021) 419 9216. From 20:00, 3-bar complex.

BRUNSWICK TAVERN, 17 Bree St, (021) 25 27 39, 08:00-03:00 (Sun from 11:00).

EIGHTEAST, 72 Waterkant St, De Waterkant, (021) 25 24 78.

Dance Bar/Disco
BRENDA'S BASH, Milton Rd, Goodwood Sports Complex, Goodwood, (083) 250 1195, monthly women's dance nights, call for schedule.

DETOUR, 27 Somerset Rd, Greenpoint, at Angels bar complex, (021) 419 9216, from 20:00.

RAINBOWS, Voortrekker Rd, at the Park Court Lodge, 1st floor, Bellville, (021) 948 0911, daily from 10:00.

Cafe
ALLADDIN COFFEE SHOP, Kloof Rd, at the Nedbank Centre, shop 7, Sea Point, (021) 439 44 28, 08:00-18:00 (Sat till 16:00), Sun 09:00-15:00.

CAFE MANHATTAN, 74 Waterkant St, De Waterkant, (021) 418 7843.

Restaurants
AFRICA CAFE, 213 Lower Main Rd, Observatory, (021) 47 95 53, 18:30-01:00.

CAFE ERTE, 265a Main Rd, Sea Point, (021) 434 6624, restaurant & coffee bar, 20:00-06:00.

CLEMENTINES, Wolfe St, in Chelsea Village, Wynberg, (021) 797 6168, intimate atmosphere.

DINNER CLUB, THE, 10 Leeuwenhog Road, Higgovale, (021) 24 08 04, private & arranged-in-advance dinner parties for 6-10 people, monthly murder mystery evenings.

ELAINE'S CURRY BISTRO, 105 Lower Main Rd, Observatory, (021) 448 1979, Mon-Fri 12:30-14:30 & 18:30-24:00 (Sat & Sun 18:00-24:00 only).

44 SOUTH AFRICA

L'ORIENT, 50 Main Rd, Three Anchor Bay, (021) 439 6572, from 19:00 (closed Mon), Southeast Asian cuisine. 🚫

LITTLE RIO, 171a Buitenkant St, Gardens, (021) 45 07 28, from 18:00.

ON BROADWAY, 21 Somerset Rd, 1st floor, (021) 418 8338, cabaret & dinner, reservations required. ♀♂

DURBAN

■ Accommodations

PALM RIDGE GUESTHOUSE, 62 Cherry Ave, Berea, Durban, Kwa-Zulu, Natal, 4001, (27-31) 282 071, (27-31) 281 013, Fax: (27-31) 304 4349. Single/double suite in a private home, private entrance & private facilities, full breakfast.

■ Bars

CLUB, THE, 301 Umbilo Rd, (031) 304 4091, bar & restaurant, membership available, closed Wed. 🍴 🎵 ♀♂

■ Dance Bar/Disco

CLUB 330, 330 Point Rd, Sat disco. 🎵 ♀♂
FELINE GROOVY, 330 Point Rd, (031) 84 96 11, women's dance night 1st Fri from 21:00. 🎵 ♀

■ Cafe

CAFE JUNGLE RENDEZVOUS, 814 Jan Smuts Hwy, Sherwood, Thai & Indonesian cuisine, serves breakfast, lunch & tea.

■ Restaurants

BISTRO 136, 136 Florida Rd, Morningside, 303 3440.

GARTH'S PLACE, 9th Ave at the Avonmore Centre, Morningside, from 18:00 (Sat, Sun from 16:00).

TWO MOON JUNCTION, 45 Windermere Rd, Morningside, (031) 303 3078, from 09:00 till late, closed Sun. 🚫

EAST LONDON

■ Dance Bar/Disco

THUMPERS, Recreation Rd, Fri & Sat from 20:00. 🎵 🕺 ♀♂

EAST RAND

■ Bars

BARN, THE, 73 6th Road, Cloverdene, (011) 968 2719. 🎵 ♂

BIRDCAGE, 50 Surprise Rd, Brentwood Park, Benoni, (011) 963 1188, daily from 10:00. 📧 🎵 ♀♂

ON THE ROCKS, 163 Meyer St, Germiston, (083) 763 7093. 📧 🎵 ♀♂

GARDEN ROUTE AREA

■ Accommodations

BLISS FLATLITS, 12 Faure Street, West Hill, Knysna, on the Cape, 6570, (27-445) 24569 (Tel/Fax)." Two self-catering cottages with private baths, expanded, full or continental breakfast, color TV, kitchenette, nearby beach & lagoon. 50% gay/lesbian clientele.

JOHANNESBURG

■ Information

AIDS INFO, (011) 725 6710, or AIDS Life Line: (0800) 0123 22.

LESBIAN FORUM, (011) 336 5081, support group for lesbians.

■ Accommodations

COTTAGES, THE, 30 Gill St, Observatory, Johannesburg, 2198, (27-11) 487 2829, Fax: (27-11) 487 2404. Separate stone & thatched cottages, private baths, country garden, no smoking in dining room, 10 minutes from gay clubs, 15% gay & lesbian clientele.

JOEL HOUSE, 61 Joel Rd nr Lily Rd, Berea, Johannesburg, 2198, (27-11) 642 4426, Fax: (27-11) 642 5221. gay-friendly guest house with restaurant, private baths, full breakfast, ceiling fans, TV lounge, nearby pool."

ROSLIN HOUSE, (27-11) 487 2402. Gay & lesbian luxury B&B guesthouse 10 minutes from Johannesburg gay nightlife, pool on premises. 🏖 ♀♂

THEME GUEST LODGE, 60 Joel Rd, across from Joel House, (011) 484 5730. 70% men, 30% women. ♂

TWIN STEEPLES, 100 Ascot Rd, Judith's Paarl, Johannesburg, 0084, (27-11) 614 7529 (Tel/Fax)." Gay-friendly B&B in a listed Victorian house, near trendy Rockey St & gay bar locations. Accommodations are NOT upmarket, but nice, comfortable & clean with shared baths. Breakfast & dinner included in extremely reasonable rates.

■ Bars

CHAMPIONS, Wolmarans St, at Loveday St, Braamfontein, (011) 720 6605, from 13:00. 🎵 🎶 ♀♂

SOUTH AFRICA

HUBCAP, 3 Urania St, Observatory, (011) 487 2402, women only Wed & Fri from 19:30.

MINNELLI'S, 185a Oxford Rd, Rosebank, (011) 442 2836, daily from 11:00. Disco Wed-Sat from 21:00.

PAUSE AWHILE, Wits Campus, at The Boz, (083) 725 9723, 1st Sat.

SASHAY SOUTH, Johannesburg St, at 5th St, La Rochelle, (011) 435 1757, from 17:00.

TOGS BAR, Putney Rd, at the Togs Sports & Rec. Centre, Brixton, (011) 837 5056, tea & coffee bar, Sun from 15:00.

Dance Bar/Disco

INIQUITY, 59a Raleigh St, Yeoville, (083) 271 4895, daily from 12:00.

KRYPTON, 17 Constantia Centre, at Tyrwhitt Ave, Rosebank, (011) 788 4708, Wed & Sat from 18:00.

QUEEN, 17 Constantia Centre, Tyrshitt Ave, Rosebank, (011) 788 4708, Fri from 18:00.

THERAPY, Henri St at Juta St, at the GASS Complex, Braamfontein, Sat from 22:00.

Restaurants

NINETY SIX DEGREES, Constantia Centre, same level as Krypton, Rosebank, (011) 442 3050.

SCOOZA MI, 4th Ave at 13th St, Parkhurst, (011) 442 7778.

Retail & Bookstores

ESTORIL, Pretoria St, Hillbrow, (011) 643 1613, gay magazines.

EXCLUSIVE BOOKS, Village Walk, (011) 884 7591, general bookstore with gay & lesbian section. Other locations: Hyde Park Corner, Hyde Park; Victoria Wharf, Waterfront, Constantia Village Shopping Centre, Constantia."

KIMBERLEY

Bars

STALLIONS ACTION BAR, Stockdale St, at Queens Hotel, cruisy, 2 bars (1 for men, 1 for women).

Restaurants

MARIO'S, Dutoitspan Road, close to Holiday Inn Garden Court, Mon-Sat 10:00-23:00.

KLERKSDORP

Bars

COTTON CLUB, North St, (018) 462 9924, from 19:00.

NYLSTROOM

Accommodations

SHANGRI-LA COUNTRY LODGE, Eersbewoond Rd, PO Box 262, Nylstroom, 0510, (27-14) 717 53 81, Fax: (27-14) 717 31 88. gay-friendly country lodge with restaurant & bar, 1 hour north of Pretoria, private baths, buffet breakfast.

PIKETBERG

Accommodations

NOUPOORT GUEST FARM, PO Box 101, Piketberg, 7320, (27) 261 5754/5856, Fax: (27) 261 5834. Email: noupoort@iafrica.com, Gay-friendly guest farm with 10 cottages, gay weekends arranged, TV lounge, conference room, BBQ, pool, sauna & basic work-out gym.

PORT ELIZABETH

Information

GAY & LESBIAN HELPLINE, (041) 335 6426, 18:00-22:00, ask for GLAC.

Bars

RICH'S, Lincoln House, 3rd floor, at Kemp & Strand Streets, Wed, Fri-Sun from 20:00.

Dance Bar/Disco

ZIPPS, Hancock St at Drury St, North End, Wed, Fri-Sat from 21:00.

Restaurants

CUYLER CRESCENT GUESTHOUSE, 19 Cuyler Crescent, (014) 55 36 72, serves breakfast & dinner, Victorian tea garden. Reservations required.

PRETORIA

Information

AIDS INFO, (012) 308 8743.

GLO-P (GAYS & LESBIANS OF PRETORIA), 255 Charles St, Brooklyn, (012) 469 888, 19:00-22:00, closed Sat-Mon. Gay library Tues 19:30-21:30.

Bars

BULL'S EYE, Hamilton St at Schoeman St, over Savers Cafe, daily from 19:00.

COCK'S EYE, 95 Gerrit Moerdyk St, Sunnyside, (012) 341 6941, pub & restaurant. ♀♂

YEARLING, THE, Rissik St at Mears St, over College Cafe, (012) 341 9293, from 20:00. 🎵 📺 ♂

SOUTH COAST

■ Accommodations
STARBASE, Port Edward, (03930) 32891. Accommodation with bar, restaurant & observatory.

■ Bars
ASTRONAUTS & CONSTELLATIONS AT STARBASE, Port Edward, (03930) 32891, bar & restaurant, Fri & Sat (bar from 19:00). 📺 ♀♂

BIRDCAGE, Main Rd beside Gypsey World, Ramsgate, (03931) 79097 or (082) 556 9875, 18:00-02:00 (Sat, Sun from 12:00). ✘ 📺 ♂

WARMBATHS

■ Accommodations
ELEPHANT SPRINGS HOTEL, 31 Sutter St, Warmbaths, 0480, (27-14) 736 21 01, Fax: (27-14) 736 35 86. Gay-friendly B&B with restaurant & bar, private baths, full breakfast. 🛏

WELKOM

■ Dance Bar/Disco
CLUB PRETENDERS, Stateway, (057) 352 4143 or (083) 262 3556, Fri & Sat from 21:00. 🎵 📺 ♂

ZIMBABWE

COUNTRY CODE: (263)

HARARE

■ Information
GALZ (GAYS & LESBIANS OF ZIMBABWE), Write: Private Bag A6131, Avondale, Harare, gay & lesbian group.

WOMEN'S ACTION GROUP, Write: Box 135, Harare, women's organization.

ZWRCN (ZIMBABWE WOMEN'S RESOURCE CENTRE & NETWORK), 288A Herbert Chitepo Ave, 737 435, library Mon-Fri 08:30-12:30, Sat 09:30-12:00. For info write PO Box 2192, Harare.

EAST ASIA
CHINA

COUNTRY CODE: (86)

COUNTRYWIDE

■ Information
LAVENDER PHOENIX, mail to: J.Lee, 14682 Charloma Dr, Tustin, CA, 92780, Chinese gay & lesbian organization, also available through email at lavender_phoenix@hotmail.com or lavenderphoenix@juno.com.

BEIJING

■ Bars
JJ'S, not a gay bar, but frequented by local gays, ask locally for address.

■ Dance Bar/Disco
NIGHTMAN DISCO, not far from the Radisson Hotel, look for red neon sign, not a gay disco, discreetly frequented by gays who stay more to the right of the DJ area. 📺

■ Cafe
HALF & HALF CAFE, San Li Tun, South 15 Bldg, Chao Yang District, (10) 6416 6919, not a gay cafe, more gay Wed, Fri & Sat evenings.

GUANGZHOU

■ Bars
FOURTY-SECOND STREET, 399 Huanshi Dong Lu, frequented by local gays. ✘

L'AFRICAIN, Dongfeng Dong Lu, at Xiniu Lu, early eveninings till late, more gays Sat.

ROCK & ROLL CLUB, near Guanhzhou & White Swan hotels, on north bank of Pearl River, more gay after 23:00. 📺

■ Restaurants
CAVE, THE, ask locally for address, restaurant & bar, many foreigners. 🍴

MILANO, 3-103 Xin Chen Bei Jie, Tianhe Dong Lu, Italian cuisine.

HONG KONG

■ Information
AIDS HOTLINE, 2898 4422, Thurs, Sat 19:00-22:00.

HONG KONG 10%, 2314 8726, gay organization with scheduled socials & events, answers in Chinese only.

HORIZONS, 2815 9268, gay organization, answers Mon-Thurs 19:30-22:30, scheduled socials.

QUEER SISTERS, 2314 4348, lesbian organization, answers in Cantonese, meets 2nd Sun at CE Top bar.

■ Bars

BABYLON, 409-413 Jaffe Rd, Kingspower Commercial Bldg, 5th floor, Wanchai, Hong Kong, 2573 3978, karaoke lounge, 20:00-02:00. ♂

CE TOP, 37-43 Cochrane St, 9th floor, Central Hong Kong, 2544 3581, karaoke bar, lounge & dance bar, 20:00-03:00. More women Sun. 🎤 ♂

CIRCUS CLUB, 2-6 Yee Woo St, Ying Kong Mansions, 11th floor, Causeway Bay, Hong Kong, 2576 5680, biggest karaoke lounge in Hong Kong, 20:00-02:00, younger crowd. ♂

FIRESIDE BAR, 37-43 Cochrane St, Cheung Hing Commercial Bldg, at CE Top bar, Central Hong Kong, 2544 3584, karaoke. ♂

G SPOT, 468 Jaffe Rd, Allways Center 3rd floor, Causeway Bay, Hong Kong, 2838 1456, karaoke lounge. ♂

GARAGE, 35 Peel St, Central Hong Kong, 2542 1488, bar & restaurant on 2 levels, 12:00-24:00 (closed Sun). ✕ ♂

H2O, 474-476 Lockhart Rd, Hop Yee Bldg, 2nd floor, Causeway Bay, Hong Kong, 2834 6451, karaoke lounge, 20:00-04:00. More women Fri-Sat. ♂

SECRET PARTY, 468 Jaffe Rd, Allways Centre, 6th floor, Causeway Bay, 2890 7731, men welcome. ♀

VELVET KARAOKE, 220 Gloucester Rd, Causeway Bay, Hong Kong, 2891 1338, karaoke lounge, from 22:00. Lesbians Mon & Wed. ♀♂

WHY NOT, 491-499 Lockhart Rd, Kyoto Plaza 12th floor, Causeway Bay, Hong Kong, 2572 7808, karaoke lounge, 20:00-02:00. ♂

XX, Lan Kwai Fong, at Club 64, Central Hong Kong, 1108 18318, women-only socials, last Sun 17:00-20:00. ♀

■ Dance Bar/Disco

CLUB 97, 9 Lan Kwai Fong, Central Hong Kong, 2810 9333, gay Fri 18:00-22:00. Horizons gay group holds Tea dance 1st Sun 18:00-21:00. 🎤 ♀♂

★ **PROPAGANDA DANCE CLUB,** 1 Hollywood Rd, lower level, Central Hong Kong, 2868 1316, disco & lounge, 21:30-03:30 (usually closed Sun). 🎤 ♂

■ Leathers/Piercing

FETISH FASHION, 52-60 Lynhurst Terrace, Central Hong Kong, 2544 1155, men's & women's rubber & leather clothing and accessories, open Mon-Sat.

KOWLOON

■ Bars

WALLY MATT LOUNGE, 9 Cornwall Ave, Tsim Sha Tsui, 2367 6874. frequented by some gays, 18:00-03:00. ✕ ▨

■ Cafe

DATELINE, 11-15 Chatham Rd, Chatham Centre, 3rd floor, 2316 2962, frequented by local gays.

SHANGHAI

■ Bars

BAHAMA MAMAS, ask locally for address, bar & cafe with younger crowd, not a gay, discreetly frequented by gays, till 04:00.

LA CAFE, ask locally for address, trendy, not a gay bar, discreetly frequented by gays, more gay after 22:00. 🎤

■ Dance Bar/Disco

DD'S, ask locally for address, DJs, not a gay bar but frequented by gays, foreigners. 🎤

JUDY'S TOO, 176 Mao Ming Lu, 6473 1417 disco, bar & restaurant, not gay but frequented by gays. ✕ 🎤

■ Restaurants

FRANKIE'S PLACE, 81 Tong Ten Rd, 6247 0886.

MALONE'S AMERICAN CAFE, 255 Tong Ten Rd, 6247 2400. ♪

JAPAN

COUNTRY CODE: (81),

GETTING AROUND JAPAN:, If you're not sure whether you'll be welcome in a bar, call first. Your language ability in Japanese, English, French, German, etc, may be

JAPAN

gh to make you welcome. Otherwise, pick a place where you can be understood & where you can understand what is going on. Not all bars listed here have English-speaking staff; many Japanese are embarassed that they don't speak English well. If you're visiting for several weeks or more, a little Japanese language study on your part may be helpful. Besides, it's a great icebreaker.

FUJISAWA

■ *Information*
KANAGAWA WOMEN'S CENTER, 1-11-1 Enoshima, Fujisawa City, (0466) 27 2111.

KYOTO

■ *Information*
AIDS POSTER PROJECT, at Artscape gay & lesbian meeting space, (075) 771 6711, call for exact address & schedule of activities. ♀♂

■ *Bars*
METRO, take the Keihan train to Marutacho Stn, take exit #2, (075) 752 4765, even Fri from 21:00, some men.
NOT STRAIGHT, (052) 935 0090, regular parties for men & women, call for schedule. ♀♂

■ *Retail & Bookstores*
SHOKADO, Nishi-iru, Nishitoin, Shimodachiuri, Kamigyo-ku, Tel/fax: (075) 441 6905, women's bookstore, Mon-Fri 10:00-17:30.

OKAYAMA

■ *Bars*
SUGATA, New Oka Bldg, B1 floor, (0862) 258 922, women-only bar, 18:00-03:00. ♀

OSAKA

■ *Information*
OSAKA GAY COMMUNITY, 6-1-26 Tenbigado, Matsubara City, (0723) 30 0870, monthly Sunday discussion groups.
WAKKATTA PLANNING, 5-3 Enoki-cho, Suita-shi, (06) 389 0044, Fax: (06) 389 1139, women's workshops, meeting rooms for rent for parties & events. They also hold their own events. If you don't speak Japanese, bring an interpreter in order to benefit from visit. Have interpreter call ahead.

WOMEN'S INFORMATION CENTER (DAWN CENTER), Otemae 2-chome, Chuo-ku, (06) 942 3821, information, library & referral center run by the city government. Can inform you of all women's organizations in the city.

■ *Bars*
DAYARUIN, 2-3-17 Higashi Shinsaibashi, Osaka-shi, Papillon Bldg 3rd fl, Chuo-ku, (06) 212 2084, women only Sat 18:30-23:30. ♀
EURIKAGO, 8-12 Kamiyama-cho, Osaka-fu, Kita-ku, 20:00-09:00 (Mon from 01:00, Sun 19:00-12:00), closed 3rd Sun. ✗ ♀
KUREY JENNY, 1-4-26 Dojima, Tamaya Bldg B1, Osaka-shi, Kita-ku, (06) 345 5284, 3rd Sat 19:00-24:00. ♀
LESBIAN NIGHT, 3-3-8 Nakazaki Nishi, Osaka-shi, Kita-ku, at Club Down, (06) 373 4919, 3rd Sun 19:00-24:00. ♀
MS. TERIOUS, 1-16-12 Nishi Shinsaibashi, Osaka-shi, New American Plaza 7 FD, Chuo-ku, (06) 281 1066, 19:00-03:00 (closed Tues), some gay men. ♀
PIPELINE, in the Takeda Bldg, lower level, Kita-ku, (06) 362 0441, women welcome. ♂
SHOW UP PUB, 2-14-10 Sonezaki, Umeda Royal Bldg 4th fl, Kita-ku, (06) 314 3935, closed Sun & national holidays. ♀

■ *Retail & Bookstores*
MS. CRAYON HOUSE, 5-3 Enoki-cho, Suita City, (06) 330 8071, Fax: (06) 330 8075, women's bookstore, 11:00-19:00, 7 days.

TOKYO

■ *Information*
INT'L FEMINISTS OF JAPAN, 3793 6241. Feminist group, write c/o AGORA, 1-9-6 Shinjuku, Shinjuku-ku, Tokyo. Unverifiable spring '97.
REGUMI STUDIO TOKYO, c/o JOKI, 3F Nakazawa Bld, 23 Araki-cho, Shinjuku, (03) 3226 8314 (tape machine), lesbian drop-in center every Sat evening. Call first, schedule changes. Women can call Meiko (044) 987 3417 before 21:00."
TOKYO INT'L DRAGON CLUB, Room 207 Nomura Bldg, 5-3 Yochoucho, Shinjuku-ku, (03) 5379 9660, Sat & Sun 10:00-23:00, meeting place for gays & lesbians, offers info to foreigners living in & traveling to Tokyo. ♀♂

TOKYO WOMEN'S FOUNDATION, Tokyo Metropolitan Government, Marunouchi Bldg 6F, 3-8-1 Marunouchi Chiyoda-ku, (03) 3213 0021, Fax: (03) 3213 0185, women's information center run by the city government.

TOKYO WOMEN'S INFORMATION CENTER, Central Plaza 15F, 1-1, Kaguragashi, Shinjuku-ku, (03) 3235 1140, women's information center run by the city government, Tues-Sat 9:00-20:00 (Sun till 17:00). Approved application necessary for use of facilities. Lobby area open to visitors for informal use."

■ Bars

BAR FRIDA, 1-7 Yotsuya, Sobi Bldg 1st fl, Shinjuku-ku, (03) 3358 7922, Sat at the Han Gallery Cafe. 🎵 ♀

HANAKO, 2-15-8 Shinjuku, Shinjuku-ku, (03) 3352 4862, friendly & cozy bar, 20:00-03:00 (closed Thurs). ♀

HUG, 2-15-8 Shinjuku, Shinjuku-ku, (03) 5379 5085, butch & femme roles strictly adhered to, 01:00-09:00 (Sat from 24:00), closed Sun. ♀

KINSMEN, 2-18-5 Shinjuku, Shinjuku-ku, Oda Bldg, 2nd floor, 3354 4949, popular bar, mostly gay/lesbian clientele, 21:00-05:00 (closed Tues). ♂

KINSWOMYN, 2-15-10 Shinjuku, Shinjuku-ku, in the Daiichi Tenka Bldg, 3rd floor, 3354 8720, women-only bar. ♀

MADAME MAR, 5-min walk from Mars Bar, ask locally for exact address, (03) 3354 7515. ♀

MADONNA, 2-15-13 Shinjuku, Shinjuku-ku, in the Fujita Bldg, 1st floor, 3354 1330, women-only bar. ♀

MARS BAR, 2-15-13 Shinjuku, Shinjuku-ku, in the Hosono Bldg, 3rd floor, 3354 7923, women-only bar, a bit expensive. Manager, Mar, speaks good English and is helpful to travelers, phone for directions." ♀

MOONSHINER, near Sunny Bar, (03) 3355 6938, call for address. ♀

NEW MARILYN, 2-28-16 Kabukicho, 4th fl, Shinjuku-ku, (03) 3200 3168, onabe bar (butch bartenders & hosts, frequented by femme lesbians & straight women), 22:00-07:30. ♀

NEW SAZAE, 2-18-5 Shinjuku, Shinjuku-ku, in the Ishikawa Bldg, 2nd floor, 3354 1745, busy after 24:00, many women." ♀♂

SALON POSITIVE, 8-13-19 Imperial Ichibankan B1, Akasaka, Minato-ku, in club Antibes, (03) 3470 7431, monthly party, women only 20:00-23:30, men welcome from 23:30. Call for schedule. ♀

SUNNY BAR, 2-15-8 Shinjuku, 2nd floor, Shinjuku-ku, 3356 0368, very small women-only bar, 14:00-05:00. ♀

TAMAGO BAR, 2-15-13 Shinjuku, Nakae Bldg III, 1st fl, Shinjuku-ku, (03) 3351 4838, karaoke bar, 21:00-05:00. ♀

■ Dance Bar/Disco

CLUB GAMOS, 2-11-10 Shinjuku, Shinjuku-ku, (03) 3354 5519, open Tues-Sun, some Tues & Wed bar only, Sat men-only dance night. 🎵 ♂

GOLDFINGER, Daikenyama Shibuya, (03) 3445 7865, ask for "Free-P," 2 dance floors. 🎵 ♀

■ Retail & Bookstores

MS. CRAYON HOUSE, 3-8-15 Kitaaoyama, Minato-ku, (03) 3406 6492, Fax: (03) 3407 9568, women's bookstore, stationery store and restaurant, also children's bookstore, women's crafts.

SABAI, 3-44-18 Koenji-minami, Suginami, (03) 3315 3715, clothing store with cafe (cafe frequented by feminist lesbian women). "

YOKOHAMA

■ Information

YOKOHAMA WOMEN'S FORUM, 435-1 Kamikuratacho Totsukaku, (045) 862 5050.

KOREA, SOUTH

COUNTRY CODE: (82),

SEOUL

■ Information

SAPPHO KOREA, CPO Box 4589, Seoul, women's group.

■ Bars

TRANCE, 136-42 Itaewon-dong, Yongsan-Gu, Itaewan., (02) 797 4310. ♂

ZIPPER, ask locally for address., ♂

ZONE, near Spartacus bar, ask locally for address., ♂

KOREA, SOUTH

■ Dance Bar/Disco
BECAUSE, in front of Trance disco, Itaewan.,

■ Cafe
WHY NOT, in front of Trance bar, Itaewan.,

TAIWAN

COUNTRY CODE: (886),

KAOHSIUNG

■ Bars
COLOUR PLATE, Tayou St 5, 2nd floor, 551 3757, karaoke lounge.

MARUI, Shing Tieb Rd 120, bar & cafe, frequented by gays & lesbians.

■ Dance Bar/Disco
SPEED, call or ask locally for address, 255 9120, karaoke disco.'

TAINAN

■ Bars
BIRD MUSIC PUB, Fu Chien Rd 300, Sec 2, 2nd floor, 299 1892.

HAN NO WA, Chinatown Theater Shopping Center, 11th floor, 220 8800, frequented by gays & lesbians, some English spoken.

■ Restaurants
FU LOW, Sha Lin Rd 1-22, 229 6535.

TAIPEI

■ Bars
MING CHUN, south side of Lane 33, near Chung Shan N Rd 22, Sec 1, 2563 7712, frequented by gays & lesbians.

MING FANG, #70, Lane 85, off Linsen North Rd, 2581 5840, karaoke bar, discreetly frequented by gays.

RE DAI YU, #5, Alley 6, lane 128, lower level, off east side of Chub Shan North Rd, Sector 2, 2562 7123, karaoke bar, discreetly frequented by gays.

SOURCE, 190 Nan Chang Rd, section 2, 2368 8797, frequented by local gays.

■ Cafe
DANTE COFFEE SHOP, call for address, NOT a gay cafe, more gay in evening.

■ Restaurants
BLUE NOTE CAFE, Roosevelt St at Shida, restaurant & jazz club, frequented by some gays & lesbians.

SOUTH ASIA
BANGLADESH

COUNTRY CODE: (880),

DHAKA

■ Retail & Bookstores
NARIGRANTHA PRABARTANA, 2/8 Sir Syed Rd., Mohammadpur, above saree and, handicraft shop., (2) 318428 or 329620, Fax: (2) 813065. Feminist bookstore and meeting place for women, 9:00-21:00.

INDIA

COUNTRY CODE: (91),

AKOLA

■ Information
SAHAYAK GAY GROUP, Write: Laxmi Narayan Sadhan, Prasad Colony, Jathar Peth, Akola 444 004.,

BANGALORE

■ Retail & Bookstores
STREELEKHA, 67, II Floor, Blumoon Complex, Mahatma Gandhi Rd, women's bookstore, library & reading room.

BOMBAY

■ Information
BOMBAY DOST, gay & lesbian group. Publishes Bombay Dost magazine, write: 105A Veena-Beena Shopping Centre, Bandra Station Rd., Bandra (West), Bombay 400 050, India."

HUMSAFAR CENTRE, (22) 972 6913, gay & lesbian drop-in center, meets Fri 18:00-21:00. Call for address.

KUSH CLUB, PO Box 57351, Bombay, 400 058, Gay & lesbian organization.

STREE SARGAM, PO Box 16613, Matunga, Bombay, 400019, Lesbian & bisexual women's collective.

CALCUTTA

■ Information
COUNSEL CLUB, gay organization, publishes Pravartak magazine, member-

ship fee, write: Post Bag 10237, Calcutta 700 019, India."

NAZ FOUNDATION INDIA TRUST, Calcutta Project, South Asian health organization. Write: NAZ, 468A Block K, New Alipur, Calcutta 700 053, India.

DELHI

■ *Information*
ARAMBH SUPPORT GROUP, gay & lesbian organization with cafe, library, small bookshop. Publishes newsletter, write: PO Box 9522, Delhi 110 095, India.

DEHLI WOMEN'S LEAGUE, 6 Bahagwan Das Rd, women's meeting place."

LUCKNOW

■ *Information*
FRIENDS INDIA, gay group, publishes bimonthly newsletter, meets Wed 17:00-18:00. Write for details: PO Box 59, Mahanagar, Lucknow 226 006, India."

MADRAS

■ *Information*
SISTERS, PO Box 26, Tambaram, Madras, 600 059, Lesbian group.

NEW DELHI

■ *Information*
AIDS BHEDBHAV VIRODHI ANDOLAN, organization doing community work involving gay men & lesbians, education, health & legal issues, etc. Write: PO Box 5308, New Delhi 110 053, India."

HELPLINE, (11) 685 9113. answers Mon, Thurs 19:00-21:00.

NAZ PROJECT, D-45 Gulmohar Park, New Delhi 110 049, (11) 667 328, South Asian health organization.

SAHELI WOMEN'S RESOURCE CENTRE, Defence Colony Flyover 105-108, New Delhi 110 024, India, women's meeting place."

SAKHI, (11) 462 8970, gay & lesbian group, write: PO Box 3526, Lajpat Nagar, New Delhi 110 024, India.

SAKHI LESBIAN COLLECTIVE, (11) 462 8970, Write SAKHI, PO Box 3526, Lajapat Nagar, New Delhi 110 024, India."

WOMEN'S NETWORK, lesbian organization, write: PO Box 142, GPO, New Delhi 110 001, India.

■ *Women's Accommodations*
NAARI, B1/7 Vishal Bhawan, 95 Nehru Place, New Delhi 19, (91-11) 646 5711, (91-11) 618 7401, Fax: (91-11) 618 7401. The first women's guesthouse in India. Offers lodgings, modern amenities, optional meals & woman-guided tours of New Delhi. ♀

SECUNDERABAD

■ *Information*
GAY INFO CENTER, Write: Owais, PO Box 1662, Secunderabad, 500 003,

NEPAL

COUNTRY CODE: (977),

KATHMANDU

■ *Information*
NEPAL QUEER SOCIETY, GPO 8975, EPC 5203, Kathmandu, Nepal, gay organization.

PAKISTAN

COUNTRY CODE: (92),

LAHORE

■ *Information*
SHIRKAT GAH, 874951, 874947. Women's resource centre, library and centre for women's organizations in Pakistan. Write to 18A Mian Mir Rd, Lahore 54840, Pakistan.

SRI LANKA

COUNTRY CODE: (94),

COLOMBO

■ *Information*
FRIENDSHIP SRI LANKA, c/o S. Gunawardane, 1049 Pannipitiya Rd, Battaramulla, Colombo, Lesbian & bisexual women's organization.

WATTALA

■ *Information*
COMPANIONS ON A JOURNEY, 27/3 Anderson Rd, Kalubowilla, (1) 82 78 69, gay & lesbian organization.

SOUTHEAST ASIA
CAMBODIA

COUNTRY CODE: (855),

PHNOM PENH

■ *Bars*

MARTINI PUB, near Olympic Stadium, ask locally for address., Not a gay bar, discreetly frequented by local gays. 🍸

SHARKY'S, ask locally for address., Not a gay bar, discreetly frequented by local gays. 🍸

INDONESIA

COUNTRY CODE: (62),

ISLAND OF BALI

■ *Bars*

CAFE LUNA, Raya Seminyak St, Seminyak area, Kuta, gays occupy indoor seating. Terrace is more hetero. 🍽

HULU CAFE, close to Padma St, Legian, bar & restaurant, 18:00-23:00 (closed Mon), drag shows Wed from 23:00. ♪ ♂

■ *Dance Bar/Disco*

DOUBLE SIX, Double Six St, Seminyak area, Kuta, many gays Sat from 24:00. 🍸 🍽

GADO GADO, Dhyana Pura St, Seminyak area, Kuta, Sun, Tues-Wed & Fri nights. 🍸 🍽

ISLAND OF JAVA

■ *Bars*

JALAN JALAN, 36-F Menara Imperium Blvd, Jln. Rasuna Said, Kuningan, Jakarta, Gay Sun evenings. ♪ 🍽

MATRA, Matraman Raya St, at the Grand Menteng Hotel, Jakarta, Not a gay bar, discreetly frequented by local lesbians, more gay men Sat am.

■ *Dance Bar/Disco*

KLIMAX, Gajah Mada St, Jakarta, more gay Sun 22:00-02:00. 🍸 ♂

NEW MOONLIGHT, Hayam Wuruk St, at Manga Besar St, Jakarta., More gays & lesbians Fri-Sun nights. 🍸

SOFIAN HOTEL DISCO, Saharjo St, Jakarta, Not a gay disco, discreetly frequented by local gays & lesbians. 🍸

★ **TANAMUR,** Tanah Abang Timur St, Jakarta, Not a gay bar, more gay Thurs-Sat, more lesbians Sun.

MALAYSIA

COUNTRY CODE: (60),

KUALA LUMPUR

■ *Bars*

BOOM BOOM ROOM, Leboh Ampang, 2nd floor., ♪

CAFE SILHOUETTE, UOA Centre, 19-A ,12, Jalan Pinang at Jalan Perak., Not a gay bar, frequented by some local gays. ♪

■ *Dance Bar/Disco*

ALIBI WOMEN'S DISCO, Central Square, Jln Hang Kasturi, women-only dance night, 1st Wed. 🍸 ♀

PENANG

■ *Bars*

FUN PUB, ask locally for address, near Babylon Boom Boom disco., Bar, cafe & disco, not gay, discreetly frequented by local gays. 🍸

■ *Dance Bar/Disco*

BABYLON BOOM BOOM, ask locally for address., Not a gay disco, discreetly frequented by local gays. 🍸

■ *Cafe*

BEACH BLANKET BABYLON, 16 Bishop St., Not gay, discreetly frequented by local gays, younger crowd.

PHILIPPINES

COUNTRY CODE: (63),

MANILA

■ *Information*

LESBIAN LINE, (2) 921 7229, Mon-Fri 18:00-22:00.

TLC (THE LESBIAN COLLECTIVE), #66-C Scout Ojeda St, Roxas District, Quezon City, (2) 97 28 60, or ask for Giney Villar at (2) 96 92 87, fax: (2) 922 5004. Discussions, social events, women from other countries welcome to attend. Ask about weekly women's parties.

UNIVERSITY CENTER FOR WOMEN'S STUDIES, Univ. of the Philippines, Diliman, Quezon City, (2) 99 50 71, center for women with courses, activities & local information.

WOMEN SUPPORTING WOMEN COMMITTEE, (632) 922 5253, Lesbian group, publishes newsletter, phone answers Mon, Wed, Fri 18:00-20:00, Sat 13:00-20:00. Write: PO Box 43-44, UP Shopping Center, UP Diliman, Quezon City.

■ Accommodations

TOWNHOUSE HOTEL, THE, Villa Carolina Townhouse, #31 201 Roxas Blvd, Tambo, Paranaque, Manila, (63-2) 833 1939, Fax: (63-2) 804 0161. Email: townhousemanila@msn.com, Small, gay-friendly, 24-room hotel on palm tree-lined Roxas Blvd, 1.5 miles from both airports, some rooms with fans, AC, TV. ♀♂

■ Bars

CLUB MAGINOO, E. Rodriguez, at Roces St, Quezon City. ♂

LIBRARY, in the area of Remedios Circle, Malate, not a gay bar, but frequented by gays, ask locally for exact address.

PIGGY & GEN GALI, beside Library bar, 2 bars with one common entrance & exit, not gay, but frequented by local gays, upscale clientele.

ZOO, THE, ask locally for address, frequented by local gays.

■ Dance Bar/Disco

★ **CHICOS,** E. Rodriquez Blvd, Quezon City, 921 1822, some hetero clientele. ♂

■ Cafe

BLUE CAFE, Nakpil St 610, Malate, close to Remedios Circle, not a gay cafe, but frequented by local gays.

SINGAPORE

COUNTRY CODE: (65),

SINGAPORE

■ Bars

CROCODILE ROCK PUB, Orchard Rd, Far East Plaza, 5th floor, not a gay bar, frequented by women.

TABOO, 21 Tanjong Pagar Rd, cafe bar with patio. ♀♂

VINCENT'S LOUNGE, 304 Orchard Rd, 6th story, at the Lucky Plaza, 7361 360. ♂

■ Dance Bar/Disco

MOONDANCE, 62/64 Tanjong Pagar, Tanjong Pagar Conservation District, 324 29 11, trendy crowd, not a gay disco, frequented by gays. More women Thurs.

MUSIC WORLD, near the Katong Shopping Center, not a gay disco, more women Thurs.

ZOO, Marina Planet South, 383 8133, gay Wed & Sat. Women's night Fri. ♂

★ **ZOUK,** 17 Jiak Kim Road, near Havelock and River Valley roads, not a gay bar, discreetly frequented by gays.

THAILAND

COUNTRY CODE: (66),

BANGKOK

■ Information

ANJAREE LESBIAN GROUP, address mail only to: Anjaree, PO Box 322, Rajdamnern, Bangkok 10200, Thailand., Group is available for exchange of info, reciprocal visits, networking. They hold a monthly open house on 2nd Sun afternoon. They will mail you directions addressed to: Post Restante, GPO, Bangkok. To receive mailed response outside Thailand, enclose an international postage voucher to cover postage for their response. DO NOT write lesbian on the envelope!

F.A.C.T. AIDS HELPLINE, (02) 574 1100, 574 3461, 09:00-24:00.

WOMEN'S ASSOC. OF THAILAND, 64 Petchabur, Bangkok, Thailand., Umbrella organization for women's groups in Thailand.

■ Accommodations

AQUARIUS, THE, 243 Hutayana, Soi Suanphlu, South Satorn Rd, Bangkok, 10120, (66-2) 286 0217, 679 3181, 679 3190, Fax (66-2) 286 2174. Email: aquarius@thaiindex.com, Guesthouse with restaurant & bar, AC, TV lounge, some rooms with color TV, room & laundry service, massage in house, private baths, women welcome." ♂

■ Bars

BE MY GUEST, Sukhumvit 31, near Utopia, frequented by some lesbians.

THAILAND

BY HEART PUB, 117/697 Sainanikhom Soi 1, frequented by lesbians.

KHRUA SILOM, Silom Alley, close to Soi 2., ♀♂

CHIANG MAI

Tours, Charters & Excursions

SONN TREKKING, (53) 814 069, in USA: (213) 962-9169, knowledgeable guide to the area, can arrange elephant rides, etc. Ask for the guide called Mister Gosonn Vonganuwong. His is the best guide service in northern Thailand and is used exclusively by Tours to Paradise."

Accommodations

CHATREE HOTEL, 11/10 Suriyawong Rd, Chiang Mai, (66-53) 279 179, Fax: (66-53) 279 085. gay-friendly hotel with restaurant, room service, AC, private baths, pool on premises.

LOTUS HOTEL, 2/25 Soi Viangbua, Tambol Chang-Phuk, Amphur Muang, Chiang Mai, 50300, (66-53) 215 376, 215 462, Fax: (66-53) 221 340. Email: mohamad@loxinfo.co.th, hotel with bar, restaurant, kiosk shops, go-go boys & drag shows, AC, phone, refrigerator, color TV, women welcome, some hetero clientele. ♂

PHUKET

Accommodations

HOME SWEET HOME GUEST HOUSE & POW-WOW PUB & RESTAURANT, 70/179-180 Paradise Complex, Moo 3, Ratuthit Rd, Patong Beach, Phuket, 83150, (66-76) 340 756, Fax: (66-76) 340 757. guesthouse with restaurant, bar & American Indian jewelry store, women welcome in guesthouse, 50% gay/lesbian in bar & restaurant, private baths, color TV, AC, telephone, maid & laundry service, VCR rental available. ♂

EUROPE
ALBANIA

COUNTRY CODE: (355),

TIRANA

Information

SHOQATA GAY ALBANIA, PO Box 104, Tirana, gay group.

Bars

LONDON, near to Hotel London, ask locally for address., Not a gay bar, very discreetly frequented by gays.

AUSTRIA

COUNTRY CODE: (43),

BREGENZ

Information

AIDS HILFE, (05574) 46 5 26.

FRAUENGETRIEBE, Schillerstr. 2, (05574) 455 38, bildungszentrum für frauen (women's info center).

GRAZ

Information

FRAUENINITIATIVE FABRIK, Plüssemanngasse 47, (0316) 47 11 79, women's organization, lesbian group meets here.

ROSALILA PANTHERINNEN, Rapoldgasse 24, (0316) 32 80 80, gay & lesbian center, Thurs from 19:00. Ask about scheduled women's cafe.

STEIRISCHE AIDS-HILFE, (0316) 81 50 50.

INNSBRUCK

Information

AIDS HILFE, (0512) 56 36 21.

FRAUENZENTRUM & FRAUENCAFE, Liebeneggstr. 15, (0512) 58 08 39, women's center, Lesbengruppe (lesbian group) meetings and Frauencafe (women's cafe) take place here.

HOSI TIROL, Innrain 100, 1st floor, (0512) 56 24 03, meetings Thurs 20:30-23:00.

Cafe

CAFE CENTRAL, Erlenstr 11, a mix of gays & heteros, 11:00-23:00

AUSTRIA

KLAGENFURT

Information
AIDS HILFE, (0463) 55 1 28.

FRAUENZENTRUM, Villacher Ring 21, (463) 51 12 48, lesbian group meets 3rd Fri from 19:00.

GAY HOTLINE, (0463) 50 46 90, Wed 19:00-21:00.

LINZ

Information
AIDS HILFE, (0732) 21 70.

FRAUENZENTRUM LINZ, Altstadt 11, (0732) 21 29, Lesbengruppe (lesbian group) meetings.

HOSI LINZ, Schubertstr. 36, (0732) 60 98 98, meetings Thurs 20:00-22:00. Rosa gay line: Mon 20:00-22:00, Thurs from 18:30. Lesbengruppe (lesbian group) meets 1st Fri from 20:00.

Cafe
COFFEE CORNER (C&C), Bethlehemstr. 30, (0732) 77 08 62, 18:00-02:00 (Sun from 17:00). ♀♂

SALZBURG

Information
AIDS HILFE, (0662) 88 14 88.

FRAUENZENTRUM UND FRAUENCAFE, Markus Sitikus Str. 17, (0662) 871 639, women's cultural center and cafe. ♀

HOSI-ZENTRUM, Müllner Hauptstrasse 11, (0662) 43 59 27, Tues from 20:00 & Wed 18:00-24:00, Fri 21:00-24:00, café Wed 19:00-24:00.

ROSA TELEFON, (0622) 43 59 27, Fri 19:00-21:00.

WIEN - VIENNA

Information
AIDS HILFE, (1) 408 61 86, Safer Sex Hotline: Mon & Fri 18:00-20:00."

FRAUENBERATUNG, (1) 586 81 50, Mon-Fri 17:00-20:00.

FRAUENZENTRUM BEISL, Währinger Str. 59, Stiege 6, 1 Stock, (1) 40 85 057, women's center, Wed & Fri 19:00-24:00."

HOSI-ZENTRUM, Novaragasse 40, (1) 216 66 04, gay & lesbian center with varying schedule of events. Tues cafe evening from 20:00, Wed Lesbengruppe (women's social) from 19:00, Thurs youth group from 17:00.

ROSA LILA TELEFON, (1) 216 66 04, Tues 18:00-20:00. Lesbentelefon (lesbian line) Wed 19:00-21:00.

ROSA LILA VILLA/TIP, Linke Wienzeile 102, (1) 58 68 150 or 58 71 778, gay & lesbian center with many activities, lending library, open Mon-Fri 17:00-20:00.

STICHWORT, ARCHIV DER FRAUEN, BIBLIOTHEK, Diefenbachgasse 38, (1) 812 98 86, archive and library for women, Mon, Tues 09:00-14:00, Thurs 15:00-20:00.

Bars
ALFI'S GOLDENER SPIEGEL, Linke Wienzeile 46, enter from Stiegengasse, (1) 586 66 08, bar & restaurant, 19:00-02:00, closed Tues. ♂

CAFE REINER, Kettenbrückengasse 4, (1) 586 23 62, bar, restaurant, cafe, daily 21:00-04:00. ♂

NANU, Schleifmühlgasse 11, (1) 587 29 87, 20:00-04:00 7 days, very few women. ♂

Dance Bar/Disco
LESBIAN DISCO, at the Frauenzentrum, Währingerstr. 59/Stiege 6, (entrance Prechtlgasse), (1) 402 87 54, 1st & 3rd Sat 21:00-05:00 (2nd Sat of month smoke-free disco from 21:00)." 🕪 ♀

WHY NOT, Tiefer Graben 22, (1) 535 11 58, Fri & Sat 22:00-04:00, Sun 21:00-02:00." 🕪 ♂

Cafe
BERG - DAS CAFÉ, Berggasse 8, enter from Wasagasse, Löwenherz bookstore location, (1) 319 57 20, daily 10:00-01:00.

CAFE SAVOY, Linke Wienzeile 36, (1) 56 73 48, 17:00-02:00, Sat 09:00-18:00 & 21:00-02:00 (Sat many women), closed Sun.

CAFE WILLENDORF, Linke Wienzeile 102, (1) 587 17 89, café & restaurant, daily 18:00-02:00, many lesbians. ♀♂

DAS POSIHIVE CAFÉ, Novaragasse 40, at the HOSI gay center, café for people with HIV or AIDS, and their friends, Tues 17:00-22:00.

DAS VERSTECK, Grünangergasse, at Nikolaigasse, (1) 513 40 53, 18:00-24:00 (Sat from 19:00), closed Sun, frequented by some gays. 🕪

FRAUENCAFE, Lange Gasse 11, (1) 43 37 54, Mon-Sat 18:00-01:00." ♀

AUSTRIA

■ Restaurants
LIVING ROOM, Franzengasse 18, at Grüngasse, (1) 585 37 07, restaurant & bar with Austrian & vegetarian cuisine, 16:00-02:00 (Sat, Sun from 10:00).

MOTTO, Schönbrunner Str. 30, (1) 587 06 72, 18:00-04:00.

ORLANDO, Mollardgasse 3, (1) 586 23 27, 17:00-02:00 (Sun from 10:00). ♀♂

■ Retail & Bookstores
FRAUENZIMMER BUCHHANDLUNG, Lange Gasse 11, (1) 406 86 78, feminist & lesbian bookshop with a wide selection of titles. Mon-Fri 09:00-18:00 & Sat till 13:00.

BELGIUM

COUNTRY CODE: (32),

AALST

■ Information
GROUP VICE VERSA, Meuleschettestr. 74, (053) 77 25 05, gay & lesbian group, café Wed from 20:30.

PINKLADIES, Michielsplaats 2, (053) 70 05 78.

■ Bars
DAENS, 6 Pontstraat., ♀

■ Restaurants
ALLEGRO, Gentsestraat., 🖾

DE VESTEN, 10 Keizersplein., 🖾

RAAR MAAR WAAR, 11 De Ridderstraat., 🖾

ST. LAZARE, 2 Consciencestraat, from 10:30 (closed Mon). 🖾

WIENERHAUS, Esplanadeplein., 🖾

AARSCHOT

■ Information
IMPULS, 47 Leuvensesteenweg, (016) 56 95 68, women's aid & resource center.

■ Restaurants
MALIBU, Dorp 2A., 🖾

SCHOLEKEN, 'T, 1 Molenstraat., 🖾

ANTWERP

■ Information
ATTHIS, Volkstraat 7, ask about women's cafe & socials. ♀

■ Women's Accommodations
KRIS'S ANTWERP WOMEN'S B & B, Dolfijnstraat 69, Antwerp, 2018, (32-3) 271 0613 or (32-3) 322 9370. Antwerp is so strategically located that your stay here will never be boring. Just get up and go to Brussels, Amsterdam or even Paris. Many interesting places are within an hour to three hours' drive or train from here. Have your own bedroom and share the bath in a big, Art Deco-style house and garden. It's close to the city center, and there are cafes, restaurants and cultural activities nearby. Your host, Kris, is a professional translator who speaks Dutch, French, English, German, Russian and Polish. Kris can give you directions to the women's bar in Antwerp, or get you invited to one of the lesbian parties that are frequently held in Antwerp. ♀

■ Bars
BORSALINO, Van Schoonhovenstr 48, from 21:00. ♂

DEN BAZAAR, Van Schoonhovenstr. 22, 12:00-05:00." ♂

LADY'S PUB, Waalse Kaai 56, from 19:00. ♀

■ Dance Bar/Disco
SHAKESPEARE, Oude Korenmarkt 24, (03) 23 70 473, mostly women, Fri-Sun 20:00-06:00. 🎵 ♀

■ Cafe
HET HESSENHUIS, Falconrui 53.,

PADDOCKS, Jezusstraat 32, 10:30-19:30 (closed Sun).

ROSKAM, Vrijdagmarkt 12, from 17:00 (Fri from 08:30, Sat & Sun from 15:00). ♀♂

■ Restaurants
CASTELLINO, Groenplaats 28, 09:00-23:00. 🖾

EILAND, 1 Isabellalei, 09:00-21:00 (closed Sun). 🖾

L'ANVERS OI, 52 Sint Jacobstraat, retaurant & bar, 18:00-22:00 (Sat till 24:00, Sun from 20:00). 🖾

LUNCH EN SUPPER, 246 L. Lozanastraat, 12:00-15:00 & 19:00-22:00 (Mon only 12:00-15:00, Sat only 19:00-22:00), closed Sun. 🖾

■ Retail & Bookstores
BOOKSHOP 'T VERSCHIL, Minderbroedersrui 42, (03) 226 08 04.

BRUGGE

Information
GAY CENTER IDEM DITO, (050) 50 78 35, café Sun 15:00-18:00, youth café Fri 20:00-23:00.

Women's Accommodations
HUIZE VITA, Gieterijstraat 45, Brugge, 8000, (32-50) 34 25 93. Visit Brugge for the flavor of old Europe. Waiting for you at our women's inn, Huize Vita, is an English-looking room named after the lesbian writer Vita Sackville-West. The double brass bed, which dates from the 19th century, has always been slept in by... women! We are famous for our homemade cake and breakfasts in bed. Our house is a five-minute walk from the city center of Brugge and a 220-minute drive from the ocean. There is a vegetarian restaurant around the corner and a supermarket close by. Whenever it's possible, we provide free pick-up from the station. We hope to hear from you very soon! ♀

Bars
HOLLYWOOD, 't Zand 24, (050) 33 72 52 tavern, bistro, 11:00-01:00 (closed Thurs).

Cafe
GOUDOU, 's Gragenstraat 44, at De Dwarskop, lesbian cafe, Thurs from 20:00. ♀

BRUSSELS

Information
AIDS LINE, 51 14 529.

INFOR-HOMO/LESBIENNES, Ave. de L'Opale 100, (02) 733 10 24, gay & lesbian meeting place & information center.

LES LESBIANAIRES, radical lesbian archives, write Isabel D'Argent, B.P. 2024, 1000 Bxl 1."

TELS QUELS, Kolenmarktstraat 81, (02) 51 24 587, Fri 20:00-22:00, first Sun 15:00-18:00.

Women's Accommodations
CHAMBRE D'HOTE, (32) (02) 420 24 56. Women's B&B, private & shared baths. Both overnight & longer stays available, call far ahead for reservations, open sporadically. ♀

GASTHOF DE GREEF, 136 Rue Th. Verhaegen, (02) 537 00 36. Women's guesthouse. ♀

Bars
CHEZ MAMAN, Grote Karmelietenstraat 7, (02) 502 86 96, 18:00-03:00 (closed Wed). ♀♂

D-LIGHT, Rue Blaes 208, (02) 511 87 89, women's night 1st Fri. ♀

SAPHO, Rue Borgval, across from Féminin disco, Fri-Sun from 22:00. ♀

TELS QUELS BAR, Kolenmarkt 81, (02) 512 3234, bar, café & gay center, mostly men, Sun-Thurs 17:00-02:00, Fri & Sat till 04:00. ♂

WINGS, Rue du Cygne 3. ♀

Dance Bar/Disco
LE FEMININ, Rue Borgval, 9, (02) 511-1709, women-only, Fri-Sun from 22:00. ♀

Huize Vita

A Romantic Room for Women

- We pamper and spoil our guests
- Non smoking
- Women only
- Vegetarian restaurant around corner
- Women - owned and -operated
- Named after English lesbian Vita Sackville-West

Brugge, Belgium

(32-50) 34 25 93

BELGIUM

SAPHO, St. Gérystr. 1, (02) 512 45 52 Thurs-Sat from 22:00. [⚧] ♀

■ Restaurants
EL PAPAGAYO, Rouppeplaan 6, 19:00-02:00.

■ Retail & Bookstores
ARTEMYS, Rue St. Jean (inside Galerie Bortier 8), next to the Central Station, (02) 512 0347, lesbian & feminist bookshop with current local information. Tues-Thurs 10:00-18:00, Fri & Sat 10:00-19:00, closed Mon. In summer open from 12:00."

GHENT

■ Information
AKSENT OP ROZE, Het Geuzenhuis, Kantienberg 19, (09) 224 35 82, lesbian organization, socials Sat 21:00-01:00."

CLG, Guinardstr. 34, (09) 25 06 52, women's info.

LESBIAN & GAY SWITCHBOARD, (09) 223 69 29. National switchboard run by the Federatie Werkgroepen Homoseksualiteit lesbian/gay organization."

LESBIES DOE FRONT, Postbus 621, 9000 Gent, (09) 223 69 29. Lesbian group with current local information for women. Organizers of the annual Lesbian Day.

■ Women's Accommodations
VROUWENHOTEL KRIS, 93 Baudelostraat, (091) 25 20 45. ♀

■ Bars
CHERRY LANE, 3 Meersenierstraat, from 20:00 (Fri-Sun from 22:00), closed Wed, ♀

LADY INN, Maaltebruggestraat 23, (09) 222 37 99, Mon-Sat 22:00-05:00. ♀

■ Dance Bar/Disco
ROLLS, Ed. Anseelplein 5., ♀⚲

■ Cafe
AKSENT OP ROZE, 'T, Geuzenhuis Bldg, Kantienberg 19, (09) 224 35 82, women's café, Sat 20:00-02:00. ♀

■ Restaurants
AVALON, 37 Geldmunt, 12:00-14:00 (closed Sun). [⚧]

BUDDHASBELLY, Hoogpoort 30, closed Sun.

LA MALCONTENTA, 7-9 Haringsteeg., [⚧]

SOL, Zwartezustersstraat 16, open Mon-Sat.

SOL Y SOMBRA, Serpentraat 5, open Wed-Sat.

VIER TAFELS, 6 Plotersgr., 11:00-14:00 & 20:00-24:00. [⚧]

WALRY, Zwijnaardsesteenweg 6, 08:00-18:00, closed Sun.

WAREMPEL, Zandberg 8, (09) 24 30 62. Women-owned restaurant, Tues-Thurs 12:00-14:00, Fri & Sat 12:00-14:00 & 18:00-22:00. [⚧]

GHENT - ANTWERP AREA

■ Accommodations
BUNGALOW 'T STAAKSKEN, Staakstraat 136/138A, Assenede, 9960, (32-9) 344 0954 (Tel/Fax). Gay-friendly B&B & self-catering bungalow, panoramic views of garden, lake & surrounding fields, 50% gay & lesbian clientele, shared baths, TV lounge, full breakfast in B&B. Color cable TV, kitchen, laundry service in bungalow." ♀⚲

HASSELT

■ Information
L.A.C.H., Lombaardstraat 20, (011) 21 20 20, gay & lesbian group.

■ Bars
MOUSTIQUE II, St. Truidersteenwg, 16, (011) 22 11 99, women on Fri-Sun from 20:00. ♀

■ Cafe
VROUWENKAFFE LILEV, Luikersteenweg 40, (011) 24 22 94, women's cafe run by women's organization, 3rd Sat of the month from 21:00.

■ Restaurants
DE LEVENSBOOM, Leopoldplein 44, 12:00-14:30 & 18:30-21:00 (Sun only 12:00-14:30), closed Mon. [⚧]

KORTRIJK

■ Information
DE NYMFEN, at Vrouwencentrum, Plein 52, (056) 20 07 13, women's center, café night Sat from 20:00. ♀

■ Bars
DE TENDER, Brugsesteenweg 21, Fri-Sun from 21:30. ♀

LEUVEN

■ *Information*
DE ROZE DREMPEL, Ierse Predikherenstraat 25, (016) 20 06 06, gay & lesbian group, café Thurs from 20:00, youth café Mon from 20:00.
LABYRINT, Martelarenlaan 109, (016) 25 55 67, lesbian group.

■ *Restaurants*
BEGIJNTJE, Naamsestraat 123, 11:30-15:00 & 17:00-22:00. ⌧
DE WITTE OLIFANT, Diestsestraat 180, 11:30-17:30 & 18:30-23:00, closed Tues. ⌧

LIEGE

■ *Cafe*
LA JUNGLE WOMEN'S CAFE, Rue Léon Mignon 20, from 22:00, closed Mon. ♀

MECHELEN

■ *Information*
LESBIAN GROUP, 74 Hanswijckstr., (015) 43 21 20, socials Mon 20:00-01:00.

NAMUR - NAMEN

■ *Accommodations*
NEW HOTEL DE LIVES, Chaussée de Liège 1178, Namur, Lives-Sur-Meuse, B-5101, (32-81) 58 05 13, Fax: (32-81) 58 15 77. Email: Francis40@infonie.be, Web: http://www.ciger.be/hotels/lives/index.html, Quiet Namur-Namen is strategically located between Brussels and Luxembourg in a spot overlooking views of the river Meuse. The New Hotel de Lives is a gay and lesbian hotel dating to the 19th century. The building has been completely renovated and has modern, private bathrooms and comfortable furnishings. Curious travelers who like to stay in one place for a few days and use a variety of day trips to see the real Belgium and Luxembourg will find this hotel an excellent base of operations. Those traveling between the gay cities of Amsterdam and Paris will be glad they stopped to experience this interesting bit of gay Belgium along the way. ♀♂

ROESELARE

■ *Cafe*
MOIRA, 4 Koornstraat, lesbian cafe Fri from 20:00. ♀

TOURNAI

■ *Dance Bar/Disco*
GEORGE SAND, 10 rue des Maux, (069) 84 14 69, Fri, Sat from 22:00, Sun 17:30-01:00. 🍴 ♀

TURNHOUT

■ *Bars*
K. W. H., Driezenstraat 23, (014) 42 35 83, socials Wed, Fri-Sun from 20:00. 🍴 ♀
■ *Cafe*
DAMESKAFEE, Buurthuis 't Stokt, Kongostr. 76, (041) 41 15 65, lesbian café, 1st Fri from 20:00. ♀

BULGARIA

COUNTRY CODE: (359),

SOFIA

■ *Information*
FLAMINGO AGENCY, PO Box 63, Sofia, 1680, (3592) 56 58 56. Gay & lesbian organization.
KISS CONTACT, PO Box 63, Sofia, 1680, (3592) 56 52 71, Gay organization

NEW Hotel de Lives

Namur - Namen
(32-81) 58 05 13

CROATIA

in Bulgaria, tourist services available to gay travelers.

CROATIA

COUNTRY CODE: (385),

ZAGREB

■ Information
INFO AIDS, (41) 171 318.
LIGMA, Berislaviceva 14, (41) 276 188, gay & lesbian human rights organization.

CZECH REPUBLIC

COUNTRY CODE: (42),

BRNO

■ Information
LAMBDA BRNO, gay & lesbian organization. Men call (05) 57 29 37. Women call 52 37 12.

■ Bars
PHILADELPHIA CLUB, Milady Horakove 1A, 17:00-04:00. ♂

■ Dance Bar/Disco
DISCO MEMPHIS, Vranovská 11, Tues-Sat 21:00-05:00. 🗓 ♀♂
H 46 (HACKO) BAR CLUB, 46 Hybesova, (05) 324 945, 17:00-02:00. 🗓 ♂
SAPFO KLUB, 24 Pekarská, close to the Autoturist building, lesbian disco, call Inge for details: (05) 523 712. 🗓 ♀
SKLIPEK U RICHARDA, Luzova 29, (05) 57 29 37, Fri & Sat 20:00-06:00, open Sept-June." 🗓 ♂

CESKA LIPA

■ Dance Bar/Disco
MARCUS, 28 Rína ul, (0425) 23 518, Tues-Sun 20:00-04:00. 🗓 ♂

CESKÉ BUDEJOVICE

■ Information
LAMBDA CESKÉ BUDEJOVICE, PO Box 33, 389 01 Vodnany, (342) 905 890, gay organization.
STOP AIDS INFO LINE, (038) 32 308.

■ Dance Bar/Disco
JIVAK, 2 Bozeny Nemcove, 2nd & 4th Sat 20:30-04:00. Only operates when local group organizes event. 🗓 ♀♂

CHEB

■ Bars
BERT, Evrobská 30, (166) 33716, daily 18:00-02:00. ♂

HRADEC KRALOVE

■ Bars
THEATER CLUB, Dlouha St, nr main theater, gay-friendly wine bar, discreetly & occasionally frequented by a few gays. 🗓

■ Dance Bar/Disco
U HROZNU, Nerudova 18, (49) 315 15, Sat 20:00-04:00, frequented by some gays.

■ Restaurants
AL DENTE, Velke Namesti, popular with gays. 🗓

LIBEREC

■ Information
STOP AIDS INFO LINE, (048) 327, ext 223.

MOST

■ Information
NADACE SOKRATES, Pionyru 2922, (047) 218 3256, gay organization with meetings & discussions Tues-Thurs 18:00-22:00. Disco Fri, Sat 20:00-05:00. Evenings call (035) 278 87; write: PO Box 9a, 434 11 Most." ♂

OSTRAVA

■ Information
KLUB LAMBDA, gay organization, PO Box 377, 730 77 Ostrava 1. Occasionally organizes activities.

■ Bars
U DZBANU, Kurí Rynek, 10:00-24:00 (Fri, Sat 20:00-04:00). ♀♂

■ Dance Bar/Disco
G KLUB, Frydecká 62, videos, 18:00-04:00 (Fri & Sat from 20:00)." 🗓 ♀♂

PRAHA - PRAGUE

■ Information
LAMBDA PRAHA, gay & lesbian organization. Men write PO Box 13, Rubensova 2180, 100 00 Prague 10. Women write Truhlárská 29, 110 00 Praha 1.
LOGOS G&L CHRISTIAN HELP LINE, (02) 2422 0327, Wed 10:00-22:00.

SOHO, Vinohradska 46, (02) 257 891, gay organization, publishes national monthly gay magazine.

WOMEN'S INFO CENTER, Klimentska 17, 231 2356, Mon 16:30-18:30 & Thurs 18:00-20:00.

■ Accommodations

PRAGUE HOME STAY, Pod Kotlárkou 14, Prague 5, 150 000, (420-2) 527 388. Phone may be altered in 1998, for information, call (420-2) 5721 0862. Lodging & kitchen privileges in a private home, some hetero clientele, easy tram ride into city, kitchen priveleges available, telephone upon request, shared baths. ♀♂

■ Bars

G&L CLUB, Lublanská 48, (02) 9000 1189 536, 19:00-22:00 (disco from 22:00), some hetero clientele. 🎵 ♀♂

PIANO BAR, Milesovska 10, from 14:00 (Sun from 15:00), small bar with artsy crowd, frequented by gays & lesbians. 🚭

RAINBOW CLUB CAFE-BAR (DUHOVY KLUB), Kamzíková 6, Old Town, below U Cerveného Páva straight bar, (420-2) 24 23 31 68. Classical & Jazz music, separate room for non-smokers, 12:00-01:00 7 days. Sandwiches, salads, pastries, liquor & coffees. ♂

STELLA, Luzicka 10, daily 17:00-04:00, large pub with younger crowd, 40% women. ♀♂

U PETRA VOKA, Na Belidle 40, near Andel metro station, occasional drag & strip shows, from 21:00. 🎵 ✖ ♂

U STRELCE, Karoliny Svetle 12, 18:00-04:00 (Fri, Sat till 06:00, popular drag shows), 20% women. 🎵 ♪ ♂

■ Dance Bar/Disco

RADOST, ul. Belehradská 120, discreetly frequented by gays (mostly expatriot American locals). Downstairs cafeteria with American breakfast & natural food items. Also bookshop with American books, posters, etc. 🎵 🚭

PROSTEJOV

■ Bars

G KLUB, Západní 5, 16:00-01:00 (Sat till 02:00), closed Sun, Mon. ♂

SOKOLOV

■ Information

GAY KLUB SOKOLOV, Slavíckova 1691, (0618) 24 254, gay organization.

TEPLICE

■ Information

GAY KLUB TEPLICE, PO Box 17, 415 03 Teplice 3, (0417) 41 058, gay organization.

DENMARK

COUNTRY CODE: (45),

AALBORG

■ Cafe

PAN BLUE GATE, Danmarksgade 27A, cafe 98 12 22 45, Tues & Wed 20:00-01:00, Thurs 20:00-02:00, Fri 22:00-04:00, Sat 22:00-05:00. 🎵 ♀♂

ÅBENRÅ

■ Cafe

PAN CAFE, Nygade 55, 74 62 11 48, cafe run by gay organization, Fri, Sat 20:00-24:00. Women meet 1st Fri from 20:00. ♀♂

ÅRHUS

■ Information

LBL, Jaegergårdsgade 42, 86 13 19 48, gay organization, Mon-Fri 11:00-15:00.

■ Bars

PAN KLUB & DISCO, Jaegergårdsgade 42, 86 13 43 80, Café: Mon-Thurs 18:00-01:00, Fri 18:00-06:00, Sat 20:00-06:00, Sun 20:00-01:00. Disco: Wed & Thurs 23:00-03:00, Fri & Sat 23:00-05:00. Women's nights Thurs. 🎵 ♀♂

■ Cafe

AKTHIVHUSET, Vestergade 5B, 86 18 16 46, HIV-group tel 86 12 43 13; HIV-café Tues & Thurs 19:00-22:00.

★ **CAFE PARADIS,** Paradisgade 7-9, frequented by gays & lesbians. 🚭

SAPPHO, Mejigade 71, women's cafe, Tues-Fri 15:00-23:00. ♀

COPENHAGEN

SEE KOBENHAVN.,

DENMARK

ESBJERG

Cafe
CAFE TULIP, Norrebrogade 102, 75 45 19 48, Thurs 19:30-22:30, party 1st Sat 20:00-24:00. ♂

FREDERICIA

Bars
CLUB 77, Dalegade 77, 75 93 12 28, Thurs 22:00-02:00, Sat 23:00-05:00. 🍴 ♀♂

KØBENHAVN - COPENHAGEN

Information
AIDS INFO, 33 91 11 19, daily 09:00-23:00.

AIDS INFO FOR GREENLANDERS IN DENMARK, 33 91 47 43, Thurs 16:00-18:00, or tape.

BOSSEHUSET, Fristaden Christiania (entrance, at Refshålevej 2), 32 95 98 72, gay meeting house, holds different events during summer, including discos with shows, cabaret, many activities for women. Phone answers Mon 20:00-22:00. 🍴 ♪ ♀♂

GREVINDE DANNER HUSET, Nansengade 1, 31 14 16 76, this shelter for battered women, often has interesting programs for lesbians & parties from time to time.

KVINDEHUSET, Gothersgade 37, 33 14 28 04, women's center with book cafe, Mon-Fri 12:00-17:30, cafe Mon & Thurs 19:00-22:00, attended by many lesbians.

LBL, Teglgårdsstraede 13, in back, 33 13 19 48, Mon-Fri 10:00-15:00. National gay & lesbian organization, also houses Radio Rosa, gay & lesbian archive, library & PAN magazine.

PAN INFO LINE, 33 13 01 12, national gay & lesbian switchboard, Thurs, Sun, Mon 20:00-23:00.

Accommodations
HOTEL WINDSOR, Frederiksborggade 30, Kobenhavn, 1360, (45) 33 11 08 30, Telefax: (45) 33 11 63 87. Email: hotelwindsor@inet.uni2.dk, Web: www.hotelwindsor.dk. Exclusively gay hotel with breakfast restaurant. Certain floors are designated for men only & have a somewhat bath house atmosphere. Shared baths, continental breakfast, color cable TV, hotel accessed by stairs, no lift. ♀♂

Bars
CAFE INTIME, Allegade 25, Frederiksberg, 38 34 19 58, intimate, old fashioned atmosphere, live piano, 17:00-02:00 (Sat from 20:00). 🍴 ♪ 🎨 ♂

MASKEN, Studiestraede 33, 16:00-02:00 (Sat, Sun open for breakfast 05:00-10:00). 🍴 ♂

NEVER MIND, Norre Voldgade 2, 22:00-06:00 (Fri, Sat till later). 🍴 ♂

★ **SEBASTIAN,** Hyskenstraede 10, 33 32 22 79, multi-level bar & cafe with changing art exhibits, daily 12:00-02:00, Gay-Time 17:00-21:00. ♪ ✖ ♀♂

Dance Bar/Disco
ALIS 'N HOLY IN WONDERLAND, dance night for women with changing dates & venues. Ask locally for current schedule. ♀ 🍴

BABOOSHKA, at Café Babooshka location, Fri & Sat women-only disco night. 🍴 ♀

★ **BLUE NOTE,** Studiestraede 31., after hours disco, showbar & café, Sat & Sun from 05:00, some hetero clientele 🍴 ♪ 📧 ♂

CLIMAX, Bernstorffsgade 3, at the Tivoli Jazz House, Fri 24:00-06:00. 🍴 ♂

CLUB AQUAPUSSY, Enghavevej, at Vega, scheduled monthly dance nights. Ask locally for exact dates. 🍴 ♀♂

JEPPES CLUB 48, Allegade 25, Frederiksberg, 31 87 32 48, disco, mostly mature lesbians, some transvestites. 🍴 ♀

PAN & PAN 2 DISCOS, Knabrostraede 3, discos held by gay organization: Pan Disco Thurs-Sat from 22:00. Pan 2 Sun-Wed from 20:00. 🍴 ♀♂

Cafe
CAFE BABOOSHKA, Turesensgade 6, 33 15 05 36, cafe, pies, cakes, men welcome, women-run, 16:00-01:00 (Thurs-Sat till 02:00). Fri & Sat women-only disco night. ✖ 🍴 ♀

KRASNAPOLSKI, Vestergade 10, 12:00-05:00. 📧

WOMEN'S CAFE, Gothersgade 37, at the Kvindehuset women's center, Mon & Thurs 19:00-22:00. ♀

Restaurants

ROSE DE TUNIS, LA, Vesterbrogade 120, 31 24 06 51, Tunisian cuisine, daily 17:00-23:00.

TEGLKROEN, Teglgårdsstraede 17.,

Retail & Bookstores

PAN BOOKSTORE & LIBRARY, Teglgårdsstraede 13, in back, 33 11 19 61, gay and lesbian bookstore & library, Mon-Fri 17:00-19:00, Sat 13:00-15:00.

KOLDING

Cafe

LOBITO GAY & LESBIAN CAFE, Dyrehavegårdvej 38, 75 54 10 23, Wed 19:00-23:00, Sat 21:00-02:00.

ODENSE

Information

LAMBDA, Vindegade 100, lower level, 66 17 76 92, gay/lesbian organization, Cafe: 4th Sat 21:00-02:00 (men-only 3rd Sat), Disco: 1st Sat 22:00-04:00.

SKAGEN

Accommodations

FINNS HOTEL PENSION, Ostre Strandvej 63, Skagen, 9990, (45) 98 45 01 55. Hotel with restaurant for guests, some hetero clientele. Telephone, library, lounge, garden, sauna, expanded continental breakfast, nearby ocean beach.

ESTONIA

COUNTRY CODE: (372),

TALLINN

Information

ESTONIAN LESBIAN UNION, Write: Eesti Lesbiliit, PO Box 3245, Tallinn, EE0090, 551 1132, fax: 221 6205, e-mail: eluell@saturn.zzz.ee. Lesbian group, publishes ELL-info newsletter & organizes parties & socials. Also has info on other local gay & lesbian services.

Bars

NIMETA BAR, Suur Karja St, Kloostri Ait, Vene St, NOT a gay bar, discreetly frequented by gays.

TALLINN, at the Tallinn hotel, lower level, 21:00-03:00, NOT a gay bar, discreetly frequented by gays.

Dance Bar/Disco

NIGHTMAN, Vineeri 4, 55 111 32 or 2 216205. Disco organized by Estonian Lesbian Union, Wed-Thurs 18:00-02:00, Fri-Sat 21:00-06:00, 2nd & 4th Wed karaoke from 23:00. Take either trams 3 or 4, or buses 5, 18 or 36 in the direction of Tondi, to Vineeri stop.

TARTU

Bars

HELLER, 15 Lossi St, gay nights alternate Saturdays.

FINLAND

COUNTRY CODE: (358),

ÅLAND

Information

VILDROSORNA GAY ORGANIZATION, PO Box 133, 22101 Mariehamn, Aland.,

HELSINKI

Information

AIDS INFO, Hietaniemenkatu 5, 4th floor, (09) 454 2070 or 454 3536.

SETA, Hietalandkatu 2B, (09) 612 32 33, Helsinki gay organization for lesbians & gays, publishes Z Magazine. Also office of Finnish nat'l organization SETA.

Bars

ESCALE, Kansakoulunkatu 3, (09) 693 1533, daily 15:00-02:00.

LOST & FOUND, Annankatu 6, bar & restaurant with dancing & cabaret entertainment.

NALLE PUB, Kaarlenkatu 3-5, (09) 701 5534, daily 15:00-02:00, frequented by women, men very welcome.

NEW FACES, Fabianinkatu 29, at Bar 52, (09) 626 940, women-only bar alt. Sat.

TOM'S CLUB, (09) 680 29 48. Club nights organized by MSC Finland (member ECMC), gay leather, rubber & fetish themes, Fri 23:00-04:00, Sat 00:00-05:00. Dress code, leather women welcome. Near H2O bar, call for exact location.

FINLAND

■ Dance Bar/Disco
★ **DTM**, Annankatu 32, next to main bus station, (09) 694 11 22, large disco, 23:00-04:00, closed Mon."

■ Saunas/Health Clubs
YRJÖNKADUN UIMHALLI, Yrjönkatu 21b, (09) 60 981. Roman-style public bathouse run by the city, discreetly frequented by gays & lesbians, men & women use separate pools & saunas. Men: Tues, Wed, Fri 14:00-20:00 (Sat 13:00-19:00). Women: Tues, Wed, Fri 14:00-20:00, closed Sun. Closed for renovation, may reopen in '99.

■ Restaurants
LOST & FOUND, Annankatu 6, (09) 680 1010, gay restaurant in Helsinki, two bars with dancing in downstairs bar, frequent shows, Mon-Fri 14:00-04:00 (Sat, Sun till 03:00), busy weekends.

■ Retail & Bookstores
BAFFIN BOOKS, Eerikinkatu 15, (09) 694 7078, gay & lesbian bookstore, 10:00-19:00 (Sat till 15:00), closed Sun."

JOENSUU

■ Information
SETA, (0) 2065 11024.

■ Bars
MOLLY'S, Torikatu 20.
PUB VANHA JOKELA, Torikatu 26, many students.

JYVÄSKYLÄ

■ Information
JYVÄSSEUDUN SETA - PINK CLUB, Yliopistonkatu 26, (014) 310 0660, gay & lesbian organization, answers Wed 18:00-21:00 (tape other times)."

■ Bars
PUB HEMINGWAY, Kauppakatu 32, not a gay bar, discreetly frequented by some gays.

KUOPIO

■ Information
KUOPION SEUDUN SETA, Tulliportinkatu 11 (3rd floor), (017) 261 95 56, gay switchboard, Thurs 18:00-20:00. Meetings Wed 18:00-20:00, Sun 15:00-17:00.

LAHTI

■ Information
PH SETA, (03) 751 79 71, gay & lesbian organization, Wed 14:00-18:00 (switchboard till 21:00), also scheduled parties.

■ Restaurants
NOPAKUN'S THAI CUISINE & CAFE, Vapaudenkatu 10, restaurant & cafe, discreetly frequented by gays & lesbians.

OULU

■ Information
OULUN SETA, Kirkkokatu 19A, (08) 376 932, gay & lesbian organization, switchboard Mon, Wed, Fri 09:00-15:00, Tues & Thurs 09:00-19:00.

■ Bars
DNC CLUB, Asemakatu 28, not a gay bar, frequented by gays.
HILPEÄ HUIKKA, Mäkelininkatu 13, bar, restaurant & nightclub discreetly frequented by gays.
MADISON, Isokatu 18, frequented by gays.

ROVANIEMI

■ Information
ROVANIEMI SETA, Hallituskatu 24, (016) 310 141, gay & lesbian organization, Fri 20:00-22:00.

■ Bars
CAN CAN NIGHTCLUB, at the City Hotel, not a gay bar, discreetly frequented by gays.

TAMPERE

■ Information
TAMPEREEN SETA, Hämeenpuisto 41A, (03) 2148 721, gay & lesbian organization, Tues & Fri 20:00-22:00 or tape.

■ Bars
★ **DISCO MIXEI**, Otavalankatu 3, (03) 222 03 64, bar & disco, 22:00-03:00 (Fri, Sat till 04:00), 80% men, 20% women.
HOSPITAL, Näsilinnankatu 22, gay-friendly & popular with gays earlier in evening.

TURKU

Information
TURUN SEUDUN SETA, Rauhankatu 1 c B 22, (02) 2550 695, gay & lesbian organization.

Bars
★ **JACK'S & MIKE'S PUB,** Kauppiaskatu 4, at Forum Bldg, inner courtyard, daily 16:00-02:00, casual atmosphere. ✘ ♀♂

VAASA

Information
VAASANSEUDUN SETA, mobile: (040) 521 0130, Fri 19:00-21:00."

FRANCE

COUNTRY CODE: (33),

NOTE ABOUT FRENCH PHONE NUMBERS:, When dialing from outside France, drop the initial "0" from the phone number. Within France, all phone numbers have 10 digits and start with "0."

ANGOULEME

Information
LIBRAIRIE DES FEMMES, 6, rue d'Arcole, 05 45 38 73 21, women's organization & Les Deux Elles disco, membership. Women's organization: 10:15-20:15 (closed Sun, Mon). Disco: daily from 20:00. 🎵 ♀

ANNECY

Dance Bar/Disco
HAPPY PEOPLE MEN'S ROOM, Route de Bourg en Brune, 04 50 22 11 54, Fri-Sun 00:00-05:00. 🎵 ♀♂

ANTIBES

Bars
LE RENDEZ-VOUS, 5 cours Massena, 04 93 34 17 77, 18:00-00:30 (summer till 02:30). 🍸 ♀♂
RELAIS DU POSTILLON, 8 rue Championnet, 04 93 34 20 77, bar & restaurant 08:00-23:00 (closed Sun pm), accommodation available. ✘ ▨

ARLES

Accommodations
APARTMENTS & STUDIOS BY SCI DE CAMARGUE, Box 7, Salin de Giraud, (33) 04 42 48 80 40, Fax: (33) 04 42 86 89 10. Apartments & studios 10 min from gay nudist beach at Piémanson. ♀♂

AVIGNON

Accommodations
MAS LA BONOTY HOTEL & RESTAURANT, Chemin de la Boniaty, Pernes Les Fontaines, 84210, (33) 04 90 61 61 09, Fax: (33) 04 90 61 35 14. Gay-owned & -operated 17th-century farmhouse surrounded by olive & lavender trees. Eight rooms, private baths, close to vinyards, pool on premises, gay/lesbian following. 🛏

Bars
LE BISTROT D'AVIGNON, 25 rue Carnot, 04 90 27 91 52, 17:00-01:00 (closed Tues). ♀♂

Dance Bar/Disco
KIPROKO, 22 Blvd Limbert, 04 90 82 68 69, weekends from 23:00. 🎵 ♀♂

Restaurants
COTÉ JARDIN, rue des Trois Carreaux, 04 90 82 26 70. ▨
PETIT BEDON, 70 rue Joseph Vernet, 04 90 82 33 98, lunch & dinner, closed Sun.

BANDOL

Accommodations
HOTEL ILE ROUSSE, 17 Bld Louis Lumière, 04 94 29 33 00, Fax: 04 94 29 49 49. 4-star luxury hotel, private beach, sea-water pool, 2 restaurants. 🛏

BAYONNE

Bars
LE JAMES DEAN, 11, rue Vieille-Boucherie, 05 59 59 19 64, 10:30-02:00. ♀♂
LE PIMM'S, Ave. Leon Bonnat, across from gardens, 05 59 25 76 22, 10:00-02:00. ♀♂

BESANÇON

Information
AIDS LINE, 03 81 81 80 00.

Bars
LE BROADWAY, 90 rue des Granges, 03 81 81 67 51, 18:00-02:00. ♀♂

FRANCE

LE SPIRAL, 3, rue Jean Petit, 03 81 81 17 90, 18:00-01:00 (Fri, Sat till 02:00), closed Sun, Mon. ♀♂

BEZIERS

■ Accommodations

CHAMBRES D'HOTE DU MOULIN, Chemin du Moulin, Poilhes, La Romaine, 04 67 93 46 22. B&B with swimming pool & terrace, some hetero clientele.

HOTEL ALMA UNIC, 41 rue Guilhemon, 04 67 28 44 31, Fax: 04 67 28 79 44. Gay-friendly hotel, nude sunbathing on the terrace.

BIARRITZ

■ Bars

OPERA CAFÉ, 31, av. de Verdun, 05 59 24 16 17, 09:00-05:00, disco from 22:00. Accommodation available. ♀♂

■ Dance Bar/Disco

LE CAVEAU, 4, rue Gambetta, 05 59 24 16 17, disco & bar with shows, 17:00-05:00. Disco from 23:00. ♂

BORDEAUX

■ Information

SAPHOLLES, 29 rue de la Boétie, 05 56 79 30 75, lesbian group, meets Thurs from 18:00.

■ Saunas/Health Clubs

SAUNA FERRÈRE, 18, rue Ferrère, 05 56 44 53 01, gay & lesbian sauna, 13:00-20:00. ♀♂

■ Restaurants

LA CAFETIÈRE, 14 rue des Faussets, 05 56 51 66 55, 20:00-24:00. ♀♂

UN MONDE A PART, 62 rue de la Devise, 05 56 48 19 92.

BREST

■ Bars

LE VILLAGE CAFE, 2 rue Duquesne, 02 98 80 05 22, bar & cafe 18:00-01:00. ♀♂

BRITTANY

■ Accommodations

HOTEL DE FRANCE, 57 Avenue Victor Hugo, Vannes, 56000, (33) 02 97 47 27 57, Fax: (33) 02 97 42 59 17. Hotel & bar in the port city of Vannes, in the heart of Brittany. Private & shared baths, continental breakfast, mostly hetero clientele with a gay/lesbian following.

■ Women's Accommodations

CHEZ JACQUELINE, c/o Jacqueline Boudillet, La Croix Cadio, St Donant, Brittany, 22800, June through Sept: (33) 02 96 73 81 22, Oct-May: Paris (33) 01 47 39 94 54. 6, rue du Port, 92110 Clichy, 01 47 39 94 54. Women-only bed & breakfast. Double rooms with shared bath. TV room. ♀

BURGUNDY REGION

■ Accommodations

LA SALAMANDRE, Au Bourg, Salornay sur Guye, 71250, (33) 03 85 59 91 56, Fax: (33) 03 85 59 91 67. Gay-owned, gay-friendly guesthouse in a restored 18th-century house surrounded by a large park with old trees. Vineyards nearby and country walks and biking routes. Private baths, expanded continental breakfast. Optional 3-course guest dinner FF 120.

LE CHATEAU QUENTIN, Route du Pont, Alluy, 58110, (33) 03 86 84 08 95. Cottage & manor house 40 km from Nevers & 300 km from Paris, private baths.

CAEN

■ Bars

LE ZING, 12 rue de Vaugeux, 02 31 93 20 30, 17:00-04:00. ♀♂

■ Dance Bar/Disco

LE PHIL ET BEA, 189 rue St Jean, 02 31 86 60 05, 22:00-04:00. ♂

■ Cafe

MELROSE CAFE, 78 rue Caponière, 02 31 86 20 53, 22:00-04:00. ♀♂

CANNES

■ Information

AIDS INFO, 04 93 68 98 31.

■ Accommodations

LE CHEVAL BLANC, 3 rue Guy de Maupassant, at Av de Grasse, 04 93 39 88 60, Fax: 04 93 38 01 50. Open Dec-Oct.

LES CHARMETTES, 47 Av de Grasse, 04 93 39 17 13, Fax: 04 93 68 08 41, mention Ferrari when making reservation.

SELECT, 16 rue Helene Vagliano, near train station, 04 93 99 51 00, Fax: 04 92 98 03 12.

TOURING HOTEL, 11 rue Hoche,

Cannes, 06400, (33) 04 93 38 34 40, Fax: (33) 04 93 38 73 34. Gay-friendly hotel in center of Cannes, private baths, continental breakfast, color TV phone, maid & laundry service, 30% gay/lesbian following.

Bars
EXTÉRIEUR NUIT, 16, rue du Suquet, 04 93 99 27 36, 1950's style bar, 18:00-02:30, closed Tues. ♀♂

LE ZANZI-BAR, 85, rue Félix-Faure, 04 93 39 30 75, daily 18:30-05:00." ♂

Dance Bar/Disco
LE SEPT, 7, rue Rouguières, 04 93 39 10 36, 23:00-06:00. ♪ 🎤 ♀♂

Restaurants
LA CROISETTE, 15, rue du Commandant André, 04 93 39 86 06. Fondues & Italian cuisine, Tues-Sat 12:00-14:30 & 19:00-22:30, Sun only 19:00-22:30, closed Mon. 🍴

LE BISTROT DE LA GALERIE, 4, rue Saint-Antoine, 04 93 39 99 38. Seafood, daily 12:00-14:00 & 19:30-23:00, closed Mon. 🍴

LE MARAIS, 9, rue du Suquet, 04 93 38 39 19, 19:30-23:00, closed Mon. ♀♂

LE TREIZE, 13, rue Perissol, 04 93 39 85 19, French & Swiss cuisine, daily 19:30-24:00. ♀♂

COGNIN

Dance Bar/Disco
SIXTIES GAY TEA DANCE, RN 6, Cognin, 04 79 69 11 22, 22:00-02:00, closed Mon. ♀♂

DIJON

Information
AIDS LINE, 03 80 30 37 77.

DINARD

Bars
PALACE CAFE, 21 bd Wilson, 02 99 46 93 50, 10:30-24:00. ♪ ♀♂

DIOU

Bars
LE BATACLAN, Ecluse de Putay, 04 70 42 90 03, Fri-Sun 23:00-04:00. ♪ 🎤 ♀♂

DOMME

Camping & RV
LA DORDOGNE CAMPING DES FEMMES, St.-Aubin de Nabirat, Domme, 24250, (33) 05 53 28 50 28. camping, 20 tent sites, 3 campers, 2 toilets, hot & cold showers, meeting rooms, TV lounge, many outdoor activities, convenient to shopping." 🏕 ♀

GIGNY SUR SAONE

Bars
LE WHY NOT, Chateau de la Colonne, 03 85 44 81 71, Sat 23:00-05:00, some hetero clientele. ♂

GRENOBLE

Information
AIDS INFO, 04 76 63 82 44.

Bars
LE QUEEN'S, 62, cours Jean-Jaurès, 04 76 46 83 44, 10:00-01:00." ♀♂

RUTLI, 9, rue Etienne Marcel, 04 76 43 21 16, 17:00-01:00 (closed Mon), bar with video area, accommodations available. ♂

Restaurants
L'ANGE BLEU, Place de Metz, 04 76 87 55 89, 12:00-14:00 & 19:00-01:00, closed Sun. 🍴

LE GRILL PARISIEN, 34, av Alsace-Lorraine, 04 76 46 77 44, 12:00-14:30 & 19:30-23:30, closed Mon. 🍴

LA GRANDE MOTTE

Bars
BAL & MASQUES, Place Paul Valéry, 04 6756 2724, bar with restaurant.

LE MANS

Information
AIDS INFO, 02 43 23 96 71.

Dance Bar/Disco
LA LIMITE, 7, rue Saint-Honoré, 02 43 24 85 54, 23:00-04:00, closed Mon, theme nights. ♪ 🎤 ♀♂

LILLE

Information
ASSOCIATION DU COTE DES FEMMES, 18 rue du Cirque, women's organization, daily 14:30-18:30, contact for women's café & library info." ♀

LES FALMANDS ROSES, 1/2, rue Denis de Pèagre, 03 20 47 62 65, gay & lesbian cultural center, 2nd Tues from 20:00.

Bars

LE LOFT, 80 bis Barthélémy Delespaul, 03 20 42 05 86, 21:00-02:00 (closed Mon). ♀♂

LE ROCAMBOLE, 11, place Jacques Louchard, Les Terrasses, Ste. Catherine, 03 20 55 12 52, 21:00-02:00. ♀♂

Dance Bar/Disco

ZÉNITH, 74 av de Flandre, Villeneuve d'Ascq, 03 20 89 92 29, from 23:00, closed Mon-Wed. 🍴 ♀♂

LORIENT

Bars

LE DROLE DE..., 26 rue Jules le Grand, 02 97 21 08 73, 15:00-01:00 (Jul-Aug from 18:00). ♀♂

LUNEL

Dance Bar/Disco

LE ZEEBOYS, Route de Nimes RN 113, between Nimes & Montpellier, 04 67 71 02 01, Thurs-Sun from 23:00. 🍴 ♪ ♀♂

LYON

Information

GAY & LESBIAN CENTER, c/o Aris, 16 rue St Polycarpe, 1st fl, Mon-Fri 19:00-21:00, local info available.

Bars

BAR DU CENTRE, 3, rue Simon Maupin, 04 78 37 40 18. very gay at night, daily 08:00-03:00 (Sun from 17:00). ♀♂

LE VERRE A SOI, 25, rue des Capucins, 04 78 28 92 44, 11:00-03:00 (Sat from 18:00), closed Sun. ♀♂

LE VILLAGE BAR, 8 rue St Georges, 04 78 42 02 19, women-only bar, from 18:00 (Sat from 20:00). ♀

SPARTAC CAFE, 3 place St Paul, 04 78 28 03 32, bar & restaurant 10:00-01:00. ♀♂

Dance Bar/Disco

LA TAVERNE II, 12, rue René-Leynaud, 04 78 28 24 28, Thurs-Sun from 22:30." 🍴 ♪ ♀♂

LE MYLORD, 112, Quai Pierre Scize, 04 78 28 96 69, 22:30-04:00, closed Sun. 🍴 ⛔

Restaurants

LES FEUILLANTS, 5, Petite-rue-des-Feuillants, 04 78 28 20 50, Tues-Sat 12:00-14:00 & 19:30-22:15 (Mon only 19:30-22:15)." ♀♂

TCHIN-TCHIN, 17, rue du Sergent-Blandon, 04 78 27 20 46, 18:00-03:00, closed Mon." ♀♂

MARSEILLE

Information

AIDS INFO, 04 91 84 74 64.

Accommodations

SAINT FERRÉOL'S HOTEL, 19 rue Pisancon, 04 91 33 12 21, Fax: 04 91 54 29 97. In pedestrian shopping area, near the opera & gay bars, rooms with bath, phone & TV. Mention Ferrari when making reservation.

Saunas/Health Clubs

WOMEN'S SAUNA CLUB SALVATOR, 20 Boulevard Salvator, 04 91 42 99 31, separate women's sauna at a men's sauna, 12:00-20:30. ♀

Restaurants

CHEZ ALEX, 43, rue Curiol, 04 91 47 80 12, Italian cuisine, 12:00-14:00 & 18:00-24:00, closed Sun. ⛔

MAULÉON D'ARMAGNAC

Dance Bar/Disco

ASSOCIATION AMAZONES, La Thébaide, (33) 05 62 09 69 55, women's disco Sat evening only in July & August. Popular with women from surrounding area. Travelers welcome. 🍴 ♀

MONTPELLIER

Accommodations

CAUSSE ET LAMAS, Route De Navas, Montdardier, 30120, (33) 04 67 81 52 77 (Tel/Fax). B&B and campground with restuarant & agricultural project, 50% gay/lesbian clientele, private & shared baths, 6 tent sites, continental breakfast in B&B only.

HOTEL ULYSSE, 338 Avenue St Maur, 04 67 02 02 30, Fax: 04 67 02 16 50. Gay-friendly hotel.

Bars

LA BODEGA, 27, rue du Fbg St-Jaumes, 04 67 41 06 98, 10:30-15:00 & 19:00-01:00, closed Mon. Bar & restaurant with patio, Spanish cuisine. ♀♂

Dance Bar/Disco

LE ROME CLUB, in the Fréjorgues Est shopping center, Mauguio, towards the airport, 04 67 22 22 70, large dance bar, 2 levels, Fri-Mon from 23:00. 🍴 ♀♂

FRANCE 69

■ *Restaurants*
LE COLOMBIER, 11, bd de l'Observatoire, 04 67 66 05 99, 12:00-14:00 & 20:00-23:30, closed Mon. Seafood a specialty. 🔲

LE VOLT FACE, 4, rue des Ecoles Laïques, 04 67 52 86 89. Restaurant & bar with garden, 17:00-23:30 (Summer also 12:00-14:00). 🔲

LES GOÉLANDS, 8, rue de la Petite-Loge, 04 67 60 60 34, 19:00-24:00, closed Wed. ♀♂

MORNAC-SUR-SEUDRE

■ *Dance Bar/Disco*
JOY'S, Rue du Port (10km from Royan), over Dream's bar & restaurant, facing harbour, 05 46 22 76 44, Sat 23:00-5:00. 🔲♀♂

MULHOUSE

■ *Dance Bar/Disco*
LE GEMEAUX, 3 rue J. Ehrmann, 03 89 66 19 60, from 23:00. 🔲♀♂

LE J.H., 32 Quai du Forst, 03 89 32 00 08, Fri-Mon 23:00-04:00. ♂

NANCY

■ *Information*
AIDS INFO, 03 83 27 91 71.

■ *Dance Bar/Disco*
LA LUNA, 27, rue de la Visitation, 03 83 36 51 40, 20:30-04:00 (Fri, Sat 22:30-05:00). 🎵♀♂

NANTES

■ *Information*
AIDS LINE, 02 40 47 99 56.

■ *Bars*
LE SECOND SOUFFLE, 1 rue Kervegan, 02 40 20 14 20, 17:00-02:00. ♀♂

PLEIN SUD, 2 rue Premion, 02 40 47 06 03, 17:00-02:00 (closed Mon), some hetero clientele. ♂

■ *Dance Bar/Disco*
LE TEMPS D'AIMER, 14, rue Alexandre-Fourny, 02 40 89 48 60, 23:00-05:00, closed Mon. 🔲🎵♀♂

NICE

■ *Accommodations*
BAHIA VISTA, Basse Corniche, Pont St Jean, Villefranche sur Mer, between Nice & Monaco, 04 93 01 32 32, Fax: 04 93 01 29 77. Comfortable & modern rooms & suites with TV, videos, bay views. Bar & swimming pool on roof, restaurant.

HOTEL DU CENTRE, 2 rue de Suisse, 04 93 88 83 85, Fax: 04 93 82 29 80. Gay-friendly hotel.

HOTEL MEYERBEER BEACH, 15 rue Meyerbeer, 04 93 88 95 65, Fax: 04 93 63 08 80. Gay-owned, gay-friendly hotel.

■ *Bars*
BAR LE RUSCA, 2, rue Rusca, 04 93 89 46 25, terrace, 18:00-02:30. ♀♂

LE MORGAN, 3, rue Claudia, 04 93 86 86 08, large bar, shows, 21:30-02:30. 🎵♂

■ *Dance Bar/Disco*
LE BLUE BOY ENTERPRISES, 9, rue Spinetta, 04 93 44 68 24, disco, videos, 2 dance floors, 2 bars, 23:00-05:00. 🔲🎵♀♂

■ *Restaurants*
CHAT GOURMAND, 1 ruelle de la Boucherie, 04 93 90 98 18, frequented by women, 19:30-01:00, closed Tues. 🔲

L'ESTAMINET, 21 rue Barla, 04 93 55 41 55, 12:00-14:00 & 19:00-22:30 (Sat only 19:00-22:30, closed Sun). ♀♂

NIMES

■ *Information*
AIDS INFO, 04 66 76 26 07.

NORMANDY

■ *Accommodations*
BED & BREAKFAST ON A SMALL ISOLATED FARM, Les Hauts Vents, St Jean le Blanc, 14770, (33) 02 31 69 67 56." Lesbian-owned B&B in a traditional, century-old Normandy farm house. 250 km from Paris, 40 km from Caen, surrounded by lush, green pastures. Horseback riding, hiking & biking trails. ♀♂

ORLEANS

■ *Dance Bar/Disco*
LE REFUGE, in nearby town of La Ferte-St-Aubin, 10 minutes by car south of Orleans on the RN 20, 02 38 64 61 60, Open Fri & Sat from 23:00 in winter; Thurs-Sun in summer. 🎵♀♂

■ *Restaurants*
LA CABANE AU CANADA, 224 rue de Bourgogne, 02 38 81 01 08, closed Sat lunch & all day Sun.

FRANCE

PARIS INTRO

■ Information

ARCHIVES LESBIENNES, 01 48 05 25 89, lesbian archives, phone Wed 16:00-20:00 or Fri 18:00-22:00 for appointment or write A.R.C.L, BP 662, 75531 Paris Cedex 11.

CANAL MIEL, lesbian info line. To receive info, call (1) 43 796 191, to give info, call (1) 43 796 607.

CENTRE GAI ET LESBIEN, 3 rue Keller (11th arrondissement), (métro: Bastille/Voltaire), 01 43 57 21 47, Fax: 01 43 57 27 93. Gay & lesbian group, cafe on premises, Mon-Sat 12:00-20:00, Sun Café Positif 14:00-19:00. Organizers of local gay events, information about other gay groups.

PARIS 1ST ARROND.

■ Bars

BANANA CAFÉ, 13, rue de la Ferronnerie, (métro: Châtelet/Les Halles), 01 42 33 35 31, daily 16:30-05:00, terrace. ♀♂

BAR DU PALMIER, 16 rue des Lombards, (métro: Châtelet/Les Halles), 01 42 78 53 53, 17:00-05:00. ♀♂

LE LONDON, 33 rue des Lombards, (métro: Châtelet/Les Halles), 01 42 33 41 45, bar, disco & restaurant, daily from 20:00. 🍽♂

LE VAGABOND, 14, rue Thérèse, (métro: Pyramides), 01 42 96 27 23, bar & restaurant 18:00-03:30 (closed Mon), some women later in evening. ♂

MYTILENE BAR, 5 rue Bertin Poirée, (métro: Châtelet or Pont Neuf), 01 40 08 06 27, 14:00-02:00 (Sun from 14:30), women-only Fri & Sat 22:00-02:00. ♀

TROPIC CAFE, 66 rue des Lombards, 01 40 13 92 62, from 16:00. ♀♂

■ Dance Bar/Disco

CLUB 18, 18, rue du Beaujolais, (métro: Palais-Royal), 01 42 97 52 13, young crowd, from 23:00 weekends. 🍽♪♀♂

■ Restaurants

AU DIABLE DES LOMBARDS, 64, rue des Lombards (métro: Châtelet), 01 42 33 81 84, restaurant & bar, American cuisine, daily from 08:00. 🚬 ☥

AU RENDEZ-VOUS DES CAMIONNEURS, 72, quai des Orfèvres, (métro: Pont Neuf), 01 43 54 88 74, 12:00-14:00 & 20:00-23:30 (Sat only 20:00-23:30). 🚬

CHEZ MAX, 47 rue Saint Honoré, 01 45 08 80 13, 12:00-14:00 & 20:00-24:00. ♀♂

L'AMAZONIAL, 3, rue Sainte-Opportune, (métro: Châtelet/Les Halles), 01 42 33 53 13, 12:00-15:00 & 19:00-00:30 (Fri, Sat till 04:00)." ♀♂

LE CHANT DES VOYELLES, 4 rue des Lombards, (métro: Châtelet/Les Halles), 01 42 77 77 07, 11:00-15:00 & 18:00-02:00. 🚬

LES PIÉTONS, 8 rue des Lombards, (métro: Châtelet), 01 48 87 82 87, restaurant & tapas bar, 11:00-02:00. 🚬

PARIS 2ND ARROND.

■ Bars

LA CHAMPMESLÉ, 4, rue Chabannais, (métro: Pyramides), 01 42 96 85 20, one room for women, one mixed, cabaret nights, 17:00-02:00 (Thurs-Sat till later), closed Sun. 🎵♀

■ Dance Bar/Disco

L'ENTRACTE, 25, bd Poissonnière (métro: Rue Montmartre, or Bonne Nouvelle), at Scorpion disco, 01 40 26 01 93, Tues-Sun from 23:00, men welcome. 🍽♀

SCORPION, 25, bd Poissonnière, (métro: Rue Montmartre), 01 40 26 01 50, from 23:45 (shows start at 03:30, Fri & Sat 04:30)." 🍽♪♂

■ Cafe

LE DÉNICHEUR, 4 rue Tiquetonne, 01 42 21 31 01, everything here is for sale, coffee, snacks & even the furniture. 🚬

■ Restaurants

AUX TROIS PETITS COCHONS, 31 rue Tiquetonne, (métro: Etienne Marcel or Les Halles), 01 42 33 39 69, open from 20:00, closed Mon. 🚬

LE LOUP BLANC, 42 rue Tiquetonne, (métro: Etienne Marcel or Les Halles), 01 40 13 08 35, dinner only, Sun brunch 12:00-18:00. 🚬

LE MONDE A L'ENVERS, 35 rue Tiquetonne, 01 40 26 13 91, 12:00-15:00 & 20:30-23:00 (Sat, Sun only 20:30-23:00), many lesbians. ♀♂

MATINÉE-SOIRÉE, 5, rue Marie-Stuart, (métro: Châtelet/Les Halles), 01 42 21 18 00, 12:00-14:30 & 19:30-22:30 (Fri, Sat 19:30-23:00). 🚬

PARIS 3RD ARROND.

Bars

LE DUPLEX, 25, rue Michel-Le-Comte, (métro: Rambuteau or Arts et Métiers), 01 42 72 80 86, 20:00-02:00, monthly art exhibits, women welcome. ♂

UNITY BAR, 176-178 rue Saint Martin, (métro: Rambuteau), 01 42 72 70 59, daily 15:00-02:00. ♀

Restaurants

AU PETIT CABANON, 7, rue Ste.-Apolline, (métro: Strasbourg-St.-Denis), 01 48 87 66 53, traditional French cuisine, open Thurs-Sat 12:00-15:00 & 19:00-01:00, many lesbians. ♀♂

L'IMPRIMERIE, 101, rue Vieille-du-Temple, (métro: Hôtel de Ville), 01 42 77 93 80, 12:00-15:00 & 20:00-24:00 (Sun only 20:00-24:00). 🍴

MADAME SANS GENE, 19 rue de Picardie, (métro: Filles du Calvaire), 01 42 71 31 71, 12:00-14:30 & 19:30-23:30 (Sun only 19:30-23:30). 🍴

PARIS 4TH ARROND.

Bars

BAR L'ACCESS SOIR, 41 rue des Blancs Manteaux, (métro: Hôtel-de-Ville), 01 42 72 12 89, 11:00-02:00 (Sat, Sun from 17:00). ♀♂

CAFE CHANTANT, 12, rue du Plâtre, (métro: Rambuteau), 01 48 87 51 04, 18:00-02:00, women welcome 21:00-23:00 during karaoke hours. ♂

L'AMNESIA, 42, rue Vieille-du-Temple, (métro: Hôtel-de-Ville or Saint-Paul), 01 42 72 16 94, snacks, 12:00-02:00, women welcome. ✕ ♂

L'OPIUM CAFE, 5 rue Elzévir, (métro: St Paul), 01 40 29 93 40, bar & restaurant, 10:00-02:00. ♀♂

LE PIANO ZINC, 49, rue des Blancs-Manteaux, (métro: Rambuteau), 01 42 74 32 42, live piano & sing-a-long. Open 18:00-02:00 (closed Mon), women welcome. 🎵 ♂

LES MAUDITES FEMELLES, 12, rue Simon-le-Franc, (métro: Rambuteau), at QG men's bar, information: 01 48 97 92 29 or 01 39 69 50 04, this hard-core lesbian group organizes lesbian sex parties, leather, chaps, vinyl, latex, uniform, etc. Call for schedule. ♀

LES SCANDALEUSES, 8 rue des Ecouffes, 01 48 87 39 26 lesbian bar, 18:00-02:00. ♀

MIXER BAR, 23 rue Sainte Croix de la Bretonnerie, (métro: Hôtel-de-Ville), 01 48 87 55 44, 16:00-02:00. ♂

OPEN CAFE, 17 rue des Archives, (métro: Hôtel-de-Ville), 01 42 72 26 18, 10:00-02:00, women welcome. ♂

Restaurants

AMADEO, 19, rue François Miron, (métro Hôtel de Ville), 01 48 87 01 02, 12:00-14:00 & 20:00-23:30 (Sat only 20:00-23:30), closed Sun. 🍴

AU BISTROT DE LA PLACE, 2 rue Place du Marché Ste. Catherine, 01 42 78 21 32, open daily, frequented by gays. 🍴

AU TIBOURG, 29 rue du Bourg Tibourg, (métro: Saint Paul or Hôtel de Ville), 01 42 74 45 25, 12:00-15:00 & 19:00-23:30. 🍴

AUBERGE DE LA REINE BLANCHE, 30, rue St-Louis-en-l'Ile, (métro: Pont-Marie), 01 46 33 07 87, daily 18:00-00:00 (Mon & Tues also 12:00-15:00, Fri-Sun from 12:00).

ECLACHE ET CIE, 10 rue St Merry, 01 42 74 62 62, daily 12:00-01:00, breakfast & lunch on weekends. 🍴

EQUINOX, 33 rue des Rosiers, (métro: Hôtel de Ville or Saint Paul), 01 42 71 92 41, 11:00-15:30 & 19:00-02:00. 🍴

FOND DE COUR, 3, rue Sainte-Croix-de-la-Bretonnerie, (métro: Hôtel-de-Ville or Saint Paul), 01 48 04 91 12, 12:30-14:00 & 19:30-23:30 (closed Sun). 🍴

L'EGLANTINE, 9, rue de la Verrerie, (métro: Hôtel-de-Ville), 01 48 04 75 58, traditional French cuisine, 11:30-14:00 & 19:30-22:00 (closed Mon), Sun brunch. ♀♂

LA CANAILLE, 4, rue Crillon, (métro: Quai-de-la-Rapée), 01 42 78 09 71, 11:45-14:15 & 19:30-24:00 (Sat, Sun only 19:30-24:00)." 🍴 ♀

LA PETITE CHAUMIERE, 41 rue des Blancs Monteaux, (métro: Hôtel-de-Ville), 01 42 72 13 90, lunch & dinner (closed Sat lunch), Sun brunch 12:00-16:00.

LE DIVIN, 41, rue Ste. Croix de la Bretonnerie, (métro: Hôtel-de-Ville), 01 42 77 10 20, 12:00-14:00 & 19:30-23:00 (Sun only 19:30-23:00), closed Mon. 🍴

LES MAUVAIS GARÇONS, 4 rue des Mauvais Garçons, (métro: Hôtel de

Ville), 01 42 72 74 97, 11:45-14:30 & 20:00-23:30 (closed Sun & Mon).

PIANO SHOW, 20, rue de la Verrerie, (métro: Hôtel-de-Ville), 01 42 72 23 81, dinner & female impersonator shows nightly from 20:30, closed Mon."

Retail & Bookstores

LE PHARMACIE DU VILLAGE, 26 rue du Temple, 01 42 72 60 72, 08:30-22:00, closed Sun.

LES MOTS A LA BOUCHE, 6, rue Sainte-Croix de la Bretonnerie, (métro: Hôtel de Ville), 01 42 78 88 30, gay & lesbian bookshop, 11:00-23:00 (Sat till 24:00), mail order available.

PARIS 5TH ARROND.

Accommodations

HOTEL DES NATIONS, 54 rue Monge, Paris, 75005, (33) 01 43 26 45 24, Fax: (33) 01 46 34 00 13. Email: hoteldesnations@compuserve.com, Web: www.hoteldesnations.com, This 3-star hotel is in the Latin Quarter's picturesque Mouffetard neighborhood between the Pantheon and Notre Dame and close to the Marais. Rooms have contemporary charm and the convenience of direct-dial phone, radio, TV, individual safekeeping. Parking is nearby. A buffet breakfast starts the day. Nearby are bicycle rentals, public gardens, a covered public pool, excellent restaurants, boutiques and department stores. Gay-friendly.

Restaurants

★ **LE PETIT PRINCE,** 12, rue de Lanneau, (métro: Maubert Mutualité), 01 43 54 77 26, 19:30-00:00 (Fri, Sat till 00:30).

Retail & Bookstores

LES AMAZONES, 4 rue des Grands Degrés, (métro: Maubert Mutualité), 01 46 34 25 67 (tel/fax), lesbian & women's books, by appointment only (call/fax during Paris business hours only).

LIBRAIRIE FOURMI AILÉE, 8 rue du Fouarre, (métro: Maubert), feminist bookshop, lesbian periodicals."

PARIS 6TH ARROND.

Restaurants

LE VIEUX CASQUE, 19, rue Bonaparte, (métro: St.-Germain-des-Prés.), 01 43 54 99 46, 19:00-23:00 (closed Sun).

Retail & Bookstores

LIBRAIRIE DES FEMMES, 74 rue de la Seine, (métro: Mabillon), 01 43 29 50 75, personnel said not to be lesbian-oriented.

PARIS 8TH ARROND.

Dance Bar/Disco

★ **LE QUEEN,** 102 avenue des Champs Elysées, (métro: George V), 01 53 89 08 89, from 24:00, call for tape of weekly programs.

Cafe

LORD SANDWICH, 134, rue du Fg-Saint-Honoré, (métro: Miromesnil), 01 42 56 41 68, Mon-Fri 11:00-16:00.

XAVIER GOURMET, 89, bd de Courcelles, (métro: Ternes), 01 43 80 78 22, 12:00-16:00 & 19:00-23:30."

PARIS 9TH ARROND.

Dance Bar/Disco

CHEZ MOUNE, 54 rue Pigalle, (métro: Pigalle), 01 45 26 64 64, Sun afternoon disco, lesbians-only from 16:30-20:00.

ENTRE NOUS, 17 rue Laferrière (métro: Saint-George), 01 48 78 11 67, Fri & Sat from 23:00.

L'EGO CLUB, 50 rue de la Chauseé d'Anten, 01 42 85 20 38, Thurs-Sun 18:00-04:00 (women-only Sun from 17:00 & Thurs), Fri & Sat men welcome.

HOTEL DES NATIONS
The Latin Quarter's Comfortable Hotel
PARIS
Tel: (33-1) 43 26 45 24

FRANCE 73

■ Restaurants
GILLES ET GABRIEL, 24, rue Rodier, (métro: Cadet), 01 45 26 86 26, 12:00-14:30 & 19:30-22:30 (Sat only 19:30-23:00), closed Sun. 🚫

LE P'TIT MONNIER, 24, rue Henry-Monnier, (métro: St-Georges), 01 40 16 02 40, traditional French cuisine, 12:00-14:30 & 19:00-22:30 (Sat only 19:00-22:30), closed Sun." 🚫

LES COLONNES DE LA MADELEINE, 6, rue de Sèze, (métro: Madeleine), 01 47 42 60 55, 12:00-15:00 & 19:00-22:30 (closed Sun). 🚫

PARIS 10TH ARROND.

■ Accommodations
HOTEL LOUXOR, 4 rue Taylor, Paris, 75010, (33) 01 42 08 23 91, Fax: (33) 01 42 08 03 30. Gay-friendly hotel, 50% gay/lesbian clientele, private shower/toilets, color TV, breakfast, quiet lounge, near main boulevards & northern & eastern railway stations.

■ Restaurants
CHALET MAYA, 5 rue des Petits Hotels, (métro: Gare de l'Est or Gare du Nord), 01 47 70 52 78, 11:30-14:00 & 19:30-01:00 (Mon only 19:30-01:00), closed Sun. ♀♂

J.O.Z., 12 rue de la Fidelité, 01 43 48 79 23, large restaurant & bar, 21:00-03:00. 🚫

PARIS 11TH ARROND.

■ Information
ARCHIVES, RECHERCHES ET CULTURES LESBIENNES, ARCL, POB 362, 75526 Paris, 11, 01 48 05 25 89, Wed 16:00-20:00, Fri 18:00-22:00 and by appt.

GROUPE DES LESBIENNES FÉMINISTES, c/o Maison des Femmes, 8 Cité Prost, 75011, Paris, (métro: Charonne), 01 43 48 24 91, lesbian feminist group.

MAISON DES FEMMES, 8 Cité Prost, 01 43 48 24 91, women's center with different meetings & socials throughout the week.

■ Accommodations
HÔTEL BEAUMARCHAIS, 3 rue Oberkampf, (métro: Filles du Calvaire or Oberkampf), Paris, 75011, (33) 01 53 36 86 86, Fax: (33) 01 43 38 32 86. Newly opened hotel in the heart of Paris, close to the Marais and Bastille Square. Our colorful rooms feature air conditioning, satelite TV, telephone, safe, etc. We offer a warm and friendly atmosphere with personal, attentive service. Gay-run, some hetero clientele, doors open 24 hours. ♀♂

■ Bars
OBJECTIF LUNE, 19, rue de La Roquette, (métro: Bastille), 01 48 06 46 05, 17:00-04:00. 🚫

■ Restaurants
MANSOURIA, 11 rue Faidherbe, (métro: Faidherbe-Chaligny), 01 43 71 00 16, women-owned Moroccan restaurant, 12:00-14:15 & 19:30-23:00 (Mon only 19:30-23:00), closed Sun. 🚫

■ Erotica
DÉMONIA, 10 cité Joly, (métro: Père Lachaise), women's domination shop, books, magazines, videos, clothing, accessories, 11:00-19:00.

PARIS 12TH ARROND.

■ Restaurants
CAVIAR AND CO, 5, rue de Reuilly, (métro: Faidherbe-Chaligny), 01 43 56 13 98, 12:00-14:00 & 19:30-24:30 (closed Sun & Mon). ♀♂

PARIS 13TH ARROND.

■ Information
MARGUERITE DURAND ARCHIVES, 79 rue Nationale, (métro: Port d'Ivry), feminist & women's studies library in existence since the late 1880's. Modern facilities & impressive resources, some personnel speak English.

■ Restaurants
LE VERDI, 27 rue de la Colonie, (métro: Tolbiac), 01 45 88 30 98, 11:30-14:00 & 19:30-23:00, closed Sat, Sun. 🚫

PARIS 14TH ARROND.

■ Dance Bar/Disco
L'ENFER, 34 rue du Départ (métro: Montparnasse), 01 42 79 94 94, dance garage, women-only Fri & Sat from 23:30. 🚫 ♀

■ Restaurants
AU FEU FOLLET, 5 rue Raymond-Losserand, (métro: Gaîté), 01 43 22 65 72, 19:30-23:30 (weekends 19:00-00:00). 🚫

PARIS 15TH ARROND.

L'ACCENT, 93, rue de Javel, (métro: Charles Michel), 01 45 79 20 26, 20:00-00:30 (closed Sun).

L'IMPASSE, 7 rue de Cadix, 01 40 45 09 81, restaurant & bar, frequented by women, 17:00-02:00 (closed Sun).

PARIS 17TH ARROND.

Bars
LA POTERNE, 17 rue Vernier, (métro: Porte de Champerret), 01 45 72 40 63, 20:00-02:00 (closed Sun-Mon). ♀

Restaurants
L'INSOLENCE, 66, rue Legendre, (métro: Rome), 01 42 29 57 96, 12:00-14:30 & 19:30-22:30 (Sat only 19:30-22:30), closed Sun & Mon.

WAGON 7, 7, rue Boursault, (métro: Rome), 01 42 93 41 57, Thurs-Sat jazz nights, 12:00-14:00 & 20:00-24:00 (Sat, Sun only 20:00-24:00), closed Mon."

PARIS 18TH ARROND.

L'ÉCHAPPÉE BELLE, 5 rue Pierre Picard, (métro: Anvers or Barbès Rochechouart), 01 42 54 61 21, Tues-Sat, lunch & dinner.

LE PERROQUET VERT, 7, rue Cavallotti, (métro: Place de Clichy), 01 45 22 49 16, 12:00-15:00 & 18:30-23:00 (Sat only 18:30-23:00), closed Sun.

LE PIERROT DE LA BUTTE, 41, rue de Caulaincourt, (métro: Lamarck-Caulaincourt), 01 46 06 06 97, traditional French cuisine, 19:30-23:15 (closed Sun).

LE POULAILLER DE LA BUTTE, 18 rue Bachelet, (métro: Jules Joffrin), 01 46 06 01 99, frequented by women.

PARIS 19TH ARROND.

LA LANTERNE, 9 rue du Tunnel, 01 42 39 15 98, 12:00-14:30 & 19:00-23:00 (Sat only 19:00-23:00).

PERIGUEUX

Dance Bar/Disco
L'AN DES ROYS, 51, rue Aubarede, 05 53 53 01 58, from 23:00 (closed Mon). Separate rooms for gays & lesbians. ♀♂

PLOUAY - BRETAGNE

Women's Accommodations
LA HULOTTIÈRE, Le Floch Aline et Jeannine, Le Longeau du Bas, Plouay, 56240, (33) 02 97 33 15 60. Three women-only cottages, fully-furnished with kitchens, dining & living rooms, private baths, BBQ, ping pong table, nearby forest, river & lake, 20 km to ocean. ♀

QUIMPER

Bars
CARPE DIEM, 54bis Ave de la Liberation, 02 98 90 00 21, 18:00-01:00 (closed Mon), frequented by gays & lesbians.

REIMS

Information
AIDS LINE, 03 26 49 96 10.

RENNES

Information
AIDS LINE, 02 99 79 06 04.

FEMMES ENTRE ELLES, 02 99 59 34 07, women's group meets Wed 19:00-20:00.

Bars
LE CARPE DIEM, 21 Blvd de Chezy, 02 99 30 15 55, 11:00-01:00 (from 15:00 weekends). ♀♂

Dance Bar/Disco
LE BATCHI, 34, rue Vasselot, 02 99 79 62 27, 23:00-05:00 (closed Mon). ♀♂

Restaurants
LA BONNE PÂTE, 6 rue Derval, 02 99 38 88 87, 12:00-14:00 & 19:00-23:00. ♀♂

ROUEN

Bars
KOX, 138 rue Beauvoisine, 02 35 07 71 97, 18:00-02:00 ♀♂

Dance Bar/Disco
L'OPIUM, 2, rue Malherbe, 02 35 03 29 36, Fri-Sun 23:00-04:00. ♀♂

Restaurants
GOURMANDINE, 236, rue Martainville, 02 35 71 95 13, 11:00-18:00 (Fri-Sun till 23:00).

FRANCE 75

ST-ETIENNE

Information
AIDS INFO, 04 77 80 75 71, weekdays 13:00-19:00."

Bars
LE CLUB, 3, place Villeboeuf, 04 77 33 56 25, 18:00-01:00. ♂

ST-MALO

Dance Bar/Disco
ANGELUS BIS, 3, rue des Cordiers, 02 99 40 13 20, video disco & cocktail bar 21:00-03:00.

ST-TROPEZ

Bars
CHEZ MAGUY, 5 rue Sibille, 04 94 97 16 12, bar & restaurant. ♂

Dance Bar/Disco
LE BAL, Residence du Nouveau Port, 04 94 97 14 70, daily 23:00-06:00 (in winter Fri-Sun only). ♀♂

Restaurants
L'ENTRECOTE 21, 12, rue du Portail-Neuf, 04 94 97 40 02, 19:30-01:00.
LE BAR A VIN, 13, rue des Feniers, 04 94 97 46 10, restaurant & bar, 19:00-01:00 (closed Sun).

SAINTES

Accommodations
HOTEL CHIMAT DE FRANCE, on route de Royan, (5 min from city center), 05 46 97 20 40, Fax: 05 46 92 22 54, hotel & restaurant.

Bars
LA BELLE EPOQUE, 11 quai de la République, 05 46 74 20 33, frequented by gays & lesbians.

Dance Bar/Disco
LE GRILLON, 12 rue Pierre Schoeffer Concoury, 05 46 74 66 98, 23:00-05:00. ♀♂
SPARTACUS, route de Royan, at Complexe St Vegas, 05 46 93 42 76, Sun 22:00-05:00, 20% women. ♂

SOUTHWEST FRANCE - RURAL

Accommodations
HILLTOP CANTEGRIVE FARM-HOUSES, Bidot Haut, St. Avit Sénieur (Bergerac), 24 440, (33) 05 53 22 01 94, Fax (33) 05 53 27 87 85. Gay-friendly & discrete, this private, centuries-old country estate is magnificently set in 50 acres (20 hectares) of field & forest 1-1/2 hours east of Bordeaux. Two self-contained, fully equipped units sleep 2-4 or 4-6 people. Modern amenities include satellite TV, fireplace & large pool. Visit prehistoric caves & fascinating châteaux, dine in quaint restaurants & participate in abundant outdoor activities. Women-oriented, but men welcome.
PITAU, Lagraulet du Gers, Gondrin, 32330, (33) 05 62 29 15 08 (Tel/Fax).

Hilltop Cantegrive Farmhouses

A Tranquil Hideaway for Women in Chateaux and Wine Country

Southwest France - Rural

(33) 553 22 01 94

FRANCE

Gay-owned & -operated guesthouse in a 1798 stone house in the countryside of Gascony, continental breakfast, shared bath, 5 tent sites, some hetero clientele. ♀♂

VILLA ROUMÉGOUS, St. Antonin Noble Val, 82140, (33) 05 63 30 60 55 (Tel/Fax). Email: jlovell@ilink.fr, A holiday house in the Aveyron Valley area with shared baths, continental breakfast. Michou and Jane have lovingly restored part of their large, comfortable house in the Aveyron Valley to enable you to relax and enjoy your holiday in this beautiful setting. The area, rich in flora and fauna, has magnificent scenery, rustic villages and plenty of calm. We're only 1 hour from the Toulouse-Blagnac airport, and 1/2 hour from the Montauban station, where the high-speed train from Paris stops. ♀♂

■ Women's Accommodations

LA RUCHE, Chez Cormenier, Charente region, Parzac, 16450, (33) 05 45 85 75 15. Women-only retreat offering B&B, self-catering cottage & camping on a beautifully renovated 400-year-old farmstead. With quiet roads, tranquil countryside & beautiful views, the area is perfect for walks & cycling. Horseriding, swimming, canoeing & kayaking are nearby. Traditional French breakfast, plus gourmet evening meals included. Regular activities are organised with the women of the area, such as walks, BBQs, dinners, dances, etc. Only 2-1/2 hours from Paris by train. ♀

MONDÈS, Courrensan, Gondrin, 32330, (33) 05 62 06 59 05 (Tel/Fax). Women-only inn & campground, double rooms with shared baths, 20 tent sites, living room with fireplace, full breakfast buffet & gourmet vegetarian dinners. 🚃 🎵 ♀

PRAT SISTERS, Maison Prat, 32150 Cutxan, Cazaubon, (33) 05 62 09 55 21. Women-only retreat & campground on a country farm, shared baths, 20 tent sites, breakfast. 🎵 ♀

ROUSSA, Courrensan, Gondrin, 32330, (33) 05 62 06 58 96, Fax: (33) 05 62 64 45 34. Women-only guesthouse in 200-year-old renovated former farmhouse, shared baths, generous breakfast & vegetarian dinner, conference room available for rent, many group activities. ♀

SAOUIS, Cravencères, Nogaro, 32110, (33) 05 62 08 56 06. Women-only guesthouse, double rooms, shared showers, garden, tent sites, expanded continental breakfast, dinner. ♀

STRASBOURG

■ Information
AIDS LINE, 03 88 75 73 63, Mon-Fri 09:00-18:00.

■ Dance Bar/Disco
WARNING BAR, 3 rue Klein, 03 88 37 99 33, 22:00-04:00, closed Mon. 🍴 ♂

■ Cafe
LA LUNE NOIRE, 8, rue Metzeral, 03 88 39 96 08, Fri, Sat 21:30-01:00, women's café with monthly dances." ♀

■ Restaurants
AU COIN DU FEU, 10, rue de la Râpe, 03 88 35 44 85, traditional French cuisine, 10:00-14:30 & 19:00-23:30 (Tue only 19:00-23:30), closed Mon." ♀♂

TERGNIER

■ Dance Bar/Disco
LA PARILLA CLUB DISCO & RESTAURANT, 38, rue Démosthène-Gaucher, 03 23 57 25 08. Disco: Fri, Sat 22:00-04:00. Bar: Tues-Sun 15:00-24:00. Restaurant: Tues-Sun 16:00-22:00. 🍴 ♀♂

VILLA ROUMEGOUS

The Real Charm of a Simple Life
Southwest France

(33-5) 63 30 60 55

TOULON

Information
AIDS INFO, 04 94 62 96 23.

Bars
EQUIPE BAR, 4 Place Gustave Lambert, 04 94 09 10 04, 2 terraces, frequented by gays, 10:00-01:00 (Sun from 17:00).
RENATO CLUB, 1 rue Etienne Dauphin, 04 94 62 30 95, winter 15:00-01:00, summer 17:00-04:00.
TEXAS, 1, rue de l'Humilité, 04 94 89 14 10, 16:30-01:00 (in summer till 03:00)."

Dance Bar/Disco
BOY'S PARADISE, 1, bd Pierre Toesca, across from train station, 04 94 09 35 90, rave, 23:00-05:00.

TOULOUSE

Information
AIDS INFO, 05 61 42 22 87.

Bars
★ BAGDAM CAFÉE, 4, rue Delacroix, 05 61 99 03 62. Cafe, restaurant & bar for women only, with theatre, exhibitions, films, concerts, lectures, discussions & women's resource center. Monthly disco, 18:00-02:00 (closed Sun, Mon). Closed for vacation mid-Aug-mid-Sept.
LA CIGUE, 6, rue de la Colombette, 05 61 99 61 87, 19:00-02:00, closed Mon.
QUINQUINA BAR, 26, rue Peyras, 05 61 21 90 73, 08:00-22:00, Sun from 18:00.
SAND'S, 31 rue de Stalingrad, 05 61 63 03 05, 16:00-02:00 (Sat 18:00-04:00).

Restaurants
CHEZ PHILIPPE, 24 Grande rue St Michel, 05 61 25 35 08.

TOURS

Information
AIDS INFO, 02 47 20 16 56.

Bars
CHEZ NELLO, 8 rue Auguste Chevalier, 02 47 39 12 11, bar & restaurant 17:00-02:00.

Dance Bar/Disco
CLUB 71, 71, rue Courteline, 02 47 37 01 54, 22:30-04:00 (closed Mon).

LA RUCHE

Experience Rural France at a 400-year-old Farmstead

Southwest France

(33) 05 45 85 75 15

VALENCE

Women's Accommodations
INANNA, La Renaude, Chastel-Arnaud, 26340, (33) 04 75 21 50 72. Women-only retreat & campground with classes available at times, rooms & tent sites, breakfast & dinner."

Bars
AMBIGU BAR, 13 Ave Gambetta, 17:00-04:00.

GERMANY

COUNTRY CODE: (49),

AACHEN

Information
ROSALINDE LESBENTREFF, Wilhelmstr. 69 at Frauen Helfen Frauen, (0241) 902 416, lesbian meeting at Women Helping Women, 1st Sun of the month, 17:00-19:00.

Bars
BAR JEDER VERNUNFT, Promenadenstr. 43, (0241) 250 39, 22:00-03:00 (closed Tues). Women only Thurs.

GERMANY

ASCHAFFENBURG

Information
FRAUENZENTRUM, Herrleinstr. 26, (06021) 243 99, women's center, Lesbentreff (lesbian social) Fri from 20:00.

AUGSBURG

Information
AIDS HILFE, (0821) 566 93.

FRAUENZENTRUM, Haunstetterstrasse 49, (0821) 58 11 00 women's center, Lesbentreff (lesbian social) Fri from 20:30.

Retail & Bookstores
ELISARA, Schmiedgasse 11, (0821) 15 43 03, women's bookstore.

BAMBERG

Cafe
CAFE ABSEITS, Pödeldorferstr., ♀

BERLIN

Information
BERLINER AIDS HILFE, (030) 883 3017 or Pluspunkt Berlin: (030) 445 86 81.

EWA FRAUENZENTRUM, Prenzlauer Allee 6, (030) 442 55 42, 442 72 57, women's center, 10:00-18:00. Lesbian group meets Wed 19:00.

FRAUENFORSCHUNGS-, BILDUNGS-, UND INFORMATIONSZENTRUM E. V., (FFBIZ), Danckelmannstrasse 47, (030) 322 10 35, information, archives, library, gallery, cultural events for women.

FRIEDE FRAUENZENTRUM, Proskauerstr. 7, Freidrichsain, (030) 442 4276 women's center.

LÄRM & LUST FRAUENMUSIKZENTRUM, Schwedenstr. 14, (030) 784 72 97, women's music center.

LESBENBERATUNG, Kulmerstr. 20a, (030) 215 20 00, lesbian information center. Mon, Tues, Thurs 17:00-20:00.

RUT, RAT UND TAT, KULTURZENTRUM, Schillerpromenade 1, (030) 621 47 53, women's cultural center, Wed-Fri 17:00-21:00.

SCHOKOFABRIK, Naunynstr. 72, (030) 615 29 99, large complex with woodworking & other workshops, 10:00-14:00 (Wed 12:00-16:00), closed Fri-Sun.

SPINNBODEN LESBENARCHIV, Burgsdorfstr. 1, (030) 465 20 21, lesbian archives, Wed & Fri 13:00-20:00.

Accommodations
ARCO HOTEL — NORDDEUTSCHER HOF, Geisbergstr. 30, Berlin, 10777, (49-30) 218 21 28, Fax: (49-30) 211 33 87. Hotel 2 blocks from Wittenbergplatz with breakfast buffet, private & shared baths, telephone, terrace, garden, small lounge, near gay bars, 50% gay/lesbian clientele.

HOTEL CHARLOTTENBURGER HOF, Stuttgarter Platz 14, Berlin, 10627, (49-30) 32 90 70, Fax: (49-30) 323 37 23. hotel with small restaurant, newsstand & hair salon, 20% gay male clientele, women welcome, mostly straight clientele, color cable TV, maid service, modern rooms, centrally located, full breakfast 5 DM extra.

PENSION NIEBUHR, Niebuhrstr 74, Berlin, 10629, (49-30) 324 95 95 or 324 95 96, Fax: (49-30) 324 80 21. Stay in a turn-of-the-century home in a quiet neighborhood, yet close to the well-known Charlottenburg district and the Kurfürstendamm, the popular main street of Berlin. A choice of international restaurants is nearby, as are shopping and nightlife. Our recently furnished rooms don't feel like hotel rooms. 50% hetero clientele. Most of our gay guests are men, but women are always very welcome.

PENSION NIEBUHR

NIEBUHRSTR. 74,
10629 BERLIN

(030) 324 95 95/6

Recently Remodeled
Rooms In A
Quiet Neighborhood

GERMANY 79

Women's Accommodations

ARTEMISIA, WOMEN ONLY HOTEL, Brandenburgischestrasse 18, Berlin, 10707, (49-30) 873 89 05, or 873 63 73, Fax: (49-30) 861 86 53. Email: Frauenhotel-Berlin@t-online.de, Women-only hotel with bar, 5 min from Ku-Damm, singles, doubles, suite, modern decor & soothing pastels, meeting rooms, TV lounge, art displays, lavish buffet-style breakfast." ♀

Bars

ARTEMISIA HOTEL BAR, at Artemisia Hotel, a place for a quiet drink in a pleasant room with a modern decor & women's art, muted music for conversation. Open 7 days 17:00-01:00. ♀

BALLHAUS BAR, Naunynstr. 27, women-only Mon-Wed. 🍽 ♀

BEGINE, Postdamer Strasse 139, (030) 215 43 25, Café und Kulturzentrum, with lite menu, live lesbian concerts, cabaret, readings, films, a different schedule each month. Open daily 18:00-01:00. Scheduled disco nights. 🍽 ✖ ♪ ♀

Dance Bar/Disco

AM WASSERTURM, Spandauer Damm 168, (030) 302 52 60, Wed, Sat from 21:00. 🍽 ♀

DIE BUSCHE, Mühlenstr. 11-12, (030) 589 15 85, Fri, Sat 21:30-06:00; Wed, Sun 21:30-05:00. 🍽 ♂

EWA FRAUENDISCO, Prenzlauer Allee 6, at EWA women's center, women's dance night Sat. 🍽 ♀

POUR ELLE, Kalkreuthstrasse 10, (030) 218 75 33, small bar & disco, from 21:00. Women's bar Tues & Thu-Sun, also for men on Mon, Wed." 🍽 ♀

Cafe

ANDERES UFER, Hauptstr. 157, (030) 784 15 78, 11:00-02:00.

CAFE ANAL, Muskauer Str. 15, (030) 618 70 64, daily from 15:00 (from 17:00 in winter), Mon women's night." ♂

CAFE SEIDENFADEN, Dircksen Str. 47, (030) 283 2783, drug- & alcohol-free women's cafe, 11:00-21:00 (Sat, Sun till 18:00), closed Mon. ♀

EWA FRAUENCAFE, Prenzlauer Allee 6, at EWA women's center, Mon-Fri 16:00-23:00. ♀

FRAUENCAFE, Glogauer Str. 22, (030) 612 31 35, Mon-Thurs 15:00-17:00. ♀

SCHOKO CAFÉ, Naunynstr 72, (030) 615 29 99, 13:00-24:00 (closed Mon), disco last Sat. Also Hamam steam bath 13:00-22:00 (Mon from 17:00). 🍽 ♀

Restaurants

ABENDMAHL, Muskauer Str. 9, (030) 612 51 70, 18:00-01:00.

ALTBERLINER BIERSTUBEN, Saarbrückenstr. 17, (030) 282 89 33, daily 12:00-02:00.

CALVADOS, Bayreuther Str. 10, (030) 213 47 79, 11:00-02:00 (Fri, Sat till 03:00), Sun 17:00-01:00."

HOFGARTEN, Regensburger Str. 5,

DAS FRAUENHOTEL
artemisia

A hotel for women, with modern, beautifully-appointed rooms • quiet cocktail bar • sumptuous breakfast buffet • close to all Berlin's sights

Tel: (49 30) 873 89 05 or Fax: (49 30) 861 86 53
E-MAIL: Frauenhotel-Berlin@t-online.de
BRANDENBURGISCHE STRASSE 18 • D 10707 BERLIN

GERMANY

(030) 218 18 83, bar & restaurant, 18:00-01:00, summer 17:00-01:00. ♉

OFFENBACH STUBEN, Stubbenkammerstr. 8, (030) 445 85 02, daily 18:00-02:00.

SLOBO'S, Heimstrasse 8, (030) 693 09 00, 17:00-01:00, closed Wed.

BIELEFELD

■ Information

FRAUENKULTURZENTRUM, FRAUENCAFE & KNEIPE, Am Zwinger 16, (0521) 686 67, women's cultural center Mon-Thurs 17:00-20:00, Frauencafé & Frauenkneipe (women's cafe & bar) Mon-Fri 16:00-24:00.

LESBENARCHIV, Am Zwinger 16, at Frauenkulturzentrum, (0521) 667 13, lesbian archives, Wed 19:00-21:00.

LESBENTELEFON, (0521) 13 83 90, Wed 19:00-21:00.

BOCHUM

■ Dance Bar/Disco

FRAUENSCHWOOF, Langendreer, at Alter Bahnhof, women's dance night 2nd Sat. [♫] ♀

■ Cafe

FRAUENCAFE TRA DI NOI, Oskar-Hoffmann-Str. 109, (0234) 30 91 69, kommunikationszentrum & gallerie, women's cafe, gathering place & gallery Tues-Sun 15:00-24:00. ♀

■ Retail & Bookstores

FRAUENBUCHLADEN AMAZONAS, Schmidstr. 12, (0234) 68 31 94, women's bookstore.

BONN

■ Information

AIDS HILFE, (0228) 21 90 21.

FRAUENMUSEUM, Im Krausfeld 10, (0228) 63 84 65, women's museum, open Mon-Sat 20:00-23:00.

LESBEN UND SCHWULENZENTRUM, Endenicher Str. 1, (0228) 63 00 39, lesbian & gay center, Mon 20:00-24:00, Sat 10:00-14:00, Sun 16:00-20:00. Women meet Tues from 20:00.

■ Bars

ZARAH L., Maxstrasse 22, (0228) 63 46 35, Wed, Thurs 21:30-02:00 & Fri, Sat from 22:00. Frauenabend (women's bar night) Mon. ♂♂

■ Retail & Bookstores

BONNER FEMINISTISCHES ARCHIV UND BÜCHEREI, Dorotheenstr. 20, (0228) 68 58 14. Feminist bookstore and archives, Tues, Thurs, Fri 14:00-18:00, Wed 14:00-20:00.

BUCHLADEN 46, Kaiserstr. 46, (0228) 22 36 08, general bookstore with a gay section, 10:00-18:30 (Sat till 14:00), closed Sun.

NORA, Kekulestrasse 35, (0228) 224 491, women's books.

BOTTROP

■ Information

LESBENTELEFON, (02041) 635 93, lesbian line, Mon 17:00-20:00."

BRAUNSCHWEIG

■ Information

LABRYS LESBENGRUPPE, (0531) 33 29 86, lesbian group, meets 1st Tues from 20:00. Call for details."

SPINSTERS FRAUENKULTURZENTRUM, Steintorwall 8, (0531) 124 641, women's info center.

■ Bars

SIR HENRY, Petersilienstr. 1-3, (0531) 434 20, 21:00-02:00, Fri & Sat till 03:00, closed Mon. ♂

■ Cafe

LILITH FRAUENCAFE, Rosenstr. 6, (0531) 79 67 60, women's cafe. ♀

■ Retail & Bookstores

FRAUENBUCHLADEN, Magnikirchstr. 4, (0531) 407 44.

BREMEN

■ Information

AIDS HILFE, (0421) 70 2012.

BELLADONNA KULTUR, KOMMUNIKATIONS UND BILDUNGSZENTRUM, Sonnenstr. 8, (0421) 70 35 34, women's culture, communications and information center.

FRAUENKULTURHAUS, Am Krummen Arm 1, (0421) 701 632, women's center, Wed 10:00-12:00.

LESBENTELEFON, (0421) 339 9046, Fri 20:00-22:00.

RAT UND TAT ZENTRUM, Theodor

Körnerstr. 1, (0421) 70 41 70, gay center, women meet Sat 17:00.

■ Bars
FRAUENKNEIPE, Lahnstr. 37-39, at Klöntje, women's bar night Fri from 20:00. ♀

■ Dance Bar/Disco
FRAUENLESBEN DISCO, Thedinghauserstr. 1156, at the Jugendfreizeitheim, Women's & lesbian disco, ask locally for exact dates. ♀

■ Cafe
FRAUEN INFO CAFE, Humboldtstr. 116, at De Colores, Tues, Thurs 15:00-19:00. ♀
FRAUENCAFE IM FRAUEN-KULTURHAUS, Am Krummen Arm 1, (0421) 70 16 32, women's cafe at women's cultural center. Lesbengruppe (lesbian group) meets 1st & 3rd Thurs from 20:00. ♀

■ Restaurants
BIENENKORB, Rembertistr. 32, (0421) 32 72 18, daily 11:00-06:00."

■ Retail & Bookstores
FRAUENBUCHLADEN HAGAZUSSA, Friesenstr. 12, (0421) 741 40, women's bookstore."

BREMERHAVEN

■ Bars
SAND, Karlsburg 9, (0471) 41 23 40, women only 2nd & 4th Wed. ♀

BRUNKEN - WESTERWALD

■ Women's Accommodations
LICHTQUELLE FRAUENBILDUNGSSTÄTTE, Hochstr. 11, Brunken, 57539, (49-2742) 71587. Lichtquelle means "Source of Light," and Lichtquelle is a place for healing, meditation and therapy. English, French and German speakers will feel comfortable at the weekend seminars, which can involve dancing, music and therapy. When there are no seminars being held, women can come for an individual retreat amidst the beautiful German countryside. There are many places for walking, and horseback riding is nearby. Therapeutic massage and biodynamics (psychic massage) are available at DM 50 for 1/4 hour. Vegetarian meals can include rice, two vegetables, tofu and seaweed. ♀

BÜCKEN

■ Women's Accommodations
FRAUENFERIENHAUS ALTENBÜCKEN, Schürmannsweg 25, Bücken, 27333, (49-4251) 7899, Fax: (49-4251) 6291. women-only retreat with classes available, shopping, swimming & sauna nearby, single, double & dorm rooms with shared baths, groceries provided. ♀

Lichtquelle

Women's Retreat

- Individual and Group Retreats • Therapeutic Massage
- Psychic Massage • Horseback Riding
- Walking in the German Countryside • Vegetarian Meals

We Speak English, French & German

Tel: (49-2742) 71587 Brunken, Germany

GERMANY

CHARLOTTENBERG

■ *Women's Accommodations*
FRAUENLANDHAUS, Holzappelerstrasse 3, Charlottenberg, 56379, (49-6439) 7531. Frauenlandhause is a bed and breakfast for women only where English, Italian and German are spoken. A large garden decorates the grounds. There are many single rooms in a recently constructed new building. Workshops are offered here on a variety of subjects, such as massage, nutrition, self-defense, Tantra, voice awareness and expression, magic, spirituality and writing. There is a sauna on premises and bicycles for guests to use when exploring the countryside. English, Italian and German are spoken here. ♀

CHEMNITZ

■ *Information*
LESBENGRUPPE, Hainstr. 34, lesbian group meets here.
LILA VILA, Kassbergerstr. 22, (0371) 326 78, Frauenbegegnungszentrum (women's info. center).

COLOGNE
SEE KÖLN.,

B&B For Women

We Speak English, Italian & German

Frauenlandhaus

- Massage
- Self-Defense
- Nutrition
- Spirituality
- Writing

Tel: **(49-6439) 7531**
Charlottenberg

DARMSTADT

■ *Cafe*
FRAUENCAFE IM FRAUENZENTRUM, Emilstrasse 10, (06151) 71 49 52, women's café in women's center, 10:00-14:00 (Thurs from 20:00). ♀

DORTMUND

■ *Information*
AIDS HILFE, (0231) 52 76 37.
LESBENTELEFON, (0231) 83 19 19, lesbian line, Sat 10:00-12:00.

■ *Cafe*
FRAUENCAFE GERÜCHTEKÜCHE, Adlerstr 30, (0231) 14 08 21, Sun 16:00-21:00. ♀
ZAUBERMAUS, Kielstr. 32b, (0231) 81 46 49, 16:00-01:00, Fri, Sat till 03:00.

■ *Retail & Bookstores*
LITFASS, Münsterstr. 107, (0231) 83 47 24, general bookshop with a gay section, Mon-Fri 10:00-20:00, Sat till 14:00.

DRESDEN

■ *Information*
AIDS HILFE, (0351) 441 6142.
LESBENTELEFON, (0351) 514 70, lesbian line Wed 19:00-22:00.
SOWIESO FRAUENZENTRUM, Angelikastr. 1, (0351) 514 70, lesbengruppe, women's center with lesbian group meetings, lesbian disco 2nd & 4th Sat.

■ *Retail & Bookstores*
FRAUENBUCHLADEN PUSTEBLUME, Martin Luther Str. 23.,

DUISBURG

■ *Bars*
CAFE BERLIN, An der Bleeck 40-42, (0203) 24 273, 16:00-02:00 (Fri, Sat till 05:00). ♀

DÜSSELDORF

■ *Information*
AIDS HILFE, (0211) 726 05 26.
FRAUENBERATUNGSTELLE, Ackerstr. 144, (0211) 68 68 54, Frauenberatung (women's info), women's bar night Thurs.
LESBEN SCHWULENZENTRUM, Lierenfelderstr. 39, (0211) 737 00 30, lesbian & gay center.

GERMANY

Accommodations
HOTEL ACON, Mintropstrasse 23, Düsseldorf, 40215, (49-211) 37 70 20, Fax: (49-211) 37 70 31. Hotel with bistro/bar, expanded continental breakfast, all private baths, color TV, centrally located, 15-min walk to gay/lesbian bars. 50% gay & lesbian clientele.

Bars
LESBENKNEIPE, Lierenfelderstr. 39, at the Lesben- und Schwulenzentrum, women's cafe at lesbian & gay center, Tues. ♀

VALENTINO, Bahnstr. 63, (0211) 36 29 59, 20:00-05:00, closed Mon. 🍸 ♀

Dance Bar/Disco
FRAUENSCHWOOF IM ZAKK, Fichtenstr. 40, popular women's disco, 1st Fri from 22:00. 🍸 ♀

LESBENSCHWOOF, Oberbilkerallee 327, at Cafe Rosa Mond, Thurs from 20:00, men welcome. 🍸 ♀

WOMEN'S DANCE NIGHT, Lierenfelderstr. 39, at the Lesben-Schwulenzentrum, last Sat. 🍸 ♀

Cafe
ROSA MOND CAFÉ, Oberbilker Allee 327, (0211) 77 54 42, women's café & bar night, vegetarian menu, Fri 20:00-24:00. ♀

Retail & Bookstores
FRAUEN-BÜCHER-ZIMMER, Becherstr. 2, (0211) 46 44 05, women's bookstore.

EDERTAL-ANRAFF

Women's Accommodations
FRAUENBILDUNGSHAUS EDERTAL-ANRAFF, Königsberger Str. 6, Anraff, 34549, (49-5621) 3218, Fax: (49-5621) 94726. women-only retreat guesthouse with restaurant & bar, numerous classes available, double room & dorms, shared baths, groceries provided, nearby pool & lake. ♀

EICHSTÄTT

Cafe
FRAUENCAFE, Luitpoldstr. 31, (08421) 65 68, women's café, Thurs 18:00-22:00. ♀

ERFURT

Dance Bar/Disco
ATLANTIZ, Zum Nordstrand 1, Wed-Sat 21:00-03:00. 🍸 ♀♂

LESBENDISCO, Thomas Müntzerstr. 20, (0361) 642 1383, lesbian disco last Sat of the month. 🍸 ♀

ERLANGEN

Information
FRAUENZENTRUM & LESBENBERATUNG, Gerberei 4, (09131) 20 80 23, women's center, lesbian information center & café.

ESSEN

Information
AIDS HILFE, (0201) 236 096.

Dance Bar/Disco
FRAUENTANZ IN DER ZECHE CARL(A), Hömannstr. 10, women's dance night, 3rd Sat from 22:00. 🍸 ♀

FLENSBURG

Information
LESBENGRUPPE, Marienkirchof 4/5, (0461) 266 11, lesbian group, meets 3rd Mon 18:00-20:00.

LESBENTELEFON, (0461) 213 47, Tues 18:00-19:00.

LUZIE'S FRAUENZIMMER, Marianstr. 29-31, women's info center, Tues-Fri 15:00-18:00.

FÖHR/WRIXUM

Women's Accommodations
KVINDEGARD FRAUENHOF, Ohl Dörp 52, 2270 Wrixum, Island of Föhr, 25938, (49-4681) 8935. women-only, self-catering guest apartments, nearby pool & ocean beach, gym, weights, sauna, steam, massage within walking distance. ♀

FRANKFURT - MAIN

Information
AIDS HILFE, (069) 43 97 04, 43 97 05.

LESBEN ARCHIV, Klingerstr. 6, at the Lesbisch-Schwules, Kulturhaus (lesbian & gay cultural center), (069) 29 30 45.

LESBENINFORMATIONS UND BERATUNGSTELLE, Alte Gasse 38, (069) 28 28 83, lesbian information center, Tues, Thurs, Fri 17:00-19:30, consultancy, seminars, info and more.

LESBISCH SCHWULES KULTURHAUS, Klingerstr. 6, (069) 29 30 44. Lesbian and gay cultural center.

SWITCHBOARD, gay & lesbian switchboard and cafe, Alte Gasse 36, (069) 28 35 35, Tues-Thurs 19:00-24:00; Fri, Sat till 01:00; Sun 15:00-24:00."

■ Bars

GRÖSENWAHN, Lenaustr. 97, at Nordenstr., (069) 59 93 56, 16:00-01:00 (Fri, Sat till 02:00). ♂

★ **LUCKY'S MANHATTAN,** Schäfergasse 27, (069) 28 49 19. 12:00-01:00, Fri & Sat till 02:00, Sun 09:00-01:00. ♂

PARAGON, Liebfrauenberg 37, (069) 20 230, from 10:00. ♂

TREIBHAUS, Elefantengasse 11, (069) 29 12 31, daily 09:00-01:00 (Fri, Sat till 02:00)." ♂

VICTORIA, Bleichstr. 38, bar & cafe. ♀

ZUM SCHWEJK, Schäfergasse 20, (069) 29 31 66, 11:00-01:00, Mon from 16:00 & Sun from 15:00. ♂

■ Dance Bar/Disco

BLUE ANGEL, Brönnerstrasse 17, (069) 28 27 72, from 23:00 (Fri, Sat from 22:00). 🎵♂

C5 INDUSTRY, Alte Gasse 5, (069) 29 13 56, Wed-Sat from 22:00. Women's night monthly. 🎵♂

LOVE BALL, Hanauerlandstr. 181, at Love House, gay Sat only. 🎵♀♂

■ Cafe

CAFE LILIPUT, Neue Kräme 29 (Sandhof-Passage), (069) 28 57 27, daily 10:00-24:00 (Sun from 14:00)." ♂

HARVEY'S, Bornheimer Landstr. 64, (069) 49 73 03, bar & restaurant, 09:00-01:00 (Fri, Sat till 02:00)." ♂

LESBIAN CAFE, Klingerstr. 6, at the gay & lesbian Kulturhaus, Sun 15:00-19:00. ♀

FREIBURG

■ Information

FEMINISTISCHES ARCHIV, Wilhelmstr. 15.,

FRAUENZENTRUM, Schwarzwaldstr. 107, (0761) 38 33 90, women's center, lesbian group Sappho meets Tues from 20:00.

LESBENTELEFON, (0761) 38 33 90, Wed 20:00-22:00.

■ Cafe

FRAUENKNEIPE, Wilhelmstrasse 15, at Jos Fritz bookstore location, women's café 1st, 3rd & 5th Fri. ♀

■ Retail & Bookstores

JOS FRITZ, Wilhelmstr. 15, (0761) 26 877, bookstore 09:00-18:30. Scheduled gay Fri evening, call for details."

GIESSEN

■ Information

LESBENTELEFON, (0641) 314 38, lesbian line, 1st Thurs 19:00-21:00.

GÖTTINGEN

■ Information

LESBENTELEFON, (0551) 455 10, lesbian line, Tues 18:00-20:00."

■ Bars

LESBENTREFF, Gronerstr. 28, enter from Nicolaistr., lesbian social 2nd Fri from 20:00. ♀

■ Cafe

LESBEN UND FRAUENCAFE, Geismarlandstr. 19, Tues from 20:30. ♀

SCHWESTERNBLICK, Immanuel Kant Str. 1, at the gay center, (0551) 770 1100, bar & café. ♀

■ Retail & Bookstores

LAURA, Burgstr. 21, (0551) 473 17, women's bookstore."

HALLE

■ Information

AIDS INFO, (0345) 364 19.

HAMBURG

■ Information

AIDS HILFE, (040) 319 6981.

INFOTELEFON VON LESBEN FÜR LESBEN, (040) 279 00 49, lesbian info line, Wed 17:00-19:00."

JUNGLESBEN ZENTRUM, Glashüttenstr. 2, (40) 430 46 24, center for young lesbians, answers Mon 16:00-18:00 & Wed 14:00-16:00. Lesbians over age of 25 call (40) 245 002. Lesbian cafe Thurs 17:00-19:00.

MAGNUS HIRSCHFIELD CENTRUM,

GERMANY

Borgweg 8, (040) 279 00 69, gay & lesbian center, 15:00-24:00 (Sun from 13:00)."

Accommodations

KÜNSTLER PENSION SARAH PETERSEN, Lange Reihe 88 (moving back to newly restored location, in early summer, '98 at Lange Reihe 50, call for exact date), Hamburg, 20099, (49-40) 24 98 26 (Tel/Fax). gay & lesbian guesthouse, 30% hetero clientele, creatively furnished rooms, B/W & color TV, shared baths, nearby lake & public pool, beverages, expanded (meatless) continental breakfast." ♀♂

Women's Accommodations

HOTEL HANSEATIN, Dragonerstall 11, Hamburg, 20355, (49-40) 341 345, Fax: (49-40) 345 825. Email: hanseatin@w4w.net, Welcome to the first women's hotel in Hamburg! Situated in a beautiful heritage building, the hotel is in the heart of the city, close to the concert hall, the trade fair grounds, the conference centre and shopping area. It's also just a few minutes away from Alster Lake. Adjoining the hotel is the women's café "Endlich" (open Monday to Saturday from 4pm and on Sunday from 9am) and a shady terrace. ♀

Bars

AMIGO BAR, Taubenstrasse 22, (040) 31 64 36, from 21:00. ♀♂

FRAUENKNEIPE, Stresemannstr. 60, (040) 43 63 77, women's bar, from 20:00 (closed Tues). ♀

IKA STUBEN, Budapest Str. 38, (040) 31 09 98, from 19:00 (Fri, Sat from 21:00), closed Mon, Tues. ♀

Dance Bar/Disco

CAMELOT, Hamburger Berg 13, (040) 317 4489, lesbian disco one Sat per month, call for schedule. ♀

FRAUENDISCO, Borgweg 8, at the Magnus Hirschfeld Zentrum, women's disco 2nd Sat from 21:00. ♀

Cafe

BISSQUIT, Lange Reihe 61, 11:00-24:00. ♀

CAFE FRADKIN, Eulenstr. 49, 10:00-24:00 (Sun from 11:00)."

CAFE MEGDONNA, Grindelalle 43, at the Denk(t)räume center, 15:00-19:00 (Mon till 21:00), closed Fri-Sun. ♀

HOTEL HANSEATIN
Exclusively for Women
Hamburg
(49-40) 341 345

FRAUENCAFE, Borgweg 8, at the Magnus Hirschfeld Zentrum, women's café, Wed 15:00-18:00." ♀

FRAUENCAFE ENDLICH, Dragonerstall 11, (040) 35 1616, women's cafe, daily from 16:00 (Sat from 21:00). ♀

FRAUENCAFE VENUS, Bismarckstr. 98, (040) 420 47 48, women's cafe at the Frauenbuchladen." ♀

FRAUENLESBENCAFE, Hospitalstr. 207, women's & lesbian cafe, Tues 18:00-24:00, ask locally to verify street number. ♀

LESBENCAFE, Glasshüttenstr. 2, at the Junglesben Zentrum, lesbian cafe, Thurs 17:00-19:00. ♀

LESBENCAFE, Borgweg 8, at the Magnus Hirschfeld Centrum, lesbian cafe. ♀

SEUTE DEERN, Kolbhöfen 15, from 17:00. ♀

Retail & Bookstores

FRAUENBUCHLADEN, Bismarckstr. 98, (040) 420 47 48, women's bookstore.

HANNOVER

Information

AIDS HILFE, (0511) 32 77 71.

LESBENTELEFON, (0511) 44 05 68, lesbian line, answers Mon 19:00-21:00.

LESBENZENTRUM, Lichtenbergplatz 7, enter from Teichstr., (0511) 44 05 68, lesbian center.

GERMANY

Dance Bar/Disco
FRAUENDISCO IM MUSIKTHEATER BAD, Am Grossen Garten 60, women's disco last Thurs of the month from 21:00. ♀

Cafe
CAFE CALDO, Bergmannstr. 7, (0511) 151 73, gay cafe, 09:30-02:00, Sat & Sun from 11:00. ♀♂

FRAUEN UND LESBENABEND IM CAFE KLATSCH, Limmerstr. 58, Linden., Women's & lesbian evening at Cafe Klatsch 2nd Mon of the month, from 20:00." ♀

Retail & Bookstores
BUCHLADEN ANNABEE, Gerberstr. 6, (0511) 131 81 39, general bookstore with gay & lesbian section, 10:00-18:00 (Sat till 14:00), closed Sun."

HEIDELBERG

Information
AIDS HILFE, (06221) 16 17 00.

Bars
FRAUENCAFE, Blumenstr. 43, women's cafe Mon 20:00-23:00, Tues till 24:00, last Wed from 19:30, Fri till 24:00, 1st & 3rd Thurs 20:00-23:00." ♀

Retail & Bookstores
FRAUENBUCHLADEN, Theaterstr. 16, (06221) 222 01, women's bookstore.

HEILBRONN

Cafe
BELLADONNA FRAUENCAFÉ, Werderstr. 159, (07131) 603 50, women's café at the Frauenzentrum (women's center)."

HOPSTEN-SCHALE

Women's Accommodations
FRAUENBILDUNGSHAUS OSTERESCH, Zum Osteresch 1, Hopsten-Schale, 48496, (05457) 15 13. Women-only retreat organised around workshops in German (some especially for lesbians) in crafts, massage, dance, feminist medicine, music, arts. Guests may stay only if attending workshop; 1 shared bath, tent sites." ♀

ISLAND OF SYLT

Accommodations
HAUS KORALLE, Nordmarkstr. 5, Westerland/Sylt, 25980, (49-4651) 27315, Fax: (49-4651) 29866. Luxurious apartments with cable TV, phone, gardens, parking, 50% gay & lesbian clientele.

KAISERSLAUTERN

Information
AIDS HILFE, (0631) 180 99.

Dance Bar/Disco
★ **NANU,** Dr. Rudolf Breitscheid Str. 58, (0631) 138 12, from 21:00 (summer months from 22:00), closed Mon, Tues & Thurs. Frequented by military personnel, more women Sat." ♂

REMBRANDT'S, (formerly Joy Club), Burgstr. 21, (0631) 95844, Thurs 20:00-01:00, Fri-Sat 21:00-04:00, Sun 19:00-24:00, gallery space for artists, men welcome." ♀

KARLSRUHE

Information
LESBENTELEFON, (0721) 69 10 70, lesbian line, Fri 20:00-22:00. Ask about scheduled lesbian socials.

Cafe
FRAUENCAFE, Rudolfstr. 17, women's cafe, lesbians meet Fri from 20:00. ♀

Retail & Bookstores
KASSIOPEIA, Marienstr. 14, (0721) 37 02 04, women's bookstore.

KASSEL

Information
FRAUENZENTRUM, Goethestr. 44, women's center with Frauenkneipe (women's bar night) 1st Fri from 21:00, Frauendisco (women's disco) 3rd Fri from 21:00."

Bars
FRAUENFRÜHSTÜCK, at The Avocado, Schönfelder Str. 3, women's breakfast 1st, 2nd & 4th Sun." ♀

Retail & Bookstores
ARADIA, Pestalozzistr. 9, (0561) 172 10, women's bookstore.

KEMPTEN

Information
FRAUENZENTRUM LILA DISTL, Hoföschle 7a, (0831) 155 86, women's center with Lesbentreff (lesbian social) 1st Mon from 20:00."

GERMANY 87

■ Bars
FRAUENTREFF, Stuibenweg 1, at Le Filou bar, (0831) 268 29, women's social Tue & Fri from 20:00. ♀

LE FILOU, Stuibenweg 1, (0831) 268 27, 20:00-01:00 (Fri, Sat till 03:00), closed Mon, Tues. ♂

■ Retail & Bookstores
FRAUENBUCHLADEN, Rathausplatz 9, (0831) 182 28, women's bookstore.

KIEL

■ Information
AIDS HILFE, (0431) 551 054.

■ Dance Bar/Disco
FRAUENDISCO, Hass Str. 22, at Pumpe, women's disco 2nd & 4th Sat. ♀

■ Cafe
FRAUENCAFE KASSANDRA, Schasstr. 4, (0431) 67 35 36. ♀

KÖLN - COLOGNE

■ Information
AIDS HILFE, (0221) 20 20 30.

LESBEN UND SCHWULENBERATUNG IM SCHULZ, Kartäuserwall 18, (0221) 9318 8080, gay & lesbian organization with socials, daily 10:00-01:00 (Fri, Sat till 03:00). Lesbengruppe (lesbian group) meets here.

■ Accommodations
HOTEL HUBERTUSHOF, Mühlenbach 30, Köln 1, 5000, (49-221) 217 386, Fax: (49-221) 21 89 55. Bed & breakfast with gay sauna. 50% gay & lesbian clientele, especially on weekends, expanded German buffet breakfast.

■ Bars
GEORGE SAND, Marsilstein 13, (0221) 21 61 62, 19:00-01:00 (Fri, Sat till 03:00). ♀♂

GLORIA CAFÉ & SHOWBAR, Apostelnstr. 11, (0221) 258 36 56, café: 09:00-01:00. Call 25 44 33 for show schedule. Scheduled lesbian disco. ♂

INDIGO, Vondelstr. 12, (0221) 32 49 88, 17:00-01:00 (Sat, Sun from 10:00). Sun brunch 11:00-16:00. ♀

KÖLSCH ROUGE, Merowingerstr. 31, (0221) 32 99 67. ♀

SCHULZ BAR, Kartäuserwall 18, at the SCHULZ lesbian/gay center, (0221) 9318 8080, daily 10:00-01:00 (Fri, Sat till 03:00). Women-only 1st Sat 10:00-01:00, women's dance night 1st Sat from 21:00-02:00. ♀♂

VAMPIRE, Rathenauplatz 5, (0221) 240 12 11, 20:00-01:00 (Fri, Sat till 03:00), closed Mon, women-owned. ♀

■ Dance Bar/Disco
ENTRE NOUS, at the Schulz gay & lesbian center, women's dance night, 1st Sat from 21:00. ♀

FRAUEN- UND LESBENDISCO, Apostelnstr. 11, at Gloria bar, (0221) 25 44 33, call for schedule. ♀

FRAUENDISCO, Berlinerstr. 77, at Mülheimer Mütze, (0221) 64 41 01, monthly women's dance on a Fri. ♀

FRAUENDISCO, Dreikönigenstr. 23, at Bürgerhaus Stollwerk, (0221) 31 80 53, monthly women's disco, call for schedule. ♀

FRAUENDISCO BÜTZE, Venlörstr. 429, (0221) 54 21 11, women's disco last Sat. ♀

LULU, Breite Str. 79, (0221) 257 5450. ♀♂

■ Cafe
QUO VADIS, Vor St. Martin 8-10, (0221) 258 1414, 11:00-01:00, closed Tues.

■ Restaurants
DOMERIE, Frankenwerft 27, (0221) 257 4044, 18:00-01:00, closed Sun.

MINELLI, Bismarckstr. 53, (0221) 510 1130, 18:00-01:00 (Fri, Sat till 03:00, Sun from 11:00).

■ Retail & Bookstores
GANYMED, Kettengasse 3, (0221) 251 110, gay bookstore, 10:00-20:00 (Sat till 16:00), closed Sun.

RHIANNON FRAUENBUCHLADEN, Moltkestr. 66, (0221) 52 31 20, women's bookstore, 10:00-18:30 (Thurs-Fri till 19:30, Sat till 15:00), closed Sun.

KONSTANZ

■ Bars
FRAUENKNEIPE, Bücklestr. 33., ♀

KOPPENWIND

■ Women's Accommodations
TARA, Bergstrasse 3, Koppenwind, 8602, (09554) 481. Retreat for women with seminars in a rural setting. ♀

KREFELD

Bars
PALETTE, Dionysusstr. 40, (02151) 77 23 94, 21:00-03:00 (Fri & Sat till 05:00), closed Thurs." ♂

LEIPZIG

Information
AIDS INFO, (0341) 232 31 26.
FRAUENKOMMUNIKATIONSZENTRUM, Ludwigstr. 115, (0341) 689 7903, Lesbengruppe (lesbian group), Lila Pause, meets here.
LESBENTELEFON, (0341) 123 3775, lesbian line.

Dance Bar/Disco
ESPLANADE, Richard Wagnerstr. 10, 28 23 30, Sun from 21:00, men welcome. 🍽 ♀
LEFT SIDE, Windscheidtstr. 51, room 5, (0341) 308 0142, women's disco Wed from 20:00. 🍽 ♀

Cafe
CAFE VISAVIS, R.-Breitscheid-Str. 33, 24hrs.

Retail & Bookstores
TIAN-FRAUENBUCHLADEN, Könneritzstr. 67, (0341) 479 74 75, women's bookstore. Lesbenclub (lesbian group) meets here Thurs 19:30.

LÜBECK

Information
AIDS HILFE, (0451) 725 51.
ARANAT FRAUEN-UND LESBEN-ZENTRUM, Dankwartsgrube 48, (0451) 738 27.

LUDWIGSBURG-EGLOSHEIM

Information
NORA FRAUENZENTRUM, Hahnenstr. 47, (07141) 343 80.

LUDWIGSHAFEN

Cafe
FRAUENCAFE, Westendstr. 17, (06210 52 84 06, women's cafe. ♀

MAINZ

Information
FRAUENZENTRUM, Walpodenstr. 10, (06131) 22 12 63, women's center with lesbian meetings: Lesbenberatung Thurs 18:30-20:00 & Lesbengruppe Thurs from 20:00; Frauencafé (women's cafe) Wed from 17:00 & Fri from 19:00; and Frauenfrühstück (women's breakfast) 3rd Sun from 10:00.

MANNHEIM

Information
AIDS HILFE, (0621) 28 600.

Bars
CLUB CAFE DUO, G2, 12., ♀
LE JARDIN, K2 31, (0621) 207 46. ♀

Dance Bar/Disco
SUBWAY, T6, 14, (0621) 10 27 79, 21:00-03:00 (Fri till 05:00, Sat till 04:00). Women welcome Wed from 20:00." 🍽 ♂

Cafe
FRAUENCAFE & LESBENSTAMMTISCH, C4, 6, (0621) 15 26 67, women's cafe. Lesbenstammtisch (lesbian social) Fri from 19:00. ♀

Retail & Bookstores
DER ANDERE BUCHLADEN, M2, 1, (0621) 217 55, general bookshop with a gay & lesbian selection, 10:00-18:30, Sat till 14:00, closed Sun.
XANTHIPPE, T3, 4, (0621) 216 63, women's bookstore.

MARBURG

Bars
HAVANNA ACHT, Lahntor 2, 234 32, Sun 20:00-01:00. ♀♂
LESBENKNEIPE, Lahntor 8, at Havanna, women's bar night, 2nd Sat. ♀

MINDEN

Information
FRAUEN LESBEN TREFFPUNKT, Umradstr. 25, (0571) 207 02, lesbian meeting.

MÖNCHEN/GLADBACH

Information
LESBENTELEFON, (02161) 219 00, lesbian line.
LILA DISTEL FRAUENZENTRUM, Lüpertzenderstr. 69, (02161) 21 900, women's center. Lesbentreff (lesbian social) 2nd & 4th Fri 20:00-22:00.

MÜNCHEN - MUNICH

Information
AIDS INFO, (089) 268 071.
KOFRA KOMMUNIKATIONS ZENTRUM FÜR FRAUEN, Baaderstr. 8, (089) 2010450, women's center with cafe, groups, vast information available, library.
LESBENTELEFON, (089) 725 42 72, lesbian line.

Accommodations
PENSION BRASIL, Dultstrasse 1, (089) 26 3417. Gay-friendly hotel above bar, shared baths, continental breakfast.

Bars
CLUB YOU, Baumgartnerstr. 15, (089) 767 01784, Sat women only. 🎵 ♀♂
MORIZZ, Klenzestr. 43, (089) 201 67 76, yuppies, 19:00-02:00 (Fri, Sat till 03:00), frequented by some women." ♂
MYLORD, Ickstattstr. 2a, (089) 260 44 48, sofas & chairs, quiet music, mostly hetero, occasionally frequented by gays, lesbians, good place to meet for quiet conversation, daily 18:00-01:00 (Sat till 03:00). ♀♂

Dance Bar/Disco
FORTUNA, Maximiliansplatz 5, (089) 55 40 70, after hours disco. 🎵 ♂
SAPPHO, Corneliusstrasse 16, (089) 202 1296, Fri & Sat women only. 🎵 ♀♂
★ **SOUL CITY**, Maximiliansplatz 5, enter from Max-Joseph-Str, (089) 59 52 72, 22:00-04:00 (Fri, Sat till later). 🎵 ♂

Cafe
RICK'S CAFEBAR, Augustenstr. 112, (089) 523 31 10, bistro-style café, 07:00-01:00, some hetero clientele. ✕ ♂
VILLANIS, Kreuzerstr. 3b, Asamhof, (089) 260 7972, bistro-style café, 10:00-01:00 (Sun from 11:00). ✕ ♂

Restaurants
MEATING, Reichenbachstr. 37, (089) 201 42 94, gay restaurant, to open in '98. ♀♂
SEITENSPRUNG, Holzstrasse 29, (089) 26 93 77, woman-owned. ♀♂

Retail & Bookstores
LILLEMORS FRAUENBUCHLADEN, Arcisstrasse 57, (089) 27 21 205, e-mail: lillemors@frauenliteratur.de; web: www.frauenliteratur.de. Women's bookstore with lesbian & feminist books in English & German and local information. Reading lounge with coffee, women only! Open Mon-Fri 10:00-18:30, Sat 10:00-14:00, closed Sun.

Erotica
LADIES FIRST, Kurfürstenstrasse 23, (089) 271 88 06, women's erotica.

MÜNSTER

Information
FRAUENGALERIE, Kettelerstr. 25, (0251) 27 92 56, women's art gallery.
LESBEN & SCHWULENZENTRUM, Am Hawerkamp 34, (0251) 665 686, gay & lesbian center, Mon 15:00-17:00 & Wed 17:00-19:00. Ask about scheduled lesbian socials.

BERKHÖFEL

North - Rhine Westphalia Area **(49-2823) 29749**

LESBENTELEFON, (0251) 194 46, lesbian line, Thurs 20:00-22:00."

■ *Bars*
LADYLIKE BIERCAFE, Maximilianstr. 2, (0251) 230 1097. ♀

WOMEN'S BAR NIGHT, Königspassage, at Königsstrasse 14, at the Star Club, 2nd Sat & 4th Fri. 🔞 ♀

■ *Retail & Bookstores*
CHRYSALIS, Buddenstr. 22, (0251) 555 05, women's bookstore."

NORTH-RHINE WESTFALIA AREA

■ *Women's Accommodations*
BERKHÖFEL, Uedemer Str. 196, Bedburg-Hau, 47551, (49-2823) 29749. In the midst of pastures & orchards, near the lower Rhine and the border between Germany and The Netherlands, this restored farmhouse offers bright, clean & welcoming guestrooms. All-vegetarian meals are served, and there is a sun-terrace & patio with deck chairs. The area has many manors & beautiful little museums. The wide, flat landscape is ideal for bicycle trips. We're a 1-hr drive from Düsseldorf, 30 mins from Nijmegen (Netherlands) & 1-1/2 hrs from Amsterdam. Lesbian-owned & -operated. ♀ See ad on page 89.

NÜRNBERG

■ *Information*
AIDS HILFE, (0911) 26 61 91.

FRAUENKUNST KULTURZENTRUM, Kleinreuther Weg 28, (0911) 35 19 70, women's art & cultural center, open Thurs-Sun.

LESBENBERATUNG, Fürther Str. 154, Rückgebäude, (0911) 32 82 62, lesbian info space, Tues 17:00-19:00.

LESBENTELEFON, (0911) 23 25 00, Wed 19:00-22:00.

■ *Bars*
SONNIGE PFALZ, Obere Kanalstr. 31, (0911) 26 23 00, 20:00-01:00 (Fri, Sat till 03:00), more women weekends, closed Mon. ♂

■ *Cafe*
CAFE WENDELTREPPE, Kleinreuther Weg 28, at Frauenkunst, Kulturzentrum, (0911) 35 19 70, women's cafe at Women's Art & Cultural Center, Thurs-Sun 20:00-01:00." ♀

CARTOON, An der Sparkasse 6, (0911) 22 71 70, 11:00-01:00, Sun from 14:00.

■ *Retail & Bookstores*
FRAUENBUCHLADEN, Kleinreuther Weg 28, at Frauenkunst-Kulturzentrum, (0911) 35 24 03, women's bookstore."

OBERHAUSEN

■ *Bars*
FRAUENKNEIPE, Am Förderturm 27, at Druckluft, women's bar night, Thurs from 19:00. ♀

OFFENBACH

■ *Information*
FRAUENZENTRUM, Grosse Hasenbachstr. 35, (069) 81 65 57, women's center & cafe with Lesbengruppe (lesbian group) meetings.

OLDENBURG

■ *Information*
AIDS LINE, (0441) 883 010, or Oldenburg Aids-Hilfe (0441) 19411.

LESBEN & SCHWULENZENTRUM, Ziegelhofstr. 83, (0441) 777 5990.

LESBENTELEFON, (0441) 777 5149, lesbian line, Thurs 20:00-22:00.

■ *Bars*
FRAUENDISCO & FRAUENKNEIPE, at Alhambra, Hermannstr. 83, Frauenkneipe (women's bar night) Wed from 17:00, disco 2nd Sat of the month from 22:30. 🔞 ♀

HEMPELS, Ziegelhofstr. 83, cafe at lesbian/gay center, (0441) 777 5990, Fri 20:00-24:00, Sun 18:00-20:00 (women only Thurs 20:00-24:00, men only Mon 20:00-24:00). ♀♂

LESBENKNEIPE, Ziegelhofstr. 83, at the lesbian/gay center, women's bar night Thurs 20:00-24:00. ♀

PULVERFASS, Heiligengeiststr. 12, (0441) 126 01, 22:00-02:00 (Fri, Sat till 05:00), closed Sun & Mon. ♂

■ *Dance Bar/Disco*
DER SCHWARZE BÄR, Donnerschweer Str. 50, (0441) 885 0737, 21:00-02:00 (Fri, Sat till 05:00), closed Sun. Mon leather night with dress code. 🔞 ♂

ROSA DISCO, at Alhambra,

Hermannstr. 83, last Sat of the month from 22:00. [♫]

Cafe

CAFE AM DAMM, Damm 36, (0442) 183 30, 11:00-24:00, Sun from 10:00, Sun natural foods breakfast.

CAFE MACHATSCHKALA, Hauptstr. 2, Kirchhatten, (04482) 8326, vegetarian cuisine, 12:00-22:00 (Sat, Sun 09:00-19:00), closed Wed.

Retail & Bookstores

VIOLETTA, Lindenstr. 18, (0441) 88 30 39, women's bookstore, 10:00-18:00 (Sat till 14:00), closed Mon."

OSNABRÜCK

Information

FRAUENARCHIV NATALIE BARNEY, Lange Str. 26, at Laischaftstr., (0541) 875 99.

FRAUENBERATUNGSTELLE, Spindelstr. 41, (0541) 25 93 13, women's information center.

LESBENTELEFON, (0541) 85 846, Thurs 18:00-20:00.

Retail & Bookstores

MOTHER JONES FRAUEN-BÜCHERCAFE, Jahnstr. 17, (0541) 437 00, women's bookstore & cafe with Lesbenstammtisch (women's meeting) Tues from 20:00.

OSTFRIESLAND

Women's Accommodations

FRAUENFERIENHOF OSTFRIES-LAND, Zum Lengener Meer 2, Friedeburg-Bentstreek, 26446, (49-4956) 4956 (Tel/Fax). women-only retreat with courses & programs, shared baths. [♿]♀

PADERBORN

Information

FRAUENBERATUNGSTELLE LILITH, Königstr. 64, (05251) 213 11, women's information center, meetings 2nd & 4th Thurs 17:00-19:00.

PASSAU

Information

LESBENTELEFON, FRAUEN-ZENTRUM UND FRAUENCAFE, Spitalhofstr. 62a, (0851) 553 67, lesbian line, women's center & cafe, line answers Thurs 19:00-20:00, women's cafe Thurs 17:30-20:00.

RECKLINGHAUSEN

Dance Bar/Disco

FRAUENSCHWOOF, Kellerstr. 10, in the Altstadtschmiede, (02361) 21 212, lesbian dance night 4th Sat. [♫]♀

REGENSBURG

Information

FRAUENZENTRUM & FRAUENKNEIPE, Prüfeningerstr. 32, (0941) 242 59, Lesbengruppe (lesbian group) meets Thurs from 20:00. Frauenkneipe (women's bar night) Tues from 20:00.

LESBENTELEFON, (0941) 241 71, lesbian line, Tues 19:00-21:00.

ROSTOCK

Cafe

CAFE TAUBENSCHLAG, Gerberbruch 14, at Am Windspiel bar, (0381) 490 2401, from 19:00. Tues women only. ♂

SAARBRÜCKEN

Information

AIDS HILFE, (0681) 31 112.

ZENTRUM FÜR LESBEN UND SCHWULE, Bismarckstr. 6, (0681) 37 49 55, center for lesbians & gays.

Bars

FRAUENKNEIPE, Bismarkstr. 6, at Lesbian & Gay center, (0681) 37 49 55, women's bar night Tues from 20:00. ♀

Dance Bar/Disco

FRAUENDISCO, Dudweilerstr., at Café Ultra, women's disco, Fri from 21:00. [♫]♀

SCHLESWIG- HOLSTEIN AREA

Women's Accommodations

HAUS AM DOM FRAUENHOTEL, Töpferstr, Schleswig, 24837, (49-4621) 21388. women's hotel in renovated 200-year-old house, private baths, telephone, reading room, winter & flower gardens & summer house, ocean nearby. ♀

GERMANY

SCHÖLLNACH

Accommodations
DIE MÜHLE (THE MILL), Englfing 16, Schöllnach, 94508, (49-9903) 562, Fax: (49-9903) 2614. mainly men, lesbians welcome, living room area, TV, bar, radio, record collection, shared baths. ♂

SOLINGEN

Information
FRAUENZENTRUM, Klemens Horn Str. 15, (02122) 172 29, lesbian group meets here.

STUTTGART

Information
AIDS HILFE, (0711) 61 08 49.

Cafe
SARAH CAFÉ FÜR FRAUEN, Johannesstr. 13, (0711) 62 66 38, women's cafe. ♀

Retail & Bookstores
GOUDOU FRAUENBUCHLADEN, Schloss Str. 66, (0711) 66 11 00, women's bookstore.

TIEFENBACH

Women's Accommodations
FRAUENFERIENHAUS TIEFENBACH SILBERSEE, Hammer 22, Tiefenbach, 93464, (49-9673) 499. women-only retreat & conference center, near swimming, shopping, sauna, bath hall, single, double & dorm rooms, 1 en suite & 3 shared baths, many outdoor activities. ♀

TRIER

Information
FRAUENZENTRUM, Saarstrasse 38, (0651) 401 19, women's center.

Bars
PALETTE, Oerenstrasse 13b, (0651) 426 09, 20:00-01:00, Fri & Sat till 02:00. ♂

Dance Bar/Disco
FRAUENDISCO FAMFATAL, Wechselstrasse, at Tuchfabrik., 🎵 ♀

TÜBINGEN

Information
LESBENTELEFON, (07071) 329 01, lesbian info line Fri 18:00-20:00."

Dance Bar/Disco
FRAUENDISCO, at Club Voltaire, Haaggasse 26b, women's disco Sat from 22:00. 🎵 ♀

Cafe
FRAUENCAFE, at Epplehaus, Karlstrasse 13, (07071) 328 62, women's cafe, Mon-Fri 20:00-24:00. ♀

Retail & Bookstores
THALESTRIS FRAUENBUCHLADEN, Bursagasse 2, (07071) 265 90, women's bookstore. Lesbenkontaktnetz (lesbian contact network) housed here.

ULM

Information
FRAUENZENTRUM, Hinter dem Brot 9, (0731) 67 775, women's center, lesbian group meets here.

VILLINGEN-SCHWENNINGEN

Bars
CLUB 46 A, Dauchingerstr. 46a, (07720) 639 09, from 21:00, closed Mon, Tues. Women's disco 2nd Fri. ♂

OZ, Hans Krauth Str 9, 58565, 18:00-01:00, frequented by gays.

WEIMAR

Information
FRAUENZENTRUM, Freiherr von Stein Allee 22, (03640) 850 186, women's center, lesbian group meets Wed from 20:00.

WIESBADEN

Information
FRAUENMUSEUM, Wörthstrasse 5, (0611) 308 17 63, women's museum, lesbians welcome.

FRAUENZENTRUM, Adlerstr. 7, women's center.

Bars
FRAUENLESBENKNEIPE, Marcobrunner Str. 9, at Café Klatsch, (0611) 44 02 66, women's bar night last Sun. ♀

Retail & Bookstores
FRAUENBUCHVERSAND UND LADEN, Luxemburgstrasse 2, (0611) 37 15 15, Fax: (0611) 37 19 13, women's bookstore.

WILHELMSHAVEN

■ *Information*
AIDS HILFE, (04421) 211 49.

■ *Cafe*
FRAUENCAFE BACKSTUBE, Albrechtstr. 10, women's café 1st Sat. ♀

WORMS

■ *Cafe*
FRAUENCAFE, Friedr. Ebertstr. 20, (06241) 524 59, women's café Mon-Thurs from 15:00. Lesbenstammtisch (lesbian group) meets 1st & 3rd Wed from 20:00. ♀

WUPPERTAL

■ *Information*
FRAUENZENTRUM URANIA, Stifstr. 12, (0202) 44 99 68, women's center.

LESBENTELEFON, (0202) 42 39 46, lesbian line, answers Mon, Tues Thurs 10:00-12:00 & 17:00-19:00, Fri only 10:00-12:00.

■ *Bars*
LESBENKNEIPE, Stiftstr. 12, at the Frauenzentrum, (0202) 44 99 68, women's bar night at the women's center, Fri from 21:00. ♀

SPEICHER, Gathe 91, (0202) 455 171, 21:00-05:00, leather group meets Thurs, lesbian group meets Wed. ♂

■ *Dance Bar/Disco*
FRAUENSCHWOOF, Stiftstr. 12, at the Frauenzentrum, women's dance night 3rd Sat at women's center. 📽 ♀

FRAUENSCHWOOF, Viehofstr. 25, (0202) 421 081, women's dance night, last Sat from 21:00. 📽 ♀

LESBENDISCO, Wiesenstr. 11, at the Autonomes Zentrum, lesbian disco 1st Sat from 21:00. 📽 ♀

■ *Retail & Bookstores*
DRÖPPEL(FE)MINA, Am Brögel 1, (0202) 877 07, women's bookstore & cafe.

WÜRZBURG

■ *Information*
LESBENTELEFON, (0931) 41 26 46, lesbian line, Mon 19:00-21:00.

ZÜLPICH-LÖVENICH

■ *Women's Accommodations*
FRAUENBILDUNGSHAUS ZÜLPICH-LÖVENICH, Prälat-Franken-Str. 13, Zülpich-Lövenich, 53909, (49-2252) 6577. Women-only retreat with courses & programs, variety of rooms with private & shared baths, garden, nearby lake, groceries available. ♀

GREECE

COUNTRY CODE: (30),
NOTE ABOUT ISLAND ADDRESSES:, The following Greek islands are so small that street addresses may not be necessary: Corfu, Lesbos, Mykonos, Paros, Rhodes, Samos & Santorini.

ATHENS

■ *Information*
EOK & AKOE-AMPHI, 21 Patission Str, 7th floor, (01) 52 39 017, gay & lesbian organizations.

■ *Accommodations*
ATHENIAN INN, 22 Haritos, Kolonaki., Reserve through Windmills Travel, (30-289) 23877 or 22066 (fax only November-March). Gay-friendly inn.

PLAKA HOTEL, 7 Kapnikareas, at Mitropoleos, Plaka., Reserve through Windmills Travel, (30-289) 23877 or 22066 (fax only November-March). Gay-friendly hotel.

■ *Bars*
BAR 21, 21 Fillia St, (01) 88 21 532, small, cozy bar open till morning, Greek music, variety of clientele. If arriving after 03:00, ring the bell. ♂

PORTA, 10 Falirou St, Makriyianni, (01) 32 49 660, both Greek & foreign music. ♀

SPYROS, Vourvachi St, at Syngrou Ave, (01) 92 23 982, till late. ♀♂

■ *Dance Bar/Disco*
ALEXANDER'S, 44 Anagnostopoulou St, Kolonaki, (01) 26 44 660, bar upstairs, disco downstairs, Greek music, very few lesbians. 📽 ♂

DOM, 112 Pireos St & 31 Ikarieon, Gazi, huge disco, closed Mon & Tues. 📽 ♀♂

FACTORY I, Panepistimiou, at Em. Benaki, male strippers. 📽 ⚥ ♂

Journeys by Sea, Inc.
(800) 825-3632
(954) 522-5865
Yacht Charters
$195 pp/day all incl.

Cafe

BRITANIA, Omonoia Sq, at Athineas, open all night, dangerous area.

DE PROFUNDIS, 1 Hatzimichali, Plaka, tea house.

KIRKI, 31 Apostolou Pavlou, Thission Sq, below Lizzard disco, Sun from 12:00, some hetero clientele. ♀

L.A., 1 Em. Benaki, mezzanine floor, at Stadiou.,

MONTPARNASSE, 32 Haritos, Kolonaki, (01) 72 90 746, till 02:00 (closed Sun), reservations required.

NEON CAFE, Omonoia Sq.,

OVAL CAFE, 5 Tossitsa St. near Exarchia Sq., cozy, feminist-run cafe & bar with light menu. ♀

STYLE, Kritis St, at Chiou St, Ag. Pavlou Square., ♀♂

Restaurants

FOTAERION, 74 Ippokratous St, (01) 36 22 362, excellent food & service, wide variety of teas, recommended by local gay group.

HOTEL ELYSIUM
Absolutely Enchanting
MYKONOS GREECE
(30-289) 23952

GASTRA TAVERNA, 1 Dimaki St, Kolonaki, (01) 36 02 757, excellent food, a bit expensive, closed July & Aug, reservations a must.

Retail & Bookstores

SELANA BOOKSTORE, Sina Str. 38, (01) 36 38 262, women's bookstore.

CORFU

Bars

SWEET MOVIE, Ag. Ioannis Peristeron, close to Benitses, (0661) 923 35, some hetero clientele. ♂

LESBOS

Accommodations

LESBOS ACCOMMODATION INFORMATION, contact Pam Taylor at, (30-289) 23877 or fax (30-289) 22066.

Women's Accommodations

ANTIOPO WOMEN'S HOTEL, (30-1) 956 3218 (Tel/Fax). Located at Sappho's birthplace, the village Skala Eressos on the island of Lesbos. The hotel has 15 doubles, 3 singles, 3 studios & 1 apartment, all with shower & WC. The 3 kilometer beach is so long that some areas practically become "women only." ♀

Bars

JIMMY'S, ♀♂

Dance Bar/Disco

SARAI, some hetero clientele. ♀♂

MYKONOS

Accommodations

COSTA'S STUDIOS, above Mykonos Town, reserve through Windmills Travel, (30-289) 23877 or 22066 (fax only November-March). gay-friendly.

FLORA'S ROOMS & STUDIOS, in Mykonos Town, reserve through Windmills Travel, (30-289) 23877 or 22066 (fax only November-March). Gay-friendly.

HOTEL ELYSIUM, School of Fine Arts, Mykonos Town, Mykonos, 84600, (30-289) 23952, 24210, 24684, Fax: (30-289) 23747. Hotel with deluxe accommodations & panoramic views of ocean & Old Town Mykonos. The 42 well-appointed rooms & 3 suites have colour satelite TV, direct-dial phones, stereo music & private baths. An American buffet breakfast is served daily. Pool on premises. Some hetero clientele. 🏊 ♀♂

MARIETTA'S STUDIOS, School of Fine Arts, Mykonos Town, reserve through Windmills Travel, (30-289) 23877 or 22066 (fax only November-March). Gay-friendly studios.

PETINOS HOTELS & APARTMENTS, in towne & Plati Yialos, reserve through Windmill Travel, (30-289) 23877 or 22066 (fax only November-March). Gay-friendly hotels & apartments.

PRESIDENT'S STUDIOS, reserve through Windmill Travel, (30-289) 23877 or 22066 (fax only November-March). Studios with double glazing, AC, color TV, kitchenette, full bathroom. In a quiet residential area of Mykonos town.

VILLA KONSTANTIN, Mykonos, 84600, (30-289) 25824/26204, (30-289) 23461, Fax: (30-289) 26205. studios & apartments, some hetero clientele, private baths, kitchen, refrigerators, maid service, nearby pool & ocean. ♀♂

■ Beaches

ELIA, mixed hetero & gay men & women, nudity permitted, 2 restaurants & tabernas nearby, bus hourly from the harbor or boat from Plati Yialos.

PARANGA BEACH, a 20-minute walk from Plati Yialos, a section is becoming a gay beach area, men & women, nudity permitted, snack bar & taberna nearby.

■ Bars

DIVA BAR, in Little Venice, the area of Mykonos on the water, perfect for sunsets. ♀♂

HAPPINESS, Fabrika bus square., Also in the same complex: Happiness Boutique with disco-type clothing, and Tapas Cafe & Bar. 🎵 ♀♂

IKAROS BAR, Matoyianni St, over Manto bar, rooftop bar, fabulous sunset views. ♀♂

KASTRO BAR, in Little Venice, the area of Mykonos on the water, (289) 23 072, sunset views & classical music. ♀♂

MANTO BAR, Matoyianni St, next to Pierro's Bar, drinks and coffee. ♀♂

MONTPARNASSE PIANO BAR, in Little Venice, piano bar & cafe with trendy crowd. 🎵 ♀♂

Mykonos Gay Reservations

Individual travelers looking for the right hotel and travel agents seeking professional assistance with reservations for valued clients now have a personal contact on Mykonos. Pam Taylor, of *Windmills Travel*, is an accommodations, transportation, and excursions expert for Mykonos, the Cycladic Islands, and Greece.

Accommodations, including first-class hotels, deluxe studios and apartments, and pensions can be arranged to suit varying price requirements. Commitment ceremonies, special accommodation package deals, and island hopping packages are also available. Pam can handle airport/port transfers and pickup; car, jeep, or motorbike rentals; plane and boat tickets; and local excursions.

Excursions include guided and unguided tours to Delos; day tours, with a guide, to Tinos and Santorini; and a day trip, via fishing boat, to an isolated beach for a beach party. **Official Tour Operator for the gay and lesbian Nine Muses Party, Sept. 7-12, 1998.**

Contact Pam at Windmills Travel & Tourism, Mykonos, Greece. Tel: (30 289) 23877/26555/26556/26557, Fax: (30 289) 22066. E-mail: windmills@travelling.gr.

GREECE

■ Dance Bar/Disco
★ **PIERRO'S BAR**, Matoyianni St, (289) 22177 Email: pierros1@otenet.gr, popular disco, many heteros."

■ Cafe
ARISTOTE CAFE BAR, Matoyianni St, close to Credit Bank, upscale, trendy cafe bar with Greek & foreign music.
TAPAS CAFE & BAR, Fabrika bus square, open for breakfast, lunch & early dinner.

■ Restaurants
APPALOOSA, 2 streets behind the Credit Bank, on Mavrogenous St,, restaurant & bar with some outside dining, reservations recommended.
DELPHINE'S, Matoyianni St, homestyle Greek cuisine.
EDEN GARDEN, international cuisine.
EL GRECO RESTAURANT, international cuisine.
GATSBY'S, indoor & garden seating.
MACCHARONI, near Lakka Square, Italian cuisine, outdoor seating.

■ Retail & Bookstores
INTERNATIONAL BOOKSTORE, near Pierro's disco, general bookstore with some gay & lesbian titles.

PAROS

■ Bars
AUGOSTA, in the town of Naoussa, NOT a gay bar, frequented by gays.
KABARNIS, across from Christo's Taberna, rooftop garden, creperie, frequented by gays.
STAVEDO, in Parikia, frequented by gays.

RHODES

■ Dance Bar/Disco
BERLIN, Orphanidou 47, near Alexia hotel.,
MEDOUSSA, in city center, discreetly frequented by gays.
VALENTINO, in Old Town.,
VEGGERA, in city center., dicreetly frequented by gays.

■ Cafe
NEORION, near the cathedral, NOT a gay cafe, discreetly frequented by gays.

SAMOS

■ Bars
BARINO, in town of Koraki.,

■ Dance Bar/Disco
★ **METROPOLIS**, trendy crowd.
★ **TOTEM**, in town of Pythagoreion, (0273) 272 50.

■ Cafe
MYKALI, at Mykali beach, (0273) 222 15, ask locally for directions, discreetly frequented by gays.

SANTORINI

■ Accommodations
GROTTO VILLAS, in Fira, reserve through Windmills Travel, (30-289) 23877 or 22066 (fax only November-March). Gay-friendly villas.
MELINA HOTEL, in Fira, reserve through Windmills Travel, (30-289) 23877 or 22066 (fax only November-March). Gay-friendly hotel.
NINE MUSES, in Perivolos/Emboriou, reserve through Windmills Travel, (30-289) 23877 or 22066 (fax only November-March). Gay-friendly hotel.
ROCCABELLA STUDIOS & APARTMENTS, in Imerovigli, reserve through Windmills Travel, (30-289) 23877 or 22066 (fax only November-March). Gay-friendly.

■ Bars
FRANCO'S, Marinatou St, classical music.

■ Dance Bar/Disco
CASABLANCA, younger crowd, discreetly frequented by gays.
JUST BLUE, in the main square, town of Fira, discreetly frequented by gays.
TROPICAL, near Franco's bar.,

THESSALONIKI

■ Information
O.P.O.TH., (031) 85 57 06 (tel/fax), gay group with scheduled activities, publishes O Pothos magazine, airs weekly radio show Sun 12:00-14:00.

■ Bars
AHUDUDU, 3 Chalkis St, (031) 83 64 44.
BACHALON, 8 Romanou St, (031) 26 86 37.

TABOO, 7 Kastritsiou St, (031) 27 91 32, may close in 1996. ♀

■ Dance Bar/Disco
FACTORY, 51 Proxenou Koromila St, expensive.
FUNKY MOBILE, 29 Papandreu St, younger crowd, frequented by gays.

■ Cafe
DE FACTO, 17 Pavlou Mela St., ♀♂
STRETTO, 18 C. Diehl St., ♀♂

HUNGARY

COUNTRY CODE: (36),

BUDAPEST

■ Information
GAY SWITCHBOARD BUDAPEST, 30 32 33 34, 16:00-20:00, run by gay & lesbian organization, English &/or German spoken.

HATTER & LABRISZ, PO Box 50, Budapest 1554, (1) 302 50 80. Gay & lesbian group "Hatter," phone answers 18:00-23:00. New lesbian group "Labrisz," meets every 2 weeks at Hatter location, call for exact address.

PLUSS AIDS INFO, 60 343 773.

■ Bars
CAFE CAPELLA, 23 Belgrad Rakpart (V), (1) 267 26 16, from 17:00, gay Wed & Sun, women welcome.

MYSTERY, 3 Nagysándor Jószef ut. (V), (1) 312 14 36, small bar, recently renovated, 21:00-04:00 (closed Sun), frequented by some women. ✕ ♂

■ Dance Bar/Disco
ANGYAL, 33 Szovetség ut. (VII), (1) 351 64 90, bar & restaurant on 1st floor, basement disco & darkroom, Thurs-Sun from 22:00. More gay Sat, more women Fri. ✕

■ Cafe
AMSTEL RIVER CAFE, 6 Parizsi ut (V), (1) 137 23 09, 09:00-23:00 (Sun from 11:00), frequented by gays.

■ Restaurants
DIVA, 1 Hevesi S. Ter (VII), in front of National Theater, gay-owned restaurant TO OPEN SUMMER '98.

FENYOGYONGYE VENDEGLO, 155 Szepvolgyi ut. (II), (1) 325 97 83, 12:00-24:00, some straight clientele. ♀♂

PIZZERIA CLUB 93, 2 Vas ut (V), (1) 138 11 19, 11:00-23:00 (Sun 17:00-01:00), many gays & lesbians after 20:00.

ICELAND

COUNTRY CODE: (354),

REYKJAVIK

■ Information
REYKJAVIK GAY CENTER (SAMTÖKIN 78), Lindergata 49, (354) 552 8539, Fax: (354) 552 7525, e-mail: gayice@mmedia.is Tel. answers Mon & Thurs 20:00-23:00, center open Mon & Thurs 20:00-23:00 with cafe, library. Very popular in winter. Open bar night Sat 21:30-02:00, Thurs cafe open till midnite, AA meetings Tues 21:00.

■ Accommodations
ROOM WITH A VIEW, Laugavegur 18, 6th floor, Reykjavik, 101, (354) 552 7262 (Tel/Fax). Email: arnike@mm.is, 1-bedroom apartments with kitchens, sleeping 1-4 persons, fully furnished, laundry facilities. Also on premises: coffee shop open daily 09:00-21:00 & bookshop selling gay magazines. ♀♂

■ Bars
★ BAR 22, Laugavegur 22, mostly gay bar with dance floor on second floor. Open nightly but most popular with gays & lesbians Thurs 23:00-01:00, Fri & Sat 18:00-03:00. ♀♂

■ Dance Bar/Disco
NELLY'S, on a very short street called Bankastraeti, disco & bar, nightly till 01:00 (Fri, Sat till 03:00), openly gay-friendly, approx. 50% gay/lesbian.

■ Cafe
KAFFI LIST, Klapparstig 28, 10:00-01:00 (weekends 11:00-03:00), serves soups, salads, tapas, coffee, desserts. Mostly straight clientele, but popular with gays & lesbians. ✕

KAFFI PARIS, Austurstrati 14, 08:00-01:00, light meals & coffee. Mostly straight clientele, but popular with gays & lesbians.

SOLON ISLANDUS, Bankastraeti 7a, very popular with gays & lesbians, but frequented by mostly hetero clientele, many artists, serves light meals & coffee. ✕

Retail & Bookstores

MAL OG MENNING, Laugavegur 18, general bookstore with some gay books.

IRELAND

COUNTRY CODE: (353),

CORK

Information

AIDS LINE, (021) 27 66 76, Mon-Fri 10:00-17:00.

GAY INFORMATION & LESBIAN LINE, (021) 27 10 87, gay Wed 19:00-21:00 & Sat 15:00-17:00, lesbian Thurs 20:00-22:00."

LESBIAN & GAY RESOURCE GROUP, see Other Place listing under retail."

Accommodations

DANNY'S B & B, 3 St. John's Terrace, upper St. John St, (021) 50 36 06. Gay & lesbian B&B. ♀♂

MONT BRETIA B & B, Adrigole, Skibbereen, West Cork, (353-28) 33 663. B&B, some hetero clientele, shared baths, TV lounge, full breakfast, organic garden, maps of area, free bicycles, 6 mi to beach. ♀♂

Women's Accommodations

AMAZONIA, Coast Road, Fountainstown, Myrtleville, Cork, (353-21) 831 115. The beach at the bottom of the hill is very safe for swimming and sports. The walking path to nearby pubs affords marvelous views of the ocean and rocky coastline. Bikes, canoes, body boards, tennis racquets and golf clubs are free for guests' use, and we can arrange horseback riding. Women-only B&B with full Irish breakfast, and optional vegetarian evening meals. ♀

Bars

LOAFERS PUB, Douglas St, women only Thurs in rear bar." ♀

OTHER PLACE, at Other Place Bookstore location, (021) 31 76 60, lesbian & gay winebar Fri-Sat, women's night 1st Fri. Cafe with tea, coffee, snacks other times.

Restaurants

OTHER SIDE CAFE, THE, 8 South Main St, (021) 27 84 70, 11:00-18:00 (closed Sun).

QUAY CO-OP, 24 Sullivan's Quay, (021) 31 76 60, 09:30-22:30 (Sun from 18:00).

Retail & Bookstores

OTHER PLACE, 7/8 Augustine St (beside Queen's Old Castle), (021) 27 84 70, gay & lesbian books, resource & information centre.

OTHER SIDE BOOKSHOP, 8 South Main St, (021) 27 84 70, 11:00-17:30 (closed Sun).

QUAY CO-OP, 24 Sullivans Quay, (021) 31 76 60. Bookstore with gay & lesbian sections, natural food shop, restaurant & women's centre.

WATERSTONE'S, 69 Patrick St, (021) 276 522, general bookstore with gay & lesbian section.

DERRY

Information

LESBIAN & GAY & FRIEND LINE, (01504) 26 3120, Thurs 20:00-22:00.

Bars

DUNGLOE, THE, Waterloo St, frequented by gays.

GWEEDORE BAR, Waterloo St, frequented by gays.

Dance Bar/Disco

MAGEE UNIVERSITY DISCO, at the Student Union, Fri. Call Friend line for hours. ♀♂

AMAZONIA

Women's B&B
Overlooking
Rolling Green
Hills & the
Atlantic

CORK • IRELAND

(353-21) 831 115

Retail & Bookstores

BOOKWORM, 16 Bishop St, (0504) 26 16 16, general bookstore with gay & lesbian titles.

DUBLIN

Information

AIDS HELPLINE DUBLIN, (01) 872 42 77, Mon-Fri 19:00-21:00, Sat 15:00-18:00.

GAY SWITCHBOARD, (01) 872 10 55, Sun-Fri 20:00-22:00, Sat 15:30-18:00.

LESBIAN LINE, (01) 872 99 11, Thurs 19:00-21:00.

LOT (LESBIANS ORGANISING TOGETHER), 5 Capel St, (01) 872 7770, Mon-Fri 10:00-18:00, women's center & library.

OUTHOUSE, 6 South William St, gay & lesbian resource center & cafe, 12:00-18:00 (Sun from 14:00). Women's night Thurs 19:00-23:00. ♀♂

Accommodations

DUNSANY BED & BREAKFAST, 7 Gracepark Gardens, Drumcondra, Dublin 9, (353-1) 857 1362, Mobile: (353-88) 695 051. A warm Irish welcome awaits at this Victorian B&B with period features. A havenin a bustling city, the house is situated in a quiet cul-de-sac with a bowling green to the front and fields behind. Dublin city with its many cultural & historical sights is easily accessible by bus, car, or on foot. We offer private & shared baths, full Irish breakfast, tea & coffee all day, and a TV lounge. 70% gay & lesbian clientele. ♀♂

FAIRFIELD LODGE, Monkstown Ave, Monkstown, County Dublin, (353-1) 280 3912 (Tel/Fax). Email: JSB@Indigo.ie, Studio apartment for 2 in a garden setting, 15 minutes by car from Dublin center & situated close to the sea. Bus stop outside the gate takes you into Dublin every 7 minutes. ♀♂

FRANKIES GUESTHOUSE, 8 Camden Place, Dublin 2, Reservations: (353-1) 478 3087 (Tel/Fax) or (353-1) 475 2182. exclusively gay, women welcome, 12 rooms with single & double beds, color TV, private & shared baths, TV lounge, full Irish breakfast, near gay venues." ♂

HORSE & CARRIAGE, THE, 15 Aungier St, Dublin, 2, (353-1) 478 3537, Fax: (353-1) 478 4010. Email: liamtony@indigo.ie, Gay-owned guesthouse, mostly men with women welcome. Private & shared baths, full breakfast, color cable TV, coffee & tea-making facilities, free admission to Incpgnito sauna, near gay bars. ♂

INN ON THE LIFFEY, 21 Upper Ormond Quay, Dublin, 7, (353-1) 677 0828, Fax: (353-1) 872 4172. Inn, mostly men with women welcome. ♂

Bars

FRONT LOUNGE, Parliament St, close to City Hall, gay Sun. ♂

OUT ON THE LIFFEY, 27 Upper Ormond Quay, (01) 872 24 80, 50% gays & lesbians. ✕ ♀♂

DUNSANY B&B

A Warm Irish Welcome

Tel: (01) 857 1362
Mobile: (088) 695 051

7 Gracepark Gardens,
Drumcondra,
Dublin 9.

IRELAND

Dance Bar/Disco

FREEDOM KLUYB ZU ZU, Eustace St, in Temple Bar, across from the Irish Film Centre, disco with upstairs bar, Mon from 23:00.

FRESH, Duke Lane, at the Buttery Brasserie, Sun 22:30-02:30.

GET OUT, 1-2 Aston Quay, at The Furnace Club USI, 2nd Sat 21:00-01:00.

H.A.M., Old Harcourt St. train station, at POD, Fri from 23:00.

KITCHEN, THE, Temple Bar, East Essex St at the Clarence Hotel, 23:15-02:30, some gays & lesbians

MILDRED, Clarendon St,, Clarendon Market at The DA Club, Tues 23:00-02:30.

MISS CANDY'S NIGHT OUT, Temple Bar, at The Kitchen, Mon gay disco night.

OSCAR'S, 27 Upper Ormond Quay, upper level, at Out on the Liffey, Wed-Sun till 24:30.

PLAYGROUND, THE, at Republica in the Earl of Kildare Hotel, Kildare St, Sun from 23:15. Venue changes, ask locally for current schedule.

POWDERBUBBLE, Old Harcourt St at Red Box, over the POD, (01) 679 7388, gay disco 2nd or 3rd Sat from 22:00, ask locally for exact schedule.

STONEWALTZ, at Griffith College, The Barracks, South Circular Rd, women's dance night, Sat 21:00-02:00.

STRICTLY HANDBAG, Dame Lane, in back of St George's St at Rí Rá, 23:15-02:30, some gays & lesbians.

WONDERBAR, Curved St, at Temple Bar Music Centre, gay dance nights, alternate Sat 21:30-02:45.

Cafe

CAFE VITAE, 67 Lower Camden St, vegetarian menu, 08:00-20:00 (Thurs-Fri till 04:00, Sat from 10:00), closed Sun.

SMALL TALK CAFE, Parliament St, near the river & Front Lounge, after hours cafe, frequented by many gays & lesbians.

Restaurants

MARK'S BROS, 7 South Great George's St, trendy coffee shop, younger crowd, 10:00-17:30.

Retail & Bookstores

BOOKS UPSTAIRS, 36 College Green, (01) 679 66 87, gay & lesbian sections 10:00-20:00, Sat till 19:00, Sun till 18:00.

WATERSTONE'S, 7 Dawson St, (01) 679 14 15, general bookstore with gay & lesbian section.

WINDING STAIR, 40 Lower Ormond Quay, (01) 873 32 92, bookshop & cafe.

GALWAY

Information

AIDS HELPLINE, (091) 56 62 66, Mon-Fri 10:00-12:00 (Thurs also 20:00-22:00).

LESBIAN LINE, (091) 56 61 34, Wed 20:00-22:00, ask about lesbian socials.

Bars

BLUE NOTE, near Dominicks St, frequented by gays & lesbians.

NEACHTAINS, Quay St, pub, frequented by gays & lesbians.

Dance Bar/Disco

LIBERATION, Salthill, at Vagabonds, 23:00-01:30.

Cafe

JAVA, Lower Abbeygate St, frequented by gays & lesbians.

Retail & Bookstores

CHARLIE BYRNE'S BOOKSHOP, Middle St, (091) 56 17 66.

KILKENNY

Restaurants

MOTTE RESTAURANT, THE, Instioge, 15 miles from city centre, (056) 586 55, 19:00-21:30 (closed Sun, Mon).

LIMERICK

Information

AIDS HELPLINE, (061) 31 66 61, answers Mon-Fri 09:30-17:30."

GAY SWITCHBOARD & LESBIAN LINE, (061) 31 01 01, switchboard Mon, Tues 19:30-21:30, lesbians Thurs 19:30-21:30, ask about scheduled meetings and local events."

TINAHELY

Accommodations

STONEYBROKE HOUSE, Ballinamanogue, Tinahely, Co. Wicklow, (353-402)

38236. Inn with restaurant & wine bar, 60 miles south of Dublin, 1-1/2 mi from Tinahely. Private & shared baths, colour TV, full breakfast, dinner. Eight entrees available from menu, including Wicklow lamb & sirloin steak, Chicken breast Stoneybroke, salmon & vegetable Kiev. ♀♂

ITALY

COUNTRY CODE: (39),

ACQUI TERME

■ Women's Accommodations
LA FILANDA GUESTHOUSE, Reg. Montagnola No. 4, Acqui Terme, 15011, (39-144) 32 39 56 (Tel/Fax). women-only cultural center & guesthouse in an Italian villa for female musicians & artists, music room & diverse yearly workshops, shared baths, 2 full equipped kitchens, living rooms, video library, large garden, nearby health center, pool & river. 🏠 ♀

BARI

■ Information
ARCI GAY, Via Celentano 81, (080) 55 43 474, gay & lesbian organization, Tues 20:00-23:00. Women meet Wed 18:00-21:00.

CLS DESIDERANDA, Via Imperatore Traiano 28, (080) 878 8983, lesbian group with monthly Sun disco.

BERGAMO

■ Information
ARCI GAY, Via Baschenis 9, (035) 230 959, gay organization, Mon 20:30-22:30, Sat 15:00-18:00. Gay line answers Fri 20:30-22:30.

■ Bars
NITE LITE, Via Baschenis 9, (035) 244 300, large bar & disco, younger crowd, some women, Thurs-Sun from 22:00. 🍽✗♂

■ Dance Bar/Disco
GET UP, Via Bianzana 46, closed Mon. 🍽 ♀♂

BOLOGNA

■ Information
ARCI GAY NAZIONALE, Piazza di Porta Saragozza 2, (051) 644 70 54, fax: (051) 644 67 22, national headquarters of Arci Gay organization, Mon-Fri 15:00-18:00.

CENTRO DI DOCUMENTAZIONE, Piazza di Porta Saragozza 2, (051) 644 68 24, library, cultural center, gay archives, open every evening.

CENTRO PER LE DONNE, Via Galliera 8, (051) 233 863, Women's organizaton with large feminist library, open daily 08:30-14:00 & 15:00-18:00 (Sat only 08:00-14:00), library Mon-Fri 08:30-14:00 (Mon & Thurs also 15:00-18:00).

GAY INFO LINE, Piazza di Porta Saragozza 2, (051) 644 68 20, answers Mon-Fri 11:00-13:00, information for all of Italy.

VISIBILIA, Via Falegnami 3c, (051) 263 592. Lesbian group & archives, Wed & Sat 20:00-23:00, holds annual film festival.

■ Bars
★ **CASSERO,** Piazza Porta Saragozza 2, (051) 644 69 02, parties, shows, 21:30-01:00. Sun disco 22:00-02:30. 🍽✗♀♂

■ Dance Bar/Disco
KINKY, Via Zamboni 1, gay & lesbian Thurs only. 🍽♂

STONEWALL, Via del Pratello 96, pub weekdays, DJ Fri, Sat, closed Mon. 🍽 ♀

■ Restaurants
PIZZERIA DA NINO, Via Volturno 9, (051) 26 0294, gay-friendly, many gays on Sunday evenings.

SPEEDY PIZZERIA, Via Saragozza 65, popular with gays & lesbians. 🍽

TRATTORIA BONI, Via Saragozza 88, popular with gays & lesbians. 🍽

TRATTORIA FANTONI, Via del Pratello 4 or 5, popular with local gays. 🍽

■ Retail & Bookstores
LIBRERIA DELLE DONNE, Via Avesella 2/2, (51) 27 17 54, women's bookstore.

BRESCIA

■ Information
ARCIGAY ORLANDO, Piazzale Arnaldo 21, gay group, meets Sun 15:00-18:00.

PIANETA VIOLA, Via Villa Glori 10, (030) 241 0604, lesbian group, meets Thurs 20:30-22:30.

■ Dance Bar/Disco
OUT LIMITS, Via Ugo Foscolo 2, in the town of Paderno Franciacorta, (030) 63

BRINDISI

Information
ATTIKA, Via Santa Chiara 6, (0831) 563 051, gay group, meets Tues & Fri 19:00-20:30. ♀♂

AVVENTATE, Via Santa Chiara 6, women's group, meets Fri 19:00-23:00.

CAGLIARI

Retail & Bookstores
CENTRO DI DOCUMENTAZIONE, Via Lanusei 15, (070) 66 68 82, women's center & library, Tues & Thurs 10:00-13:00 & 16:00-20:00, Wed & Fri 10:00-13:00.

CATANIA

Information
OPEN MIND CENTRO INIZIATIVO GAY LESBICA, Via Gargano 33, (095) 532 685, daily 17:00-20:00 (Mon social).

Bars
NIEVSKY, Scalinata Alessi 13, pub, popular with gays Fri & Sat (80% gay), otherwise mostly straight. ♀♂

SOTTO SOPRA, Via Santangelo Fulci 9, pub & food. ♀♂

Dance Bar/Disco
PEGASUS, in summer: Viale Kennedy 80, zona playa; in winter: Via Canfora 11., Disco affiliated with Arci Gay group. ♀♂

CREMONA

Information
ARCIGAY ARCILESBICA LA ROCCA, via Speciano 4, (0372) 20484, gay organization, meets Fri 21:30-24:00.

DESENZANO

Dance Bar/Disco
ART CLUB, Via Mantova, inside Centro Comerciale Garda., (030) 999 1004, gay Fri, Sat, some heteros Fri. ♀♂

FABRO SCALO - CHIUSI

Camping & RV
TERRADILEI, 05010 Fabro Scalo (Chiusi), (39-763) 835 241 (Tel/Fax). Women-only camping retreat with vegetarian restaurant, coffee bar, 1 room, trailer rental, unlimited tent space, some RV parking, inside & outside showers, nearby pool & lake, full breakfast. Open April-Oct. ♀

FIRENZE - FLORENCE

Information
AZIONE GAY E LESBICA, Via San Zanobi 54 (red number), (055) 476 557 meetings 16:00-20:00. Bar Wed-Sun 16:00-02:00, women meet Thurs 21:00.

Accommodations
DEI MORI B&B, Via Dante Alighieri 12, Florence, 50122, (39-55) 211 438. Email: deimori@bnb.it, B&B in a 19th-century building in central Florence with view of Il Duomo. No elevator, 47 steps to 2nd floor location.

MORANDI ALLA CROCETTA, Via Laura 50, Firenze, 50121, (39-55) 2344747, Fax: (39-55) 2480954. Email: Hotel.Morandi@dada.it, Web: www.dada.it/Hotel.Morandi, gay-friendly guesthouse, variety of rooms with color satellite TV, AC, phone, refrigerator, private baths."

Women's Accommodations
B N B, Borgo Pinti 31, 3rd floor, Florence, 50121, (39-55) 248 0056, Fax: (39-55) 247 9654." Email: bnb@mail.cosmos.it, Web: www.bnb.it, Women-only B&B with 4 rooms & 2 baths (2 rooms have sinks), rooms have views of Il Duomo. ♀

Bars
PICCOLO CAFFE, Via Borgo Santa Croce, open daily, usually 30% women, many women Fri evening till 01:00. ♂

SATANASSA, Via Pandolfini 26, watch for the red number, garage entrance, (055) 243 356, 22:00-03:00 (Fri, Sat till 06:00), closed Sun & Mon. Thurs & Fri women's night. ♀♂

Cafe
PICCOLO CAFFE, Via Borgo Santa Croce, gay-friendly, day bar, closes at 01:00

Restaurants
LE COLONINE, Borgo Santa Croce, near Piccolo Caffee, Mon-Sat.

Retail & Bookstores
LIBRERIA DELLE DONNE, Via Fiesolana 2/b, (055) 24 03 84, women's bookstore, 09:00-13:00 & 15:30-19:30 (closed Mon till 15:30).

ITALY 103

GENOVA

Information
ARCI GAY GENOVA, Via San Luca, 11/4, (010) 246 7506, group meets Mon 21:00-23:00, Fri 17:30-19:30.

Accommodations
BARABINO, Via Sanpierdarena 99, Genova, 16121, (39-10) 411 384. gay-friendly hotel, single & double rooms, 50% gay & lesbian clientele, more gays among large theater clientele on weekends."

MINI HOTEL, Via Lomellini 6, (010) 246 5876. Gay-friendly hotel.

Bars
LA CAGE, Via Sampierdarena, 167/R, (010) 645 45 55, Tues-Sun 22:00-04:00.

Dance Bar/Disco
L'ALTRA NOTTE, in town of Arenzano, about 10 km from Genoa.,

ISOLA D'ELBA

Accommodations
CASA SCALA, Loc. Filetto No 9, Marina di Campo, Isola d'Elba, 57034, (39-565) 977 777, Fax: (39-565) 977 770. cottage with workshops, women only, kitchen, refrigerator, shared baths, nearby ocean beach, continental breakfast with workshops only. ♀

LECCE

Information
ARCIGAY ARCILESBICA ARCOBALENO, Via Francesco Milizia 56b, (0832) 312 511, Sat, Sun only after 20:00.

MILANO - MILAN

Information
ARCI GAY CENTRO D'INIZIATIVA GAY, Via Torricelli 19, (02) 5810 0299. Gay center with archives, library, group meetings, afternoon & evening 7 days (archives Omologie/Fondo Olivari also Wed 21:00-24:00).

CDM, Via Cicco Simonetta 15, (02) 805 18 08, lesbian group, socials Sun 15:00-20:00.

TELEFONA AMICO & AMICA LINES, (02) 8940 1749, answers 20:00-24:00, gay line Tues, Thurs, Fri. Lesbian line Wed.

Bars
★ **AFTER LINE,** via Sammartini 25, (02) 669 2130, bar & disco, 17:00-02:00, closed Tues.

CICIP E CICIAP, Via Gorani 9, (02) 86 72 02, bar & restaurant from 20:00, circolo culturale e politico (cultural & political center for women), women only. ♀

L'ELEPHANTE, Via Melzo 22, (02) 2951 8768, bar & restaurant, Sun brunch 12:00-16:00 (closed Mon). ♂

LA BIRRERIA UNO ALTERNATIVA, Via Borsieri 14, (2) 6900 3271. ♀♂

MOLTO, Via Borgogna 7, bar & cafe.

NO TIES, Via Giacosa 58, private club. ♀♂

QUERELLE, Via de Castillia 20, (02) 683 900 or 552 10359, bar run by Arci Gay organization, 21:00-02:00 (closed Mon). Third Mon of month women only. ♀♂

RECYCLE, Via Calabria 5, (02) 376 1531, Wed & Thurs men & women. Fri-Sun women only. ♀♂

Dance Bar/Disco
MAN TO MAN, Viale Umbria 120, at Killer Plastic, (02) 733 996, gay only Thurs 23:00-06:00. Monthly lesbian night.

★ **NUOVA IDEA,** Via de Castillia 30, (02) 689 27 53, Thurs-Sun 21:30-02:00, women welcome.

SEGRETA, Piazza Castello 1, (02) 860 307, from 22:30, closed Mon & Tues.

SOTTOMARINO GIALLO, Via Donatello 2, (02) 2940 1047, disco for women-only with 2 floors, quieter bar upstairs. Unverifiable spring '98. ♀

Restaurants
CICIP E CICIAP, Via Gorani 9, (02) 86 72 02, women's restaurant & a social local for local women.

DUE AMICI, via Borsieri 5, (metro #2, Garibaldi stop, exit to G. Pepe St.), (02) 668 46 96. Gay-friendly restaurant & bar with patio dining in summer, 20:00-03:00, except Wed evening.

LA RISOTTERIA, Via Dandolo 2, (02) 5518 1694, 20:00-23:00 (closed Sun).

LA VILLETTA DI ELISA, Viale Bezzi 86, (02) 498 2376, gay-friendly, expensive, 19:00-03:00, patio dining.

Retail & Bookstores
LIBRERIA BABELE, Via Sammartini,

ITALY

23, (02) 669 2986 (tel/fax), gay & lesbian bookshop, Mon-Sat 09:30-19:30.
LIBRERIA DELLE DONNE, Via Dogana 2, (02) 874 213, women's bookstore, 9:30-13:00 & 15:30-19:00 (closed Mon till 15:30 & Sun).

MODENA

■ Bars
WOVOKA CLUB, Via Canaletto 152D, (059) 313 244, 21:00-02:00 (Tues, Fri, Sat 22:30-04:00), Sat women-only dance night. 🎵🍸♀♂

NAPOLI - NAPLES

■ Information
ARCI GAY ANTINOO NAPOLI, Vico S. Geronimo 17/20, (081) 552 8815, gay & lesbian organization, Mon-Fri 16:00-20:00. Women meet Sat 10:30-13:00.

■ Bars
FERDINAND STRASSE, Piazza Porta Nova 8, (081) 206 390, gay in the evenings from 21:00, cultural discussions take place, 20% women. ♂

■ Dance Bar/Disco
BASIS, Gradini Amadeo 12, open Tues, Thurs & Sat (days change frequently), opens irregularly. 🎵🍸♂
DIABOLICA, Via Nicolò Tommaseo, on 1st corner, taking Via Parenope form Piazza Vittoria, gay Sat only, 20% women. 🎵♂
QUEEN, Via Sgambati 47 (exit freeway at Camaldoli), metro: Rione Alto, Sat only. 🎵♀♂

PADOVA

■ Information
ARCI GAY, Via Santa Sofia 5, (049) 876 2548, Monday 21:30-23:00.

■ Bars
FLEXO, ask locally for address, video bar, 21:00-02:00 (women last Tues 21:00-02:00), closed Mon-Tues. ♂

■ Dance Bar/Disco
BLACK & WHITE DISCO BAR, Viale Navigazione Interna 38/A, zona industriale nord, (049) 776 414, private club, join for 15,000 Lire or get membership to Arci Gay, 80% men, open 7 days in summer, in winter closed Mon & Tues. 🎵♂
FABBRICA, Via Giulia 59, in Perarolo, 3km outside Padova, dance bar. 🎵♂

PALERMO

■ Information
ARCI GAY ORLANDO, Via Genova 7, (091) 335 688, fax: (091) 611 3245, gay line, 17:00-19:30 (women answer Mon).

■ Bars
HEMINGWAY, Piazza Ignazio Florio, 80% women. ♀
I GRILLI, Piazza Valverde, in Palermo's old section, pub, many tables outside with nice atmosphere. ♀♂
IT, Via S. Oliva 38, pub, 15,000 Lire for membership to enter, open evenings 7 days (better after 21:00), also Sun afternoons. ♂
LORD GREEN, Via Parisi, pub, 50% straight, 50% gay/lesbian.

■ Dance Bar/Disco
ANGELO AZZURRO, Via S. Martino, in sector called Bocca di Falco, nearly 100% men, but women welcomed if they show up. 🎵♂

PARMA

■ Dance Bar/Disco
ANDROMEDA, Via Gramsci 5, in the town of Soragna, (0524) 597 204, Fri, Sat 22:00 till 02:00 or 03:00, 90% men. 🎵♂

PERUGIA

■ Information
ARCI GAY, Via Fratti 18 (Apollo 2), (075) 572 3175, gay & lesbian organization, Wed, Fri & Sat from 21:30. Women meet Thurs.

PESCARA

■ Bars
HEROES, Via E. Flaiano 21, 21:00-02:00, unverifiable spring '97. ♂

PISA

■ Information
ARCI GAY, Via della Croce Rossa 7, (050) 576 420 Mon-Wed 21:00-24:00, lesbians meet Fri.

■ Bars
G.A.O., Via della Croce Rossa 7, at Arci Gay location, (050) 576 420, Thurs-Sun 21:00-01:00. ♀♂

ITALY 105

PONSACCO

Dance Bar/Disco
INSOMNIA, in the small town of Ponsacco, not far outside Pisa, gay-friendly disco, winter gay Fri, summer gay Sat.

PROCIDA ISLAND

Accommodations
HOTEL CELESTE RESIDENCE, Via Rivoli 6, Isola di Prócida, Napoli, 80079, (39-81) 896 7488, Fax: (39-81) 896 7670. Email: procida@mbox.vol.it or procida@pointel.it, Web: www.pointel.it/celeste, Hotel on the island of Prócida, a 1-hour ferry ride from Naples. Guests occupy their own private apartments, restaurant & bar on premises, buffet breakfast, interior gardens & terraces with panoramic views, 200 meters from beach.

RAVENNA

Information
ARCI GAY ANDROMEDA, Via Castel San Pietro 71, (0544) 66170, Sun & Wed evenings after 21:00.

RIMINI - RICCIONE

Accommodations
GARNI CECCARINI 140, Viale Ceccarini 140, Riccione, Gay-friendly hotel.

Dance Bar/Disco
CLASSIC CLUB, Via Feleto 11, Rimini, (0541) 731 113, disco & piano bar, video, 70% men; summer: 7 days 23:00-06:00, winter: Sat only 23:00-06:00.

ROMA - ROME

Information
AIDS INFO, (06) 638 0365.

ARCI GAY PEGASO, Via Primo Acciaresi 7, (06) 41 73 0752, gay & lesbian organization, answers Sat 18:00-20:00.

CENTRO ARCOBALENO (RAINBOW CENTER), (06) 581 9593, answers Mon-Fri 21:00-23:00.

CENTRO SOCIALE GARAGE, Via Gustavo Modena 92, near Piazza Sonnino, gays meet Sun, couselling & help Thurs.

CIRCOLO MARIO MIELI, Via Corinto 5, (06) 541 39 85, Mon-Fri from 18:00, bar, shows & video evenings, mostly men.

COORDINAMENTO LESBICO ITALIANO, Via S. Francesco di Sales 1/A, (06) 686 4201, lesbian organization.

Accommodations
HOTEL GRANDI, Via Acchile Grandi 7, For information, contact Max's Bar at 70 30 15 99.

HOTEL SCALINATA DI SPAGNA, Piazza Trinità dei Monti 17, Roma, 00187, Bookings: (39-6) 679 3006 or 699 40896, Fax: (39-6) 699 40598. Gay-friendly bed & breakfast, 20%-30% gay & lesbian clientele, rooms have modern conveniences, near Borghese Garden, 5 min to gym, steam, sauna, Jacuzzi, steps away from Spanish Steps, expanded continental breakfast.

Bars
APEIRON CLUB, Via dei Quattro Cantoni 5, (06) 482 88 20, 22:30-02:00 (closed Sun).

IL SETTIMO CIELO, gay bar on gay beach near Ostia., On the beach road, 2km north of Tor Vaianica and just a little south of the nude beach, Il Buco. Beach volleyball and other activities, music. Officially open June thru late Sept, but opens on any warm, sunny weekend. Open days and, in summer, some evenings.

SHELTER, Via dei Vascellari 35, pub, 20:30-02:00, some hetero clientele.

Dance Bar/Disco
ANGELO AZZURRO, Via Cardinal Merry del Val 13, (06) 580 04 72, 23:00-04:00 (Sat till 05:00), Fri women only. Opens infrequently.

FRUTTA E VERDURA, Via Principe Umberto 38, (06) 446 4862, drag cafe, 22:00-03:00.

JOLIE COEUR, Via Sirte 5, (06) 8621 5827, women's night Sat only from 22:00.

PALADIUM, Via del Comercio 36, gay Fri only 22:30-04:00 (name changes frequently).

Saunas/Health Clubs
IXTASIA, Via Ombrone 1, mixed hetero, gay & lesbian with men's & women's days.

ITALY

■ Restaurants
ISOLA DEL SOLE, Lungotevere Arnaldo da Brescia, (06) 320 1400, 13:00-15:00 & 20:30-24:00 (closed Mon). ⚥

■ Retail & Bookstores
AL TEMPO RITROVATO, Via dei Fienaroli, (06) 654 37 49, women's bookshop & local info.

LA BANCARELLA, Piazza Alessandria 2, (06) 8530 3071, gay & lesbian bookstore.

LIBRERIA BABELE, Via dei Banchi Vecchi 116, (06) 687 66 28, gay & lesbian bookstore, Mon-Sat 9:30-19:30.

TAORMINA

■ Accommodations
HOTEL VILLA SCHULER, Via Roma 17, Taormina/Sicily, 98039, (39-942) 23481, Fax: (39-942) 23522. Email: schuler@tao.it, Web: http://www.cys.it/schuler, Gay-friendly bed & breakfast hotel & bar, variety of spacious guest quarters, private & shared baths, TV lounge, solarium, nearby ocean beach, expanded continental breakfast.

■ Bars
MARENGO, Vico F. Paladini 4, (0942) 239 45, 20:00-03:00 (closed Thurs), 50% gay & lesbian.

MARRAKECH, Piazzetta Garibaldi, (0942) 625 692, 20:00-03:00 (closed Wed), patio, live music in summer, mostly gay, many heteros.

★ **SHATULLE,** Piazzetta Paladini 4, (0942) 211 41, 20:00-03:00 (closed Mon), 50% gay & lesbian with a large straight following.

TYKE, Piazzetta Paladini 8, 20:00-03:00 (closed Tues), 50% gay & lesbian.

■ Dance Bar/Disco
★ **LE PERROQUET,** Piazza S. Domenico 2, (0942) 244 62, cabaret, lounge, 70% men. July-Sept daily from 21:30 till late, rest of year Sat & Sun only 21:30-03:30. 🎵 ✗ ♂

■ Restaurants
LA PIAZZETTA, Via Paladini 5, (0942) 626 317, 12:30-15:00 & 19:30-24:00, closed Mon.

TORINO - TURIN

■ Information
CIRCOLO OUT! MAURICE, Via della Basilica 3/5, (011) 521 1116, gay & lesbian group, archives & library. Mon-Fri 10:00-12:00 & 15:00-18:00, Sat 09:00-12:00 & 16:00-19:00, Sun 18:00-20:00. Call for women's nights

INFORMAGAY, (011) 436 50 00, gay info line, AIDS info, answers Tues & Sat 17:00-20:00 & 21:00-23:00 (Fri lesbian line).

■ Bars
CIRCOLO BRIDGE, Via Maria Auseliatrice 46bis, (011) 436 4952, 21:00-04:00 (closed Tues). ♀

IL MALE, Via Lombardore 10, (011) 284 617, pub, 20:00-03:00, 70% men. ♂

MAIN STREET, Via Valperga Caluso 15, (011) 657 905, gay Tues only. 🎵 ♀♂

ROUTE 66, Via Silvio Pellico 4, (1) 669 9588. ♀

■ Dance Bar/Disco
EPIC GAY CLUB, Via Martiri della Libertà, Località Borgaretto, (011) 358 3346, 22:30-02:00 (Sat till 04:00), 90% men. 🎵 ♂

IL CENTRALINO, Via delle Rosine 16, gay Fri & Sun, 70% men, 30% women. 🎵 ♀♂

LE MUST, Via Porta Palatina 23., 🎵 ♂

QUARTIERE LATINO, Via Principessa Clotilde 82, Fri women only, Sat gay & lesbian. 🎵 ♀♂

■ Retail & Bookstores
LIBRERIA LUXEMBURG, Via C. Battisti 7, (011) 561 3896, general bookstore with a small gay section.

TRIESTE

■ Information
ARCI GAY ARCOBALENO, Strade di Rozzol 7-9, (040) 941 708.

TUSCANY - RURAL

■ Accommodations
PRIELLO BED & BREAKFAST, Caprese Michelangelo, Arezzo, 52033, (39-575) 791 218 (Tel/Fax). Email: a.voglino@agora.stm.it, 1-1/2 hours E of Florence & 1-1/2 hrs W of Rimini. A B&B on a working farm on the site of an ancient monastery high in the mountains of Tuscany. Mainly gay & lesbian. ♀♂

UDINE

■ Information
AIDS INFO, (0432) 26859.

ARCI GAY NUOVI PASSI, Via Gorghi, (0432) 454 68, gay & lesbian organization, gay line Mon & Wed 20:00-22:00.

VENEZIA - VENICE

Information
ARCI GAY NOVE, Campo San Giacomo dell'Orio, S. Croce, (041) 721 842, gay & lesbian group, meetings Mon, Wed, Fri 18:00-24:00, Thurs 21:00-23:00."

VERONA

Information
CENTRO D'INIZIATIVA OMOSESSUALE PINK, Via Scringari 7, (045) 801 2854, gay & lesbian organization, meets Mon, Tues & Fri evenings, Sat afternoon

Bars
CAMPOFIORE, Via Campofiore, more gays in evening, be discreet.

DOLCE & BANANA, Via XX Settembre 68, Mon-Sat 09:00-14:00 & 16:00-02:00, frequented by gays.

MIRO, near Porta Leone, more gay in evening, many tourists by day.

VIAREGGIO

Dance Bar/Disco
FRAU MARLEEN, Viale Europa, Torre del Lago, (0584) 34 22 82, very mixed hetero/gay, younger crowd, Sat & Sun from 23:30, hours may increase in summer.

LATVIA

COUNTRY CODE: (371),

RIGA

Information
AIDS INFO, 522 222.

Bars
EIGHT-O-EIGHT (808), 8 A. Kalnina St, Wed-Sun from 18:00.

PURVS, 60 Matisa St, (7) 311 717, 19:00-07:00, closed Mon.

Cafe
CAFE OSIRIS, 31 Krisjan Barona St, (7) 243 002, 08:00-01:00 (Sat, Sun from 10:00), not a gay cafe, discreetly frequented by gays.

SYMPOSIUM, 84-1 Dzirnavu St, (7) 242 545, 11:00-01:00, not a gay cafe, discreetly frequented by gays.

LITHUANIA

COUNTRY CODE: (370),

KAUNAS

Bars
MEFISTOFELIS, ask locally for address., Not a gay bar, discreetly frequented by local gays, 21:00-06:00, Fri-Sat disco.

VILNIUS

Bars
AMSTERDAM, Profsajungu Ramai, Not a gay bar, discreetly frequented by local gays, 12:00-06:00, Sat disco.

LUXEMBOURG

COUNTRY CODE: (352),

LUXEMBOURG

Information
AIDS LINE, (352) 406 251.

Bars
BIG MOON, 14, rue Vauban, (352) 43 17 46.

CAFE DE LA GARE, 58 rue Fort Neippberg, 40 65 99. 2 levels, frequented by gays.

CHEZ GUSTY, rue d'Eich., (352) 43 12 23.

CHEZ MANDA, rue Vaubon, mostly women, men welcome.

Dance Bar/Disco
CAFE CONQUEST, 7 rue du Palais de Justice, Techno music, good mix of gays & straights.

PULP, 36 Blvd d'Avranches, 49 69 40. DJs, techno music, frequented by gays.

NETHERLANDS

COUNTRY CODE: (31),

ALDEBOARN

■ Accommodations
DE GRUPSTAL, Wjitteringswei 67, Aldeboarn (FRL), 8495 JM, 05663 1465, Fax 05663 1238, Holiday retreat with special lesbian activities, mainly hetero clientele, accommodations for 45 people & camping, write for information.

ALKMAAR

■ Information
COC INFO LINE, Bierkade 14A, (072) 511 16 50, ask about scheduled bar nights."

AMSTERDAM

■ Information
AIDS LINE, (020) 685 0055.

DORA, organization providing travel information for women of all ages traveling in Europe & overseas. Also provides contacts with women who want to share their knowledge about destinations they have visited. Write: Postbus 14735, 1001 LE Amsterdam, The Netherlands. Tel: (020) 638 0765 answers Tues 14:00-16:00, Wed 19:00-22:00.

GAY & LESBIAN SWITCHBOARD, (020) 623 65 65, 10:00-22:00.

HET VROUWENHUIS, Nieuwe Herengracht 95, (020) 625 20 66, call for opening hours.

INTERNATIONAL WOMEN'S LIBRARY, 4 O.B. Plein, (020) 624 21 34, call for opening hours.

LESBIAN ARCHIVES, Eerste Helmerstr. 17, (020) 618 58 79.

■ Tours, Charters & Excursions
VAARSCHOOL GRIETJE, Prinsengracht T/O 187, Amsterdam, Tel/Fax: (31-20) 625 91 05. Sail the small canals of Holland, Belgium or France on "The Grietje." Seven-day sails are scheduled from end of July-early Sept. The vessel has a living room, kitchen & sleeps up to 4 women. There is no electricity or hot shower, but hot shower available almost daily. ♀

■ Accommodations
AMSTERDAM HOUSE BV, Amstel 176a, Amsterdam, 1017 AE, (31-20) 62 62 577, Fax: (31-20) 62 62 987, USA: (904) 677-5370, (800) 618-1008, Fax: (904) 672-6659. Gay-friendly apartment hotel with houseboats. Available for short- and long-term business or leisure stays. Most apartments overlook the Amsterdam canals and both apartments and houseboats are spacious and luxuriously furnished. Accommodations include kitchen, refrigerator, telephone, color TV and private baths. Secretarial services, fax, answering machines, and photocopiers are also available. We are close to the main railway station and other transport intersections and afford easy access to the Amsterdam International Airport and downtown amenities."

AMSTERDAM TOFF'S, Ruysdaelkade 167, Amsterdam, 1072 AS, (31-20) 67 38 529, Fax: (31-20) 66 49 479. self-catering serviced apartments, 50% gay/lesbian clientele, colour cable TV, phone, kitchen, beverage making facilities, VCR on request.

C & G BED & BREAKFAST HOUSE, 2nd Leliedwarsstraat 4, PO Box 15889, Amsterdam, 1001 NJ, (31-20) 422 7996 or (31-20) 5300 8800. Mobile: (31-20) 653 713452 (for calls within Amsterdam, dial "0" before the "6"). Private housing in two well-furnished modern houses in central Amsterdam. Continental breakfast, roof garden, near gay bars & many tourist attractions. Women welcome. ♂

CENTRE APARTMENTS AMSTERDAM, Heintje Hoekssteeg 27, PO Box 15889, Amsterdam, 1001 NJ, (31-20) 627 25 03, Fax: (31-20) 625 11 08. Mobile: (31-20) 653 713452 (for calls within Amsterdam, dial "0" before the "6"). Fully-furnished 2- & 3- room apartments & studios for 3, fully equipped kitchens, modern bathrooms, near Centraal Station. ♀♂

FREELAND HOTEL, Marnixstraat 386, Amsterdam, 1017 PL, (31-20) 622 75 11 or 627 75 78, Fax: (31-20) 626 77 44. hotel, women welcome, private baths, full Dutch breakfast, color cable TV, telephone, meeting rooms." ♂

HOTEL "THE VILLAGE", 25 Kerkstraat, Amsterdam, 1017 GA, (31-20)

626 9746, Fax: (31-20) 625 4081. Centrally located hotel with residents' bar, café, restaurant, 50% gay/lesbian, private baths, Dutch breakfast. Gay-owned.

HOTEL AERO, Kerkstraat 49, Amsterdam-C, 1017 GB, (31-20) 622 77 28, Fax: (31-20) 638 8531. hotel with bar & gay-sex shop, women welcome, newly-renovated rooms with modern conveniences, private & shared baths, full breakfast. ♂

HOTEL CLEMENS, 39 Raadhuisstraat, Amsterdam, 1016 DC, (31-20) 624 60 89, Fax: (31-20) 626 9658. gay-owned hotel near Royal Palace, 60% gay/lesbian clientele, private & shared baths." ♀♂

HOTEL NEW YORK, Herengracht 13, Amsterdam, 1015-BA, (31-20) 624 30 66, Fax: (31-20) 620 32 30. bed & breakfast hotel, women welcome, private & shared baths, modern, comfortable decor, centrally located, ocean beach nearby, Dutch breakfast." ♂

HOTEL SANDER, Jacob Obrechtstraat 69, Amsterdam, 1071 KJ, (31-20) 6627574, Fax: (31-20) 6796067. This attractive 4-star hotel with bar is situated 1 block from the Van Gogh Museum and the Concertgebouw and is a 10-minute walk from the Kerkstraat gay area. Rooms include colour cable TV, direct-dial phones, radio, individual safe and en suite WC & shower. Room rates include expanded continental breakfast. Mostly gay & lesbian with some hetero clientele. ♀♂

HOTEL THE GOLDEN BEAR, Kerkstraat 37, Amsterdam, 1017 GB, (31-20) 624 47 85, Fax: (31-20) 627 0164. Email: goldbear@xs4all.nl, Web: http://www.xs4all.nl/~goldbear, Comfortable rooms with single through queen beds, private & shared baths, expanded continental breakfast, guests have own room keys, near gay bars." ♂

HOTEL WILHELMINA, Koninginne Weg 167-169, Amsterdam, 1075 CN, (31-20) 662 5467, Fax: (31-20) 679 2296, Telex: WILHL NL. Email: wilhlhtl@euronet.nl, gay-friendly hotel, centrally located, variety of rooms, color cable TV, private & shared baths, full Dutch breakfast."

ITC HOTEL, Prinsengracht 1051, Amsterdam, 1017 JE, (31-20) 623 0230, Fax: (31-20) 624 5846. hotel with bar, in heart of Old Amsterdam, near gay nightlife of Rembrandtplein & Kerkstraat. Most rooms have private baths, and all are pleasantly furnished in a modern style. Other attractions are a late breakfast and your own front door key. Women welcome. ♂

LILIANE'S HOME; GUESTHOUSE FOR WOMEN ONLY, Sarphatistraat 119, Amsterdam, 1018 GB, (31-20) 627 4006 (Tel/Fax). guesthouse for women only, shared baths, color cable TV, breakfast, beverage-making facilities, maid & laundry service. ♀

MAES B & B, Herengracht 26, Amsterdam, 1015 CB, (31-20) 427 5156, Fax: (31-20) 427 5166. Email: maesbb94@xs4all.nl, Web: http://www.xs4all.nl/~maesbb94/, Bed & breakfast, expanded continental breakfast, coffee/tea-making facilities, private baths, 5-10 min. walk to gay bars, some hetero clientele." ♀♂

RIVERSIDE APARTMENTS, Weteringschans 187 E, Amsterdam, 1017 XE, (31-20) 627 9797, Fax: (31-20) 627 9858. Email: geuje@worldonline.nl, Gay-friendly apartment rentals in & around Amsterdam, 50% gay/lesbian clientele, near entertainment & restaurants. Amenities vary according to type of accommodation."

Amsterdam House

Feel at home away from home

In The USA
Tel: (904) 677-5370
Fax: (904) 672-6659
Toll Free: (800) 618-1008

Amstel 176a
1017AE Amsterdam

Tel: (31-20) 62 62 577
Fax: (31-20) 62 62 987

RUBENS BED & BREAKFAST, Rubensstraat 38bv, Amsterdam, 1077 MS, (31-20) 662 9187 (tel/fax). Email: rubensbb@xs4all.nl, Web: http://www.xs4all.nl/~rubensbb, Owned & operated by 2 Dutch guys, this private apartment is in a 1930s neighbourhood, just outside the old city centre. Recently renovated, it is brought back to its original Art Deco style. The B&B's 2 rooms share a small state-of-the-art bathroom with shower & heated floor, and both rooms open up to a balcony with morning sun. Major museums & tourist attractions are within walking distance (or a few tram stops), and the Beethovenstraat shopping area is nearby. The exhuberant Amsterdam nightlife is not far away either. Expanded continental breakfast, 50% gay/lesbian clientele.

SINGEL SUITE — THE BED & BREAKFAST SUITES, Singel 420, Amsterdam, 1016 AK, (31-20) 625 8673, Fax: (31-20) 625 8097. Overlooking one ot the prettiest canals in the heart of Amsterdam, our guests find someting better than the average hotel: luxury, comfort and privacy. Our two apartments are 17th century in style, but throrougly modern in luxury and comfort, and located near the best-known clubs and restaurants. One has a Jacuzzi-bath bathroom next to a private patio.

SUNHEAD OF 1617, Herengracht 152, Amsterdam, 1016 BN, (31-20) 626 1809, Fax: (31-20) 626 1823. Email: sunhead@xs4all.nl, bed & breakfast, some hetero clientele, some rooms overlooking canal, private baths, full breakfast, afternoon snacks, color cable TV, VCR, video tape library, phone, maid & laundry service. ♀♂

WESTEND HOTEL & COSMO BAR, Kerkstraat 42, Amsterdam, 1017 GM, (31-20) 624 80 74, Fax: (31-20) 622 99 97. bed & breakfast with bar, women welcome, comfortable double rooms with shared baths, color TV upon request, men's bars & sauna nearby. ♂

■ Bars

CLIT CLUB, 472 Prinsengracht, Thurs 21:00-02:30. Location changes frequently, check locally for current address." ♀

DE STEEG, 10 Halvemaansteeg, Dutch sing-alongs with live singers, 16:00-01:00, Fri & Sat till 03:00. ♂

GETTO, Warmoesstraat 51, Wed-Sun 16:00-01:00. Women Tues from 17:00. ♂

HELLEN'S DANCE, Kerkstraat 52, 22:00-04:00 (Fri, Sat till 05:00). 🎵 ♀

★ **MANKIND,** 60 Weteringstraat, (020) 638 47 55, 11:00-01:00, Fri & Sat till 02:00. ♂

MIX CAFE, 50 Amstel, (020) 420 33 88, 20:00-03:00 (Fri, Sat till 04:00)." ♀♂

OUDE VEERHUIS, 8 Singel, (020) 624 32 81, 09:00-01:00 (Fri, Sat till 02:00). ♂

SAAREIN, 119 Elandsstraat, 15:00-01:00 (Fri, Sat till 02:00, Mon from 20:00). ♀

VAN DEN BERG, 95 Lindengracht, (020) 622 27 16, women's cafe, restaurant, bar, dancing, regular shows, gay men welcome, daily 16:00-01:00." 🎵 🎶 ♀

■ Dance Bar/Disco

COC DISCO, BAR & CAFÉ, 14 Rozenstraat, (020) 623 40 79, Wed-Sun 13:00-17:00 & 20:00-24:00. Call for schedule of men's & women's disco nights."

COC VROUWENDISCO, at COC coffeeshop, 14 Rozenstraat, women's disco night. Call for scheduled Sat disco." 🎵 ♀

DE BRUG, 676 Keizersgracht, disco for lesbians over 35 years, 1st Fri." 🎵 ♀

★ **EXIT,** 42 Reguliersdwarsstraat, (020) 625 87 88, disco & 2 bars, 23:00-04:00 (Fri, Sat till 05:00). 🎵 ♂

★ **HOMOLULU,** 23 Kerkstraat, (020) 624 63 87, disco & restaurant, ring the bell, daily 22:00-04:00, women's disco nights 1st Sun & 3rd Fri of the month." 🎵 ✕ ♀♂

HOMOLULU WOMEN'S NIGHTS, at Homolulu disco, 1st Sun & 3rd Fri 20:00-01:00." 🎵 ♀

ROXY LADY, 465 Singel, at the Roxy disco location, women's disco 3rd Sun 18:00-23:00. 🎵 ♀

VIVELAVIE, 7 Amstelstraat, (020) 624 01 14, 15:00-01:00, Fri, Sat till 03:00." 🎵 🎶 ♀

■ Cafe

★ **LE MONDE,** 6 Rembrandtplein, (020) 626 99 22, breakfast, lunch, dinner, patio, popular with gays & lesbians 08:00-22:00, till 24:00 during summer." ♀♂

★ **SAAREIN,** 119 Elandsstraat, (020) 623 49 01, women-only cafe, 15:00-01:00 (Fri, Sat till 02:00, Mon from 20:00). ♀

NETHERLANDS 111

SARAH'S GRANNIES, 176 Kerkstraat, (020) 624 01 45. Breakfast & lunch cafe with light meals, Mon-Fri 09:30-17:00, Sat from 10:30. B&B available for non-smoking women." ♀

■ Restaurants

AMSTERDAM, 6 Watertorenplein, 11:00-01:00 (Fri, Sat till 02:00).

BALDUR, 76 Weteringschans, (020) 624 46 72, non-smoking vegetarian restaurant popular with lesbians, daily 17:00-22:00. 🗷 ♀

BISTRO CONTRA 73, 24 Karperstraat., 🗷

CAMP CAFE, 45 Kerkstraat, 11:00-01:00.

CARLITA'S CANTINA, 121 Ceintuurbaan, (020) 675 69 30, 17:00-24:00. 🗷

COSTELICK MAEL, 'T, 115 1st C. Huygensstraat, 17:00-24:00. 🗷

DE APPLEGAARD, 105 Wittenkede.,

DE HUYSKAEMER, 137 Utrechtstraat., 🗷

DE JAREN, 20-22 Nieuwe Doelenstraat, (020) 625 5771. 🗷

GEMINI, 11 Thorbeckeplein, open 11:00-01:00 (Sat, Sun till 02:00).

GERARD, 23 Geldersekade, 17:30-23:00 (closed Tues). 🗷

GRIET MANSHANDE, 10 Keerpunkt, from 18:00, closed Tues.

HARVEST, 25 Govert Flinckstraat, (020) 676 9995, vegetarian cuisine, Tues-Sat 17:30-22:30.

HEMELSE MODDER, 9 Oude Waal., 🗷

INDRAPURA, 42 Rembrandtplein, (020) 623 73 29, Indonesian cuisine. 🗷

INTERMEZZO, 28 Herenstr., 17:30-22:00 (Fri, Sat 18:00-22:30)."

JARDIN PARISIEN, 30A Utrechtstraat, 16:00-24:00. 🗷

JEAN JEAN, 12 1st Anjeliersdwarsstraat, 18:00-22:30, closed Mon. 🗷

KILIMANJARO, 6 Rapenbplts., 17:00-22:00 (closed Mon). 🗷

LE GARAGE, 54 Ruysdaelstraat, 12:00-14:00 & 18:00-23:00 (Sat, Sun 18:00-23:00 only).

LETO, 114 Haarlemmerdijk, 17:00-22:00, closed Mon."

LOMBOK, 12 Halve Maansteeg., 🗷

MAXIES BRASSERIE, 100 PC Hoofstraat, 11:00-21:30 (closed Sun, Mon). 🗷

SINGEL SUITE
The Bed & Breakfast Suites

Luxury • Comfort • Privacy
In the heart of Gay Amsterdam

(31-20) 625 86 73

MEMORIES OF INDIA, 88 Reguliersdwarsstr., (020) 623 5710, 17:00-23:00. 🗷

PORTUGALIA, 35 Kerkstraat, 17:00-23:00. 🗷

RA KANG THAI, 29 Elandsgracht, closed Mon.

SATURNINO, 5 Reguliersdwarsstraat.,

SAY SATÉ, 26 Amstelstr., (020) 625 75 60, open till 01:00 (Fri, Sat till 02:00)." 🗷

SCHOOIERTJE, 'T, 190 Lijnbaansgracht, (020) 638 40 35, Sat-Thurs 10:00-22:00. 🗷

SLUISJE, 'T, 1 Torensteeg, near Spuistraat, (020) 624 08 13, steakhouse, 17:00-01:00 (closed Wed). 🗷 ⊻

SLUIZER, 41 Utrechtsestraat, (020) 622 63 76, indoor & terrace dining 10:00-24:00. 🗷

SUKHOTHAI, 147 Ceintuurbaan, 17:30-24:00.

TEMPO DOELOE, 75 Utrechtsestraat, (020) 625 67 18, Indonesian cuisine, 18:00-23:00." 🗷

■ Retail & Bookstores

ANTIQUARIAAT LORELEI, 495 Prinsengracht, (020) 623 43 08, Tues-Fri 12:00-18:00, Sat till 17:00.

BOEKENCASA, 133 Haarlemmerdijk, (020) 622 58 92, alternative bookstore with women's section.

DESMET, 4a Plantage Middenlaan, cinema with scheduled gay movies on weekends, not erotic.

VROLIJK BOOKSTORE, 135 Paleisstraat, (020) 623 51 42, gay & lesbian bookshop, books in many languages, cards, art posters & magazines, Mon-Fri 10:00-18:00, Thurs till 21:00, Sat till 17:00.

VROUWENINDRUK, 5 Westermarkt near Westerkerk, (020) 624 50 03, secondhand books on women's sexuality, herstory, feminism. Most books are in Dutch, many in English, 11:00-18:00 (Mon from 13:00).

XANTIPPE, 290 Prinsengracht, (020) 623 58 54, one of Europe's largest selections of women's & lesbian books, many in English. Stop by & ask us for local info, 10:00-18:00 (Mon from 13:00, Sat till 17:00), closed Sun."

ARNHEM

■ Information
COC GAY ORGANIZATION, Nieuwstad 50, (026) 442 31 61, Thurs 19:00-21:00, Sat 14:00-16:00.

IRIS, Willemsplein 21, lesbian group."

■ Retail & Bookstores
HELLEVEEG, Bentinckstraat 36, (026) 451 54 31, women's bookstore, Tues-Sat 10:00-18:00 (Thurs till 21:00).

BERGEN OP ZOOM

■ Information
COC GAY ORGANIZATION, Blokstallen 4, (0164) 2542 35, bar nights Fri 21:00-02:00, Sun 18:30-23:00, every 3rd Sat 21:00-02:00.

BREDA

■ Information
COC GAY ORGANIZATION, St. Annastraat 10, (076) 522 66 62, Sat 12:00-16:00, 2nd Sat 21:00-03:00, 4th Wed 20:30-24:00. Vrouwencafe (women's cafe) 2nd & 4th Fri from 21:00." ♀♂

■ Restaurants
PORTO BELLO, 2 Kastelplein.,

DELFT

■ Bars
DELFT WERKGROEP HOMOSEXUALITAT BAR, Lange Geer 22, (015) 2146 893. Gay & lesbian organization with gay bar (women welcome), Sun, Wed & 3rd Thurs 20:00-01:00, Fri 21:00-02:00. Potterie lesbian evening 1st Sat of the month 21:00-02:00. 🍴♪♀♂

DEN HAAG - THE HAGUE

■ Information
AIDS INFO, (070) 354 1610, Tues, Thurs 19:00-21:00.

COC GAY ORGANIZATION, Scheveningseveer 7, (070) 365 90 90, bar nights Wed 17:00-00:30, Thur 20:00-00:30, Fri & Sat from 21:00l.

■ Restaurants
DER VERLIEFDE KREEFT, Bleyenburg 9-11, 18:00-23:00. 🍴

HAAGSE GRAAF, Gortstr. 12, Mon-Sat 12:00-21:00. 🍴

WALONG, 286 Fred. Hendriklaan, 12:00-22:00.

WILHELM TELL, Ln. van Meerdervoort 324, 18:00-24:00 (closed Wed). 🍴

■ Retail & Bookstores
TRIX, Prinsestraat 122, (070) 364 50 14, women's bookstore, Mon 13:00-17:00, Tues-Fri 10:00-17:30, Sat 10:00-17:00.

EINDHOVEN

■ Information
COC GAY ORGANIZATION, 54 Hendrikstraat, (040) 245 57 00, bar nights Tues, Thurs, Fri 21:00-01:00, Sun 15:00-18:00.

■ Bars
SHAKESPEARE, Kloosterdreef 108, 20:00-02:00. ♀

TOLERANT, Stratumsedijk 103a, Wed-Sun 21:00-02:00. ♀

■ Restaurants
ANCIENNE BELGIQUE, Stratumsdijk 23-I, 11:30-22:00 (Sat, Sun from 17:00). 🍴

DE PEPERMOLEN, 259 Leenderweg, 10:00-21:00.

OLD VALLEY, THE, 18 St. Antoniusstraat, 17:00-22:00 (Sun from 14:00), closed Tues.

PEACOCK, THE, 208 Heuvelgalerie, 09:00-18:00 (Fri till 21:00), closed Sun.

SALA THAI, Staringstraat 31, open Tues-Sun. 🍴

■ Retail & Bookstores
BOEKENNEL, Grote Berg 11, (040) 243 06 39, women's bookstore.

NETHERLANDS

ENSCHEDE

Information
COC GAY ORGANIZATION, Walstraat 12-14, (053) 430 51 77, bar nights Thurs 20:00-24:00, Fri 20:00-02:00, Sat 16:30-20:00, Sun 16:00-22:00.

Bars
STONEWALL, Walstraat 14, (053) 431 70 14, Fri 19:30-02:00, Sat 15:30-20:30, Sun 16:00-22:00. Sat women only 21:00-02:00. ♂

Restaurants
HANS & HEINZ, Walstraat 5.,
LA PETITE BOUFFE, Deuringerstraat 11, 17:30-22:30, closed Mon, Tues.

GRONINGEN

Bars
DE KONINGEN, O. Boteringestraat 60, (050) 314 59 62, 20:00-01:00 (Fri, Sat till 02:00), closed Sun, Mon." ♀
WOMEN'S BAR NIGHTS, Kraneweg 56, at the COC lesbian/gay center, (050) 313 26 20, 2nd, 3rd & 4th Sat 22:00-02:00. ♀

Restaurants
BISTANGO, Poelestraat 14, from 12:00.
DE BENJAMIN, 33 Kl. Leliestraat, 17:30-23:00, closed Sun & Mon.
DE TWEE DAMES, 64 Zuiderdiep, from 16:00, closed Sun & Mon.
DE ZEVENDE HEMEL, 7 Zuiderkerkstraat, from 17:00.
LE PETIT CHEF, Kerklaan 13.,

Retail & Bookstores
TRUI, Folkingestraat 14, (050) 313 62 66, women's bookstore.

HAARLEM

Information
COC GAY ORGANIZATION, Oudegracht 24, (023) 532 54 53, bar nights Wed & Thurs 20:00-01:00, Fri 16:00-03:00, Sat 22:00-03:00.

LEEUWARDEN

Information
COC GAY ORGANIZATION, Noordvliet 11, (058) 2124 908, bar night Sat 21:00-01:00. Women's bar nights 1st & 3rd Fri.

Women's Country House
(Vrouwen Buiten Verblijf)

Oud-Annerveen
Netherlands

♀

(31-598) 491578

NIJMEGEN

Information
AIDS INFO, (024) 322 8556.
COC GAY ORGANIZATION & LESBIAN ARCHIVES, In de Betouwstraat 9., (024) 323 42 37, Tues, Wed, Fri 13:30-17:00. Lesbian Archives call: 323 44 59, Mon-Wed 14:00-17:00."

Bars
METS, Grotestraat 7, (024) 323 95 49, 12:00-02:00 (Sun from 14:00, Mon from 10:00), women welcome."

Dance Bar/Disco
DE MYTHE, Platenmakersstr 3, (024) 322 01 55, disco & bar from 20:00 (Sat, Sun from 15:00), closed Mon-Wed. ♀♂

Retail & Bookstores
VROUWENBOEKHANDEL DE FEEKS, Van Welderenstraat 34, (024) 323

93 81. Women's bookstore specializing in women's literature & women's studies, with a large selection of lesbian titles in Dutch & in English. Open 10:00-18:00 (Mon from 13:00, Thurs till 21:00, Sat till 17:00), closed Sun. Ask about current local info.

OUD ANNERVEEN

■ Women's Accommodations
WOMEN'S COUNTRY HOUSE (VROUWEN BUITEN VERBLIJF), Tolweg 38, Oud-Annerveen, 9655 PG, (31-598) 491578." Email: vbv@xs4all.nl, Web: http://www.xs4all.nl/~vbv, Our women-only country house in the province of Drenthe, is between the towns of Groningen & Assen (28 kilometers from Groningen). This beautiful country setting is ideal for walking, cycling, swimming & other water sports. Here, women come to meet other women, enjoy a vacation, to work, study or to participate in weekend classes. Part of our program of activities is open to women who speak English or German. Activities taking place at the house which are not mentioned in our English-language leaflet are only for Dutch-speaking women. Most of our guests do speak English and/or German, so staying at the house should be no problem for English-speaking women. See ad on page 113.

ROTTERDAM

■ Information
AIDS INFO, (010) 436 5811.
COC GAY ORGANIZATION, Schiedamsesingel 175, (010) 414 15 55, bar nights Thurs 22:00-24:00, Fri 21:00-01:00, Sat 22:00-01:00, 1st Sun 15:00-18:30.

■ Bars
KEERWEER, 14 Keerweer, (010) 433 46 15, some heteros, 15:00-04:00, till 05:00 on weekends. ♂
MARIETJES MINI BAR, Noordplein 119, 15:00-01:00 (Fri, Sat till 02:00), closed Sun & Mon. ♀

■ Dance Bar/Disco
★ **GAY PALACE DISCO,** 139 Schiedamsesingel, (010) 414 14 86, 23:00-04:00 (till 05:00 on weekends)."

■ Restaurants
DE MOSSELMAN VAN SCHEVENINGEN, Mariniersw. 74a, (010) 404 56 50.
DE RAADSKELDER, Walenburgerweg 66, Wed-Mon 17:30-22:30.

SCHIEDAM

■ Restaurants
CHEZ PIERRE, 429A Rotterdamsedijk, 11:00-01:00 (Fri, Sat till 02:00).

TILBURG

■ Information
VROUWENCENTRUM, Nieuwlandstr. 43, (013) 5421 896, women's center with scheduled socials and activities.

■ Bars
COC BAR NIGHTS, Koestr. 73, (013) 535 9050, gay organization, bar nights Thurs 20:00-22:00, Fri 19:00-24:00, Sat 21:00-01:00. Women-only 2nd Sat." ♂
MY WAY, L. van Vechelstr. 1, (013) 536 78 27, 21:00-03:00 (Sun, Wed till 02:00), closed Mon & Tues.

■ Restaurants
KHROEWA THAI, 51 Korvelseweg, (013) 544 4364, 16:00-23:00.

UTRECHT

■ Information
COC GAY ORGANIZATION, 221 Oudegracht, (030) 231 88 41, bar nights Thurs 20:00-01:00, Fri & Sat 21:00-02:00, Sun 20:30-02:00.
GROEP 7152, Mariaplaats 14, (030) 273 25 37, women's organization. Women's bar night 2nd Sat 21:00-01:00.

■ Bars
WOLKENKRABBER, 47 Oudegracht, (030) 231 97 68, bar with patio, 16:00-02:00.

■ Dance Bar/Disco
BODYTALK, 64 Oudegracht, (030) 231 57 47, mainly men with lesbians welcome, Fri-Sun from 23:30.
DE ROZE WOLK, 45 Oudegracht, (030) 232 20 66, younger crowd, 23:00-04:00, Fri & Sat till 05:00.

■ Retail & Bookstores
SAVANNAH BAY, Telingstraat 13, (030) 231 44 10, women's bookstore.

POLAND

WAGENINGEN

Retail & Bookstores
SHIKASTA, Junusstraat 1A, (0317) 4215 38, women's bookstore.

ZWOLLE

Information
AIDS INFO, (038) 455 1603.

NORWAY

COUNTRY CODE: (47),

BERGEN

Information
LLH, 55 31 21 39, gay & lesbian organizaton. Call for current local information.

Bars
CAFE OPERA, Engen 24, 55 23 03 15. ♀♂
FINCKEN CAFÉ, Nygårdsg. 2A, 55 32 13 16, 12:00-00:30 (Sun from 18:00). ♂

KRISTIANSAND

Information
LLH, 38 02 00 48, gay & lesbian organization. Call for current local information.

Cafe
KAFÉ KILDEN, Rådhusgaten 11, 38 02 96 20, not a gay cafe, frequented by some gay & lesbian clientele.

OSLO

Information
AIDS INFO, 22 33 70 15, toll-free in Norway 800 34 000.
LLH (LANDSFORENINGEN FOR LESBISK OG HOMOFIL FRIGJORING), St. Olavs Plass 2, 22 36 19 48, center, bar and café, Mon-Fri 09:00-16:00.

Beaches
HUK, nude gay beach on the peninsula of Bygdoy. Take bus #30 to Bygdoy from central station (Jernbanetorvet), Wesselsplass just behind the Parliament bldg, or from Nationaltheatret.
SVARTKULP, gay beach on a small lake just north of Olso. Take the Sognsvannbanen (#13 northbound) from Nationaltheatret underground station to the terminal station Sognsvann, then ask for directions.

Bars
POTPURRIET, Ovre Vollgate 13, 22 41 14 40, bar & restaurant, 16:00-06:00.

Dance Bar/Disco
CLUB CASTRO, Kristian 4, 21:00-04:00, 7 days. ♀♂

Retail & Bookstores
TRONSMO BOKHANDEL, Kristian Augustsgate 19, 22 20 25 09, left wing bookstore with gay & lesbian section.

STAVANGER

Information
LLH, Jelsagt. 34, PO Box 1502, Kjelvene 4004 S Stavanger, 51 53 14 46, gay & lesbian organizaton, Mon 18:00-20:00, Wed 19:00-22:00, youth group Fri 19:00-21:00, cafe Sat 13:00-15:00. Call for other activities.

Cafe
CAFE STING, Valbjerget 3, 51 53 24 40, frequented by many gays, especially on weekends.

TROMSØ

Information
LLH, Stakkevollveien 24, 77 68 56 43, gay & lesbian organizaton."

TRONDHEIM

Information
LLH, Kjopmannsgata 12, 73 52 42 26, gay & lesbian organization."

POLAND

COUNTRY CODE: (48),

BIELSKO BIALA

Dance Bar/Disco
PANORAMA DISCO, ul. Konopnickiej 5, from 17:00 (closed Mon-Tues). ♂

GDYNIA

Bars
U IRENY, ul Folwarczna 2, from 14:00, disco Fri-Sun from 17:00 (closed Sun). ♂

JELENIA GÓRA

Dance Bar/Disco
GALERY, ul. Wroclawska 67, at Galery restaurant, (075) 2 1694, disco & restau-

POLAND

rant, frequented by gays, accommodation available. 🏨 ✕ 🆔

KATOWICE

■ Bars
APERITIF BAR POLONIA, ul. Kochanowskiego, at the Polonia hotel., ♂
MAXIM, ul. Mariacka 14, from 18:00. 🏨 ♂

KRAKOW

■ Bars
SAUNA CLUB, ul. Rejtana 4, bar & disco. 🏨 ♂

■ Cafe
JAMA MICHALIKA, ul. Florianska, used as a meeting place by local gays & lesbians, mainly afternoons & evenings, open daily 10:00-22:00. 🆔

LÓDZ

■ Bars
JEFFERS, ul. Bazarowa 6, (042) 54 23 05, 19:00-22:00, dance bar from 20:00. 🏨 ✕ ♂

■ Cafe
BAGDAD CAFE, ul Jaracza 45, not gay, discreetly frequented by gays.
DADA, ul Moniuszko, not gay, discreetly frequented by gays.

PLOCK

■ Bars
U ADAMA, ul Kolejowa 3., ♂

■ Restaurants
WRZOS, ul Nowy Rynek.,

POZNAN

■ Information
LAMBDA POZNAN, (061) 537 655, info line answers Fri 17:00-20:00.

■ Bars
FENDO, ul. 27 Grudnia 22, bar & cafe. ♂

■ Dance Bar/Disco
QUEENS CLUB, ul. Karwoskiego 5, Fri, Sat 20:00-04:00. 🏨 ♂

WARSZAWA - WARSAW

■ Information
LAMBDA WARSZAWA, Krakowskie Przedmiescie 24/26, gay organization.

RAINBOW KLUB, ul. Sniadeckich 1/15, (02) 628 52 22, gay group with current local info, Fri 16:00-22:00. Women answer Wed 18:00-21:00.

■ Bars
KOZLA CLUB, ul. Kozla 10/12, relaxed & intimate ambiance, open until last customer leaves bar.
RED CLUB, ul Marszalkowska 9-15, bar, disco & restaurant. 🏨 ✕ ♂

■ Dance Bar/Disco
★ **RUDAWKA,** ul. Elblaska 53, (22) 633 1999, very popular, crowded restaurant, bar & disco with small dance floor, Fri 22:00-05:00, 80% men, 20% women (some hetero women)." 🏨 ✕ ♂

WROCLAW

■ Bars
EDEN CLUB, ul. Myslowicka 31, (071) 346 6333, bar with disco Fri-Sat from 21:00. 🏨 ♂

■ Dance Bar/Disco
OSCAR, ul. Piotra Skargi 18a, from 18:00. 🏨 ♂

PORTUGAL

COUNTRY CODE: (351),

ALGARVE

■ Accommodations
CASA MARHABA, Rua de Benagil, Alfanzina, Lagoa, 8400, (351-82) 358720 (Tel/Fax). bed & breakfast with bar, women welcome, private baths, expanded continental breakfast, TV lounge, video facilities. 🛌 ♂
CASA PEQUENA, Apartado 133, Praia da Luz, Lagos, Algarve, 8600, (351-82) 789068 (24-hr tel/fax). Email: mop02352@mail.telepac.pt, Guesthouse with TV lounge, video, pool & Jacuzzi on premises, expanded continental breakfast, private bath adjacent to room, ocean nearby, women welcome." 🛌 📺 ♂
RUBI MAR GUESTHOUSE, Rua da Barroca 70, first floor, (082) 763 165, Fax: (082) 767 749. Gay-friendly.

■ Bars
CHAPLIN'S, Rua Dr. Jose Antonio Santos 8365, Armaçao de Pera, Lagos., ♀

PORTUGAL 117

LAST RESORT, Rua Lançarote de Freitas 30a, (082) 768 219, cocktail bar. ♂

LUISOL, Rua de Sao Jose 21, Lagos, (082) 761 794. ♂

PRIVILEGIO, CC Arcadas de Sao Joao, at Aveiros beach, in town of Albufeira, (089) 589 96, open 7 days. ♣♂

TWICE AS NICE, Rua M. de Albuquerque, Areias de Sao Joao, in town of Albufeira, (089) 542 907, from 21:00. ♂

■ Cafe

LA ROSE, Vila Magna, Montechor, in Albufeira, (089) 542 285. ▨

AVEIRO

■ Bars

OPÇAO, Avda. Fernandes Lavrador 214, in town of Barra, Ilhavo, (034) 360 519. ✘♂

LISBOA - LISBON

■ Information

AIDS INFO, (01) 395 7978, (01) 395 7973 or (01) 795 8296.

ILGA-PORTUGAL, Rua Sao Lazaro 88, (01) 254 5383, write: Apartado 21281, 1131 Lisbon Codex.

■ Accommodations

IMPALA HOTEL APARTMENTS, Rua Filipe Folque 49, (01) 314 8914, Fax: (01) 357 5362. Gay-friendly, reasonably priced, comfortable accommodation, not fancy.

PENSAO ALEGRIA, Praça da Alegria 12, Lisbon, 1250, (351-1) 347 5522, Fax: (351-1) 347 8070." Gay-owned & -staffed, 60% hetero & 40% gay/lesbian clientele, more gay in winter. 25 rooms, all have shower or bath, some have WC, must share WC. ▨

PENSAO LONDRES, Rua D. Pedro V 53, (01) 346 2203. Gay-friendly.

■ Bars

AGUA NO BICO, Rua de Sao Marçal 170, (01) 347 2830. 21:00-02:00. ♂

PORTAS LARGAS, Rua da Atalaia 105, (01) 346 6379, 20:00-03:00. ♀♂

■ Dance Bar/Disco

ALCANTARA MAR, Rua da Cozinha Económica 11, (01) 363 6432, late-night disco from 04:00, mainly hetero, gays welcome, closed Mon & Tues. ▨ ▨

BRIC A BAR, Rua Cecilio de Sousa 82, (01) 342 8971, 22:00-04:00, closed Mon. ♣ ♂

FRAGIL, Rua da Atalaia 128, in the Bairro Alto, (01) 346 9578, frequented by many gays, 23:00-04:00. ▨ ▨

KEOPS, Rua da Rosa 157, 24:00-04:00, more gay on weekends. ▨ ▨

KINGS & QUEENS, Rua da Cintura do Porto de Lisboa, Armazem H, Naves A & B, from 23:00 (Mon, Tues from 22:30), very gay after 04:00, closed Sun. ▨

KREMLIN, Escadinhas da Praia, (close to Avda 24 de Julho), 22:30-04:00 (Fri, Sat 18:00-08:00), frequented by gays. ▨

MEMORIAL, Rua Gustavo de Matos Sequeira 42-A, (downstairs), (01) 396 8891, very smokey, good music, closed Mon. ▨ ♣ ♀

★ **TRUMPS,** Rua da Imprensa Nacional 104-B, (01) 397 1059, younger crowd, 23:00-06:00 (shows 02:30 Wed, Sun), closed Mon. ▨ ♣ ♂

■ Cafe

BRASILEIRA DO CHIADO, Rua Garret 120, cafe & restaurant, 08:00-02:00, more gay later in afternoon. ✘ ▨

ESPLANADA PASSEIO DA AVENIDA, Avenida da Liberdade near Restauradores, outdoor cafe on both sides of the street, occasionally frequented by gays." ▨

ROSSO, Rua Ivens 53, (01) 347 1524, 09:00-02:00, discreetly frequented by local gays.

■ Restaurants

ALCÂNTARA CAFE, Rua Maria Holstein 15, (01) 362 1226, 20:00-03:00.

BOTA ALTA, Travessa da Queimada 35-37, closed Sun. ♀♂

CANTINHO DAS GAVEAS, Rua das Gaveas 82-84, Bairro Alto, (01) 342 6460, Portuguese cuisine. ▨

CASANOSTRA, Travessa do Poço da Liberdade 60, (01) 342 5931, 30-40% gay clientele, closed Mon. ▨

CONSENSO, Rua da Academia das Ciencias 1-1A, (01) 346 8611, Portuguese cuisine, 20:00-01:00.

FIDALGO, Rua da Barroca 27, (01) 342 2900, 10:00-24:00, closed Sun.

FREI CONTENTE, Rua de Sao Marçal 94, (01) 347 5922, Portuguese cuisine. ▨

118 PORTUGAL

GRÉMIO, Rua do Grémio Lusitano 26, (01) 346 88 68, 18:00-02:00.

MASSIMA CULPA, Rua da Ataláia 35-37, (01) 342 0121, Italian cuisine.

PAP AÇORDA, Rua da Ataláia, Bairro Alto, (01) 346 4811, 80-90% gay clientele.

POE-TE NA BICHA, Travessa da Agua da Flor 36, Bairro Alto, (01) 342 5924. ♀♂

PRAÇA DAS FLORES, Praça das Flores 30A, (01) 395 6887, restaurant & showbar.

REPÚBLICA, Rua Nova da Trinidade 19, (01) 347 2580, 13:00-15:00 & 19:00-24:00, closed Sat.

TRIVIAL, Rua da Palmeira 44a, (01) 347 3552, Portuguese cuisine, lunch & dinner, 40% gay clientele.

WILLIAM TELL, Rua da Barroca 70, (01) 342 23 45, 20:00-01:00, closed Mon.

PORTO

■Bars
GLAM CLUB, Rua Dr. Barbosa de Castro, closed Mon, Tues. ♀♂

MOINHO DE VENTO, Rua Sá de Noronha 66, (02) 31 68 83, daily 21:30-02:00, women welcome. ♂

MY WAY, Rua do Heroismo 333, at Centro Comercial Stop, loja 145, (02) 576 739. ♂

POLL, Rua Formosa 400., ♂

SETUBAL

■Cafe
CAFE GARBO, Rua Deputado Henriques Cardoso 63, (065) 535 089, restaurant & bar. ♂

RUSSIA

COUNTRY CODE: (7),

MOSCOW

■Information
MOSCOW AIDS CENTER, 14/2 8th ul. Sokolinoy Gory, (metro: Semionovskaya), (095) 365 56 65, Mon-Fri 09:00-18:00.

■Dance Bar/Disco
★ **CHAMELEON,** 14 Presnensky Val, (metro: Ulitsa 1905 Goda), (095) 253 63 43, very large disco, 22:00-07:00. ♂

★ **CHANCE,** ul. Volochaevskaya 11/15 (metro: Ploshchad, Ilicha), at the DK Serp i Molot, (095) 298 62 47, disco & bar, daily 23:00-06:00, male dancers & strippers, popular disco Fri & Sat. ♂

DELFINY, Rakhmanovsky Pereulok 1/24, (metro: Teatralna or Kuznetski Most), (095) 200 55 66, 18:00-07:00, shows Wed. ♂

★ **DYKE,** Trubnaya Ploshchad 4 (metro: Trubnaya Ploshchad), at the Three Monkeys Club, (095) 163 80 02, very popular women-only night, Sat 18:00-23:00. ♀

PROPAGANDA, Bolshoy Zlatoustinsky Pereulok 7, (metro: Kitay Gorod), (095) 924 57 32, 20:00-05:00, trendy crowd. ♀♂

TITANIK, Leningradsky Prospekt 31 (metro: Dinamo), at the Stadion Yunykh Pionerov, (095) 213 45 81, not a gay disco, but popular with upscale gays, 23:00-06:00.

★ **UTOPIYA,** ul. Bolshaya Dmitrovka 2, (metro: Pushinskaya/Tverskaya), at Rossiya Cinema, (095) 229 0003, not a gay disco, but popular with younger gays, 23:00-06:00.

■Restaurants
★ **ANGELICOS,** Bolshoy Karetny Pereulok, (metro: Tsvetnoy Bulvar), (095) 299 36 96, elegant restaurant, reasonable prices, Mediterranean cuisine, 11:30-02:00. ♀♂

★ **ROSSINI,** ul. Gasheka 7, Dukat Plaza II Business Center, (metro: Mayakovskaya), (095) 785 02 60, restaurant & cafe, italian cuisine, 11:00-01:00.

ST. PETERSBURG

■Information
SAFO, (812) 156 65 75, lesbian organization, for information write: c/o Natalia Ivanova, P.O. Box 113, 198096 St. Petersburg, Russia.

■Bars
CAT, ul. Stremiannaya, (metro: Mayakovskaya), (812) 311 33 77, intimate cafe, popular evenings, 11:00-01:00. ♀♂

■Dance Bar/Disco
DZHUNGLI, ul. Blokhina 8, (812) 238 80 33, Fri-Sat 24:00-06:00. ♂

■Restaurants
CAT, 24 ul. Karavannaya (metro: Nevsky Prospekt), (812) 315 39 00, 12:00-02:00.

LITERATURNOYE CAFE, 18 Nevsky Prospekt, (metro: Nevsky Prospekt), (812) 312 8543, upscale, Russian & international cuisine.

METROPOL, ul. Sadovaya 22.,

SADKO, ul. Brodsky at Nevsky Prospekt.,

SLOVAKIA

COUNTRY CODE: (42),

BRATISLAVA

■ *Information*
GANYMEDES BRATISLAVA, gay organization, PO Box 4, 830 00 Bratislava 3."
INFO LINE, (7) 25 38 88, information & help line, Mon, Thurs 18:00-20:00.

■ *Cafe*
CAFE AXON, Gorkého ul., Sun 09:00-02:00, some heteros. ♂
GALERIA GREMIUM, Gorhéko ul., near National Theatre, café & art gallery, some heteros. ♂

KOSICE

■ *Information*
GANYMEDES KOSICE, PO Box G13, posta 1, 043 43 Kosice, gay organization.

PRIEVIDZA

■ *Information*
GANYMEDES PRIEVIDZA, Medzibriezky 10, 971 01 Prievidza, gay organization.

SLOVENIA

COUNTRY CODE: (386),

LJUBLJANA

■ *Information*
GALFON LESBIAN & GAY INFO LINE, (061) 132 40 89, 19:00-22:00.
ROZA KLUB, MAGNUS & LL GROUPS, Kersnikova 4, (061) 132 40 89, Fax: (061) 329 188. Three organizations are housed here: Roza Klub gay & lesbian organization, meets Tues & Thurs 12:00-14:00. Magnus gay group, publishes monthly magazine Kekec. LL lesbian group.

WOMEN'S HELPLINE, (061) 9782 or (061) 44 19 93.

■ *Dance Bar/Disco*
ROZA DISCO, at Roza Klub location, Kersnikova 4, dance night Sun 22:00-04:00. 🍺 ♀♂

■ *Cafe*
CAFE GALERIJA, Mestni Trg 5, 10:00-24:00, not gay, frequented by local gays.
TIFFANY, Masarykova 24, 21:00-24:00 (Fri, Sat till later). ♂

MARIBOR

■ *Bars*
THEATRICAL CAFE, Slomskov Trg, NOT a gay bar, discreetly frequented by gays.

PIRAN

■ *Bars*
PORTA CAMPO, IX Korpusa, 08:00-23:00, NOT a gay bar, discreetly frequented by gays.

SPAIN

COUNTRY CODE: (34),

ALICANTE

■ *Bars*
DRAKE EL PIRATA, Juan Herrera 21, a mix of gays, lesbians & heteros.
EMBRUJO, Velázauez 48., ♀
HORUS, César Elguezábal 9, a mix of gays, lesbians & heteros.
PARIPÉ, Barón Finestrat 3., ♀♂

BADAJOZ

■ *Bars*
AIRE, Plaza Conquistadores, mix of gays, lesbians & heteros.
ANAS, Plaza de Cervantes 17, mix of gays, lesbians & heteros.

BALEARIC ISLANDS
IBIZA - IBIZA TOWN

■ *Bars*
WAUNAS, Calle Mayor 9., ♀♂

■ *Dance Bar/Disco*
AMNESIA, Carretera San Antonio, km 6., 🍺

SPAIN

ANFORA, Calle San Carlos 5, large disco downstairs, bar upstairs. [!] ♂
PACHÁ, Avenida 8 de Agosto., [!]
PRIVILEGE, Carretera San Antonio, km 7., [!]

■ Restaurants
CHEZ FRANÇOISE, Plaza del Parque.,
EL BISTRO, Sa Carrosa 15.,
EL OLIVO, Plaça de la Vila, (971) 30 06 80. ⊠

MALLORCA - PLAMA

■ Accommodations
HOTEL ROSAMAR, Avenida Joan Miro 74, Palma de Mallorca, 07015, (34-71) 732723, Fax: (34-71) 283828. Email: rosamar@ocea.es, gay-friendly hotel with bar, recently-refurbished near bars & beach, single & double rooms, private baths, continental breakfast, mainly hetero clientele."

■ Bars
BACCUS, Lluis Fabregas 2., ♀♂
BRUIXERIES, Estanc 9, La Llonja, mix of gays, lesbians & heteros.
CA'N JORDI, Plaza Mediterráneo 2-4, videos. [!] ♪ ♀♂
LA YEDRA, Avenida Joan Miró 47, (971) 73 74 93. ♂

BARCELONA

■ Information
CASAL LAMBDA, Calle Ample 5, (93) 412 72 72, gay organization, 17:00-21:00 (Fri till 23:00), closed Sat, Sun."
COORDINADORA GAY Y LESBIANA, Buenaventura Muñoz 4.,
K LA DONA, Gran Vía 549 4o, 1a, (93) 323 33 07, Thurs 20:00.
REVISTA LABERINT, Calle Roselló, 256, (93) 21 56 336, feminist women's magazine with current local information.
TELEFONO ROSA, toll-free in Spain (93) 900 601 601, Mon-Fri 18:00-22:00. AIDS info Fri 21:00-23:00."

■ Tours, Charters & Excursions
BCN TURÍSTIC, (34) 93442 4076, Fax: (34) 93442 0270. Email: BCNTUR@santdersupernet.com, Web: http://www.web-show.com/Barcelona/BCNTUR, Hotels from one to five stars. Apartments in Barcelona, Sitges and other coastal resorts.

■ Accommodations
HOTEL CALIFORNIA, Calle Raurich 14, (93) 317 77 66, Fax: (93) 317 54 74. Gay-friendly hotel, rooms with bath, AC, phone, TV.
HOTEL REGENCIA COLON, Calle Sagristans 13-17, (93) 318 98 58, Fax: (93) 317 28 22. Gay-friendly hotel close to Barcelona's Gothic quarter with single thru triple rooms, private bath, phone, TV, minibar, safe & hairdryers.

■ Bars
AURORA, Aurora 7, 22:00-03:00 (Fri, Sat also 06:00-12:00), frequented by gays.
BAHIA, Calle Séneca 12, 21:30-03:00. [!] ♀♂
BLENDED 104, Calle Mariano Cubí 55, (93) 200 71 26, 19:00-03:00. [♪] ♀♂
CAFE DE LA CALLE, Calle Vic, 11, 18:00-03:00. ♀♂
CHEEK TO CHEEK, Muntaner 325, 19:00-03:00. ♀♂
DANIELS, Calle Cardona 7, at Mariano Cubí & Laforja, (93) 209 99 78, disco & bar. [!] ♀
ENTREACTE, Lleida 23, 20:00-03:00, frequented by gays.
ESTE BAR, Calle Consell de Cent 257, 22:00-03:00. ♀♂
IMAGINE, Calle Mariano Cubí, 4, 23:00-04:00 (Sun from 19:30). [!] ♀♂
LA ROSA, Brusi 39, (93) 414 61 66, 20:00-03:00. ♀♂
MEMBERS, Calle Séneca, 3, (93) 237 12 04, 20:00-03:00. ♀♂
PADAM PADAM, Calle Rauric 9, (93) 302 50 62, 19:00-03:00. ♀♂
SATANASSA, Aribau 27, 22:00-03:00. [!] ♀♂
THESEO, Comte Borrell 119, 08:30-02:30, frequented by gays.

■ Dance Bar/Disco
CLUB FELLINI, Estació de França, 24:00-05:00. [!] ♀♂
GOOD MORNING, Badajoz 150., [!] ♀♂
HEY DAY, Calle Bruniquer 59-61, (93) 450 36 75, 24:00-06:30. [♪] [!] ♀♂
METRO, Calle Sepúlveda 185, (93) 323 52 27, video disco, 24:00-05:00. [♪] [!] ♀♂

SPAIN 121

PICASSO, Paralelo 106, 01:30-06:00.

Cafe
CAFE DE LA OPERA, Ramblas, 74, outdoor café frequented by some gays.
LA ILLA, Carrer Reig i Bonet 3, Metro Joanic, lesbian cafe, 20:00-03:00.

Restaurants
AIRE, Enric Granados 48, 11:30-24:00.
COLIBRÍ, Riera Alta 33, (93) 442 30 02.
LA MOSSEGADA, Diputació 214, (93) 454 72 75.
LA VERONICA, Avinyó 30, pizzeria.
THESEO, Comte Borrell 119,

Retail & Bookstores
ANTINOO, Anselm Clave 6, (93) 301 90 70, gay & lesbian books.
ANTINOVS, Josep Anselm Clavé 6, bookshop & cafe, frequented by gays & lesbians.
COMPLICES, Cervantes 2, Tel/Fax: (93) 412 72 83, gay & lesbian bookshop with books in Spanish & English, mail order, 10:30-20:30 (Sat from 12:00), closed Sun."
PROLEG LIBRERIA DE MUJERES, Calle Daguería 13, (93) 319 24 25, women's bookstore with feminist & lesbian books in Catalan & Spanish, current local information avaiable here, 10:00-20:00.

BENIDORM

Dance Bar/Disco
LA TERRAZA, Avda de la Penetración.,

BILBAO

Information
AGERIAN LESBIANEN TALDEA, (94) 415 54 83, lesbian info.
ALDARTE, Buenos Aires 2, 3-izq, (94) 423 72 96, lesbian & gay organization with counselling & support services, film & book libraries.
EHGAM, Calle Escalinatas de Solokoetxe 4, (94) 415 07 19, gay & lesbian center, library & local information, Mon-Fri 20:00-22:00.""

Bars
EL CONVENTO, Esperanza 14,
OTXOA PUB, Heros 9, at Lersundi, (94) 424 18 48.

Accommodation-Find Service
(Barcelona, Sitges, Coastal Resorts)
- Hotels (from 1 to 5 star)
- Apartments
- Individuals & Groups

Guided Walking Tours of Barcelona's Old City

- English
- French
- German
- Spanish

Mornings, by Appointment

BCN TURÍSTIC

Email: BCNTUR@santandersupernet.com
Web: http://www.web-show.com/Barcelona/BCNTUR

Tel: (34) 93442 4076
Fax: (34) 93442 0270

SPAIN

TXOKOLANDAN, Calle Escalinatas de Solokoetxe 4, Fri & Sat at the EHGAM gay center, 24:00-03:00.

■ Dance Bar/Disco
CRISTAL, Buenos Aires 5, a mix of gays & heteros.
DISTRITO, Alameda de Recalde 18, a mix of gays & heteros.

CADIZ

■ Bars
CAFE PONIENTE, Calle Beato Diego de Cadiz 18.

■ Cafe
EL VEINTE, Cánovas del Castillo 27.,

CANARY ISLANDS GRAN CANARIA - PLAYA DEL INGLES

■ Accommodations
VISTA BONITA VILLAS, (34-28) 141 618, Fax: (34-28) 140 539. Fully-furnished terraced villas, mostly men with women welcome."

■ Bars
CENTER STAGE, Yumbo Center, 2nd floor, small, 70% men.

■ Restaurants
AUBERGINE, Yumbo Center, 1st floor.,
BEI LELO, Yumbo Center, 2nd floor.,
EL CHACO, La Sandía Center, 2nd floor.,

CANARY ISLANDS LA PALMA - SANTA CRUZ DE LA PALMA

■ Accommodations
APARTAMENTOS LA FUENTE, Calle Pérez de Brito 49, Santa Cruz de la Palma, (34-22) 415636 (Tel/Fax). gay-friendly self-catering apartments, maid service, color TV, telephone, central location, nearby ocean beach."

CANARY ISLANDS TENERIFE PUERTO DE LA CRUZ

■ Dance Bar/Disco
HEAVEN, Avda Generalísimo.,
LEPANTO, Avde. Generalísimo 11.,

CORDOBA

■ Bars
CAFE BAR JUDA LEVI, Plaza de Judá Leví 1.,

GIJON

■ Bars
LA BRUXA CURUXA, Calle Celestino Junquera 1.,

GRANADA

■ Information
NOS, (958) 20 06 02, gay organization.

■ Bars
EL BODEGÓN, Arco de Elvira.,
LA SABANILLA, Plaza Bib, la Rambla, mix of gays, lesbians & heteros.
LA SAL, Santa Paula, mix of lesbians & heteros.
LA VIÑA II, La Colcha, mix of gays, lesbians & heteros.
LAS FÁBULAS, Lavadero·de la Cruz.,

■ Restaurants
LA CABINA, Pza San Miguel, lower level.,
TASCA DEL PIE DE LA VELA, Carr. Darro 25.,

ISLAS BALEARES
SEE IBIZA & MALLORCA,

ISLAS CANARIAS
SEE GRAN CANARIA, LA PALMA & TENERIFE,

JAEN

■ Bars
LA NOCHE, Avenida Andalucía 22, 22:30-04:00, closed Mon.

LA CORUÑA

Bars
ALFAIATE, Plaza de España, mix of gays, lesbians & heteros.
MISA DE UNA, Travessia del Orzán., ♀♂

Dance Bar/Disco
OHALÁ, Santa Cristina., 🎵
PACHÁ, Santa Cristina., 🎵

LERIDA

Bars
ASSIS, Carretera Comarcal 1313, (973) 29 01 52, Fri & Sat 21:00-03:00. 🎵🎵♀♂
BRAZIL, Calle Alcalde Costa 63, 20:00-02:30. 🎵♀♂

MADRID

Information
COLECTIVO GAY DE MADRID (COGAM), Fuencarral 37, (91) 522 45 17.
GAY INFORM, (91) 523 00 70, daily 17:00-21:00.

Accommodations
HOSTAL HISPANO, Hortaleza 38, 2nd fl, Madrid, 28004, (34-1) 531 4871, Fax: (34-1) 521 8780. Gay-friendly hotel, private & shared baths, color TV, telephone, laundry facilities, TV lounge, 1 block to gay bars. ♀♂

Bars
A DIARIO, Zurita 39, a mix of gays, lesbians & heteros. 👠
CACHITO, Libertad 4, a mix of gays, lesbians & heteros.
CANDILEJAS, Bailén 16, a mix of gays, lesbians & heteros. 👠
CHUECA'S FRIENDS, Plaza Cueca 9., ♀♂
CORAZÓN LOCO, Plaza Santiago 1, a mix of gays, lesbians & heteros. 👠
EL BARBERILLO DE LAVAPIES, Calle Salitre 43, (metro Lavapiés), (91) 228 18 15, bar & cafe, 80% women, men welcome. ♀
EL MOJITO, Calle del Olmo 6 (metro: Antón Martín), 21:00-03:00, some hetero clientele. ♀♂
ENCLAVE, Pérez Galdós 4, a mix of gays, lesbians & heteros.
FRAGIL, Lavapiés 17, (metro Tirso de Molina)., ♀
FRÁGOLA, Calle Buenavista 42 (metro: Antón Martín)., ♀♂
LA ARCALLATA, Apodaca 10, a mix of gays, lesbians & heteros.
LA BOHEMIA, Plaza de Chueca (metro: Chueca)., ♀
LA BOMBACHA, Corr. Alta San Pablo 33., ♀
LA LUPE, Torrecilla del Leal 12, a mix of gays, lesbians & heteros.
LA SIXTA, Calatrava 15, a mix of gays, lesbians & heteros.
LA VENTURA, Olmo 31, a mix of gays, lesbians & heteros.
LUCAS BAR MIX, San Lucas 11, a mix of gays, lesbians & heteros. 👠
MOSKITO, Torrecilla del Leal 13., ♀♂
NO SE LO DIGAS A NADIE, Ventura de la Vega 7, a mix of gays, lesbians & heteros.
PRISCILLA, San Bartolomé 12, a mix of gays, lesbians & heteros.
PUNTO DE ENCUENTRO, Colmenares 3, a mix of gays, lesbians & heteros.
SMOKE, San Bartolomé 11., 👠♀♂
TRUCO, Gravina 10., ♀
WHY NOT, San Bartolomé 7, a mix of gays, lesbians & heteros.

Dance Bar/Disco
BLACK & WHITE, Calle Libertad 34, (metro Chueca), (91) 531 11 41, 20:00-05:00. 🎵🎵♀♂
GRIFFIN'S, Calle Villalar 8 (metro: Banco de España)., 🎵♀♂
LA ROSA, Tetuán 27, (91) 531 01 85. 🎵♀♂
MEDEA, Calle Cabeza 33, (metro Antón Martín)., 🎵♀
SACHA'S, Plaza de Chueca 1 (metro: Chueca)., 🎵👠♀♂

Cafe
ACUARELA, Gravina 8, a mix of gays, lesbians & heteros. ☕
ARTE ALTERNATIVO, Gravina 10, a mix of gays, lesbians & heteros. ☕
CAFE GALDOS, Calle Pérez Galdós 1 (metro: Chueca), (91) 532 12 86. ♂
KAPPA, Olmo 26, a mix of gays, lesbians & heteros. ☕
LA SASTRERÍA, Hortaleza 74, a mix of gays, lesbians & heteros. ☕
LATINO, Augusto Figueroa 47, bar & restaurant, a mix of gays lesbians & heteros. ☕

MAD, Virgen de Peligros 4, a mix of gays, lesbians & heteros. 🏳
URANIA'S, Fuencarral 37., ♀♂
XXX, Reina at Clavel, a mix of gays, lesbians & heteros. 🏳

■ Restaurants
A BRASILEIRA, Calle Pelayo 49.,
CASA VALLEJO, San Lorenzo 9.,
CHEZ POMME, Calle Pelayo 4.,
CORNUCOPIA, Calle Flora 1, (metro: Sol or Opera), (91) 547 6465, gay-owned & -operated, American haute cuisine, 13:30-16:00 & 20:30-24:00.
DIVINA LA COCINA, Colmenares 13.,
EL 26 DE LIBERTAD, Calle Libertad 26.,
EL ARMARIO, San Bartolomé 7.,
EL MARQUÉS, Jesús del Valle 36.,
EL MARSOT, Calle Pelayo 6, (91) 531 07 26.
EL RINCÓN DE PELAYO, Calle Pelayo 19.,
EL TRASTERO, Calle Pelayo 19, (91) 532 65 75.
IL CAMINETTO, Hernán Cortés 19.,
KALAS, Amnistía 6.,
LA DAMA DUENDE, La Palma 63.,
LA DAME NOIRE, Calle Pérez Galdós 3.,
LA DOLCE VITA, Cardenal Cisneros 58.,
LA TRASTIENDA, Calle Pez 2.,
LATINO, Augusto Figueroa 47, at Latino bar.,
LOS GIRASOLES, Calle Hortaleza 106.,
SARRASÍN, Calle Libertad 8.,

■ Retail & Bookstores
BERKANA, Calle Gravina 11, (91) 532 13 93, gay & lesbian bookstore with books in Spanish & English.
LIBRERIA DE MUJERES, Calle San Cristóbal 17 (metro: Sol), (91) 521 70 43, women's bookstore with feminist & lesbian literature, current local information, 10:00-14:00 & 17:00-20:00.
SIC LIBROS SL, Cáceres 42, 4th floor A, (91) 473 41 58, mail order gay & lesbian books.

MALAGA

■ Bars
TORERO, TORERO, Plaza San Francisco 8.,

■ Dance Bar/Disco
MOLOKKO, San Lorenzo 19., 🍴

■ Cafe
TRICLINIUM, Peña Juan de la Encina 6.,

MURCIA

■ Bars
PISCIS, Enrique Villar 13., 🍴 🔑 ♂

■ Dance Bar/Disco
DISCOTECA METROPOL, Calle San Andrés 13., 🍴 🎵 ♂

■ Cafe
CAFE BAR ODEON, Calle de la Fuensanta 5, 17:00-01:00. ✗ ♂
ITACA, Mariano Vergara 6, mix of gays, lesbians & heteros.

OVIEDO

■ Accommodations
CASA LORENZO, c/o David Braddy, Palo Alto Travel, 535 Ramona #7, Palo Alto, CA, 94301, (415) 323-2626, (800) 359-3922, Fax: (415) 323-2684. Gay-owned inn in the town of S. Pedro de la Ribera, a 30-minute drive northwest of Oviedo in the province of Asturias. One room, 2 suites, shared baths, expanded continental breakfast, 50% gay & lesbian clientele.

■ Bars
NOCHES, Río Caudal 7, a mix of gays, lesbians & heteros.

■ Cafe
SEVILLA, Cimadevilla 9., ♀♂
TAMARA, Altamirano 6, at La Santa Sede leather bar., ♀♂

SALAMANCA

■ Bars
CARMEN, ask locally for address. ♀

■ Dance Bar/Disco
MARÍA, Avenida de Mirat 36, mix of gays, lesbians & heteros. 🍴

■ Cafe
ARETINO, Plaza del Corrillo, mix of gays, lesbians & heteros.

SAN SEBASTIAN

■ Retail & Bookstores
SOLANA ELORZ, Fuenterrabia 19, (93) 421 17 45, gay & lesbian books.

SANTIAGO DE COMPOSTELA

Bars
CAFE DE MARY, Plaza de la Quintana, mix of gays, lesbians & heteros.
RUA NOVA, Nova 36, mix of gays, lesbians & heteros.
TARASCA, Entremuros 13, mix of gays, lesbians & heteros.
ULTRAMARINOS, Casas Reales, mix of gays, lesbians & heteros.

SEVILLA

Information
ASAMBLEA DE MUJERES DE SEVILLA, Calle Alberto Lista 16, lesbian group with feminist info for all of southern Spain."

Bars
EL PASEO, Paseo de Colón 2., ♀
GALERÍA TORNEO, Torneo 64, mix of gays, lesbians & heteros.
ISBILIYA, Paseo Colón 2., 🍽 ♀♂

Retail & Bookstores
LIBRERIA FULMEN, Calle Zaragoza 36, (95) 422 71 78, women's bookstore with current local information."

SITGES

Accommodations
HOTEL MONTSERRAT, Espalter 27, Sitges, 08870, (34-3) 894 03 00, Fax: (34-3) 894 50 50. 2-star hotel with bar, private baths, buffet breakfast, 50% gay & lesbian clientele, more gays in summer.
HOTEL ROMÀNTIC I LA RENAIXENÇA, Carrer de Sant Isidre 33, Sitges, 08870, (34-3) 894 8375, Fax: (34-3) 894 8167. Bed & breakfast hotel with bar & solarium, some hetero clientele, antique furnishings, private baths, continental & buffet breakfasts, nearby pool & ocean beach, centrally located to all gay bars." ♀♂

Bars
MITJA LLUNA, Santa Tecla 8, 18:00-03:00. ♀♂
PARROT'S, Plaza Industria 2, 17:00-03:00. ♀♂

Dance Bar/Disco
RICKY'S, San Pablo 23, mix of gays, lesbians & heteros. 🍽

Cafe
ELSA'S, Calle Parellades 86, 09:00-19:00. 🚭

Restaurants
CASA HIDALGO, San Pablo 12.,
EL CANDIL, Carreta 7.,
EL CASTELL, Carreta 21.,
EL TRULL, Pasaje M. F. Clará 16., 🚭
EL XALET, Isla de Cuba 35.,
OLIVER'S, Isla de Cuba 39.,

TARRAGONA

Accommodations
MONTYMAR, Av Principe de España, Apdo (Box) 113, Miami Playa, Tarragona, 43892, (34-77) 81 05 30. In this small village on the Mediterranean coast, between mountains and the sea, our Spanish-Moorish-style house is just 600 meters from the beach. All rooms face the quiet patio. Local restaurants feature Spanish, French and German specialties. Boat rentals are available. Day trips to Barcelona, Tarragona and Tortosa are easy by train. ♀

TORREMOLINOS

Bars
CANDELA, La Nogalera (local 13), mix of gays, lesbians & heteros.
MALU, La Nogalera (local 1103), 20:30-03:00, women welcome." ♂
POURQUOI PAS, La Nogalera (local 713)., ♀♂

Restaurants
EL COMEDOR, Plaza de los Tientos 4.,

VALENCIA

Information
LAMBDA, Calle Salvador Giner 9, (96) 391 20 84, gay & lesbian group."

Bars
ADN, Calle Angel Custodio 9., 🍽 ♀♂
CONTRAMANO, Calle Murillo 12., ♂
DONA DONA, Angel Custodio., ♀
METAL, Plaza Picadero Marqués de Dos Aguas 3., 🍽 ♀♂

Dance Bar/Disco
VENIAL, Quart 26, from 24:00 till late. 🚹♀♂

Cafe
LA SEU, Santo Caliz 7., ♀♂
TÁBITA, Angel Custodio 15., ♀

Retail & Bookstores
EL COBERTIZO, Plaza Vicente Ibarra 4, (96) 391 37 21, gay & lesbian books.
SAL DE CASA LIBRERIA DE DONES, Emperador 7, (96) 352 76 98, women's bookstore.

VALLADOLID

Bars
CATTO'S, Santuario 3., ♀

VITORIA

Bars
MOET & CO, Los Herrán 46., ♀♂

ZARAGOZA

Bars
LA MAGDALENA, Calle Mayor 48, mix of gays, lesbians & heteros.
LA NOCHE, Fita 11, mix of gays, lesbians & heteros.
YORUBA, Heroísmo 36., ♀

Cafe
CAFE DEL MERCADO, Muralla Romano, mix of gays, lesbians & heteros.
LA INFANTA, San Jorge, mix of gays, lesbians & heteros.
SOPA DE LETRAS, San Félix, mix of gays, lesbians & heteros.
TULI TULI, El Carmen 16., ♀♂

Retail & Bookstores
LIBRERIA DE MUJERES, San Juan de la Cruz 4, 45 26 52, women's bookstore.

SWEDEN

COUNTRY CODE: (46),

COUNTRYWIDE

Information
SWEDISH GAY ONLINE, www.gaymap.com. Opening in 1998.

BORÅS

Information
RFSL, Magasingatan 1, (033) 10 69 70, cafe, pub & party run by gay organization. Cafe Tues 19:00-01:00, pub 2nd Fri 21:00-01:00, party last Sat 22:00-02:00. ♀♂

BORLÄNGE

Women's Accommodations
KVINNOHÖJDEN, FEMINIST STUDY CENTER & GUESTHOME, Storsund 90, Borlänge, 78194, (46-243) 223707 (Tel/Fax, when faxing call first). Feminist study center & guesthome in rural Sweden, room for 50 women. Week-long courses held in summer, weekend courses rest of year (most courses in Swedish, inquire about other languages). Women are expected to participate in cooking & household activities. No drugs or alcohol." ♀

ESKILSTUNA

Information
RFSL, Noreusgatan 5, (016) 51 00 69, cafe run by gay organization Mon 19:00-21:00.

FALUN

Information
RFSL, Brittsarsvägen 7, (023) 284 85, cafe run by gay organization Wed 19:00-21:00. ♀♂

GÄVLE

Information
RFSL, Fjärde Tvärgatan 19-21, (026) 18 77 18, cafe, pub & parties run by gay organization. Cafe Tues, Thurs 19:00-21:00, pub Fri 21:00-01:00 (except on Fri before a party), party 1st Sat 21:30-02:00. ♀♂

GÖTEBORG

Information
AIDS INFO, (031) 603 442.
RFSL CENTRE, Esperantoplatsen 7, (031) 711 61 51. Gay & lesbian center, address may change in '98.

Bars
GRETAS, Drottninggatan 35, bar & cafe from 16:00 (Sat from 12:00, Sun from 13:00). ♀♂

Dance Bar/Disco
NEMO, Bellmansgatan 7, (031) 13 20 42, Thurs & Fri from 20:00. 🚹♂
★ **PARK LANE**, Avenyn 36-38, Fri-Sat till 05:00, frequented by gays. 🚹

SWEDEN 127

TOUCH, Esperantoplatsen 7, (031) 711 14 20, disco, restaurant, bar: Wed from 21:00; disco: Fri, Sat 21:00-02:00; women's disco: 2nd Fri. Address may change in '98. 🏳️‍🌈 ✖ ♀♂

WOMEN'S DISCO AT TOUCH, women's disco night at Touch Disco, (031) 711 14 20, 2nd Fri 21:00-02:00. 🏳️‍🌈 ✖ ♀

■ *Cafe*

CAFE HELLMAN, Esperantoplatsen 7 (RFSL Centre), (031) 711 61 51, Mon-Fri 12:00-19:00, Sun 19:00-22:00. Mon & Wed Youth Cafe 19:00-22:00. Address may change in '98. ♀♂

■ *Retail & Bookstores*

ROSA RUMMET, Esperantoplatsen 7 (RFSL Centre), (031) 711 61 51, gay & lesbian bookshop, Wed & Sun 19:00-22:00. Address may change in '98.

HALMSTAD

■ *Information*

RFSL, Stålverksgatan 1, (035) 21 48 00, gay organization Mon & Wed 19:00-22:00, call for cafe & party schedule. ♀♂

HELSINGBORG

■ *Information*

RFSL, Pålsgatan 1, (042) 12 35 32, 11:00-17:00. Pub & cafe run by gay organization (pub Fri 22:00-02:00, cafe weekdays 11:00-18:00 & even Sun 16:00-20:00.

■ *Dance Bar/Disco*

CLUB EMPIRE (RFSL DISCO), at RFSL Centre, (042) 12 35 32, RFSL disco, pub & café. Disco: 2nd & 4th Sat 22:00-03:00; Pub: Fri 22:00-02:00; Cafe: weekdays 11:00-18:00 & 2nd & 4th Sun 16:00-20:00 🏳️‍🌈 ♀♂

■ *Cafe*

HILDAS CAFE, Kungsgatan 16, (042) 28 01 37, cafe known for its salads, baked potatoes & pies, 11:00-18:00 (Sat 10:00-15:00), closed Sun

K & COMPANY, Nedre Långvinkelsgatan 9, (042) 18 78 35, intimate, small cafe with art gallery, 09:00-18:00 (Sat 10:00-13:00), closed Sun.

■ *Erotica*

KOSMOS, Furutorpsgatan 73, (042) 14 16 16. ♂

JÖNKÖPING

■ *Information*

RFSL, Västra Holmgatan 14, (036) 71 84 80, disco, bar & cafe run by gay organization. Cafe Thurs 19:00-22:00, disco 2nd Sat 21:00-02:00.

KALMAR

■ *Information*

RFSL, (0480) 859 55, gay organization, call for schedule cafe, pub & party schedule. Phone answers Thurs 20:00-22:00. ♀♂

KARSTAD

■ *Information*

RFSL, Älvdalensgatan 8c, (054) 15 20 90, cafe run by gay organization Wed 19:00-21:00. ♀♂

KRISTIANSTAD

■ *Information*

RFSL, Norra Kanalgatan 2, (044) 10 65 90, pub Fri 20:00-24:00. ♀♂

LINKÖPING

■ *Information*

RFSL, Nygatan 58, behind Hotel Brask, (013) 31 20 22, Tues 19:00-22:00.

■ *Bars*

RFSL BAR NIGHTS, Nygatan 58, (013) 13 20 22, cafe Tues 19:00-22:00, Wed, Thurs 13:00-16:00, pub: even Fri 21:00-01:00; disco: Sat 22:00-02:30 (alternate weeks women's dance night). ♀♂

LULEÅ

■ *Information*

RFSL, (0920) 226 166, gay organization with scheduled activities.

LUND

■ *Bars*

RFSL GAY PARTIES, (040) 611 99 51, parties run by gay organization, call for schedule. ♀♂

■ *Restaurants*

PETRI PUMPA, Petri Kyrkogata 7, (046) 13 55 15, 11:30-01:00 (kitchen closes at 22:00). 🍽️

SWEDEN

MALMÖ

■ Information
AIDS INFO, Noah's Ark: (040) 611 52 15; Positiva Gruppen: (040) 79 161."
MALMÖ GAY JOUR, (040) 611 99 44, gay/lesbian phone line Fri 19:00-24:00.
RFSL, Monbijougatan 15, (040) 611 99 62, gay organization with scheduled activities 11:00-16:00.

■ Bars
VICTORS, Lilla Torget, bar & café, 18:00-01:00. 🚻

■ Dance Bar/Disco
FYRAN DISCO, Snapperupsgatan 4, (040) 23 03 11, Sat 23:00-03:00. SLM leather group meets here odd Fri 23:00-03:00. 👖♂
INDIGO, Monbijougatan 15, (040) 611 99 62, RFSL disco & pub. Disco: Fri, Sat 22:00-02:00 (women's dance night 1st Sat); Pub: Wed 21:00-24:00. 👖♂

■ Cafe
GUSTAV ALBERT, Gustav Adolfs Torg 43, (040) 611 22 72, 09:00-01:00, patio in summer. 🚻

■ Restaurants
RESTAURANG G, Gustav Adolfstorg, (040) 23 94 00, restaurant with outdoor seating, 11:00-01:00 (Sat, Sun till 03:00).

NORRKÖPING

■ Information
RFSL, Västgötegatan 15, (011) 23 81 50, cafe & disco held by gay organization. Disco 2nd & 4th Sat 22:00-03:00. Cafe Wed 18:00-21:00. ♀♂

NYKÖPING

■ Bars
RFSL BAR NIGHT, Östra Kyrkogatan 15, (0155) 21 02 29, gay organization's cafe night, Thurs 19:00-21:00. ♀♂

ÖREBRO

■ Information
RFSL, Slottsgatan 19b, (019) 14 42 32, cafe & parties run by gay organization. Cafe weekdays 13:00-16:00 (Tues also 19:00-22:00), parties 2nd & last Sat 21:00-02:00. ♀♂

ÖSTERSUND

■ Information
RFSL, Rådhusgatan 64, (enter from Gränsgatan), (063) 10 06 68, cafe & parties run by gay organization. Cafe Tues & Wed, party 1st Sat 21:00-02:00. ♀♂

PITEÅ

■ Information
RFSL, Aronsgatan 11, (0911) 925 70, gay organization's evening cafe, and parties last Sat.

SKÖVDE

■ Information
RFSL, Storgatan 12a, (0500) 41 06 63, cafe & party run by gay organization. Cafe Thurs & Sun 18:00-21:00, party 1st Sat. ♀♂

STOCKHOLM

■ Information
AIDS LINE, (020) 78 44 40.
KVINNOHUSET (WOMEN'S BUILDING), Blekingegatan 67b, (metro: Skanstull), (08) 64 32 200, lesbian & feminist center with book café, activities.
LESBISK NU! (LESBIAN NOW! CENTRE), Kocksgatan 28, (metro: Medborgarplatsen), (08) 641 86 16, bar, café at women's centre. Café: Tues, Thurs 18:00-21:00. Bar: 2nd Sat 20:00-01:00. ♀
POSITHIVA GRUPPEN, Magnus Ladulåsgatan 8, (metro: Mariatorget, exit at Torkelknutssongatan), (08) 720 19 60, HIV/AIDS info, Tues-Fri & Sun from 15:00, Sat from 20:00. ♂
RFSL, Sveavägen 57-59, (metro: Rådmansgatan), (08) 736 02 12, gay organization, houses RFSL library, cafe, bookshop & a variety of other community services Mon-Fri 10:00-18:00.

■ Bars
BAREN 2 LIKE (2 OF A KIND), Wollmar Yxkullsgatan 7, daily 18:00-01:00. ♂
BOTTLE & GLASS, Hornsgatan 136, (08) 845 610, neighborhood pub 16:00-01:00 (Sat, Sun from 14:00), frequented by some gays. 🍴 🚻
FLAP BAR, St Eriksgatan 56, (08) 654 79 00, private club, membership at door,

SWEDEN

Thurs-Sun 18:00-01:00, disco Wed, Fri, Sat 20:00-03:00.

HÄCKTET, Hornsgatan 82, at Restaurant Bysis, (08) 84 59 10, bar & restaurant, patio in summer, gay Wed-Fri.

★ **HJÄRTER DAM,** Polhemsgatan 23, (08) 65 35 739, private club, evenings.

KINKS & QUEENS, Kungsholmsgatan 20, at the Cavern Club (metro: Rådhuset), not a gay bar, but frequented by gays, Sat from 23:00.

MINGLE, Sveavägen 47, bar, restaurant & disco, Thurs-Sat 17:00-03:00 (disco from 22:00).

SAPPHO BAR, Kocksgatan 28, at Lesbisk Nu center, (metro: Medborgarplatsen), (08) 641 86 16, women-only bar, alternate Sat 20:00-01:00.

SLM, Wollmer Yxkullsgatan 18, (metro: Mariatorget), (08) 643 31 00, strict leather, rubber, uniform, western dress code, Wed, Fri & Sat 21:00-03:00. Last Thurs of the month: meeting of LASH lesbian fetish/leather club from 21:00-01:00.

Dance Bar/Disco

BITCH-GIRL CLUB, Gula Gången, Kolingsborg, (metro: Slussen), (08) 720 52 05, bar & disco, call for schedule.

KARUSELL, Rosenlundsgatan 33, (metro: Skanstull or Mariatorget), (08) 720 03 32, Fri 17:00-03:00, Sat 19:00-03:00.

★ **PATRICIA,** Stadsgårdskajen 152, (metro: Slussen), (08) 74 30 570, gay bar nights on a boat, Sun 18:30-05:00. Variety of discos from 80's to techno, 4 different bars (5 in summer) on 3 levels with restaurant Sunday. Deck has view of Stockholm.

Cafe

CAFE G, Sveavägen 57., at RFSL Huset, (08) 30 99 33, 12:00-20:00 (Sat, Sun till 18:00).

DICK FARMER, Drottningholmsvägen 9, (08) 652 11 19, 09:00-20:00 (Sat 12:00-16:00), closed Sun.

GOLDEN LADIES, Sveavägen 57, cafe for mature lesbians at RFSL Huset, Thurs from 17:00, dinners 1st Fri,"

MÄRTHA'S CAFE, Kocksgatan 28, at Lesbisk Nu center, (metro: Medborgarplatsen), (08) 641 86 16, women-only cafe Tues & Thurs 18:00-21:00.

STRING KAFE, Nytorgsgatan 38, (08) 714 85 14, cafe & '40s- & '50s-style furniture store, frequented by gays & lesbians.

Restaurants

MOONCAKE, Luntmakarg 95, (08) 16 99 28, from 17:00 (Sat, Sun from 12:00), closed Mon & occasionally in summer.

NILS EMILS BAKFICKA, Folkungagatan 126, (08) 641 33 87, 11:00-14:00 & 17:00-22:00 (Sat 13:00-22:00), closed Sun.

SJÖGRÄS, Timmermansgatan 24, (08) 84 12 00, California cuisine, 17:00-24:00 (closed Sun).

Retail & Bookstores

ANTIKT GAMMALT & NYTT, Mäster Samuelsgatan 11 &, Hantverkarg 34, (08) 678 35 30, gay-owned antique store with jewelry, including partnership rings, 11:00-18:00 (Sat till 14:00), closed Sun.

INTERPRESSBUTIKEN, Drottningg 35, (08) 411 11 93, magazine store with gay magazines & coffee bar overlooking the city, 07:00-19:00 (Sat till 17:00, Sun 11:00-17:00).

KVINNOBOKHANDELN MEDUSA, Wollmar Yxkullsgatan 33, (metro: Mariatorget), (08) 84 50 07, women's bookshop with women's events, 10:00-18:00 (Fri from 11:00, Sat till 14:00), closed Sun. Importers of many books from US & England."

ROSA RUMMET, Sveavägen 57 (RFSL-huset complex), (08) 736 02 15, gay & lesbian bookstore, Mon-Thurs 15:00-20:00, Fri 15:00-18:00, Sat & Sun 13:00-16:00.

SERGEL GULD, Sergelgatan 12, (08) 21 69 68, sells engagement & partnership rings, reseller of "Gay rings."

VELVET VIDEO, Bondeg 46, (08) 640 40 64, wide selection of videos for sale & rent, including many gay & lesbian videos11:00-20:00 (Sun from 14:00).

Leathers/Piercing

CRIME, Borgargatan 6, (metro: Hornstull), (08) 720 6777, lesbian-owned leather/rubber shop, including specialties for women.

SWEDEN

■ Erotica
SECRETS, Tulegatan 2, (metro: Odenplan), exotica boutique run by women for women. ♀

SUNDSVALL

■ Information
RFSL, Skolhusalléen at Östra Långgatan, (060) 17 13 30, disco, bar & cafe run by gay organization. Cafe Sun & Wed 19:00-22:00, disco 2nd & last Sat 22:00-02:30, bar Fri (& weekends when there is no disco) 22:00-02:30. ♀♂

TROLLHATAN

■ Information
RFSL, Stritsbergsgatan 8, (0520) 41 17 66, cafe & party run by gay organization. Cafe Wed 19:00-22:00, Thurs 15:00-19:00, party last Sat 21:00-02:00. Closed Jun-Aug. ♀♂

UMEA

■ Information
RFSL, Östra Esplanaden 5, (090) 774 710, gar organization's cafe & disco. Cafe: Wed 19:00-22:00, disco: 1st & 3rd Sat 21:00-01:00. ♀♂

UPPSALA

■ Information
RFSL, (018) 69 23 96, cafe, pub & parties run by gay organization, call for schedule. ♀♂

VÄSTERÅS

■ Bars
RFSL, Emausgatan 41e, (021) 11 80 41, pub & café run by gay organizaton. Cafe Tues, call for pub & party schedule. ♀♂

VÄXJÖ

■ Information
RFSL HUSET, CAFE & TELEFONJOUR, Östregårdsgatan 8, (0470) 208 08, Café Sun 17:00-20:00 & Wed 19:00-22:00, parties last Sat 21:00-02:00. Gay line answers Wed 19:00-22:00.

■ Cafe
NOAH'S ARK - RÖDA KORSET CAFÉ, Kungsvägen 66, (0470) 193 81, HIV+ café Wed 18:00-21:00. ♂

VISBY

■ Information
RFSL, (0498) 26 85 84, gay organization, call for schedule of parties & pub nights (ask for "Gay Info"). ♀♂

SWITZERLAND

COUNTRY CODE: (41),

AARAU

■ Information
FRAUENBERATUNG, (062) 822 7901, women's line.

FRAUENZENTRUM, Kronengasse 5, (062) 824 0114, Frauentreff (women's social), Thurs 19:00-23:00."

BASEL

■ Information
AIDS HILFE, (061) 692 21 22.

FRAUENBIBLIOTHEK, Rössligasse 9, (061) 641 60 62, women's library, Sat 14:00-18:00.

FRAUENZENTRUM, Klingentalgraben 2, (061) 681 33 45, women's center, Frauenbar (women's bar) Tues from 18:30. Houses Lesben Initiative Basel (LIBS), LIBS Lesbenbar (lesbian bar night) 1st Tues, women's library Tues 18:00-21:00.

HABS INFO LINE, (061) 692 66 55, Wed from 20:00.

LESBENBERATUNG, (061) 681 33 45, lesbian info line, Wed from 20:00. Ask about lesbian bar night 1st Wed from 20:00.

SCHWULEN & LESBENZENTRUM, Gärtnerstrasse 55, (061) 631 55 88, SchLez gay organization, Wed from 20:00, disco Fri & Sat 22:00-03:00.

■ Accommodations
WHITE HORSE HOTEL, Webergasse 23, Basel, 4005, (41-61) 691 57 57, Fax: (41-61) 691 57 25. Gay-owned hotel with bar, in city centre, private showers & WCs, expanded continental breakfast, colour TV, phone. 20-50% gay & lesbian following.

■ Bars
DUPF BAR, Rebgasse 43, (061) 692 00 11, 16:00-01:00 (Fri till 03:00). ♂

ELLE ET LUI, Rebgasse 39, (061) 692 54 79, 19:00-03:00 (closed Sun). ♂

SCHLEZ & KEGELKINO, Gärtnerstr. 55, (061) 631 55 88, cafe & bar run by gay & lesbian organization, disco Fri & Sat from 22:00, Lesbenbar (lesbian bar) Thurs from 20:30, lesbian disco Sat 22:00-03:00, lesbian brunch Sun from 12:00. 🎵♀♂

ZISCH BAR, Klybeckstr. 1b (in the Kaserne), Tues 18:00-24:00.

■ Dance Bar/Disco
ISOLA CLUB, Gempenstrasse, 60, Fri 21:00-01:00, Sat 22:00-03:00. ♂

■ Retail & Bookstores
ARCADOS BUCHLADEN & VIDEOTHEK, Rheingasse, 69, (061) 681 31 32, gay bookshop, 14:00-19:00, Sat 11:00-17:00, closed Sun, Mon.

BERN

■ Information
FRAUENBEITZ SPINNE, Langmauerweg 1 at Frauenzentrum (women's center), (031) 331 07 73, Lesbenabend (lesbian evening) Tues-Thurs from 18:00, Fri from 20:00, Sat till 00:30, disco & bar last Sat of the month 20:00-02:00. 🎵

FRAUENBERATUNGSTELLE, Laupenstrasse 2, (031) 381 2701, women's line, answers Mon-Tues & Thurs-Fri 09:00-12:00.

FRAUENBIBLIOTHEK, Seftigenstr. 11, at Villa Stucki, (031) 371 44 40, women's library, Wed 15:00-17:00, Sat 10:00-12:00.

FRAUENZENTRUM BERN, Langmauerweg 1, (031) 331 07 73, houses Lesbeninitiative Bern (LIB) (lesbian initiative).

HAB INFO LINE (ANDERLAND), (031) 331 63 53, Sun 20:00-22:00. AnderLand gay center located at Mühleplatz 11, 5th floor.

■ Dance Bar/Disco
ANDERLAND, SCHWULES BEGEGNUNGSZENTRUM BERN, Mühlenplatz 11, 5th floor, (031) 311 11 97 or 311 63 53, disco & bar at gay center, Sun-Fri evenings. Scheduled women's dance nights.

🎵✖♂

WELLE FRAUENDISCO, Sandrainstrasse 25, at Gaskessel, (031) 372 49 00, women's disco 3rd Fri. 🎵♀

■ Restaurants
BRASSERIE LORRAINE, Quariergasse 17, (031) 322 39 29, frequented by women.

■ Retail & Bookstores
FRAUENBUCHLADEN, Münstergasse 41, (031) 312 12 85, women's bookstore, 09:00-18:30 (Sat till 16:00, Mon 14:00-18:00).

GENEVE - GENEVA

■ Information
AIDS INFO, (022) 700 15 00.

CENTRE FEMMES NATALIE BARNEY, 30, av. Peschier, (022) 789 26 00, women's center & lesbian switchboard. Permanence téléphonique tous le mercredi (answers Wed) 18:30-20:30 or tape. Prêt des livres, consultation de revues, livres en anglais, français, allemand & italien (library & reading room with books in English, French, German & Italian). Bar nights Fri & Sat from 22:00. Bal (dancing) 1st & 3rd Sat of the month 22:00-03:00.

DIALOGAI GAY CENTER & INFO LINE, 11, rue de la Navigation, (022) 906 40 40, Fax 906 40 44, Wed 20:00-22:00, 90% men. Sun brunch in winter 12:00-14:00. AIDS café group 2nd & last Tues 20:00-22:00 (meal prepared last Tues by group members). Home to a library & many diverse gay groups. Info line Wed 19:00-22:00.

■ Bars
BAR UNDERGROUND, 22 Grand Rue, (022) 311 13 15, frequented by gays, 17:00-22:00.

CHEZ BRIGITTE, 12, rue Prévost-Martin, 21:00-04:00. ♂

L'INTERDIT, 18, Quai du Seujet., ♂

LA BRETELLE, Rue des Étuves 17, (022) 732 75 96, 17:00-02:00, dancing Fri, Sat, men welcome. 🎵♫♀

WOMEN'S BAR NIGHT, at the Centre Femmes Natalie Barney, Fri & Sat from 22:00. ♀

■ Dance Bar/Disco
LE DECLIC, 28 Bld du Pont d'Arve, (022) 720 59 14. 🎵♫♂

■ Cafe
CHARLES DUBOIS CONFISERIE, 49,

bd Carl-Vogt, (022) 328 01 24, pastry shop, NOT gay, discreelty frequented by gays. 2nd location: 4, car. de Villeruese, Tel: (022) 736 80 64.

YVES QUARTIER, 24, rue Voltaire, (022) 44 53 21, café, patisserie, confiserie (pastry shop).

■ Restaurants
L'ÉVIDENCE, 13 rue des Grottes, (022) 733 61 65, bar & restaurant, frequented by gays, 06:00-01:00 (Sat, Sun from 11:00)."

■ Retail & Bookstores
L'INÉDITE, 18, ave Cardinal Mermillod, Carouge, (022) 343 22 33, feminist bookshop with a small selection of lesbian books, 09:00-12:00 & 14:00-18:30 (Mon only 14:00-18:30), Sat 10:00-13:00."

KONSTANZ

■ Dance Bar/Disco
EXCALIBUR, Augustinerplatz, gay disco Sun.

LUZERN

■ Information
AIDS HILFE, (041) 410 68 48.

HALU GAY & LESBIAN GROUP, Geissensteinring 14, at Uferlos gay & lesbian center, (041) 360 14 60, meetings Wed from 20:00. Gay & lesbian disco 1st Sat.

ZEFRA FRAUENZENTRUM, Mythenstrasse 7, (041) 210 73 10, women's center, library open Wed 14:00-16:00, Thurs & Fri 18:00-20:00, info office Thurs 09:00-11:00, women's bar night Fri 20:00-24:00.

■ Dance Bar/Disco
RÄGEBOGE, Züricherstrasse 43, women's disco 3rd Sat.

ST-GALLEN

■ Information
FRAUENBIBLIOTHEK, Davidstr. 42, (071) 222 65 15, women's library, Mon 16:00-20:00, Wed, Thurs 14:00-18:00, Sat 12:00-16:00.

■ Bars
FRAUENBEIZ, Engelgasse 22, at Restaurant Schwarzer Engel, (071) 23 35 75, women's bar night, even Thurs from 19:30.

HOPPALA BAR, Linsebühlstr. 96, (071) 222 7222, bar & restaurant with patio, from 16:00 (Sun from 18:00).

■ Dance Bar/Disco
LA LUNA, Im Sihltobel, women's disco 3rd Sat.

PEPPERMINT BAR, St. Jakobstr. 103, (71) 245 24 98.

SOLOTHURN

■ Information
FRAUENZENTRUM, Prisongasse 4, (032) 622 7374, women's center.

WINTERTHUR

■ Information
FRAUENZENTRUM, Steinberggasse 61, (052) 212 2650, women's center, coffees Tues, Fri 09:00-11:00.

■ Retail & Bookstores
FRANXA BUCHHANDLUNG, Lagerhausstrasse 15, (052) 212 3880, feminist bookstore, 10:00-18:30 (Mon from 13:00, Sat till 16:00), regular readings & exhibitions.

ZÜRICH

■ Information
AIDS INFO, (01) 291 37 20, Tues, Thurs 09:00-13:00, Wed 14:00-18:00.

FRAUEN LESBEN ARCHIVE, Quellenstr. 25, (01) 237 39 49, women's & lesbian archives, Wed 18:00-20:00, Sat 16:00-18:00.

FRAUENZENTRUM, Mattengasse 27, (01) 272 85 03, women's center. Library open Tues-Fri 18:00-20:00. Pudding Palace Frauenbeiz (women's pub) Tues-Fri 12:00-14:00 & 18:00-22:00, Sat from 18:00, bar night Fri from 22:00.

HAZ INFO LINE & CENTER, Sihlquai 67, 3rd floor, (01) 271 22 50, Tues-Fri 19:30-23:00, Sun 12:00-14:00.

INFRA, (01) 272 8844, women's info line, Tues 15:00-19:30.

LESBENBERATUNGSSTELLE, (01) 272 73 71, Thurs 18:00-20:00.

■ Accommodations
HOTEL GOLDENES SCHWERT, Marktgasse 14, Zürich, 8001, (41-1) 266 1818, Fax: (41-1) 266 1888. Email: hotel@gaybar.ch, Web: http://

www.gaybar.ch/hotel, Hotel with bar & disco, some hetero clientele, single, double, theme rooms & suite, all private baths. ♀♂

■ Bars

CHNELLE 4, Feldstr. 108, from 16:00 (closed Mon). ♂

LA BAL, Beethovenstrasse 8., ♀

PUDDING PALACE FRAUENKNEIPE, at Frauenzentrum, Mattengasse 27, (01) 271 56 98, Tues-Fri 12:00-14:00 & 18:00-22:00 with bar night continuing Fri from 22:00. ♀

SFINX, Löwenstrasse 2, women-only bar. ♀

TRÜBLI GROTTO BAR, Zeughausgasse 67, (01) 242 87 97, bar & restaurant, daily 14:00-24:00, gay after 20:00. ♀

VENUS BAR, Badenerstrasse 219, some hetero clientele. ♀

■ Dance Bar/Disco

AMAZINE LESBIAN NIGHT, Stadthausquai 13, at Cincecitta, ask locally for exact times. 🏠 ♀

HEARTBREAKER FRAUENDISCO, Neugasse 56, women's disco. 🏠 ♀

KANZLEILA, Kanzleistrasse 56, at the Kanzleiturnhalle, large women's disco. 🏠 ♀

LES NOUVELLES FRAUENDISCO, Sihlquai 240, women's disco 2nd Sat from 22:00 (address is hard to find & this disco is not held regularly). 🏠 ♀

ZABI, Leonhardstrasse 19, inside StuZ, disco night run by gay organization, Fri 23:00-03:00. 🏠 ♀♂

■ Cafe

CAFE MARION, Mühlegasse 13, 07:00-19:00.

CAFE ODEON, Limmatquai 2, (01) 251 16 50, cafe and bar frequented by many gays, especially popular late in the evening, light menu, open 07:00-02:00, Fri, Sat till 04:00." 🍴

CAFE TABU, Josefstr. 142, (021) 272 85 86, 07:30-19:00 (Sat, Sun 10:30-17:00), closed Mon. ♂

HOT POT CAFE, Badenerstrasse 138, 06:45-22:30 (Sat 08:00-16:00), closed Sun. ♂

■ Fitness Centers

LADY FIT, Universitätstr. 33, (01) 252 3333, women's fitness center.

■ Restaurants

DON CAMILLO, Seestrasse 31, (01) 926 6585, Italian cuisine, closed Mon.

JOHANNITER, Niederdorfstrasse 70, 251 46 00, between 22:00-02:00 enter through Carrousel bar in rear. 🍴

RESTAURANT KUTSCHERHALLE, Müllerstrasse 31, (01) 241 53 15, frequented by women.

SUNSET THAI, Birmensdorferstr. 488, (01) 463 6570, Thai cuisine.

■ Retail & Bookstores

FRAUENBUCHLADEN, Gerechtigkeitsgasse 6, (01) 202 62 74, feminist bookstore, Mon 14:00-18:30, Tues-Fri 09:00-18:30, Sat 09:00-16:00.

RAINBOW BOOKSHOP, Hildastr. 5, (01) 242 0182, Thurs 15:00-21:00, Sat 11:00-16:00.

SEC 52 BUCHLADEN, Josefstrasse 52, (01) 42 18 18, general bookstore with gay section.

TURKEY

COUNTRY CODE: (90),

ANKARA

■ Bars

KILIM, Sili Meydani, close to Airport Disco., 🏠 ♂

Z BAR, Sakarya Cadessi., ♂

ANTALYA

■ Bars

ALWAYS BAR, in the harbour area, ask local gays for exact address, 24:00-04:00. 🏠 ♂

ISTANBUL

IN ISTANBUL:, Take taxis from bar to bar, or go with someone trustworthy who knows the way. Although bars are close to each other, neighbourhoods may not be safe at night. Bouncers tend to be friendly & fluent in English and, when asked, will be happy to instruct taxi drivers to take you where you want to go.

■ Information

AIDS LINE, 435 2047.

LAMDA ISTANBUL, gay organization meets Sun 15:00, ask local gays for address.

SISTERS OF VENUS, write: MBE 165, Kayisdag Cadessi 99, Ziverbey, Istanbul,

TURKEY

Turkey., Lesbian group with newsletter, local information.

■ Bars

BARBAHCE, Siraselviler Cadessi, Soganci Sok. 7, 1st floor, Taksim, bar & restaurant. ✘ ♂

CLUB 14, Abdulhakhamit Cadessi, Belediye Dukkanlari 14, Taksim, (212) 256 2121. Difficult to find, ask someone who knows the area how to find this bar. Busy weekends 24:00-04:00, videos. ♂

FASIL, Rihtim Cadessi, Kadikoy., ✘ ♂

FIVE-KAT, Siraselviler Cadessi, Soganci Sok. 7, 5th floor, Taksim, (212) 293 3774, bar & restaurant with upscale clientele, 18:00-02:00 (closed Sun). ✘ ♂

HAN CAFE, Cumhuriyet Cadessi, Taksim Square, bar & cafe, 09:00-02:00. ♂

KEMANCI MANDALA, Siraselviler Cadessi 69, Taksim, (212) 245 3048, NOT a gay bar, discreetly frequented by gays, especially on 3rd level.

ROXY, Siraselviler Cadessi, Arslanyatagi Sok. 9, Taksim, (212) 249 4839, NOT a gay bar, frequented by some gays & lesbians.

SAFAATHANE, Istiklal, Atlas Sinemasi Pasaji, (212) 251 2245, NOT a gay bar, discreetly frequented by gays.

■ Dance Bar/Disco

TWENTY - NINETEEN, Abdulhakhamit Cadessi, Taksim, beside Club 14 bar, 01:00-06:00. ♂

TWENTY - TWENTY, Oto Sanayi, in Maslak, (212) 285 1896, 01:00-07:00, discreetly frequented by gays.

■ Cafe

BORSA, Cumhuriyet Cadessi, Taksim Square, 09:00-24:00. ✘ ♂

CAFE PIA, Istiklal Cadessi, Bekar Sok., discreetly frequented by gays & lesbians. ✘

KAKTUS, Istiklal Cadessi, Imam Adnan Sok. 4, Taksim, (212) 249 5979, discreetly frequented by gays & lesbians. ✘

■ Restaurants

DURAN SANDWICHES, in Taksim Square.,

■ Retail & Bookstores

MEPHISTO, Istiklal Cadessi, Taksim, general bookstore with gay & lesbian titles.

PANDORA, Istiklal Cadessi, Buyukparmakkapi Sok 3, Taksim, (212) 245 1667, general bookstore with gay & lesbian titles.

U K - ENGLAND

COUNTRY CODE: (44),

THE PHRASE "PUB HOURS" USED IN LISTINGS MEANS:, 11:00-17:00 & 17:30-23:00, Sun 12:00-14:00 & 19:00-22:30. Some pubs are now open all day.

AVON

■ Accommodations

LODGE AND THE KEEP, THE, Banwell Castle, Banwell, Avon, BS24 6NX, (44-1934) 823 122, Fax: (44-1934) 823 946. Bed & breakfast, women welcome, Victorian style rooms with private baths, color TV & TV lounge, gardens, full breakfast, The Keep restaurant. ♂

BATH

■ Accommodations

KENNARD HOTEL, THE, 11 Henrietta Street, Bath, Avon, BA2 6LL, (44-1225) 310472, Fax: (44-1225) 460054. Email: kennard@dircon.co.uk, A true Georgian Town House, this charming small hotel was originally built in 1794. The 13 bedrooms are individually furnished for your comfort & the original Georgian kitchen is now a delightful garden-style bistro. Quietly situated in Henrietta Street, its city centre location is just over Pulteney Bridge, minutes from the Ab

The Kennard Hotel
Charm & Character

Bath
(44-1225) 310 472

bey and Roman Baths and with easy access from London or the Station. Mostly hetero clientele with a gay/lesbian following.

LEIGH HOUSE, Leigh Road West, Bradford-on-Avon, Wiltshire, BA15 2RB, (44-1225) 867835. Gay-owned & -operated 16th century farmhouse on 6 acres, deep in the heart of the West Country. Private baths, full breakfast, collection of rare-breed animals & fowl. Some hetero clientele. ♀♂

■ Dance Bar/Disco
SISTERS, at Sportsman, women-only dance night, last Fri from 20:00. 🏠 ♀

BEDFORD

■ Information
AIDS INFO, (01582) 48 44 99.
GAY & LESBIAN SWITCHBOARD, (01234) 21 89 90, Tues, Thurs 19:30-22:00.

■ Dance Bar/Disco
ECLIPSE, Bedford Rd, at the Saxon Club, Kempston, (01234) 34 68 38, last Fri from 19:00. 🏠 ♀

BIRMINGHAM

■ Information
AIDS LINE, (0121) 622 15 11, Mon-Fri 11:00-22:00.
FRIEND, (0121) 622 73 51, 19:30-21:30, ask about men's & women's socials.
LESBIAN & GAY SWITCHBOARD, (0121) 622 65 89, 7 days 19:00-22:00.
LESBIAN LINE, (0121) 622 65 63, Tues lesbian social nights, from 19:30
WOMEN'S ADVICE & INFORMATION CENTRE, at the Devonshire House, High St, in Digbeth, (0121) 773 6952, Tues, Thurs 10:00-16:00.

■ Accommodations
FOUNTAIN INN, THE, 102 Wrentham St, Birmingham, West Midlands, B5 6QL, (44-121) 622 1452, Fax: (44-121) 622 5387. In USA call (407) 994-3558, Fax: (407) 994-3634. guesthouse inn with bar & pub food, women welcome, refurbished, quality rooms with coffee/tea making facilities, 10 min walk to RR Sta, shopping, entertainment, 5 min to gay pubs & discos (The Fountain), full or continental breakfast. ♂

VILLAGE, THE, 152 Hurst Street, Birmingham, B5 6RY, (44-121) 622 4742. hotel with gay bar, private baths, tea & coffee making facilities, TV. ♂

■ Bars
FOX, THE, 17 Lower Essex St, (0121) 622 12 10, pub with patio, 19:00-23:00 (Sun pub hours), women welcome. 🏠 ♂
PARTNERS, Hurst St, (0121) 622 47 10, pub, 15:00-23:00 (Fri, Sat from 13:00), Sun pub hours, women welcome." ♂
PELICAN BAR, 87 Bar St, Hockley Hill, (0121) 55 46 721, 19:00-23:00, men welcome. ♀
SUBWAY CITY, Livery St, (0121) 23 30 310, 7 days, Sun men only. 🪩 ♂
VILLAGE INN, 152 Hurst St, (0121) 622 4742, 12:00-23:00 (Sun pub hours), patio. Black lesbian & gay group meets 1st Wed. ♂

■ Dance Bar/Disco
NIGHTINGALE, Kent St, at the Essex House, (0121) 622 17 18, disco, bar & restaurant complex, Mon-Thurs 22:00-02:00 (Fri, Sat from 21:00), Sun 21:00-24:00. 🏠 ♂

■ Restaurants
OVER 18 RESTAURANT, Kent St, across from Route 66 bar, (0121) 622 6717. ♀♂

BLACKPOOL

■ Information
AIDS INFO, (01253) 29 28 03.

■ Accommodations
ABBEYVILLE, 39 High St, Blackpool, FY1 2BN, (44-1253) 752-072. Bed & breakfast, gay-friendly, singles, doubles, with color TV, tea/coffee making facilities, centrally located, breakfast with optional dinner. ♀♂

ASHBEIAN HOTEL, 49 High St, Blackpool, FY1 2BH, (44-1253) 26301 (Tel/Fax). May change in 1998 to: (44-1253) 626 301 (Tel/Fax). Small, intimate guesthouse with full breakfast, private baths. Across street from beach, near shopping, theatres & restaurants. 10-20% gay & lesbian clientele.

BELVEDERE HOTEL, 77 Dickson Rd, Blackpool, FY1 2BX, (44-1253) 24733. Hotel with bar, private & shared baths, TV, coffee & tea-making facilities. near other gay bars. ♀♂

UK - ENGLAND

BROOKLYN HOTEL, THE, 7 Wilton Parade, North Shore, Blackpool, FY1 2HE, (44-1253) 27003, Fax: (44-1253) 24622. Hotel with restaurant & bar. Private baths, full breakfast, near gay bars. 50% gay/lesbian clientele.

CHAUCER HOUSE, 59 High St, Blackpool, FY1 2BN, (44-1253) 299 099. Exclusively gay & lesbian B&B, 7 rooms, private & shared baths, full English breakfast. ♀♂

COLINS HOTEL, 9-11 Cocker St, Blackpool, FY1 1SF, (44-1253) 20 541. hotel with residents' bar, private & shared baths, women welcome. ♂

CROMPTON HOTEL, 20 Cocker St, Blackpool, FY1 2BY, (44-1253) 291 583 (Tel/Fax) Gay-owned hotel with residents' bar, private & shared baths, concessions to Flamingo dance bar. 50% gay & lesbian clientele.

DALMENY HOTEL, 44 Palatine Rd, Blackpool, (44-1253) 25560. Hotel with full English breakfast, private & shared baths, full English breakfast, concession to Flamingo gay dance bar, 25% gay/lesbian clientele.

DUDLEY HOUSE HOTEL, 27 Cocker St, Blackpool, SY1 2BZ, (44-1253) 20988. Hotel with private & shared baths, full English breakfast, some hetero clientele. ♀♂

EDWARD HOTEL, 27 Dickson Road, Blackpool, FY1 2AT, (44-1253) 24271." Gay-owned & -operated B&B hotel with private & shared baths, full breakfast, near gay bars & clubs. ♀♂

GLENROY HOTEL, 10 Trafalgar Rd, Blackpool, FY1 6AW, (44-1253) 344607. gay-owned hotel, 50% gay & lesbian clientele, color TV, beverage-making facilities, private baths, nearby pool & ocean beach, full breakfast, dinner."

KINGSMEAD GUEST HOUSE, 58 Lord St, Blackpool, FY1 2BJ, (44-1253) 24496, Fax: (44-1253) 292 634. Email: evanswarburton@msn.com, Gay-owned & -operated B&B guesthouse with shared baths, full breakfast included with evening meal optional. Complimentary concessions to Flamingo club. 50% gay/lesbian.

LEXHAM HOTEL, 14 Banks St, Blackpool, FY1 1RN, (44-1253) 27158." private & shared baths, 5 minutes from city centre, B&B available.

LONSDALE HOTEL, 25 Cocker St, Blackpool, FY1 2BZ, (44-1253) 21628. gay-owned licensed hotel with private baths, colour satellite TV, near gay bars, concession to Flamingo dance bar, 50% gay clientele, more gay weekends.

LYNWOOD HOTEL, 4 Trafalgar Rd, Blackpool, FY1 6AW, (44-1253) 346156, ask for Robin. Hotel with licensed bar lounge, colour TV, central heat, concessions to Flamingo dance bar, 50% gay/lesbian clientele.

MARDI GRAS HOTEL, 41/43 Lord St, Blackpool, FY1 2BD, (44-1253) 751 087, Fax: (44-1253) 231 79 Hotel with all ensuite baths, full English breakfast, women welcome. ♂

OSCARS HOTEL, 23 Lord St, Blackpool, FY1 2BD, (44-1253) 290 700 (Tel/Fax), call before faxing. Gay & lesbian hotel with licensed bar for residents, private & shared baths, colour TV, near gay bars. ♀♂

PIERROTS, 45 High St, Blackpool, FY1 2BN, (44-1253) 28125. Gay-owned B&B guesthouse, shared baths, beverage making facilities, TV lounge, nearby ocean beach, full English or continental breakfast. 50% gay & lesbian clientele."

PRIMROSE HOTEL, THE, 16 Lord St, Blackpool, Lancashire, FY1 2BD, (44-1253) 22488. gay-owned hotel with bar, 60% gay/lesbian clientele, beverage-making facilities, private & shared baths, TV lounge, continental or full English breakfast, concession to Flamingo." ♀♂

ROYALE, THE, 18 Regent Road, Blackpool, Central, FY1 4LY, (44-1253) 26623. Guesthouse with licensed bar, private baths, 75% gay/lesbian clientele. ♀♂

SANDOLIN GUEST HOUSE, 117 High St, Blackpool, FY1 2DW, (44-1253) 752 908. Gay-owned, gay-friendly hotel, tea & coffee-making facilitiesprivate & shared baths, concessions to local clubs.

SANDYLANDS GUEST HOUSE, 47 Banks St, North Shore, Blackpool, FY1 2BE, (44-1253) 294 670 (Tel/Fax)." Gay-owned, gay-friendly guesthouse with shared baths, near bars, mostly hetero clientele, about 40% gay on weekends. ◪

SHERWOOD HOTEL, 412-414 North Promenade, Blackpool, FY1 2LB, (44-1253) 351 898." Gay-owned hotel with theatre bar, sea views, private & shared

UK - ENGLAND 137

baths, 70% hetero & 30% gay clientele. Popular with gay & lesbian families with children.

Women's Accommodations

AMALFI HOTEL, 19-21 Eaves Street, Blackpool, Lancashire, FY1 2NH, (44-1253) 22971. hotel with residents' bar, full English or vegetarian breakfast, shared baths, 98% women. " ♀

Bars

BASE COFFEE BAR, 4 Springfield Rd, (01253) 29 61 96, 10:00-19:00. ♂

Dance Bar/Disco

★ **FLAMINGO,** 176 Talbot Rd, (01253) 249 01, large dance bar complex, Mon-Sat till 02:00, Sun day & eve. till late.

BOLTON

Information

LESBIAN LINE, (01204) 39 46 10, Thurs 19:00-22:00.

Bars

CHURCH, 174 Crook Street, (01204) 52 18 56, women welcome (Thurs women-only)."

GEORGE, 92-94 Great Moor St, (01204) 36 19 79, 11:00-23:00, women welcome. ♂

★ **STAR & GARTER,** 11 Bow St, (01204) 259 26, pub, women welcome." ♂

BOURNEMOUTH

Information

AIDS LINE, (01202) 29 73 86.

HELPLINE, (01202) 31 88 22, Mon-Fri 19:30-22:30, or tape. Ask about women's group meetings."

Accommodations

AARON HOUSE, 18 Purbeck Road, The West Cliff, Bournemouth, BH2 5EF, (44-1202) 292 865. Gay-owned, gay-friendly hotel in a newly renovated Victorian building, private & shared baths, a 1-minute walk to gay nightlife, 40% gay clientele.

BEECH CRESCENT, Branksome Park, Poole, (44-1202) 762092 (Tel/Fax)." Gay-owned & -operated guesthouse near beach, full array of amenities, private bath, full breakfast, women welcome. ♂

BONDI, 43 St Michael's Rd, Bournemouth, BH2 5DP, (44-1202) 554893. gay-owned B&B near sea & shopping, colour TV, beverage-making facilities, shared baths, residents' lounge, color satellite TV, 50% gay & lesbian clientele.

CHINE BEACH HOTEL, THE, 14 Studland Road, Alum Chine, Bournemouth, BH4 8JA, (44-1202) 767 015, Fax: (44-1202) 761 218. Hotel with public bar & full restaurant on the beach, full English breakfast, private baths, colour TV, pool on premses. 50% gay & lesbian clientele.

CLAREMONT HOTEL, THE, 89 St. Michael's Road, West Cliff, Bournemouth, BH2 5DR, (44-1202) 316 668 (Tel/Fax), or mobile: (44-585) 137 756." Gay-owned hotel with private & shared baths, more hetero clientele weekdays, more gay on weekends.

CREFFIELD, THE, 7 Cambridge Road, Bournemouth, BH2 6AE, (44-1202) 317 900. Exclusively gay late Edwardian B&B with all en-suite baths, full breakfast & two rooms with 4-poster beds. Full central heating, conservatory, large private garden & near all venues & shopping. Women welcome. ♂

HEDLEY HOTEL, THE, 125 West Hill Rd, Bournemouth, BH2 5PH, (44-1202) 317 168. Gay-friendly hotel, 20%-30% gay clientele, full English breakfast, private & shared baths.

LLOYDS HOTEL, 123 West Hill Rd, Bournemouth, BN2 5PH, (44-1202) 291 112. Gay-owned hotel wtih 50% gay & lesbian clientele, more gay in winter, private & shared baths.

NEWARK HOTEL, 65 St. Michaels Rd, West Cliff, Bournemouth, BH2 5DP, (44-1202) 294989. gay-friendly hotel with licensed restaurant, 50% gay/lesbian clientele, color TV, private & shared baths, TV lounge, full breakfast. "

ORCHARD HOTEL, THE, 15 Alumdale Rd, Alum Chine, Bournemouth, BH4 8HX, (44-1202) 767 767. hotel with full residents' liquor license, color TV, private baths, TV lounge, nearby ocean beach, full English breakfast." ♀♂

WESTOVER GARDENS HOTEL, 5/7 Westover Road, Bournemouth, BH1 2BY, (44-1202) 556 380 (Tel/Fax). Gay-owned, gay-friendly hotel with licensed residents-only bar, full English breakfast, 20% gay & lesbian clientele.

UK - ENGLAND

■ Bars
QUEENS HALL PUB, 14 Queens Rd, Westbourne, (01202) 76 44 16, pub hours." 🏨 🎵 ♂

BRADFORD

■ Information
AIDS INFO, (01274) 73 43 54.
GAY & LESBIAN SWITCHBOARD, (01274) 72 22 06, Tues, Thurs-Sat 19:30-21:30.
LESBIAN LINE, (01274) 30 55 25, Thurs 19:00-21:00, or tape.

■ Bars
GUYS & DOLLS, Westgate, Bradford Centre, women-only Sun 20:00-23:00. 🏨 ♀
NEW EDITION, 10 Worthington St, (01274) 49 35 49," women's nights every other Thurs 21:00-02:00. ♀

■ Dance Bar/Disco
CHECKPOINT, (01274) 49 35 49, women's dance night every other Fri, call locally for address. 🏨 ♀

BRIGHTON

■ Information
AIDS INFO, (01273) 69 32 66, Mon-Fri 10:00-17:00.
BRIGHTON WOMEN'S CENTRE, 10 St Georges Mews, (01273) 60 21 41, Lesbian Strength social group meets 2nd & 4th Tues from 19:30.
LESBIAN LINE, (01273) 60 32 98, Tues & Fri 20:00-22:00, ask about scheduled monthly lesbian bar nights.
RAINBOW CENTRE TRUST, 2A Brading Rd.,

■ Accommodations
ALPHA LODGE PRIVATE HOTEL, 19 New Steine, Brighton, E Sussex, BN2 1PD, (44-1273) 609 632, Fax: (44-1273) 690 264. guesthouse with a steam-room suite, centrally located, overlooking the sea, singles, doubles, beverage-making facilities, color TV, full English breakfast, nearby pool & beaches, women welcome. ♂
ASHLEY COURT GUEST HOUSE, 33 Montpelier Rd, Brighton, BN1 2LQ, (44-1273) 739916. B&B guesthouse, some hetero clientele, full English breakfast, private sinks & showers in rooms, ocean beach nearby. ♀♂
BANNINGS GUEST HOUSE, 14 Upper Rock Gardens, Brighton, BN2 1QE, (44-1273) 681403. A women-only guesthouse in Brighton's gay area, run by 2 gay men who enjoy entertaining & provinding a safe environment for women. All rooms have showers, some en-suite rooms available, full vegetarian English breakfast, close to venues. ♀
BARRINGTON'S PRIVATE HOTEL, 76 Grand Parade, Brighton, BN2 2JA, (44-1273) 604 182. hotel with bar, 50% gay/lesbian clientele, luxury rooms, private showers, shared baths, colour TV, full English breakfast."
CATNAPS PRIVATE GUEST HOUSE, 21 Atlingworth St, Brighton, E Sussex, BN2 1PL, (44-1273) 685 193, Fax: (44-1273) 622 026. guesthouse, women welcome, 7 rooms, shared baths, TV lounge, nearby pool & ocean beach, full English breakfast, welcoming tea & coffee." ♂
COURT CRAVEN HOTEL, 2 Atlingworth St, Brighton, BN2 1PL, (44-1273) 607710, Fax: (44-1273) 607 710. Hotel with bar, women welcome, showers in rooms." ♀♂
GEORGE IV HOTEL, 34 Regency Square, Brighton, BN1 2FJ, (44-1273) 321 196. Gay-run, comfortable accommodation in a beautiful 5-floor Regency building, 100 yards from the sea & a 5-minute walk to gay venues. Rooms have full ensuite baths, colour TV, phone & tea- & coffee-making facilities. ♀♂ ♀♂
HUDSONS GUEST HOUSE, 22 Devonshire Place, Brighton, E Sussex, BN2 1QA, (44-1273) 683 642, Fax: (44-1273) 696 088. elegant, comfortable, well-equipped rooms, including tea/coffee making facilities, near shopping, restaurants, Royal Pavilion, beaches, proper English breakfast, vegetarians welcome." ♀♂
PORTLAND HOUSE HOTEL, 55-56 Regency Square, Brighton, East Sussex, BN1 2FF, (44-1273) 820 464, Fax: (44-1273) 746 036. hotel with bar, 50% gay/lesbian clientele, rooms with modernconveniences, beverage-making facilities, full English or continental breakfast, near ocean beach.
SHALIMAR HOTEL, 23 Broad St, Marine Parade, Brighton, Sussex, BN2 1TJ,

UK - ENGLAND

(44-1273) 605 316 (Tel/Fax). hotel with backroom resident's bar, women welcome, private & shared baths, colour TV, beverage-making facilities, phone, nearby ocean beach, full breakfast. ♂

SINCLAIRS GUEST HOUSE, 23 Upper Rock Gardens, Brighton, BN2 1QE, (44-1273) 600 006 (Tel/Fax) and (44-1831) 248 361. Bed & breakfast guesthouse, women welcome, colour TV, beverage-making facilities, private & shared baths, full English breakfast. ♂

WHITE HOUSE HOTEL, THE, 6 Bedford St, Brighton, East Sussex, BN2 1AN, (44-1273) 626266 (Tel/Fax). B&B hotel near gay village & nudist beach, 50% gay/lesbian clientele, private & shared baths, full breakfast.

■ Women's Accommodations

ONLY ALTERNATIVE LEFT, THE, 39 St Aubyn's, Hove, Sussex, BN3 2TH, (44-1273) 324739. Women-only B&B, private & shared baths, continental breakfast buffet. ♀

■ Bars

BLUE MOON, 37 New England Rd, (01273) 70 90 40, Fri, Sat 19:30-23:00. 📺 ♀

COWLICK, Brunswick St East, at Sanctuary Cafe, (01273) 77 00 02, Sun women's & lesbian night. ♀

JUST SISTERS, 205-209 Kingsway, at the Excelsior Hotel, Hove, women's night Sat 20:30-01:00. ♀

LEGENDS BAR, 31-32 Marine Parade, at the New Europe Hotel, (01273) 62 44 62. 📺 🎵 ♂

QUEEN'S HEAD, 10 Steine St, (01273) 60 29 39, pub, women welcome. Leather group meets 1st Sat 21:00-23:00. 🎵 ✕ 📺 ♂

VILLAGE, 74 St James' St, (01273) 62 22 60, lounge upper level, disco lower level, 20:00-02:00 (Thurs-Sat from 14:00), Sun pub hours. ♂

■ Dance Bar/Disco

CLUB CHEEKY, 15 King's Rd, at Zenon's, (01273) 32 68 48, women's dance night, Fri 22:00-02:00. 📺 ♀

CLUB REVENGE, 32 Old Steine, opposite Palace Pier, (01273) 60 60 64, large dance bar, Mon-Thurs 22:30-02:00, Fri, Sat from 22:00 (Fri uniform & leather nights, upper level)." 📺 ♂

DYNAMITE BOOGALOO, 37 West St, at the Joint, Thurs." 📺 ♂

PINK PROMOTIONS, (01903) 72 36 25, floating women's disco at various locations on the South Coast, call for exact date & location." 📺 ♀

★ **WILD FRUIT,** 78 West St, at Paradox, (01273) 32 16 28, 1st Mon 22:00-02:00, women welcome. 📺 ♂

■ Cafe

ALBATROSS CAFE, 27 Middle St, (01273) 32 94 62, 11:00-17:00 (closed Sun), call about women-only nights, some lesbian/gay nights. ♀

■ Restaurants

COOK & FIDDLE, 183 Kings Rd Arches, (01273) 73 95 30.

■ Retail & Bookstores

CARDOME, 47a St James' St, (01273) 69 29 16, gay cards, etc.

OUT!, 4 & 7 Dorset St, (01273) 62 33 56, gay & lesbian bookstore, also videos, toys, rubber, leather, etc., 10:00-18:00 (Fri, Sat till 20:00), Sun 11:00-17:00.

BRISTOL

■ Information

GAY & LESBIAN SWITCHBOARD, (0117) 942 08 42, daily 19:30-22:30."

LESBIAN LINE, (0117) 929 08 55, Thurs 19:30-22:00, ask about scheduled women's dance nights."

■ Bars

ELEPHANT, THE, St Nicholas St, (0117) 949 99 01, women welcome. ♂

GRIFFIN, THE, Colston St, (0117) 927 24 21, pub, women welcome. Leather group meets 1st Fri & 3rd Sat from 21:00. ♂

JUST, 1 Fiennes Ct, at Fairfax St, (0117) 930 46 75, 22:00-02:00 (Sun 21:00-01:00), closed Mon. ♀♂

■ Dance Bar/Disco

VIBES, Bath Rd, at the Parkside Hotel, lesbian disco night 1st Sat 21:00-02:00. 📺 ♀

■ Cafe

LILAC CAFE, Horley Rd, at St. Werburgh's Community Centre, lesbian cafe 2nd Sun 15:00-18:00. ♀

■ Retail & Bookstores

GREENLEAF BOOKSHOP, 82 Colston St, general bookstore with gay & lesbian section.

BURNLEY

Bars
MCNEILS, Guy St, in Padiham, (01282) 77 48 77, Sun, Mon, Thurs from 20:00. ♀♂

BURY SAINT EDMONDS

Bars
DOG & PARTRIDGE, Newmarket Rd, Barton Mills, (01638) 71 27 61, 19:00-23:00 (Sun till 22:30). Disco 1st Sat of the month. 🍴 ♂

CAMBRIDGE

Information
CAMBRIDGE FRIEND, (01223) 24 60 31.
LESBIAN LINE, (01223) 31 17 53, Fri 19:00-22:00.
WOMEN'S RESOURCE CENTRE, Hooper St, (01223) 32 11 48, lesbians meet odd Thurs 19:30."

Accommodations
PEAR TREE HOUSE, Chapel Road, West Row, Mildenhall, Suffolk, 1P28 8PA, (44-1638) 711 112 (Tel/Fax). Gay-owned & -operated 1770 country guesthouse with private & shared baths, full breakfast. ♀♂

Dance Bar/Disco
SISTER ACT, monthly women's disco, call leslbian line for info. 🍴 ♀
TASTY, Hills Rd, at Q-Club, (01223) 51 59 57, 2nd Thurs 22:00-01:00. 🍴 ♀♂

CANTERBURY

Information
EAST KENT FRIEND & GAY HELPLINE, (01843) 58 87 62, Tues 19:30-22:00. Gay Helpline: (01843) 45 48 68, Wed 20:00-08:00.
LESBIAN LINE, (01227) 46 45 70, Fri 19:00-22:00, ask about scheduled lesbian disco & bar nights.

Accommodations
FOXDEN, 5 Landon Rd, off Beltinge, Herne Bay, Kent, CT6 6HP, (44-1227) 363 514. A spacious 1920's home in a peaceful residential area 7 mi from Canterbury. Fine furnishings, private & shared baths, substantial breakfast, garden with fishponds, walk-through aviary. Walk to town centre, sea, cliff walks. Gay-owned, mostly hetero clientele.

CHELTENHAM

Information
AIDS LINE, (01242) 22 46 66, Mon, Wed 19:00-21:00.

CHESTER

Information
AIDS INFO, (01244) 40 04 15, 19:00-22:00.

CHESTERFIELD

Information
AIDS INFO, (01246) 55 94 31.

CHICHESTER

Bars
★ BUSH, THE, 16 The Hornet, (01243) 78 29 39, frequented by local gays. 🚫

COLCHESTER

Dance Bar/Disco
THELMA'S, Church St, at the Colchester Arts Centre, (01206) 57 73 01, 1st Fri 21:00-01:30. 🍴 ♀♂

CORNWALL

Accommodations
GLENCREE PRIVATE HOTEL, 2 Mennaye Rd, Penzance, Cornwall, TR18 4NG, (44-1736) 362026 (Tel/Fax). In US call (407) 994-3558, Fax: (407) 994-3634. Gay-owned guesthouse with drink license, 50% gay & lesbian clientele, private & shared baths, full English breakfast, beverage making facilities, colour TV, nearby pool & ocean beach."
PENRYN HOUSE, The Coombes, Polperro, Cornwall, PL13 2RQ, (44-1503) 272 157. Hotel in a Cornish fishing village, 30 minutes north of the city of Plymouth. Full English breakfast, ensuite baths, 50% gay & lesbian & 50% hetero clientele.
ROSEHILL IN THE FERN, Roseworthy, Camborne, Cornwall, TR14 0DU, (44-1209) 712 573. guesthouse, some hetero clientele, spacious double rooms, private baths, colour TV, full breakfast, extra charge for evening meal." ♀♂
RYN ANNETH, Southfield Place, St Ives, Cornwall, TR26 1RE, (44-1736) 793 247. bed & breakfast, cozy, comfortable

rooms, shared baths, lounge, full breakfast, nearby ocean beach." ♀♂

WOODBINE VILLA, Fore St, Grampound, near Truro, Cornwall, TR2 4QP, (44-1726) 882 005. bed & breakfast in a private home with sauna & gym, women welcome, shared baths, TV lounge with fireplace, full English breakfast." ♂

■ *Women's Accommodations*
CAPISTRANO, 1 Chy-an-Dour Square, Penzance, Cornwall, TR18 3LW, (44-1736) 364 189. women-only bed & breakfast, comfortable, homey room with sea view, color TV, beverage-making facilities, kitchen privileges, full breakfast, nearby pool & ocean beach." ♀

COTSWOLDS

■ *Accommodations*
CRESTOW HOUSE, Stow-on-the-Wold, Gloucestershire, GL54 1JY, (44-1451) 830 969, Fax: (44-1451) 832 129. Email: 100620.773@compuserve.com, Gay-friendly bed & breakfast in an 1870 country manor house, a 2hr drive from London. Antique furnishings, 12-foot ceilings, private baths, expanded English breakfast, colour TV, heated swimming pool."

COVENTRY

■ *Information*
AIDS LINE, (01203) 22 92 92.
COVENTRY FRIEND, (01203) 71 41 99, Mon-Fri 19:30-21:30."

■ *Dance Bar/Disco*
INDULGENCE, Lower Precinct, at Browns, gay dance night 1st Tues. ♀♂

■ *Retail & Bookstores*
WEDGE BOOKSHOP, 13 High St, general bookstore with gay & lesbian section.

CUMBRIA

■ *Women's Accommodations*
FAWCETT MILL FIELDS, Gaisgill, Tebay, Penrith, CA10 3UB, (44-15396) 244 08 (tel/fax) At England's largest women-only space, a creek, complete with footbridge & pattering waterfall, runs beside a venerable stone house surrounded by wooded acres so private that nudity is permitted. Women travellers are welcomed to this bit of unique, quiet England, where a series of 12 women's events are held each year. These include a lesbian bonfire weekend, Christmas & Easter events, a walking holiday, therapeutic lesbian workshops & circle dancing weekends. Packages for the events include all meals.

But you don't have to sign up for a special event in order to enjoy it here. The self-catering cottage & 2 b&b rooms in the main house are quite often available. And guests who simply want to enjoy the enchanting English setting are welcome to participate (or not) in whatever event is in progress at the time. ♀

Fawcett Mill Fields

- Lesbian Bonfire Weekend
- Christmas & Easter
- Therapeutic lesbian Workshops
- 12 Women's events per year
- Space often available for B&B
- Largest Women's facility in the UK

Cumbria
(44-15396) 24408
TEL/FAX

DARTFORD

■ Bars
A BIT ON THE SIDE, 201 Lowfield St, at Fox & Hounds, entrance at Phoenix Pl, (01322) 29 05 19. ♀♂

DERBY

■ Information
AIDS LINE, (01332) 29 07 66, 24hrs.
DERBY FRIEND, (01332) 349 333, Wed 19:00-22:00.

DERBYSHIRE

■ Accommodations
HODGKINSON'S HOTEL & RESTAURANT, South Parade, Matlock Bath, Derbyshire, DE4 3NR, (44-1629) 582 170, Fax: (44-1629) 584 891. Gay-owned hotel & hairdressing salon, 50% gay/lesbian, 50% hetero clientele, 6 double rooms, private baths, tea/coffee making facilities, sauna, full English breakfast."
OLD STATION HOUSE, THE, 4 Chatsworth Rd, Rowsley, Derbyshire, DE4 2EJ, (44-1629) 732 987. B&B, 60% gay & lesbian & 40% hetero clientele, 3 doubles, 1 shared bathroom, 1 toilet, TV lounge, full breakfast."

DEVON

■ Accommodations
BRIDGE STREET COTTAGE, Bridge Street, Sidmouth, EX10 0RU, (01395) 597 419. Thatched cottage with 3 double guest rooms in an ancient Saxon village in East Devon. ♀♂
MAYFAIR HOTEL & YE OLDE COTTAGE INNE, Lynway, Lynton, North Devon, EX35 6AY, (44-1598) 753 227. Hotel & inn with restaurant & bar, private baths, full English breakfast, color TV, stunning views of N Devon coast, near National Trust Coastal Path, Exmoor & beaches, 70% gay/lesbian clientele. ♀♂
POLLARDS, People's Park Road, Crediton, EX17 2DA, (44-1363) 777 613. Private house, women welcome, comfortably furnished rooms, beverage-making facilities, private baths, TV lounge, full English breakfast. ♂
TOR DOWN HOUSE, Belstone, Okehampton, Devon, EX20 1QY, (44-1837) 840 731. bed & breakfast guesthouse in Dartmoor National Park. Comfortable double rooms with four-poster beds, color TV, private baths, tea/coffee tray, full breakfast."

DONCASTER

■ Information
WOMEN'S CENTRE, 21 Cleveland St, social group for lesbians meets here.

DORSET

■ Accommodations
SUNRIDGE HOTEL, THE, Bleke Street, Shaftesbury, Dorset, SP7 8AW, (44-1747) 853 130, Fax: (44-1747) 852 139. Hotel with restaurant & bar, private baths, full breakfast, situated close to town centre. Mostly hetero with a gay & lesbian following.

EASTBOURNE

■ Accommodations
BATEMANS GUEST HOUSE, (44-1323) 640 756." Gay-owned, popular with lesbians. 2 suites with ensuite bathrooms, full English breakfast, 3- second walk to gay bar. ♀♂
FAIRLIGHT HOTEL, 41 Silverdale Rd, Eastbourne, East Sussex, BN20 7AT, (44-1323) 721 770. Gay-Friendly hotel & licensed bar near town center & the sea, private baths, colour TV, full English breakfast, games room, large garden."

■ Bars
HARTINGTON, THE, 89 Cavendish Place, (01323) 64 31 51. ♀♂

EXETER

■ Information
AIDS LINE, (01392) 41 16 00, Mon-Fri 19:00-22:00.

GLOUCESTER

■ Information
GLOUCESTER FRIEND, (01452) 30 68 00, Mon, Wed, Thurs 19:30-22:00."

GREAT YARMOUTH

■ Dance Bar/Disco
KINGS WINE BAR, 42 King St, (01493) 85 53 74, gays in the rear bar. 🍽 ♂

HARLOW

■ Information
HARLOW LESBIAN & GAY SWITCHBOARD, (01279) 63 96 37, Tues, Thurs, Sun 20:00-23:00, Fri 20:00-24:00. Women answer Sun."

RUBY'S LESBIAN & GAY CENTRE, Wych Elm, (01279) 45 16 77, 19:00-23:00, Thurs till 24:00, Fri-Sat till 02:00. Call for scheduled men-only & women-only Wed.

HASTINGS - E. SUSSEX

■ Information
AIDS LINE, (01424) 42 99 01.

HASTINGS BEFRIENDERS & LESBIAN LINE, (01424) 44 47 77, Wed 19:00-21:00.

■ Accommodations
SHERWOOD GUEST HOUSE, 15 Grosvenor Crescent, St Leonards-on-Sea, Hastings, E Sussex, TM38 0AA, (44-1424) 433 331. 30% gay/lesbian clientele, private & shared baths, color TV, beverage-making facilities, morning call for breakfast, near ocean beach.

HUDDERSFIELD

■ Information
AIDS LINE, (01484) 43 24 33.

LESBIAN & GAY SWITCHBOARD, (01484) 53 80 70, Sun & Tues 19:00-21:00. Ask about women's socials."

■ Bars
GREYHOUND, THE, 16 Manchester Rd, (01484) 42 07 42. ♀♂

HULL

■ Information
AIDS INFO, (01482) 32 70 60.

HULL FRIEND, (01482) 44 33 33, Mon & Thurs 20:00-22:00, Sat 19:00-21:00, ask about scheduled events.

LESBIAN LINE, (01482) 321 43 31, Mon 19:00-21:00, or tape."

■ Bars
POLAR BEAR, THE, 229 Spring Bank, (01482) 32 39 59, frequented by gays, many women."🚳

■ Retail & Bookstores
PAGE ONE BOOKS, 9 Princess Ave, (01482) 34 19 25, general bookstore with women's & gay section.

IPSWICH

■ Information
AIDS LINE, (01473) 23 20 07, Tues, Fri 19:30-22:00.

GAY & LESBIAN SWITCHBOARD, (01473) 23 22 12, Tues & Sat 19:30-21:30."

■ Bars
QUEEN'S HEAD, 1 Civic Dr, (01473) 25 41 59 discreetly frequented by local gays.

■ Dance Bar/Disco
OLIVE LEAF, THE, St Helen St, (01473) 25 86 33, Lesbian group meets alternate Mon. ♀

ISLE OF WIGHT

■ Information
HELP LINE, (01923) 52 51 23, Wed & Sat 19:30-22:00 or tape.

■ Accommodations
BERRY BROW HOTEL, Shanklin, (44-1983) 862 825, Fax: (44-1983) 865 995. Gay-friendly hotel with all ensuite baths, special discount gay weekend breaks, including ferry fare. 🚳

EDGECLIFFE HOTEL, THE, 7 Clarence Gardens, Shanklin, Isle of Wight, PO3 6HA, (44-1983) 866 199 (Tel/Fax). Gay-owned hotel with bar & small fitness room, private & shared baths, full breakfast, colour TV, coffee & tea-making facilities. Close to cliff edge walk & ocean, 33% gay & lesbian clientele.

■ Women's Accommodations
RIDGE COTTAGE, Sandy Way, Shorwell, Isle of Wight, PO30 3LN, (44-1983) 740 980." Women-only B&B 1-1/2 miles from the coast, surrounded by peaceful downland. Private & shared baths, full or continental breakfast, supper optional, coffee & tea-making facilities, log fire, colour TV. ♀

■ Restaurants
COTTAGE RESTAURANT, 8 Eastcliff Rd, Shanklin Old Village, (01983) 86 25 04. 🚳

LAKE DISTRICT

■ Accommodations
HOLLY PARK HOUSE, 1 Park Rd, Windermere, Cumbria, LA23 2AW, (44-

15394) 42107, Fax: (44-15394) 48997. Gay-owned & -operated guesthouse with bar, 1 mile from lake & near many areas of natural beauty, 5-min walk to bus & train station. Private baths, full breakfast, colour TV, coffee & tea-making facilities. Gay/lesbian following.

LANCASHIRE

■ Accommodations
HOLMERE HALL HOTEL, Milnthorpe Road, Carnforth, Lancashire, LA5 9SN, (44-1524) 735353 (Tel/Fax). gay-friendly 17th-century coaching inn & romantic period restaurant in a country setting, an artist's or walker's paradise, private & shared baths, full English breakfast, call for directions. Renovating after fire. To reopen in '98.

LANCASTER

■ Information
GAY & LESBIAN SWITCHBOARD, (01524) 84 74 37, Thurs & Fri 19:00-21:00, ask about lesbian socials.

■ Dance Bar/Disco
WOMEN'S DISCO, Penny St, Farmers Arms, women-only disco, Fri from 20:00.

LEAMINGTON SPA

■ Bars
SLUG & LETTUCE, Clarendon St, (01926) 33 93 66, women's bar night every other Sun 19:00-22:30. ♀

LEEDS

■ Information
AIDS LINE, (0113) 242 32 04. "
GAY SWITCHBOARD & LESBIAN LINE, (0113) 245 35 88, 19:00-22:00. Women answer Tues 19:30-21:30.

■ Bars
★ **NEW PENNY**, Call Lane, pub with shows, women welcome.
OLD RED LION, Meadow Lane, near Leeds Bridge, pub, women welcome. ♂
QUEENS COURT, Lower Briggate, (0113) 245 9449, 21:00-02:00.
TRASH, Roundhay Rd, in Astoria, (0831) 55 72 20, every other Fri 22:00-02:00, many women. ♀♂

■ Dance Bar/Disco
★ **CONFETTIS**, at Primos 2 bar location, (0113) 238 09 99, 1st Tues 14:00-06:00. After hours breakfast at Primos 2 bar 02:00-06:00. ♂

LEICESTER

■ Information
AIDS INFO, (0116) 255 99 95.
GAY & LESBIAN LINES, (0116) 255 06 67, Mon-Fri 19:30-22:00, women answer Tues.

■ Bars
MAGAZINE, Newark St, (0116) 254 05 23, bar, frequented by gays. Women-only evenings every other Wed.

■ Cafe
LESBIAN & GAY LINE COFFEE BAR, 15 Wellington St, Thurs, Fri 12:00-14:00, Sat 10:30-17:00. Women-only Wed 12:00-14:00. ♀♂

LINCOLN

■ Information
AIDS LINE, (01522) 51 39 99, Tues & Thurs 09:00-17:30. Mon, Wed, Fri till 19:00.
LESBIAN & GAY SWITCHBOARD, (01522) 53 55 53, Thurs & Sun 19:00-22:00. Women answer Tues."

LIVERPOOL

■ Information
AIDS LINE, (0151) 709 90 00, Mon-Wed & Fri 19:00-21:00.
LIVERPOOL FRIEND LINES, (0151) 708 95 52, 19:00-22:00, women answer Tues & Thurs.

■ Bars
★ **PACO'S BAR**, 25 Stanley St, (0151) 236 97 37, 2 bars. ♂

■ Dance Bar/Disco
GARLANDS, 8-10 Eberle St, (0151) 236 33 07, 12:00-21:00 (Fri, Sat till 02:00), closed Sun. ♂

LONDON INTRO

PUB HOURS, A FREQUENTLY-USED TERM IN LONDON, MEANS A PUB, is open Mon-Sat 11:00-23:00, Sun 12:00-15:00 & 19:00-22:30. Special note is made when a pub is open all day.

UK - ENGLAND

■ Information
AIDS INFO, (0800) 61 62 12 (toll-free national line); Body Positive (0171) 373 91 24; Positively Women (0171) 713 02 22.
BLACK LESBIAN & GAY HELPLINE, (0171) 620 38 85, Tues & Thurs 11:00-17:30.
LESBIAN & GAY SWITCHBOARD, (0171) 837 73 24, 24hrs.
LESBIAN LINE, (0171) 251 69 11, Mon & Fri 14:00-22:00, Tues-Thurs 19:00-22:00.
NORTH LONDON LINE, (0171) 607 83 46.
SHAKTI, South Asian Lesbian & Gay Network, meets 2nd & 3rd Sun 15:00 & scheduled monthly socials. Call for details (0171) 837 73 41.

LONDON EARLS COURT

■ Accommodations
BROMPTON'S GUEST HOUSE, PO Box 629, London SW5 9XF. Tel: (44-171) 373 6559, Fax: (44-171) 370 3583. Email: brompton@dircon.co.uk. Exclusively gay (mostly men). Ten tastefully-decorated rooms with direct-dial phones, coffee and teamaking facilities, TV, private and shared baths. Located in heart of Gay London. ♂
NEW YORK HOTEL, THE, 32 Philbeach Gardens, Earls Court, London, SW5 9EB, (44-171) 244 6884, Fax: (44-171) 370 4961. Hotel, spacious, well-decorated rooms with modern conveniences, most with en suite bathrooms, Jacuzzi, expanded continental breakfast, 90% men, women welcome. ♂

■ Bars
BRANDED, at the Garage, upper level, across from Highbury & Islington tube, alt Fri 22:00-03:00. 🍴 ♀

■ Restaurants
NEW YORK RESTAURANT, at the New York Hotel, (0171) 244 68 84, open 19:30-23:30.
ROY'S RESTAURANT, 234 Old Brompton Rd, (0171) 373 99 95. ♀♂

LONDON EAST

■ Information
WOMEN'S CENTRE, 109 Hoe St, (0181) 520 53 18, lesbian social odd Thurs 19:30-22:00.

Bromptons
GUESTHOUSE
in the Centre
of Gay London
(44-171) 373 6559

■ Bars
H20, 130 Balls Pond Rd, (0171) 354 06 11, from 16:00 (Fri-Sun from 14:00). Different themes & DJs nightly, scheduled rubber, fetish & underwear nights. 🍴 🍴 📺 ♂
HER SHE BAR, 88-89 Cowcross St, at Jacomo's, (0171) 553 76 41. ♀
RAW, 120 Romford Rd, at The Pigeons, (0181) 534 19 55 Sat 21:00-02:00. 🍴 ♀♂
WOODMAN, THE, 119-121 Stratford High Rd (Stratford tube), (0181) 519 8765, traditional pub, pub hours, cabaret, 70% men. ♪♂

■ Dance Bar/Disco
POPSTARZ, 121 Holborn, at Leisure Lounge, big gay Indian rock & pop night, Fri 22:00-05:00. 🍴 ♀♂
REFLECTIONS, 8 Bridge Rd, (Stratford tube), Stratford, (0181) 519 12 96, pub with cabaret & weekend disco, 21:00-02:00 (Fri, Sat till 05:00), Sun 12:00-01:00. 🍴 🍴 🍴 ♀♂
TURNMILLS, 63b Clerkenwell St, (Farringdon tube), popular venue with a changing schedule of special nights. Ask locally for schedule. 🍴 ♂

■ Restaurants
LE TIGRE ET LA GRENOUILLE, 261 Bethnal Green Rd, (Bethnal Green tube), (0171) 729 0829 French cuisine.

LONDON NORTH

■ Women's Accommodations
HELEN AND KATE'S B & B, (44-181) 809 0891." London's only women's inn for women who want to see London while staying in a private women's home. Two available rooms with shared bath/shower, buffet breakfast. ♀

■ Bars
BAR 269, 269a West End Lane, West Hampstead, intimate cabaret, 18:00-23:00 (Sun 12:00-15:00 & 19:00-22:30). 🏠♫♂

BLACK CAP, 171 Camden High St (Camden Town tube), (0171) 428 27 21 dance bar & cabaret nightly. Upstairs quiet bar (Shufflewick's), daily 12:00-02:00, Sun till 24:00; Downstairs cabaret & dancing, from 21:00. 📺♫♀♂

CLUB KALI, 1 Darmouth Park Hill, at Dome, South Asian club meets 3rd Fri. Arabic, Hindi & house music. 📺♀♂

DUE SOUTH, 35 Stoke Newington High St, (0171) 249 75 43, from 16:00 (Sat, Sun from 13:00).Thurs women only. 📺♂

DUKE OF WELLINGTON, 119 Balls Pond Rd (Dalston Kingsland BR), (0171) 249 37 29, pub, Mon-Sat 12:00-24:00, Sun pub hours, some hetero clientele." ♂

KING EDWARD V I, 25 Bromfield St, (Angel tube), (0171) 704 07 45, cafe upstairs, patio, daily 12:00-24:00 (Sun till 23:30)." ✕ ♂

OAK, THE, 79 Green Lanes, use bus route, (0171) 354 2791, live bands, disco weekends, popular with women. Women-only 21:00-02:00. ✕ ♀♂

RAM BAR, 39 Queens Head St, (0171) 154 0576. 🏠♂

SHAKTI, 1 Dartmouth Park Hill, at the Dome, club for gay & lesbian Asians, last Fri. 📺♀♂

■ Dance Bar/Disco
CLUB V, Highbury Corner, at The Garage (Highland & Islington tube), (0171) 607 18 18, 21:00-03:00, gay & lesbian dance night alternate Sat, Indian rock music. 📺♀♂

GIRLZONE, 240 Amherst Rd, at Trenz, Fri 22:00-04:00. 📺♀

KISS, 79 Green Lanes, at The Oak, women-only 21:00-02:00. 📺♀

■ Restaurants
OF A FEATHER, 4 New College Parade, (0171) 722 4272, British cuisine, 12:00-15:00 & 18:00-23:30 (closed Sat, Sun).

■ Retail & Bookstores
COMPENDIUM BOOKSHOP, 234 Camden High Street, (Camden Town tube), (0171) 485 89 44, general bookshop with gay & lesbian section.

GAY'S THE WORD BOOKSHOP, 66 Marchmont St, (Russell Sq tube), (0171) 278 76 54. Gay & lesbian books, magazines, newspapers, tapes, Mon-Sat 10:00-18:30 (Sun 14:00-18:00).

HOUSMAN'S, 5 Caledonia Rd, (0171) 837 44 73, radical bookshop, 10:00-18:30 (closed Sun).

KILBURN BOOKSHOP, 8 Kilburn Bridge, (0171) 328 70 71, general bookstore with gay & lesbian titles.

■ Erotica
SH!, 43 Coronet St, (0171) 613 54 58, erotica exclusively for women, closed Sun.

LONDON SOUTH

■ Information
BLACK LESBIAN & GAY CENTRE, 5 Westminster Bridge Rd, (0171) 620 38 85.

WOMEN'S CENTRE, 13 Woodside Green, Croydon, lesbian group meets Thurs 20:00.

■ Accommodations
NUMBER SEVEN GUESTHOUSE, 7 Josephine Ave, London, SW2 2JU, (44-181) 674 1880, Fax: (44-181) 671 6032. Email: hotel@no7.com, Web: http://www.no7.com, An exclusively gay & lesbian guesthouse, voted Hotel/Guesthouse of the Year in 1994 & 1995 by readers of The Pink Paper. All rooms have private bathroom en-suite, tasteful furnishings, cable TV, and direct-dial phones. Free parking and car service available. Situated in a tree-lined avenue just five minutes' walk to gay clubs and 10 minutes by tube to the theatre district and the Soho gay village. ♀♂

■ Bars
CHUNKKIES, 349 Kennington Lane, (Vauxhall tube), at Dukes bar, (0171) 793 09 03, for large men & women. ♂

UK - ENGLAND 147

DIVA DIVE, 64 Wilton Rd, lesbians over 30 yrs old. 🏠 ♀
FATHER RED CAP, 319 Camberwell Rd, (0171) 708 4474, cabaret, 12:00-24:00 (Fri, Sat till 01:00, Sun till 23:00). Women in upper level bar 21:00-02:00. 🍴 ♀♂
ORANGE, THE, 118 Lower Rd, (Surrey Quays tube), (0171) 237 22 24. Bar, disco, cabaret, 19:30-24:00 (Thurs-Sat till 01:00) 🎵 🏠 ♂
PRINCESS OF WALES, 18 Wilmount St, (Woolwich Arsenal British Rail), (0181) 316 02 29 11:00-23:00 (Sun12:00-22:30). 🎵 ♂
PROHIBITION BAR, 2a Sunny Hill Rd, at the Greenhouse cafe bar., ♀♂
VIXENS AT VAUXHALL, 372 Kennington Lane (Vauxhall tube), at the Royal Vauxhall Tavern, (0171) 582 08 33, pub dance night Fri 19:00-02:00. 🏠 🎵 ♀
WOOLWICH INFANT, 9 Plumstead Rd, (Woolwich Arsenal British Rail), (0181) 854 37 12 pub hours, Mon women-only. 🎵 🏠 ♀♂

■ *Dance Bar/Disco*
BULK, at The Hoist location, Thurs night for big men & women and their admirers. Buffed-out strippers, cruisy. 🏠 ♂
DIAMONDS, at Jacque of Clubs, 47 Ossory Rd, near Old Kent Rd, (0171) 252 0007, Sat 21:00-04:00. 🏠 ♀
FRIDGE, THE, Town Hall Parade, Brixton Hill, (Brixton tube)., (0171) 326 5100. men's & women's theme nights, constantly changing. Call for current schedule.Thurs women-only, Sat Love Muscle. 🏠 🍸 ♀♂

■ *Restaurants*
GREEN ROOM, 62 Lavender Hill, Battersea, (Clapham Jct BR), (0171) 233 46 18. Vegetarian & vegan cuisine, daily 19:00-late (Sat also 12:00-16:00), live jazz Fri." 🎵 🏠

■ *Retail & Bookstores*
INDEX BOOK CENTRE, 10-12 Atlantic Rd, Brixton, general bookstore with gay & lesbian titles.

LONDON WEST

■ *Accommodations*
ARGYLE HOUSE, in Ealing, West London, (Ealing Broaday tube), (44-181) 987 9461, Fax: (44-181) 995 1813. Email: info@argyle.co.uk, Web: www.argyle.co.uk, Elegant Edwardian house, shared baths, continental breakfast. Gay men & lesbians welcome.
HESPER LEWIS HOTEL, 111 Ebury St, Belgravia, London, SW1 W9QU, (44-171) 730 2094, Fax: (44-171) 730 8697. Gay-owned B&B hotel, 50% gay & lesbian clientele, private & shared baths, TV, mini-bars, coffee & tea-making facilities. 🏠

■ *Bars*
BLARNEY STONE, 48a High St, (0181) 992 15 68 gay Irish pub, 20:00-23:00 (Sun 15:00-22:30). 🎵 ♀♂
GEORGE MUSIC BAR, 114 Twickenham Rd (Isleworth BR), (0181) 560 1456, traditional pub with cabaret, pub hours. 🏠 🍸 ♀♂
GIRLFRIEND, 30 Lisle St, (181) 809 1777, Thurs. ♀
QUEEN'S ARMS, 223 Hanworth Rd (Hounslow Central tube), Hounslow, (0181) 570 9724, pub with cabaret nightly, pub hours. 🎵 ♀♂
REEVES, 48 Shepherd's Bush Green, at Reeves Hotel, (0181) 740 11 58. ♀
SHE'S OUT, 4 George St (enter from Manchester St), at Westmoreland Arms, 2nd Sat 19:30-23:00. ♀
TED'S PLACE, 305a Northend Rd, (West Kensington tube), (0171) 385 93 59, from 19:00 (closed Mon), Sat disco, many women, TV & TS. Women-only Fri from 20:00. 🏠 ♀♂

Number Seven
GUESTHOUSE

Best UK Gay Hotel

7 Josephine Ave • LONDON
(44 181) 674 1880

UK - ENGLAND

VALE BAR, 99 Chippenham Rd, Maida Vale, (0171) 286 72 24 11:00-23:00 (Fri 12:00-24:00, Sun 12:00-22:00). ♀♂

■ Dance Bar/Disco
GREYHOUND, Junction 5, M4, near A4 Colnbrook Bypass., 🎵 ♀♂

MFSB, 10 Beak St, at Cairo Jacks (Oxford Circus tube), Sun 21:00-01:00. 🎵

■ Restaurants
BALANS WEST, 239 Old Brompton Rd, 08:00-01:00, 7 days. 🍽

LA LIBERTÉ, 32 Philbeach Gardens, at the New York Hotel, French & English cuisine. 🍽

LE GOURMET, 312 Kings Rd, 7 days. 🍽

LO SPUTINO, 130 Kings Rd, bar & restaurant. 🍽

LONDON WEST END

■ Accommodations
CLONE ZONE LUXURY APARTMENTS, 64 Old Compton St, Soho, London, W1, Reservations: (44-171) 287 3530, Fax: (44-171) 287 3531. This self-contained, modern apartment is equipped with many amenities including AC, phone, fully fitted kitchen, bathroom with bath and shower and a spacious lounge. It is situated in the heart of London's lesbian & gay area, two floors above, but completely separate from, the Clone Zone shop. Women welcome. ♂

NOEL COWARD HOTEL, 111 Elbury St, Belgravia, London, SW1W 9QU, (44-171) 730 2094, Fax: (44-171) 730 8697. Terrace house hotel, once home of Noel Coward. Private & shared baths, full English breakfast, some hetero clientele. ♀♂

RUSSELL LODGE GUEST HOUSE, 20 Little Russell St, London, WC1A 2HN, (44-171) 430 2489, Fax: (44-171) 430 0755. B&B with private & shared baths, continental breakfast, cable TV, a 5 min walk to gay bars. ♂

SOHO GUESTROOMS & APARTMENTS, Charing Cross Road at Oxford St, (underground: Tottenham Court Road), Reservations: (44-973) 167 103. Tel/Fax: (44-171) 497 7010. Web: www.leedsnet.com/accom1.htm, Three deluxe guestrooms, suite with balcony or self-contained private apartments in a unique West End location! Daily, weekly or monthly rates include breakfast, 24-hour unlimited tea, coffee, juices, etc. Also included are wine, chocolates, fruit on arrival, colour TV, alarm-clock/radio, hair dryer, toiletries, giant towels, steam iron and free, unlimited laundry facilities. Some hetero clientele. ♀♂

■ Bars
A TRULY WESTERN EXPERIENCE, 16-22 Great Russell St, at Central Club., 🎵 U ♀♂

BAR AQUDA, 13 &14 Maiden Ln, (Covent Garden tube), (0171) 557 9891. 🍽 ♀♂

BAR, THE, 36 Hanway St, (Tottenham Court tube), (0171) 580 98 11 DJs Wed-Thurs, Sat. 🎵 ♂

BOX, THE, 32-34 Monmouth St, Seven Dials, (0171) 240 58 28, cafe, brasserie & bar, Mon-Sat 11:00-23:00, Sun 12:30-22:30. Sun 19:00-23:00 women only. 🍽 ♀♂

CANDY BAR, 4 Carlisle St, men welcome as guests. Changing schedule of special nights, ask locally for schedule. ♀

DRILL HALL, THE, 16 Chenies St (Goodge St tube), (0171) 631 13 53, women only Mon 17:30-23:00, also women-only at the Greenhouse vegetarian restaurant next door, downstairs. 🍽 ♀

EDGE, THE, 11 Soho Square, Soho, (Tottenham Court Rd. tube), (0171) 439 13 13, continental café & bar, 12:00-01:00, Sun 12:00-22:30. 🍽 ♀♂

FIRST OUT, 52 St. Giles High St, (Tottenham Court Rd tube), (0171) 240 80 42, cafe bar, 10:00-23:00 (Sun 12:00-22:30). Women-only Thurs (men welcome as guests). 🎵 🍽 ♀♂

FREEDOM, 60 Wardour St (Piccadilly Circus tube), (0171) 734 0071, cafe, bar & theater, 2 floors, stylish bar serving food & fancy drinks, downstairs bar open late, 10:00-22:30 (Sun till 23:00). 🎵 ♀♂

GIRL FRIDAY, 52 St. Giles High St, at First Out (Tottenham Court tube), women's night Fri 20:00-23:00, men welcome as guests. ♀

MADAME JO JO'S, 8-10 Brewer St (Piccadilly Circus tube), (0171) 734 24 73, showbar with major drag extravaganza mainly for hetero audience, Mon-Sat 22:00-03:00. 🍽 🎵 🎶 ✈

RETRO BAR, 2 George Ct, (Charing Cross tube), 12:00-23:00 (Sun till 22:30), DJs. ♂

★ **SEVENTYNINE CXR,** 79 Charing Cross Rd, (Tottenham Ct Rd or Leicester Square tubes), (0171) 734 0769, 13:00-02:00 (Sun 13:00-22:30), variety of gay & lesbian clientele. 🍽 ♂

SHAHARA, 4-5 Neals Yard, at Euton's, (0171) 379 68 77, very upscale women-only piano bar." ♀

WALTZING WITH HILDA, Great Russell St, at the Central Club Hotel, ballroom dancing, Fri 20:30-23:30 (classes 19:00-20:30). 🍽 ♀

WOW BAR, 15 Golden Sq, at the Global Bar, Sat 20:00-24:00. ♀

■ Dance Bar/Disco

ACE OF CLUBS, at 52 Piccadilly, (Piccadilly tube), (0171) 408 44 57, women-only dance night Sat 21:30-04:00. 🍽 ♀

DUCKIE, Great Queen St, Connaughts Brasserie, (0171) 582 0833, Fri 22:00-03:00. 🍽 ♂

★ **G. A. Y.,** 157 Charing Cross Rd (Tottenham Ct tube), at Astoria, (0171) 734 69 63, large dance bar, gay nights Mon, Thurs & Sat 22:30-04:00, trendy crowd. 🍽 ♀♂

★ **HEAVEN,** The Arches, Villiers St (Charing Cross, or Embankment tube), (0171) 930 20 20, gigantic complex with huge disco and multiple other bar venues and a changing schedule of special nights for gays & lesbians, Tues & Wed 22:30-03:00, Fri & Sat 21:30-03:00. Call for current schedule of men's, women's & mixed nights. 🍽 ♪ 🎵 ♂

MIS-SHAPES, 37 & 39 Oxford St, at Plastic People, Indie pop music, 22:00-02:00. 🍽 ♀♂

RENEGADE RANCH, Great Russell St, at Central Club Hotel, c&w dance bar, Fri from 20:00. ∪ 🍽 ♂

SALSA ROSADA, 1A Dean St, (0171) 287 96 08 gay salsa dance club, alternate Sat 21:00-02:00, classes on Wed. 🍽

SOUNDSHAFT, Hungerford Ln, popular venue with a changing schedule of special nights. Ask locally for schedule. 🍽 ♂

CENTRAL LONDON
In The Heart Of The West-End On The Soho and Covent Garden borders
DELUXE GUESTROOMS/APARTMENTS

DAILY, WEEKLY & MONTHLY RATES
including breakfast, free laundry, unlimited refreshments plus wine, chocolates & fruit
Call JAMES at SOHO GUESTROOMS on:
+44(0) 973 167 103
or Tel/Fax: +44(0) 171 497 7010

■ Restaurants

BALANS, 60 Old Compton St, (Leicester Square tube), (0171) 437 52 12, 08:00-05:00. ♀♂

NUSA DUA, 11 Dean St, near Soho Square, (0171) 437 3559, Indonesian cuisine, 7 days. 🔲

ROSSANA'S, 17 Strutton Ground, off Victoria St, (0171) 233 17 01, restaurant & bar, vegetarian cuisine, Wed-Fri 19:00-23:00 women-only. " ♀

■ Retail & Bookstores

RAINBOW, 52 Dean St, gay gift shop.

SILVER MOON, 64-68 Charing Cross Rd, (Leicester Square tube), (0171) 836 79 06, feminist bookshop, 10:00-18:30 (Thurs till 20:00, Sun 12:00-20:00).

LOUGHBOROUGH

■ Bars

WOMEN'S BAR NIGHT, Fennel St, at the Labour Club, (01509) 23 56 10, even Mons 20:30. ♀

MANCHESTER

■ Information

AIDS LINE, (0161) 237 97 17.

LESBIAN & GAY SWITCHBOARD, (0161) 274 39 99, daily 16:00-22:00."

MANCHESTER GAY CENTRE, 49-51 Sidney St, (0161) 274 38 14.

UK - ENGLAND

■ Accommodations
CARLTON HOTEL, 153 Upper Chorlton Rd, Whalley Range, Manchester, M16 7SH, (44-161) 881 4635. Hotel located above a gay men's sauna (separate entrance). 15 rooms with private & shared baths, full English breakfast, colour TV. TV lounge & bar area for guests, hotel is 1-1/2 miles from city centre & gay bars." ♀♂

CLONE ZONE MANCHESTER HOLIDAY APARTMENT, 39 Bloom St, Manchester, M1 3LY, (44-161) 236 1398, Fax: (44-161) 236 5178. apartment in the heart of the gay & lesbian village, 2 floors above Clone Zone store, color TV, bath/shower, kitchen, tea/coffee-making facilities, near tourist attractions & metro, bus & rail stations. ♀♂

REMBRANDT HOTEL, 33 Sackville St, Manchester, M1 3LZ, (44-161) 236 1311, Fax: (44-161) 236 4257. hotel with 2 gay bars & restaurant, women welcome, shared baths, full English breakfast, color TV." ♂

ROYAL CROWN HOTEL, 37 Swan St, (0161) 8394424. Hotel with bar, 20%-30% gay & lesbian clientele on weekends, color TV, minutes from clubs, pubs, full English breakfast, phone 24 hours.

■ Bars
AUSTIN'S, 63 Richmond St, in back of New Union Pub, (0161) 236 15 47, daily 22:00-02:00, closed Sun. ♂

MANTO, 46 Canal St, (0161) 236 26 67, café bar & art gallery, 12:00-23:30 (Sun 12:00-23:00). After hours breakfast Fri-Sat 02:00-06:00. ♂

NEW YORK, NEW YORK, 98 Bloom St, (0161) 236 65 56, 12:00-23:00. Upper level men-only Fri-Sat 20:00-02:00. 🍴♂

★ **REMBRANDT HOTEL BAR,** 33 Sackville St, (0161) 236 24 35, 236 11 31, hotel, bar & restaurant, lesbians welcome, open daily 11:00-23:00, Sun lunch. Fri women-only upstairs bar. ✕ ♀♂

SAPPHO'S BAR, at Rembrandt Hotel (upstairs), women-only, Fri." ♀

STAR & GARTER, 18-20 Fairfield St, (0161) 273 67 26, 3rd Fri. ♀♂

UNIVERSAL, Canal St, below Blooms Hotel, at Village Edge, women's bar night, Sat 22:00-02:00. 🍴♀

■ Dance Bar/Disco
CENTRAL PARK, Sackville St, (0161) 237 59 19, pub & cabaret, late dance night Sun 02:30-12:00, women-only disco Fri upstairs. 🎵🍴♀♂

CLIMAX, 11-13 New Wakefield St, at Generation X, (0161) 236 48 99, women-only dance night, 1st Thurs 22:00-03:00. 🍴♀

GLIDE, 42 Charles St, (0161) 273 37 22. 🍴♂

PARADISE FACTORY, 112 Paradise St, (0161) 273 5422, 4-floor dance club, Fri-Sat from 20:00, Fri women-only on top level. 🍴♂

SARSPARILLA, 112 Paradise St, at Paradise Factory, lesbian disco Sat 22:00-03:00. 🍴♀

TIME, 48 Princess St, (0161) 237 99 24,"" Ask about gay & lesbian dance nights. Call 2 days ahead for membership. 🍴⚥

■ Cafe
★ **BLOOM STREET CAFE,** 39 Bloom St, (0161) 236 34 33, closed Sun ♀♂

THAT CAFE, 1013 Stockport Rd, Levenshulme, (0161) 432 46 72, cafe, Tues-Sat from 18:00, Sun 12:00-15:00. ⚥

■ Restaurants
BALEARICA, 42 Charles St, at Glide, (0161) 273 37 22, restaurant & bar, Mediterranean cuisine. ♂

BLUE RESTAURANT, 29 Sackville St, (0161) 236 00 74, till 24:00. ⚥

■ Retail & Bookstores
FRONTLINE, 1 Newton St, radical bookstore with gay & lesbian section, 10:00-18:00 (Sat from 09:00), closed Sun.

MIDDLESBROUGH

■ Information
AIDS LINE, (01642) 24 45 58.

LESBIAN LINE, (01642) 21 79 55, Mon 20:00-22:00.

MIDDLESBROUGH FRIEND, (01642) 24 88 88, Tues & Fri 19:30-21:30.

NEWCASTLE-UPON-TYNE

■ Information
AIDS INFO, (0191) 232 28 55, Mon-Fri 10:00-19:00, Sat till 16:00."

LESBIAN LINE, (0191) 261 22 77, Tues 19:00-22:00.

NEWCASTLE FRIEND, (0191) 261 85 55, Mon-Fri 19:00-22:00.

UK - ENGLAND

■ Accommodations
CHEVIOT VIEW GUEST HOUSE, 194 Station Rd, Wallsend, Newcastle, NE28 8RD, (44-191) 262 0125, mobile: (0378) 863 469, Fax: (44-191) 262 2626. guesthouse with cocktail bar for residents, women welcome, private & shared baths, colour TV, full English breakfast, pool & ocean beach nearby. ♀♂

■ Bars
BARKING DOG, THE, 15 Marlborough Crescent, (0191) 221 0775, upstairs bar women-only Wed & Fri." ♀

POWERHOUSE, Blenheim St at Waterloo St, (0191) 261 45 07, gay Mon, Thurs-Sat 22:00-01:00, back bar men only, some hetero clientele." 🍴 ♂

STRINGS, 29 Blenheim St, (0191) 232 35 30, pub, many women. 🍴 ✖ 🚫

■ Dance Bar/Disco
ROCKSHOTS, Waterloo St, (0191) 232 96 48, gay Mon, Wed, Thurs 23:00-02:00, Sat till 03:00, women welcome." 🍴 ♂

■ Retail & Bookstores
ALLEYCAT BOOKS COOP, 46 Low Friar St, (0191) 221 17 50, radical bookstore with gay & lesbian titles.

NORFOLK

■ Accommodations
BRIARS, Riverside, Reedham, Norwich, NR13 3TF, (44-1493) 700054 (Tel/Fax)." Guesthouse located midway between Norwich & Great Yarmouth. Rooms with private bathscolour TV, VCR. Private baths, full breakfast, some hetero clientele. ♀♂

NORTHAMPTON

■ Information
GAY & LESBIAN LINES, Men (01604) 359 75, Tues 18:30-21:30. Women 25 08 87, Wed 18:30-21:30. Ask about socials.

LESBIAN & GAY RESOURCE CENTRE, 61-69 Derngate, at Charles House, (01604) 28 986.

■ Bars
FUDGE, 39 Sheep St, at Kabana's, (01604) 78 76 41, 1st Fri. 🍴 ♂

NORWICH

■ Information
AIDS LINE, (01603) 61 58 16, Thurs 20:00-22:00, Sat 11:00-15:00, Sun 14:00-16:00."

NORWICH FRIEND & LESBIAN LINES, (01603) 62 80 55, Fri & Sun 19:00-21:00. Lesbian Line Tues 19:00-21:00.

■ Accommodations
LORD RAGLAN, THE, 30 Bishopbridge Road, Norwich, Norfolk, NR1 4ET, (44-1603) 623 304. B&B with gay bar, colour TV, 24-hr privacy access, coffee & tea-making facilities, short walk to city center. Mostly men with women welcome. ♂

■ Bars
CASTLE, 1 Spittlefields, near Ketts Mill, men welcome. ♂

CLOUDS, above 14/16 Lower Goat Lane, gay Sun from 20:00. ♂

LORD RAGLAN, THE, 30 Bishopbridge Rd, (01603) 62 33 04, 12:00-14:00 & 19:00-23:00 (Sun pub hours). ♂

■ Dance Bar/Disco
FIRST OUT, King St, at The Waterfront, (01603) 63 27 17, dance bar 1st Tues 20:00-24:30. 🍴 ♀♂

JIGSAW CLUB, Oak St, at The Talk club, Fri 22:00-02:00, men welcome. 🍴 ♀

■ Retail & Bookstores
BOOKMARK BOOKSTORE, 83 Unthank Rd, (01603) 76 28 55, general bookstore with gay & lesbian titles.

GREEN CITY CENTRAL, 42-46 Bethel St, general bookstore with gay & lesbian titles.

JT BOOKS, Dove St, (01603) 63 06 36, general bookstore with gay & lesbian section.

NOTTINGHAM

■ Information
GAY & LESBIAN SWITCHBOARD, (0115) 941 14 54, Mon-Fri 19:00-22:00.

LESBIAN CENTRE, 30 Chaucer St, in the Women's Centre, (0115) 948 36 97, scheduled events, lesbian group meets Fri 19:30-22:00, disco 1st Fri from 21:00. Univerifiable spring '97."

LESBIAN LINE, (0115) 941 06 52, Mon & Wed 19:30-21:00.

■ Bars
CELLO'S, Meadow Lane Stadium, at the Meadow Club, (0115) 961 73 89, women-only with no-smoking bar 4th Sat. ♀

OLDHAM

Information
LESBIAN & GAY SWITCHBOARD, (0161) 678 94 48, Tues 19:00-21:00, ask about socials.

OXFORD

Information
AIDS LINE, (01865) 24 33 89.

GAY SWITCHBOARD, (01865) 79 39 99, 19:00-21:00.

LESBIAN LINE, (01865) 24 23 33, Wed 19:00-21:00.

OXFORD GAY & LESBIAN CENTRE, North Gate Hall, St Michael's St, (01865) 20 02 49, gay organization with disco, café & bar. Men-only Thurs 20:00-23:00; Fri women's disco night from 20:00; Sat disco 21:00-02:00. Café: Sat 12:00-16:00.

Retail & Bookstores
INNER BOOKSHOP, 111 Magdalen Rd, (01865) 24 53 01, alternative bookshop with gay & lesbian section, 10:00-17:30 (closed Sun)."

PETERBOROUGH

Information
AIDS LINE, (01733) 623 34, Tues & Thurs 19:30-21:30.

PETERBOROUGH FRIEND, (01733) 614 99, Tues & Thurs 19:30-21:30, or tape.

PLYMOUTH

Information
AIDS INFO, (01752) 66 36 09.

Retail & Bookstores
IN OTHER WORDS, 72 Mutley Plain, Devon, (0752) 663 889, general bookstore with gay & lesbian books and magazines.

PORTSMOUTH

Information
LESBIAN LINE, (01705) 87 69 99, Thurs 20:00-22:00.

Bars
DD'S, 164 Twyford Ave, at The Stamshaw Hotel, lower level, women-only bar Mon, Thurs & Sat 19:00-23:00, Sun lunch (closed 2nd Sat). ♀

TWO-WANDAZ, Eastgate St, at the Network Club, women's disco nights 1st & 3rd Thurs, 21:00-01:00. [♿] ♀

Dance Bar/Disco
FARPIES, Trafalgar Pl, Clive Rd, at the Fratton Community Centre, women-only disco, 2nd Sat 20:00-23:00, call lesbian line for details. [♿] ♀

PRESTON

Information
GAY SWITCHBOARD & LESBIAN LINE, (01772) 25 11 22, men answer Tues, Thurs, Fri 19:30-21:30, women answer Wed 19:30-21:30.

Restaurants
CANNONS, 37 Cannon St, (01772) 561 74, 11:00-14:00 & 19:00-23:00 (closed Sun, Mon).

READING

Information
AIDS LINE, (01734) 57 61 64, Mon-Thurs 17:00-21:00 or tape."

LESBIAN & GAY LINE, (01734) 59 72 69.

Bars
WYNFORD ARMS, 110 Kings Rd, 19:30-23:00 (Sat day & evening, Sun pub hours). ♀♂

ST. ALBANS

Information
AIDS INFO, (01462) 45 47 44, Mon-Fri 19:00-21:00.

SALISBURY

Information
GAY & LESBIAN SWITCHBOARD, (01722) 41 50 51, Wed 19:30-22:30, ask about scheduled cafe night.

SCARBOROUGH

Bars
BACCHUS, 7a Ramshill Rd, Fri & Sat. ♀♂

UK - ENGLAND

SHEFFIELD

Information
AIDS LINE, (0114) 275 55 00, Mon-Fri 19:00-22:00.

GAYPHONE, (0114) 258 81 99, Mon-Wed 19:30-21:30, ask about gay socials."

WOMEN'S CULTURAL CLUB, Paternoster Row, Workstation, (0114) 272 18 66, 11:00-23:00, scheduled socials, events, women's bar nights.

Bars
COSSACK, THE, 45 Howard St, (0114) 272 28 89, pub & disco, Fri women only. 🕍♂

Dance Bar/Disco
PLANET, 429 Effingham Rd, (0114) 244 90 33, 22:00-03:30 (Sun till 01:30), closed Mon & Tues. Women-only dance night last Wed. 🕍♂

QUEEN'S HOTEL, 85 Scotland St, (0114) 272 69 09, hotel with scheduled women-only dance nights. 🕍 ♀♂

SHREWSBURY

Bars
PEACH TREE, 21 Abbey Foregate, (01743) 35 50 55, gay Mon. ♀♂

Dance Bar/Disco
OVER THE BORDER, (01743) 36 86 91, Wed 19:30-22:30, line dancing. 🕍 ♀♂

Cafe
FRUIT BOWL, 1a Wyle Cop Steps, unit 3, Reilley Centre, Sat 12:00-17:00. ♀♂

SHROPSHIRE

Accommodations
COCKFORD HALL, Cockford Bank, Clun, Shropshire, SY7 8LR, (44-1588) 640 327, Fax: (44-1588) 640 881. Gay-friendly, luxury Georgian B&B, rural retreat on 20 acres above historic town of Clun. Full breakfast, 3-course dinner by arrangement at extra charge, all private baths.

SOMERSET

Accommodations
BALES MEAD, West Porlock, Somerset, TA24 8NX, (44-1643) 862565. country house B&B, private & shared baths, expanded continental or full breakfast, color TV, central heating, panoramic views of sea & countryside, 50% gay/lesbian clientele.

MANOR HOUSE FARM, Prestleigh, nr Shepton Mallet, Somerset, BA4 4NJ, (44-1749) 830 385 (Tel/Fax). Email: gayboyz2@aol.com, Web: http://users.aol.com/gayboyz2, bed & breakfast with restaurant, private & shared baths, TV lounge, coffe/tea making facilities, full breakfast." ♀♂

SOUTHAMPTON

Information
LESBIAN LINE, (01703) 40 51 11, Tues & Thurs 19:30-22:00.

SOLENT GAY SWITCHBOARD & AIDS INFO, (01703) 63 73 63, Mon-Fri 19:30-22:00.

Bars
ATLANTIC QUEEN, Bugle St, (01703) 22 91 46, piano bar, women welcome. ♂

NEW VIC, Northam Rd, Northam, (01703) 33 39 63, women-only 3rd Fri. ♀

STEPPING OUT, Compton Walk, at The Box, women-only Sat 20:00-02:00. 🕍 ♀

Retail & Bookstores
OCTOBER BOOKS, 4 Onslow Rd, (01703) 22 44 89, general bookstore with gay section.

SOUTHEND-ON-SEA

Information
AIDS LINE, (01702) 39 17 50, answers Mon-Fri 18:00-21:30.

SOUTHEND GAYLINE, (01702) 48 03 44.

STOCKPORT

Dance Bar/Disco
NEW INN, THE, 93 Wellington Rd South, (0161) 480 40 63. disco Fri & Sat, pub weekdays. 🕍♂

SUTTON-IN-ASHFIELD

Accommodations
CENTRAL HOTEL, 1 Station Rd, Sutton in Ashfield, Nottinghamshire, NG17 5FF, (44-1623) 552 373, Fax: (44-1623) 443 106. Gay-owned hotel with 20% gay & lesbian clientele, colour TV, late keys, private & shared baths.

SWANSEA

Information
WOMEN'S CENTRE, 228 High St.,

TORQUAY

Accommodations

CLIFF HOUSE HOTEL AT THE BEACH, St. Marks Rd, Meadfoot Beach, Torquay, TQ1 2EH, (44-1803) 294 656, Fax: (44-1803) 211 983. Luxury hotel overlooking ocean with restaurant & bar, rooms have bygone elegance with modern amenities, colour TV, coffee/tea making facilities, Jacuzzi, steam room, massage, gym, full English breakfast.

RAVENSWOOD HOTEL, 535 Babbacombe Rd, Torquay, South Devon, TQ1 1HQ, (44-1803) 292 900 (Tel/Fax). hotel & residents' bar, 20% gay/lesbian clientele, private & shared baths, full English breakfast, dinner optional, color cable TV, late night keys.

RED SQUIRREL LODGE, Chelston Rd, Torquay, TQ2 6PU, (44-1803) 605 496, Fax: (44-1803) 690 170. Email: squirrel@mail.zynet.com.co.uk, gay-friendly hotel with bar, elegant Victorian rooms, colour TV, beverage-making facilities, private baths, gardens, nearby ocean beach, full English breakfast."

TYNE - WEAR

Accommodations

STRATFORD LODGE, 8 Stratford Grove Terrace, Heaton, Newcastle upon Tyne, NE6 5BA, (44-191) 265 6395, mobile: (44-831) 879182. bed & breakfast, shared baths, colour satellite TV, beverage-making facilities, expanded continental breakfast, massage & solarium.

WARWICK

Bars

ANTELOPE INN PUB, Birmingham Rd, at The Antelope Inn, (01926) 49 90 35, from 19:00, 80% men, 20% women.

WARWICKSHIRE

Accommodations

ELLESMERE HOUSE, 36 Binswood Ave, Royal Leamington Spa, Warwickshire, CV32 5SQ, (44-1926) 424 618. Victorian bed & breakfast homestay, women welcome, spacious rooms with antique furnishings, private baths, color TV, full English breakfast.

WELLINGBOROUGH

Information

GAY INFO LINE, (01933) 271 1871, Thurs 19:00-22:00. Ask about gay & lesbian socials.

Bars

GAY & LESBIAN SOCIALS, 14 Havelock St, at Anchor House.,

WELLS-NEXT-THE-SEA

Accommodations

WARHAM OLD POST OFFICE COTTAGE, c/o Three Horseshoes Free House, In Warham near Wells-next-the-Sea, NR23 1NL, (44-1328) 710 547. Gay-owned bed & breakfast with restaurant & bar near North Norfolk Coast, private & shared baths, full English breakfast, TV lounge, 20% gay & lesbian clientele.

Bars

THREE HORSESHOES, Bridge Street, Warham, 4 miles from Walsingham, gay-friendly pub, frequented by gay men & women.

WOLVERHAMPTON

Information

AIDS LINE, (01902) 64 48 94, Mon, Tues & Thurs 09:00-17:00, Wed & Fri till 12:00.

Bars

BABE, Temple St, at the Dorchester Club, 1st Thurs.

GREYHOUND, 14 Bond St, (01902) 209 16, pub, women welcome.

LORD RAGLAN, Great Brickkiln St, (01902) 228 87, till 02:00 (Sun till 24:00).

YORK

Information

AIDS LINE, (01904) 63 95 95.

LESBIAN LINE, (01904) 64 68 12, Fri 19:00-21:00 or tape, ask about local lesbian group.

Accommodations

BULL LODGE, 37 Bull Lane, Lawrence St, York, YO1 3EN, (44-1904) 415522 (Tel/Fax). guesthouse, gay-friendly, comfortable rooms with beverage-making facilities, near pool & leisure center, full English breakfast, optional evening meal.

■ Bars
MILK & HONEY, Mickelgate, at the York Arts Centre, (01904) 62 71 29, 1st Fri 21:00-02:00. ♀♂

YORK ARMS, THE, 26 High Petergate, near the Minster, many gays. 🏳

■ Dance Bar/Disco
GUPPY'S, The Old Brit, Nunnery Lane, women's dance bar twice monthly, contact lesbian line for schedule." 🏳 ♀

YORKSHIRE

■ Accommodations
INTERLUDES, 32 Princess St, Old Town, Scarborough, North Yorkshire, Y011 1QR, (44-1723) 360 513, Fax: (44-1723) 368 597. Email: interludes@mcmail.com, Web: www.interludes.mcmail.com, This elegant Georgian townhouse with sea views is peacefully situated in a conservation area, yet close to beach & town centre. The hotel is licensed, and, because of our connections with the theatre, has a theatrical theme. Bedrooms are well equipped. Scarborough, an attractive resort, is an ideal centre for exploring nearby N. Yorkshire Moors Nat'l Park and the historical towns of York and Whitby. 50% gay & lesbian clientele

SUN HOTEL, 124 Sunbridge Rd, Bradford, W Yorkshire, BD1 2ND, (44-1274) 737 722, Fax: (44-1274) 738 364. Hotel with gay & lesbian pub, shared baths (planning en suite facilities), English breakfast, color TV, near Lake District. ♀♂

U K - NORTHERN IRELAND

COUNTRY CODE: (44),

BELFAST

■ Information
AIDS LINE, (01232) 24 92 68.

CARA FRIEND, (01232) 32 20 23, Mon-Wed, Fri 19:30-22:00.

LESBIAN LINE, (01232) 23 86 68, Thurs 19:30-22:00.

■ Dance Bar/Disco
CROW'S NEST, Skipper St, near High St., 🏳 ♂

INTERLUDES hotel

Your Theatrical Seaside Escape

Scarborough North Yorkshire

(44-1723) 360 513

■ Cafe
QUEER SPACE, 3 Botanic Ave, 1st floor, (01232) 32 34 19, cafe, library & community center.

■ Retail & Bookstores
MISS-TIQUE, 27 Gresham St., till 18:00 (Thurs till 20:00), closed Sun.

DERRY

■ Information
GAY & LESBIAN LINE, (01504) 26 44 00.

■ Dance Bar/Disco
M&MS OUTBURST, Waterloo St, at Gweedore Bar, Thurs 22:00-01:00. 🏳 ♀♂

■ Retail & Bookstores
BOOKWORM, 16 Bishop St, (01504) 26 16 16, gay & lesbian selection.

U K - SCOTLAND

COUNTRY CODE: (44),

ABERDEEN

■ Information
ABERDEEN LESBIAN GROUP, Shoe Ln near Queen St, at the Women's Centre, (01224) 62 50 10, Wed 20:00-22:00."

AIDS HELPLINE, (01224) 57 40 00, or Body Positive Grampian: (01224) 40 44 08, 24hr tape.

UK - SCOTLAND

GAY & LESBIAN SWITCHBOARD, (01224) 63 35 00.

WOMEN'S CENTRE, Shoe Lane, (01224) 625 010, lesbians welcome, 09:30-16:00. Ask about women's socials.

■ Bars
CASTRO BAR & CLUB, 47 Netherkirkgate, (01224) 62 44 72, 17:00-02:00 (Sat, Sun till 03:00). ♂

CLUB 2000, 62 Shiprow, (01224) 59 69 99. ♂

AVIEMORE

■ Accommodations
AUCHENDEAN LODGE HOTEL, Dulnain Bridge near Grantown-on-Spey, Inverness-Shire, PH26 3LU, (44-1479) 851 347 (Tel/Fax). An Edwardian country hunting lodge, now an elegant, gay-friendly inn with restaurant, private & shared baths, full breakfast, furnished in antiques, with spectacular views, skiing, walking, fishing, golfing.

AYR

■ Information
GAY & LESBIAN SWITCHBOARD, (01292) 61 90 00, Mon, Wed, Fri 19:00-22:00, or tape."

DUMFRIES - GALLOWAY

■ Information
LESBIAN & GAY LINE, (01387) 691 61, Thurs 19:30-21:30 or leave message, ask about schedule for lesbian & gay group meetings in local hetero bars and special disco nights."

DUNDEE

■ Information
LESBIAN & GAY SWITCHBOARD, (01382) 202 620, Mon 19:00-22:00.

■ Bars
★ **DEVA'S,** 75 Seagate, (01382) 2268 40, Mon-Sat 11:00-24:00. ♀♂

XS, St Andrew's Lane, in back of Liberty club, (01382) 20 06 60, 19:00-24:00 (Sun till 23:00). ♀♂

■ Dance Bar/Disco
LIBERTY NIGHTCLUB, 124 Seagate, (01382) 200 660, 23:00-02:30, closed Mon-Tues. ♂

EDINBURGH

■ Information
GAY & LESBIAN SWITCHBOARD, (0131) 556 40 49, 7 days 19:30-22:00.

LESBIAN & GAY COMMUNITY CENTRE, 58a-60 Broughton St, (0131) 557 26 25, 11:00-23:00 (Sun from 12:00), this centre houses several gay businesses."

LESBIAN LINE, (0131) 557 07 51, Mon & Thurs 19:30-22:00.

WOMEN'S CENTRE, 61a Broughton St, (0131) 557 3179, ask about lesbian & feminist group meetings Tues 20:00-21:30, social for lesbians over 45, first Sat 13:00-17:00."

■ Accommodations
AMARYLLIS GUEST HOUSE, THE, 21 Upper Gilmore Place, Edinburgh, EH3 9NL, (44-131) 229 3293 (Tel/Fax). Guesthouse with some hetero clientele, private & shared baths, full breakfast, coffee/tea-making facilities." ♀♂

ARIES GUEST HOUSE, 5 Upper Gilmore Place, Edinburgh, EH3 9NW, (44-131) 229 4669. Small lesbian-owned & -run guesthouse in central Edinburgh. Private & shared baths, full Scottish breakfast, minutes to Princess Street, castle & Old Town, near gay bars. Some hetero clientele. ♀♂

ARMADILLO GUEST HOUSE, THE, 12 Gilmore Place, Edinburgh, EH3 9NQ, (44-131) 229 6457. guesthouse, some hetero clientele, shared baths, color TV, beverage-making facilities, phone, laundry facilities. ♀♂

GARLANDS GUEST HOUSE, 48 Pilrig St, Edinburgh, EH6 5AL, (44-131) 554 4205 (Tel/Fax)." Gay-friendly B&B with color TV, private baths, coffee & tea-making facilities.

MANSFIELD HOUSE, 57 Dublin St, Edinburgh, EH3 6NL, (44-131) 556 7980 (Tel/Fax). centrally located guesthouse, variety of elegantly furnished rooms, color TV, private & shared baths, continental breakfast." ♀♂

REGIS HOUSE, 57 Gilmore Place, Edinburgh, EH3 9NT, (44-131) 229 4057. gay-friendly guesthouse, private & shared baths."

UK - SCOTLAND

■ Bars
CC BLOOM'S, 23 Greenside Place, (0131) 556 9331, bar with disco & restaurant, 19:00-03:00 (Sat, Sun from 14:00).

DIVINE DIVAS, 15 Calton Rd, at The Venue, upstairs, (0131) 556 8997, women only 4th Fri 21:00-03:00.

FRENCH CONNECTION, 89 Rose St Lane North, (0131) 225 7651, small bar, 12:00-01:00 (Sun from 13:00)."

LORD NELSON BAR, 9-13 Nelson St at Linden Hotel, (0131) 557 43 34, open till 01:00, popular Sun afternoon." ♂

ROUTE 66, 6 Baxter's Place, (0131) 524 0061 12:30-01:00 (Sun from 15:00).

■ Dance Bar/Disco
TACKNO, 36-39 Market St, at Club Mercado, (0131) 226 4224, last Sun 23:00-04:00, frequented by gays.

TASTE, 36 Blair St, at the Honeycomb, (0131) 220 4381, 23:00-03:00, DJs.

■ Cafe
BLACK BO'S, 57-61 Blackfriars St, (0131) 557 6136, vegetarian cuisine, 12:00-14:00 & 18:00-22:30.

BLUE MOON CAFE, 36 Broughton St, (0131) 557 2788, a center for gay and lesbian socializing, 09:00-01:00 (Fri, Sat till 01:30, Sun till 24:00). ♀♂

CAFE KUDOS, 22 Greenside Place, (0131) 556 4349, 12:00-01:00, some hetero clientele. ♂

CAFE LUCIA, 13-29 Nicholson St, at the Edinburgh Festival Theatre., (0131) 662 1112, frequented by gays & lesbians, 10:00-22:00.

CITY CAFE, 19 Blair St, (0131) 220 0125, 11:00-23:00.

CYBERIA, 88 Hanover St, (0131) 220 4403, café with internet access, 10:00-22:00 (Sun 12:00-19:00), frequented by gays.

NEXUS CAFE BAR, 60 Broughton St, at the Lesbian & Gay Community Centre, (0131) 478 7069, 11:00-23:00. ♀♂

OUTHOUSE CAFE, Broughton Street Lane, (0131) 557 6668, 12:00-01:00 (Sun from 12:30), frequented by gays.

■ Restaurants
CLAREMONT BAR & RESTAURANT, 133-135 E Claremont St.,

LOVEATE BISTRO, 1-7 Montrose Terrace, at the Stag & Turret, (0131) 478 7231, 12:00-15:30 & 17:00-19:00.

■ Retail & Bookstores
BOBBIES BOOKSHOP, 220 Morrison St, (0131) 538 7069, general bookstore with gay & lesbian section, Mon-Sat 10:00-17:30.

OUT OF THE BLUE, 36 Broughton St, (0131) 478 7048, gay & lesbian bookshop, 12:00-21:00.

PJ'S WATCHES & GIFTS, 60 Broughton St, at the Gay & Lesbian Center, (0131) 558 8174, 12:00-19:99 (Sun till 17:00).

FALKIRK

■ Bars
DROOKIT DUCK, Graham's Rd, (01324) 613 644, discreetly frequented by some gays."

■ Restaurants
PIERRE'S, 140 Grahams Rd, (01324) 63 58 43, French cuisine, discreetly frequented by gays.

FIFE

■ Bars
CLUB XS, 27 Canmore St, (01383) 62 17 00, bar & disco, 15:00-24:00 (Sat from 17:00, Sun from 19:00). ♂

GALASHIELS

■ Restaurants
GREENS DINER, 4 Green St, (01896) 757 667, discreetly frequented by local gays, 10:00-22:00 (Mon, Tues till 17:00), closed Sun.

GLASGOW

■ Information
BODY POSITIVE, (0141) 332 5010.

GAY & LESBIAN CENTRE, 11 Dixon St, (0141) 221 7203, this center houses several gay businesses, 10:00-22:00.

LESBIAN LINE, (0141) 552 3355, Wed 19:00-22:00. Ask about scheduled socials.

WOMEN'S LIBRARY, 109 Trongate, 4th & 5th floors, (0141) 552 8345, fiction, nonfiction, postcards & information, Tues-Fri 13:00-18:00, Sat 14:00-17:00.

■ Accommodations
GLASGOW GUEST HOUSE, 56 Dumbreck Road, Glasgow, G41 5NP, (44-

UK - SCOTLAND

141) 427 0129 (Tel/Fax)." Gay-owned guesthouse with 60% gay/lesbian hotel, full Scottish or vegetarian breakfast, private & shared baths. ♀♂

■ Bars
AUSTIN'S, 183a Hope St, (0141) 332 2707, 16:00-24:00 (Sat, Sun from 14:00). ♪ 🖻 ✕ ♀♂

COURT BAR, 69 Hutcheson St, (0141) 552 2463, small, gay in evenings, Mon-Sat 11:00-24:00, Sun 20:30-23:00." 🖾

★ **DELMONICA'S BAR,** 68 Virginia St, (0141) 552 4803, pub, daily 12:00-24:00. ♪ ✕ ♀♂

POLO LOUNGE, 84 Wilson St, (0141) 553 1221, 12:00-01:00 (Fri-Sun till 03:00), piano & jazz bar. ♂

SADIE FROST'S, 8-10 West George St, (0141) 332 8005, 12:00-24:00, upscale bar with some hetero clientele. ✕ ♂

VICTORIA BAR, 157-159 Bridgegait, (0141) 552 6040, 11:00-24:00 (Sun from 12:30), frequented by gays & lesbians.

■ Dance Bar/Disco
★ **BENNETS DISCO,** 80-90 Glassford St, (0141) 552 5761, gay Wed-Sun 23:00-03:00 (closed Mon). 🏨 ♪ 🖻 ♀♂

■ Cafe
CAFFE LATTE, 58 Virginia St, (0141) 553 2553, 11:00-24:00 (Sun from 11:30).

OVER THE RAINBOW BISTRO, 6 Kersland St, (0141) 357 3739, cafe & bistro, frequented by gays.

QC'S, 11 Dixon St, at the gay & lesbian center, (0141) 204 5418, 10:00-22:00 (Sun 11:00-18:00). ♀♂

■ Retail & Bookstores
PJ'S WATCHES & GIFTS, 11 Dixon St, (0141) 226 9977, 12:00-19:00 (Sun till 18:00).

INVERNESS

■ Bars
NICO'S BAR & BISTRO, at the Glen Mhor Hotel, Ness Bank, (01463) 234 308, discreetly frequented by gays, more gays Wed & Fri 21:00-23:00." 🖾

ISLE OF BUTE

■ Accommodations
ARDMORY HOUSE HOTEL, Ardmory Road, Ardbeg, Isle of Bute, PA20 0PG, (44-1700) 502 346, Fax: (44-1700) 505 596. Email: Ardmory.House.Hotel@DIAL.PIPEX.COM, Gay-friendly hotel with restaurant & bar, 60 minutes from Glasgow, 30 minutes Wemyss Bay ferry, full breakfast, dinner available, private baths, garden, color TV, telephone, gay male following.

KILMARNOCK

■ Bars
KAYPARK TAVERN, 27-29 London Rd, (01563) 523 623, more gays Mon (in lounge area)." 🖾

STIRLING

■ Information
FORTH FRIEND, (01786) 4712 85, Mon 19:30-21:30. Ask about group meetings alternate Wed.

■ Bars
BARNTON BISTRO, 3 Barnton St, (01786) 461 698, discreetly frequented by gays, younger crowd, 10:30-23:45 (Fri, Sat till 24:45, Sun from 12:00). ✕ 🖾

U K - WALES

COUNTRY CODE: (44),

ABERYSTWYTH

■ Information
LESBIAN & GAY LINE, (01970) 62 17 18, Tues 18:00-20:00.

■ Women's Accommodations
WOMEN'S LODGINGS, (44-1974) 202 231. Women-only accommodation, 1 double room with shared bath in a private home, 9 miles south of Aberystwyth. ♀

■ Bars
BOAR'S HEAD, Queens Rd, (01970) 62 61 06, more gays Fri & Sat.

AMMANFORD - DYFED

■ Accommodations
APPLE COTTAGE, (44-1269) 824072. self-contained stone cottage, men welcome, fully-equipped kitchen, color TV, linens, open fire range, oil central heat, hot water, thermostatically-controlled shower. ♀

UK - WALES

BANGOR

Information
GAY & LESBIAN LINE, (01248) 35 12 63, men answer Fri 19:00-21:00, women answer Tues 19:00-21:00.

BRECON BEACONS

Accommodations
TYBESTA TOLFRUE, Brecon, (44-1874) 611 115. B&B in the heart of Brecon Beacons National Park, full breakfast, color TV, coffee/tea-making facilities, TV lounge, maid service, nearby pool & gym. ♀♂

CARDIFF

Information
AIDS LINE, (01222) 22 34 43, Mon-Fri 10:00-22:00.

CARDIFF FRIEND, (01222) 34 01 01, Tues-Sat 20:00-22:00.

LESBIAN LINE, (01222) 37 40 51, Tues 20:00-22:00.

Accommodations
COURTFIELD HOTEL, 101 Cathedral Rd, Cardiff, CF1 9PH, (44-1222) 227 701 (Tel/Fax). gay-friendly hotel with restaurant & bar, tastefully-decorated rooms with tea making facilities, private & shared baths, pool nearby, full Welsh breakfast, vegetarian cuisine available."

Bars
COURTFIELD HOTEL BAR, bar & restaurant in gay-friendly hotel, mainly hetero clientele be discreet.

WOW CLUB, Bute Terrace, 21:00-02:00 (closed Sun, Mon), Tues women-only. ♀♂

LAMPETER

Women's Accommodations
SILVERWEED B&B, Post Office House, Park-y-rhos, Cwmann, Lampeter, Dyfed, SA48 8DZ, (44-1570) 423 254. Women-only B&B in village of Park-y-rhos, 2 miles from Lampeter. Jewelry-making courses available, vegetarian breakfast, light lunch on course days. Cambrian Mountains nearby, 16 miles to sea. ♀

LLANDUDNO

Bars
BROADWAY BOULEVARD, Mostyn Broadway, (01492) 87 96 14, alternate Mon 20:30-00:30. ♂

NEWPORT

Information
AIDS LINE, (01633) 22 34 56, Wed 19:30-21:00.

POWYS

Accommodations
FACHWEN GANOL, Llwydiarth, Llangadfan, Powys, SY21 0QG, (44-1938) 820 595. Women-only guesthouse in a 17th-century Welsh farmhouse, shared baths, full English breakfast, lounge, books, games, large garden, 15 miles to Shropshire border, 10 miles to Snowdonia, 30 miles from the West Coast. ♀

SNOWDONIA NAT'L. PARK

Accommodations
DEWIS CYFARFOD, Llanddferfel, near Bala, Gwynedd, LL23 7DR, (44-1678) 530 243. Women's guest house, en suite baths, TV, beverage-making facilities, full or continental breakfast, art tuition available for groups or individuals, painting & sculpture also available. ♀

PENNANT HALL, Beach Road, Penmaenmawr, Conwy, LL34 6AY, (44-1492) 622 878. Hotel with restaurant & bar, private baths, expanded continental breakfast, colour TV, Jacuzzi, ocean nearby, women welcome. ♂

Bars
JACK'S HYDRO, Beach Rd, at Pennant Hall, Penmaenmawr, (01492) 62 28 78, hotel bar. ♂

SWANSEA

Information
AIDS LINE, (01792) 45 63 03, Thurs 15:00-20:00.

LESBIAN LINE, (01792) 65 19 95, Wed 19:00-21:00.

Dance Bar/Disco
PALACE CLUB, THE, 154 High St, near the station, (01792) 45 79 77, 22:00-02:00 (Sun 19:00-22:30), ask about women's dance nights. ♀♂

UKRAINE

COUNTRY CODE: (380),

KIEV

■ Bars
BUDAPESHT, ul. Leontovicha 13 (metro: Kreshchatik), at Budapesht casino, 23:00-06:00, discreetly frequented by gays. ☿ ✕ ▨

★ **CHICAGO,** ul. Raisy Okipnoy 3 (metro: Levoberezhnaya), (044) 517 41 48, 19:00-06:00, discreetly frequented by gays. ☿ ✕ ▨

DNIPRO, ul. 1/2 Kreshchatik, at the Dnipro Hotel, bar & restaurant, not gay, but discreetly frequented by gays in evening, especially on weekends. ✕

GABRIELLA, Ploshchad Leninskogo Komsomola 42, (metro: Levoberezhnaya), at the Dnepr Hotel, hotel casino bar, 22:00-06:00, discreetly frequented by gays. ☿ ✕ ▨

KRASNOYE Y CHERNOYE, Prospekt Pobedy 44 (metro: Universitet), at the Lybed Hotel, from metro take trolleybus 5 to hotel, 16:00-24:00, discreetly frequented by gays. ☿ ✕ ▨

SPLIT, ul. Proreznaya 24 (metro: Kreshchatik), at Split casino, 23:00-06:00, discreetly frequented by gays. ☿ ✕ ▨

■ Dance Bar/Disco
DISCO NA KIKVIDZE, ul. Kikvidze 33, at the "obshezhitiye" (hostel), irregularly held Sat disco, 21:00-05:00. Closes occasionally, ask locally for current schedule. ♫ ✕ ♂

■ Cafe
FLAMINGO, ul. Sorokaletiya Oktiabria 70, (metro: Liebedskaya), at Hotel Mir, (044) 264 92 03, from metro take trolleybus 11, 12 or 4 to Hotel Mir, 16:00-24:00, discreetly frequented by gays." ☿ ✕ ▨

MIDDLE EAST
ISRAEL

COUNTRY CODE: (972),

EILAT

■ Dance Bar/Disco
PROPAGANDA, at city entrance, across from Paz gas station., ♫ ♂

PROPAGANDA, at the Shalom Center, lower level, across from airport, (052) 767 449, ask for Shahar, Sat from 24:00, frequented by gays. ♫ ▨

TEDDY'S BAR, beside Ophira Park, frequented by gays. ♫ ▨

HAIFA

■ Information
ISHA LE ISHA, 47 Hillel St, (04) 853 0159, feminist organization, KLAF lesbian feminist group meets here, many activities & outdoor events are held.

KLAF, (04) 853 0159, lesbian feminist community meets at a feminist organization Isha Le Isha, 47 Hillel St.

LAVENDER LINE, (04) 851 0966, lesbian line, Thurs 17:30-20:30.

SOCIETY FOR THE PROTECTION OF PERSONAL RIGHTS (SPPR), 6 Nordau St, 3rd fl, (04) 8672 665, branch of main group in Tel Aviv.

WHITE LINE, (04) 8525 252, gay & lesbian helpline, Mon & Thurs 19:00-23:00.

JERUSALEM

■ Information
INFO & AIDS LINE, (02) 537 3906, Tues 20:00-22:00. Aids line answers Sun 20:00-22:00.

KLAF, PO Box 6360, Jerusalem 91062, (02) 625 1271, lesbian feminist community, answers Sun 19:00-21:00 or tape.

OTHER TEN PERCENT, THE, PO Box 6916, Jerusalem 91068, Israel, (02) 5818 414, student group, meets Wed at 20:15 at Mount Scopus campus of Hebrew University, Goldschmidt Bldg, room 306.

■ Cafe
TMOL SHILSHOM, 5 Solomon St, in pedestrian zone Nahlat Shivah, rear entrance, (02) 6232 758, coffee shop & book

store with poetry readings, sing-alongs. 10% gay group's social Wed 23:00.
ZIG ZAG, 3 Hama'alot St, (02) 625 3446, frequented by gays & lesbians.

TEL AVIV

Information

AIDS HELPLINE, (03) 560 4576, Mon & Thurs 19:30-22:00.

KLAF, PO Box 22997, TA 61228, (03) 699 5606, a lesbian feminist community, meets alternate Sun at SPPR community center, publish Kelaf Hazak newsletter, many activities & outdoor events are held.

SOCIETY FOR THE PROTECTION OF PERSONAL RIGHTS (SPPR), 28 Nehmani St, lower level, (03) 629 3681, 620 4327, Sun-Tues, Thurs 19:30-22:30 (Wed 20:00 for gays & lesbians under 22 yrs). The only gay & lesbian community center in the Middle East. Organizes social & cultural events for the gay, lesbian & bisexual community in Israel, umbrella organization for various groups. Organizes disco parties, call for location. Write PO Box 37604, Tel Aviv 61375. SPPR branch in Haifa.

WHITE LINE, (03) 629 2797, gay, lesbian helpline, Sun, Tues-Thurs 19:30-23:30. Women: (03) 525 9555, Mon 19:30-23:00."

Bars

ABBIS, 40 Geulah, (03) 510 1219. Daily from 20:00, 80% men.

HE & SHE, 8 Hashomer, 2nd floor, (03) 510 0914, 2 bars & disco, 60% women.

Dance Bar/Disco

DIP, 3 Ahuzat Bayit St, beside Shalom Tower, Sat from 21:30.

FIFTY-FOUR SALOME, 54 Salome St, Thurs from 24:00.

LEMON, 17 Nagarim St, at Eliphelet St, (03) 681 3313, gay Mon only.

X-PLAY, 58 Allenby St, gay Fri only.

ZMAN AMITI, 22 Eilat St, call SPPR gay group for schedule of gay dance nights.

Cafe

NORDAU CAFE, 145 Ben Yehuda St, (at Arlozorof St), (03) 524 0134, coffee shop & restaurant, frequented by many gays & lesbians.

Restaurants

BESI HATIVIYUT, 34 Yermyahu, (03) 604 2373, gay-friendly natural food & dairy restaurant with blintzes, pancakes. Open 09:00-24:00 daily.

Retail & Bookstores

AVI SOFFER GALLERIES, Kikar Kedumim, Old Jaffa, (03) 683 1054; 2nd location: 238 Dizengoff St, Tel Aviv, Tel: (03) 546 0184. Gay-friendly arts & crafts galleries.

BENI'S PHARMACY, 174 Dizengoff St, (03) 522 2386, gay-friendly pharmacy.

LEBANON

COUNTRY CODE: (961),

BEIRUT

Dance Bar/Disco

EQUINOX, in town of Jounieh, mostly hetero wtih some gay clientele.

L'ORANGE MECHANIQUE (OM), in the Sin el Fil area,, hard to find, best to take a servis taxi. Mix of gays, lesbians & heteros, occasional "men only if accompanied by women" door policy.

LE SECRET, in town of Jounieh, mostly hetero with some gay clientele.

PACIFIC REGION
AUSTRALIA

COUNTRY CODE: (61),

AUS. CAPITAL TERR.
CANBERRA

Information

AIDS COUNCIL & GAY INFO LINE, (61-2) 6257 2855. Mon-Fri: AIDS council answers 09:00-17:00; Gay info line answers 18:00-22:00.

LESBIAN LINE, (61-2) 6247 8882, Mon 18:00-20:30.

Accommodations

CARRINGTON OF BUNGENDORE, THE, PO Box 39, Bungedore, NSW, 2621, (06) 238 1044, Hotel & restaurant 30 minutes from Canberra, B&B available, gays & lesbians welcome.

NORTHERN LODGE, Northbourne Ave, (2) 6257 2599. Bed & breakfast.

Bars
TILLY'S, 96 Wattle Street, at Bigelow St, Lyneham, smoke-free bar & cafe, live bands. 🎵 ♀

Dance Bar/Disco
HEAVEN NIGHTCLUB, Garema Place, (2) 6257 6180, alternative club with 80% gay & lesbian clientele, occasional male dancers, drag shows every Sat, closed Mon. 🎵 ♀♂

MERIDIAN CLUB, 34 Mort St, Braddon, (2) 62489 966, dance bar & lounge, Tues-Thurs 18:00 till late, Fri 17:00 till late, Sat 20:00 till late, occassional strippers. Women-only nights Wed. 🎵 ♀♂

Restaurants
REPUBLIC, Allara St, modern Australian cuisine.

NEW SOUTH WALES
BERRY

Accommodations
TARA COUNTRY RETREAT, 219 Wattamolla Rd, Berry, NSW, 2535, (61-2) 4464 1472, Fax: (61-2) 4464 2265. Email: rods@ozemail.com.au, Web: http://www.ozemail.com.au/~rods, Guesthouse & campground with restaurant, bar & shops, beverage-making facilities, shared baths, TV lounge, Jacuzzi, gym equipment, nearby ocean beach, full country breakfast." ♀♂

BLUE MOUNTAINS

Information
BLUE MOUNTAINS GAY LINE, (047) 821 555.

Accommodations
ALLENDALE COTTAGE, Blackheath, (61-47) 878 270. Luxury suite with private bath with sunken 2-person spa, fireplace & sun deck.

BALMORAL GUEST HOUSE, 196 Bathurst Road, Katoomba, NSW, 2780, (61-47) 822 264, Fax: (61-47) 826 008. gay-friendly B&B guesthouse with bar & restaurant, full breakfast, private & shared baths, AC, color TV, VCR, Jacuzzi, nearby pool, 20% gay & lesbian clientele.

BYGONE BEAUTYS COTTAGES, 20-22 Grose St, Leura, NSW, 2780, (61-47) 84 3117, (61-47) 84 3108, Fax: (61-47) 84 3078. Gay-friendly B&B cottages with restaurant, private baths, full breakfast, color TV, VCR, kitchen, refrigerator, beverage-making facilities.

CHALET, THE, 46-50 Portland Ave, Medlow Bath, 2780, (047) 881 122. Hotel & restaurant.

CRABAPPLE COTTAGE, 9 Beattie St, Leura, (047) 841 899. Country cottage with full breakfast, spa bath.

COFFS HARBOUR

Accommodations
SANTA FE LUXURY BED & BREAKFAST, The Mountain Way, Coffs Harbour, NSW, 2450, (61-66) 537 700, Fax: (61-66) 537 050. gay-friendly B&B, 50% gay & lesbian clientele, private baths, full breakfast, colour TV, VCR, video tape library, ceiling fans, laundry facilities, pool on premises.

HUNTER VALLEY

Accommodations
POKOLBIN VILLAGE RESORT, in Hunter Valley vineyards area, Resort & conference center, accommodation & winerey tours.

NEWCASTLE

Bars
WICKHAM PARK HOTEL BAR, Maitland Rd, Wickham Park, pub, open daily. ♀

Dance Bar/Disco
ISLINGTON BARRACKS, 139 Maitland Rd, Islington, (049) 69 1848, pub with dance bar in rear, alternative, many gays & lesbians, 60% gay & lesbian.

NORTHERN NEW SOUTH WALES

Accommodations
RIVER OAKS B & B C/O BILL SCHREURS, 53-59 Broken Head Rd, Byron Bay, NSW, 2481, (61-26) 6685 8679, Fax: (61-2) 6685 5636. B&B, mostly men with women welcome, private & shared baths, continental breakfast, colour TV, VCR, video tape library, heated pool on premises. ♂

Women's Accommodations

A SLICE OF HEAVEN RURAL RETREAT FOR WOMEN, Lot 3 Pacific Highway, Stokers Siding, Mail to: PO Box 5077, South Murwillumbah, NSW, 2484, (61-66) 779 276, mobile: (61-15) 590 299. Email: spower@medeserv.com.au, Web: http://www.powerup.com.au/~qldq/soh.html, A rural women's retreat in tropical northern New South Wales, near Byron Bay and Coolangatta with salt-water, billabong-style swimming pool and 10-woman hot spa, tennis court, pool table, mini gym, croquet and volleyball. Bushwalks are a favorite pastime in these parts. We serve gourmet meals and even have Thai cooking classes. For women of mature age, we hold courses in Growing Old Disgracefully, which are full of new ideas for getting the most out of life. B&B is in-house or in a separate studio adjacent to the games room. ♀

RYLSTONE

Women's Accommodations

STRINGYBARK FARM CABINS & CAMPING, PO Box 78, Rylstone, NSW, 2849, (61-63) 791 182. 2 cabins, women only, private bath. ♀

SYDNEY

Information

AIDS INFO, (02) 9283 3222.
GAY & LESBIAN LINE, (02) 9207 2800, 16:00-24:00.
LESBIAN LINE, (02) 9557 4337.
LESBIAN SPACE COMMUNITY CULTURAL CENTRE, 43 Bradford St, Newtown, (02) 9519 3870, drop in Sat 11:00-17:00, drum 15:00-17:00.
NEWTOWN WOMEN'S CENTRE, 523 King St, Newtown, (02) 9550 6993.
PRIDE CENTRE, (2) 9331 1333.
WOMEN'S LIBRARY, Garden St, Alexandria Town Hall, Alexandria, (02) 9319 0529.

Accommodations

BRICKFIELD HILL BED & BREAKFAST INN, 403 Riley St, Surry Hills, Sydney, NSW, 2010, (61-2) 9211 4886, Fax: (61-2) 9212 2556. Email: fields@zip.com.au, Four-storey Victorian terrace house in a residential part of Sydney's gay district. Near Oxford St & the city, some rooms with balconies & views, expanded continental breakfast, private & shared baths, some hetero clientele. ♀♂

CHELSEA GUEST HOUSE, 49 Womerah Ave, Darlinghurst, NSW, 2010, (61-2) 9380 5994, Fax: (61-2) 9332 2491. Email: xchelsea@ozemail.com.au, Web: www.citysearch.com.au/syd/chelsea, For travellers weary of large hotels, this classic terrace house in one of the Darlinghurst's tree-lined streets is the answer. We offer 6 beautifully appointed guestrooms with fresh, crisp, cotton sheets, tea and coffee-making facilities, shared baths and continental breakfast.

See ad on next page

If You Want To Be Pampered, Our Place Is For You!

A Slice of Heaven
Rural Retreat for Women

- Swimming Pool • 10-Woman Spa
- Croquet & Volleyball • Gourmet Dinners
- Growing Old "Disgracefully" Courses
- Comfortable Accommodations

Tel: (61-66) 779 276

CHELSEA GUEST HOUSE
Elegance & Style in the Heart of Sydney

(61-2) 9380 5994
xchelsea@ozemail.com.au

The many cafes and restaurants of Oxford Street are within walking distance. Complimentary use of Bayswater Gym. Gay-owned, some hetero clientele. ♀♂

COOGEE SANDS MOTOR INN, 161 Dolphin St, Coogee, (61-2) 9665 8588, Fax: 9664 1406. Gay-friendly.

DORCHESTER INN, 38 Macleay St, Potts Point, Sydney, NSW, 2011, (61-2) 9358 2400, Fax: (61-2) 9357 7579. Serviced apartments ideally located, close to popular sightseeing & nightlife. Private baths, color TV, AC, phone, nearby ocean & pool, some hetero clientele.

FURAMA HOTEL CENTRAL, 28 Albion St, Surry Hills, Sydney, NSW, 2010, (61-2) 9281 0333, Fax: (61-2) 9281 0222. Gay-friendly, modern hotel with restaurant & bar, 128 luxurious rooms offering complete privacy & convenience. Located minutes from central train station, short walk to Darling Harbour, theatres & city centre. Amenities include private baths, indoor heated pool, colour TV, AC.

FURAMA HOTEL DARLING HARBOUR, 68 Harbour Street, Darling Harbour, Sydney, NSW, 2000, (61-2) 9281 0400, Fax: (61-2) 9281 1212. Gay-friendly hotel with restaurant. Located opposite Sydney Entertainment Centre, near Chinatown, short stroll to major theatres, cinemas & major tourist attractions. All private baths, AC, 24-hr room service, colour TV and more.

GOVERNORS ON FITZROY B & B, 64 Fitzroy St, Surry Hills, NSW, 2010, (61-2) 9331 4652, Fax: (61-2) 9361-5094. Email: governor@zip.com.au, bed & breakfast, individually decorated double rooms, private & shared baths, spa, 4 blks from heart of gay area (Oxford St), 20 min drive to ocean, full breakfast, tea/coffee." ♀♂

MANOR HOUSE BOUTIQUE HOTEL, 86 Flinders St, Darlinghurst, Sydney, NSW, 2010, (61-2) 9380 6633, Fax: (61-2) 9380 5016. Two-story terrace mansion with 18 boutique accommodations, restaurant & bar. All private baths, buffet breakfast, pool on premises. Near Oxford St and gay venues. Mostly men with women welcome. ♂

MEDINA EXECUTIVE APARTMENTS, 359 Crown St, Surry Hills, Sydney, NSW, 2010, (61-2) 9360 6666, Fax: (61-2) 9361 5965. Email: medina@s055.aone.net.au, gay-friendly five-star serviced apartments, mostly hetero with a gay & lesbian following, restaurant & pool on premises, private baths, AC, colour TV, VCR, maid & laundry service, gym, rooftop tennis court.

MEDUSA HOTEL, 267 Darlinghurst Rd, Darlinghurst, Sydney, NSW, 2010, (61-2) 9331 1000, Fax: (61-2) 9380 6901. Email: info@medusa.com.au, Web: www.medusa.com.au, The innate elegance of this luxury hotel turns heads with bold, vivid colors and a vibrant blend of the historic and the modern. Eighteen individually styled studios feature state-of-the-art facilities, cutting-edge interiors, enormous beds, natural fibre linen, organic toiletries and sumptuous evening chocolates. In the centre of Darlinghurst, Sydney's new focal point, the hotel is around the corner from Oxford Street and minutes from the downtown business district. Medusa's service evokes personality, performance and sleek sophistication. Our lively team of people are alert and care for your needs. Guest comfort and privacy is top priority ♀♂

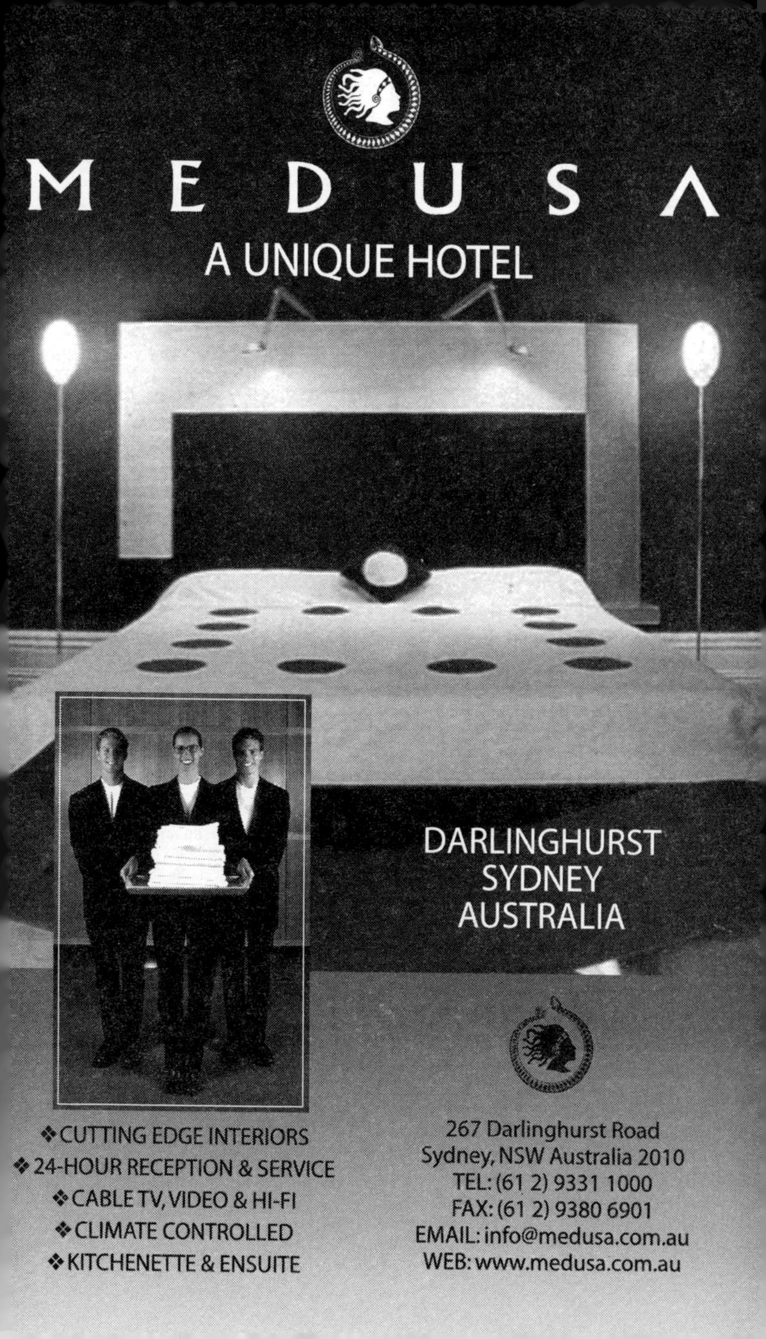

MEDUSA
A UNIQUE HOTEL

DARLINGHURST
SYDNEY
AUSTRALIA

- ❖ CUTTING EDGE INTERIORS
- ❖ 24-HOUR RECEPTION & SERVICE
- ❖ CABLE TV, VIDEO & HI-FI
- ❖ CLIMATE CONTROLLED
- ❖ KITCHENETTE & ENSUITE

267 Darlinghurst Road
Sydney, NSW Australia 2010
TEL: (61 2) 9331 1000
FAX: (61 2) 9380 6901
EMAIL: info@medusa.com.au
WEB: www.medusa.com.au

NEW SOUTH WALES

NEWINGTON MANOR, 10-14 Sebastopol St, Marrickville, NSW, (02) 9560 4922, fax: 9550 9789. Guesthouse with gay male following, double rooms with private baths, color TV, phone, spa, pool, continental & expanded continental breakfast.

OBSERVATORY HOTEL, THE, 89-113 Kent St, Sydney, NSW, 2000, (61-2) 9256 2222, Fax: (61-2) 9256 2233. Gay-friendly hotel with restaurant, bar, gift shop & health & leisure club, mostly straight with a gay & lesbian following, colour cable TV, VCR, video tape library, pool on premises, nearby health club.

PARK LODGE HOTEL, 747 South Dowling St, Moore Park, Sydney, NSW, 2016, (61-2) 9318 2393, Fax: (61-2) 9318 2513. Email: pklodge@geko.net.au, Web: http://www.geko.net.au/~pklodge/, Victorian-style boutique hotel, continental breakfast, private baths, color TV, VCR rentals, telephone, refrigerator, pool & ocean nearby, 50% gay & lesbian clientele.

SOUTHERN CROSS HOTEL, THE, Cnr Elizabeth & Goulburn Sts, Sydney, NSW, 2000, (61-2) 9282 0987, Fax: (61-2) 9211 1806. Toll free in Australia: (1-800) 221 141. Gay-friendly hotel with gay & lesbian following, private baths.

SULLIVANS HOTEL, 21 Oxford St, Paddington, Sydney, NSW, 2021, (61-2) 9361 0211, Fax: (61-2) 9360 3735. Email: sydney@sullivans.com.au, A small, stylish hotel, offers great value, a delightful garden courtyard and an intimate atmosphere. Amenities include are private baths, direct-dial telephones, AC and colour TV. Breakfast is served daily in our breakfast cafe, and there is ample covered parking available. Conveniently situated in central Paddington, near Oxford Street's excellent shops, restaurants, cafes, cinemas and art galleries. Gay-friendly.

SYDNEY STAR ACCOMMODATION, 275 Darlinghurst Rd, Darlinghurst, NSW, 2010, (61-414) 677 778 (24-hour mobile phone), Fax: (61-2) 9331 1000. You'll always feel welcome. Sydney Star combines all the style and elegance of a European pensione with the service and security of a modern hotel. We're a short stroll from restaurants, cafes, galleries and boutiques. Single, twin and double suites are available, each with kitchen and colour TV. Some hetero clientele. Member AGLTA. ♀♂

VICTORIA COURT SYDNEY, 122 Victoria Street, Sydney-Potts Point, NSW, 2011, (61-2) 9357 3200, Fax: (61-2) 9357 7606. Toll-free in Australia: (1800) 63 05 05. Email: vicsyd@ozemail.com.au(qn), Web: www.VictoriaCout.com.au, Two Victorian houses, restored and modernized, comprise this gay-friendly B&B hotel. The focal point is a courtyard conservatory where free-flying birds accompany breakfasting guests. Rooms have ensuite bathrooms, colour TVs & phones. Located in Potts Point, the heart of Sydney's bohemian scene.

■ Women's Accommodations

HELEN'S HIDEAWAY, PO Box 113, Darlinghurst, NSW, 2010, (61-2) 9360 1678, Fax: (61-2) 9360 4865." Lesbian-owned & -operated women-only B&B, shared baths, buffet breakfast, TV lounge, atrium, close to bars, restaurants & galleries. ♀

VITA'S PLACE, PO Box 249, Rozelle, NSW, 2039, (61-2) 9810 5487." This private, self-contained haven for women travellers is close to Sydney Harbour, restaurants, galleries, parks and markets. The sunny garden studio has an ensuite bath, double bed, ceiling fan, TV, linen and towels, and

---

SULLIVANS
★★★
HOTEL

Experience the Charm!
Sydney, NSW

(61-2) 9361 0211

French windows looking out onto a private and leafy walled courtyard with gas BBQ and outdoor dining. A separate fully equipped kitchen has microwave, crockery, utensils, refrigerator, tea and coffee. We're situated on the Balmain Peninsula, a convenient 20-minute bus or ferry ride to the heart of Sydney. ♀

■ Bars

ANNIE'S BAR, Bourke St at Arthur St, behind Carrington Hotel, Surry Hills, (02) 9360 4714, 17:00-24:00 (Sat from 18:00, Sun 12:00-22:00), some hetero clientele. ♂

BANANA BAR, at the Taylor Square Hotel, 1-5 Flinders St, Darlinghurst, (02) 9360 6373 upscale cocktail bar, 15:00-03:00 (Mon till 01:00, Sun till 24:00). ♀♂

BANK HOTEL BAR, 324 King St, Newtown, (02) 9557 1692, Wed women's pool competition. ♀

BASE BAR, 267 Oxford St, under the Beauchamp Hotel, (02) 9331 2575, in basement, from 12:00. ♂

BEAUCHAMP HOTEL BAR, 267 Oxford St, Darlinghurst, (02) 9331 2575, 12:00-24:00 (Sat till 02:00), mainly gay. ♂

BERESFORD HOTEL BAR, 354 Bourke St, Surry Hills, (02) 9331 1045, bar & disco, open mostly daytime 06:00-14:00. Alternative disco in the rear.

CAESARS BAR, 388 Parramatta Rd, behind Petersham Inn, Petersham, (02) 9569 4448, from 14:00 (Sun till 22:00). ♀♂

CLEVELAND HOTEL BAR, 433 Cleveland St, Surry Hills, (02) 9698 1908, alternative club with a large gay clientele, 11:00-02:00 (Thurs till 03:00, Fri-Sat till 05:00, Sun 12:00-24:00). ♀

GREEN PARK HOTEL BAR, 360 Victoria St, Darlinghurst, (02) 9380 5311, 10:00-01:00 (Sun till 24:00), 60% gay clientele. ♂

LANSDOWNE HOTEL BAR, 2 City Road, Chippendale, (02) 9211 2325, from 21:00, good mix of gays, lesbians & heteros.

LAVA BAR, 2 Oxford St, at the Burdekin Hotel, Darlinghurst, top floor cocktail bar with DJ, gay & straight crowd, Wed & Fri from 17:00, Sat & Sun from 19:00.

LEICHHARDT HOTEL, 126 Balmain Rd, Leichhardt, (02) 9569 1217, 10:00-24:00 (Sun-Mon from 12:00). ♀

LIZARD LOUNGE, 34 Oxford St, at the Exchange Hotel, 1st floor, Darlinghurst, (02) 9331 1936, upscale cocktail lounge, 17:00-03:00. Many women, especially for cocktail hour. ♀♂

NUBAR, 134 Oxford St, at Oxford Hotel, lower level, Darlinghurst, (02) 9331 3467, 17:00-02:00 (Fri, Sat till 03:00, Sun 15:00-24:00). ♀♂

OXFORD COCKTAIL BAR (GILLIGAN'S), at the Oxford Hotel, (02) 9331 3467, upstairs Gilligan's upscale cocktail bar, downstairs is gay men's pub with DJ, from 17:00 (Sun till 24:00). ♀♂

★ **OXFORD HOTEL BAR,** 134 Oxford St, Darlinghurst, (02) 9331 3467, cruise bar, 17:00-02:00 (Fri, Sat till 03:00, Sun till 24:00). ♂

STONEWALL HOTEL, 175 Oxford St, Darlinghurst, (02) 9360 1963, 12:00-03:00 (Thurs-Sun till 05:00). ♀♂

■ Dance Bar/Disco

BOOTSCOOT C&W LINE DANCING NIGHTS, at the Imperial Hotel, Erskineville, (02) 9388 1236 or 9550 9937, Tues-Thurs 20:00-23:00, Sat 14:00-17:30. ♀♂

EXCHANGE HOTEL, 34 Oxford Street, Darlinghurst, (02) 9331 1936, 2 dance bars, drag shows weekends.

HELLFIRE CLUB, 111 Regent St, S/M club, 22:00 till dawn. Action-packed, call to verify night.

SYDNEY STAR ACCOMMODATION

SYDNEY (61-414) 677 778

A Stylish Private Accommodation

NEW SOUTH WALES

IMPERIAL HOTEL, 35 Erskineville Rd, Erskineville, (02) 9519 9899, from 14:00 (Fri,Sat till 08:00). Disco & cabaret in front bar where women play pool on weekends. ♪ 🏨 ♀♂

★ **MIDNIGHT SHIFT,** 85 Oxford Street, Darlinghurst, (02) 9360 4319, bar & upstairs disco, from 12:00 (Sun 06:00-24:00). 🏨 ♪ ♂

NEWTOWN HOTEL, 174 King Street, Newtown, (02) 9557 1329, upstairs piano bar, dance bar & cabaret, 10:00-24:00 (Sat from 11:00, Sun till 22:00). ♪ ♂

★ **PHOENIX,** basement of Exchange Hotel, enter from Oxford St, Darlinghurst, (02) 9331 1936, underground, alternative, progressive music, from 22:00 (Sun from 21:00), closed Mon, cruisy Thurs & Sun. 🏨 ♪ ♂

★ **THE OTHER SIDE,** at The Site, 171 Victoria St, Pott's Point, women's weekly dance night, Sun from 19:00. Largest running women's dance club in Sydney. 🏨 ♀

■ Cafe

BILL'S 2, corner of Fitzroy & Crown St, Surrey Hills, major meeting place for gays & lesbians. ♀♂

GREEN IGUANA CAFE, 6 King St, Newtown, (02) 9516 3118, from 08:00. 🆗

LESBIAN LINE CAFÉ, 164 Flood St, Leichhardt, (02) 9550 0910, Fri 20:00-22:00. ♀

★ **ONE NINETY ONE CAFE,** 191 Oxford St, Darlinghurst, (02) 9326 1166, frequented by gays & lesbians." 🆗

■ Restaurants

ANGKOR WAT, 227 Oxford St, Darlinghurst, (02) 9360 5500, Cambodian cuisine. 🆗

BALKAN RESTAURANT, 209 Oxford St, Darlinghurst, (2) 9360 4970, "the meat overdose restaurant." 🆗

BISTRO MONCUR, 116 Queen St, Woollahra, (02) 9363 2782, French cuisine.

CANTINE, 191-195 Oxford St, Taylor Square, Sun from 23:00. 🆗

GOODFELLAS, 111 King St, Newtown, (02) 9557 1175, from 18:30. 🆗

HARVEST VEGETARIAN RESTAURANT, 71 Evans St, Rozelle, (02) 9818 4201, vegetarian cuisine. 🆗

LUSH, at the Manor House Hotel.,

O CALCUTTA, 251 Victoria St, Darlinghurst, (02) 9360 3650. 🆗

SIROCCO, 23 Craigend St, Darlinghurst, Morrocan cuisine. 🆗

TRASITS ON CROWN, 413 Crown St, Surrey Hills, (2) 9319 0748, Thai cuisine. 🆗

YIPI YI YO, 290 Crown St, Darlinghurst, (2) 9332 3114, American Southwestern cuisine. 🆗

■ Retail & Bookstores

BOOKSHOP DARLINGHURST, THE, 207 Oxford St, Darlinghurst, (02) 9331 1103, wide selection of gay & lesbian books, magazines & cards, open Mon-Sat 10am-10pm, Sun noon-9pm.

BOOKSHOP NEWTOWN, THE, 186 King St, Newton, (02) 9514 244, gay & lesbian books, magazines & cards, open Mon-Sat 9am-9pm, Sun noon-9pm.

FEMINIST BOOKSHOP, THE, Shop 9, Orange Grove Plaza, Balmain Road, Lilyfield, (02) 9810 2666. Books by, for and about women, centre for information & resources, 10:30-18:00 (Sat till 16:00), closed Sun.

GLEEBOOKS, 49 Glebe Point Rd, Glebe, (02) 9660 2333, general bookstore with gay & lesbian section, daily 09:00-21:00. 2nd-hand books at 191 Glebe Point Rd location.

■ Erotica

FANTASY LANE, 320 King St, Newtown.,

PURR EFFECT, 62 Oxford St, Paddington, (02) 9332 1370, leather clothes & accessories for women.

WOLLONGONG

■ Dance Bar/Disco

CHEQUERS, 341 Crown St (access via car park roof), at the Picadilly Shopping Centre, (042) 263 788, Thurs-Sat from 19:00. 🏨 ♪ ♀♂

NORTHERN TERRITORY
ALICE SPRINGS

■ Information

AIDS INFO, (08) 89531 118.

GAY LINE, (08) 89532 844, info on social groups, monthly dances.

■ Cafe

SWINGERS CAFE, Gregory Terrace, near Todd St, gay-friendly cafe with espresso & lite menu. 🆗

QUEENSLAND

DARWIN

Information
AIDS INFO, 6 Manton St, (8) 8941 1711, Mon-Fri 10:00-17:00.

Dance Bar/Disco
PANDORA'S, at the Don Hotel, enter at Litchfield St, (8) 8948 1069, Thurs-Sat 20:00-04:00 in rear bar, DJ, occasional drag shows.

Restaurants
UNCLE JOHN'S CABIN, Gardiner St, gay bar with attached straight restaurant.

QUEENSLAND
BRISBANE

Information
AIDS INFO, 32 Peel St, S. Brisbane, (07) 3844 1990, 09:00-17:00 Mon-Fri.

LESBIAN LINE, (07) 3839 3288, Tues & Sun 19:00-22:00.

Accommodations
EDWARD LODGE, 75 Sydney St, New Farm, Brisbane, QLD, 4005, (61-7) 3254 1078, Fax: (61-7) 3254 1062. B&B guesthouse. Large, comfortably furnished guest rooms with telephones, private baths, expanded continental breakfast, 24-hr tea/coffee facilities, Jacuzzi. Convenient to public transport, restaurants, cafes, gay venues and park. Women welcome.

SPORTSMAN HOTEL, 130 Leichhardt St, Spring Hill, Brisbane, QLD, 4000, (61-7) 3831 2892, Fax: (61-7) 3839 2106. Constructed in the late 1800s & remodeled in the late 1960s. Rooms are comfortable but not recommended for long stays. Shared baths, continental breakfast, 3 bars, a Bistro & entertainment on Friday nights.

Bars
CLUB LIBERTINE, private fetish club with men's & women's SM parties. For info, send SASE to PO Box 5036, West End 4101 Brisbane.

SPORTSMAN HOTEL BAR, 130 Leichhardt St, Spring Hill, (07) 3831 2892, bar & hotel, daily 18:00-01:00, Sun disco 16:00-24:00. Bears 3rd Sat, leather night 1st Sat.

Dance Bar/Disco
BARN, at Waterloo Hotel, Ann St at Commercial St, women's dance night 3rd Sun.

BEAT NIGHTCLUB, Ann St, Fortitude Valley, dance bar downstairs (mix of gays & straights), upstairs lounge (mostly "trannies"), popular Sun afternoon.

BROADWAY HOTEL BAR, Logan Rd, Woolloongabba, pub, open Sun afternoon.

KD'S, 470 St Paul's Terrace, at Jubilee Hotel, Fri women's dance night.

SANDPIT, at Melbourne Hotel, Melbourne St, South Brisbane, women's dance night 2nd Fri.

WICKHAM HOTEL BAR, 308 Wickham St, Fortitude Valley, (07) 3852 1301, disco & restaurant.

Cafe
G SPOT, 129 Leichardt,

Restaurants
BOUNDARY STREET BRASSERIE, 145b Boundary St, West End, (07) 3844 3811.

CAFE BABYLON, 142 Boundary St, West End, (07) 3846 4505, dinner daily (Fri, Sun also lunch).

MORAY CAFE, at Moray St & Merthyr Rd, New Farm, (07) 3254 1342, café & wine bar, open daily."

Retail & Bookstores
BRISBANE WOMEN'S BOOKSHOP, 15 Gladstone Rd, Highgate Hill, (07) 3844 6650. Women's & lesbian books, non-sexist children's books, jewelry, T-shirts, cards, music, Mon-Fri 09:30-17:30, Sat 10:00-02:00, Sun 11:00-15:00. Monthly coffeehouse in courtyard."

EMMA'S BOOKSHOP, 82a Vulture St, West End, (07) 3844 4973, general bookshop with gay & lesbian section.

RED BOOKS, Brunswick St, Fortitude Valley, general bookstore with some gay & lesbian books.

BUNDABERG

Accommodations
MENGYUAN, Lot 24, Woodswallow Dr, MS 882, Gin Gin, QLD, 4671, (61-71) 573 024, Fax: (61-71) 573 025. Email:

QUEENSLAND

fod@ozemail.com.au, B&B guesthouse on 25 acres of working property with gardens, chickens, some cattle. North of Brisbane & 40 minutes east of Bundaberg & coast, easy access to Great Barrier Reef, whale watching & turtle rookeries. Some hetero clientele. ♀♂

CAIRNS

Information
AIDS INFO, (070) 511 028, 24hrs.

Accommodations
EIGHTEEN TWENTY-FOUR JAMES, 18-24 James St, Cairns, QLD, 4870, (61-70) 514 644, Fax: (61-70) 510 103. Email: 18_24james@internetnorth.com.au., Web: http://www.eagles.bbs.net.au/james, Gay-owned & -operated plantation-style hotel in a tropical rainforest. Licensed restaurant & bar on premises, and complimentary tropical poolside breakfasts are served. Guestrooms feature private baths, AC, phones and TV with free in-house movies. Fully tiled salt-water pool on premises. ♂

FIFTY-FOUR CINDERELLA STREET, 54 Cinderella St, Cairns, QLD, 4878, (61-70) 550 289, Fax: (61-70) 559 383. Email: dsdelmont@c131.aone.net.au, Superb accommodation, creative cuisine & absolute beachfront at a fairy tale women-only hideaway, 10 minutes from Cairns & the airport on Reddens Island at the mouth of the Barron River on Machans Beach. Amenities at this B&B guesthouse include full breakfast, private & shared baths & color TV. Spend idyllic days in the large garden, the rock swimming pool with waterfall, or use the private beach access. Cairns offers magnificent rainforests & some of the best reef diving in the world. ♀

LUGGER BAY BEACH RESORT, Explorers Drive, South Mission Beach (via Cairns), QLD, 4852, (61-740) 688 400, Fax: (61-740) 688 586. Email: lugger@ozemail.com.au, Web: http://www.ozemail.com.au/~lugger, Built expressly as a luxury gay and lesbian resort, Lugger Bay Beach Resort features unique pole-style tree houses which overlook both rainforest and sea views and have private modern bathroom facilities. Here, it's your choice to relax and forget the world or to fill each day with a different adventure outing, perhaps to the rainforest or the Great Barrier Reef, Cairns or Mission Beach. Lugger Bay's many amenities and services include a gym, massage, hairdressing, personal guides and much more. Just below the resort grounds, there are three beautiful beaches to choose from. ♀♂

TURTLE COVE RESORT CAIRNS, Captain Cook Hwy, PO Box 158, Smithfield, Cairns, Far North QLD, 4878, (61-7) 4059 1800, Fax: (61-7) 4059 1969. Email: gay@turtlecove.com.au, Web:

Lugger Bay Beach Retreat
Quality Rainforest Retreat With All Reef and Adventure Experiences
(61-7) 40 688400
via Cairns, QLD

Escape to Turtle Cove
Gay Heaven On The Beach In Tropical North Queensland
Email: gay@turtlecove.com.au
http://www.turtlecove.com.au
Tel.: (61-7) 4059 1800
Fax: (61-7) 4059 1969

SOUTH AUSTRALIA

http://www.turtlecove.com.au, Beachfront resort with restaurant, bar, resort shop & private gay beach. Private baths, colour TV, in-house video, video tape library, telephone, AC, refrigerator, tropical & continental buffet breakfast, pool & Jacuzzi. Rainforest and barrier reef tours.

Women's Accommodations
WITCHENCROFT, Write: Jenny Maclean, PO Box 685, Atherton, QLD, 4883, (61-740) 912 683 (Tel/Fax). Email: jj@bushnet.qld.edu.au, Women-only guesthouse on 5-acre organic farm, 2 apartments with kitchens, baths, color TV, garden, nearby rivers & lakes, vegetarian cuisine or self-cater."

Dance Bar/Disco
CLUB TRIX, 53 Spence St, (070) 518 223, open Tues-Sun.

LAKE COOTHARABA

Accommodations
LE BATEAU IVRE GUESTHOUSE & UNITS, 25 Urunga Parade, Boreen Point, QLD, 4565, (61-7) 5485 3164, (61-7) 5485 3482. Guesthouse & 2 fully self-contained units, color & B&W TV, VCR, ceiling fans. Guesthouse: expanded continental breakfast, shared bath. Units: private baths. Gays & lesbians welcome.

MALENY

Accommodations
ZAMAZ, Montville Rd, (074) 594 3422, fax 594 3005. Gay-friendly country house with restaurant & tea rooms, 50% gay/lesbian clientele, private baths, summer house, drawing room, CD library, gardens, tennis court.

NOOSA

Accommodations
NOOSA COVE, 82 Upper Hastings St, Noosa, QLD, 4567, (61-7) 5449 2668, Fax: (61-7) 5447 5373. Guest house & holiday apartments near national park & Alexandria nudist beach, private baths, near gay nightclub, restaurant, women welcome.

NOOSA HEADS

Accommodations
LAKES HOLIDAY APARTMENTS, **THE,** 1/273 Weyba Rd, Noosaville, QLD, 4566, (61-7) 5449 8605." Luxurious holiday apartment resort, landscaped gardens, BBQ, pool on premises.

SURFERS PARADISE

Bars
SHOOTERS, Orchid Ave, The Mark Bldg, level 1, mix of gay & bi clientele, 7 days.

Dance Bar/Disco
BENSONS NITE CLUB, Orchid Ave, gay Wed only.

MEETING PLACE, THE, Paradise Centre, level 1, Gold Coast Hwy, enter beside Hark rock Cafe, (04) 1122 0284, Tues-Sun from 20:00, male strippers, drag shows nightly.

Cafe
GLOBAL CAFE, 3070 Gold Coast Hwy, 92 4192, European style cafe, closed Sun.

Retail & Bookstores
LAVENDER MUSIC, Orchid Ave, Shop 4, The Mark Arcade, (07) 5538 1533, wide variety of music, including local & import lesbian, gay & alternative, etc.

TOWNSVILLE

Accommodations
SANDY'S ON THE STRAND, PO Box 193, Townsville, QLD, 4810, (61-07) 4772 1193 (Tel/Fax). Gay-owned & -operated beachfront B&B with bay views, AC, private baths, continental breakfast. Walking distance to casino, city centre, beach across road, pool on premises.

Bars
DIANA'S, at Hermit Park Hotel, upper level, (077) 214 143, Fri, Sat from 20:30.

Retail & Bookstores
MARY WHO BOOKSHOP, 155 Stanley St, (077) 71 38 24, general bookstore with a gay & lesbian section.

SOUTH AUSTRALIA
ADELAIDE

Information
AIDS INFO, (08) 8363 2000.

GAY & LESBIAN COMMUNITY LIBRARY, 64 Fullarton Rd, enter from Gray St, Norwood, (08) 8362 3106, 09:30-17:30 (Sat 14:00-17:00), closed Sun.

SOUTH AUSTRALIA

Rochdale B&B
Spacious Rooms With Private Baths
Adelaide
(61-8) 8379 7498
jonespk@ozemail.com.au

GAYLINE, (08) 8362 3223, daily 19:00-22:00 (Sat, Sun 14:00-17:00)."

LESBIAN LINE, (08) 8207 7680.

WOMEN'S STUDIES RESOURCE CENTRE, 64 Pennington Terr., N Adelaide, (61-8) 267 3633, fax: (61-8) 267 2997. Mon-Thurs 9am-6pm, Fri 9am-5pm, Sun 2pm-5pm.

Accommodations

CITY APARTMENTS, 70 Glen Osmond Rd (office), Parkside, SA, 5063, (61-8) 8274 1222, Toll-free within Australia: (800) 888 501, Fax: (61-8) 8272-7371. serviced townhouses & apartments, gay & lesbian following, quality ranging from economy to superior, private courtyards, suburban & downtown locations close to shopping, art gallery, beach, continental breakfast 1st morning."

GREENWAYS APARTMENTS, 45 King William Rd, North Adelaide, SA, 5006, (61-8) 8267 5903, Fax: (61-8) 8267 1790. Holiday apartments, straight-friendly, fully-furnished kitchenette apts, AC, color TV, pool 3/4 mi, close to city center, shopping, entertainment, ocean beach 15 mi."

ROCHDALE B & B, 349 Glen Osmond Rd, Glen Osmond, SA, 5064, (61-8) 8379 7498, Fax: (61-8) 8379 2483. Email: jonespk@ozemail.com.au, Adelaide's only accommodation provider for gay men and women, Rochdale is a private, traditional bed and breakfast in a typical late 1920s Adelaide residence. The two spacious and well-appointed guestrooms have private baths and an air of understated elegance. Wood panelling is used extensively throughout the formal living areas. Open fires warm the study, lounge and one of the guestrooms. The gardens provide areas suited to quiet, secluded, relaxing reading and alfresco dining. A short stroll takes you to a district of shopping and restaurants.

Bars

BEANS BAR, 258 Hindley St, (08) 8231 9614, many women, from 21:00 (Fri, Sun from 20:00), 17:00-21:00, closed Mon.

DROOPY ROSE, 168 Gouger St, cabaret club with drag shows & other entertainment, not all gay clientele

EDINBURGH CASTLE HOTEL BAR, 233 Currie St, (08) 8410 1211, like an English pub, 11:00-24:00 (Sun 14:00-20:00), usually 70% men.

QUEER LOUNGE, 213 Hindley St, at Cargo Club, (08) 8231 2327, 1st Thurs, live bands.

SEMAPHORE HOTEL BAR, 17 Semaphore Rd, Semaphore, pub atmosphere, 7 days, 60% women.

STIX POOL HALL, 123 Gouger St, closed Sun.

Dance Bar/Disco

MARS BAR, 120 Gouger St, (08) 8231 9639, Mon-Sat from 22:30, DJ, drag shows Fri, 60% men, 40% women.

PLANET, 77 Pirie St, alternative dance bar, 20% gay, more gay Wed.

Q-BAR & POOL HALL, 274 Rundle St, level one, gay only Sun 23:00-04:00.

Cafe

CAFE ANTICO, 176 Henley Beach Rd, Torrensville, open late.

Restaurants

BRENNO'S, 125a The Parade, Norwood, (08) 8332 6000, closed Sun.

DON'S TABLE, 136 The Parade, Norwood, (08) 8634 3488.

EROS, 275-277 Rundle St, (08) 8223 4022.

EXCELSIOR, THE, at Hotel Excelsior, 110 Coglin St, Brompton, (08) 8346 2521, seafood, oysters, curries, soups, beef, etc.

LIME & LEMON, 89 Gouger St, (08) 8231 88 76, Thai cuisine, lunch Mon-Fri, dinners nightly. 🟥

MANSE, THE, 142 Tynte St, North Adelaide, (08) 8267 4636.

QUEEN STREET CAFE, 12 Elizabeth St, Croydon, (08) 8346 1811, closed Sun, Mon.

RANG MAHAL, 125 Gilles St, (08) 8223 5597, closed Sun, Mon.

SECRETS SUPPER HOUSE, 73 Melbourne St, North Adelaide, (08) 8367 0300, from 19:00.

SESTRI RESTAURANT & GALLERY, 6 Semaphore Rd, Semaphore, (08) 8242 3322, closed Mon.

SEVILLE IN SPAIN, 143 O'Connell St, North Adelaide, (08) 8267 3820.

SKETCHES CAFE, 121 The Parade, Norwood, (08) 8364 6422.

STAR CAFE, 230 The Parade, Norwood, (08) 8364 5900.

SWEET WATER, 187 Rundle St, (08) 8223 68 55, Thai cuisine. 🟥

■ Retail & Bookstores

EUROPA BOOKSHOP, 238 Rundle St, (08) 8223 2289, general bookstore with gay & lesbian titles.

IMPRINTS BOOKSHOP, 80 Hindley St, (08) 8231 4454, general bookstore with a gay & lesbian section. 🟥

MURPHY SISTERS BOOKSHOP, 240 The Parade, Norwood, (08) 8332 7508. Women's, lesbian & gay books, journals, music with browsing section & coffee room, current local information, 09:30-05:00 (Thurs till 20:00, Sat 10:00-16:00), closed Sun.

SISTERS BY THE SEA, Shop 1, 14 Semaphore Rd, Semaphore, 314 7088," women's bookstore, open daily.

■ Erotica

CLUB FEMME, 73 Hindley St, 8410 0636, men's & women's erotica, pride videos.

TASMANIA
BEACONSFIELD

■ Accommodations

YORKTOWN MANOR, PO Box 138, Beaconsfield, TAS, 7270, (61-363) 834 647 (tel/fax). Gay-friendly.

DEVONPORT

■ Accommodations

TRELAWNEY BY THE SEA, 6 Chalmers Lane, Devonport, 7310, (61-364) 243 263 (tel/fax). Gay-friendly.

HOBART

■ Information

AIDS INFO, (3) 6224 1034.

GAY INFO LINE, (3) 6334 8179.

■ Accommodations

CORINDA'S COTTAGES, 17 Glebe St, Glebe, Hobart, TAS, (61-03) 62 34 1590, Fax: (61-03) 62 34 2744. An award-winning National Trust Classified property in the heart of Hobart, these historic outbuildings are now delightful gay-owned, self-contained cottages. Private baths, expanded continental breakfast, 5-min drive to gay bars.

FORGE, THE, Brookbank, Richmond, 7025, (61-3) 62602 216, Fax: (61-2) 602 699. Gay-friendly.

MAVISTA COTTAGES, PO Adventure Bay, Bruny Island, 7150, (61-362) 931 347 (tel/fax). Gay-friendly.

■ Bars

BAVARIAN TAVERN, 281 Liverpool St, gay bar Sun from 20:00, gay dance night 1st Sat 21:00-03:00, occasional drag shows. 🎵 ♀♂

■ Dance Bar/Disco

JUICE, at the Fruit Juice Bar, 7 Watchburn St, Hobart, Sun from 15:00. ♀♂

LA CAGE II, 53 Collin St, Hobart, Thur-Sat 23:00 till late. ♀♂

LAUNCESTON

■ Accommodations

BRICKFIELDS TERRACE, 64 & 68 Margaret St, Launceston, TAS, 7250, (61-03) 6330 1753, Fax: (61-03) 6330 2334. Gay-friendly terraces with private baths, expanded continental breakfast, color TV, phone, fully equipped kitchen, handmde Tasmanian fudge.

EDENHOLME GRANGE, 14 St Andrews St, Launceston, 3250, (61-363) 346 666, Fax: (61-363) 343 106. Gay-friendly.

TASMANIA

NORFOLK REACH, PO Box 56, Exeter, TAS, 7275, (61-363) 947 681 (tel/fax). Gay-friendly.

PLATYPUS PARK FARM, 343 Brisbane St, Launceston, TAS, 7250, (61-363) 561 873 (tel/fax). Gay-friendly.

Bars

TRAMSHED BAR, 3 Earl St, at the Great Northern Hotel, Wed from 20:00, gay-friendly drinks nite, no dancing. ♀♂

Dance Bar/Disco

VENUE AT ST JAMES HOTEL, THE, 122 York St, Fri from 20:30, live show & DJ.

SWANSEA

Accommodations

COOMBEND COTTAGES, RSD 14, Swansea 7190, (61-362) 578 256, Fax: (61-362) 578 484, gay-friendly.

VICTORIA

DAYLESFORD

Accommodations

BALCONIES, THE, 35 Perrins St, Daylesford, VIC, 3460, (61-3) 53 48 1322 (Tel/Fax). Web: http://www.spacountry.net.au/balconys, B&B with in-house dinner, private & shared baths, cooked or continental breakfast, beverage-making facilities, TV lounge, video library, indoor heated pool (nudity permitted) on premises. ♀♂

DOUBLE NUT, Howe St, Daylesford, VIC, (61-354) 483 981. Gay-owned guesthouse with private baths. Mostly hetero clientele.

HOLLY LODGE, Grenville St, Daylesford, (61-353) 48 3670. B&B guesthouse. ♀♂

LINTON HOUSE, 68 Central Springs Rd, Daylesford, VIC, 3460, (61-353) 482 331. gay-friendly studio-style accommodations, private bath.

POOLWAY COTTAGES, Borsa Crescent, Hepburn Springs, VIC, (61-353) 481 049. Six self-contained cottages, woman-owned, gay-friendly.

VILLA VITA, Main Road, Kingston, VIC, (61-353) 456 448. B&B, mostly women with men welcome, private shower/WCs, buffet breakfast, TV lounge, VCR, video tape library, laundry facilities, nearby pool, river & lake. ♀

Women's Accommodations

AVALON MISTS, Mt. Franklin Rd, 5 min outside Daylesford, (61-354) 764 337." Women-only. ♀

Dance Bar/Disco

SPUDS CLUB, Midland Hwy, Neewlyn, 53 45 7300, gay restaurant which becomes a dance bar Sat 22:00. ♀♂

Cafe

NOT JUST MUFFINS, 26-28 Albert St, 53 48 3711, 08:00-14:00 (closed Tues).

Restaurants

DOUBLE NUT, Howe St, 53 48 3981, variety of cuisines with a Swiss accent.

GEELONG

Dance Bar/Disco

TWO FACES, 73 Yarra St, upstairs, gay Fri. ♀♂

WOOL EXCHANGE, 44 Corio St, (052) 242 400. ♀♂

MELBOURNE

Information

AIDS INFO, (03) 9347 6099.

ALSO FOUNDATION, 35 Cato St, 1st floor, Prahran, (03) 9510 55 69, gay organization, many gay & lesbian groups meet here.

GAY & LESBIAN SWITCHBOARD, (03) 9510 5488, 18:00-22:00.

Accommodations

CALIFORNIA MOTOR INN, 138 Barkers Rd, Hawthorn, VIC, 3122, (61-3) 9818 0281, Fax: (61-3) 9819 6845. Toll free in Australia: (1800) 331166. Gay-friendly motel with restaurant & bar, color TV, direct dial phones, AC, coffee/tea-making facilities, pool on premises, 50% gay & lesbian clientele.

FITZROY STABLES, 124 Victoria St, Fitzroy, Melbourne, VIC, 3065, (61-3) 9415 1507. Fully self-contained, fully furnished apartment, private bath, color TV, telephone, kitchen, ceiling fans. Mostly women, men welcome. ♀

ONE SIXTY-THREE DRUMMOND STREET, 163 Drummond Street, Carlton, Melbourne, VIC, 3053, (61-3) 9663 3081, Fax: (61-3) 9663 6500.

Guesthouse, private & shared baths, expanded continental breakfast, 24hr self-serve tea & coffee, TV lounge with colour TV, ceiling fans, laundry facilities, maid service.
PALM COURT BED & BREAKFAST, 22 Grattan Place, Richmond, Melbourne, VIC, 3121, (61-3) 9427 7365 (Tel/Fax), Mobile: (0419) 777 850. B&B with expanded continental breakfast, private & shared baths, women welcome. ♂

■ Bars
BARRACUDA, 64 Smith St, Collingwood, (03) 9419 2869 cocktail bar, dance bar & restaurant. 🍴♀♂
CANDY BAR, 162 Greville St, Prahran, (03) 9529 6566, bar & cafe with DJ, 50% gay. No dance floor, but later in evening everyone starts dancing around wherever. 🍴▨
DIVA BAR, 153 Commercial Rd, South Yarra, (03) 9824 2800, bar & cafe, daily 16:00-03:00 (closed Sun, Mon). ♪♀♂
DT'S HOTEL BAR, 164 Church St, Richmond, (03) 9428 5724, pool table, games, 11:30-01:00 (Sun till 23:00). 🍴♂
DUKE HOTEL BAR, St Kilda Rd, at Martin St, St Kilda, (03) 9534 4666, from 17:00 (Sun from 12:00). ♀♂
GIRL BAR, 5 Martin St, at Subway, St Kilda, gays, lesbians & "trannies," 70% women Fri nite only. ♀♂
GLASSHOUSE HOTEL BAR, 51 Gipps St, Collingwood, (03) 9419 4748, from 12:30-01:00 (Fri, Sat till 03:00). 🍴♀♂
JOCK'S, 9 Peel St, Collingwood, (03) 9417 6700, 18:00-01:00 (Sun 16:00-23:30), cabaret showd (NOT usually drag shows). 🍴♂
Q&A, 211 Gertrude St, at the Builders Arms, Fitzroy, gay Thurs 19:00-01:00, punk, alternative grunge "Indie" crowd, dance floor. 🍴♀♂
RASCALS HOTEL BAR, 194 Bridge St, Richmond, (03) 9429 9491, local pub with female bands, 7 days. 🍴♀
ROYAL HOTEL BAR, 41 Spensley St, at the Royal Hotel, Clifton Hill, (03) 9489 8716, Thurs-Sat from 20:00 women's nights.
★ **STAR HOTEL BAR,** 176 Hoddle St, Collingwood, (03) 9417 2696, 19:00-01:00 (Fri, Sat till 03:00), large gay & lesbian clientele. ♀♂

TOOTSIE'S, 34 Inkerman St, at Newmarket Hotel, St Kilda, (03) 9534 2385, Sat 21:00-01:30, glam galore! ♪♀♂
★ **VM'S,** 199 Commercial Rd, South Yarra, (03) 9827 6611, burned, to reopen late 1998. 🍴♀♂

■ Dance Bar/Disco
BARRACUDA, 64 Smith St, Collingwood, (03) 9419 2869 dance bar, restaurant & cocktail bar. 🍴♀♂
COMING OUT, 22-24 Bay St, Port Melbourne, (03) 9646 2677, Fri till 03:00. Women's dance nights, venues change frequently, call for current locations & times. 🍴♀
GREYHOUND HOTEL BAR, 1 Brighton Rd, St Kilda, (03) 9534 4189, gay Sat only 19:00-01:00, dance party. 🍴♀♂
JANE'S BAR, 19 Commercial Rd, at the Dome nightclub, S Yarra, (03) 9529 8966, drag heaven at The Dome, Sat night. ♪🍴
MONKEY, Lower Esplanade, in back of Palace, St Kilda, Sun from 24:00. 🍴♀♂
★ **PEEL DANCE CLUB,** Peel & Wellington Sts, Collingwood, (03) 9419 4762, video dance bar, daily from 22:00. 🍴♂
★ **PLUSH,** at The Lounge, 243 Sanston Walk, (03) 9663 2916, Thurs gay dance nite from 23:00, house music, alternative drag entertainment. 🍴♀♂
THREE FACES, 143 Commercial Rd, South Yarra, (03) 9826 0933, Thurs-Sun from 21:00, cabaret cocktail bar upstairs, dance bar & drag shows downstairs. ♪ 🎭🍴♀♂
URANUS, at Joey's Ministry of Sound, Commercial Rd, at Grattan St, Prahran, (03) 9534 1819, recovery bar, 04:00 Sun till Sun afternoon. 🍴♀♂
VELVET UNDERGROUND, 19 Park St, S. Melbourne, Fri-Sun from 20:00, alternative dance bar, popular with gays. 🍴▨

■ Cafe
BLUE ELEPHANT, Commercial Rd, near Izett St, South Yarra.. ♀♂
CAFE 151, 151 Commercial Rd, Prahran, (03) 9826 5336, daily from 12:00. ♀♂
CAFE FARGO, 406 Brunswick St, Fitzroy, (03) 9416 2599, 07:00-24:00 (Fri-Sun till late). ♀♂
COL'S CAFE, 70 Smith St, Collingwood., ▨
GALLEON CAFE, 9 Carlisle St, St Kilda, (03) 9534 8934, 09:00-24:00. ▨

VICTORIA

RAMJET'S, Commercial Rd, near Porter St., ♀♂
SANDGROPER'S, Commercial Rd, near Porter St, South Yarra., ♀♂

Restaurants
BARRACUDA, 64 Smith St, Collingwood, (03) 9419 2869 restaurant, cocktail bar & dance bar. ♀♂

CHINTA RIA, Commercial Rd, near Izett St, Prahran, Malaysian cuisine. Second location: 94 Acland St, St Kilda. Both locations very popular with gays. 🍴

GLOBE CAFE, 218 Chapel St, Prahran, (03) 9510 8693, daily. 🍴

KING & I, 103 Lonsdale St, Thai cuisine, 7 days.

ROCOCO, 226-228 Coventry St, S. Melbourne, (03) 9696 0001, restaurant & bar, modern Australian cuisine. 🍴

SUKHOTHAI, 490 High St, Northcote, (03) 9489 5551, Thai cuisine, daily from 17:30. Second location: 234 Johnson St, Fitzroy, 9419 4040. 🍴

THAI LOTUS, 106 Hoddle St, Collingwood, (03) 9417 4555, Thai & Australian cuisine, closed Mon. 🍴

Retail & Bookstores
HARES & HYENAS, 135 Commercial Rd, South Yarra, (03) 9824 0110, gay & lesbian bookshop. Second location 110 Smith St, Collingwood, (03) 9419 4445.

MORNINGTON PENINSULA

Accommodations
CAPE SCHANCK LODGE BED & BREAKFAST, 134 Cape Schanck Rd, Cape Schanck, VIC, (61-3) 5988 6395 (Tel/Fax). Email: graem@alphalink.com.au, Gay-friendly B&B 1 hr south of Melbourne on the tip of the Mornington Peninsula. Popular with women looking for a peaceful retreat from the city, 2 wings allow for greater privacy. Private baths, pool, silver-service dinners on request, shiatsu massage & sauna packages, 10% lesbian following.

NEWBURY

Accommodations
BLUE MOUNT B & B, Kearneys Rd, Newbury -Trentham, VIC, 3458, (61-354) 241 296. Gay-friendly B&B, 50% hetero clientele, private baths, full breakfast, beverage-making facilities, colour TV, video library, private cottage garden, nearby mineral spas, wineries, horseback riding.

STRATHBOGIE RANGES

Women's Accommodations
WHISPERING WINDS, PO Box 286, Euroa, VIC, 3666, (61-357) 981 608. a hand-built mudbrick, stone & timber cottage for women only, located in northeast Victoria, 2hrs from Melbourne, 1 loft bedroom (linen provided), potbelly stove heating in winter, lovely scenery, many nearby activities. ♀

WARRNAMBOOL

Accommodations
KING'S HEAD, PO Box 658, Warrnambool, VIC, 3280, (61-3) 5561 4569, Fax: (61-3) 5562 4085. Email: kinghead@ansonic.com.au, Web: http://www.ansonic.com.au/kingshead, Good mix of gays & lesbians, private & shared baths. ♀♂

WESTERN AUSTRALIA
PERTH

Information
AIDS INFO, (8) 9429 9900.

GAY & LESBIAN LINE, (8) 9328 9044, Mon-Fri 09:00-12:00 & 19:30-22:30.

Accommodations
COURT HOTEL, 50 Beaufort St, Perth, WA, 6000, (61-8) 9328 5292, Fax: (61-8) 9227 1570. hotel with restaurant & gay bar, some hetero clientele, private & shared baths, TV lounge, & laundry facilities, nearby sauna & gym. ♀♂

LAWLEY ON GUILDFORD, THE, 72 Guildford Rd, Mount Lawley, WA, 6050, (61-8) 9272 5501 (Tel/Fax), mobile (61-41) 299 5178. B&B with expanded continental breakfast, private & shared baths, color TV, AC, public phone, TV lounge, Jacuzzi, grass tennis court, enclosed conservatory. ♀♂

PENNY'S BY THE SEA, PO Box 208, 96A Stanley St, Scarborough, Sunset Coast, WA, 6019, (61-8) 9341-1411, Fax: (61-8) 9245-1073, Mobile: (015) 1969 30. Apartments with kitchens, available by day or week, clean & comfortable, private baths, nearby pool & ocean beach. ♀♂

NORTH ISLAND 177

SULLIVANS HOTEL, 166 Mounts Bay Road, Perth, WA, 6000, (61-8) 9321 8022, Fax: (61-8) 9481 6762. gay-friendly hotel, private baths with showers.

SWANBOURNE GUEST HOUSE, 5 Myera St, Swanbourne, Perth, WA, 6010, (61-8) 9383 1981, mobile (041) 893 2994, Fax: (61-8) 9385 4595. Web: www.ozemail.com.au/~ksetra/sgh.html, B&B guesthouse, women welcome, private & shared baths, continental breakfast, colour TV, VCR, beverage-making facilities, nearby pool, ocean, river & lake. ♂

■ Bars

COURT HOTEL BAR, 50 Beaufort St, (8) 9328 5292, daily 10:00-24:00 (Sun 12:00-21:00), DJ in the pub, Wed women only.

★ **DIVEBAR,** 232 William St, Northbridge, (8) 9328 1822, bar with snack bar. ♂

■ Dance Bar/Disco

CONNECTIONS, 81 James Street, Northbridge, (8) 9328 1870, 60% men, 40% women, Tues-Sat 22:00-06:00 (Tues men only, Thurs women only), Sun 20:00-24:00. ♂

■ Cafe

COOD ST CAFE, in suburb of Mt Lawley, popular with gays & lesbians.

■ Restaurants

ORIEL CAFE & BRASSERIE, in suburb of Subiaco, gay-friendly.

■ Retail & Bookstores

ARCANE BOOKSHOP, 212 William St, Northbridge, (8) 9328 5073. Bookstore with lesbian, feminist & gay literature, general books, calendars, postcards, 10:00-17:30 (Sat till 17:00), Sun 12:00-16:00.

PACIFIC REGION
NEW ZEALAND

COUNTRY CODE: (64),

NORTH ISLAND
AUCKLAND

■ Information

AIDS INFO, (0800) 802 437 (24hrs), (09) 358 00 99.

AUCKLAND GAY & LESBIAN COMMUNITY CENTRE, 44-46 Ponsonby Rd, 1st floor, (09) 302 0590. Unverifiable spring '97.

GAY & LESBIAN LINE, (09) 303 35 84, 10:00-22:00 (Sat, Sun from 17:00). Women answer evenings Mon, Wed & Sat.

PRIDE CENTRE, 33 Wyndham St, (09) 302 05 90.

WOMANLINE, (09) 3765 173, answers Mon-Fri 11:00-20:30.

■ Accommodations

ASPEN LODGE, 62 Emily Place, Auckland, North Island, (64-9) 379 6698, Fax: (64-9) 377 7625. Email: aspenlodge@xtra.co.nz, gay-friendly budget bed & breakfast hotel 5 min from downtown, shared baths, TV lounge, continental breakfast, complimentary tea, coffee.

BUDGET INN TALOFA, 508 Great North Rd, Grey Lynn, (09) 378 8872. Gay-friendly hotel with bar & restaurant, private baths.

HERNE BAY B&B & SERVICED APARTMENTS, 4 Shelly Beach Rd, Herne Bay, Auckland, (64-9) 360 03 09, Fax: (64-9) 360 0389. B&B & fully self-contained serviced apartments, very centrally located at the edge of the gay area. A 5-min walk to cafes & shops. 50% gay & lesbian clientele. ♀♂

PARITUHU BEACHSTAY, 3 King Edward Parade, Devonport, Auckland, (64-9) 445 6559 (Tel/Fax). Email: parituhu@iprolink.co.nz, Web: home.iprolink.co.nz/Parituhu, B&B with double room, private bath. No smoking in house, TV, laundry facilities, phone, fax, e-mail, computer, near Devonport shops, cafes & beach. Some hetero clientele. ♀♂

PARK CENTRAL THE DARLINGHURST, 52 Eden Crescent, Auckland City, 1001, (64-9) 366 3260, (0800) 944 400, Fax: (64-9) 366-3269. Email: darlinghurst@parkcentral.co.nz, Deco-style apartment hotel in ceity centre, modern city apartments with traditional hotel service. Private baths, harbor views. Gay/lesbian following.

■ Bars

SURRENDER DOROTHY, 175 Ponsonby Rd, Shop 3, (09) 376 4460, 18:00-01:00 (Sat, Sun from 12:00). ♂

NORTH ISLAND

■ Dance Bar/Disco
KASE, THE, 340 Karangahape Rd, 3 bars, Wed-Sat from 18:00 (disco from 22:00).

LEGEND, 335 Karangahape Rd, (09) 377 60 62, from 16:00.

■ Restaurants
RYBURN'S BAR & GRILL, North Rd, Clevedon, (09) 292 8111.

SALSA BAR & CAFE, 137a Richmond Rd, Ponsonby, (09) 378 81 58, 15:00-23:30 (closed Sun).

■ Retail & Bookstores
ONEHUNGA BOOK EXCHANGE, 163 The Mall, Onehunga, (09) 622 1766, general bookshop with new & secondhand gay titles, 09:00-17:30 (Fri till 19:00, Sat till 14:00).

WOMEN'S BOOKSHOP, THE, 228 Dominion Rd at Valley Rd, Mt Eden, (09) 6307 162, feminist & lesbian books & magazines Tues-Sat from 10:00.

BAY OF ISLANDS

■ Accommodations
ORONGO BAY HOMESTEAD, Aucks Road, RD1, Russell, Bay of Islands, (64-9) 403 7527, Fax: (64-9) 403 7675. Email: orongo.bay@clear.net.nz, Guesthouse with gourmet dining room & historic wine cellar, on 17 acres of bush, lake & lawns, sweeping views, 50-min flight from Auckland. Full breakfast with champagne, all private baths. Central to many outdoor activities, beaches & game fishing. 50% gay & lesbian clientele.

COROMANDEL

■ Accommodations
HARBOUR VIEW MOTEL, 2050 Long Bay Rd, Coromandel, (64-7) 866 8690 (Tel/Fax). 6 1-BR units with full kitchen, harbour views.

FEATHERSTON

■ Women's Accommodations
PETRA KIRIWAI FARM, RD 3, Featherston, (64-6) 307 7899. women-only guesthouse on 350 acres of land, near ocean & lake, mostly lacto-vegetarian cuisine, private & shared baths, laundry facilities. ♀

HAMILTON

■ Information
AIDS INFO, (07) 838 557.
GAYLINE, (07) 854 9631, Wed 20:00-22:00.

■ Bars
NEXT DOOR BAR, 10 High St, Frankton, (07) 847 8635, 17:30-03:00 (closed Mon, Tues.)

■ Retail & Bookstores
BOOKSHOP 242, 242 Victoria St, gay magazines.
GOLDMINE BOOKSHOP, 312 Victoria St, general bookshop with gay section.

HUNTERVILLE

■ Beaches
VINEGAR HILL, from Christmas to the week after New Year's, large crowds of gays & lesbians. 5km north of Hunterville off State Hwy 1. Camping at the downriver end, bring a tent. Loosely-organized activities.

NAPIER/HASTINGS

■ Information
GAYLINE, (06) 8357 482, 17:00-08:00.

■ Accommodations
CORNUCOPIA LODGE, 361-363 State Highway 5, Eskdale, Napier, 4021, (64-6) 836 6508, Fax: (64-6) 836 6518. Email:

CORNUCOPIA LODGE

A Refreshing Luxury Wine-Country Retreat

NAPIER · NEW ZEALAND

North Island

(64-6) 836-6508

cornucopia@clear.net.nz, Fruit and nut trees surround this fully self-contained lodge featuring expansive views over gardens & grapvines, pastures & forest-planted hills. The sunny verandah overlooks the garden, and the dining room features views over the Linden Estate Winery. Meals can be prepared in our state-of-the-art kitchen with turbo oven, microwave & dishwasher. The town of Napier is only 15 km away and offers many excellent restaurants, bars, stores & tourist sights.

PROVIDENCIA GUEST HOUSE, Middle Rd, RC2, Hastings, (06) 877 2300. Gay-friendly.

Retail & Bookstores

CLARK'S CIVIC CT BOOKSHOP, Station St, Napier, general bookstore with a gay & lesbian section.

PALMERSTON NORTH

Information

GAYLINE & LESBIAN LINE, (06) 358 5378, 24hrs.

Bars

MANAWATU GAY RIGHTS ASSN BAR NIGHTS, (06) 358 5378, Fri from 20:00, Sat from 21:30, ask about women-only nights.

Retail & Bookstores

WOMEN'S SHOP, Square Edge, Church St, (06) 358 2644, women's bookstore & crafts, good information resource for travelling lesbians.

ROTORUA

Information

AIDS SUPPORT, (03) 348 1199.

GAYLINE, (07) 348 3598, Tues 19:00-21:00.

Accommodations

TROUTBECK, 16 Egmont Rd, PO Box 242, Ngongotaha, Rotorua, (64-7) 357 4795, Fax: (64-7) 357 4780. Email: troutbeck@troutbeck.co.nz, Web: http://nz.com/webnz/troutbeck, Homestay 5 km from Rotorua on 1/2 acre of landscaped garden on banks of Waiteti Stream, fly fish for trout Dec-May from the garden's edge. Shared baths, full breakfast & optional dinner NZ $15. Close to thermal areas, Maori culture & golf courses. Women welcome. ♂

THAMES COAST

Accommodations

TE PURU COAST VIEW LODGE, 468 Thames Coast Road, Te Puru, Coromandel Peninsula, (64-7) 868 2326, Fax: (64-7) 868 2376. Web: 100036.2460@compuserve.com, Gay-friendly lodge 15 min north of Thames. Situated on a Maori archeaological site & has views of the Firth of Thames & Coromandel ranges, private baths, fully licensed restaurant on premises.

The Mermaid
Wellington's Guesthouse for Women

❖ Latest info on Women's accommodation and events nationwide
❖ Antique, Art Deco and Contemporary furnishings
❖ 10 mins walk to cafes, offices, shops & theatres
❖ Luxurious robes, towels and fragrant soaps
❖ King, Queen and double beds
❖ Private and shared facilities

**Ph/Fax (644) 384 4511-mermaid@sans.vuw.ac.nz
1 Epuni St, Aro Valley, Wellington, New Zealand**

NORTH ISLAND

WELLINGTON

■ Information
AIDS INFO, (04) 3816 640.
GAY SWITCHBOARD, (04) 3850 674, daily 19:30-22:00.
LESBIAN LINE, (04) 3898 082, Tues, Thurs 19:00-22:00.

■ Accommodations
AMBASSADOR TRAVEL LODGE, 287 The Terrace, (64-4) 484 5697, Fax: (64-4) 485 7215. Centrally located B&B, mainly straight clientele, comfortable, well-furnished, single rooms thru villas, full breakfast & dinner.

■ Women's Accommodations
MERMAID, THE, 1 Epuni St, Aro Valley, Wellington, (64-4) 384 4511 (Tel/Fax). Email: mermaid@sans.vuw.ac.nz, Early 1900s wooden building in one of Wellington's older historical areas. Women only. Individually decorated double and single rooms, shared & private bathrooms. TV, VCR, fresh fruit, complimentary wine. Large deck, guests' lounge with pool table. Breakfast included. Great atmosphere! ♀ See ad on page 179.

■ Bars
BOJANGLES, 52 or 60 Dixon St, (04) 384 8445. ♂
CHEQHERZ, 105 Vivian St, at Seranno's, upper level, 2nd Sun 17:00-24:00. ✗ ♀
RUBY RUBY, 19 Edward St, (04) 384 5211, 11:00-03:00. ♂

■ Cafe
EVERGREEN COFFEE BAR, 144 Vivian St, (04) 385 1510, after hours. ♀♂

■ Restaurants
BRASSERIE FLIPP, 103 Ghusnee St, (04) 385 9493.

■ Retail & Bookstores
AFTERNOONS & COFFEE SPOONS, shop 6, 165 Riddiford St, Newtown., Women's shop with new & used books, videos, music, t-shirts, sarongs, jewelry, crafts, etc. Coffee, tea, muffins & cakes. 11:00-19:00 (Sun till 15:00), closed Mon.

SOUTH ISLAND
CHRISTCHURCH

■ Information
GAY INFO LINE, (03) 3793 990, 24hrs.

■ Accommodations
DOROTHY'S BOUTIQUE HOTEL, 2 Latimer Square, Christchurch, (64-3) 365 6034, Fax: (64-3) 365 6035.
TOTARA VALE RETREAT, Totara Vale, Dawbers Road, Le Bons Bay, RD3, Akaroa, (64-3) 304 7172, Fax: (64-9) 304 7182. Accommodation on the Banks Peninsula on 100+ acres. Spa on premises, home-cooked meals available.

■ Women's Accommodations
BUSHLINE LODGE, c/o Bushwise Women, PO Box 28010, Christchurch, (64-3) 332 4952 (Tel/Fax), (64-3) 738 0077, or mobile: (64-3) 25 360 926. Email: bushwise@bushwise.co.nz, Web: http://www.bushwise.co.nz, This women-only B&B on the West Coast of New Zealand is the ideal retreat for women seeking time out in a women's space and ambiance. Our 3 rooms have private & shared baths & we serve expanded continental breakfast. This unique lodge is situated in a spectacular area, ideal for bushwalkers, bird lovers, rafting, caving, gold-panning & year-round trout fishing. Bookings essential. ♀
FRAUENREISEHAUS (THE HOMESTEAD), 272 Barbadoes St, Christchurch, 1, (64-3) 366 2585. Women-only backpackers hostel in a very spacious, 2-story, 100-year-old house near the city centre. Accommodation for 70 people in single, twin & bunk rooms & self-contained apartments. Five large, sunny kitchens are fully-equipped & stocked with crockery, glasses, cutlery, cooking utensils & free herbs & spices. Bedrooms are spacious & clean. Linen, duvets, pillows, local phone calls, washing facilities & bicycles are provided free. There are ample shower & toilet areas & plenty of hot water. We don't limit the number of showers as many hostels do. ♀

■ Restaurants
BAR PARTICULAR, 51 Lichfield St, (03) 3650 781, restaurant, bar & cafe, from 17:00 (closed Sun, Mon).

Retail & Bookstores

KATE SHEPPARD WOMEN'S BOOKS, 145 Manchester St, (03) 790 784, feminist, spiritual & new age titles, also music, posters, cards & jewelry, also gay men's titles, Mon-Thur 09:00-17:30, Fri 09:00-21:00, Sat 10:00-13:00.

DUNEDIN

Information

GAYLINE, (03) 477 2077, 24hrs, ask about coffee evenings 2nd & 4th Fri."

LESBIAN LINE, (03) 4772 077, Tues 17:30-19:30.

Bars

BATH ST BAR, Bath St, gay & lesbian bar night, last Wed from 21:00. ♀♂

QUEER SPACE, Upper Morney Place, at the Tangente Cafe, Thurs 19:30-23:00. ♂

INVERCARGILL

Information

GAYLINE, (03) 216 6344, evenings, weekends.

LESBIAN LINE, 218 3877, 19:00-21:00.

Accommodations

HOME INN STEAD, 58 Milton Park Rd, Invercargill, (64-3) 216 3610, Fax: (64-3) 216 7838. Homestay with double rooms, breakfast, modern amenities.

NELSON

Information

AIDS INFO, (03) 546 1731, Mon-Fri 08:00-16:00.

Accommodations

PALM GROVE GUEST HOUSE, Cambria St, at Tasman St, (03) 548 4645.

TE PUNA WAI LODGE, 24 Richardson Street, Nelson, 7001, (64-3) 548 7621 (Tel/Fax). Early Victorian villa with mountain & sea views, luxurious ensuite marble baths, expanded continental breakfast. Five min from waterfront restaurants. 50% gay & lesbian clientele.

Women's Accommodations

HECATE HOUSE, 181 Nile St East, Nelson, (64-3) 546 6890, Fax: (64-3) 546 6895. Women-only guesthouse with hot tub, double & single rooms, separate lounge, kitchen & bathroom facilities, non-smoking. ♀

Restaurants

RIBBETTS RESTAURANT, 20 Tahunanui Dr, (03) 548 6911.

QUEENSTOWN

Accommodations

HOME INN STEAD, 6 Lockey Rd, Fernhill, (64-3) 442 5470, Fax: (64-3) 216 7838. Gay homestay with private & shared baths, modern amenities, continental breakfast.

Bushline Lodge
Women-Only B&B
West Coast
New Zealand
Christchurch
(64-3) 332 4952

Come Stay With Us at Frauenreisehaus
frauenreisehaus
the homestead
Christchurch, New Zealand
(64-3) 366-2585

PACIFIC REGION ISLANDS
COOK ISLANDS

COUNTRY CODE: (682),

RAROTONGA

Accommodations
MANUIA BEACH HOTEL, PO Box 700, Rarotonga, (682) 22461, fax: 22464. On one of Rarotonga's best white-sand beaches by the lagoon, you'll stay in a Polynesian-style thatched bungalow with stylish decor, private bathroom, refrigerator, minibar and ceiling fans.

TAMURE RESORT HOTEL, PO Box 483, Rarotonga, (682) 22415, fax: 24415. Rooms overlook the lagoon and the Pacific, 100 yards from a coral reef, with patio, individual AC, private bathroom and refrigerator, tropical gardens and a cocktail bar on the premises.

FIJI ISLANDS

COUNTRY CODE: (679),

NADI

Accommodations
WEST'S MOTOR INN, THE, Martintar, Nadi, (679) 720 044, Fax: (679) 720 071. Gay-friendly hotel with restaurant, piano bar & gift shop, 10 min drive from Nadi Town & Nadi airport. Private & shared baths, AC, phone, large pool on premises, airport shuttle.

TAVEUNI

Accommodations
MARAVU PLANTATION RESORT, PO Box Matei, Taveuni Island, (679) 880 555, Fax: (679) 880 600. Resort cottages with restaurant & bar, private baths, ceiling fans, pool on premises.

FR. POLYNESIA - TAHITI

COUNTRY CODE: (689),

MOOREA ISLAND

Accommodations
RESIDENCE LINAREVA, PO Box 1, Haapiti, Moorea, (689) 56 15 35 (Tel/Fax). At the foot of lush, green hills, is a tropical lagoon paradise with floating pub & restaurant for gay, lesbian and other visitors from faraway. Each typical Tahitian grass bungalow features deluxe accommodations with private shower-bath, kitchenette, color TV, ceiling fans & is decorated with traditional crafts."

PAPEETE

Bars
HOTEL PRINCESSE HEIATA BAR, address not needed, 3 281 05, late-night disco popular after the other nightclubs have closed and frequently open till dawn, women welcome.

★ **PIANO BAR,** rue des Ecoles, 3 228-24, popular disco for gay men & women, drag shows featured, open till about 2am, sometimes later.

GUAM

COUNTRY CODE: (671),

DEDEDO

Bars
CLUB SOPHIA, 2F Dededo Center (Route 1), 653 8602, 22:00-02:00, discreetly frequented by gays.

Deluxe Accommodations in a tropical lagoon paradise

Residence LINAREVA

Floating pub & restaurant

PO Box 1 • Haapiti-Moorea

Tel/Fax (689) 56 15 35
French Polynesia

TAMUNING

Dance Bar/Disco
★ **UNDERGROUND/CLUB PARADISE,** Marine Drive, near Blockbuster Video, 646 1578, big, trendy dance club, mostly gay clientele.

TUMON

Bars
JAKOB'S, 340 San Vitores Rd, in front of Guam Visitors Bureau, 646 9510, small karaoke lounge, 21:00-02:00, some Japanese spoken. ♂

CANADA
ALBERTA
BANFF

Information
GAY LINE, (403) 760-2888.

CALGARY

Information
GAYLINE, (403) 234-8973. 7-10pm or tape 7 days. 24hr info line 234-9752.
LESBIAN INFO LINE, (403) 265-9458. 7:30-9:30pm Mon & Wed or tape. Information available on women's collective.

Accommodations
BLACK ORCHID MANOR, 1401-2 St NW, Calgary, AB, T2M 2W2, (403) 276-2471. Email: lthrman@canuck.com, B&B in an Edwardian home with antique furnishings, shared baths, full cooked breakfast, 1hour to Banff National Park & museums. ♀♂
CALGARY WESTWAYS GUEST HOUSE, 216 25th Ave SW, Calgary, AB T2S0L1, (403) 229-1758, Fax: (403) 228-6265. Email: calgary@westways.ab.ca. Web: http://www.westways.ab.ca. This 1914 heritage home offers 4 tastefully-appointed bedrooms with private baths. After active days, guests can relax in a hot tub or on the secluded deck. Breakfasts are a choice of a traditional English, Canadian or health-conscious breakfast prepared by an awardwinning chef. We're just a 10--minute walk from bars and restaurants and a 20-minute walk to downtown. Bus and tram stops are nearby. ♂
FOXWOOD BED & BREAKFAST, THE, 1725-12 Street SW, Calgary, AB, T2T 3N1, (403) 244-6693. Edwardian character home in the heart of Calgary, shared baths, color cable TV, 2 rooms wtih VCRs, full breakfast, near gay bars, 1 hour to Olympic ski area. Some straight clientele. ♀♂

Bars
MONEY PENNIES, 111 15th Ave SW, (403) 263-7411. Bar & restaurant, pool table, days: 75% men, evenings 50/50. ♀♂
ROOK'S BAR & BEANERY, 112 16th Ave NW, (403) 277-1922, dance club, 90% women, men welcome. ♀

Restaurants
FOLKS LIKE US BISTRO, 110 10th St NW, at Kensington Rd, (403) 270-2241. Eclectic mix from cottage pies to veggie chilies, Middle Eastern, sandwiches, salads, some meat dishes. Women-owned.
MONEY PENNIES, 111 15th Ave SW, (403) 263-7411. Bar & restaurant. ♀♂
VICTORIA'S, 306 17th Ave SW, (403) 244-9991. Frequented by gays late evenings. Weekend brunches.

Retail & Bookstores
A WOMAN'S PLACE BOOKSTORE, 1412 Centre Street S, (403) 263-5256. Feminist, lesbian & gay men's titles.
RAINBOW MERCANTILE, 306-310 17th Ave SW, pride items, open Thurs-Sat evenings.

Calgary Westways Guest House
You're At Home...
(403) 229-1758

ALBERTA

EDMONTON

Information
AIDS HELPLINE, 11456 Jasper Ave, Rm 201, (403) 488-5742.
GAY & LESBIAN COMMUNITY CENTER, #103, 10612 124th St, (403) 488-3234, info line (403) 988-4018.
GAY LINE, (403) 486-9661. Tape with local info.
WOMANSPACE & LESBIAN LIFELINE, 9930 106th St, (403) 482-1794. Lesbian meetings 2nd Tues. Monthly women's dances, lesbian library, events.

Accommodations
LABYRINTH LAKE LODGE, Site 2 Box 3, RR1, Millet, AB, T0C 1Z0, (403) 878-3301. Fully-equipped cabin (sleeps 12) on 160 acres in the country with secluded lakefront. Canoes, bikes, skis & more. 50 minutes from Edmonton. Gay men welcome. ♀

Dance Bar/Disco
BUDDYS, 10116 124th St, (403) 488-6636. Dance pub with Sat women's night. ♀♂
ONE-O-ONE DISCOTHEQUE, 10045 109 St, (403) 413-3476. Open 8pm-3am daily. ♪ ☒ 🕪 ♀♂
ROOST, THE, 10435 104th St, near 104th Ave, (403) 426-3150. strippers. 🕪 ☒ ✕ ♀♂

Restaurants
GARAGE RESTAURANT, 10242 106th St, attached to Boots, (403) 423-5024, burgers, fries, chicken, wings, straighter crowd for lunch.
JAZZBERRY'S TOO, 10116 124th St, home cooking. ☒

Retail & Bookstores
ORLANDO BOOKS, 10640 Whyte Ave, (403) 432-7633. General bookstore with large gay, lesbian & women's section.

GRAND PRAIRIE

Information
GAY & LESBIAN COMMUNITY CENTER, (403) 539-3325. Ask about Open Closet Drop-in Center Thurs-Sat 7:30pm-9:30pm.

Dance Bar/Disco
ATTIC, 112 101st St., Mainstream alternative club, techno music, semi-popular with gay crowd. 🕪

LETHERIDGE

Information
GAY ALLIANCE, (403) 329-4666. Socials, discussions, events, Wed 7-10pm.

RED DEER

Information
GAY & LESBIAN ASSN. OF CENTRAL ALBERTA, (403) 340 2198. Wed 7-9pm or tape, coffee house 2nd Wed 7-10pm.

Dance Bar/Disco
THE OTHER PLACE (TOP), Bay 3 & 4, 55794 47th St, (403) 342-6440. 4pm-3am Tues-Sun, dance bar with DJ. 🕪 ♀♂

BRITISH COLUMBIA

FERNIE

Accommodations
FERNIE WESTWAYS GUEST HOUSE, Box 658, 202-4a Avenue, Fernie, BC, V0B 1M0, (250) 423-3058, Fax: (250) 423-3059." Email: fernie@westways.ab.ca, Our 1908 Heritage home presents spacious bedrooms, hardwood floors, high ceilings, private & shared baths, and views of the Rocky Mountains. Full breakfast is served in the elegant dining room. We're 5 minutes from Fernie Snow Valley Ski Resort and walking distance to shops. Just south of Banff, Fernie is a refreshing alternative to the busier Rocky Mountain resorts. ♀♂

Fernie Westways
Guest House
Comfort, Elegance, Warmth

(250) 423-3058

KELOWNA

■ Information
OKANAGAN RAINBOW COALITION, (250) 860-8555. Scheduled Gay & lesbian dance nights, coffeehouses, potlucks, volleyball on the beach, picnics on long weekends. Coffee Mon 7pm-10pm. Lesbians meet Wed. Travelers welcome to participate.

■ Bars
KNOBBY'S, 235 Queensway, Lounge & restaurant, discreetly frequented by gays & lesbians.

■ Dance Bar/Disco
JUNIOR'S, Leon Ave, near Gotcha's niteclub., Gay-friendly alternative dance club.
SPLASHES CABARET, 275 Leon Ave, (250) 762-2956. Young crowd, discreetly frequented by gays & lesbians.

NANAIMO

■ Bars
NEIGHBOURS, 70 Church St, bar entrance on Front St, (250) 716-0505. Video lounge, Mon-Fri 5pm-1am, Sat 6pm-1am, Sun 5pm-midnite, longer hours in summer. ♀♂

SALT SPRING ISLAND

■ Accommodations
BLUE EWE, 1207 Beddis Rd, Salt Spring Island, BC, V8K 2C8, (250) 537-9344. Gay & lesbian inn with many female clientele. ♀♂

GREEN ROSE AT SCOTT POINT, 388 Scott Point Dr, Salt Spring Island, BC, V8K 2R2, (250) 537-9927. Private suite with kitchenette, sitting room, private bath. 50% gay & lesbian clientele, ocean & nearby lake, minutes from ferry terminal.

SUMMERHILL GUEST HOUSE, 209 Chu-An Drive, Salt Spring Island, BC, V8K 1H9, (250) 537-2727, Fax: (250) 537-4301. Email: summerhill@saltspring.com, B&B overlooking the ocean, 50% gay & lesbian clientele. Private baths, full breakfast, many outdoor activities.

SUNNYSIDE UP BED & BREAKFAST, 120 Andrew Place, Salt Spring Island, BC, V8K 1X3, (250) 653-4889. Accommodations with ocean view, 50% gay & lesbian clientele. ♀♂

TOFINO

■ Accommodations
WEST WIND GUEST HOUSE, THE, 1321 Pacific Rim Hwy, Mail: Box 436, Tofino, BC, V0R 2Z0, (250) 725-2224, Fax: (250) 725-2212. Email: Westwind@island.net, Private cottage & suite near beaches & Pacific Rim National Park. Telephone, hot tub, universal gym, bicycles, private covered parking. ♀♂

■ Women's Accommodations
WIND RIDER, A GUEST HOUSE FOR WOMEN, Box 548, 231 Main St, Tofino, BC, V0R 2Z0, Administration: (250) 725-3230, Reservations: (250) 725-3240, Fax: (250) 725-3280. Email: whole@island.net, Women's guesthouse in downtown Tofino. Dorm-style with private room available, shared bath, AC, Jacuzzi, outside deck. Sunset views & view of Clayoquot Sound & Meares Island. ♀

VANCOUVER

■ Information
AIDS HELPLINE, (604) 681-2122. Mon-Fri 10am-9pm, Sat 10-6.
GAY & LESBIAN CENTRE, 1170 Bute, (604) 684-5307. Helpline: (604) 684-6869. 7pm-10pm 7 days, or (800) 566-1170 (within BC).
LESBIAN CENTER, 876 Commercial Dr, (604) 254-8458. Thurs & Fri 11am-6pm, Sat noon-4pm.

■ Accommodations
ALBION GUEST HOUSE, THE, 592 West Nineteenth Ave, Vancouver, BC, V5Z 1W6, (604) 873-2287, Fax: (604) 879-5682. Email: hle@bht.com, B&B 5 minutes from downtown. Double rooms with private & shared baths, some with color TV or VCR & video tape library. Full breakfast, non-smoking establishment." ♀♂

COLIBRI BED & BREAKFAST, 1101 Thurlow St, Vancouver, BC, V6E 1W9, (604) 689-5100, Fax: (604) 682-3925. Email: smokry@ibm.net, Conveniently

the ROYAL HOTEL

VANCOUVER'S GAY HOTEL & PUB

(604) 685-5335

located bed & breakfast, some hetero clientele. Airy, cheerful rooms with shared baths. Full breakfast, secure parking & nearby pool & ocean." ♀♂

COLUMBIA COTTAGE GUEST HOUSE, 205 West 14th Ave, Vancouver, BC, (604) 874-5327, Fax: (604) 879-4547. Email: goobles@msn.com, Web: http://www.novamart.com/columbia, B&B minutes from everything, 20% gay/lesbian clientele. 1920's-style rooms with private baths & full breakfast. English country garden."

DUFFERIN HOTEL, 900 Seymour St, Vancouver, BC, V6B 3L9, (604) 683-4251, Fax: (604) 683-0611. Hotel with gay bar & restaurant, Private baths. 50% men.

NELSON HOUSE, 977 Broughton St, Vancouver, BC, V6G 2A4, (604) 684-9793, Fax: (604) 684-4141. **No boring old B&B!** Every spacious corner guestroom suggests a different travel itinerary. Will it be Sailors, Vienna, Klondyke, or Hollywood? The third-floor studio suite, with Far Eastern ambience, a fireplace, deck, kitchen and Jacuzzi ensuite, is especially appealing. We are often complimented on our breakfast food, fun and conversation. Visit awhile. After all, Vancouver is right on the doorstep. ♀♂

O CANADA HOUSE, 1114 Barclay St, Vancouver, BC, V6E 1H1, (604) 688-0555, Fax: (604) 488-0556. Web: http://www.bbcanada.com/919.html, Gay-friendly Victorian B&B with private baths, full gourmet breakfast, complimentary snack bar, short walk to beaches, 3 blocks to gay bars. Some straight clientele.

ROYAL HOTEL, THE, 1025 Granville St, Vancouver, BC, V6Z 1L4, (604) 685-5335, Fax: (604) 685-5351. With low prices and adequate accommodations for budget-minded travelers. An "oldie but a goodie," this downtown hotel has been recently renovated, offering accommodations that are the cleanest and most reasonably priced on the strip. Constructed in 1912, its exterior is accented with flower-filled window boxes. Contemporary interior furnishings create a comfortable atmosphere. The hotel bar, recently renovated, is a popular gay night spot. ♀♂

RURAL ROOTS BED AND BREAKFAST, 4939 Ross Road, Vancouver-Mt. Lehman, BC, V4X 1Z3, (604) 856-2380, Fax: (604) 857-2380. Email: rroots@uniserve.com, Web: http://cimarron.net/canada/bc/rdrr/html, B&B on a heather farm with gardens & orchard, Color TV, private & shared baths, full breakfast, hot tub. ♀♂

WEST END GUEST HOUSE, 1362 Haro St, Vancouver, BC, V6E 1G2, (604) 681-2889, Fax: (604) 688-8812. Gay-friendly B&B. Unique, beautiful rooms with Victorian ambiance, private & shared baths. Guest lounge, expanded continental breakfast & nearby ocean beach."

YWCA HOTEL RESIDENCE, 733 Beatty St, Vancouver, BC, V6B 2M4, (604) 895-5830, Fax: (604) 681-2550; in BC & Alberta: (800) 663-1424. Email: ywcavan_hotel@bc.symatico.ca, Hotel with international craft shop, private & shared baths, gay men welcome.

■ *Women's Accommodations*

HAWKS AVENUE BED & BREAKFAST, 734 Hawks Avenue, Vancouver, BC, V6A 3J3, (604) 253-0989. A women-only heritage townhouse in Strathcona neighbourhood. Quiet, comfortable accommodation, close (10 min) to downtown theatres, shopping and restaurants, Gastown, Chinatown and Commercial Dr. Delicious breakfast, local calls free,

on-street parking & public transport. Reasonable rates. Non-smokers preferred. ♀
YWCA, 580 Burrard St, (604) 683-2531, Fax: 684-9171. Hotel at the YWCA. Mostly straight women with lesbians & gay men welcome.

■ Bars
DENMAN STATION, 860 Denman St, (604) 669-3448. 75% men, 25% women. 🏠[!]♪♂
DUFF PUB, THE, 900 Seymour St, in the Dufferin Hotel, (604) 683-4251. Bar & restaurant in the Dufferin Hotel featuring live bands weekly drag shows, male strippers Sun. ♪🖼[!]♀♂
GIRL TO GIRL NIGHTS, at Homers bar, women's nites Tues & Thurs. ♀
HOMER'S, 1249 Howe St, (604) 689-2444. Relaxed lounge with 3 pool tables, full sound system, balcony, serving lite menu. Women's night Tues & Thurs. ♀♂
MS T'S, 339 W Pender St, near Homer, (604) 682-8096. [!]∪♀♂
ROYAL HOTEL PUB, 1025 Granville, at the Royal Hotel, (604) 685-5335. Afternoon pub, live bands, closes at 11pm. ♪[!]♂
UNCLE CHARLIE'S BAR & GRILL & CHUCK'S PUB, 455 Abbott St, at Heritage House Hotel (side entrance)., Uncle Charlie's: 1st floor bar & restaurant. Chuck's is men's drinking bar, drag & leather events. 👅🖼♂

■ Dance Bar/Disco
★ **CELEBRITIES,** 1022 Davie St, at Burrard, (604) 689-3180. Getting lots of younger straight crowd, gayer Wed & Sat. [!]🖼♀♂
FLYGIRL & HER-SHE BAR, 1545 W 7, (604) 875-9907. Scheduled women's dance nites, call for dates. [!]♀
LOTUS CLUB, 455 Abbott St, at Heritage House Hotel, downstairs, (604) 685-7777. Tues-Sat from 8pm, Fri women-only. [!]♪♀
MARS, 1320 Richards St, (604) 662-7702. Mainstream club, gay Fri only. [!]
URBAN CHOCOLATE, at the Waldorf Hotel, monthly women's dance night. [!]♀

■ Cafe
CAFE DU SOLEIL, 1393 Commercial Dr & 2096 Commercial Dr, (604) 254-1145 & (604) 254-1195. 🖼
★ **EDGE EXPRESSO BAR,** 1148 Davie St, (604) 685-3417. Big with bar crowd, lots of smokers. Cruisy late evenings.
★ **HARRY'S OFF COMMERCIAL,** 1716 Charles St, (604) 253-1789. Coffeehouse with sandwiches, many women.
SPUNTINO CAFFEE, 1103 Davie, (604) 688-9658. Restaurant, bakery & cafe, great lunches. 🖼
VICIOUS CIRCLE, 2062 Commercial Dr, (604) 255-7629. Licensed cafe & laundromat.

Hawks Avenue
Bed & Breakfast for Women

734 HAWKS AVENUE, VANCOUVER, BC,
CANADA V6A 3J3 (604) 253-0989

Heritage townhouse, quiet, comfortable accommodation
10 min. to downtown, theatres, shops & restaurants, Gastown,
Chinatown, delicious breakfast, street parking, public transport
Reasonable Seasonal Rates. Non-smokers preferred

For reservations and more information please call Louise
(604) 253-0989 No credit cards accepted

Restaurants

ALLEGRO CAFE, 888 Nelson St, (604) 683-8485. Mediterranean cuisine, inspired chef, varied menu. 🌈

★ **CAFE LUXY,** 1235 Davie St, (604) 681-9976. Italian cuisine, good food & atmosphere, large portions. 🌈

CHATTERS, 23180 Gilley Rd.,

DEDE'S, 1030 Denman St, (604) 688-6264. Contemporary cuisine, lunch, brunch, dinner, & cocktails. 🌈

DELANEY'S ON DENMAN, 1039 Denman, (604) 662-3344. ♀♂

DELILAH'S, 1739 Comox, (604) 687-3424. Elegant, upscale continental cuisine. Trendy & excellent. 🌈

DENIRO'S BISTRO, 1007 Mainland St, (604) 684-2777. Funky with great martinis. 🌈

DOLL & PENNY'S CAFE, 1167 Davie St, (604) 685-3417.

ELBOW ROOM CAFE, 500 block of Davie St, (604) 685-3628. Brunch & lunch only. Many gays for Sat, Sun brunch." 🌈

HAMBURGER MARY'S, 1202 Davie St, (604) 687-1293.

LE VEGGIE, 1095 Denman St, (604) 682-3885. Chinese vegetarian cuisine.

MILESTONES, on Denman., Casual dining, curly fries & burgers, curry dishes. 🌈

PURPLE ONION, 15 Water St, (604) 602-9442. Healthy, gourmet, light snacks to meals, early evening till 1:30am. 🌈

★ **STEFHO'S,** ask locally for address., Greek cuisine, gay-friendly. 🌈

TAKI'S TAVERNA, 1106 Davie St, (604) 682-1336. Greek restaurant. Gay-friendly, a "must" in Vancouver. 🌈

TSUNAMI SUSHI, 238-1025 Robson & Burrand, upper level, (604) 685-5244.

WAAZUBEE, 1622 Commercial Dr, (604) 253-5299. Cocktails, Asian-influenced cuisine, Sat & Sun brunch. 🌈

Retail & Bookstores

LITTLE SISTER'S, 1238 Davie St, (604) 669-1753, fax: (604) 685-0252, books by mail: (800) 567-1662, E-mail: lsisters@netfinder.com. Gay & lesbian books, cards, videos.

RAINBOW'S END, 573 E Hastings St, (604) 254-6442. Thrift store & transgender boutique.

WOMEN IN PRINT, 3566 W 4th Ave, (604) 732-4128, Fax: (604) 732-4129. Feminist bookstore.

WOMYNSWARE, 896 Commercial Dr, at Venables, (604) 254-2543, Fax: (604) 254-5472, www.womynsware.com. Women's sexuality items, "vibes, dills, lubes, latex & more."

VICTORIA

Information

AIDS HELPLINE, 733 Johnson St #304, (250) 384-4554. Mon-Thurs 9am-9pm, Fri till 5pm.

Accommodations

CLADDAGH HOUSE BED & BREAKFAST, 1761 Lee Ave, Victoria, BC, V8R 4W7, (250) 370-2816, Fax: (250) 592-0228. B&B, some straight clientele, private & shared baths, hearty breakfast, Irish Milsèan confectionery, pool nearby. ♀♂

OAK BAY GUEST HOUSE, 1052 Newport Ave, Victoria, BC, V8S 5E3, (250) 598-3812, (800) 575-3812, Fax: (250) 598-0369. Email: OakBay@bedsbreakfasts.com, Web: http://bedsbreakfasts.com/OakBay, Gay-friendly B&B. Variety of rooms with private & shared baths, TV lounge, library, full breakfast, nearby ocean beach.

OCEAN WILDERNESS, 109 West Coast Rd RR#2, Sooke, BC, V0S 1N0, (250) 646-2116, (800) 323-2116, Fax: (250) 646-2317. Email: ocean@sookenet.com, Web: www.sookenet.com/ocean, Gay-friendly B&B inn. Large, beautifully-decorated rooms, hot tub, full breakfast, wake-up coffee. Nearby ocean beach, river.

WEEKENDER BED & BREAKFAST, THE, 10 Eberts St, Victoria, BC, V8S 5L6, (250) 389-1688. B&B within steps of the ocean along Victoria's scenic drive. Spacious rooms with private baths, continental breakfast. ♀♂

Women's Accommodations

BACK HILLS GUESTHOUSE FOR WOMEN, THE, 4470 Leefield Rd, Victoria, BC, V9C 3Y2, (250) 478-9648. Email: backhill@islandnet.com, Women-only guesthouse with full breakfast, 3 rooms, 2 shared baths. Beaches & hiking nearby. ♀

Bars

BJ'S LOUNGE, 642 Johnson St, at Broad, (250) 388-0505. Daily noon-2am (Sun till midnite). Piano bar & video lounge, all ages.

G SPOT, 910 Store St, (250) 382-7768, bar, dancing, art gallery, run by Women's Creative Network.

Dance Bar/Disco

RUMOURS, 1325 Government St, near Johnson, (250) 385-0566. Dance bar, cabaret, strippers Thurs, women's nights 3rd Fri.

Restaurants

BENT MAST, THE, in the Ames Bay area, (250) 383-6000. Call for location.

DILLETTANTE'S CAFE, 787 Forte St, (250) 381-3327. Eclectic fare, brunch, lunch.

FRIENDS OF DOROTHY, 615 Johnson St, (250) 381-2277. Restaurant with Wizard of Oz decor, 11:30am-10pm 7 days, Sun champagne brunch 11:30am-3pm.

MILKY WAY CAFE, 560 Johnson St, Mediterranean cuisine, breakfast-dinner.

Retail & Bookstores

EVERYWOMAN'S BOOKS, 635 Johnson St, near Douglas, (250) 388-9411. Women's bookstore open Mon-Sat.

WEST KOOTENAYS

Accommodations

BEACH HOUSE, THE, PO Box 1375, Kaslo, BC, V0G 1M0, (250) 353-7676, Fax: (250) 879-4547. Email: rdwilson@nel.auracom.com, Guesthouse retreat on lake with private beach, 50% gay & lesbian clientele. Private baths, full gourmet breakfast. Nearby natural hot springs.

WHISTLER

Accommodations

WHISTLER RETREAT, THE, 8561 Drifter Way, Whistler, BC, V0N 1B8, (604) 938-9245 (Tel/Fax). Email: whistler@axionet.com, Discovering The Whistler Retreat, brings downhill and cross-country skiing, snowshoeing, snowmobiling, hiking, mountain biking, swimming sunbathing, golf, tennis, canoeing, and horseback riding to your doorstep. This spacious alpine home, located on a mountainside just 5 minutes north of Whistler Village, has spectacular mountain views, 3 fireplaces, queen-sized beds, an outdoor Jacuzzi, a sauna, and a pool table. We offer a full breakfast each morning which is preceded by coffee, fresh fruit and freshly-baked muffins all awaiting you when you wake up. Whistler, a world-renowned mountain resort, has been rated one of the best places in the world to ski by *Snow Country Magazine* and *SKI Magazine*.

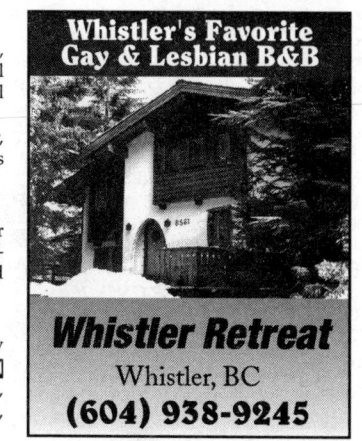

Whistler's Favorite Gay & Lesbian B&B

Whistler Retreat
Whistler, BC
(604) 938-9245

MANITOBA
BRANDON

Information

GAYS & LESBIANS OF BRANDON & ELSEWHERE, (204) 727-4297. Monthly socials 3rd Fri. Phone line, 7pm-9pm."

WINNIPEG

Information

AIDS INFO LINE, (204) 945-2437 or (800) 782-AIDS (inside Manitoba). "

GAY & LESBIAN RESOURCE CTR, 1-222 Osborne St S, office: 474-0212. Info line: (204) 284-5208."

WOMEN'S RESOURCE CENTER, 1910 Pembina Hwy, (204) 269-6836. Mon-Fri 9am-4:30pm. Call first."

190 MANITOBA

■ Accommodations
MASSON'S B & B, 181 Masson St, Winnipeg, MB, R2H 0H3, (204) 237-9230 (Tel/Fax). Gay-owned & -operated B&B in a Victorian setting, shared baths, full breakfast, some hetero clientele. ♀♂

TWIN PILLARS, 235 Oakwood Ave, Winnipeg, MB, R3L 1E5, (204) 284-7590, Fax: (204) 452-4925. Email: tls@escape.ca, Gay-friendly B&B, shared bath, color TV, expanded continental breakfast, 25% gay & lesbian clientele.

WINGED OX GUESTHOUSE, 82 Spence St, Winnipeg, MB, (204) 783-7408 (Tel/Fax). Email: winged-ox@gaycanada.com, Smoke-free B&B, convenient downtown location, shared baths, full breakfast, some hetero clientele. ♀♂

■ Dance Bar/Disco
CLUB 200, 190 Garry Street, (204) 943-6045. Dance bar & cabaret, restaurant, 60% men, 40% women, some straight clientele. 4pm-2am, closed Sun. 🎵 ♪ ✕ ♀♂

GIO'S SOCIAL CLUB, 272 Sherbrooke, (204) 786-1236. Disco & lounge, 75% men, 25% women. Private club, male strippers, travelers welcome. 8pm-2am (Fri till 3:30am). Wed karaoke, most popular Fri. 🎵 ♂

HAPPENINGS SOCIAL CLUB, 274 Sherbrooke St, near Portage (upstairs), (204) 774-3576. Nightly dance bar and lounge. Private club, travelers welcome, male strippers Thurs. On Sat for after hours, till 3:30am, 50% straight. 🎵 📺 ♀♂

MS PURDY'S WOMEN'S CLUB, 226 Main St, (204) 989-2344. Disco. Men welcome Fri & Sat, closed Sun & Mon. 🎵 ♪ ♀

■ Cafe
PANIC CAFE, on Broadway., 🍴

■ Restaurants
BIG RUBY'S BISTRO, 102 Sherbrooke, (204) 775-0188. 🍴

CLUB 200 RESTAURANT, at the Club 200, 190 Garry St, (204) 943-6045. Closed Sun. Burgers, nachos, etc. ♪ 🍷 ♀♂

■ Retail & Bookstores
MCNALLY-ROBINSON BOOKSELLERS, Grant Park Shopping Center, (204) 453-2644, Fax: (204) 452-0749. General bookstore with coffee shop & gay section, Mon-Fri 9:30am-9:30pm, Sat 9:30am-6:00pm, Sun noon-5pm.

NEW BRUNSWICK
AULAC

■ Accommodations
GEORGIAN HOUSE, 114 Mount Whatley Loop, Aulac, NB, E4L 2M2, (506) 536-1481. B&B, shared bath, some straight clientele." ♀♂

FREDERICTON

■ Information
GAYLINE, (506) 457-2156. Tues & Thur 6:30pm-8:30pm, info on support groups and social activities, library and newsletter called Flag Mag.

■ Dance Bar/Disco
KURT'S PHOENIX RISING, 377 King St, (506) 453-0740. Gay bar on 2nd floor with pool table, open Tues-Sun from 8pm. 3rd fl: Alternative dance bar with 50% gay/lesbian clientele, 9pm-2am Fri & Sat. Lower level: Bona fide gay bar. 🎵

MONCTON

■ Dance Bar/Disco
TRIANGLE, 264 St George St, (basement of Nat'l Bank bldg)., (506) 857-8779. Dance bar with gay/straight crowd. 🎵 ♀♂

SAINT JOHN

■ Accommodations
MAHOGANY MANOR, 220 Germain St, Saint John, NB, E2L 2G4, (506) 636-8000, Fax:(506) 636-8001. Email: leavittr@nbnet.nb.ca, Gay-owned B&B, gay & lesbian following, private baths, full hot breakfast.

■ Dance Bar/Disco
BOGART'S, 9 Sydney St, (506) 652-2004. Dance bar, Wed-Sun 8pm-2am, DJ Thurs-Sat, 60% men, 40% women. Ladies nite 3rd Fri. 🎵 ♪ ♀♂

NEWFOUNDLAND
ST JOHN'S

■ Accommodations
ABBA INN 3-STAR TRAVEL LODGING ST. JOHN'S, 36 Queen's Rd, St. John's, NF, A1C 2P9, (709) 754-0047, (800)

563-3959. Email: abba@thezone.net, Web: http://www.bbcanada.com/1873.html, Gay-friendly B&B inn with private & shared baths, full breakfast.

BANBERRY HOUSE, 116 Military Rd, St John's, NF, A1C 2C9, (709) 579-8006, Fax: (709) 579-3443. Email: captain_quintana.msn.com, Gay-owned B&B with mainly straight clientele, in an old Victorian with 5 guest rooms, all private baths, full gourmet breafkast.

■ *Dance Bar/Disco*
ZONE, THE, 216 Water St., Small disco. 🍺 ♀♂

NOVA SCOTIA
ANNAPOLIS VALLEY

■ *Women's Accommodations*
PUMPKIN ECOLOGICAL WIMMIN'S FARM & RETREAT, RR #5, Bridgetown, NS, B0S 1C0, (902) 665-5041. Rural ecological womyn's guesthouse & organic farm in a quiet space & rustic surroundings. Full vegetarian breakfast, lunch & supper available for extra fee. ♀

BEAR RIVER

■ *Accommodations*
LOVETT LODGE INN, PO Box 119, Bear River, Nova Scotia, NS, B0S 1B0, (902) 467-3917. 50% gay & lesbian clientele.

HALIFAX

■ *Bars*
PURPLE PENGUIN, 1541 Barrington St., Bar & restaurant. ♀♂
RAINBOW ROOM, 2104 Gottingen St, (902) 423-2956. Conversation bar. ♀♂

■ *Dance Bar/Disco*
REFLECTIONS CABARET, 5184 Sackville St, at Barrington, (902) 422-2957. Gets busy later on weekends. 🎵♂

MARGARETVILLE

■ *Accommodations*
TALISMAN B & B, THE, 6 Seaman St, Margaretville, NS, B0S 1N0, (902) 825-2531. B&B near Bay of Fundy with shared bath, full breakfast. Mostly hetero with a gay female following.

PEGGY'S COVE

■ *Accommodations*
OLD FISHER HOUSE B & B, THE, 204 Paddy's Head Road, RR 1, Box 1527, Indian Harbour, NS, B0J 3J0, (902) 823-2228 (Tel/Fax). B&B in an island home, 40 min drive from Halifax. Two rooms with queen beds & oceanfront views, 1 shared bath. Full breakfast, private beach for swimming, kayaks on premises, motorhome available to rent for excursions, dolphin & whale watching nearby. Some hetero clientele, open May-Oct. ♀♂

ONTARIO
BRIGHTON

■ *Accommodations*
BUTLER CREEK BED & BREAKFAST, RR7, Hwy 30-202, Brighton, ON, K0K 1H0, (613) 475-1248, Fax: (613) 475-5267. Gay-owned B&B in the countryside halfway between Toronto & Ottawa, 15% gay & lesbian clientele.

GUELPH

■ *Information*
AIDS LINE, (519) 763-2255, Mon-Fri 11am-8pm, Sat 12pm-4pm.
GUELPH OUTLINE, (519) 836-4550, 7pm-10pm, Fri & Sat 6pm-9pm.

■ *Dance Bar/Disco*
GAY & LESBIAN DANCES., Call Outline for schedule. 🍺 ♀♂

HAMILTON

■ *Information*
AIDS LINE, (905) 528-0854, (800) 563-6919 (southern Ontario). Mon-Thurs 9-9pm, Fri 10am-7pm.

■ *Camping & RV*
CEDARS TENT & TRAILER PARK, PO Box 195, Millgrove, ON, L0R 1V0, (905) 659-7342 or 659-3655. Campground with clubhouse, 600 campsites with shared shower facilities. ♀♂

■ *Bars*
CLUB 121 BAR, 121 Hughson St N, (905) 546-5258. Bar & restaurant, DJ & live bands upstairs, snack in back bar. 🍺 ✖ ♂

ONTARIO

WINDSOR BAR & GRILL, 31 John St N, (905) 308-9939. Bar & restaurant. 🚫

Dance Bar/Disco
CLUB SODA, 31 John St. N (upstairs)., 🍽️♀♂

EMBASSY CLUB, THE, 54 King St East, (905) 522-7783. High energy dance bar open 7 days, 60% men, 40% women. 🍽️♀♂

Restaurants
CAFE 121 RESTAURANT, 121 Hughson St N, (905) 546-5258. Bar & restaurant, steak, chicken, Sun brunch. ♀♂

LA SPAGHETT, 970 Upper James, (905) 318-8211. 🚫

Retail & Bookstores
GOMORRAH'S BOOKS, 158 James St South, (905) 526-1074, (888) 338-8278. Gay & lesbian books, gifts, pride items, jewelry, cards, adult toys, etc.

WOMEN'S BOOKSTOP, 333 Main St W, (905) 525-2970. Feminist bookstore with lesbian section.

KINGSTON

Dance Bar/Disco
CLUB 477, 477 Princess St, (613) 547-2923. Alternative dance bar, game room, lounge, 7 days, DJ Thurs-Sat. Winter 6:30pm-2am, Summer 4pm-2am, weekends till 3am. 🍽️✖️♀♂

KITCHENER

Dance Bar/Disco
CLUB RENAISSANCE, 24-A Charles W, (519) 570-2406. Wed-Sun 9pm-3am. 🍽️✖️♀♂

ROBIN'S NEST, in the old Farmer's Bldg, Cambridge, (519) 621-2688. At Cambridge fairgrounds, 15 miles from Kitchener. Disco Sat, c&w dancing alt Sun afternoons. Seasonal, usually closed in summer. Sat 8pm-2am. 🍽️♀♂

LONDON

Information
AIDS HOTLINE, 200-343 Richmond St, (519) 434-8160. Mon-Thur 9-9, Fri 9-5."

GAY LINE, (519) 433-3551. Mon, Thurs 7-10pm.

Bars
JUNCTION, at Club London complex, (519) 438-2625. Cruise bar attached to the Club London, leather meeting last Sat. 🚫♂

Dance Bar/Disco
APARTMENT, 186 Dundas St, (519) 679-1255. Dance bar. 🍽️♀♂

HALO BAR, 649 Colborne St, at Pall Mall, (519) 433-3762. Private club & community center, dance bar Wed, Fri, Sat. Also Options upstairs quiet bar Sat from 9pm, coffeehouse Mon, most popular for men on Sat. Mon-Thurs 7pm-midnite, Fri-Sat 9pm-2am." 🍽️♀♂

INFINITY, 192 Dundas St, (near The Apartment bar)., 🎵🍽️♀♂

SINS, Clarence between York & King., 🍽️♀♂

Restaurants
BLACKFRIARS CAFE, 46 Blackfriars St, (519) 667-4930. Breakfast thru dinner, international cuisine. 🚫 🎵

GREEN TOMATO, 172 King St, (519) 660-1170. 🚫

MARLA JANE'S, 460 King St, (519) 858-8669. 🚫

VERANDAH CAFE, 546 Dundas., 🚫

Retail & Bookstores
MYSTIC BOOKSHOP, 616 Dundas St, (519) 673-5440. New Age, holistic, self-help, books, candles, incense, etc. 11am-6pm (closed Sun).

WOMANSLINE BOOKS, 573 Richmond Street, (519) 679-3416. Feminist & lesbian bookstore, 10am-6pm (Thurs-Fri till 8pm), closed Sun.

MAYNOOTH

Women's Accommodations
WILDEWOOD, Box 121, Madawaska Rd, Maynooth, ON, K0L 2S0, (613) 338-3134. Guesthouse with shared baths, full breakfast. The gay male owners have found that women "love the way we pamper them. They love having nothing to decide other than when to open the wine." ♀

NIAGARA FALLS

Accommodations
DANNER HOUSE BED & BREAKFAST, 12549 Niagara River Parkway, Niagara Falls, ON, L2E 6S6, (905) 295-5166, Fax: (905) 295-0202." Email:

comniag@vaxxine.com, Web: http://www.vaxxine.com/danner, Gay-owned & -operated B&B with private baths, full breakfast, AC, nearby 30km recreational trail. ♀♂

FAIRBANKS HOUSE BED & BREAKFAST, 4965 River Rd, Niagara Falls, ON, L2E 3G6, (905) 371-3716. Email: FBH@mergetel.com, Gay-owned Victorian B&B on 1/2 acre overlooking the Niagara River, a 1-min walk to Niagara Falls viewpoint & casino. Rooms with private baths, full breakfast & a separate, private living room for guests' use. 50% gay/lesbian clientele.

OTTAWA/HULL

Information

AIDS SUPPORT LINE, (613) 238-4111 or 238-5014.

GAYLINE TELEGAI, (613) 238-1717. Mon-Fri 7:30pm-10:30pm, Sat, Sun 6-9pm."

PINK TRIANGLE SERVICES, 71 Bank St #203, (613) 563-4818. Gay & lesbian lending library, open M-Sat.

WOMEN'S CENTRE, University of Ottawa, 85 Hastey Ave, Room 08A, (613) 564-6853.

Accommodations

RIDEAU VIEW INN, 177 Frank St, Ottawa, ON, K2P 0X4, (613) 236-9309, (800) 658-3564, Fax: (613) 237-6842. Email: rideau@istar.ca, Web: http://home.istar.ca/~rideau/, B&B in a large Edwardian home built in 1907. Relax in front of the fireplace in the living room or take a walk to nearby restaurants, bars and tourist attractions. We have seven well-appointed guest rooms, two of which have private baths. In the morning, enjoy a hearty breakfast in the gracious dining room. Ours is the only gay-owned and -operated B&B in Ottawa.

Women's Accommodations

GABRIELLE'S GUESTHOUSE, 40 Gilmour St, Ottawa, ON, K2P 0N4, (613) 237-0829 (Tel/Fax). Women-only B&B in downtown Ottawa, 2 doubles, shared bath, expanded continental breakfast. ♀

LE JARDIN DES TREMBLES, 29 rue des Chardonnerets, Hull, QC, J9A 2A6, (819) 595-8761, Fax: (819) 595-0515.

Rideau View Inn

Victorian Elegance in the Heart of Ottawa

(800) 658-3564
HTTP://HOME.ISTAR.CA/~RIDEAU/

Email: cw002@freenet.carleton.ca, Women-only B&B minutes from downtown Ottawa with shared bath, continental breakfast, TV lounge & video tape library. ♀

Bars

CENTRETOWN PUB, 340 Somerset St West, near Bank, (613) 594-0233. Video bar & restaurant with patio, 75% men. ♂

LOOKOUT BAR & BISTRO, 41 York St, (613) 789-1624. Bar & small restaurant. ♀♂

MARKET STATION, 15 George St, Ottawa, (613) 562-3540. Bar & restaurant, downstairs games room. Lunch, dinner, weekend brunch. 60% men, 40% women. ♀♂

SILHOUETTE PIANO BAR, 340 Somerset St West, at Centretown Pub, downstairs., 🎵 ♀♂

Dance Bar/Disco

CORAL REEF, 30 Nicholas St, inside parking ramp, (613) 234-5118. Open Fri only, 8pm-2am. 🎵 ♀

FRANKIE'S, 303 Frank St, (613) 233-9195. 2nd floor dance floor, fireside lounge, pool tables, pinball, daily from 3pm. 3rd floor women's bar. Sat male dancers, monthly fetish night. ♀♂

ICON, 366 Lisgar St., Dance bar with show bar downstairs, young techno crowd. ♂

ONTARIO

PUB DE LA PROMENADE, 175 Promenade du Portage, Hull, (819) 771-8810. Trendy dance bar, popular with trendy gays & straights, mostly francophones. 🏳️‍🌈
Q, 363 Bank St, Opening June '98. ♂♀

■ Cafe
SCREAMING MIMI'S, 369 Bank., Lite menu & coffees.

■ Restaurants
★ LE BISTRO BIS, 9 Richmond Rd., Continental cuisine with Asian flair, large gay following.
LE BOULANGER FRANCAIS (THE FRENCH BAKER), 119 Murray St, (613) 789-7941. Sandwiches, espresso.
MANGIA RESTAURANT, 121 Clarence St, (613) 562-4725. Antipasto, pasta & pizza.
URBAN BISTRO, THE, 87 Holland Ave, (613) 798-1652. Lunch, dinner, weekend brunch.

■ Retail & Bookstores
AFTER STONEWALL, 370 Bank St, (613) 567-2221 (Moved to this new address June '98, after Nov call info. for new tel #) Gay & lesbian bookstore, pride items, cards, books galore, 10am-6pm (Fri till 9pm, Sun noon-4pm).
MOTHER TONGUE, 1067 Bank St, (613) 730-2346. Women's bookstore with large lesbian section.
ONE IN TEN, 216 Bank., Cards & gifts, to open June '98.
WILDE'S, 367 Bank St, (613) 234 -5512. Rubber, leather, fetish.

PETERBOROUGH

■ Information
RAINBOW SERVICE ORGANIZATION, (705) 876-1845. Men's & women's meetings & dances, nightly after 5:30pm, Sat & Sun all day.

■ Dance Bar/Disco
FRIENDS BISTRO, 450 George St N., Dancing, pool tables, coffee lounge. ♂

■ Retail & Bookstores
INNER CIRCLE BOOKS, Unit 3, 188 Hunter St W, (705) 743-3393. General bookstore with a large gay & lesbian section.

PORT SYDNEY

■ Accommodations
DIVINE LAKE NATURE'S SPORT & SPA RESORT, Port Sydney, ON, P0B 1L0, (705) 385-1212, Fax: (705) 385-1283. Information & reservations (Canada & USA): (800) 263-6600. Email: divinelk@vianet.on.ca, Web: www.divinelake.com, Gay-friendly resort with bar, 2 lounges & restaurant, cottages & chalets. Full breakfast, fireplaces & kitchenettes available, color TV/VCR, health spa with steam/herbal sauna, massages, many outdoor activities.

STRATFORD

■ Accommodations
BURNSIDE, 139 William St, Stratford, ON, N5A 4X9, (519) 271-7076, Fax: (519) 271-0265 Gay-friendly B&B, shared baths, TV lounge with color cable TV, VCR. Full breakfast, whirlpool tub. 50% gay & lesbian clientele."
MAPLES OF STRATFORD, THE, 220 Church St, Stratford, ON, N5A 2R6, (519) 273-0810. Gay-friendly B&B 3 blocks from the center of town & within walking distance of all theatres. Private & shared baths, continental breakfast. 50% gay & lesbian clientele.

SUDBURY

■ Retail & Bookstores
MARIGOLD'S BOOKS & THINGS, 5 Elgin St, (705) 675-2670. "A women's bookstore where all are welcomed." Tues-Sun, sometimes Mon.

THOUSAND ISLANDS

■ Accommodations
BOATHOUSE COUNTRY INN, 17-19 Front St, Rockport, ON, K0E 1V0, (613) 659-2348 (Tel/Fax), (800) 584-2592. Email: rockport@boathouse-heritage.on.ca, Web: www.boathouse-heritage.on.ca, Gay-friendly inn with restaurant, bar & boat tours. Private baths, suites with full breakfast. ♀♂

THUNDER BAY

■ Retail & Bookstores
NORTHERN WOMAN'S BOOKSTORE, THE, 65 S Court St, (807) 344-7979.

RAINBOW BOOKS, 264 Bay St, (807) 345-6272. Gay & lesbian bookstore with some straight titles.

TORONTO

■ Information

519 CHURCH STREET COMMUNITY CENTER, 519 Church St, (416) 392-6874. 9am-10:30pm (Sat noon-5pm, Sun 9am-5pm).

AIDS HOTLINE, (416) 392-2437, (800) 668-2437 (inside Ontario). 9am-11:30pm (Sat, Sun 11am-4pm).

TORONTO AREA GAYS & LESBIANS (TAGL), (416) 964-6600, 7pm-10pm Mon-Sat.

WOMEN'S CENTER, 49 St George St, (416) 978-8201. Lesbian groups, etc.

■ Accommodations

ABERDEEN GUEST HOUSE, 52 Aberdeen Ave, Toronto, ON, M4X 1A2, (416) 922-8697, Fax: (416) 922-5011. Email: aberdeengh@aol.com, Guesthouse with shared bath, near gay village, 50% gay/lesbian clientele.

ALLENBY GUEST HOUSE, 223 Strathmore Blvd, Toronto, ON, M4J 1P4, (416) 461-7095. Email: azroyalvil@aol.com, Guesthouse & apartments, private & shared baths, expanded continental breakfast.

BANTING HOUSE, 73 Homewood Ave, Toronto, ON, M4Y 2K1, (416) 924-1458, Fax: (416) 924-3304. Email: bantinghs @aol.com, Web: www.bbcanada.com/1960.html, Gay-owned & -operated B&B 2 blocks from the gay & lesbian village. Shared baths, expanded continental breakfast, AC, short walk to bars & restaurants, some hetero clientele. ♀♂

CATNAPS 1892 DOWNTOWN GUESTHOUSE, 246 Sherbourne St, Toronto, ON, M5A 2S1, (416) 968-2323, Reservations: (800) 205-3694, Fax: (416) 413-0485. Email: catnaps@onramp.ca, Centrally-located B&B guesthouse. Color cable TV, AC, shared baths, laundry facilities & expanded continental breakfast. ♀♂

CAWTHRA SQUARE B & B, 10 Cawthra Square, Toronto, ON, M4Y 1K8, (416) 966-3074, (800) 259-5474, Fax: (416) 966-4494. Email: host@cawthra.com,

Cawthra Square B & B

"...where the heart is..."

(416) 966-3074
www.cawthra.com
Toronto, Canada

Web: http://www.cawthra.com, Our elegant Edwardian or Victorian homes are beautiful retreats in the heart of Toronto's vibrant gay village. The salon, with fireplace and grand piano, looks out onto a quiet, tree-shaded street. Spacious guest rooms provide private terraces and a continental breakfast is served in a bright country kitchen. Shops, restaurants, cafes & nightclubs are nearby. Toronto's best theatres, museums and galleries are all at your doorstep. ♀♂

DUNDONALD HOUSE, THE, 35 Dundonald Street, Toronto, ON, M4Y 1K3, (416) 961-9888, (800) 260-7227, Fax: (416) 961-2120. Email: dundonal@idirect.com, Web: http://www2.cglbrd.com/dundonald, Gay & lesbian B&B in a quiet tree-lined area of downtown Toronto. Seven bedrooms, shared baths, full breakfast, AC, hot tub, sauna, touring bikes. Near gay venues, walking distance to Yonge St. ♀♂

HOUSE ON MCGILL, THE, 110 McGill St, Toronto, ON, M5B 1H6, (416) 351-1503 (Tel/Fax). For fax, call ahead to alert computer. Gay-owned & -operated Victorian B&B close to Toronto's gay village & theatre district, shared bath, expanded continental breakfast, bicycle loan. Some hetero clientele. ♀♂

196 ONTARIO

MANFRED'S MEADOW RESORT, RR #1, Grand Valley, ON, L0N 1G0, (519) 925-5306. Guesthouse, shared baths. 🏕️🐾♀♂

MIKE'S ON MUTUAL, 333 Mutual St, Toronto, ON, M4Y 1X6, (416) 944-2611, Fax: (416) 944-3938. Gay & lesbian B&B in a non-smoking private home, a very short walk from gay bars & shops. Shared baths, expanded continental breakfast. ♂

TWO ABERDEEN, 2 Aberdeen Ave, Toronto, ON, M4A 1X2, (416) 944-1426 ,Fax: (416) 944-3523. Email: aberdeen@interlog.com, B&B with private & shared baths, full breakfast, 50% gay/lesbian.

WINCHESTER GUEST HOUSE (FORMERLY SAPHO'S CHOICE), 35 Winchester, Toronto, ON, M4X 1A6, (416) 929-7949 (Tel/Fax). Guest house with one private and three shared baths. Open year-round. ♀♂

■ *Bars*

BAR BABYLON, 553 Church St, 3rd floor, (416) 923-2626. "Martini bar," fireplace, chesterfields. Restaurant, dance bar, lounge. 🚫

BYZ, 499 Church St, (416) 922-3859. Upscale martini bar & restaurant, daily from 5:30pm, drag queen hostess. 🚫

PEGASUS BILLIARD LOUNGE, 491 Church St, (416) 927-8832. Pool hall. ♀♂

QUEEN'S HEAD PUB, 263 Gerrard St E, above Pimbletts, (416) 929-9525. Pub & restaurant. 🍴♀♂

TANGO & CREWS TORONTO, 508 Church St, (416) 972-1662. 🎵 ♀

★ **WOODY'S/SAILORS,** 467 Church Street, (416) 972-0887. Preppie conversation bar, sweaters & cologne, 70% men & lipstick lesbians. 🍴✕♂

■ *Dance Bar/Disco*

BOOTS/WAREHOUSE/SELBY LOUNGE, 592 Sherbourne St, in the Hotel Selby bldg, (416) 921-0665, (416) 921-3142. Largest gay dance club in Toronto. Selby Lounge is cocktail club. Courtyard adjacent. ♂

EL CONVENTO RICO, 750 College St, (416) 588-7800. Latin night club open Tue-Sun. Men's night Sun. 🎵 🚫 ♀♂

★ **POPE JOAN,** 547 Parliament St, (416) 925-6662. Dance bar & restaurant. 🎵 ♀

STUDIO 619, 619 Yonge St, 2nd floor, in the back lane, (416) 922-3068. Dance club, lite menu, 70% men, bingo Fri & Sat. 🎵🍴♂

■ *Cafe*

PAM'S TEA & COFFEE, 585 Church St, (416) 923-7267. 🚫

SECOND CUP, 546 Church St, (416) 727-8377. Popular after bars close. 🚫

SWEET CITY BAKERY, 16 Banigan Dr, between Yone & Bay Sts, (416) 423-0039. Bakery & cafe serving baked goods & deserts. Mon-Fri 6:30am-6pm, Sat & Sun 8am-4pm. 🚫

ZELDA'S, 208 Queen St West, (416) 598-4719. 🚫

■ *Restaurants*

BYZANTIUM, 499 Church St, (416) 922-3859. Mediterranean cuisine. 🚫

CAFE CALIFORNIA, 538 Church St, (416) 960-6161. 🚫

LE CHAROLAIS, 577 Parliament St, (416) 963-5097. French cuisine, lunch, dinner. 🚫

LIVING WELL, 692 Yonge St, (416) 922-6770. 🚫

MANGO, 580 Church St, (416) 922-6525. 🚫

NEIGHBORS, 9 Isabella St, (416) 960-1200. Bar & restaurant.

PIMBLETT'S, 263 Gerrard St E, above Queen's Head Pub, (416) 929-9525. Restaurant & bar. 🚫 🍷

PJ MELLON'S, 489 Church St, (416) 966-3241. Lunch, dinner, Sun brunch 11:30am. 🚫 🍷

RIVOLI, Queen St, near Spadina, (416) 596-1908. Bar & restaurant overlooking Queen St West. 🚫

SLACK ALICE, 562 Church St, (416) 962-6255, trendy. 🍷 🚫

SPIRAL, 582 Church St, (416) 964-1102. Asian continental cuisine, martini & margarita menu. 🚫

TRATTORIA IL FORNO, 459 Church St., Italian cuisine. 🚫

WILDE OSCAR'S, 518 Church St, (416) 921-8142. Restaurant & bar, continental cuisine, Sat, Sun brunch. 🚫 🍷 ♀♂

■ *Retail & Bookstores*

EX LIBRIS, 467 Church St, 2nd Floor, (416) 975-0580. Gay & lesbian new & used books.

GLAD DAY BOOKS, 598-A Yonge St, (upstairs), (416) 961-4161. Gay & lesbian bookstore.

LEE'S GLITZ, 455 Church St, (416) 975-1343. Cards & gifts.

OMEGA CENTRE, THE, 29 Yorkville Ave, (416) 975-9086. Self-discovery bookstore with self-help resources on AIDS & an extensive alternative healing section.

OUT ON THE STREET, 551 Church St, (416) 967-2759. Cards, gifts, t-shirts & magazines.

THIS AIN'T THE ROSEDALE LIBRARY, 483 Church Street, (416) 929-9912. General bookstore with a gay & lesbian section.

TORONTO WOMEN'S BOOKSTORE, 73 Harbord, near Spadina, (416) 922-8744. Feminist & lesbian bookstore in central Toronto.

■ Erotica

GOOD FOR HER, 181 Harbord St, (416) 588-0900. Women-only hours: Thurs 11am-2pm, Sun noon-5pm.

WARKWORTH

■ Accommodations

BAXTER'S BED & BREAKFAST, RR1, Warkworth, ON, K0K 3K0, (705) 924-1230, (888) 398-6550, Fax: (705) 924-1231. Email: baxter@accel.net, B&B with some straight clientele, 2 rooms with 1 private & 1 shared bath. ♀♂

WINDSOR

■ Information

LESBIAN & GAY HOTLINE, (519) 973-4951. 24hr tape, Mon, Thurs Fri 8-10pm. Women Tues 7:30-9:30pm.

■ Dance Bar/Disco

HAPPY TAP, 1056 Wyandotte St E, (519) 256-2737. Nude male dancers, 75% men, 25% women.

★ **NOSTALGIA,** 634 Chilver at Wyandotte, Wed-Sat (may change nights), very popular weekends.

QUEBEC

CHICOUTIMI

■ Bars

LE VERÇO, 564 boul. Saguenay ouest, (418) 690-5354. Thurs-Sun 9pm-3am. ♀♂

DRUMMONDVILLE

■ Bars

NUANCE, 336 rue Lindsay, 2nd floor, (819) 471-4252. Wed-Sun. ♀♂

HULL

SEE OTTAWA, ONTARIO.,

JONQUIÈRE

■ Cafe

BAR AU CLAIR DE LUNE, 3876 St Laurent, (418) 695-9687.

MONT-TREMBLANT

■ Accommodations

VERSANT OUEST BED & BREAKFAST, 110 Chemin Labelle, Mont-Tremblant, QC, J0T 1Z0, (819) 425-6615 (Tel/Fax), (800) 425-6615. Email: verso@cil.qc.ca, Web: www.embuscade.qc.ca/VersantOuest.htm, B&B in a ski resort, 1-1/2 hours from Montreal, walking paths & river nearby, mainly gay & lesbian clientele, full breakfast, shared baths. ♀♂

MONTRÉAL

■ Information

CONCORDIA WOMEN'S CENTER, 2020 rue Mackay, basement annex P-03, (514) 848-7431. Drop-in space, mainly anglophones (English-speaking). Weekday hours, scheduled evening events. Women's calendar of events available. ♀

GAIE ÉCOUTE, (514) 521-1508. French language gay info line.

GAY LINE ENGLISH, (514) 990-1414, 6:30pm-10pm, 7 days.

■ Accommodations

ALACOQUE BED & BREAKFAST, 2091 St-Urbain, Montreal, QC, H2X 2N1, (514) 842-0938, Fax: (514) 842-7585. B&B in a 1900 town house with private & shared baths, full breakfast, laundry & kitchen facilities, 10 minute walk to gay bars. 50% gay/lesbian clientele.

AU STADE B & B, POB 42, Stn M, Montréal, QC, H1V 3L6, (514) 254-1250, voice box #1. Fax available. B&B near gay & lesbian community. Shared bath, TV lounge, small gym, fax facilities & continental breakfast. ♀♂

AUBERGE INN, 1646 Amherst, Montreal, QC, (514) 526-5846, Fax: (514) 597-1430. Gay-owned B&B with shared bath, continental breakfast, phone, AC, some hetero clientele. ♀♂

CHABLIS GUEST HOUSE, 1641 rue St-Hubert, Montreal, QC, H2L 3Z1, (514) 527-8346., Fax: (514) 596-1519. Gay-friendly guesthouse with private & shared baths, continental breakfast, gay male following.

CHÂTEAU CHERRIER B & B, 550 rue Cherrier, Montréal, QC, H2L 1H3, (514) 844-0055, (800) 816-0055, Fax: (514) 844-8438. Email: chateau.cherrier@sympatico.ca, B&B in private home, some straight clientele. Rooms individually decorated in period furniture, full breakfast. Downtown near pool, quartier latin, gay village. ♀♂

GINGERBREAD HOUSE BED & BREAKFAST, 1628 St. Christophe, Montreal, QC, H2L 3W8, (514) 597-2804, Fax: (514) 526-4636. Email: gingerbread house@gai.com, Gay-owned & -operated B&B with shared bath, expanded continental breakfast, color cable TV, women welcome. ♂

HOTEL MANOIR DES ALPES, 1245 rue St-André, (514) 845-9803, reservations only: (800) 65-2929. Free parking, color TV, phone, AC & continental breakfast.

HOTEL ST.-ANDRÉ, 1285 rue St.-André, Montréal, QC, H2L 3T1, (514) 849-7070, Fax: 849-8167, reservations only: (800) 265-7071. A 2-star, inexpensive, small hotel with all private baths, queen beds, TV & phone, continental breakfast served in room, 40% gay & lesbian.

LA CONCIERGERIE GUEST HOUSE, 1019 rue St.-Hubert, Montréal, QC, H2L 3Y3, (514) 289-9297, Fax: (514) 289-0845. Web: http://www.gaibec.com, B&B near Ste Catherine, Old Montreal & gay village, women welcome. Comfortable rooms in Victorian homes. Expanded continental breakfast. Massage by appointment, Jacuzzi, nearby gym." ♂

LE CHASSEUR GUEST HOUSE, 1567 rue St.-Andre, Montréal, QC, H2L 3T5, (514) 521-2238, (514) 849-2051, (800) 451-2238. A charming European bed and breakfast, centrally located in Montréal. Gay bars, restaurants, Old Montréal, the Latin Quarter and trendy boutiques are all nearby. Our staff will provide a wealth of information and will spare no expense to make your stay easy-going and relaxing. *Le Chasseur,* a step in the right direction. The bed and breakfast "recommended by friends for friends. ♂

MAISON CHABLIS, 1639 St Hubert, Montreal, QC, H2L 3Z1, (514) 527-8346, Fax: (514) 596-1519. B&B with restaurant, private & shared baths, continental breakfast, AC, color cable TV. Mostly hetero with a gay male following.

PENSION VALLIÈRES, 6562, Delorimier St, Montréal, QC, H2G 2P6, (514) 729-9552. B&B, color cable TV, ceiling fans, private & shared baths, full breakfast, 95% women, men welcome. ♀

RUTA BAGAGE, 1345 rue Sainte-Rose, Montreal, QC, H2L 2J7, (514) 598-1586. B&B with 4 rooms with queen or double beds, shared baths, continental breakfast. Mostly gay & lesbian clientele. ♀♂

■ Women's Accommodations

LA DOUILLETTE, 7235 de Lorimier St, Montréal, QC, H2E 2N9, (514) 376-2183. Private home with small garden, furnished with antiques. Each room is supplied with local maps & information about current events. Full breakfast, shared bath, women only. ♀

LINDSEY'S BED & BREAKFAST FOR WOMEN, 3974 Laval Ave, Montréal, QC, H2W 2J2, (514) 843-4869. Women-only B&B with private & shared baths, expanded continental breakfast. ♀

■ Bars

BAR LA POMPE, 151 rue Champlain, St Jean sur Richelieu, (514) 346-9512. Sun tea dance, 3pm-3am. ♂

BAR LANCELOT, 1997 boul. Ste-Adèle, St-Adèle, Gay complex with bar & restaurant, accommodations, swimming pool, terrace. ♂

CATS, 5322 boul St Laurent, (514) 278-CATS. Bar & restaurant, terrace, 7 days. ♀

CLUB DATE, 1218 rue Ste-Catherine est, near Montcalm, (514) 521-1242. Piano bar, Fri-Sun, karaoke nights Mon & Tues. ♂

★ L'ENTRE-PEAU CABARET, 1115 rue Ste-Catherine Est, (metro: Beaudry), (514) 525-7566. Show bar with large straight following. ♂

L'UN ET L'AUTRE, 1641 Amherst., Bar & restaurant, rooms for tourists by the week, mostly gay. ♂

LOUNGE, THE, 1333 rue Ste-Catherine Est, above the Saloon Cafe., Live music nightly from 8pm, Sun shows at 7pm. Women's nite Sun 5-9pm. ♀♂

MYSTIQUE, 1424 rue Stanley, (514) 844-5711. Women welcome. 🐱 ♂

★ **O'SIDE,** 4075-B St Denis, (metro: Sherbrooke), (514) 849-7126. Cafe bistro with light menu, pool table, dance nights every 2 weeks, women only. Packed on weekends. 🍴 ♀

★ **SKY PUB,** 1474 rue Ste-Catherine Est, (metro: Papineau or Beaudry), (514) 529-6969. Girls in the Sky night Thurs. ♀♂

■ Dance Bar/Disco

BAR LA MAIN GAUCHE, 470 rue Mondor, Ste Hyacinthe, (514) 774-5556. Dance club, terrace, 7 days. 🍴 ♀♂

CABARET SAPHO, 217 rue Frontenac, (metro: Frontenac), (514) 523-0292. Cabaret & dance bar, live singers on weekends. Slightly older crowd. 🍴 ♀

CLUB BOLO, 960 Amherst, Fri-Sun only, C&W dancing. ∪ 🍴 ♂

GROOVE SOCIETY, 1296 Amherst., Gay Thurs only. 🍴 ♂

MISSISSIPPI CLUB, 1592 rue Ste-Catherine Est, (514) 523-4679. Wed Woolco, mixed; Fri mixed; Sat women only, Sun entertainment. 🍴 ♀♂

SECRET, LE, 3029 boul Labelle, at Hotel Up-North, Prevost, (514) 224-7350. Disco. 🍴 ♀♂

★ **SISTERS,** 1456 rue Ste-Catherine Est, at Station C complex (metro: Beaudry), (514) 524-9947. Thurs-Sat 22:00-03:00, early 20's crowd. 🍴 ♀

★ **SKY CLUB,** 1474 rue Ste-Catherine Est, (metro: Beaudry or Papineau)., Disco, bar, cabaret & restaurant. 🍴 ♪ ♀♂

■ Saunas/Health Clubs

BAIN COLONIAL BATHS, European sauna, straight during the day, gayer at night, Tues 1pm-10pm women only.

■ Restaurants

BAZOU, 1271 rue Albert, (514) 526-4940. Nouvelle cuisine. 🔪

BOZ-ART, 1493 rue Amherst, (metro: Beaudry), (514) 522-6144. Popular with gay women. 🔪

★ **CAFE LES ENTRETIENS,** 1577 Laurier est, (514) 521-2934. Healthy food, quiche, etc, 9:30am-midnite, popular with gays. 🔪

CAFE UNIVERSAL, 1030 rue Cherrier Est, (514) 598-7136. Deli. 🔪

CHABLIS, 1639 St-Hubert, (metro: Berri-UQAM), (514) 523-0053. French cuisine. 🔪 ⍷

CLIN D'OEIL CAFÉ, 1429 rue Amherst, (514) 528-1209. Popular Sun brunch." 🔪

★ **CLUB SANDWICH,** 1578 rue Ste-Catherine Est, (metro: Papineau), (514) 523-4679, 24hrs. ♀♂

L'ANECDOTE, 801 rue Rachel est, at St.-Hubert (metro: Mont Royal), (514) 526-7967. Snack bar, burgers, beer, many women. 🔪

L'ARMORICAIN, 1550 rue Fullum, (514) 523-2551. French cuisine, upscale. 🔪

L'EXCEPTION, 1200 rue St-Hubert, (metro: Berri-UQAM), (514) 282-1282. Casual cuisine. 🔪

L'UN ET L'AUTRE, 1641 Amherst, (metro: Beaudry), (514) 597-0878. Bar & bistro. Bar good for cocktail hour. ♂

MAESTRO S.V.P., 3615 St-Laurent, (514) 842-6447; or 3017 Masson, (514) 722-4166. Steaks, oysters, shrimp & other seafood. 🔪

MOZZA, 1208 rue Ste-Catherine Est, (metro: Beaudry), (514) 524-0295. Mostly pasta. 🔪

O'SIDE, 4075-B rue St-Denis, at O'side bar, (514) 849-7126. Women-only cafe bistro, lite menu, pool table, dancing Sat nite, packed on weekends. ♀

OGATO, 1301 rue Ste-Catherine Est, (514) 528-6222. Dessert only & only cakes.

PARYSE, LA, 302 Ontario est, at Sanguinet (metro: Berri-UQAM), (514) 842-2040. Many women, closes early some evenings, call first. ♀♂

PIAZZETTA, 1101 rue Ste-Catherine Est, (514) 526-2244. Square pizza. 🔪

★ **PICCOLO DIAVOLO,** 1336 rue Ste-Catherine Est, (514) 526-1336. Italian cuisine. 🔪

★ **PIZZADELIC,** 1329 rue Ste-Catherine Est, (metro: Beaudry), (514) 526-6011. 🔪

★ **PLANÉTE, LE,** 1451 rue Ste-Catherine Est, at Plessis, (514) 526-1336. Creative, varied menu, very fine cuisine. 🔪

ROTISSERIE ST-HUBERT, 1019 rue Ste-Catherine Est, (514) 385-5555. Chicken BBQ. 🔪

QUEBEC

★ SALOON CAFE, 1333 rue Ste-Catherine Est, (metro: Beaudry), (514) 522-1333. Cafe & restaurant. ♀♂

Retail & Bookstores
LIBRAIRIE L'ANDROGYNE, 3636 St-Laurent, at Prince Arthur, (514) 842-4765. Gay and lesbian bookstore, with books in both French & English. Also an excellent source of local information for newcomers to Montreal. Open daily. Ask for free catalogue.

NICOLET-SUD

Accommodations
L'AUBERGELLE, 445 rang St-Alexis RR 1, Nicolet Sud, QC, J3T 1T5, (819) 293-6215. Gay-friendly B&B in a rural area, midway between Montreal & Quebec, full breakfast, popular with bicyclists, river behind house.

QUÉBEC

Accommodations
BED & BREAKFAST IN OLD QUEBEC, 35 Rue des Remparts, (418) 655-7685. Gay-friendly B&B. Variety of accommodations with various conveniences, private & shared baths, TV lounge, full brunch.

LE 727 GUEST HOUSE, 727 rue d'Aiguillon, Québec, QC, G1R 1M8, (418) 648-6766, (800) 652-6766. Guesthouse in Old Quebec with, private & shared baths, continental breakfast, women welcome. ♿ ♂

LE COUREUR DES BOIS, 15 rue Ste.-Ursule, Québec, QC, G1R 4C7, (418) 692-1117, (800) 269-6414. An historical, early French-Canadian guesthouse within the walls of Old Québec. Seven individually furnished rooms emphasize cleanliness and comfort and share three baths. Breakfast of croissants, fresh fruit, cheese, muffins, sweet breads and assorted beverages. ♀♂

Bars
AMOUR SORCIER, L', 789 Côte Ste-Geneviève, (418) 523-3395. ♀

Dance Bar/Disco
★ BALLON ROUGE, 811 rue St-Jean, at St-Augustin, (418) 529-6709. Large disco, avant garde music, terrace. 🅗 ♂
L'ÉVEIL, 710 rue Bouvier, (418) 628-0610. Pool table, men welcome. ♀

Cafe
KOOKENING KAFE, 565 rue St-Jean, (418) 521-2121. Sandwiches, coffees. 🌱

Restaurants
BURGER CLUB, 469 rue St-Jean, (418) 525-4766. Women-owned & -operated. 🌱
LA PLAYA, 780 rue St-Jean, (418) 522-3989. West Coast cuisine, pastas, nightly specials, terrace for summer. Large straight following. ♀♂
LE COMMENSAL, 860 rue St Jean, (418) 647-3733. Vegetarian food. 🌱
ZORBA, across from Diana restaurant., Popular after bars close, 90% gay.

Retail & Bookstores
EMPIRE LYON, 873 rue St-Jean, (418) 648-2301. Gay video store with cafe, books & clothing.

ST-CUTHBERT

Bars
CHEZ LINDA EN HAUT, 3189 Pointe Ste-Catherine, (514) 836-1601. ♂

ST-GEORGES-EST

Dance Bar/Disco
L'IMPAK, 8450 boul. La Croix, (418) 227-5594. Small disco. ♂

ST-JEAN BAPTISTE

Bars
LE PATELINO, (418) 736-5432. 🅗 ♂

STE-HYACINTHE

Restaurants
BISTROT MONDOR, 1400 Cascades Ouest, (514) 773-1695. 🌱

SHERBROOKE

Women's Accommodations
CHEZ LA SALAMANDRE, 155 Rte 253, Sawyerville, QC, J0B 3A0, (819) 889-2504. Women-only secluded guesthouse retreat, accommodates 1-6, 1 shared bath. Canoeing & skiing 30-45 mins away, 5 min to nearby lake, horseback riding. Professional therapeutic massage available. ♀

Bars
LES DAMES DE COEUR, 54 rue King est, (819) 821-2217. Cafe & bar, mostly women with men welcome (Fri women only, Sat more men). 🅗 ♀♂

TROIS RIVIERES

■ Accommodations
LE GÎTE DU HUARD B & B, 42 rue St-Louis, CP 1381, Vieux Trois-Rivieres, QC, G9A 1T5, (819) 375-8771. Gay-friendly B&B in the heart of the city's historic section, along waterfront promenade with views of St. Lawrence River. Private baths, AC, TV, continental breakfast, kitchen facilities.

■ Bars
CAFE BAR LE LIEN, 1572 rue Royal, (819) 370-6492. 7 days 1pm-3am, drag shows Sun.

■ Dance Bar/Disco
L'INTRIGUE, 1528 Notre Dame, at St-Antoine, (819) 693-1979.

SASKATCHEWAN

MOOSE JAW

■ Information
LESBIAN & GAY COMMITTEE, (306) 691-5187.

PRINCE ALBERT

■ Information
LAMBDA NORTH, (800) 358-1833.

RAVENSCRAG

■ Accommodations
SPRING VALLEY GUEST RANCH, Box 10, Ravenscrag, SK, S0N 0T0, (306) 295-4124. gay-owned B&B & campground with restaurant, shared bath. 50% gay & lesbian clientele.

REGINA

■ Information
AIDS HOTLINE, (306) 924-8420. 9am-5pm.
PINK TRIANGLE INFORMATION LINE, (306) 525-6046. Tues & Fri 8:30pm-11:30pm. Lavender Social Club (306) 586-5066 or 565-6295, dances 3rd Sat at Oddfellows Hall.

■ Dance Bar/Disco
OSCAR'S & BRIXX, 1422 Scarth St, (306) 522-7343. Disco lounge, game room with darts, pool table, cards, music theme nights, 8:30pm-3am, 7 days. Queer Gear gay store inside open Tues, Thurs-Sat.

SASKATOON

■ Information
AIDS LINE, (306) 242-5005 or (800) 667-6876.
GAY INFO, 203-220 3rd Ave S, at Gay & Lesbian Health Services., (306) 665-1224 (in SK: 800) 358-1833) Drop in Mon-Wed noon-4:30pm, Thurs & Fri noon-10pm.

■ Accommodations
BRIGHTON HOUSE B & B, 1308 5th Ave N, Saskatoon, SK, S7K 2S2, (306) 664-3278. Lesbian-owned B&B, expanded continental breakfast, private & shared baths, 5% gay/lesbian clientele.

■ Dance Bar/Disco
DIVA'S, 110-220 3rd Ave S, alley entrance off 3rd Ave, (306) 665-0100. Private club, 70% men, 30% women. 8pm-2am 7 days.

■ Retail & Bookstores
CAFE BROWZE, 269-B 3rd Ave S, (306) 664-BOOK (2665). Bookstore cafe. Lunch, dinner, desserts & full liquor, gay & lesbian books & magazines. Mon-Sat 10am-11pm, Sun 11:30am-11pm.

■ Erotica
OUT OF THE CLOSET, 203-220 3rd Ave S, at Gay & Lesbian Health Services., Shop for lesbians & gay men. Magazines, pride flags, t-shirts, wet lube, etc. Mon-Wed 12-4:40, Thurs & Fri 12-9, Sat 12-5:30.

SWIFT CURRENT

■ Information
GAY & LESBIAN SUPPORT GROUP, (306) 778-6245 or 778-0033.

YUKON

WHITEHORSE

■ Information
GAY & LESBIAN ALLIANCE, (867) 667-7857. Holds gay dances & meetings in Whitehorse, pop. 20,000.

■ Retail & Bookstores
MAC'S FIREWEED BOOKSTORE, 203 Main St, (867) 668-6104. General bookstore. Will special order gay & lesbian titles.

CARIBBEAN/ATLANTIC ISLANDS

CUBA

HAVANA

■ *Accommodations*
GAY & LESBIAN GUESTHOUSE, Contact Milu Tours: (49-30) 217 6488, Fax: (49-30) 214 3374. There is a new gay & lesbian guesthouse in Havana. For information, contact Milu Tours (49-30) 217 64 88, fax: (49-30) 214 3374. ♀♂

DOMINICAN REPUBLIC

CABARETE

■ *Women's Accommodations*
PURPLE PARADISE, Mail: Hell Von Gogh, EPS D#184, PO Box 02-5548, Miami, FL, 33102, (809) 571-0637, Fax: (809) 571-0691. Relax on an endless sandy beach, chill out in the Jacuzzi or slide into the pool nestled in lush gardens. Our airy, Spanish-style villa on the north coast of the Dominican Republic has bright, sunny rooms, all with private baths and two with private entrances. Women only. ♀

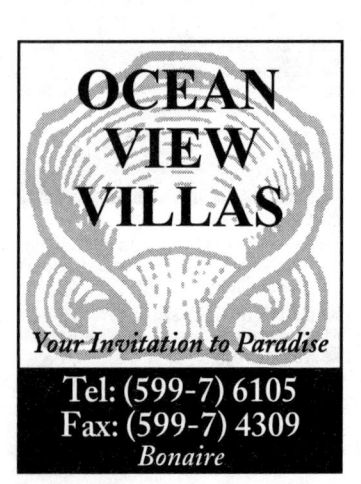

DUTCH WEST INDIES

BONAIRE

■ *Accommodations*
OCEAN VIEW VILLAS, Kaya Statius Van Eps 6, Bonaire, (599-7) 6105, Fax: (599-7) 4309. Stay at these award-winning apartments in Bonaire, an arid, spartan island, surrounded by a spectacular underwater world teeming with exotic creatures. Furnished in pickled oak with pastel accents, apartments have secluded rear patios for private sunbathing & outdoor showers. Kitchens are fully equipped with all the conveniences of home. There is AC, but guests usually prefer the refreshing, cool tradewinds. Some straight clientele. ♀♂

CURAÇAO

■ *Information*
APEX, PO Box 855, Curaçao, Netherlands Antilles, (599-9) 575 6969. Email: apex@caribbe.an, Gay youth organization, answers 6pm-10pm, weekends all day. Gives travelers info on gay meeting places.

■ *Cafe*
CAFE DES ARTISTES, ask locally for address, NOT a gay cafe, discreetly frequented by gays & lesbians.

SABA

■ *Accommodations*
CAPTAIN'S QUARTERS, Windwardside, Saba, (5994) 62201, (800) 446-3010, Fax: (5994) 62377. Email: SabaCQ@megatropic.com, Web: http://saba-online.com, Sixteen-room Victorian gay-friendly guesthouse in a tropical paradise. A short 10-minute flight from St Maarten, Saba, The Unspoiled Queen of the Caribbean," offers spectacular scuba, hiking and relaxation in a storybook setting of Dutch "Gingerbread" villages that will remind you of "Switzerland with Palm Trees." All rooms with stunning ocean views, many with antique/four-poster beds. Convenient to all diving, village shopping and the 1,064 steps to the top of Mt. Scenery & tropical rainforest. Little nightlife, less cruising, this is a perfect romantic getaway. Dive packages available.

OCEAN VIEW VILLAS

Your Invitation to Paradise

Tel: (599-7) 6105
Fax: (599-7) 4309
Bonaire

ST MAARTEN

Bars

PINK MANGO, in the Laguna Beach Hotel on French side of island, in city of Marigot., Hard to find, go around the back, knock at the doo.

FRENCH WEST INDIES
ST BARTHELEMY

Accommodations

HOSTELLERIE DES TROIS FORCES, Vitet 97133, St. Barthelemy, Direct: (590) 276-125, Fax: (590) 278-138. Gay-friendly inn with French & Creole restaurant & bar, private cottages with various conveniences, massage, nearby ocean beach, continental breakfast.

PUERTO RICO
AGUADA

Accommodations

SAN MAX, PO Box 1294, Aguada, PR, 00602, (787) 868-2931. Guesthouse with rooms 85 miles from San Juan, studio apartment, private baths.

Bars

JOHNNY'S BAR, ask at San Max Guest House for directions., women welcome, pool table.

AGUADILLA

Dance Bar/Disco

FACTORY CLUB, Punto Boringuen Shoppin Center, C Belt, Base Ramey, (787) 890-1530. Huge mega club, liver performances by famous local talent, closed Mon-Wed.

AÑASCO

Bars

EL QUINQUE DE CONFE JR., in town of Añasco, past town center, a bit into the mountains, pool tables, music, open daily 3pm-1am.

BAYAMON

Dance Bar/Disco

GILLIGAN'S, Av. Betances D-18, at Hnas. Davila, (787) 786-5065. Private club, gay, daily stripper shows (Thurs male strippers), many pool tables.

Journeys by Sea, Inc.
(800) 825-3632
(954) 522-5865
Yacht Charters
$195
pp/day all incl.

CAGUAS

Dance Bar/Disco

KENNY'S, Rio Piedras to Caguas Highway, Km 232, exotic country club atmosphere on a mountaintop, swimming pool, food service, Fri-Sat.

HORMIGUEROS

Dance Bar/Disco

FACES PUB, Carretera 2 km 164, Casa Blanca, Big new mega club, closed Mon-Tues.

ISABELA

Dance Bar/Disco

VILLA RICOMAR, Bo. Jobas, Carretera 459, Sector La Sierra, entrance across from Brendy Pizza, Mega club, huge patio, performances, dancing, open Fri-Sun.

Restaurants

HAPPY BELLY'S ON THE BEACH, Playa Jobos on the beach, outrageous burgers & pastas, frozen drinks. Live jazz Thurs & Fri.

ISLA VERDE

Restaurants

FIESTA BURGER, 6 Isla Verde Ave, (787) 727-3080.

LAJAS

Bars

MILAGROS PLACE, Carretera 16, Km 3.4, many pool tables, typical rural bar with large gay following.

LUQUILLO BEACH

Restaurants

KIOSKO 10, ELY'S PLACE, in Luquillo Beach, about 40 miles outside of San Juan., Oyster bar with many gay customers.

PIÑONES

Dance Bar/Disco
BEBO'S PUB, Carretera 187, Torreuela Baja, Piñones., Wed-Sun from 5pm, Sun tea dance, 60% women.

PONCE

Dance Bar/Disco
MICHELANGELOS, Carretera 10, towards Adjuntas, km 13.7, Closed Mon-Wed.

SAN GERMAN

Bars
HACIENDA EL COSQUI, 30 Minillas, Carretera 102 km 38.,

Dance Bar/Disco
NORMAN'S BAR, Carretera 318, Barrio Maresua, San German., Salsa & marengue, lost of pool tables, 50% men, 50% women.

SAN JUAN

Information
AIDS INFO, (787) 751-5858.

Accommodations
ATLANTIC BEACH HOTEL, Calle Vendig #1, Condado, San Juan, PR, 00907, (787) 721-6900, Fax: (787) 721-6917. Hotel with restaurant & bar, some straight clientele. 37 double rooms, Jacuzzi, ocean beach, 10 min from historical section. Many restaurants, nightspots nearby. Mostly male clientele.

EMBASSY GUEST HOUSE - CONDADO, 1126 Calle Seaview-Condado, San Juan, PR, 00907, (787) 725-8284 or (787) 724-7440, Fax: (787) 725-2400. Guesthouse on the beach with restaurant & bar, some straight clientele. Color TV, AC, ceiling fans & private baths.

L'HABITACION BEACH GUEST HOUSE, 1957 Calle Italia, Ocean Park, San Juan, PR, 00911, (787) 727-2499, Fax: (787) 727-2599. Email: habitationbeach@msn.com, Web: http://www.freeyellow.com/members3/habitationbeach/, Gay & lesbian B&B on the gay Ocean Park Beach with bar & restaurant.

NUMERO UNO GUEST HOUSE, Calle Santa Ana #1, Ocean Park, San Juan, PR, 00911, (787) 726-5010, Fax: (787) 727-5482. Guesthouse with restaurant & bar, private baths, expanded continental breakfast, AC, pool & ocean beach on premises, near gay nightlife, 50% gay/lesbian clientele.

OCEAN PARK BEACH INN, Calle Elena 3, Ocean Park, San Juan, 00911, (787) 728-7418 (Tel/Fax), reservations: (800) 292-9208. Overlooking a turquoise sea, our inn offers a tropical retreat for men and women. All rooms surround a lush courtyard with hundreds of plants and flowers, songbirds, ocean surf... A quiet oasis, steps from restaurants, bars and shopping. Rooms have private baths, AC, refrigerator or kitchenette. A verandah, TV lounge and complete bar invite guests to relax. Complimentary tropical breakfast and beach equipment, year-round weekly rates.

OCEAN WALK GUEST HOUSE, Calle Atlantic No 1, Ocean Park, San Juan, PR, 00911, (787) 728-0855 or (800) 468-0615, Fax: (787) 728-6434. Guesthouse on the beach with cafe & bar, some straight clientele in season, 50% straight off season, women welcome, variety of rooms with private baths, continental breakfast.

SEABREEZE VACATION APARTMENT RENTALS, 1505 Loiza St #277, San Juan, PR, 00911, (787) 723-1888 (Tel/

Tropical Gardens by the Ocean

Ocean Park Beach Inn

San Juan (800) 292-9208

VIRGIN ISLANDS

Fax). Apartment rentals close to beach. ♀♀♂

Bars
BEACH BAR, at Atlantic Beach Hotel., Outdoor bar on the beach, popular early afternoon, Sun Tea Dance 5pm.

CAFE MATISSE, 1351 Ashford Ave, gay-friendly bar in a restaurant. Bar becomes gay on Tues for Alternative night.

CAFE VIOLETA, Fortaleza 56, Little private rooms for cocktails, oldest gay-oriented establishment in San Juan, mixed gay/straight.

DOWNSTAIRS LOUNGE, at the Condado Inn.,

RIVERA HERMANOS, 157 Calle San Sebastian, liquor store with some open-air seating, woman-owned, you can drink there, closed Sun.

Dance Bar/Disco
ABBEY NIGHTS AT LASER, 251 Calle Cruz, Old San Juan, Gay Thurs only.

ASYLUM SUNDAYS, Avda Ponce de Leon, Santurce, (787) 723-3416. Gay dance night with live performance art.

BOCCACIO, Calle Z between Avenida Ponce de Leon & Avenida, Muñoz Rivera in Hato Rey., Across from fire dept, disco with outdoor patio and patio bar. Fri, Sat only from 10pm, $12 entry for all-you-can-drink, 50% men, 50% women.

CLUB MILLENIUM, Ashford Ave, in Condado Plaza, Gay Mon only.

COLORS, Roosevelt Ave, Hato Rey, Salsa, merengue, upscale Latin crowd.

★ **CUPS,** Calle San Mateo 1708, Santurce, (787) 268-3570, disco."

EROS, 1257 Ponce de Leon, Parada 18, Santurce, (787) 722-1131. Wed-Sun, younger crowd, 70% men. Club kids dress up in wild costumes, all-out drag shows, strippers, real performance, real productions.

LA LAGUNA NIGHTCLUB, Calle Barranquitas 53, Condado., Private after hours dance club with strippers & live entertainment, open daily from 10pm.

Restaurants
ALLEGRO RISTORANTE, 1350 Roosevelt Ave, Hato Rey, (787) 793-0190. Italian cuisine.

CAFE BERLIN, 407 San Francisco, Plaza Colon, Old San Juan, (787) 722-5202. Huge gay following.

CAFE MATISSE, 1351 Av. Ashford, Condado, (787) 723-7910. Continental cuisine, live entertainment Wed.

CARUSO ITALIAN RESTAURANT, 1104 Ashford Ave, Condado, (787) 723-6876. Italian cuisine.

LA FONDA DE CERVANTES, Wilson Ave 1464, Condado, in Hotel Iberia, (787) 722-5380. Exotic European cuisine with Spanish influence.

LAS OLAS, 1 Calle Venedig, at Atlantic Beach Hotel, (787) 721-6900, breakfast & lunch. ♀♂

OCEAN WALK RESTAURANT, at the Ocean Walk guest house.,

PARROT CLUB, 363 Calle Fortaleza, (787) 725-7370.

TERRACE, at Condado Inn Hotel., ♀♂

Retail & Bookstores
SCRIPTUM, 1129-B Ashford Ave, at Calle Venedig, Condado., Gay bookstore.

VIRGIN ISLANDS - B V I
COOPER ISLAND

Accommodations
COOPER ISLAND BEACH CLUB, Cooper Island, British VI, USA office: PO Box 512, Turners Falls, MA, 01376, (413) 863-3162, (800) 542-4624 (USA office), Fax: (413) 863-3662. Email: info@cooper-island.com, Web: http://www.cooper-island.com, Experience an island 1-1/2 miles by 1/2 mile, where there are no roads, nightclubs, malls or fast-food outlets. Your principal activities will be sunning, swimming, snorkeling, reading, writing and enjoying relaxing meals. Our beachfront restaurant and bar offer dramatic sunset views. Our twelve rooms are on the beach, with open-plan living room, kitchen, balcony, bath and shower that is almost outdoors! Gay-friendly.

TORTOLA

Accommodations
FORT RECOVERY ESTATE, Box 239, Road Town, Tortola, (284) 495-4354, (800) 367-8455 (wait for ring), Fax: (284) 495-

4036. Email: FTRHOTEL@caribsurf.com, Web: www.fortrecovery.com, Gay-friendly luxury seaside villa resort with chef on premises, private baths, continental breakfast, private beach, freshwater pool on premises.

PROSPECT REEF, PO Box 104, Road Town, Tortola, in USA: (800) 356-8937. Direct fax: (809) 494-5595. Village resort with pub, private yacht harbour, panoramic views. Spacious accommodations with room service. Superb snorkeling & sailing, dive & sightseeing trips arranged. Town centre, shopping & airport nearby.

VIRGIN ISLANDS - U S

■ Accommodations

RENT A VILLA, (800) 533 6863, (973) 533-6863, Fax: (973) 740-8833. Rent privately owned villas in the USVI by the week or month, full amenities, 10-20% gay/lesbian clientele.

ST CROIX

■ Accommodations

CORMORANT BEACH CLUB & HOTEL, 4126 La Grande Princesse, St. Croix, USVI, 00820, (340) 778-8920, (800) 548-4460, Fax: (340) 778-9218. Email: infor@cormorant-stcroix.com, Web: www.cormorant-stcroix.com, Enjoy a turquoise ocean view from your private balcony... step out your door and onto the palm-studded white sand beach or into our beachside fresh-water pool. Play tennis, snorkel or just doze in a hammock. Watersports, deep sea fishing, golf and horseback riding are nearby. Duty-free shopping and fine restaurants in nearby Christiansted. Bar & restaurant on premises. Gay-friendly.

ON THE BEACH, 127 Smithfield, Frederiksted, St. Croix, USVI, 00840, (340) 772-1205 or (800) 524-2018 (Toll-free reservations), Fax: (340) 772-1757. The premier gay destination in the Caribbean. Twenty immaculate suites located directly on a beautiful white sandy beach. Two freshwater pools. Kitchens in all units, plus free continental breakfast. Half mile to town. Exclusively gay & lesbian clientele. Member IGLTA. Our 20th year!

■ Bars

LAST HURRAH, King St, Frederiksted, (973) 772-5225. Bar & restaurant with Hollywood theme. ♂

■ Restaurants

CAFE DU SOLEIL, Strand St, Frederiksted., Oceanfront continental cuisine, upstairs location with ocean view.

ST JOHN

■ Accommodations

SUNSET POINTE IN ST. JOHN, Address of office: 45A King St, Christiansted, St. Croix, USVI, 00820, (340) 773-8100 or (340) 773-2449, Fax: (340) 773 3547. Rental house & cottage, color cable TV, fully equipped kitchen, house has pool, 50% gay/lesbian clientele."

ST THOMAS

■ Accommodations

BLACKBEARD'S CASTLE, PO Box 6041, St Thomas, USVI, 00804, (809) 776-1234, (800) 344-5771, Fax: (809) 776-4321. Our tower, a national historic site, was built in 1679 to scan for pirates & enemy ships. It provides a spectacular backdrop

---

ON THE BEACH

US Virgin Islands Oceanfront Resort.

This **is** Gay/Lesbian Paradise!
- Spectacular View ■ Beach Snorkeling
- Oceanfront Pool ■ Friendly & Relaxed
- Rooms/Suites w/Kitchens

800 -524-2018

for an oversized fresh water pond & terrace. The views are exceptional! This intimate inn's spacious, quiet guest rooms provide all the expected amenities.
HOTEL 1829, PO Box 1567, Govt Hill, St. Thomas, USVI, 00804, (809) 776-1829, Fax: 776-4313, (800) 524-2002. Gay-friendly hotel with restaurant & bar, private baths.

Beaches
MORNING STAR BEACH., Frequented by many gays especially on Sun.

Dance Bar/Disco
R&R NIGHT CLUB & LEMON GRASS CAFE, on Back Street, at Baker Square., Fri & Sat only: Dining room converts to dance club about 10pm. Busy by 11pm, 80%-90% gay & lesbian.

Restaurants
BLACKBEARD'S CASTLE, at Blackbeard's Castle hotel., Open while rebuilding after hurricane. Come enjoy our new, intimate atmosphere."
OLD STONE FARMHOUSE, at Mahogany Run Golf Course., Rebuilding, due to reopen in 1996.

WEST INDIES
BARBADOS

Information
INFO SERVICE, (246) 428-7635 or (246) 428-2510. Answers 8am-8pm, ask for Fran! For detailed local gay information.

Accommodations
ROMAN BEACH APTS, Oististown Christ Church, Barbados, (246) 428-7635, (246) 428-2510. Ten gay-friendly peaceful & private beachfront studio apartments with kitchens & private bathrooms. Not fancy, but clean and comfortable, and the price is right: US $45-$60/night winter, US $35-$50/night summer.

Beaches
ACCRA BEACH, Christ Church, NOT a gay beach, it is a public beach surrounded by hotels, restaurants, bars, but frequented by gays.

Bars
COACH HOUSE, in the St James area on west coast of island, NOT a gay bar, just one of the bars frequented by all visitors to the island Live bands.
HARBOR LIGHTS, Bay St, Bridgetown., NOT a gay bar, just one of the bars frequented by visitors to the island. Dance bar, patio & dancing under the moonlight.
SHIP'S INN, St Lawrence Gap, Christ Church on the south coast, NOT a gay bar, just one of the bars frequented by visitors to the island, live bands some nights.

Restaurants
WATERFRONT CAFE, the Wharf, in Bridgetown., Restaurant & bar with entertainment nightly. NOT a gay business. One of the restaurants frequented by visitors to the island.

BLACKBEARD'S Castle
Restaurant — Hotel — Piano Lounge
and all that jazz

P.O. Box 6041 • St. Thomas
U.S.V.I. • 00804

(809) 776-1234
(800) 344-5771

JAMAICA

Accommodations

HOTEL MOCKING BIRD HILL, PO Box 254, Port Antonio, Jamaica, (876) 993-7267, (876) 993-7134, Fax: (876) 993-7133. Email: mockbrd@cwjamaica.com, Elegant, charming retreat with restaurant, bar & gallery studio featuring women artists. Mixed clientele. Ceiling fans, private baths, TV lounge & pool. Hiking & tours. Nearby are rainforests, mountains and numerous waterfalls, romantic coves and beautiful beaches.

LIGHTHOUSE PARK, PO Box 3, Negril, Jamaica, (876) 957-0252. Gay-friendly seaside cabanas, a stone house & tent spaces. Double rooms, private & shared baths. House has kitchen privileges, communal kitchen available. Gay/lesbian following of 40% gay artist & musician types.

SEAGRAPE VILLAS, Ocho Rios, Jamaica, (773) 693-6884, (800) 637-3608, Fax: (847) 297-6882. Email: sgvillas@aol.com, 3 four-bdrm villas with cook & maid, gay-friendly, pier access beach available. ♀♂

TREASURE POINTE VILLA, Mail c/o PO Box 424, Bethany Beach, DE, 19930, (800) 442-9697, (302) 539-4003. Gay-friendly, fully-furnished & staffed villa.

LATIN AMERICA
ARGENTINA

COUNTRY CODE: (54),

BUENOS AIRES

Bars

BACH BAR, Cabrera 4390, Palermo Viejo, popular with younger crowd, from 22:00 (closed Wed). ♀♂

CENTRO CLUB SNOB, Hipólito Yrigoyen 1115, (01) 384 6271, Thurs-Sat from 24:00, 50% gay & lesbian & 50% hetero clientele.

D. GALA, Paraguay 459, 50% gay & lesbian & 50% hetero clientele, more gay Wed & Sun.

EL OLMO, Santa Fe, at Pueyrredon, not a gay bar, more gay 22:00-02:30. Also after-hours café for breakfast, 07:00.

ELEGANT, Ecuador at Santa Fé, discreetly frequented by gays.

INVITRO, Azcuenaga 1007, (01) 824 0932, 60% men, 40% women.

MANHATTAN CON G, Anchorena 1347, from 22:00 (closed Thurs). ♂

OVIEDO, Avda Pueyrredón at Santa Fé, discreetly frequented by gays.

PIOLA, Libertad, between Marcelo .T de Alvear & Avenida Santa Fe, bar & restaurant, popular with gays Wed & Sun evenings, 50% gay & 50% straight clientele.

Hotel Mocking Bird Hill
Port Antonio, Jamaica.
Tel: 876-993-7134/7267 Fax: 876-993-7133. E-MAIL: mockbrd@cwjamaica.com

ARGENTINA

TADZIO, Anchorena 1122, (01) 961 7180, closed Tues. Wed. Breakfast Sat & Sun.

TODO, Laprida 1528, (01) 827 5449.

Dance Bar/Disco

ANGELS, Viamonte 2168, from 24:00 (closed Mon-Wed).

BUNKER, Anchorena 1170, large disco, Wed, Fri-Sun from 24:00, some straight clientele.

CUARTO (IV) MILENIO, Alsina 934, disco & restaurant, 60% men, 40% women, open Fri from 01:00.

ENIGMA, Suipacha 927, in shopping center, women's disco, open only on weekends, men welcome.

POSH, Cabrera 3046.,

VAI VEN, Pte. Peron 18-1.,

Restaurants

KATMANDÚ, Córdoba 3547, (01) 963 1122, from 20:00 (closed Sun).

KATTILA, Suipacha 880, (01) 394 7663, from 10:30.

TE MATARE RAMIREZ, Paraguay 4062, (01) 831 9156.

CORDOBA

Accommodations

HOSTAL DE LA LUNA, Monsenor Pablo Cabrera s/n, Cruz Chica, La Cumbre, Cordoba, CC 74 CP 5178, (54-548) 51877 (Tel/Fax). Gay-friendly B&B with 5 guestrooms, color TV, phone, private baths, full gourmet breakfast & complimentary evening wine or afternoon tea. Dinner is optional. Pool on premises.

Bars

BEEP, Sucre 173, from 22:30, mix of gays, lesbians & heteros.

UNIVERSO PUB, Blvd Las Heras 116, from 24:00, mix of gays, lesbians & heteros.

Dance Bar/Disco

HANGAR 18 DISCO, Blvd Las Heras 118, Fri-Sun from 00:30, mix of gay, lesbian & hetero clientele.

LA PIAF, Obispo Ceballos 45, San Martín.,

CORRIENTES

Bars

CONTRAMARCHA, Paímbre 5000.,

LA PLATA

Dance Bar/Disco

BACK DISCO, Calle 35 & Calle 5, Fri & Sat.

MAR DEL PLATA

Bars

DICROICA, Bolivar 2152, open all year.

Dance Bar/Disco

EXTASIS, Corrientes 2044, (023) 920 338, Fri & Sat.

MENDOZA

Bars

LA JUNGLA, Salta 1843, bar & cafe.

Dance Bar/Disco

LA REDENCIÓN, Bandera de los Andes, 5241 Guaymallén.,

RIO NEGRO

Dance Bar/Disco

LOS FAUNOS, calle Venezuela, at Camino de Circunvalación, in Cipolletti,

ROSARIO

Bars

CONTRATO BAR, Alvear 40 bis, Thurs-Sun from 23:00.

INIZIO, Mitre 1880, from 22:00.

Dance Bar/Disco

STATION G, Avda. Rivadavia 2481.,

SALTA

Bars

ESTACION TEQUILA CLUB, San Luís 348, from 22:00.

NOSOTROS DISCO, Juan M. Guemes 11, in barrio Don Emilio, (087) 224 035.

Dance Bar/Disco

O'CLOCK DISCO, La Rioja, at Santa Fé, Fri-Sun.

SANTA FE

Bars

TUDOR TABERNA PUB, Javier de la Rosa 325, Barrio de Guadalupe, bar with Sat disco.

TUCUMAN

■ *Dance Bar/Disco*
MADONNA, San Martín 986.

BOLIVIA

COUNTRY CODE: (591),

LA PAZ

■ *Bars*
CAFE BRASIL, Avda. Héroes del Acre 1762, between Conchitas & Castrillo, in San Pedro, cruise bar with dancing on weekends, vast majority male clientele.

BRAZIL

COUNTRY CODE: (55),

BELEM

■ *Bars*
GO FISH, Tv. Castelo Branco 1269.

■ *Dance Bar/Disco*
MIX, Rua Almirante Wandenlock 985, Fri, Sat from 23:00.

BELO HORIZONTE

■ *Bars*
CANTINA DO LUCAS, Av. Augusto de Lima 223/18,
QUEEN SCOTCH, Rua Gonçalves Dias 2217, from 19:00, closed Mon.

■ *Dance Bar/Disco*
BLOW UP, Rua Tenente Brito Mello 267, Thurs-Sun from 22:00.
★ **FASHION**, Rua Tupis 1240, near Araguari, Barro Preto, (031) 271 3352.
YES DISCO, Rua Maranhao 1123, (031) 225 6854.

BRASILIA

■ *Bars*
BEIRUTE, CLS 109, Bloco A, loja 02, Asa Sul.,
CAFE CASSIS, CLS 214, Bloco B, loja 22, Asa Sul.,
CAFE SAVANA, CLN 116, Bloco A, loja 04, Asa Norte, (06) 347 9403.
COFFEE HOUSE, SHN, Galeria do Hotel Manhattan, loja 10.,

MARTINICA CAFE, CLN 303, Asa Norte, from 18:00, closed Mon.
SPHAERA, CLN 203, Bloco D, loja 67-73.,

■ *Dance Bar/Disco*
NEW AQUARIUS, SDS Edificio Acropo L., Bloco N, loja 12, (06) 312 42 23, Fri, Sat from 23:00.

CAMPINAS

■ *Bars*
DOUBLE FACEM, Rua Barao de Jaguara 358, (019) 236 7361, Fri-Sun from 22:00.
HASÉS, Av. José de Souza Campos 735, (019) 255 1552, Fri-Sun from 22:00.

■ *Dance Bar/Disco*
CLUB, THE, Rod. Campinas Mogi Mirim, km 105.5, (019) 253 6380, Fri & Sat.

CURITIBA

■ *Bars*
AGNUS DEI, Rua Visconde do Rio Branco.,
NICK HAVANA BAR, Rua Francisco Torres 272, (041) 263 4884, piano bar.
OPÇAO, Rua Benjamin Constant 180, (041) 322 1180.
OUTDOOR, Rua Sen. Xavier da Silva 242, (041) 973 4341, viedos, from 20:00, closed Mon, Tues.
SONHO MEU, Rua 24 de Maio 540, from 20:30, closed Mon, Tues.

■ *Retail & Bookstores*
LILITH FEMINIST BOOKSHOP, Rua Bruno Filgueira 1921, women's bookstore.

FLORIANOPOLIS

■ *Bars*
ESCOTHILA, Rua Arista Garibaldi 253, from 20:00 (closed Sun, Mon), frequented by gays & lesbians.
FABRICA DE ARTE, Rua Nunes Machado 104, (048) 224 1102, Tues-Sat from 20:00, discreetly frequented by gays.
ILHEUS, Rua O. Cunha, from 22:00, closed Mon.
PARADA OBRIGATORIA, Av das Randeiras, Lagoa da Conceiçao, from 20:00, closed Mon.
POINT BAR, Av Dom Manuel 30.,

BRAZIL 211

■ Dance Bar/Disco
HOMINUS, Escadaria do Rosario, 🏠 ♂
IBIZA CLUB, Praia dos Ingleses, north side, Fri, Sat from 22:30. 🏠 ♀♂

FORTALEZA

■ Beaches
JERICOACOARA, difficult to find, ask locally for directions.

■ Bars
BAR DO JOCA, Av Beira Mar 3101, barraca 205a, (085) 261 4006, 7 days. ♂
EUROTUNEL, Av 13 de Maio 2400, Benfica, closed Sun. ♂
GRAFITT BAR, Av 13 de Maio 2400, lofa 02, Benfica., ♂
TABU, Avenida Santos Dumont 1673, in Aldeota, Fri & Sat. 🏠 ♂

■ Dance Bar/Disco
AXE BABA, Av. Tristao Gonçalves 1615, closed Mon. 🏠 ♂
BROADWAY, Rua Carolina Sucupira 455, Aldeota, Fri-Sun. 🏠 ♂
HANGAR 7 NIGHT CLUB, Av Monsenhor Tabosa 1101, Praia de Iracema, Fri & Sat. 🏠 ♂
MEDHUZA, Rua Oswaldo Cruz 46, Beira Mar, (085) 295 4127, Fri & Sat. 🏠 ♂
STYLE, Rua Senador Pompeu 1493, closed Mon. 🏠 ♂

GUARULHOS

■ Dance Bar/Disco
CASA DO SOM, Praça dos Estudantes 174, (011) 208 0222, Fri & Sat 22:30—4:30, Sun 16:30-22:30. 🏠 ♀♂

MANAUS

■ Dance Bar/Disco
IS, Blvd. Dr. V. de Lima 33, (081) 228 6828, Fri-Sun from 22:00. 🏠 ♂

PORTO ALEGRE

■ Bars
CLAUDIO'S, Avenida Joao Pessoa, near Avenida Venancio Aires, open until very late. ♂
DOCE VICIO, Rua Vieira de Castro 32, 3 levels, bar with restaurant & terrace. ♀♂
LOCAL HERO, Rua Venancio Aires 59, near Rua José Patrocínio, Wed-Sun. 🏠 ♪ ♂

■ Dance Bar/Disco
★ **ENIGMA,** Rua Pinto Bandeira 485, Fri-Sun. 🏠 ♂
FIM DE SECULO, Rua Plinio 427, gay Thurs only. 🏠 ♂
VITRAUX, Rua da Conceiçao, at Alberto Bins, Fri-Sun, many women. 🏠 ♀♂

RECIFE

■ Dance Bar/Disco
DAZIBAO, Rua Progresso 336, (081) 231 2492. 🏠 ♪ ♂
DOUTOR FROID, Rua das Ninfas, Boa Vista, (081) 423 1875. 🏠 ♀♂

RIBERAO PIRES

■ Dance Bar/Disco
SCHLOSS, Rua Guaracy 171, Ouro Fino Paulista, (011) 742 0168, disco, bar & gallery. 🏠 ♂

RIO DE JANEIRO

■ Information
BARRALES CULT, PO Box 37517, Rio de Janeiro, Tel/Fax: (021) 385 2121, lesbian group.
NOSS, Rua Visconde de Pirajá 127/201, Tel/fax: (021) 227 5944, social health organization involved in HIV/AIDS issues & outreach services, publishes bimonthly newspaper Nós Por Exemplo.

■ Bars
POINT MIX, Estr. do Itaubangua 1681, from 21:00. ♀

■ Dance Bar/Disco
BOHEMIO, Rua Santa Luzia 760, Cinelandia, (021) 240 7259. 🏠 ♪ ♀♂
ELEVEN FORTY (1140), Rua Capitao Menezes 1140, Fri-Sun from 22:00. 🏠 ♂
GAVIOTA, Rua Rodolfo de Amoedo 347, in Barra da Tijuca, Fri & Sat from 23:00, Sun from 20:30. 🏠 ♂
INCONTRUS, Praça Serzedelo Correia 15, Copacabana, (021) 257 6498, from 22:00. 🏠 ♪ ♂

SALVADOR

Information

GRUPO GAY DA BAHIA, Rua do Sodré 45, in Dois de Julho, city center, 243 4902.

Bars

ALAMBIQUE, Rua J. de Deus 25, 1st floor, (071) 322 5470, from 19:00.

ANCORADOURO, Rua Pinto de Aguiar 24, Fri-Sat from 20:00, Sun from 15:00.

ARTES & MANIAS, Av Senior Costa Puro 809.

BANZO, Largo do Pelourinho.

CANTINA DA LUA, Terreiro de Jesus 2, Praça da Sé, not a gay bar, discreetly frequented by gays.

CHARLES CHAPLIN, Rua Carlos Gomes 141, younger crowd.

EMPORIO, Avenida 7 de Setembro 3809, in Porto da Barra, (071) 247 5881, many women.

FLORAIS DE BAR, Largo de Mariquita, (071) 335 4701.

LADY FALCAO, Av Lermanja 35, (071) 371 5312, closed Mon.

MAO DUPLA, Rua Alfredo de Brito 39.

QUINTAL DO RASO DA CATARINA, Av. 7 do Setembro 1370, 18:00-03:00 (closed Sun), NOT a gay bar, but discreetly frequented by gays.

SUMMER 2000, Avenida Pinto de Aguiar 25, in Patamares, (071) 231 9980, Fri, Sat from 20:00, Sun from 15:00.

VOLLUPIA, Praia de Stella Maris, in back of Super Mix, (071) 974 2666, closed Mon.

Dance Bar/Disco

★ **BANANA REPUBLICA,** Rua Braulio Xavier 2, in Vitoria, (071) 237 3079, disco, patio, live music, Thurs-Sun from 23:00.

BIZARRO DISCO DANCING, Rua Augusto França 55, in Dois de Julho, (071) 321 5373, open summers Thurs-Sun from 23:00.

IS KISS, Rua Carlos Gomes 30, in the city center.

MIK OZONE, Rua Augusto França 55, (071) 321 5373, Thurs-Sun from 23:00.

NEW LOOK BAR, Rua Nilton Prado 24, on Gamboa, (071) 336 4949, Thurs-Sun from 23:00, go go boys, live music on 2nd level.

USINA DANCING, Av. Vasco da Gama 250, (071) 382 3368, some hetero clientele.

SANTA MARIA

Bars

BIG LUCAO, Praça Saldanha Marinho, (055) 221 6996.

Dance Bar/Disco

OVER BUSY, Rua Riachuelo 244, (055) 222 7541, Thurs-Sun from 22:00.

REFUGIO DOS DEUSES, Rua Dr. Bozano 936, (055) 222 7541.

ZAMAH, Avenida Presidente Vargas 1030, (055) 221 4769, Fri, Sat from 24:00.

SAO PAULO

Bars

ALIBI, Praça Roosevelt 134.

CANECA DE PRATA, Av Vieira de Carvalho 55, (011) 223 6420.

CASA DA VILA, Rua Girassol 310, Vila Madalena, (011) 210 5216, gay men welcome, some hetero clientele.

CHOPP ESCURO, Rua Marquês de Itù 152, in Vila Buarque, (011) 221-0872, 7 days.

CORSARIO, Praça Roosevelt 252, (011) 256 5371.

CUBE, Rua Consolaçao 2967, Jardins, (011) 932 1854, bar & restaurant, 19:00-02:00 (closed Sun).

FERRO'S BAR, R Martinho Prado 119, (011) 258 0004, bar & restaurant, frequented by lesbians.

FLAG, Rua da Consolaçao 3055, Jardins, bar & restaurant, daily from 19:00.

MADE IN KUSDRA, Rua Nestor Pestans, from 19:00.

★ **PAPARAZZI,** Rua da Consolaçao 3046, (011) 881 6665.

PITTOMBA, Rua da Consolaçao 3161, Jardins, (011) 852 4058, daily from 19:00.

PRETA'S BAR, Rua Santo Antonio 579, Bela Vista, closed Mon.

PRIDE, Al. Itu 176, Jardins, (011) 853 1213, karaoke lounge & videos.

CHILE 213

QUARTELL, Rua da Consolaçao 2518, Jardins, (011) 258 8090, from 19:00 (Sun from 18:00), closed Mon. ♂

QUATRO (4) POR ACASO, Av Santo Amaro 5394, (011) 241 4907, bar & restaurant, 21:00-01:00. ♀

RED POINT, Rua Frei Caneca 135, closed Mon. ♪✕♂

RITZ, Alameda Franca 1088, (011) 280 6808, NOT a gay bar, discreetly frequented by gays.

ZWEI, Rua Original 139, Vila Madalena, (011) 211 7528, bar & restaurant, from 20:00 (closed Mon, Tues), men welcome. ✕♀

▇ *Dance Bar/Disco*

ALVORADA, Rua Tabapoa 1236, (011) 820 6774, from 21:00, closed Sun. ♪ 🎵 ♂

ATENAS NIGHT DANCE, Praça J. Mesquita 73, (011) 221 6268, Sat from 22:00, Sun from 19:00. 🎵 ♀♂

DISCO FEVER, Rua Augusta 2203, Jardins, (011) 852 6345, from 23:00, closed Mon-Wed. 🎵 ♂

TUNNEL, Rua dos Ingleses 355, Jardins, (011) 285 0246, Fri, Sat from 23:00, Sun from 19:00. 🎵 ♀♂

Z CLUB, Alameda Jaú 48, Jardins, (011) 283 0033, many womenThurs-Sun, men welcome. 🎵 ♀

CHILE

COUNTRY CODE: (56),

LA SERENA

▇ *Bars*
BEST, Balmaceda 3390, Paradero 6 1/2, La Pampa, (51) 24 26 07. 🎵 🎶 ♀♂

▇ *Dance Bar/Disco*
REMAKING, Avda Francisco de Aguirre 062., 🎵 ♀♂

▇ *Restaurants*
LA MÍA PIZZA, Avda del Mar 2100.,

SANTIAGO

▇ *Information*
AIDS INFO, (2) 633 69 66.

CENTRO DE ESTUDIOS DE LA MUJER, Purísima 353, (2) 77 11 94, women's center & archives.

CENTRO LAMBDA CHILE, Agustinas 2085, at Avda Brasil, Santiago Centro, 687 35 95 gay & lesbian organization.

MOVILH, Santa Rosa 170-A, Santiago Centro, (2) 632 43 09. Gay & lesbian organization, 18:00-22:30 (Sat 17:00-21:00), active in civil & human rights causes, organizes public marches, producers/directors of Chile's gay radio program "Triángulo Abierto," provides local information. Write: MOVILH, Casilla 52834, Correo Central, Santiago. E-mail: movilh@entelchile.net.

▇ *Bars*
BAR DE WILLY, Paseo Las Palmas, Av. Providencia, 11 de Septiembre, Providencia, 22:00-04:00. ♪♀♂

BAR DIONISIO, Bombero Nuñez 111, Barrio Bellavista, (2) 737 60 65, from 21:00 (closed Sun). ♀♂

DELOS, Avda Las Condes 9177, Las Condes, (02) 202 0360. Pub, piano bar & restaurant. Pub & piano bar from 18:00, restaurant from 19:30. ✕ ♂

SEVEN-SEVEN-SEVEN (777), Alameda 777, Santiago Centro, bar & restaurant, frequented by gays. 🎵

YO CLAUDIO, Av. Santa Lucía, Santiago Centro.,

▇ *Dance Bar/Disco*
BUCANEROS, TELOS, new gay disco, to open Spring '97, ask locally for address. 🎵 ♀♂

BUNKER, Calle Bombero Nuñez 159, (2) 737 1716, Thurs-Sat 24:00-04:30, stippers, mostly gay with a large straight following. 🎵 ♪ 🎶 ♀♂

DELOS, Avda Las Condes 9179, Las Condes, (02) 202 0360, from 23:00. 🎵 ♂

FAUSTO, Av. Santa María 0832, Providencia, (2) 777 1041, from 21:30, closed Sun. 🎵 ♂

LA TRIANON, Avenida Santo Domingo, at Baquedano, at La Trianon Restaurant, Mon from 23:00. ✕ ♪ 🎵 ♀♂

NAXOS, Alameda B. O'Higgins 776, Santiago Centro., 🎵 🎶 ♂

QUASAR, Coquimbo 1458, (2) 671 1267, Sat from 24:00. ♪ 🎵 ♀♂

QUEEN SANTIAGO, General Santiago Bueras 128, Santiago Centro, (2) 639 87

03, disco & bar, 23:30-05:00 (Fri, Sat till 06:30, Sun from 23:00).

Cafe
LA HOLANDESA, Avda Santa Rosa 31, at Alameda B. O'Higgins, Santiago Sur, fuento de sode (soda fountain), not a gay cafe, frequented by gays & lesbians later at night.

QUEEN COFFEE, San Martín 527, Santiago Centro.

TAVELLI, Avda Providencia, between Andrés de Fuenzalida, & Las Urbanas, Providencia, not a gay cafe, frequented by gays & lesbians.

Restaurants
HA - WHA, Merced, at José Miguel de la Barra, city center, restaurant & bar.

HAMBURGER PLACE, Paseo Ahumada, at Agustinas, Santiago Centro, not a gay restaurant, more gays & lesbians later in evening.

LA PIZZA NOSTRA, Avda Providencia 1975, at Avda Pedro de Valdivia, Providencia, Italian cuisine, many tourists.

LA TRIANON, Avenida Santo Domingo, at Baquedano, bar & restaurant.

LOMIT'S, Alameda B. O'Higgins, at Irena Morales, next to the Hotel Crowne Plaza, not a gay restaurant, more gays & lesbians later in evening.

PROSIT, Providencia 21, in front of Plaza Valledano, not gay, frequented by gays & lesbians.

Retail & Bookstores
LILA LIBRERIA, Providencia 1652, local 3, at Padre Mariano, Providencia, (2) 236 81 45 women's bookstore and meeting place.

MIMESIS, Calle Portugal 48, Torre 6, local 13, (2) 222 5321, gay & lesbian bookstore, 09:00-18:00 (Sat till 14:00).

VALPARAISO

Information
SOCIEDAD HOMOSEXUAL SURGENTE (SHOMOS), Independencia 2446, gay & lesbian group, AIDS info.

Bars
TACONES, Huito 301, at Brasil, 22:00-02:00.

Dance Bar/Disco
FOXY DISCO, Independencia 2446, Fri, Sat 23:30-05:00.

SOVIET, Arlegui 346, in town of Viña del Mar, Thurs-Sat 23:00-05:00.

COLOMBIA

COUNTRY CODE: (57),

BOGOTA

Information
GAY INFO LINES, (1) 507 7000 or (1) 506 6000.

Bars
ENJALME Y LOMA, Via la Calera, km 4., upscale with a younger, trendy crowd.

MILENIO, Calle 58 #6-12, (1) 255 5452, trendy & upscale bar & restaurant.

STUDIO 77, Transversal 18 #77-21, frequented by some gays.

TERTULIA BAR, Calle 63 #14-81, women-only bar.

Dance Bar/Disco
ALTO SAN ANTONIO, km 6 via La Calera, (1) 211 5523, disco & restaurant.

BOYS CLUB, Avda Caracas 37-68, large disco & bar, techno & latino music, mix of gays & heteros.

Restaurants
MILENIO, at the Milenio bar location.

COSTA RICA

COUNTRY CODE: (506),

ALAJUELA

Information
ASOCIACION TRIANGULO ROSA, (506) 234 2411, gay & lesbian community center, scheduled meetings & socials.

Bars
MARGUISS, 250 meters south of Llobet stores, city center, from 18:00 (closed Mon).

LAKE ARENAL

Women's Accommodations
LEA'S COSTA RICA HAVEN, (011-506) 694 4093, Fax: (011-506) 695 5387. In USA call Lea (808) 575-2957. 1BR house overlooking lake. Private on 2 acres of land in the rainforest of north-central Costa

Rica, $25 nightly, volcano views. Local swimming, kayaking, fishing, windsurfing, hot springs, nearby restaurants, men welcome.

PUNTARENAS

Women's Accommodations

CASA YEMAYA, downtown Puntarenas, across from beach, (506) 661 0956 (Tel/Fax). Frequent thunderstorms interrput phone service every 2 days, so please call back. Web: http://www.cybershack.com/friends/yemaya, Women-only guesthouse. Accommodations are 3 rooms with fans, and amenities include hot water, use of kitchen & laundry facilities. There is great access to the Nicoya Peninsula. We offer local trip & event planning & travel counseling. Reservations recommended. Note: Thunderstorms tend to interrupt phone service, so please try again and again.

QUEPOS

Accommodations

COSTA LINDA, on road in back of 1st beach in Manuel Antonio, (506) 777 0304. Gay-friendly youth hostel/guesthouse, 20 rooms.

HOTEL CASA BLANCA DE MANUEL ANTONIO S.A., Apdo 194, Quepos-Manuel Antonio, 6350, (506) 777-0253 (Tel/Fax). Email: cblanca@sol.racsa.co.cr, Web: http://bertha.pomona.edu/cblanca/, Exclusively gay & lesbian hotel & guesthouse with private baths, all rooms have ceiling fans & some rooms with A/C. Suites and apartments have kitchenette. Near gay beach.

Bars

BISTRO TROPICAL, ask locally for address, gay-friendly, frequented by gays for after hours.

COCKATOO BAR, at the Eclipse Hotel, terrace bar, daily from 17:00.

VELA BAR, Calle Manuel Antonio, 77 04 13, bar & restaurant on the beach, frequented by gays.

Dance Bar/Disco

ARCO IRIS, in downtown Quepos, ask locally for directions, not a gay bar, gay crowd later in evenings after 23:00, especially weekends.

Casa Blanca
MANUEL ANTONIO
(506) 777-0253
The Hotel Is NOT the Main Attraction Here!

MAR Y SOMBRA, beachside disco at Playa Espadilla, not gay, but frequented by many gays, disco mostly on weekends in-season.

MARACAS, near the dock, in city center, huge dance bar, gay crowd later in evening.

Restaurants

DULÚ, Km 1 on the highway to Quepos, (506) 777 1297, restaurant & bar, Creole & Costa Rican cuisine, from 18:00 (closed Wed).

LA BOQUITA, in the Sansa Building, 2nd floor, city center, discreetly frequented by gays after bars close.

SAN JOSE

Information

AIDS INFO, 26 8972.

Accommodations

APARTMENTS SCOTLAND, Ave 1, Calle 27, San Jose, (506) 223-0033, (506) 257-4374, Fax: (506) 257-5317. Web: http://www.yellowweb.co.cr/scotland.html, gay-friendly apartment hotel, convenient to shopping, 50% gay/lesbian clientele, full 1-bedroom apartments with linens, kitchen utensils, color TVs, phones.

COSTA RICA

HOTEL COLOURS - THE GUEST RESIDENCE SAN JOSE, c/o Colours Destinations, 255 W 24th St, Miami Beach, FL, 33140, (800) ARRIVAL (277-4825), (305) 532-9341, Fax: (305) 534-0362. Local San Jose (506) 296 1880. Email: newcolours@aol.com, Web: http://www.colours.net, Experience this newly expanded & completely renovated resort! The vibrant tropical "colours," private baths, a new pool, Jacuzzi & gardens make this the best the "Capitol City" has to offer. New administration ensures the most complete service available. Total enjoyment from lounging poolside to touring in a supportive, attentive atmosphere. Bar/restaurant on premises. Now also Colours — The Lodge at the beaches of Nosara! 🏖 🛗 ♀♂

HOTEL KEKOLDI, Avenida 9, Calle 3 Bis, across from INVU, San José, (506) 223-3244, Fax: (506) 257-5476. Email: kekoldi@sol.racsa.co.cr, Web: www.costaricainfo.com/kekoldi.html, Gay-friendly B&B, continental breakfast with tropical fruits, TV, local info provided, tours/trips arranged.

JOLUVA GUESTHOUSE, Calle 3B, between avenues 9 and 11 #936, San Jose & Manuel Antonio Beach, (506) 223 7961, Fax: (506) 257 7668. USA reservations & info (800) 298-2418. Email: joluva@sol.racsa.co.cr, Web: www.hotels.co.cr/joluva.html, USA reservations/info: (800) 298-2418. B&B, women welcome, continental breakfast with tropical fruits, color cable TV, local info provided, tours/trips arranged. ♂

■ Bars

ALFONSINA Y EL MAR, across from Complejo Convoy, Tibás, (506) 235 6303 bar & restaurant, from 19:00 (closed Sun), shellfish a specialty, woman-owned.

BOCHINCHE, 11th St, between 10th & 12th Ave, video bar & restaurant, Wed-Sat from 19:00, 95% men. ♂

BUENAS VIBRACIONES, Paseo de los Estudiantes, in front of Mas X Menos parking lot, city center, open daily, 90% women. ♀

KARMA, Avenida 8, between calle 5 & 3, 70% women. ♀

PUCHOS/BARIL DORADO, 11th St, between Avenidas 8 & 10, 17:00 till 10:00 next day, small bar, after midnight knock on door. 🛗 ♀♂

■ Dance Bar/Disco

★ **DEJA VU/SINNERS,** Calle 2 between Avenidas 14 & 16, (506) 223 3758. Deja Vu: dance bar Wed-Sun; Sinners: bar, open Tues-Sun, 70% men, 30% women, many straights. 🍴 🎵 ♂

★ **LA AVISPA,** 834 Calle 1, between Avenidas 8 & 10, (506) 223 5343, open Tues-Sun (except Thurs), giant screen TV, 60% men, 40% women, lesbian-owned. Women-only last Wed. 🍴 ✂ ♀♂

■ Restaurants

KASHBAH, 150 meters north of Hotel Europa, (506) 258 0774, restaurant & bar, 11:00-23:00 (Fri-Sun till 24:00). ♀♂

LA ESQUINA, adjacent to the Hotel Colours, bar & restaurant, international cuisine. ♀♂

LA PERLA, Avenida 2 at Calle Central, bar & restaurant, 24hrs. 🚭 🍸

SAN PEDRO

■ Bars

LA TERTULIA, 100 meters east & 150 meters north of the church, in San Pedro, (506) 225 0250, from 18:00 (closed Sun), a variety of music, 80% women, frequented by some men. ♀

Colours
SAN JOSE
• Stunning New Pool
• Jacuzzi • Gardens
(800) ARRIVAL
http://www.colours.net

Retail & Bookstores

CLARA LUNA, 150 meters south of Univ. of Costa Rica, woman-owned general bookstore with gay & lesbian titles.

SANTA ANA

Bars

CASA MIA, 19:00-02:00 (Sun from 15:00), woman-owned bar, call or ask locally for address.

TAMARINDO

Accommodations

CABINA MARIELOS, (506) 653 0141. Gay-friendly, woman-owned accommodation across the street from the beach, clean rooms, kitchen facilities, turtle tour reservations.

TILARAN

Accommodations

VILLA DECARY, Nuevo Arenal, 5717 Tilaran, Guanacaste, Fax: (506) 694-4330 or (506) 694-4132. 5-BR B&B & cottage overlooking Lake Arenal, with private baths, full breakfast, ceiling fans, 50% gay/lesbian clientele.

EL SALVADOR

COUNTRY CODE: (503),

SAN SALVADOR

Dance Bar/Disco

ESCAPE, Condominio Blvd Los Heroes, near Olimpo disco location.

OLIMPO DISCOTEC, Condominio Juan Pablo Segundo, Colonia Miramontes, dance club with show bar, Sat only.

ORACULOS, Condominio Blvd Los Heroes, 225 0427, Thurs-Sat.

GUATEMALA

COUNTRY CODE: (502),

ANTIGUA

Dance Bar/Disco

LA CASBAH, Calle del Arco, 2 levels, more gays & lesbians Thurs.

Restaurants

GIL'S, 6a Calle Oriente #3, across from picturesque Parque Union., Authentic, hearty American cooking, gay-friendly. Open 10:30am.

GUATEMALA

Bars

ENCUENTROS, Avda 6, in city center.

Dance Bar/Disco

METROPOLIS, Calle 6, Zona 1.

★ **PANDORAS BOX,** in city center, videos, 2 levels.

TRILOGIA, Avda 4, Zona 1.

HONDURAS

COUNTRY CODE: (504),

PUERTO CORTES

Accommodations

HOTEL PLAYA, on Puerto Cortes Beach., Very popular gay-friendly hotel.

SAN PEDRO SULA

Dance Bar/Disco

CONFETIS, Avda. Circunvalación, male strippers, 50% gay & lesbian, 50% hetero clientele.

TEGUCIGALPA

Information

PRISMA GAY & LESBIAN INFO, men call Juan Carlos: 327 304; women call Rosalina: 329 345.

Accommodations

HOTEL LA RONDA, in Barrio La Ronda, 378 151. Gay-friendly hotel, 50% men, 50% women.

HOTEL PRADO, next to the cathedral in downtown Tegucigalpa, 370 121. Gay-friendly hotel, 50% men, 50% women.

Bars

BRIK BRAK, on the pedestrian mall in city center, video bar & restaurant, 24hrs, discreetly frequented by gays.

EL CLOSET, Colonia El Prado, left from Krispy Chicken, open Thurs-Sat. Thurs & Sat men's cruise bar, Fri lesbian night.

★ **ENCUENTROS,** beside Parque Valle, in city center, 60% gay, 40% lesbian clientele.

HONDURAS

VAQUEROS, Blvd Morazan, in La Epoca shopping center, younger crowd, 50% gay & lesbian, 50% hetero clientele.

■ Restaurants
PICA DELI, beside the Ministry of Finance building, (Ministerio de Hacienda), open-air cafeteria, umbrella tables, live piano music, open daytime only, 20% gay clientele.

TELA

■ Accommodations
GRAN HOTEL PRESIDENTE, on Tela Beach in downtown Tela, 482 821. Gay-friendly hotel, 50% men, 50% women.

MEXICO

For much more detailed information on Mexico, see Ferrari Guides' GAY MEXICO.

COUNTRY CODE: (52),

ACAPULCO

■ Accommodations
CASA CONDESA, PO Box D-247, Acapulco, GRO, 39851, (52-74) 841616, Fax: (52-74) 811183." Email: jamesallen@unforgettable.com, B&B, cottage & private apartment with 4 rooms, full breakfast.

CASA LE MAR, Lomas del Mar 32-B, Acapulco, 39690, (52-74) 84 10 22 or (52-74) 84 68 54. Fax: (52-74) 84 68 54. B&B in a private, open-air luxury villa, patio with pool, sun deck, wet bar, private baths, full breakfast, pool on premises, women welcome.

■ Dance Bar/Disco
DISCO DEMAS, Privada Piedra Picuda 17, behind Carlos & Charlies, (74) 84 1370, open daily, male strippers.

LA MALINCHE, Calle la Picuda 216, (74) 84 9221, male strippers.

RELAX, Lomas del Mar 4, Fracc. Club Deportivo, (74) 82 04 21, video dance bar, drag shows, male strippers.

■ Restaurants
LA BISTROQUET, Calle Andrea Doria 5, (074) 84 68 60. Gay-owned, gay-friendly restaurant, international cuisine.

LA TORTUGA, Lomas del Mar 5A, restaurant & bar, daily 10:00-02:00.

MARISCOS PIPO, Plaza Canada, (74) 84 0165, seafood, till 21:30.

AGUASCALIENTES

■ Bars
IMPERIAL BAR, Moreles & Juan de Montoro, from the Plaza de las Armas, Not a gay bar, but frequented by local gays.

■ Dance Bar/Disco
MANDILES DISCO, Blvd Lopez Mateos 730, close to Convencion del 1914, between Aguacate, & Chabacano, (49) 15 3281. The hot spot for gays & lesbians.

BAJA CALIFORNIA SUR

■ Accommodations
LA CONCHA BEACH RESORT, Kilómetro 5 Carretera a Pichilingue, La Paz, BCS, CP 23010, In USA: (619) 260-0991, Fax: (619) 294-7366 or (800) 999-BAJA (2252). Gay-friendly hotel with restaurant & gift shop, private baths, color cable TV, phone, AC, pool on premises. Condos have kitchen.

CABO SAN LUCAS

■ Accommodations
CABO SAN LUCAS ACCOMMODATIONS, contact Gay Baja Tours, (52-61) 72 8329.

■ Bars
RAINBOW BAR, Blvd. de la Marina 39-E, on the marina across, from Planet Hollywood, next to Shrimp Bucket, (114) 314 55. Gay bar, everyone welcome, dance music, videos, Latino & techno ambiance, younger crowd, daily 20:00-03:00.

■ Dance Bar/Disco
TENAMPA, close to the Cabo San Lucas air strip, no official address, taxi is best., After hours, where locals go when all other bars are closed, busiest 03:00-07:00, varied clientele, gay & straight.

■ Restaurants
ALFONSO'S, Plaza Bonita, across marina from Rainbow Bar., (114) 320 22, daily 07:00-23:00 (off-season, call for hours), nouvelle Mexican cuisine.

JAZMÍN, Calle Morelos,, between Saragosa & Obregón, San José del Cabo,

CANCUN

■ Bars
PICANTE, Avda Tulum 20, Zona Centro, small dance floor. 🈁♂

■ Dance Bar/Disco
KARAMBA, Avda. Tulúm 9, Altos, (98) 84 00 32, 22:00-02:00 (closed Mon). 🎵🈁 🈁♂

CIUDAD DE MEXICO

■ Bars
ANSIA, Algeciras 26, Centro Armand, across from Galerias Insurgentes, Thurs-Sat from 21:30, strippers. 🎵🈁♂

ANYWAY, THE DOORS & EXACTO, Monterrey 47, Col. Roma, Complex with 3 venues, daily from 21:00, strippers. Many women at The Doors. 🎵🈁♂

★ **BUTTERFLIES**, Eje Central at J.M. Izazaga 9, daily till 03:00, videos. 🎵♂

CAZTZI, Carlos Arellano 4, Ciudad Satélite, open Wed-Sat. 🎵🈁♂

★ **EL NUMERITO**, Plaza de la República 9, (5) 703 2218 strippers. 🎵🈁🈁♂

ENIGMA, Morelia 111, Colonia Roma, (5) 207 7367, drag shows where women dress like men, closed Mon, men welcome. 🎵🈁 ♀

LA CITA, Tacuba 58, at Isabela la Católica, (5) 521 5804, bar, restaurant & disco 🎵🈁🈁♂

■ Dance Bar/Disco
ARCANOS, Roberto Martínez Poniente 422, strippers, closed Mon, Tues. 🎵🈁🈁 ♂

COLIBRÍ, Puebla 163C, Colonia Roma, disco & bar, closed Mon. 🈁♂

DREAMS, Reforma Norte 76, across from Feria del Disco, mix of gays & heteros, closed Sun-Wed. 🎵🈁🈁

EL DON, Tonalá 79 corner of Alvaro Obregón, Col. Roma, (5) 207 0872, open Fri, Sat. 🎵🈁♂

PRIVATA, Avda Universitaria 1909, (5) 661 5939, rave-style music, open till 03:00, busier after 23:30. 🈁🈁♂

SIXTY-EIGHT (68) VERSALLES, Versalles 68, Col. Juárez, (5) 566 7476, gay Sun only, DJ. 🈁♂

■ Restaurants
LA CAFETERA, Rio Nazas 68-B.,
MARIA BONITA, Antojería Cuernavaca 68, Condesa.,
MERLIN, Culican 52.,
MESON D'MISS, Tlacotalpan 18, Col. Roma.,
PLATA, Juan Escutia 24, Condesa.,
TABERNA GRIEGA, Algeciras 26-W-8.,
THE DOORS, Monterrey 47, Col. Roma.

■ Retail & Bookstores
LAS SIRENAS, Avenida de la Paz 57, San Angel, 500 93 86, women's bookstore.

COZUMEL

■ Accommodations
LA CASA NOSTRA, 15 Avenida Sur 548, Cozumel, Quintana Roo, (987) 212 75, e-mail: jenhan@cozumel.czm.com.mx. Gay-friendly hotel inn with apartments, campground, bar & vegetarian/natural foods restaurant, almost all private baths, nearby ocean beach.

■ Dance Bar/Disco
CARLOS & CHARLIE'S, on the main strip near the pier, upstairs, dance bar & restaurant, NOT a gay bar, but discreetly frequented by visiting gays & lesbians. 🈁🈁

CUERNAVACA

■ Accommodations
CASA AURORA, Arista No. 12, Centro, Cuernavaca, Mor., 62000, (52 73) 18 63 94. A B&B or guesthouse with private & shared baths, continental breakfast or 3 meals. There is a small garden & each room has a terrace with a hammock. Some hetero clientele. ♀♂

■ Dance Bar/Disco
SHADEE, Avda Adolfo López Mateos, across from gas station DIF, (73) 183 963, disco, bar & restaurant, from 21:00, occasional drag shows. 🎵🈁♂

ENSENADA - BAJA CALIFORNIA NORTE

■ Accommodations

VILLA PLAYAS, 1129 Granito, Playas de Tijuana, BCN, Direct: (52-66) 30 1298 (Tel/Fax) or 80 1052. Voice mail: (619) 236-0989. Email: warren@cyberheads. com, B&B, boarding house & retirement home 7 miles from border, gay bars & discos, beaches nearby. Private bath across hall for guests' use, expanded continental breakfast, other meals optional. Mostly men with women welcome. Some hetero clientele. 🖪 ♂

■ Dance Bar/Disco

COYOTE CLUB, Blvd. Costero 1000 #4 & 5, at Diamante, (61) 77 3691, state-of-the-art nightclub, video bar with monitors, dance on lower level, garden patio, 9pm-3am (closed Mon-Wed), women welcome. 🍴 ♂

■ Restaurants

MARISCOS CALIFORNIA, Calle Ruiz, at Calle Segunda., Traditional Baja California seafood specialties, burritos Monterrey, green chili rellenos, shrimp & clams, 9am-8pm (closed Sun). ♀♂

GUADALAJARA

■ Information

GRUPO LESBICO PATLATONALLI, (3) 632 05 07, lesbian group, write: Apartado Postal 1-663, Col. Centro, C.P. 4410.

■ Accommodations

RAY AND BIS BED AND BREAKFAST GUESTHOUSE, 4063 Galaxia, Col. Lomas Altas, Guadalajara, Jalisco, 45120, (52-3) 813 08 42 direct. USA (773) 348-3948. Email: sharpening@aol.com, B&B guesthouse, some straight clientele, complete breakfast in garden, private & shared baths, color TV, maid service, 15-20 mins. to gay bars. 🖪 ♀♂

■ Bars

ANGELS, Avda La Paz 2030, Col Americana, (3) 615 2525, bar & restaurant, 20:00-03:00 (closed Mon-Tues), younger crowd. 🚻 🍴 ♀♂

ARIZONA, Avda La Paz 1985, Col. Americana, gay Thurs-Sun 22:00-03:00, strippers. ♪ 🚻 ♂

BAR MASKARA, Maestranza 238, daily 09:00-02:00. ♂

CHIVAS, Calle Degollado 150, at López Cotilla, daily 08:00-03:00. Address may change in '98. ♂

PANCHOS JR., Galeana 180-A, downtown, (3) 613 5325, daily 21:00-03:00. ♀♂

■ Dance Bar/Disco

LA MALINCHE, Alvaro Obregón 1230, Sector Libertad, 20:00-05:00. ♪ 🚻 🍴 ♂

MONICAS, Alvaro Obregón 1713, Sector Libertad., 22:00-02:00 (closed Mon, Tues). 🍴 ♪ ♂

S.O.S., La Paz 1985, Sector Hidalgo, Zona Rosa, (3) 826 2196, disco & bar, 21:30-04:00 (Wed & Sun from 19:00), closed Mon, Tues. 🍴 ♪ ♂

LA MANZANILLA

■ Accommodations

VILLA MONTAÑA, c/o Daniel Clarke, PO Box 16343, Seattle, WA, 98116, (206) 932-7012, Fax: (206) 932-7012. Email: outlandaventures@foxinternet.net, Gay-friendly villa 2-1/2 hours south of Puerto Vallarta. This one-story hilltop villa sleeps 4 comfortably & is creatively expandable to sleep 6. Idyllic bay & village views, private baths, linens provided. ♀♂

LEON

■ Bars

SAN LUÍS, Calle República, close to Zaragoza & López Mateos, daily 09:00-24:00. ♂

■ Dance Bar/Disco

BAGOA'S, Mar Báltico 1332 at Alfredo Valadéz, Col. Rinconada del Sur, (47) 71 0153, Fri, Sat till 03:00. 🚻 🍴 ♂

MAZATLAN

■ Bars

LA ALEMANA BAR, Zaragoza between Benito Juárez &, Serdán, Zona Centro, 09:00-24:00. ♂

NAVY BAR, in back of Corsario Bar, mix of gays & heteros.

PEPE TORO, Avda de las Garzas 18, Dorada, (69)14 41 76, 21:00-03:00 (closed Mon-Wed), occasional strippers & drag shows. ♪ 🚻 🍴 ♂

SALON ROSA, Isla Asada 4, 2nd floor, 18:00-02:00.

Dance Bar/Disco
CORSARIO BAR, Calle 17 de Spetiembre, at Paseo Clausen, Zona Centro, till 05:00, frequented by gays & lesbians.

Restaurants
PATRICK'S, Camerón Sábado 333-10, Centro Comercial Las Palmas, Zona Dorada, 11:00-05:00, American cuisine.
ROCA MAR, Avda del Mar, near Señor Frogs.,

MERIDA

Dance Bar/Disco
KABUKI, Avda Jacinto Canek 381.,
STATUS, Calle Calos, in back of cinema, gay Thurs & Sat. Lesbian only Sun.

MEXICALI

Bars
★ CINCO ESTRELLAS, Jalisco, near 3rd St, Wed-Sun 19:00-02:00 (Sat till 03:00), 80% lesbian.
REY DE COPAS, on Tuxtla Gutiérrez (4th St), mix of lesbians & heteros.
TARUINO'S BAR, Avda Zuazua 480, Zona Centro, 10:00-02:00 (Fri, Sat till 03:00), some lesbians.

MEXICO CITY
SEE CIUDAD DE MEXICO,

MONTERREY

Dance Bar/Disco
VONGOLE, Blvd Pedrera 300, Wed-Sat from 22:00.

MORELIA

Bars
CON LA ROJAS, Aldama 343, zona centro, (43) 12 1578, upscale clientele, 21:00-02:00 (closed Sun-Wed).

PLAYA DEL CARMEN

Bars
BABYLON, Calle 6, in Plaza Playa, 5 days from 22:00.

PUEBLA

Dance Bar/Disco
DISCO GAROTOS, 22 Oriente #602, Xanenetla, Fri, Sat 21:00-03:00.
KEOPS, 14 Poniente 101, San Andres Cholula, (12 km from Puebla), (22) 47 0368, dance & show bar, Thurs-Sun from 22:00.

PUERTO VALLARTA

Accommodations
ARCO IRIS, 115 Paseo de los Delfines, Fracc. Conchas Chinas, Puerto Vallarta, JAL, 48390, (52-322) 15579, Fax: (52-322) 15586. In US or Canada: (800) 682-9974. Email: arcoiris@pvnet.com.mx, **Come enjoy the service** at this newest gay hot spot on the Mexican Riviera, featuring air-conditioned rooms, apartments, houses, private pools and views from every room that can't be beat. Full **tropical breakfast** and **sunset margaritas** are included. Play, cruise or relax either here or at nearby gay beach and bars. Ask for Thom or Randy. Some hetero clientele.

BOANA TORRE MALIBU, Amapas 328, Puerto Vallarta, in USA contact: (619) 297-3646, (800) 936-3646, Fax: (619) 297-3642. 1-BR suites with kitchenettes &

ARCO IRIS
Puerto Vallarta

Your Place In the Sun

(800) 682-9974

222 MEXICO

Casa Fantasia
Where Your Dreams Become Reality
Puerto Vallarta
(52-322) 2 19 04
US RESERVATIONS
(503) 233-8118

balconies with views. Pool bar, mainly gay with some straight clientele.
CASA DE LOS ARCOS, PO Box 239BB, Puerto Vallarta, Jalisco, 48300, (52-322) 259 90 (Tel/Fax). In USA: (800) 424-3434, ext. 277, ask for Ron. Email: csarcos@tag.acnet.net, Our vacation villa has an incredible vista of Vallarta & the beaches of Los Muertos & El Dorado, and jungle foliage bordering our back garden provides a backdrop for colorful tropical birds. The villa accommodates up to 8 guests in two 1- or 2-bedroom suites. Amenities include AC, ceiling fans, color cable TV, on-premises pool & ocean. It can be arranged for a cook to come into your suite & prepare dinner for you. Some hetero clientele.
CASA DOS COMALES, Calle Aldama 274, (52-322) 320 42. Gay-friendly B&B & apartments, private baths, AC, continental breakfast, indoor pool on premises.
CASA FANTASÍA, Apartado Postal #387 Centro, Puerto Vallarta, Jalisco, CP 48300, (52-322) 2 19 04, Fax: (52-322) 2 19 23. For US reservations: (503) 233-8118. Email: casafanta@aol.com, A jewel in Puerto Vallarta's gay district, this B&B guesthouse with bar & restaurant consists of 3 separate traditional Old-World-style Mexican haciendas. Common areas are elegant, yet informal, and the 8 large bedrooms have private full baths & king or twin beds. The terrace provides a staffed bar for guests & their friends adjacent to the swimming pool. Mostly men with women welcome, some straight clientele.
CASA NAUTIQUE, Marina Vallarta, Puerto Vallarta, in USA: (818) 753-1982 (Tel/Fax), (888) 867-2723. Email: mh777@aol.com, Townhouse in a marina resort on a private island. Nautical & tropical interiors, private baths, AC, kitchen, bar, cable TV, stereo/CD with speakers in living room & master bedroom. Pool on premises. Walk to shops, restaurants & nightlife. 50% gay/lesbian clientele.
CASA PANORÁMICA, Apdo. Postal 114, Puerto Vallarta, Jalisco, 48300, (800) 745-7805, Fax: (808) 324-1302 in USA. Or call direct (52-322) 23656. Email: CasaPano@pvnet.com.mx, B&B in a private 7 bedroom villa, bay views, private baths, full breakfast. Pool on premises & complete housekeeping services.
DOIN IT RIGHT / TRANSFORMATIONAL JOURNEYS, 1010 University Ave C-113-741, San Diego, CA, 92103, (619) 297-3646, (800) 936-3646, Fax: (619) 297-3642." Email: gaypvr@aol.com, THE gay Vallarta specialist with over 175 villas, condos and gay properties from moderate to luxury. Call us for every-

Mission San Francisco
Your Private Casa Overlooking the Bay
Puerto Vallarta
(916) 933-0370

thing from an inexpensive hotel room to a private villa with cook included. Airport greets, private tours, local excursions. Our "purple sheet," a 6-page listing of Vallarta businesses, with maps, is free to our clients. ♀♂

GARZA BLANCA VILLAS & LA PALAPA, Km 7 Carretera a Barra de Navidad, Zona Hotelera Sur, Puerto Vallarta, JAL, 48300, (52-322) 80338, (52-322) 20977, Fax: (52-322) 80752. Villas & condominiums.

LA HACIENDA DEL PAVO REAL, Calle Milan 274, Colonia Versalles, Puerto Vallarta, (52-322) 50358. Email: pavoreal@zonavirtual.com.mx, Web: http://www.traveldata.com/inns/data/lahacien.html, Puerto Vallarta's newest gay guesthouse, a tropical paradise, is situated on one half acre, without hills, and is easy walking distance (just steps) to central Puerto Vallarta's great shopping, beaches and restaurants. Our large, pineapple-shaped swimming pool is surrounded by lush vegetation. There is a lounge, bar and breakfast nook which overlooks the tropical grounds and swimming pools. All rooms are air-conditioned and have cable TV. ♂

LOS CUATRO VIENTOS, Matamoros 520, (52-322) 201 61. Women-owned hotel. ♀

MISSION SAN FRANCISCO RENTAL HOMES, (916) 933-0370 (Tel/Fax). Email: mpizza@madre.com, Web: www.quiknet.com/~mpizza, Luxury furnished homes with ocean views, six blocks to gay beach and bar. Only US $195-US $495 per home, per week. Also available in Mexico City: one-bedroom luxury furnished apartment at US $595 per month. Gay-friendly.

PACO PACO DESCANSO DEL SOL HOTEL, Pino Suarez #583, Apdo Postal 245, Col. Emiliano Zapata, Puerto Vallarta, Jalisco, 48301, (52 322) 252 29, Fax: (52 322) 267 67. Gay hotel with rooftop bar, 3 blocks from the beach. Cloth-

Quinta Maria Cortez

eclectic beachfront retreat

PLAYA CONCHAS CHINAS
PUERTO VALLARTA, MEXICO

For Reservations, Call:
(888) 640-8100 *Toll-free*
or (801) 536-5850

THE Gay Vallarta SPECIALIST

Doin It Right

VILLAS
CONDOS
GAY
HOTELS

(619) 297-3646
(800) 936-3646
Email: gaypvr@aol.com

ing-optional sunbathing by dipping pool, all private baths.

PALAPAS IN YELAPA, c/o Antonio & Lucinda Saldaña, Apartado Postal 2-43, Puerto Vallarta, Jalisco, (52-322) 491 97. 5 palapas (cabins), 50% gay/lesbian clientele, private showers & toilets, nearby river & ocean, Spanish & English spoken.

QUINTA MARIA CORTEZ, 132 Calle Sagitario, Playa Conchas Chinas, US reservations: PO Box 1799, Salt Lake City, UT, 84110, in USA: (801) 531-8100, (888) 640-8100, Fax: (801) 531-1633. Email: res@quinta-maria.com, A beachfront retreat, this "Mexaterranean Villa" consists of six suites on seven levels, rising above the white-sand beach. Accommodations feature eclectic European-style decor with private bath, phone & most include a kitchenette & balcony. Mid-level is a common area with a sitting room, fireplace, terrace & palapa-roofed dining area — all with gorgeous ocean views. 50% gay & lesbian clientele. See ad on page 223.

VALLARTA CORA, Calle Pilitas #174, Colonia Emiliano Zapatas, Puerto Vallarta, Jalisco, 48380, (52-322) 32815 (Tel/Fax). In USA & Canada: (619) 297-3646, (800) 936-3646, Fax: (619) 297-3642. Email: coragay@pvnet.com.mx, Web: http://www.members.aol.com/charter935/amadeus.index.html, Hotel/apartment with 14 units on four floors. All units have 1 bedroom, 1-1/2 bath, daily maid service, equipped kitchens, AC or fans, and balcony. Pool on premises is clothing-optional at night. Some lesbian clientele.

■ Women's Accommodations

HOLLY'S MEXICO, Mail to: PO Box 13197, South Lake Tahoe, CA, 96151, (530) 544-7040, (800) 745-7041." Email: hollys@oakweb.com, Web: hollysplace.com, Cottage 35-34 minutes north of Puerto Vallarta in the town of Sayulit, private & shared baths, ocean views, men welcome. ♀

■ Bars

APACHE CLUB, Olas Altas 439, at Fnco. Rodriguez, cocktail, martini & hors d'oeuvres bar, 11:00-02:00 (Sun 17:00-01:00). ♀♂

ARIA PIANO LOUNGE, Pino Suarez 210, at Fnco Madera, piano lounge, 18:00-02:00. ♂

■ Dance Bar/Disco

CLUB PACO PACO, Ignacio L. Vallarta 278, at Venustiano Corranza, (52-322) 218 99. One of the best dance bars in Vallarta, 2nd floor has pool table. 1st floor with disco nightly 20:00-06:00, drag shows & strippers on weekends. Cantina has 15:00-20:00 happy hour. Mostly men with women welcome.

LOS BALCONES, Juárez 182 at Libertad, 246 71, dance bar & restaurant, ask about possible Thurs women's night.

POR QUE NO?, Morelos 101, lower level, 70's & 80's music, pool table. ♂

■ Restaurants

ADOBE CAFE, Basilio Badillo 252, closed Tues & Jun-Sept.

BOMBO'S, Corona 327, Col. El Cerro, 251 64, upscale restaurant & bar, 16:30-23:00.

★ **CAFE DES ARTISTES,** Guadalupe Sanchez 740, 232 27, upscale dining, Mexican & French cuisine. Live music.

CHEZ ELENA, Matamoros 520, garden restaurant with patio dining & rooftop bar.

CHILE'S, Pulpito 122, 11:00-18:00, burgers, hot dogs, sandwiches, etc. Closed mid-Jul thru mid-Oct.

CUIZA, Isla Rio Caule,, West Bridge, American cuisine, 09:00-24:00, closes during month of July.

LA TUNA GRILL, Fnco. Rodríguez 136, Col. Emiliano Zapata, near Playa de los Muertos, 210 84, closed Mon.

LE BISTRO, Isla Rio Caule 16-A, Art Deco dining, fusion cuisine.

RED CABBAGE, Calle Rio Ribera 206-A, regional Mexican cuisine.

SAN MIGUEL DE ALLENDE

■ Women's Accommodations

BED & BREAKFAST IN SAN MIGUEL DE ALLENDE, c/o Greta Waldas, Apdo #205, San Miguel de Allende, GTO, (52) 465 23279. Women-only B&B, 4 hours

from Mexico city in charming colonial town with artist colony, room with private bath, friendly, much to see & do. ♀
GRETA'S, Apartado #205, San Miguel de Allende, GTO, (465) 232 79. Women-only B&B, private baths. ♀

■ Bars
LA LOLA, Ancha de San Antonio 31, (415) 24050, bar & restaurant, 13:00-02:00 (closed Mon). 🍸

TIJUANA

■ Information
GAY & LESBIAN LINE & AIDS INFO, 88 02 67.

■ Bars
CLUB EXTASIS, at the Viva Tijuana Shopping Center,, near the border, Fri & Sat from 20:00, Sun from 18:00. Lesbian night Thurs from 20:00. 🎵 🍽 🍸 ♂
EL TAURINO, Calle C #579 (Niños Héroes), north of Calle I, cantina, open daily (Fri, Sat till 05:00), frequented by some women. ♂

■ Dance Bar/Disco
EMILIO'S, Calle 3 #1810-11, enter at Parking América, 75% gay. 🎵 🍽
★ **MIKE'S,** Avda. Revolución 1220, near Calle 6, till 05:00 (closed Wed), occasional male strippers. 🎵 🍽 🍸 ♂
NOA NOA, Calle D (Avda Miguel Martínez), north of Calle Primera, disco & show bar. 🍸 🎵 ♀♂
NUEVO LOS EQUIPALES, calle Séptima, south of Avda. Revolución, dance & show bar, occasional male strippers. 🍸 🎵 🍽

■ Restaurants
LA COSTA, Calle 7, between Avdas Revolución & Constitución, seafood. 🍽

VERACRUZ

■ Bars
YESTERDAY, Mártires de Tlapacoyan 40, lesbian bar. ♀

ZACATECAS

■ Information
CLOSET SOR JUANA, (492) 376 78, women's group, organizes a women's week.

■ Bars
NIVEL 7, Tacuba 125, Plaza de Armas, daily till 03:00, 50% gay. 🍸

■ Dance Bar/Disco
ESCÁNDALO, Esplanada La Feria, (492) 414 76, Fri & Sat 21:00-03:00, DJ. 🎵 🍽 🍸 ♀♂

NICARAGUA

COUNTRY CODE: (505),

MANAGUA

■ Retail & Bookstores
GALERIA DE ARTE EL AGUILA, Carretera Sur 6 1/2 Sur, 650 524 or 650 525, art gallery.

PANAMA

COUNTRY CODE: (507),

PANAMA CITY

■ Bars
BOYS BAR, ask locally for address, mostly men, more women on weekends. 🍸 ♂

PARAGUAY

COUNTRY CODE: (595),

ASUNCION

■ Bars
AUDACE, Ayolas at Manduvirá., 🍸 ♂
LA BARCA, Puente Franco 564., 🍸 ♂
SPIDER, Perú 568 at Azará., 🍸 ♂

PERU

COUNTRY CODE: (51),

LIMA

■ Information
MHOL, Mariscal Miller 828, Jesús Marí, Lima 11., (1) 4 33 63 75, Fax: (1) 4 33 55 19, Mon-Fri 09:00-13:00 & 16:00-20:00. Gay & lesbian info, AIDS info, activities throughout the year.

■ Bars
PAULINA'S BAR, Centro Comercial San Felipe #60, (1) 4 61 90 09, women-only bar. 🍸 ♀

PERU

TWIST, Avenida Diagonal, Mira Flores, 2 blocks from Gitano disco, snack bar, 12:00-24:00, frequented by many gays & lesbians.

Dance Bar/Disco

CANYU, Calle Kuilca 1, 22:00-05:00, gay & lesbian, but mostly transvestites. disco from 23:00.

EL TALLER, República de Panama, at Avenida Angamos, Thurs-Sat from 22:00.

★ **GITANO,** Calle Berlin, biggest & best disco in Lima, sometimes difficult to get in.

IMPERIO, Avenida Girón Camaná, quadra 1, 21:00-06:00 (closed Mon).

PERSEO, Avenida Aviación #2514, San Borja, 7 days, 23:00-05:00.

SPLASH, Los Pinos #124, Miraflores.

VOGLIA, Avenida Ricardo Palma 336, Miraflores.

URUGUAY

COUNTRY CODE: (598),

MONTEVIDEO

Information

GUÍA TRIÁNGULO AMATISTA, PO Box 6346, Montevideo, 11000, (598) 275 1670, gay organization with local information, publishes gay guide to Uruguay.

Bars

AVANTI, Avenida Daniel Fernández Crespo 2181, at Calle Lima, from 21:00.

Cafe

BRASILEIRO, Ituzaingó 1447, at 25 de Mayo, 08:00-20:00.

CASA GANDHI, Juan Benito Blanco 975, 19:00-02:00, closed Mon.

LA RONDA, Ciudadela 1182, at Soriano.

SOROCABANA, Carlos Quijano 1377, 08:00-24:00.

Restaurants

DOÑA FLOR, Blvd Artigas 1034, 12:30-15:00 & 20:30-24:00 (Sat dinner only), closed Sun.

LA POSADA DEL PUERTO, at the pedestrian thoroughfare Pérez Castellanos, & Yacaré, near the port., 11:30-24:45 (Sun till 16:00).

LO DE CARLOTA, Stgo. de Chile 1270, 12:00-14:00 & 21:00-01:00 (Sat only 21:00-02:00), closed Sun.

MERCADO DEL PARQUE, on Rambla Wilson, across from Rodó Park, 12:00-02:00.

VENEZUELA

COUNTRY CODE: (58),

CARACAS

Bars

LA TORTILLA, Calle San Antonio, a few meters from, El Gran Cafe, Savana Grande.

TASCA DON SOL, Blvd Savana Grande, near Calle de la Puñalada.

Dance Bar/Disco

DISCOTECA ACERO, Avda Principal de las Mercedes, about 10 min walk from Tamanaco Hotel, sector las Mercedes, 50% men & 50% women.

★ **ICE PALACE,** Avda Luís Roche, next to Cine Altamira, Altamira sector, 50% men & 50% women.

LA PUNCH, Centro Comercial Cediaz, Avda Casanova, near Calle de la Puñalada, street level, (1 block from Avda Savana Grande), 65% men, 35% women.

MY WAY, Avda Principal de las Mercedes, about 10 min walk from Tamanaco Hotel.

ZZ, Avda Libertador, corner of Avda Las Acacias, Edificio La Linea, street level, Savana Grande, 65% men, 35% women.

MARACAY

Bars

BEER GARDEN PARK, east side of Plaza Bolivar, bar & restaurant with popular patio bar, live music, screened from the street, 65% men, 35% women.

Dance Bar/Disco

TOWN TAVERN, Centro Comercial 19 de Abril, at corner of Avda 19 de Abril & Calle Boyacá.

MARGARITA ISLAND

■ Dance Bar/Disco
MOSQUITO COAST, in alley behind Bellavista Hotel., 🍽 ♀♂
SOUTH BEACH, Calle Malavé, between Calle Batiño & Calle Cedeño., 🍽 ♀♂

MERIDA

■ Bars
COPACABANA, Avda Lora, at Calle Carabobo, small bar with mainly local crowd. ♂

EL SOL DISCOBAR, Calle 25 Ayacucho, between Avda Lora & Avda Independencia, gay after 22:00. No gays earlier, 99% men, but women welcome. 🍽 ♂

SAN CRISTOBAL

■ Bars
EL TRIGAL, Carrera 4, downtown, mainly locals. ♂
END PUB, THE, Carrera Nueve, at Calle Nueve, downtown., ♂

■ Dance Bar/Disco
PUB, THE, Centro Comercial Paseo La Villa, Avda Guayana, 90% men, 10% women. 🍽 ♂

■ Cafe
FUENTE DE SODA LA BOHEME, Centro Civico San Cristobal, at Carrera Séptima, not gay, but a cruisy mainstream sidewalk cafe, frequented by many gays. 🚫

VALENCIA

■ Bars
EL PUMA, Calle Urdaneta, between Calle Libertad, Calle Independencia, 1/2 block east of the cathedral, small bar, local crowd. ♂

■ Dance Bar/Disco
LOKURAS, next to baseball stadium at east side of, Avda Bolivar, 50% men & 50% women. 🍽 ♀♂

ALABAMA 227

UNITED STATES COUNTRYWIDE

■ Information
HIV AIDS TREATMENT INFORMATION SERVICE, (800) HIV-0440. 9am-7pm (EST), TDD.

ALABAMA
BIRMINGHAM

■ Information
AIDS LINE, (205) 322-4197. Mon-Fri 9am-5pm or tape. Statewide line (800) 228-0469.

GAY & LESBIAN INFO LINE, (205) 326-8600. Mon-Sat 6 or 7 till 10pm.

■ Bars
IVY, 731 29th St So., Live music. 🎵 ♀
JOE BAR, 731 29th St South, (205) 252-3237. Martini bar, piano bar. ♂
MISCONCEPTIONS TAVERN, 600 32nd St S, (205) 322-1210, small bar, noon-3am (Sat till 2am), 70% men, 30% women. 🎱 ♂
SOUTHSIDE PUB, 2830 7th Ave, (205) 324-0997. Bar & restaurant. ✕ ♀

■ Dance Bar/Disco
BILL'S CLUB, 208 N 23rd St, near 2nd Ave, (205) 254-8634. Cabaret show, country line dancing, sports bar. 🍽
CLUB 21, 117-1/2 21st Street N, near 2nd Ave N, (205) 322-0469. Dance & show bar, Thurs-Sat, popular Thurs, younger crowd, 50% gay clientele (50% men, 50% women). 🍽 🎵 ♀♂
TOOL BOX, 5120 5th Ave S, (205) 595-5120. Cruise bar & dance bar, country line dance Sat & Wed, hosts Birmingham Leather Club meetings Wed. Cruise bar in basement. 50% men/women, weekends 70% men. 🍽 ♂

■ Restaurants
ANTHONY'S, 2131 7th Ave S, (205) 324-1215. Continental cuisine, gay friendly. 🚫

■ Retail & Bookstores
LODESTAR BOOKS, 2020 11th Ave S, (205) 939-3356, fax (205) 933-1595. Gay, lesbian & women's books, gifts, cards, music, rainbow items.

ALABAMA

PLANET MUZICA, 725 29th St S, (205) 254-9303, Fax: 254-9295. General record store with jewelry, gifts & gay & lesbian magazines.

DOTHAN

■ Dance Bar/Disco
CHUCKIE BEE'S, 100 Block S St Andrews, directly across from Civic Ctr, (334) 794-0230. Three level dance & show bar with game room, Mon-Sat from 7pm, occasional male strippers.

GADSDEN

■ Dance Bar/Disco
NITRO, 2461 E Meighan Blvd, (205) 492-9724. A place for nighttime explosions. From 8pm Wed-Sat.

HUNTSVILLE

■ Dance Bar/Disco
VIEUX CARRE, 1204 Posey, (256) 534-5970. Dance & show bar, 60% men, 40% women. Daily from 7pm, 4pm on Sun."

■ Retail & Bookstores
RAINBOW'S LTD, 522 Jordan Lane, (256) 536-5900. Gay & lesbian bookstore. T-shirts, jewelry, local info.

MOBILE

■ Bars
ON THE ROCKS, Conception near Conti., ♀

■ Dance Bar/Disco
B-BOB'S, 6157 Airport Blvd #201, near Hillcrest, West Mobile, (334) 341-0102. Hi-energy dance club, DJ, 7 days from 5pm till late, 50% men, 50% women, occasional male & female strippers. Gift shop inside.
SOCIETY LOUNGE, 51 S Conception St, at Conti, (334) 433-9141. Dance & show bar, 50% men & 50% women.

MONTGOMERY

■ Bars
AREA 51, 211 Lee St, (334) 264-5933. Private club, dance bar, shows on Sun, 7 days from 7pm (Sun from 5pm).

■ Dance Bar/Disco
PLEX, 121 Coosa, (334) 269-9672.

TUSCALOOSA

■ Bars
MICHELLE'S, in same building as Michael's bar, 2201 6th St, Mon-Sat from 6pm.

■ Dance Bar/Disco
NEW MICHAEL'S LOUNGE, 2201 6th St, (205) 758-9223. 24hrs (except Sat closes 2am), closed Sun. Top billboard music hits, 50% men, 50% women."

■ Retail & Bookstores
GAY RAINBOW STORE, 519 College Park, (205) 349-5725. Gay & lesbian books, rainbow & pride items.

ALASKA

ANCHORAGE

■ Information
AIDS HELPLINE, (907) 276-4880, (800) 478-2437. Mon-Fri 9am-5pm, with person on call other times.
GAY & LESBIAN HELP LINE, (907) 258-4777. 6-11pm 7 days.
WOMEN'S RESOURCE CENTER, 111 W 9th Ave, (907) 276-0528. Weekdays 8:30am-5pm.

■ Accommodations
AURORA WINDS, AN EXCEPTIONAL B & B RESORT, 7501 Upper O'Malley, Anchorage, AK, 99516, (907) 346-2533, (800) 642-9640, Fax: (907) 346-3192. Email: awbnb@alaska.net. Luxurious B&B. Private baths, color TV & phones. Billiards room, TV lounge, exercise room & expanded continental or full breakfast."
CHENEY LAKE BED & BREAKFAST, 6333 Colgate Dr, Anchorage, AK, 99504, (907) 337-4391, Fax: (907) 338-1023. Email: cheneybb@alaska.net. Gay-friendly B&B on Cheney Lake, private baths, continental breakfast, color TV, VCR, phone, maid service, gay & lesbian following.

■ Bars
RAVEN, THE, 618 Gambell St, at 6th, (907) 276-9672. CD juke box, pool tables, darts, pinball.

■ Dance Bar/Disco
WAVE, THE, 3101 Spenard Rd, (907) 561-

9283, Fax: (907) 563-9920. E-mail: wave@alaska.net. Dance club with coffee house upstairs, drag show Wed. 50/50 men & women, some straight clientele.

Restaurants
O'BRADY'S, Dimond Center, (907) 344-8033. 2nd location: Chugach Sq, (907) 338-1080. Gay-friendly homestyle bar & restaurant.

Retail & Bookstores
CAPRI CINEMA, Tudor & Dale, in the mall., (907) 561-0064. Cinema plays gay films often. Coffeeshop next door is frequented by gays & lesbians.

FAIRBANKS

Accommodations
ALTA'S BED AND BREAKFAST, PO Box 82290, Fairbanks, AK, 99708, (907) 389-2582. Email: picaro@mosquitonet.com, B&B, some straight clientele. Private & shared baths, TV lounge, Jacuzzi & full breakfast.

FAIRBANKS HOTEL, 517 Third Ave, Fairbanks, AK, (907) 456-6411, (888) 329-4685, Fax: (907) 456-1792. Email: fbxhotl@alaska.net, Art Deco-style hotel in downtown with private & shared baths, all rooms with pedestal-style sinks, mostly straight clientele with a gay/lesbian following.

Dance Bar/Disco
PALACE SALOON, inside & on east side of Alaskaland Park in, Gold Rush Town, near Airportway & Peeger Rd, (907) 456-5960. Gay late evening Fri & Sat, DJ.

GUSTAVUS

Accommodations
GOOD RIVER BED & BREAKFAST, Box 37, Gustavus, AK, 99826, (907) 697-2241 (Tel/Fax). Email: river@thor.he.net, Web: http://thor.he.net/~river, Spectacular Glacier Bay. Sixteen tidewater glaciers, whales, fishing, kayaking, nature walks, wilderness, and a great place to stay. Elegant log house, comfy beds, handmade quilts, fresh bread, reasonable rates. Rusic log cabin also available. Free bikes to explore unique town. Come see. 50% gay clientele.

HOMER

Accommodations
ISLAND WATCH B & B, PO Box 1394, Homer, AK, 99603, (907) 235-2265. Email: kyle@xyz.net, Gay-friendly B&B (30% gay & lesbian). Farm setting with horses & sheep, only 5 minutes from downtown. Cabin, suite & 1 handicap-accessible room. Full breakfast with fresh eggs.

JUNEAU

Information
SOUTHEAST ALASKA GAY & LESBIAN ALLIANCE, (907) 586-GAYS (4297). Returns taped messages, monthly meetings & scheduled brunches, video nites.

ARIZONA

BULLHEAD CITY

Bars
LARIAT SALOON, 1161 Hancock Rd, (520) 758-8479. 70% men, 30% women, DJ Fri.

COTTONWOOD

Accommodations
MUSTANG BED & BREAKFAST, 4257 Mustang Dr., Cottonwood, AZ, 86326, (520) 646-5929. B&B with private & shared baths, continental breakfast & movie theater."

FLAGSTAFF

Information
AIDS OUTREACH, (520) 779-9498, office staffed 10am-2pm Mon-Fri.

Accommodations
CHALET IN THE PINES, PO Box 25640, Munds Park, AZ, 86017, (520) 286-2417. B&B at Pinewood Country Club, 15 miles from Flagstaff, AZ. Expanded continental & full breakfast, private & shared baths, pool nearby, women welcome.

HOTEL MONTE VISTA, 100 North San Francisco St, Flagstaff, AZ, 86001, (520) 779-6971, (800) 545-3068, Fax: (520) 779-2904. Gay-friendly hotel with restaurant & bar. Antique reproductions, color cable TV, ceiling fans, telephone and private baths.

ARIZONA

SOUTHWEST INN at Eagle Mountain

Phoenix, AZ

(800) 992-8083

Bars
CHARLIE'S, 23 N Leroux, at Aspen., NOT a gay bar. Frequented by some gays & lesbians.

Retail & Bookstores
ARADIA BOOKS, 116 W Cottage, (520) 779-3817. Feminist, lesbian & gay books & local info, 10:30-5:30 Mon-Sat, closed Sun.

JEROME

Accommodations
COTTAGE INN, THE, PO Box 823, Jerome, AZ, 86331, (520) 634-0701, (888) 562-0701. Gay-friendly B&B, private baths, full breakfast, 10-15% gay/lesbian following.

Bars
PAUL & JERRY'S, on Jerome's main street., Not gay, but a very open atmosphere with many gays in later evenings, live bands.

PHOENIX

Information
GAY & LESBIAN COMMUNITY CENTER & AIDS LINE, 3136 N 3rd Ave, (602) 234-2752. Walk-in 10am-8pm.
LESBIAN & GAY SWITCHBOARD, (602) 234-2752, TDD 234-0873. 10am-10pm 7 days.
LESBIAN RESOURCE PROJECT, at the Gay Center, (602) 266-5542.

Accommodations
CASA DE MIS PADRES, 5965 E Orange Blossom Lane, Phoenix, AZ, 85018, (602) 675-0247, Fax: (602) 675-9476. Email: casadmp@aol.com, Gay-owned & -operated B&B with suites & 1 cottage, private baths, expanded continental breakfast, heated pool. Women welcome, straight-friendly.
LARRY'S B & B, 502 W Claremont Ave, Phoenix, AZ, 85013-2974, (602) 249-2974. Centrally-located B&B, women welcome, some straight clientele. Color TV, AC, private & shared baths, Jacuzzi, pool & full breakfast."
MARY CLAIRE II, THE, 303 E Patrician Dr, Tempe, AZ, 85282, (602) 967-2767. B&B with private bath, full breakfast, Jacuzzi, pool on premises. One mile from downtown Tempe, 15 min from downtown Phoenix.
SOUTHWEST INN AT EAGLE MOUNTAIN, 9800 N. Summer Hill Blvd, Fountain Hills, AZ, 85268, (602) 816-3000, (800) 992-8083, Fax: (602) 816-3090. Email: eminfo@swinn.com, Web: www.southwestinn.com, Beautiful, new Santa Fe-style property located 1/4 mile east of Scottsdale on the Eagle Mountain Golf Course. This gay-friendly boutique

Continued on page 232

Aradia Women's Bookstore
Women's Books & Music, Non-Sexist Children's Books, Health & Sports Spirituality, Mail Order, Holistic Health & Environmental Books.

116 West Cottage • Flagstaff 86001 • (520) 779-3817

CASTLE SUPERSTORES®

New Times Best of Phoenix

(800) 344-9076

Visit Our New Website:
www.castlesuperstores.com

America's Safer Sex Superstores® Because We Care®

- Video Sales • Video Rentals • Playful Greeting & Post Cards • Leather Goods & Apparel • Restraints • Latex Garments • Rubber Goods • Wildest Selection of Adult Toys • Gag Gifts • Novelties • Games • Condoms • Lubes • Books & Magazines • T-Shirts • Whips & Chains • Wrapping Papers • Calendars • Novels • Sensual Oils • Sexy Lingerie & more & more ...

OPEN 24 HOURS · 365 DAYS
Rediscover America's Favorite Pastime

(602) 231-9837
5501 E. Washington St.

(602) 266-3348
300 E. Camelback Rd.

(602) 995-1641
8802 N. Black Canyon Hwy.

(602) 986-6114
8315 E. Apache Trail

ARIZONA

hotel has 42 deluxe rooms & suites with fireplaces, private decks & 2-person whirlpool tubs. Every room has a private deck or patio facing the 60-mile views of mountain terrain & the Sonoran desert. Grounds include pool, spa, golf, meeting rooms and a magnificent lobby building. Totally non-smoking.

Bars

JC'S FUN ONE LOUNGE, 5542 N 43rd Ave, Glendale, (602) 939-0528. Occasional shows, 50% men, 50% women.

MARLYS', 15615 N Cave Creek Rd, (602) 867-2463. Live bands, 50% men, 50% women.

PARK, THE, 3002 N 24th St, (602) 957-6055. Upscale electronic player piano, huge patio, show bar with male strippers.

POOKIES CAFE, 4540 N 7th St, (602) 277-2121. Bar & restaurant.

ROSCOE'S ON 7TH, 4531 N 7th St, (602) 285-0833. alternative sports pub.

★ **WINKS,** 5707 N 7th St, (602) 265-9002. Show bar, yuppie types, women welcome. Lunch Mon-Fri, Sun brunch 10am. Popular happy hour.

Dance Bar/Disco

★ **AIN'T NOBODY'S BIZNESS, (THE BIZ),** 3031 E Indian School Rd, (602) 224-9977. Dance club, no cover charge. Variety of specials & events.

CASH INN, 2120 E McDowell Rd, near Squaw Peak Parkway, (602) 244-9943. C&W dance bar, women. Tues-Fri 4pm-1am, Sat 2pm-1am, Sun noon-1am.

DESERT ROSE, 4301 N 7th Ave, (602) 265-3233. C&W dance bar.

INCOGNITO LOUNGE, 2424 E Thomas, near 24th St, (602) 955-9805.

JY'S, 4343 N 7th Ave, (602) 263-8313.

NASTY HABITS, 3108 E McDowell Rd, (602) 267-8707. Dance bar with 8 music video screens, comfortable atmosphere, a variety of entertainment, open 12 noon daily. Mostly women with gay men welcome.

Cafe

CAFE UNIQUE/UNIQUE ON CENTRAL, 4700 N Central Ave #105, (602) 279-9691. Coffees, smoothies, desserts.

Restaurants

EDDIE'S GRILL, 4747 N 7th St, (602) 241-1188. Gay friendly.

POOKIE'S CAFE, 4540 N 7th St, (602) 277-2121. Bar & restaurant, American grill, kitchen open 11:30am-11pm, music video bar.

Retail & Bookstores

CHANGING HANDS BOOKSTORE, 414 S Mill Ave, Tempe, (602) 966-0203. General bookstore with a gay & lesbian section.

OBELISK BOOKSTORE, 24 W Camelback suite A, (602) 266-BOOK (2665). Gay & lesbian bookstore.

UNIQUE ON CENTRAL, 4700 N Central Ave, (602) 279-9691. Gay & lesbian cards, gifts, books, jewelry & art gallery.

Erotica

★ **CASTLE SUPERSTORE,** 5501 E Washington St, (602) 231-9837, (800) 344-9076. Large selection of gay books, magazines, videos, and much, much more. Open 24 hrs, 365 days a year.

CASTLE SUPERSTORE, 8802 N Black Canyon Hwy, near Dunlap, (602) 995-1641, (800) 344-9076. Large selection of gay books, magazines, videos, and much, much more. Open 24 hrs, 365 days a year.

CASTLE SUPERSTORE, 300 E Camelback Rd, near Central, (602) 266-3348, (800) 344-9076. Large selection of gay books, magazines, videos, and much, much more. Open 24 hrs, 365 days a year.

CASTLE SUPERSTORE, 8315 E Apache Trail, Mesa, (602) 986-6114, (800) 344-9076. Large selection of gay books, magazines, videos, and much, much more. Open 24 hrs, 365 days a year.

PRESCOTT

Retail & Bookstores

SATISFIED MIND, 113 W Goodwin St, (520) 776-9766. Retail bookstore with a gay & lesbian section.

SEDONA

Accommodations

APPLE ORCHARD INN OF SEDONA, 656 Jordan Road, Sedona, AZ, 86336, (520) 282-5328, (800) 663-6968, Fax: (520) 204-0044. Email: appleorc@sedona.net,

Web: www.appleorchardbb.com, Experience natural beauty on nearly 2 acres overlooking Wilson Mtn & Steamboat Rock. In the heart of Sedona, on the site of the historic Jordan Apple Farm, our totally renovated inn is a short walk to world-renowned galleries, fine dining & shopping. Our custom-designed rooms flavored with the Old West, offer modern luxuries such as Jacuzzi tubs and private patios.

CASA TIIGAVA, 840 Jordan Rd, Sedona, AZ, 86339, (520) 203-0192, (888) 844-4282, Fax: (520) 204-1075. Email: tiigava@sedona.net, Web: www.casatiigava.com, B&B with boutique featuring works of local artists. Full breakfast, private baths. ♀♂

COZY CACTUS, 80 Canyon Circle Dr, Sedona, AZ, 86351, (520) 284-0082, (800) 788-2082, Fax: (520) 284-4210. Gay-friendly B&B at foot of Castle Rock. Private baths, AC, TV lounge & continental breakfast.

HUFF 'N PUFF STRAW BALE INN, THE, 4320 E Beaver Creek Rd, Rimrock, AZ, 86335, (520) 567-9066. Inn in a non-toxic home with private baths, continental breakfast, some straight clientele. Tours to indian ruins arranged. ♀♂

MARTI'S GUEST RANCH, 989 South Main St, #A601, Cottonwood, AZ, 86326, (520) 634-4842, Fax: (520) 634-1405.

Relax in the restful, romantic atmosphere of our newly designed 7-room Inn
• S E D O N A •
(800) 663-6968

Email: MartiMac@Sedona.net, Come relax and enjoy yourself in a private, rustic guest cottage located on a hsistorical 65-acre ranch beside Oak Creek. Watch the sun set as ducks, geese and heron settle for the night on the banks of cool, splashing Oak Creek. Or take a quick drive to a gaming casino or to Sedona or Old Town Cottonwood. Your cottage includes 2 bedrooms, equipped kitchen stocked with coffee, tea and condiments, cable TV with VCR and movies. ♀♂

SOUTHWEST INN AT SEDONA, 3250 W. Highway 89A, Sedona, AZ, 86336, (520) 282-3344, (800) 483-7422, Fax: (520) 282-0267." Email: info@swinn.com, Web: http://www.swinn.com, You'll be pampered at this combination B&B/Small Luxury Hotel. All rooms have fireplaces & decks or patios facing beautiful red rock views. We've an outdoor pool & spa and a fun-loving staff. Complimentary deluxe continental breakfast is served mornings including fresh-baked muffins, bagels, fruits, cereal, juices, etc. We have concierge services, nature & adventure specialists, privacy, cleanliness & outstanding customer service. Gay-friendly, totally non-smoking.

■ *Women's Accommodations*
PARADISE BY THE CREEK B & B, 215 Disney Lane, Sedona, AZ, (520) 282-7107, Fax: (520) 282-3586. Email:

canyonct@sedona.net, B&B on the shores of Oak Creek overlooked by Cathedral Rock, private & shared bath, continental breakfast, men welcome. ♀

PARADISE RANCH, 135 Kachina Dr, Sedona, AZ, 86336, (520) 282-9769. For women only. Intimate, beautiful, private guesthouse with fully equipped kitchen (coffee & tea provided). Healing center with outdoor hot tub. There is a tepee and non-traditional sweat lodge on premises. We offer hypnotherapy, star chamber experiences, transpersonal therapy, workshop facilities and specialized rituals and ceremonies. We are dedicated to spreading the light of the Goddess. ♀

SAPPHO'S OASIS, PO Box 1863, Sedona, AZ, 86339, (520) 282-5679. Email: Oasis42773@aol.com, B&B guesthouse with continental breakfast, Jacuzzi, private baths, men welcome. 🏳️‍🌈 ♀

■ Retail & Bookstores

FLAGS, KITES & FUN, 202 Hwy 179, (520) 282-4496. Gay-friendly souvenir shop handling gay flags, windsocks, and rainbow products.

TUCSON

■ Information

AIDS HOTLINE, (520) 326-AIDS (2437) 9am-10pm, or call Wingspan Gay Center at (520) 624-1779.

TORTUGA ROJA

BED & BREAKFAST

2800 EAST RIVER ROAD
TUCSON, ARIZONA 85718

(800) 467-6822   (520) 577-6822

WINGSPAN GAY & LESBIAN CENTER, 300 E 6th St, (520) 624-1779, 11am-7pm Mon-Sat.

■ Accommodations

ADOBE ROSE INN BED & BREAKFAST, 940 N Olsen Ave, Tucson, AZ, 85719, (520) 318-4644, (800) 328-4122, Fax: (520) 325-0055. Email: aroseinn@aol.com, Gay-friendly B&B in an adobe house with one foot-thick walls and furniture of native lodgepole pine. Near U of A campus. 🏳️‍🌈

CASA ALEGRE BED & BREAKFAST INN, 316 East Speedway Blvd, Tucson, AZ, 85705, (520) 628-1800, (800) 628-5654, Fax: (520) 792-1880. Distinguished 1915 craftsman-style bungalow, minutes from the University of Arizona and downtown Tucson, has private baths, TV, VCR and a decor reflecting Tucson's history. The Arizona sitting room opens onto a serene patio and pool area. A scrumptious full breakfast is served in the sun room, formal dining room, and on the patio. Shopping and dining are nearby. Gay-friendly. 🏳️‍🌈

CASA TIERRA ADOBE BED & BREAKFAST INN, 11155 West Calle Pima, Tucson, AZ, 85743, (520) 578-3058 (Tel/Fax). Gay-friendly bed and breakfast inn in a remote desert setting near the Desert Museum. Great for hiking and birding. Double rooms with private baths, microwave and fridge, outdoor Jacuzzi. Full vegetarian breakfast served.

CATALINA PARK INN, 309 East 1st St, Tucson, AZ, 85705, (520) 792-4541, Fax: (520) 792-0838, Reservations: (800) 792-4885. Gay-friendly historic B&B inn. Color TV, AC, telephone, private baths, continental breakfast, 20% gay/lesbian clientsle.

DILLINGER HOUSE BED & BREAKFAST, 927 N. 2nd Ave, Tucson, AZ, 85705, (520) 622-4306 (Tel/Fax). Email: DILNGR@AOL.COM, Gay-owned B&B with increasing gay & lesbian clientele, 2 self-contained guest cottages, private baths, expanded continental breakfast, Jacuzzi. Close to gay venues, museums & shops. Some straight clientele. ♀♂

HOTEL CONGRESS, 311 E Congress, Tucson, AZ, 85701, (520) 622-8848, (800) 722-8848, Fax: (520) 792-6366. Email: hotel@hotcong.com, Gay-friendly hotel with cafe & bar. Double rooms with private baths, TV lounge.

MONTECITO HOUSE, PO Box 42352, Tucson, AZ, 85733, (520) 795-7592. My home, not a business Mostly lesbian clientele, some gay men, some straight clientele. One double with private bath, others share. Discussions at breakfast over fresh grapefruit juice from the tree in my yard, RV parking, TV lounge. Open year-round. ♀

SANTUARIO INN TUCSON, PO Box 57538, Tucson, AZ, (520) 519-0390, Fax: (520) 519-1374." Gay-owned & -operated retreat with Kuriyama relaxation therapy center, private baths, full breakfast, some straight clientele. ♀♂

TORTUGA ROJA BED & BREAKFAST, 2800 E River Rd, Tucson, AZ, 85718, (520) 577-6822, (800) 467-6822. B&B with beautiful mountain views, on a 4-acre cozy retreat in the Santa Catalina Mountain foothills. Minutes to many hiking trails, close to upscale shopping and an easy drive to the University, gay bars and most tourist attractions. A variety of guest quarters offer modern conveniences with private baths. Some accommodations include fireplaces and kitchens. Expanded continental breakfast, pool and spa on premises. Discounts available for extended stays. ♀♂

■ Women's Accommodations

HILLS OF GOLD BED & BREAKFAST, 3650 W. Hills of Gold, Tucson, AZ, 85745, (520) 743-4229 (Tel/Fax)." Email: hillsgold@theriver.com, Experience the Southwest at a single private suite, for women only, on 4 acres of Sonoran desert, 10 minutes from downtown Tucson. Hike Sabino Canyon, visit the Desert Museum, explore Kitt Peak Observatory, or relax right here. Your suite has a bedroom, sitting area, bath and private deck with mountain views. Enjoy the shared areas of our home — covered porches, hot tub, pool, gas grill and library. Your choice of a hearty Southwestern or expanded continental breakfast is included, and box lunches and dinners can be arranged. ♀

■ Dance Bar/Disco

★ **AIN'T NOBODY'S BIZNESS,* (THE BIZ),** 2900 E Broadway, (520) 318-4838. Dance club, no cover, variety of events & specials. ♀

HOURS, 3455 E Grant Rd, at Palo Verde, (520)) 327-3390. C&W dance bar, patio, 65% women, 35% men." ♀

IT'S ' BOUT TIME (IBT'S), 616 N 4th Ave, near 5th St, (520) 882-3053. Dance bar, weekly drag shows, patio, college crowd, 80% men. ♂

NEON MOON, 5150 E Speedway, (520) 881-7500. Occasional drag shows. ♂

STONEWALL & EAGLE, 2921 N 1st Ave, (520) 624-8805. Dance club in front, the Eagle drinking bar in rear, 60% men. ♀♂

HILLS OF GOLD
BED & BREAKFAST

We Are The Gold At The End Of The Rainbow

Tucson • Arizona

(520) 743-4229

ARIZONA

■ Cafe
CUP CAFE, 311 E Congress, at Hotel Congress., ◼

RAINBOW PLANET, 606 N 4th Ave, (520) 620-1770. ♀♂

■ Retail & Bookstores
ANTIGONE BOOKS, 411 N 4th Ave, (520) 792-3715. Women's bookstore with cards, jewelry, music. Large gay men's section, too.

UNIQUE ON CENTRAL, 2900 E Broadway #142, (520) 318-4307. Gay & lesbian cards, gifts, books, jewelry & art gallery.

ARKANSAS
EUREKA SPRINGS

■ Accommodations
ARBOUR GLEN B&B VICTORIAN INN & GUESTHOUSE, 7 Lema, Eureka Springs, AR, 72632, (501) 253-9010, (800) 515-GLEN(4536). Email: arbglen@ipa.net, B&B, 50% gay & lesbian clientele. Suites with private bath & modern amenities. Full gourmet breakfast. Lake on premises. ◼

CEDARBERRY B & B INN, 3 King's Hwy, Eureka Springs, AR, 72632, (501) 253-6115 or (800) 590-2424. B&B near lake & river, 50% gay & lesbian. Choice of suites, 2 with Jacuzzi. Limited kitchen privileges, full gourmet breakfast.

DAIRY HOLLOW HOUSE, 515 Spring Street, Eureka Springs, AR, 72632-3032, (501) 253-7444, (800) 562-8650, Fax: (501) 253-7223. Email: 74762.1652@compuserve.com, Web: http://www.dairyhollow.com, Gay-friendly Ozark inn, 1 mile from downtown Eureka Springs, with restaurant & shop with books by owners. Rooms & suites with private baths, full breakfast, AC, Jacuzzi. Gay & lesbian following.

GREENWOOD HOLLOW RIDGE, Rte 4, Box 155, Eureka Springs, AR, 72632, (501) 253-5283. B&B with double rooms & apt, Jacuzzi & full breakfast. Guests have CC privileges for golf, tennis. Near lake, Passion Play, country & western shows. ◼ ♀♂

MAPLE LEAF INN BED & BREAKFAST, 6 Kingshighway, Eureka Springs, AR, 72632, (800) 372-6542, (501) 253-6876. B&B, private baths, 50% gay & lesbian clientele.

POND MOUNTAIN LODGE & RESORT, Rt 1 Box 50, Eureka Springs, AR, 72632, (501) 253-5877, (800) 583-8043. Web: www.eureka-usa.com/pondmtn/, Gay-friendly B&B resort with stables & cabin. Suites with modern amenities, private Jacuzzi, private bath. Full buffet breakfast, pool on premises. 50% gay & lesbian clientele. ◼

ROCK COTTAGE GARDENS, 10 Eugenia St, Eureka Springs, AR, 72632, (501) 253-8659 or (800) 624-6646. B&B, 50% gay & lesbian clientele. Cottages with private baths, full breakfast."

SWEET SEASONS, PEABODY HOUSE & EDGEWOOD MANOR, (800) 210-5683, (501) 253-6555, Fax: (501) 253-8833. Sweet Seasons private cottages; Peabody House & Edgewood Manor deluxe tourist lodgings. Gay-owned.

WOODS, THE, 50 Wall St, (501) 253-8281. 3 cottages, Jacuzzis. 50% gay and lesbian, 50% straight clientele.

■ Women's Accommodations
GOLDEN GATE COTTAGE, Rte 7 Box 182, Eureka Springs, AR, 72631-9225, (501) 253-5291. Women-only guesthouse in a tree-shaded, peaceful setting on the lake only ten minutes from Eureka Springs. Cottage rooms with or without kitchenette. Private entrance, color TV, VCR & movie library, AC, ceiling fans, king beds, private baths, outdoor hot tub. Rates: $40-$55 (discounts for longer stays). A walking trail passes between lake and cliffs. Boat marina, with boat rentals, nearby. No children, no pets. ♀

■ Bars
CENTER ST BAR & GRILLE, 10 Center St, (501) 253-8102. Caribbean & Mexican restaurant & bar. Gay-owned & -operated, live entertainment Fri & Sat. ◼ ◼ ✕ ♪

CHELSEA'S, 10 Mountain St, (501) 253-6723, Gay-friendly beer garden, pub & restaurant, closed Sun. ◼ ◼ ♪ ◼

■ Restaurants
AUTUMN BREEZE, Hwy 23 South, 1/4 mile south of the 23/62 intersection, (501) 253-7734. Prime rib, rack of lamb, vegetarian stir fry, chocolate soufflé. ◼

ERMILLO'S, ask locally for address, lunch dinner, Italian home cooking, gay-friendly. ◼

JIM & BRENT'S BISTRO, 173 S Main St, (501) 253-7457. Eclectic American dining.

Retail & Bookstores
EMERALD RAINBOW, 45 1/2 Spring St, (501) 253-5445. Rainbow & new age items, metaphysical books, gifts. Organizers of Diversity wknd with gay dances, etc.

FAYETTEVILLE

Dance Bar/Disco
EDNA'S, S. School at Mountain, highly mixed crowd, many community events, C&W nights.

RON'S PLACE, 523 W Poplar St, (501) 442-3052. Dance bar 9pm-2am, private club.

Retail & Bookstores
DICKSON ST USED BOOKS, 325 W Dickson St, (501) 442-8182. General used bookstore with women's section."

PASSAGES, 200 W Dickson, (501) 442-5845. Book & gift shop with gay & lesbian books, music & jewelry.

FT SMITH

Dance Bar/Disco
LEGENDS OF ARKANSAS, 917 N A St, (501) 782-4190, Fax: (501) 471-5881. Gay-owned/operated dance club. Thurs-Sun 9pm-5am.

HOT SPRINGS

Dance Bar/Disco
OUR HOUSE, 660 E Grand, (501) 624-6868. Dance & show bar with restaurant, 50% men, 50% women. Closed Sun.

LITTLE ROCK

Bars
SILVER DOLLAR, 2710 Asher Ave, near Woodrow, (501) 663-9886. Closed Sun, men's night Mon.

Dance Bar/Disco
ANNEX/701 AT BACKSTREET, 1021 Jessie Rd, next door to Discovery III, (501) 664-2744. (Same building as 501 at Backstreet.) DJ weekends, live entertaiment Fri & Sat.

★ DISCOVERY III, 1021 Jessie Rd, near River Front, (501) 664-4784. Private club, Sat 9pm-5am, huge weekend straight crowd.

MISS KITTY'S BACKSTREET, 1021 Jessie Rd, (501) 664-2744. open 7 nights, 9pm-5am.

Retail & Bookstores
WOMEN'S PROJECT, 2224 Main St, (501) 372-5113. Book and gift shop, lending library. Many workshops, support groups for lesbians. Monthly coffeehouse, yearly retreat.

OZARKS

Information
GLORP (GAY & LESBIAN OZARK RURAL PEOPLE), (501) 895-4959.

TEXARKANA

Information
ARKANSAS AIDS PROJECT, (501) 773-1994.

CALIFORNIA
ANAHEIM - ORANGE COUNTY

Accommodations
COUNTRY COMFORT BED & BREAKFAST, 5104 E Valencia Drive, Orange, CA, 92869-1217, (714) 532-4010, Fax: (714) 997-1921. Email: gerilopker@aol.com, B&B near Disneyland, KnottsBerry, beaches & nightlife. All the comforts of home. Private bath, full breakfast.

APPLE VALLEY

Dance Bar/Disco
VICTOR VICTORIA'S, 22581 Outer Hwy 18, (760) 240-8018. DJ Thurs-Sat, open Mon-Sat 6pm-2am, Sun 2pm-2am, 50% men, 50% women. Sun beer bust with BBQ buffet.

ARCATA

Retail & Bookstores
NORTHTOWN BOOKS, 957 H St, (707) 822-2834. General bookstore with gay & lesbian selection.

CALIFORNIA

BAKERSFIELD

Information
GAY LINE, (805) 328-0729. Info tape & variable live staffing.

Bars
PADRE HOTEL BAR, 1813 H St, (805) 322-1419. Piano bar, gay-friendly with 20% gay clientele.

Dance Bar/Disco
CASABLANCA, 1030 20th St, (805) 324-1384. 7pm-2am, closed Mon.

BERKELEY

Accommodations
ELMWOOD HOUSE B & B, 2609 College Avenue, Berkeley, CA, 94704-3406, (510) 540-5123 (Tel/Fax), (800) 540-3050. Email: elmwoodhse@aol.com, B&B 4 blocks from U of CA Berkeley, Elmwood shopping district, mostly straight clientele. Three double rooms, one triple. Continental breakfast & nearby pools.

Retail & Bookstores
BOADECIA'S BOOKS, 398 Colusa Ave, Kensington, 1 block outside Berkeley limits, (510) 559-9184, boadbks@norcov.com. Half women's, half gay/lesbian books.

GAIA, 1400 Shattuck Ave, (510) 548-4172. Books, music, jewelry, goddess items, percussion instruments.

GOOD VIBRATIONS, 2504 San Pablo Ave, (510) 841-8986. Toys, books, videos and more for women.

MAMA BEARS CULTURE CENTER, see listing in Oakland.,

SHAMBHALA BOOKSELLERS, 2482 Telegraph Ave, (510) 848-8443. Religious & metaphysical books, tapes, some cards & sacred arts."

BIG BEAR LAKE AREA

Accommodations
BEAR CLAW CABINS, 586 Main St, Big Bear Lake, CA, 92315, (909) 866-7633, Fax: (909) 866-1454. Gay-friendly furnished cabins, 20% gay/lesbian clientele.

SMOKETREE RESORT, 40154 Big Bear Blvd, PO Box 2801, Big Bear Lake, CA, 92315, (909) 866-2415 or (800) 352-8581. Gay-friendly B&B and cabins, on 1-1/2 acres in the San Bernardino Mtns near Big Bear Lake. Main lodge: 5 B&B suites, private baths, color TV. 25 cabins vary in size from 2-person to a 14-person abode. Continental breakfast, 2 pools,

Women's Accommodations
BEAR PAUSE CABIN, 43345 Sheephorn Dr, lower Moonridge area, Big Bear Lake, CA, (760) 754-6747, (888) GO WOMEN, Fax: (760) 754-8066. Email: eventsrus@aol.com, Secluded 2-bedroom cabin, 2 miles from Big Bear Lake, with bathroom, microwave, TV, VCR, phone, near hiking, skiing, boating, etc. ♀

HOLLAND HUES, c/o Stacey Peyer, 19545 Sherman Way #57, Reseda, CA, 91335, (310) 559-5931 or (818) 349-3336. 2-bdrm cabin, men welcome. ♀

CALISTOGA

Accommodations
BACKYARD GARDEN OASIS - A B&B INN, 24019 Hilderbrand Dr, Middletown, CA, (707) 987-0505, Fax: (707) 987-3993. Email: bygoasis@jnb.com, Three cottages with private baths, near Calistoga spa, Harbin hot springs, 20 min to Napa Valley wineries, 2 mi to Twin Pines Casino.

CATHEDRAL CITY
SEE PALM SPRINGS/CATHEDRAL CITY LISTINGS,

CHICO

Information
STONEWALL ALLIANCE COMMUNITY CENTER & AIDS INFO, 341 Broadway, 3rd fl #300, (530) 893-3336. Office: Tues-Fri 4-7pm, Sat noon-4pm. Recorded local info: 893-3338.

CLEARLAKE AREA

Accommodations
SEA BREEZE RESORT, 9595 Harbor Dr, (Mail: PO Box 653), Glenhaven, CA, 95443, (707) 998-3327. Gay-friendly, lakefront resort cottages with full kitchen, color cable TV, AC & private baths. Private beach, lighted pier.

Camping & RV
EDGEWATER RESORT, 6420 Soda Bay Rd, Kelseyville, CA, 95451, (707) 279-0208, Fax:(707) 279-0138 Women-owned

CALIFORNIA

RV resort with cabins, full RV hook-ups & tent sites, clubhouse, general store, laundry facilities.

COMPTCHE

Accommodations
WITTWOOD, 8161 Flynn Creek Rd, Comptche, CA, 95427, (707) 937-5486. Gay-friendly retreat with gay female following, shared baths.

DAVIS

Information
UCD WOMEN'S CENTER, North Hall 1st fl, U of California, (916) 752-3372. Mon-Fri 8am-5pm, lesbian support groups, library.

EL CERRITO

Dance Bar/Disco
CLUB SALSA DANCE CLUB, (510) 428-2144. Women's dance nights 2nd Sat. Salsa lessons 7:30pm, dancing 8pm-11pm. Smoke- & alcohol-free. Call for current location.

EL MONTE

Bars
SUGAR SHACK, 4101 Arden Dr, (626) 448-6579.

EL SERENO

Dance Bar/Disco
PLUSH PONY, 5261 Alhambra Ave, (213) 224-9488. Latino bar for women, men welcome.

EMERYVILLE

Retail & Bookstores
HEADLINES, 5719 Christie Ave, in Powell St Plaza, (510) 547-3324. Clothing & gifts.

EUREKA

Accommodations
ABIGAIL'S ELEGANT VICTORIAN MANSION B&B LODGING ACCOMM., 1406 C Street, Eureka, CA, 95501, (707) 444-3144, Fax: (707) 442-5594. Gay-friendly Victorian B&B, exclusively non-smoking, full breakfast, Finnish sauna.

CARTER HOUSE VICTORIANS, 301 L St, Historic Old Town, Eureka, CA, 95501, (707) 444-8062, (800) 404-1390, Fax: (707) 444-8067. Gay-friendly B&B inn with dinner restaurant. Color TV, private & shared baths & full breakfast."

Dance Bar/Disco
CLUB WEST, 535 5th St, (707) 444-2582. Gay Sun evening only. Unverifiable spring '98, check first.

Retail & Bookstores
BOOKLEGGER, 402 2nd St, (707) 445-1344. General bookstore with women's & gay books (used and new).

FORESTVILLE
SEE RUSSIAN RIVER.,

FT BRAGG

Retail & Bookstores
WINDSONG BOOKS & RECORDS, 324 N Main, (707) 964-2050. Mostly used books, crafts, large women's section.

FRESNO

Information
COMMUNITY INFO & AIDS LINE, (209) 264-AIDS (2437), 8am-5pm or tape. Call for all local gay & lesbian info."

Dance Bar/Disco
EL SOMBRERO, 3848 E Belmont Ave, (209) 442-1818.
PALACE SALOON, 4030 E Belmont Ave, near 11th, (209) 264-8283. Dance & show bar, 70% women, 30% men.

Restaurants
EXPRESS CAFE, 708 N Blackstone Ave, same building as Fresno Express men's bar., (209) 233-1791. Mon-Sat dinner 6pm-9pm, Sun brunch 10am-3pm.

Retail & Bookstores
VALLEY BOOKS & GIFTS, 1118 N Fulton, (209) 233-3600. Women's, lesbian & gay books.

CALIFORNIA

GOLD COUNTRY - SIERRA FOOTHILLS

■ Accommodations

RANCHO CICADA, PO Box 225, Plymouth, CA, 95669, (209) 245-4841. Web: www.gaymall.com, Clothing-optional camping resort with cabins. Tents on raised platforms, separate men/women restroom facilities with hot showers, wash basins & flush toilets. Be discreet when contacting resort.

GRASS VALLEY

■ Accommodations

KENTON MINE LODGE, PO Box 942, Alleghany, CA, 95910, (916) 287-3212. Gay-friendly inn with cabins, private & shared baths."

GUALALA

■ Retail & Bookstores

GUALALA BOOKS, 39145 S Hwy 1, (707) 884-4255. General bookstore with gay, lesbian and feminist sections.

GUERNEVILLE

SEE RUSSIAN RIVER.,

HAYWARD

■ Dance Bar/Disco

DRIFTWOOD LOUNGE, 22170 Mission Blvd, (510) 581-2050. Dance bar, DJ some weekends.

RAINBOW ROOM, 21859 Mission Blvd, (510) 582-8078. DJ Fri & Sat.

★ **TURF CLUB**, 22517 Mission Blvd, (510) 881-9877. 70% men, summer BBQ's, patio.

IDYLLWILD

■ Accommodations

PINE COVE INN, THE, 23481 Hwy 243, Idyllwild, CA, 92549, (909) 659-5033, toll-free (888) 659-5033, Fax: (909) 659-5034. B&B, 50% gay & lesbian clientele, private baths."

WILKUM INN BED & BREAKFAST, 26770 Hwy 243, PO Box 1115, Idyllwild, CA, 92549, (909) 659-4087, (800) 659-4086. Gay-friendly B&B with a gay & lesbian following, private & shared baths, expanded continental breakfast. "

JULIAN

■ Accommodations

LEELIN WIKIUP B & B, 1645 Whispering Pines, PO Box 2363, Julian, CA, 92036, (760) 765-1890, (800) 6WIKIUP (694-5487), (800) LAMAPAK (526-2725), Fax: (760) 765-1512. Email: linda@wikiupbnb.com, Web: wikiupbnb.com, Gay-friendly B&B home with pet llamas on premises. 3 rooms, private baths. 1/2-day lunch llama treks available for guests.

LAGUNA BEACH

■ Accommodations

CASA LAGUNA BED & BREAKFAST INN, 2510 South Coast Hwy, Laguna Beach, CA, 92651, (714) 494-2996, (800) 233-0449, Fax: (714) 494-5009. Gay-friendly B&B country inn located in Southern California's gay capital. 60 miles south of LA and 30 miles south of Disneyland, Laguna boasts scenic shorelines and crystal white beaches. The Casa offers unique accommodations in a tropical hillside setting, overlooking the Pacific Ocean. Pool and sun decks, 21 rooms, suites and cottages with kitchens.

Casa Laguna Bed & Breakfast Inn

2510 S. Coast Highway
Laguna Beach, CA 92651

(800) 233-0449

CALIFORNIA 241

Expanded continental breakfast. Near gay bars, restaurants, entertainment."

COAST INN, 1401 S Coast Hwy, Laguna Beach, CA, 92651, (714) 494-7588, (800) 653-2697, Fax: (714) 494-1735. Email: coastinn@msn.com, Web: http://www.boomboomroom.com, 100% gay & lesbian oceanfront resort hotel with private beach, restaurant, disco, Coast Inn Cafe & and the famous Boom Boom Room. Rooms with cable color TV, private baths & sunning decks.

■ *Beaches*
WEST ST BEACH, opposite West St.,

■ *Bars*
MAIN STREET, 1460 S Coast Hwy, near Mountain, (714) 494-0056. Piano bar, 90% men, 10% women. Remodeling & changing in '98.

WOODY'S, 1305 S Coast Hwy, (714) 376-8809. Bar & restaurant, piano bar.

■ *Dance Bar/Disco*
★ **BOOM BOOM ROOM,** 1401 S Coast Hwy (PCH), at the Coast Inn Hotel, (714) 494-7588. Dance bar.

■ *Restaurants*
COTTAGE RESTAURANT, THE, 308 N Coast Hwy, (714) 494-3023. Breakfast, lunch, dinner in a romantic setting. Sunday brunch on patio, reservations accepted.

■ *Retail & Bookstores*
DIFFERENT DRUMMER BOOKSHOPPE, 1294-C South Coast Hwy, (714) 497-6699, Fax: (714) 497-0471. Gay and lesbian bookstore.

JEWELRY BY PONCE, 1417 S Coast Hwy, (714) 497-4154, (800) 969-7464. Gay & lesbian jewelry, watches & gifts.

■ *Erotica*
GAY MART, 168 Mountain, (714) 497-9108. Toys, lubes, videos, t-shirts & cards.

LAGUNITAS

■ *Cafe*
LAGUNITAS SWING CAFE, 7282 Sir Francis Drake Blvd, (415) 488-1689. Women's nights Fri 6pm-11pm, soups, salads, sandwiches, espresso smoothies.

LAKE ARROWHEAD

■ *Accommodations*
SPRING OAKS B & B, PO Box 2918 (mail), 2465 Spring Oak Dr, Running Springs, CA, 92382, (909) 867-7797, (800) 867-9636. Web: http://www.innguide.com/springoaks/index.html, Gay-friendly adult mountain retreat with guided hikes, workshops & concerts. Ceiling fans, private & shared baths, full breakfast, spa & massage."

LAKE TAHOE AREA

■ *Information*
GAY NETWORK LINE, (530) 541-4297. Local gay info.

■ *Accommodations*
ALPENGLOW TOWNHOUSES, PO Box 11966, Zephyr Cove, NV, 89448, (702) 588-0044 (Tel/Fax), (888) 325-7456.
Email: alpglow@aol.com, Luxury townhouses with views of Lake Tahoe, close to Heavenly Valley ski area. Near Tahoe Rim Trail hiking & backpacking, backcountry skiing, snowshoeing, etc. Full kitchens, gay-friendly, gay-owned.

BAVARIAN HOUSE, THE, PO Box 624507, Lake Tahoe, CA, 96154, (800) 431-4411, (530) 544-4411. Guesthouse with rustic, mountain decor 4 blocks from ski lift, 1 mile from Tahoe casino nightlife. Two large decks, king-sized bed, TV, VCR, private bath. Greatroom has river rock fireplace and vaulted, beamed ceiling. Separate 3-bedroom, 2-bath chalet for couples.

INN ESSENCE, 865 Lake Tahoe Blvd, South Lake Tahoe, CA, 96150, (530) 577-0339, Fax: (530) 577-0118, (800) 57 TAHOE. Email: innessence@aol.com, B&B guesthouse with color cable TV, VCR, telephone, Jacuzzi, shared bath. Full gourmet breakfast.

LAKESIDE B 'N B TAHOE, Box 1756, Crystal Bay, NV, 89402, (702) 831-8281, Fax: (702) 831-7FAX (7329). Email: TahoeBnB@aol.com, Lakeside B&B. Private & shared baths, color TV, VCR, Jacuzzi, full breakfast.

NYVADA B & B, Box 6835, Stateline, NV, (702) 588-5559. B&B. Single rooms &

Holly's

A SPECIAL PLACE
FOR ALL WOMEN
Lake Tahoe, California

COZY CABINS

916-544-7040
www.hollysplace.com

CALIFORNIA 243

apartment, TV in living room, weights, Jacuzzi, massage, full breakfast. ♀♂

SIERRAWOOD GUEST HOUSE, PO Box 11194, Tahoe Paradise, CA, 96155-0194, (530) 577-6073, (800) 700-3802. Email: Swooddave@aol.com, Guesthouse. Cozy, rustic rooms with private & shared baths, fireplace, TV lounge, hot tub, nearby lake. Full breakfast & dinner.

■ Women's Accommodations

HOLLY'S, PO Box 13197, South Lake Tahoe, CA, 96151, (530) 544-7040, (800) 745-7041. Email: hollys@oakweb.com, Web: hollysplace.com, Vacation place for women, 2 blocks to lake, 2 miles to casinos & near all outdoor recreation. Guest rooms & cabins with private baths, kitchens, color TV/VCR, fireplaces, lofts, skylights & ceiling fans. Recreation/conference room, video library, free bikes, volleyball, barbecue grills, ping pong & horseshoes." ♀

■ Dance Bar/Disco

FACES, 270 Kingsbury Grade, Stateline, NV (South Lake Tahoe), (702) 588-2333. Hi-energy dance bar, DJ weekends, limited gaming, daily 5pm-2am, Fri & Sat 5pm-4 or 5am.

LANCASTER

■ Dance Bar/Disco

BACKDOOR, 1255 W Ave I, (805) 945-2566. C&W nights Wed, DJ Fri & Sun, 50% men, 50% women. Unverifiable spring '98.

LONG BEACH

■ Information

BEING ALIVE (AIDS INFO), 994 Redondo Ave, (562) 434-9022. Hours change. AIDS support, referral, info & drop-in.

CENTER LONG BEACH, THE, 2017 E 4th St, (562) 434-4455. 9am-10pm (Sat 10am-6pm, Sun 3pm-9pm).

■ Bars

BIRDS OF PARADISE, 1800 E Broadway, (562) 590-8773. Pool & darts.

CLUB BROADWAY, 3348 E Broadway, (562) 438-7700. Jukebox & pool table, 20% men, 80% women.

FALCON, 1435 E Broadway, at Falcon, (562) 432-4146.

■ Dance Bar/Disco

★ **EXECUTIVE SUITE,** 3428 E Pacific Coast Hwy, at traffic circle, (562) 597-3884. Women's dance bar open 7 days. Club LBC house music & hip hop nite (Chicago-style house party) Wed. ♀

QUE SERA SERA, 1923 E 7th St, near Cherry, (562) 599-6170. Live bands. ♀

■ Restaurants

OMELETTE INN, 108 W 3rd St, (562) 437-5625. Breakfast & lunch.

TWO UMBRELLAS CAFE, 1538 E Broadway, (562) 435-7364. Breakfast & lunch.

WONG'S ON BROADWAY, 1506 E Broadway, (562) 432-0816. Chinese cuisine, gay-friendly.

■ Retail & Bookstores

DODD'S BOOKS, 4818 E 2nd St, near St Joseph's, (562) 438-9948. General bookstore with gay & lesbian section.

PEARLS BOOKSELLERS, 224 Redondo Ave, (562) 438-8875. Women's bookstore with men's section & 3rd-world women's crafts.

LOS ANGELES INTRO

■ Information

AIDS INFO, (213) 876-2437. AIDS project LA (ALPA) (213) 962-1600. Being Alive (213) 667-3262. Shanti (213) 962-8197.

BI-LINE, BI-SOCIAL CENTER, PAN-SOCIAL CENTER, (213) 873-3700 or (818) 989-3700 (24hrs), For all ages, races, sexual orientation & gender identities.

LA GAY & LESBIAN COMMUNITY SERVICES CENTER, 1625 N Schrader Blvd, Los Angeles, (213) 993-7400.

TRIKONE, (408) 270-8776. South Asian gay groups, meets monthly, publishes quarterly magazine. Write for details: PO Box 21354, San Jose CA 95151.

WOMEN'S CENTERS, Los Angeles Metro list."

WOMEN'S REFERRAL SERVICE, (818) 995-6646. Mon-Fri 9am-5pm referrals to women professionals.

CALIFORNIA

Visit Los Angeles
(800) CARITAS
Caritas B&B Network

Accommodations
CARITAS BED & BREAKFAST NETWORK, (800) CARITAS, (312) 857-0801, Fax: (312) 857-0805. B&B, home-stay accommodations service. Member: IGLTA

Dance Bar/Disco
CLUB FORBIDDEN, (310) 669-5957. Moving Latino dance night, call to verify location.
DEDE'S WOMEN'S DANCE CLUB, (310) 433-1470. Scheduled women's dance parties. Call Hotline for current schedule & location.

Retail & Bookstores
BOOKSTORES (GAY & LESBIAN), See West Hollywood.,

LA HOLLYWOOD

Information
WOMEN'S RESOURCES, (213) 993-7400. Housed in the Gay & Lesbian Center.

Bars
MING'S DYNASTY, 5221 Hollywood Blvd, (213) 462-2039. Gay Asian bar.

Dance Bar/Disco
CIRCUS DISCO, 6655 Santa Monica Blvd, (213) 462-1291. Thurs-Sat.
LA PLAZA, 739 La Brea Ave, (213) 939-0703. 8pm-2am, 7 days, Mon women's night, drag shows nightly 10:15pm & midnight.
PEDRO'S GRILL, 1739 N Vermont, (213) 660-9472. Gay Wed only, salsa, merengue, live bands.
PROBE, 836 N Highland Ave, near Willoughby, (213) 461-8301. Different format nightly, call for gay nights.

Fitness Centers
HOLLYWOOD GYM, 1551 N La Brea, (213) 845-1420. 24hrs.

Restaurants
OFF VINE, 6263 Leland Way, (213) 962-1900. Casual continental cuisine.
THREE-SIX-O RESTAURANT & LOUNGE, 6290 Sunset Blvd, (213) 871-2995.

LA METRO

Bars
REDHEAD BAR, 2218 E 1st St, East LA, (213) 263-2995.

Dance Bar/Disco
CATCH ONE DISCO, 4067 W Pico Blvd, near Norton, (213) 734-8849 or 737-1159. Male & female exotic dancers, jazz, blues, 9pm-4am Fri & Sat, 9pm-3am Sun.
JEWEL'S ROOM, 4067 W Pico Blvd, downstairs from Catch One Disco, (213) 734-8849. Show bar & lounge, 50% men, 50% women, 3pm-2am daily. Security parking.
LA FACTORIA, 5515 Wilshire Blvd, (at the El Rey Theater), (310) 281-6838.

LA SILVERLAKE

Bars
CASITA DEL CAMPO, 1920 Hyperion Ave, (213) 662-4255. Restaurant & bar, Mexican cuisine.
COBALT CANTINA, 4326 Sunset Blvd, (213) 953-9991. Dining room with patio, full bar. Cal-Mex cuisine, some straight clientele. Popular with women especially for women's Wednesday.
LITTLE JOY, 1477 Sunset Blvd, at Portia, (213) 250-3417.

Dance Bar/Disco
SALSA CON CLASE, (626) 576-0720, (626) 282-0330. Dance party, live bands, DJ, salsa lessons, male & female dancers. Call hotline for details

Cafe
COFFEE TABLE, 2930 Rowena Ave, (213) 644-8111.

Restaurants
CREST COFFEESHOP, 3725 Sunset Blvd, at Lucile, (213) 660-3645.
EL CONQUISTADOR, 3715 Sunset Blvd, Great margaritas.
ZEN RESTAURANT, 2609 Hyperion Ave, (213) 665-2929. Japanese restaurant & sushi bar, many gays on weekends.

CALIFORNIA 245

LA VALLEY

■ Bars
GOLD 9, 13625 Moorpark, near Woodman, Sherman Oaks, (818) 986-0285. TV, CD jukebox, pool, darts.

OXWOOD INN, 13713 Oxnard St, near Woodman, Van Nuys, (818) 997-9666. Cocktails, dancing, pool, darts, DJ on weekends. Open Mon-Thur 3pm-2am, Fri-Sun 2pm-2am.

VENTURE INN, 11938 Ventura Blvd, Studio City, (818) 769-5400. Bar & rest., 50% men, 50% women, Sun brunch.

■ Dance Bar/Disco
ESCAPADES, 10437 Burbank Blvd, at Strohm, North Hollywood, (818) 508-7008. Dance club with entertainment, 50% men, 50% women.

INCOGNITO VALLEY, 7026 Reseda Blvd, Reseda, (818) 996-2976. Video dance bar, DJ Wed-Sat, 70% men, women welcome.

■ Restaurants
VENTURE INN, 11938 Ventura Blvd, at Venture Inn bar, Studio City., Sun brunch.

LA WEST HOLLYWOOD

■ Information
JUNE MAZER LESBIAN COLLECTION, 626 N. Robertson Blvd. (2nd Floor), (310) 659-2478. Sun 12-4pm, Tues 11am-3pm, Wed 6-9pm & by appointment.

SOUTHERN CALIFORNIA WOMEN FOR UNDERSTANDING, (805) 644-7298.

■ Accommodations
GROVE GUEST HOUSE, THE, 1325 N Orange Grove Ave, Los Angeles - West Hollywood, CA, 90046, (213) 876-8887, Fax: (213) 876-3170. Toll-free reservations: (888) L.A.-GROVE (524-7683). Luxurious 1-bedroom home in quiet historical district. Full kitchen (stocked), cable TV, VCR, video tape library, gas BBQ, pool & spa.

HOLLOWAY MOTEL, 8465 Santa Monica Blvd, West Hollywood, CA, 90069, (213) 654-2454, (888) 654-6400, Fax: (213) 848-7161. Centrally-located motel, some straight clientele. Color TV, AC, phones & private baths. Walking distance to most attractions, 30 minutes to major southern CA attractions.

LE MONTROSE SUITE HOTEL DE GRAN LUXE, 900 Hammond St, West Hollywood, CA, 90069, (310) 855-1115, (800) 776-0666, Fax: (310) 657-9192. Web: http://www.travel2000.com, Gay-friendly, European-style hotel with restaurant. Suites include sunken living room, cozy fireplace, refrigerator, color TV with VCR and twice-daily maid service, multiline phone with dataport, fax machines, and voice mail services. Most

WEST HOLLYWOOD

Perhaps You've Heard of Us
le montrose
SUITE HOTEL DE GRAN LUXE
800-776-0666
INTERNET ADDRESSES: http://www.travelweb.com
http://www.travel2000.com

WEST HOLLYWOOD

Stay Someplace New. Again.
Le Parc
SUITE HÔTEL DE LUXE
800-578-4837
IntenetAddess:
http://www.travel2000.com/h/united_s/californ/west_hol/leparcwh.usa/L.htm

suites include a kitchenette, and many offer private balconies with breathtaking city views. Enjoy the rooftop heated pool and the lighted tennis. Complimentary bicycles are available. ♿ 🏊 See ad page 245.

LE PARC HOTEL, 733 N. West Knoll Dr, West Hollywood, CA, 90069, (310) 855-8888, Reservations USA only: (800) 578-4837, Fax: (310) 659-7812. Web: http://www.travel2000.com, Set in a peaceful residential neighborhood, you'll feel like you're miles away from the action, when in reality you are conveniently right in the middle of it. Our 154 luxury suites provide a living room with fireplace, balcony, kitchenette, VCR, multiline phones and cable TV. We offer twice-daily maid service, room service, free morning newspaper a private guest restaurant, a gym, sauna, rooftop pool, jacuzzi and tennis and basketball courts. Gay-friendly. See ad page 245.

LE RÊVE HOTEL, 8822 Cynthia Street, West Hollywood, CA, 90069, (310) 854-1114, (800) 835-7997, Fax: (310) 657-2623. Gay-friendly boutique hotel, walking distance to most gay bars, junior suites with fireplaces, phones, private baths. 🏊

RAMADA HOTEL WEST HOLLYWOOD, 8585 Santa Monica Blvd, West Hollywood, CA, 90069, (310) 652-6400, (800) 845-8585, Fax: (310) 652-2135. Hotel with restaurant, bar & clothing shop, rooms & suites with private baths, color cable TV, AC, pool on premises. Located in the center of West Hollywood, within walking distance of gay bars, restaurants, shops and entertainment, 50% gay and lesbian clientele. 🏊

SAN VICENTE INN & RESORT, 845 San Vicente Blvd, West Hollywood, CA, 90069, (310) 854-6915, Fax: (310) 289-5929. Centrally located B&B inn. Color TV, AC, telephone, refrigerator, private & shared baths. Expanded continental breakfast, pool on premises. 🏊 ♂

■ Bars

LUNA PARK, 665 N Robertson Blvd, (310) 652-0611. Gay-friendly bar with cabaret & restaurant, live bands 🎵 🍴

★ **REVOLVER**, 8851 Santa Monica Blvd, at Larrabee, (310) 550-8851. Video bar, after hours weekends, variety of videos. ♀♂

■ Dance Bar/Disco

CHERRY, 657 N Robertson Blvd., 🍺 ♀

CLUB 7969, 7969 Santa Monica Blvd, near Laurel, (213) 654-0280. Dance club, live entertainment, changing venues, call first. 🍺 🍴 🎵 ♀♂

★ **GIRL BAR**, (213) 460-2531. Women's dance party extravaganzas. Call for monthly schedule. 🍺 🍴 ♀

LOVE LOUNGE, Video dance bar, different venues nightly, ask locally for exact schedule. 🍺

★ **MICKEY'S**, 8857 Santa Monica Blvd, (310) 657-1176. Dance bar, occasional videos, lunches, patio. 🍺 ♂

★ **PALMS, THE**, 8572 Santa Monica Blvd, (310) 652-6188. Dance bar, mostly women, gay men welcome. Patio, Sunday buffet. 🎵 🍺 ♀

■ Restaurants

ABBEY, THE, 692 N Robertson Blvd, (310) 289-8410. Gay-owned and -operated. 🍴

BENVENUTO CAFE, 8512 Santa Monica Blvd, (310) 659-8635. Pasta, pizza, cappuccino. Delivery. Large gay & lesbian following. 🍷 🍴

RAMADA
West Hollywood

(800) 845-8585

CAFE D'ETOILE, 8941-1/2 Santa Monica Blvd, (310) 278-1011. Continental cuisine. 🍷 ♀♂

FIGS, 7929 Santa Monica Blvd, (213) 654-0780. Home cooking, gay-friendly. 🍴▨

FRENCH QUARTER AT FRENCH MARKET, 7985 Santa Monica Blvd, at Laurel, (213) 654-0898. Patio-style continental cuisine. 🍴♀♂

HEIGHTS CAFE, THE, 1118 N Crescent Heights Blvd, (213) 650-9688. Breakfast, lunch, dinner.

LUNAPARK, 665 N Robertson Blvd, (310) 652-0611. Bar with cabaret & restaurant, continental cuisine. 🎵 ♀♂

MELROSE PLACE BAR & GRILL, 650 N La Cienega, (310) 657-2227. ▨

TANGO GRILL, 8807 Santa Monica Blvd, (310) 659-3663. Argentine cuisine. 🍴▨

YUKON MINING CO, 7328 Santa Monica Blvd, (213) 851-8833. Coffee shop, 24hrs. 🍴♀♂

▪ Retail & Bookstores

A DIFFERENT LIGHT BOOKS, 8853 Santa Monica Blvd, near San Vicente, (310) 854-6601. Gay & lesbian bookstore.

BOOK SOUP, 8818 Sunset Blvd, (310) 659-3110. General bookstore with gay & lesbian section.

DON'T PANIC, 802 North San Vicente Blvd, (800) 45-PANIC. Gay & lesbian T-shirts.

DOROTHY'S SURRENDER, 7985 Santa Monica Blvd, in the French Market Place, (213) 650-4111. Gift shop.

HER BODY BOOKS, 433 S Beverly Dr, (310) 553-5821." Feminist bookstore.

UNICORN ALLEY, 8940 Santa Monica Blvd, (310) 652-6253. Gay pride items, videos.

UNICORN BOOKSTORE, 8940 Santa Monica Blvd, (310) 652-6253.

▪ Erotica

DRAKE'S II, 8932 Santa Monica Blvd, (310) 289-8932. Gay & lesbian movie rentals, adult toys novelties.

DRAKE'S MELROSE, 7566 Melrose Ave, near Curson, (213) 651-5600, Gay & lesbian movie rentals, 24hrs.

PLEASURE CHEST, 7733 Santa Monica Blvd, near Genesee, (213) 650-1022. Gay & lesbian movies, magazines & more."

WEST LA - SANTA MONICA

ALSO BEACH CITIES, CULVER CITY, MAR VISTA, VENICE & MALIBU.,

▪ Accommodations

MALIBU BEACH INN, 22878 Pacific Coast Hwy, Malibu, CA, 90265, (310) 456-6444, Fax: (310) 456-1499, (800) 4-MALIBU or Canada: (800) 255-1007. Gay-friendly ocean front hotel. Rooms with modern conveniences & private baths. Expanded continental breakfast.

▪ Beaches

WILL ROGERS GAY BEACH., In Santa Monica, take Channel Rd to the tunnel under Pacific Coast Hwy, park near tennis courts.

▪ Bars

BRASSERIE, 2214 Stoner Ave, West LA, (310) 477-2844. 🎵♂

FRIENDSHIP, 112 W Channel Rd, near Pacific Coast Highway, Santa Monica, (310) 454-6024. Beach bar. 🎬🎵♂

JJ'S PUB, 2692 S La Cienega Blvd, near Alvira, Culver City, (310) 837-7443. More gay in evenings, 30% women. 🎬🍴♂

PINK, THE, 2810 Main St, Santa Monica, (310) 392-1077. Bar with changing special events, call for schedule. ♂

▪ Dance Bar/Disco

CONNECTION, 4363 Sepulveda, Culver City, (310) 391-6817. Big-screen TV, DJ or bands on weekends, darts, pool table, big-screen TV, men welcome. 🍴🎵 ♀

▪ Restaurants

LOONEY'S, 2920 Lincoln Blvd, Santa Monica (between Ocean Park & Rose), (310) 314-9957. They're looney about lesbians. ▨

TRILOGY, 2214 Stoner Ave, West LA, (310) 477-2844. Wed-Sun 6pm-10pm, drag shows nightly. 🎵♀♂

248 CALIFORNIA

■ Retail & Bookstores
SISTERHOOD BOOKSTORE, 1351 Westwood Blvd, at Rochester, (310) 477-7300. Women's bookstore with music, cards, crafts by & about women, resource center, 10am-8pm daily.

■ Erotica
LOVE BOUTIQUE, 2924 Wilshire Blvd, Santa Monica, (310) 453-3459. Women-owned & -operated erotic store, intimate videos, small selection of lesbian & gay videos, games. We do home parties for women to display our products.

LA SOUTH BAY
INCLUDES HAWTHORNE, REDONDO BEACH, INGLEWOOD.,

■ Accommodations
PALOS VERDES INN, 1700 S Pacific Coast Hwy, Redondo Beach, CA, 90277, (310) 316-4211, (800) 421-9241 (USA), Fax: (310) 316-4863. Email: 1700s@aol.com, Gay-friendly hotel, private baths.

■ Bars
DOLPHIN, 1995 Artesia Blvd, Redondo Beach, (310) 318-3339. Beach bar, 50% men, 50% women.
EL CAPITAN, 13825 S Hawthorne Blvd, Hawthorne, (310) 675-3436.

■ Dance Bar/Disco
BABYLON, 2105 Artesia Blvd, Redondo Beach, (310) 793-9393. DJ after 9pm nightly.

MARINA DEL REY

■ Accommodations
MANSION INN, THE, 327 Washington Blvd, Marina del Rey, CA, 90291, (310) 821-2557, (800) 828-0688, Fax: (310) 827-0289. B&B inn with courtyard cafe, 50% gay & lesbian clientele. Private baths, color TV, refrigerators, expanded continental breakfast & nearby beach.

MENDOCINO COUNTY

■ Accommodations
ANNIE'S JUGHANDLE BEACH B & B INN, 32980 Gibney Ln, Ft. Bragg, CA, (707) 964-1415, Fax: (707) 961-1473. B&B cottage in an 1880's Victorian farmhouse, private baths, full breakfast, near Jughandle State Reserve, gay & lesbian following."
INN AT SCHOOLHOUSE CREEK, THE, 7051 N Highway One, Little River, CA, 95456, (707) 937-5525, (800) 731-5525, Fax: (707) 937-2012. Email: al@binnb.com, Web: www.binnb.com, Gay-friendly inn on 10 acres of gardens, private baths, ocean views.
SEA GULL INN B & B, 44594 Albion St, PO Box 317, Mendocino, CA, 95460, (707) 937-5204, (888) 937-5204. Gay-friendly B&B, private baths.
TOLL HOUSE RESTAURANT & INN, 15301 Hwy. 253, PO Box 268, Boonville, CA, 95415, (707) 895-3630, Fax: (707) 895-3632 or (707) 895-3999. Gay-friendly inn with restaurant & bar, private baths.

■ Women's Accommodations
SALLIE & EILEEN'S PLACE, Box 409, Mendocino, CA, 95460, (707) 937-2028 Women-only studio cottage & guesthouse. Kitchens, fireplace in A-frame, sun decks, hot tub. Three miles to ocean & river beaches.
WILDFLOWER RIDGE, Box 685, Albion, CA, 95410, (707) 937-3720, Reservations (510) 735-2079. Women-only cottage, private bath.

■ Retail & Bookstores
BOOK LOFT, 45050 Main St, Mendocino, (707) 937-0890. General bookstore with women's, lesbian & gay section. Metaphysical books.

MENLO PARK

■ Retail & Bookstores
TWO SISTERS BOOKSHOP, 605 Cambridge Ave, (650) 323-4778. Women's books, cards & gifts, goddess art, jewelry, music tapes, CDs, crafts, crystals, posters, T-shirts, weekly events & workshops. 11am-9pm, Sat 10am-5pm, Sun noon-5pm.

MODESTO

Dance Bar/Disco
BRAVE BULL, 701 S 9th St, (209) 529-6712. 60% men, 40% women, 7pm-2am, Sun drag shows.

MUSTANG CLUB, 413 N 7th St, (209) 577-9694. Est. 1966, 11am-2am summer, 2pm-2am winter, patio, drag shows Sun, ladies nite Wed & 3rd Fri of month.

Cafe
ESPRESSO CAFE, 3025-D McHenry Ave, (209) 571-3337. Espresso, pastas, lite menu.

MONTE RIO
SEE RUSSIAN RIVER.,

MONTEREY

Women's Accommodations
MISTY TIGER, THE, (408) 633-8808. Women-only guesthouse in a contemporary home, 15 minutes from downtown Monterey & 5 minutes from the sea. .

Bars
FRANCO'S NORMA JEAN BAR, 10639 Merritt St, Castroville, (408) 633-2090, 633-6129. Restaurant & bar, open Sat only. Huge disco & Latin music, 60% men, 40% women, women come earlier in evening.

LIGHTHOUSE BAR & GRILL, 281 Lighthouse, (408) 373-4488.

Dance Bar/Disco
AFTER DARK, BACKLOT, 214 Lighthouse Ave, near Reeside, (408) 373-7828. Video dance bar, 70% men, 30% women.

MORRO BAY - SAN LUIS OBISPO

Information
GAY & LESBIAN ALLIANCE (GALA), 1306A Higuera St, San Luis Obispo, (805) 541-4252. Networking, dances, picnics, newsletter. They have info on numerous other local groups. Mon-Fri 5:30pm-8:30pm.

WOMEN'S RESOURCE CENTER, 1009 Morro St #201, San Luis Obispo, (805) 544-9313. For all women, meetings, network center, monthly newspaper called Women's Press.

Women's Accommodations
AMBER HILLS, 7720 Rocky Rd, Paso Robles, CA, (805) 239-2073. B&B in a country setting, private bath, expanded continental breakfast, color cable TV, AC, nearby pool & ocean, men welcome.

CASA DE AMIGAS, 1202 8th St, Los Osos, CA, 93402, (805) 528-3701. B&B, private bath.

Cafe
LINNAEA'S CAFE, 1110 Garden St, San Luis Obispo, (805) 541-5888. Healthful cuisine, lunch.

Restaurants
BIG SKY MODERN FOOD, 1121 Broad St, San Luis Obispo, (805) 545-5401.

Retail & Bookstores
VOLUMES OF PLEASURE, 1016 Los Osos Valley Rd, Los Osos, (805) 528-5565, 528-3701. General bookstore with large gay, lesbian & women's sections & info center. Mon-Sat 10am-6pm, Sun 11am-4pm.

MOUNTAIN VIEW

Bars
DAYBREAK, 1711 W El Camino Real, (415) 940-9778. DJ Fri-Sat, Karaoke Thur & Sat. 30% men & 70% women."

NAPA VALLEY

Retail & Bookstores
ARIADNE BOOKS, 3780 Bel Aire Plaza, (707) 253-9402. Metaphysical, health, recovery book center with women's books & espresso bar.

OAKLAND

Information
GAY SWITCHBOARD & PACIFIC CENTER, 2712 Telegraph Ave, (510) 841-6224. Mon, Tues, Fri 8-10pm, Wed 4-6pm. Group meetings."

Dance Bar/Disco
★ **BENCH & BAR,** 120 11th St, near Oak, (510) 444-2266.

CABEL'S REEF, 2272 Telegraph Ave, (510) 451-3777.

★ **WHITE HORSE,** 6551 Telegraph Ave, at 66th St, (510) 652-3820. 50% men, 50% women.

WOMEN'S COUNTRY NIGHTS, 3903 Broadway/40th St, at Masonic Hall, (510) 428-2144. Every Fri, 80-100 women. Lessons 7:30-8:30pm, dancing 8:45-11:30pm. Smoke-, alcohol- & perfume-free, no experience or partner needed.

Retail & Bookstores

MAMA BEARS CULTURE CENTER, 6536 Telegraph Ave, at 66th, (510) 428-9684, (800) 643-8629, Fax: (510) 654-2774. A full-service women's bookstore and coffee bar. It's comfortable and spacious. Open every day 10:30am-8pm, including Sundays and holidays. Centrally located 20 minutes from San Francisco. Mail-order available.

OCEANSIDE

Bars

CAPRI LOUNGE, 207 N Tremont St, (760) 722-7284. 95% men, women welcome.

Dance Bar/Disco

GREYSTOKES GRILL, 1903 S Coast Hwy, (619) 757-2955. Dance bar, DJ & piano bar Fri & restaurant with burgers, chicken sandwiches, steaks. 60% women, 40% men.

ORANGE COUNTY

SEE ALSO ANAHEIM.,

Information

AIDS LINE, (714) 534-0961, 10am-6pm Mon-Fri.

GAY & LESBIAN COMMUNITY CENTER, 12832 Garden Grove Blvd, #A, Garden Grove, Office: (714) 534-0862. 10am-10pm weekdays.

Accommodations

HUNTINGTON BEACH HOUSE BED & BREAKFAST, 609 Main St, Huntington Beach, CA, 92648, (714) 536-7818, Fax: (714) 536-7818. B&B & cottage with private & shared baths, full breakfast weekends, continental breakfast weekdays. Cottage has color TV, ceiling fans, kitchen, coffee/tea-making facilities. 25% gay/lesbian clientele.

Bars

TIN LIZZIE SALOON, 752 St Clair, Costa Mesa, (714) 966-2029.

Dance Bar/Disco

EL CALOR, 2916 W Lincoln, at Beach Blvd, Anaheim, (714) 527-8873. Gay Wed only with drag show, disco with Latin, house & techno.

★ **HAPPY HOUR,** 12081 Garden Grove Blvd, near West St, Garden Grove, (714) 537-9079. Live bands, videos.

LION'S DEN, 719 W 19th St, at Federal, Costa Mesa, (714) 645-3830. DJ Tue, Fri-Sun. 60% men, 40% women. Sat ladies night.

★ **OZZ SUPPER CLUB,** 6231 Manchester, Buena Park, (714) 522-1542. Hi-en-

---

THE HAPPY HOUR

SUNDAYS
$5 Beer Bust, 2pm-6pm
TUESDAYS
Free Pool 7pm-11pm, $1.75 Beer
WEDNESDAYS
$1.75 Bottle Beer, Schnapps,
Well Drinks, 6pm-10pm
THURSDAYS
Karaoke, Sing with Delby
9pm-Midnight
FRIDAYS
DANCE, DANCE, DANCE
D.J.
SATURDAYS
D.J.

12081 Garden Grove Blvd.
Garden Grove, CA 92643
(714) 537-9079

CALIFORNIA

ergy dance bar, DJ nightly, piano lounge, cabaret, restaurant, 60% men, 40% women. Open Wed-Mon (many women Wed & Sun), Mon men's C&W & Wed ladis C&W nites, Thurs male strippers.

PALM SPRINGS - CATHEDRAL CITY

Information
AIDS LINE, (760) 323-2118.

Accommodations
ARUBA RESORT APARTMENTS, 671 S Riverside Dr, Palm Springs, CA, 92264, (760) 325-8440 (Tel/Fax), (800) 84-ARUBA. Resort hotel, 50% gay & lesbian clientele. Color TV, VCR, AC, kitchens, king beds & private baths. Pool & Jacuzzi on premises. Small pets permitted, member IGTA."

DESERT PALMS INN, 67-580 E Palm Canyon Dr, Palm Springs, CA, 92234, (800) 801-8696, (760) 324-3000, Fax: (760) 770-5031. Inn with restaurant, bar & shops, women welcome. Private baths, color TV, AC, business services, Jacuzzi & pool."

HEDY'S HIDEAWAY, (310) 652-9600, (800) GAY-0069, Fax: (310) 652-5454. B&B, private bath, full American breakfast.

INN OF THE THREE PALMS, 370 W Arenas Rd, Palm Springs, CA, 92262, (760) 323-2767, (800) 611-PALM (7256). Resort hotel in downtown Palm Springs, Jacuzzi & pool on premises, walk to gay bars, 50% gay/lesbian clientele.

MIRA LOMA HOTEL, THE, 1420 N Indian Canyon Dr, Palm Springs, CA, 92262, (760) 320-1178, Fax: (760) 320-5308. Motel, private baths, continental (wkdays) & full (wknds) breakfast, pool on premises, 50% gay/lesbian clientele.

PRISCILLA'S APARTMENTS, 528 S Camino Real, Palm Springs, CA, 92264, (760) 416-0168 (Tel/Fax), (888) 289-9555. Apartmets with TV, VCR, pool on premises, some straight clientele.

The Palm Springs Private Hotel For Women

BEE CHARMER INN

- Pool and Private Courtyard
- Outdoor Misting System
- Refrigerators and Microwaves
- Cable Television
- Air Conditioning
- Continental Breakfast
- Minutes from Clubs, Restaurants, Hiking, Golf, and Tennis

For Reservations or Brochure Call: **(760) 778-5883**
1600 East Palm Canyon Dr., Palm Springs, CA 92264 • e-mail: beecharmps@aol.com

CALIFORNIA

Women's Accommodations
BEE CHARMER INN, 1600 E Palm Canyon Dr, Palm Springs, CA, 92264, (760) 778-5883. Email: beecharmps@aol.com, Private women's hotel with 14 rooms decorated in southwestern pastels. Located in the heart of Palm Springs, minutes from clubs, restaurants, recreational venues, and attractions of the fabulous gay desert. Nonsmoking rooms include private baths, color TVs, microwaves, refrigerator/honor bar, phone & AC. French doors open poolside, where continental breakfast is served each morning. ♀ See ad on page 251.

Transportation
RAINBOW CAB CO., (760) 327-5702. Gay-owned & -operated cab company.

Bars
BACKSTREET PUB, 72-695 Hwy 111, A-7, Palm Desert., (760) 341-7966 Small dance floor & games, 70% men, 30% women.

DATES POOLSIDE BAR, at the Villa Resort, 67-670 Carey Rd, Cathedral City, (760) 328-7211. Popular Sat & Sun brunch, Sun T dance 2pm-6pm. ♀♂

LOVE SHACK, THE, at the Sundance Saloon, 36737 Cathedral Canyon, Cathedral City, (760) 321-0031. Ladies bar from 5pm. ♀

RAINBOW CACTUS CAFE BAR, 212 S Indian Ave, Palm Springs., Bar & restaurant. ♂

SWEETWATER SALOON, 2420 N Palm Canyon Dr, Palm Springs, (760) 320-8878. 11am-2am 7days, pool table, darts, pub food till midnite. ♂

Dance Bar/Disco
AMNESIA, 68-449 Perez Rd, Big dance club.

★ **CC'S ON SUNRISE,** 1775 E Palm Canyon Dr, (760) 778-1234. Large venue, 2 dance floors, 5 pool tables. ♂

SUNDANCE SALOON, 36737 Cathedral Canyon, in Cathedral City, (760) 321-0031. Hi NRG dance club. ∪♀♂

Restaurants
BLUE ANGEL, 777 E Tahquitz Canyon Hwy, Palm Springs, (760) 778-4343. Seaks. ♀♂

BLUE COYOTE GRILL, 445 N Palm Canyon Dr, Palm Springs., Mexican & Southwestern cuisine. Lunch, dinner, patio dining, gay-friendly."

DATES CAFE, 67-670 Carey Rd, at Villa Hotel, Cathedral City., ♀♂

GOLDEN TRIANGLES, 68-805 Hwy 111, Cathedral City, (760) 324-9113. Thai & French cuisine.

IGUANA GRILL, at Desert Palms Inn., ♀♂

MICHAEL'S CAFE, 68-665 Hwy 111, Cathedral City., Gay-friendly, breakfast & lunch."

MORTIMER'S, 2095 N Indian Canyon, Palm Springs, (760) 320-4333. Upscale, elegant, expensive continental fare.

RAINBOW CACTUS CAFE, 212 S Indian Ave, Palm Springs., Bar & restaurant. ♂

RED TOMATO, 68-784 Hwy 111, Cathedral City, (760) 328-7518. Pizza & pasta, dinner only."

★ **SHAME ON THE MOON,** 69-950 Frank Sinatra Dr, Rancho Mirage, (760) 324-5515. Northern Italian, patio dining, reservations advised 2-3 weeks ahead. ♀♂

WILD GOOSE, 67938 Hwy 111, Cathedral City, (760) 328-5775. Award-winning continental cuisine, dinner only."

Retail & Bookstores
GAY MART, 305 E Arenas Rd, Palm Springs, (760) 320-0606. Cards, swimsuits, T-shirts, videos.

Leathers/Piercing
BLACK MOON LEATHER, 68-449 Perez Rd, Cathedral City, (760) 328-7773, 770-2925. Gay department store.

Erotica
PEREZ VIDEOS & BOOKS, 68-366 Perez Rd, Cathedral City, (760) 321-5597, 24hrs.

PALO ALTO

Information
STANFORD LESBIAN, GAY, BISEXUAL COMMUNITY CENTER, (650) 723-1488 events tape, (650) 725-4222 live. Mon-Fri noon-6pm.

Retail & Bookstores
STEPPING STONES — THE

CALIFORNIA 253

ARTIFACTORY, 226 Hamilton Ave, (650) 853-9685. Feminist bookstore & artist's gallery, Tues-Sat 10am-6pm.

PASADENA

Dance Bar/Disco
CLUB 3772, 3772 E Foothill Blvd, (818) 578-9359. C&W dance lessons Tues, live entertainment Fri & Sat, men welcome.

ENCOUNTERS, 203 N Sierra Madre Blvd, (818) 792-3735. Video dance bar, 85% men, 15% women, patio.

Restaurants
CAFE SOL, 1453 N Lake Ave, (626) 797-9903.

HOLLY ST. BAR & GRILL, 175 E Holly St, (818) 440-1421. American cuisine.

PASO ROBLES

Women's Accommodations
CAMP LLAMA B & B, Box 116, Lockwood, CA, 93932, (408) 385-6755 (tel/fax). Spend the night enroute between LA & San Francisco, 1/2 hour from Paso Robles, midway between LA & SF on Hwy 101. Room with queen bed on a llama ranch. Private baths, bountiful breakfast. Stroll amongst the llamas before departing or stay on for a hike with llamas. ♀

PETALUMA

Retail & Bookstores
BOOSHA, 125 Petaluma Blvd, (behind Starbucks), (707) 773-4602. Card, gifts, jewelry.

PLEASANT HILL

Information
RAINBOW COMMUNITY CENTER, (510) 210-0563. For central Contra Costa County.

POMONA

Bars
MARY'S, 1047 E 2nd St, (909) 622-1971. Bar & restaurant, 70% women, 30% men.

Dance Bar/Disco
ROBBIE'S, 390 College Plaza East, (909) 620-4371. 70% men, 30% women, male

Women's Llama Treks

- Day Hikes • BBQ • B&B •
- Hot Tub Soaks •

Paso Robles, California

(408) 385-6755

CAMP LLAMA

strippers weekends, female strippers Thurs, upstairs cabaret, Sun buffet. 🎵 📺 ♀♂

Restaurants
MARY'S, 1047 E 2nd St, at Mary's bar., Dinner, soups, sandwiches." 🍸 ♀♂

REDDING

Bars
FIVE O ONE, THE, 1244 California St, (916) 243-7869. DJ weekends, 60% men, 40% women. ✖ 🎵 ♀♂

REDWOOD CITY

Bars
SHOUTS BAR & GRILL, 2034 Broadway, (650) 369-9651. jukebox, pool table, 65% men, 35% women. 🎵 ♂

Retail & Bookstores
BEANS ON BROADWAY, 2209 Broadway, (650) 369-3335. Cafe, gifts, cards, women's art gallery & women's books, Tues-Sat 12pm-9pm.

RIVERSIDE

Bars
MENAGERIE, 3581 University, (909) 788-8000. DJ Fri-Sun, Wed & Sun beer busts, karaoke Mon, 50% women Mon. 🏨 🎵 ♂

Fern Falls

Romance amidst redwoods!

- natural waterfall
- swimming hole
- creek & gardens
- private cabins
- fireplaces
- spa & nudity
- pets OK

Close to Guerneville

(707) 632-6108

PO Box 228 · Cazadero CA 95421

RUSSIAN RIVER

Accommodations
APPLEWOOD INN AND RESTAURANT, 13555 Hwy 116, Guerneville, CA, 95446, (707) 869-9093, (800) 555-8509. Email: stay@applewoodinn.com, Web: http://applewoodinn.com, B&B, mostly straight clientele. Comfortable, elegant rooms with private baths. Hot tub, massage, full breakfast & other meals on request." 🍽

FERN FALLS, 5701 Austin Creek Rd, PO Box 228, Cazadero, CA, 95421, (707) 632-6108, Fax: (707) 632-6216. Choose from four cottages or a suite in the main house. A curved deck looks over the on-premises creek and ravine. Amenities include color cable TV, VCR, kitchen, refrigerator, and fireplaces in the cottages. An ozonator spa is on the hill. Nearby enjoy wine tasting, horseback riding, canoeing on the Russian River, or hiking in the redwood forests. 🐾 ♀♂

FIFE'S RESORT, 16467 River Rd, Guerneville, CA, 95446, (707) 869-0656, toll-free in CA only: (800) 7FIFES1, Fax: (707) 869-0658. Gay-owned & -operated cottage, cabins & tent sites. Restaurant, gay bar & disco on premises. Mostly men with women welcome. ♂

GOLDEN APPLE RANCH, 17575 Fitzpatrick Lane, Occidental, CA, 95465, (707) 874-3756, Fax: (707) 874-1670. Art gallery lodge with 50% gay & lesbian clientele. Suites, apts & cottage. Phone, private baths, & most suites with satellite color TV. Continental breakfast. Nearby river & ocean beaches.

HIGHLAND DELL INN BED & BREAKFAST, 21050 River Blvd, Box 370, Monte Rio, CA, 95462-0370, (707) 865-1759, (800) 767-1759. Email: highland@netdex.com, Victorian lodge on the river, 50% gay & lesbian (sometimes more). Large, comfortable rooms with private & shared baths, TV lounge, weights, expanded continental breakfast. UNDER CONSTRUCTION. To open May '97. 🍽

HIGHLANDS RESORT, PO Box 346, 14000 Woodland Dr, Guerneville, CA, 95446, (707) 869-0333, Fax: (707) 869-0370. Email: highlands@wclynx.com,

CALIFORNIA

Web: www.travel.org/HighlandsResort, Inn and campground. Variety of guest quarters, 20 tent sites, TV lounge, massage, hot tub, continental breakfast.

HUCKLEBERRY SPRINGS, PO Box 400, Monte Rio, CA, 95462, (707) 865-2683, (800) 822-2683. Email: hucksprings@netdex.com, Deluxe cottages, 50% gay & lesbian. Each residence uniquely decorated. Wood stoves, TV lounge, Jacuzzi, massage, full breakfast & nearby river.

INN AT OCCIDENTAL, THE, 3657 Church St, Occidental, (707) 874-1311, (800) 551-2292. Gay-friendly inn with restaurant. Large airy rooms, private baths & full breakfast.

JACQUES' COTTAGE, 6471 Old Trenton Road, Forestville, CA, 95436, (707) 575-1033, (800) 246-1033, Fax: (707) 573-8911. Email: jacques@wco.com, Web: www.wco.com/~jacques, Cottage, women welcome.

MOUNTAIN LODGE RESORT, PO Box 169, 16350 1st St, Guerneville, CA, 95446, (707) 869-3722, Fax: (707) 869-0556. Resort, 50% gay & lesbian clientele. Condo-style suites with modern conveniences, Jacuzzi."

RIO VILLA BEACH RESORT, 20292 Hwy 116, Monte Rio, CA, 95462, (707) 865-1143, Fax: (707) 865-0115. Email: riovilla@sonic.net, Web: http://sonic.net/~riovilla, Beach resort, 50% gay & lesbian clientele. Charming, spacious rooms, color/B/W TVs, outdoor fireplace, beach access. Continental breakfast on weekends.

RIVER VIEW RETREAT, PO Box 204, Guerneville, CA, 95446, (707) 869-3040 (Tel/Fax). Email: hermpc@sonic.net, Vacation rental home with 2 bedrooms, views, balcony overlooking river.

RUSSIAN RIVER RESORT, PO Box 2419, Guerneville, CA, 95446, (707) 869-0691, (800) 41 RESORT (737678), Fax: (707) 869-0698. Resort, restaurant & bar, private baths.

STILLWATER COVE RANCH, 22555 Coast Hwy 1, Box 5, Jenner, CA, 95450, (707) 847-3227. Gay-friendly accommodations & restaurant, private baths.

TWIN TOWERS RIVER RANCH, 615 Bailhache Ave, Healdsburg, CA, 95448, (707) 433-4443. Gay-friendly B&B with 2 rooms & 2 efficiency apartments built into a barn structure. Gays & lesbians especially welcome.

VILLA MESSINA, 316 Burgundy Rd, Healdsburg, CA, 95448, (707) 433-6655, Fax: (707) 433-4515. A landmark bed and breakfast inn. Enjoy unsurpassed comfort and hospitality, panoramic 360 degree views from vineyards to the geysers. Twenty minutes from downtown Guerneville, yet a world away. Antiques, fine linens, TV, VCR, telephones, Jacuzzi, fireplace and superb Sonoma breakfast."

VILLAGE INN, PO Box 850, Monte Rio, CA, 95462, (707) 865-2304, (800) 303-2303. Hotel with restaurant & bar, 50% gay & lesbian clientele. Variety of rooms with private & shared baths. To reopen.

WILLOWS, THE, PO Box 465, 15905 River Rd, Guerneville, CA, 95446, (707) 869-2824, (800) 953-2828, Fax: (707) 869-2764. Bed & breakfast & camping on the river. Double rooms with TVs, private & shared baths. Hot tub, sauna, expanded continental breakfast, coffee & tea. Canoe use, 120 tent sites, toilets & showers."

■ Bars

MT'S BULL PEN, 16251 Main St, Guerneville,. Sports bar.

RAINBOW CATTLE CO, 16220 Main St, near Armstrong Woods, Guerneville, (707) 869-0206. 80% men, 20% women.

RIVER BUSINESS, 16225 1st St, Guerneville, (707) 869-0885, Very "LA", pool table, closed Tue.

TRIPLE R, PO Box 2419, at Russian River Resort, (707) 869-0691. Indoor & outdoor lounges, 60% men, 40% women."

■ Dance Bar/Disco

MOLLY'S COUNTRY CLUB, 14120 Old Cazadero Rd, near River Rd, Guerneville, (707) 869-0511. C&W bar & restaurant with steaks, etc, 50% men, 50% women."

■ Restaurants

BURDON'S, 15405 River Rd, near Riverside, Guerneville, (707) 869-2615. Restaurant & bar, continental cuisine.

CAPE FEAR, Hwy 116, in Duncan's

Mills, Breakfast thru dinner, steaks & burgers.

CAT'S PLACE, Hwy 116, in Guernwood Park, Women-run cafe diner inside another restaurant called Georgia's Hideaway.

CHEZ MARIE, 6675 Front St, Forestville, (707) 887-7503. Sonoma County French cuisine.

FARMHOUSE INN RESTAURANT, River Rd, Forestville, (707) 887-3300. Awardwinning chef.

JOHN ASH & CO, 4330 Barnes Rd, at River Rd, Santa Rosa, (707) 527-7687.

MOLLY'S COUNTRY CLUB, 14120 Old Cazadero Rd, at Molly's Country Club, (707) 869-0511.

NORTHWARD ROADHOUSE, 19400 Hwy 116, Monte Rio at Northwood Golf Course, (707) 865-2454. California cuisine.

SWEET'S RIVER GRILL, 16251 Main St, Guerneville, (707) 869-3383. Restaurant & cocktail lounge.

VILLAGE INN, PO Box 850, at Village Inn resort, Forestville, (707) 865-2304. Sun brunch.

SACRAMENTO

Information

AIDS LINE, (916) 448-AIDS (2437), Mon-Fri 9am-5pm, or tape.

LAMBDA COMMUNITY CENTER, 920 20th St, (916) 442-0185.

WOMEN'S CENTER, 6000 J Street, in Student Services Center, (916) 278-7388.

Accommodations

HARTLEY HOUSE INN, 700 Twenty-Second St, Sacramento, CA, 95816-4012, (916) 447-7829, (800) 831-5806, Fax: (916) 447-1820. Email: randy@hartleyhouse.com, Web: http://www.hartleyhouse.com, B&B, 50% gay & lesbian clientele. Variety of rooms with colonial flavor & modern conveniences, library, full breakfast, beverages, snacks."

Bars

JOSEPH'S T&C, 1455 De Paso Blvd, (916) 483-1220. Bar & restaurant, small dance floor, lunch, dinner, 10am-2am, 7 days.

MIRAGE, THE, 601 15th St, at F St (916) 444-3238. Sports bar, pool table, darts, popular with women, dancing Sat.

Dance Bar/Disco

★ **FACES,** 2000 K St, at 20th, (916) 448-7798. Video, dance & cruise bar, patio bar. Women's night Wed, free BBQ Sun, C&W dancing early evening.

Cafe

GRETA'S CAFE, 1831 Capitol Ave, (916) 442-7382. Popular with women, especially for breakfast.

NEW HELVETIA COFFEEHOUSE, 19th St, between L & Capitol.,

Restaurants

BARRETTA'S, 1221 Alhambra Blvd, (916) 737-0694.

ERNESTO'S, 16th & S Sts., Mexican cuisine.

HAMBURGER MARY'S, 1630 J St, (916) 441-4340.

Retail & Bookstores

HER PLACE, 6635 Madison Ave, Carmichael, (916) 961-1058. Metaphysical bookstore, goddess & spirituality items.

JUDY'S GIFTS & BOOKS, 2231 J Street, (916) 443-3236. Recovery bookstore with a small gay & lesbian selection.

LIONESS BOOKS, 2224 J St, (916) 442-4657. Feminist bookstore with gay & lesbian literature. Music, gifts & cards.

OPEN BOOK, THE, 910 21st St, (916) 498-1004. Gay & lesbian bookstore & coffeehouse, 7 days, 9am-midnight.

POSTCARDS ETC, 2101 L St, (916) 446-8049. Cards & gifts.

ST HELENA

Accommodations

INK HOUSE BED & BREAKFAST, THE, 1575 St. Helena Hwy at Whitehall Ln, St. Helena, CA, 94574, (707) 963-3890. B&B, mainly straight clientele. Rooms decorated with antique furniture. Panoramic view of NAPA Valley, expanded continental breakfast. Pool & lake nearby.

SAN BERNARDINO

Information
GAY & LESBIAN HOTLINE, (909) 882-4488. 6:30pm-10pm, 7-days.

Bars
LARK, 917 Inland Center Dr, (909) 884-8770. Jukebox, pool table, opens 10 or 11am.

SAN DIEGO

Information
AIDS FOUNDATION S.D., 4080 Centre St, Hillcrest, (619) 686-5000, Linea en Español: 686-5001.

AIDS INFO, San Diego (619) 291-1400, La Mesa (619) 668-6286. Being Alive organization.

CENTER FOR WOMEN'S STUDIES & SERVICES, 2467 E St, Golden Hill, (619) 233-3088.

GAY & LESBIAN INFO LINE, (619) 692-2077. Mon-Sat 9am-10pm or tape. Center at 3916 Normal St. Info Line (619) 692-GAYS 6pm-10pm daily."

LESBIAN & GAY MEN'S COMMUNITY CENTER, 3916 Normal St, (619) 692-GAYS, 693-2077. 9am-10pm. Walk-in till 6pm.

Accommodations
BALBOA PARK INN, 3402 Park Blvd, San Diego, CA, 92103, (619) 298-0823, (800) 938-8181, Fax: (619) 294-8070. Web: www.balboaparkinn.com, Is the finest Bed & Breakfast Inn, located in the Hillcrest area. 26 distinctive, immaculate and beautifully appointed suites. Free continental breakfast, HBO & local calls. When you want to stay at the very best, stay with us.

BANKER'S HILL BED & BREAKFAST, 3315 Second Ave, San Diego, CA, (619) 260-0673, (800) 338-3748, Fax: (619) 260-0674. Email: bhbb@inreach.com, Web: http://home.inreach.com/BHBB/, B&B walking distance to Hillcrest. Suites available, hot tub, expanded continental breakfast, pool on premises.

BAYVIEW GALLERY BED & BREAKFAST, 2005 Loring St, San Diego, CA, (619) 581-3331, E-mail: fritzklein@aol.com. B&B with private & shared baths, some straight clientele.

Visit San Diego
(800) CARITAS
Caritas B&B Network

BEACH PLACE, THE, 2158 Sunset Cliffs Blvd, San Diego, CA, 92107, (619) 225-0746. Suites for one to four people, women welcome. Accommodations include a living room, bedroom, kitchenette, private bath, closed circuit television and private deck, with a Jacuzzi in the courtyard. We are four blocks from the beach, minutes from the Hillcrest area and close to all San Diego attractions. Nightly and weekly rates.

CARITAS BED & BREAKFAST NETWORK, (800) CARITAS, (312) 857-0801, Fax: (312) 857-0805. B&B, home-stay accommodations service. Member: IGLTA

DMITRI'S GUESTHOUSE, 931 21st St, San Diego, CA, 92102, (619) 238-5547. Enjoy San Diego's most popular gay guesthouse, overlooking downtown in one of San Diego's historic turn-of-the-century neighborhoods. We offer a variety of accommodations, heated pool &

BALBOA PARK INN
San Diego's Finest Bed & Breakfast
Comprised of 26 Individually Designed Suites • Fireplaces & Jacuzzis • Close to all the Action • Located in a Quiet Residential area next door to the Zoo, Balboa Park and the heart of the Hillcrest Area.

When You Care To Stay At The Very Best San Diego Has To Offer

(800) 938-8181
(619) 298-0823 Fax: (619) 294-8070

spa, continental breakfast daily at poolside. We pride ourselves on creating a relaxed and comfortable atmosphere for the gay & lesbian traveler. Reasonable rates, women most welcome.

HILLCREST INN, THE, 3754 5th Ave, San Diego, CA, 92103, (619) 293-7078, (800) 258-2280, Fax: (619) 293-3861. Hotel, some straight clientele. Double rooms with modern conveniences, kitchenettes, patios, snack machines & nearby ocean beach.

KASA KORBETT, 1526 Van Buren Ave, San Diego, CA, 92103, (619) 291-3962, (800) 757-KASA (5272), Fax: (619) 298-9150. B&B in a 70-year-old craftsman-design home, private & shared baths, expanded continental breakfast, 4 blocks to gay bars, pool & ocean nearby.

KEATING HOUSE, 2331 Second Ave, San Diego, CA, 92101-1505, (619) 239-8585, (800) 995-8644, Fax: (619) 239-5774. B&B, 50% gay & lesbian. Individually decorated rooms with private & shared baths, gardens, full breakfast. Nearby ocean beach.

PARK MANOR SUITES HOTEL, 525 Spruce St, San Diego, CA, 92103, (619) 291-0999, (800) 874-2649, Fax: (619) 291-8844. Hotel with private baths, 60% gay/lesbian clientele."

PEA SOUP ANDERSEN'S INN, 850 Palomar Airport Rd, Carlsbad, CA, 92008, (800) 266-7880, (760) 438-7880, Fax: (760) 438-1015. Gay-friendly hotel with restaurant, bar, disco & shops. Private baths.

■ Transportation
SUNSET LIMOUSINES, (619) 294-9156.

■ Bars
★ **FLICKS,** 1017 University Ave, near 10th, (619) 297-2056. Video social bar with music videos. Male & female dancers, live comedy, dating game.

MATADOR, 4633 Mission Blvd, near Emerald, Pacific Beach, (619) 483-6943. Beach bar, women welcome. Very popular Sun eve.

THIRTY-EIGHT THIRTY-EIGHT 5TH, 3838 5th Ave, (619) 543-0300. From 6pm, 7 days, singers, drag shows, karaoke, appetizers.

■ Dance Bar/Disco
★ **CLUB BOMBAY,** 3175 India St, (619) 296-6789. Video dance bar, live entertainment, karaoke, patio.

CLUB MONTAGE, 2028 Hancock St, (619) 294-9590. Hi engergy video dance bar, 3 levels, 5 rooms, rooftop patio. Wed, Fri, Sat from 9pm, after hours till 4am Sat.

FLAME, 3780 Park Blvd, near University, (619) 295-4163. Southern California's hottest women's nightclub. High energy dance club 7 nights a week. Three bars, large dance floor. Diverse nightly entertainment. Our exclusive Ultra Suede Lounge every Saturday. Tuesday unofficial men's night. San Diego's most popu-

---

DANCING

COCKTAILS

POOL

The Hottest Women's NightClub on the Planet

the 7 flame

3780 Park Blvd.
SAN DIEGO, CA
(619) 295-4163

lar drag review Friday nights. For a good time call (619) 295-4163.

★ **KICKERS,** 308 University Ave, Hillcrest, (619) 491-0400. C&W dance bar, patio, videos. Best Thurs & Sat, Hamburger Mary's restaurant on patio.

Cafe

★ **DAVID'S PLACE,** 3766 Fifth Ave, Hillcrest, (619) 294-8908. Coffeehouse, patio garden, after hours Fri & Sat. "A positive place for positive people and their friends."

EUPHORIA, 1045 University Ave, (619) 542-0445.

LIVING ROOM, 1417 University Ave, (619) 291-8518.

STARBUCK'S, 5th & Robinson.

Restaurants

BAYOU BAR & GRILL, 329 Market St, (619) 696-8747. Upscale, Creole & Cajun, lunch & dinner, gay-friendly.

BIG KITCHEN, 3003 Grape St, (619) 234-5789. Breakfast, lunch.

CAFE ELEVEN, University & Normal.

CALIFORNIA CUISINE, 1027 University Ave, (619) 543-0790. Expensive, beautiful presentation.

CITY DELI, 535 University, (619) 295-2747. Popular with local gays.

CREST CAFE, 425 Robinsons, near 5th, Hillcrest, (619) 295-2510. Modern cafe with large gay clientele.

HAMBURGER MARY'S, 308 University, at Kickers, (619) 491-0400. Lunch & dinner.

JIMMY CARTER'S, 3172 5th Ave, (619) 295-2070. Dinner-style.

MARK'S ON 4TH, 4th Ave.

MIXX, 5th Ave., Very popular with gays & lesbians.

MOONSTRUCK CAFE, 3843 Richmond St, (619) 295-6620.

TASTE OF SZECHUAN, 670 University Ave, (619) 298-1638.

Retail & Bookstores

BLUE DOOR BOOKSTORE, 3823 5th Ave, Hillcrest, (619) 298-8610. General bookstore with strong gay & lesbian sections.

GAY MART, 6th & University.

OBELISK THE BOOKSTORE, 1029 University Ave, Hillcrest, (619) 297-4171. Gay & lesbian bookstore with cards, jewelry & T-shirts.

RAINBOW ROOM, 141 University Ave, (619) 296-8222. Rainbow store, 10am-10pm.

SIXTH AT PENN THEATER, 6th at Penn., Gay & lesbian theater.

Leathers/Piercing

CRYPT AT WOLFS, 3404 30th St, at Wolfs bar, (619) 574-1579. Leather store featuring an extensive line of leathers, lubes, safe-sex toys & magazines. Thurs-Sun 9pm-2am.

CRYPT ON WASHINGTON, 1515 Washington St, in Hillcrest, (619) 692-9499. Magazines, safe-sex toys, gifts, leather repair, body jewelry, piercing, 10am-10pm (Sun 2-10pm)."

Erotica

NORTH PARK ADULT VIDEO, 4094 30th St, at Polk, (619) 284-4724.

SAN FRANCISCO INTRO

Information

BAY AREA CAREER WOMEN, (415) 495-5393. Mon-Fri 9am-5pm. Write 55 New Montgomery St, Suite 321, San Francisco, CA 94105."

EUREKA VALLEY HARVEY MILK MEMORIAL BRANCH LIBRARY, 3555 16th St, (415) 554-9445. Comprehensive gay & lesbian collection.

WOMEN'S BATHS, see South Van Ness, Mission Area.

WOMEN'S CENTER, at Women's Bldg., See South Van Ness, Mission Area."

Accommodations

CARITAS BED & BREAKFAST NETWORK, (800) CARITAS, (312) 857-0801, Fax: (312) 857-0805. B&B, home-stay accommodations service. Member: IGLTA

JOIE DE VIVRE INC., San Francisco, CA, (415) 835-0300, (800) 738-7477. Web:

CALIFORNIA

www.joiedevivre-sf.com, Great rates at San Francisco's unique gay-friendly accommodations. Luxurious B&Bs to Union Square charmers to popularly priced motor lodges.

MI CASA SU CASA, PO Box 10327, Oakland, CA, (510) 268-8534, USA toll-free (800) 215-CASA (2272), Fax: 268-0299. International and domestic home exchange and hospitality network for lesbian, gay and gay-friendly travelers. ♀♂

Transportation

REGENCY LIMOUSINE, (415) 922-0123, (800) 922-0123, fax: (415) 922-7602. Gay-owned & -operated.

Restaurants

TAVOLINO, 401 Columbus Ave at Vallejo, in North Beach area, near Fisherman's Wharf, Italian cuisine, gay-friendly.

Retail & Bookstores

WOMEN'S BOOKSTORES, see South Van Ness, Mission Area.

Erotica

WOMEN'S EROTICA, see South Van Ness, Mission Area.

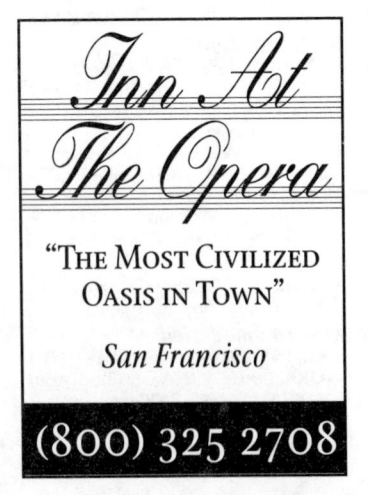

SF WESTERN DISTRICTS
(Includes Alamo Square, Haight, Pacific Hts.,Fillmore areas)

Accommodations

ALAMO SQUARE BED & BREAKFAST INN, 719 Scott St, San Francisco, CA, 94117, (415) 922-2055, (800) 345-9888, Fax: (415) 931-1304. Web: http://www.alamoinn.com., Victorian B&B with cozy guest rooms & luxurious, suites. All private baths, full breakfast, free off-street parking. Gay-friendly & owner-operated.

BOCK'S BED & BREAKFAST, 1448 Willard St, San Francisco, CA, 94117, (415) 664-6842, Fax: (415) 664-1109. B&B, some straight clientele. Various units from plain to deluxe with beverage service & continental breakfast. Pool nearby, beach 3 miles. ♀♂

CHATEAU TIVOLI, 1057 Steiner St, San Francisco, CA, 94115, (415) 776-5462, (800) 228-1647, Fax: (415) 776-0505. Web: www.citysearch.com/sfo/chateautivoli, B&B, 50% gay and lesbian. Spacious rooms with fireplaces, stained glass, stunning views. Expanded continental breakfast Mon-Fri, full champagne breakfast Sat, Sun.

INN 1890, 1890 Page St, San Francisco, CA, 94117, (415) 386-0486, (888) INN-1890 (466-1890), Fax: (415) 386-3626. Email: inn1890@worldnet.att.net, Web: http://adamsnet.com/inn1890, Gay-owned & -operated B&B in a Queen Anne Victorian, expanded continental breakfast, private & shared baths, 10 min. from the Castro, 50% gay & lesbian.

INN AT THE OPERA, 333 Fulton St, San Francisco, CA, 94102, (415) 863-8400, (800) 325-2708, Fax: (415) 861-0821. Twenty-nine guestrooms and 18 suites, each decorated in pastel colors with queen-sized canopy beds and oversized pillows. Gusets enjoy twice-daily maid service, daily valet and room service. Complimentary breakfast is served in the inn's restaurant which, in the evening, is transformed into an elegant club-like setting, where people sit in conversational clusters of cushy chairs

---

Inn At The Opera

"THE MOST CIVILIZED OASIS IN TOWN"

San Francisco

(800) 325 2708

and sofas, drinking flutes of champagne and aperitifs.

METRO HOTEL, THE, 319 Divisadero St, San Francisco, CA, 94117, (415) 861-5364, Fax: (415) 863-1970. Hotel with restaurant in historic district, 50% gay & lesbian. Variety of rooms with new interiors, color TVs, private showers, English garden.

RED VICTORIAN, 1665 Haight S, San Francisco, CA, 94117, (415) 864-1978. Gay-friendly B&B with Gallery of Meditative Art & Meditation Room. Economy to luxury rooms, private & shared baths, continental breakfast, non-smoking.

Women's Accommodations

CARL STREET UNICORN HOUSE, 156 Carl St, San Francisco, CA, 94117, (415) 753-5194. B&B near downtown, some straight clientele, men welcome. Rooms decorated with antiques, TV lounge, continental breakfast. ♀

ONE IN TEN, (415) 664-0748. Women-only guesthouse with kitchen privileges. In San Francisco's Sunset district across the street from the ocean, 3 blocks from Golden Gate Park. Surfing, nature trails. 1 block from streetcar. ♀

Bars

TRAX, 1437 Haight St, (415) 864-4213. Pool tables, happy hour, 75% men. ♂

Restaurants

BLUE MUSE, 409 Gough St, (415) 626-7505. Restaurant & bar. California cuisine with French influence, weekend brunch. Breakfast, lunch, dinner. ♂

CHARPE'S, 131 Gough St, (415) 621-6766. American cuisine, Sun brunch 11am-3pm. ♀♂

SF CASTRO

Accommodations

BECK'S MOTOR LODGE, 2222 Market St, San Francisco, CA, 94114, (415) 621-8212, (800) 227-4360, Fax: (415) 241-0435. Gay-friendly motor lodge, 1-1/2 blocks from Castro area. Comfortable rooms, color TVs/HBO, phones, coffee-makers. Beach 3-1/2 miles.

CASTILLO INN, 48 Henry St, San Francisco, CA, 94114, (415) 864-5111, (800) 865-5112, Fax: (415) 641-1321. B&B, private & shared baths, expanded continental breakfast. Mostly men with women welcome. ♂

DOLORES PARK INN C/O BERNIE H. VIELWERTH, 3641 Seventeenth St, San Francisco, CA, 94114, (415) 621-0482. B&B, 50% gay & lesbian clientele. Shared baths.

EIGHTEENTH STREET GARDEN HIDEAWAY, 4628 18th St, San Francisco, CA, (415) 626-1421 (Tel/Fax). Email: bhenry@slip.net, Web: www.webwidget.com/bob., Furnished, non-smoking garden apartment, private entrance, BBQ grill. ♀♂

INN ON CASTRO, 321 Castro St, San Francisco, CA, 94114, (415) 861-0321. The innkeepers invite you into a colorful and comfortable environment filled with modern art and exotic plants. Meet fellow travelers from around the world over a memorable breakfast. We're just 100 yards north of the corner of Market & Castro, where the neighborhood is quiet, yet a stone's throw from the Castro Theater and dozens of bars, shops and restaurants. ♀♂

LE GRENIER, 347 Noe St, San Francisco, CA, 94114, (415) 864-4748. B&B, private bath, some straight clientele. ♀♂

LEMON TREE HOMESTAYS, PO Box 460424, San Francisco, CA, 94146, (415)

SAN FRANCISCO's Newest & Grandest Guest House

THE PARKER HOUSE
"Historic Guest House and Gardens"

- *Private Baths, Cable TV, In-Room Modem/Voicemail*
- *Relaxing Library with Fireplace and Piano*
- *Large Breakfast Room, Sunning Deck, Expansive Gardens*

Contact Us Today for Color Brochure, Rates, and Availability

520 Church Street • San Francisco, CA • 94114

1-888-520-PARK

http://members.aol.com/Parkerhse/sf.html

861-4045. B&B in a Mediterranean-style home near Mission Dolores, private or shared bath, continental breakfast. ♂

PARKER HOUSE, THE, 520 Church St, San Francisco, CA, 94114, (415) 621-3222, toll-free: (888) 520-PARK (7275). Email: parkerhse@aol.com, Web: http://members.aol.com/PARKERHSE/sf.html, Castro's newest, most beautiful guesthouse, this renovated 1909 Edwardian mini-mansion has expansive gardens & lawn areas, fern dens, statues, fountains & walking paths. Rooms feature private baths, cable TV, modem ports, voice mail, king- or queen-sized beds and expanded continental breakfast. We're steps away from bars, cafes, restaurants, Dolores Park & streetcars. Hosts Bob and Bill will take care of everything! ♂ See ad on page 261.

TWENTY-FOUR HENRY GUESTHOUSE, 24 Henry St, San Francisco, CA, 94114, (800) 900-5686, (415) 864-5686, Fax: (415) 864-0406. Email: walterian @aol.com, Guesthouse, private & shared baths, extended continental breakfast, private phone, answering machine. ♀♂

WILLOWS, THE, 710 14th St, San Francisco, CA, 94114, (415) 431-4770, Fax: (415) 431-5295. Email: Vacation @WillowsSF.com, Web: www.WillowsSF.com, Your Haven within the Castro. Housed in a 1904 Edwardian, *The Willows B&B Inn* derives its name from the handcrafted willow furnishings which grace each room. Complementing these unique pieces are country antiques, willow chairs and headboards, warm earthtones, wooden shutters, fresh flowers, telephones, shared baths and expanded continental breakfast. ♀♂

■ Women's Accommodations

NANCY'S BED, (415) 239-5692. Women-only accommodations with shared bath. ♀

■ Bars

HARVEY'S, 500 Castro St, (415) 431-4278. Gay memorabilia bar & restaurant with photos & items reminiscent of gay personalities & events. Lunch bar menu. Wonderful drag shows. 🎵 ♀♂

METRO, 3600 16th St, at Market, (415) 703-9750. Video bar, karaoke nites & Chinese restaurant. Preppie, ivy-league clientele. ♂

■ Dance Bar/Disco

★ **CAFE, THE,** 2367 Market St, (415) 861-3846. Dance bar, pool table, balcony overlooking the Castro shopping area. Patio. ♀♂

■ Fitness Centers

MARKET STREET GYM, 2301 Market St, at Noe, (415) 626-4488. Visitors welcome, daily & weekly memberships. Bodybuilding, Jacuzzi & juice bar. Men & women.

WOMEN'S TRAINING CENTER, 2164 Market St, near Sanchez, (415) 864-6835. Weight training, free weights.

THE WILLOWS BED & BREAKFAST INN

Your Haven within the Castro, for Business or Pleasure

For brochure or reservations please call **(415) 431-4770**

FAX **(415) 431-5295**

http://www.WillowsSF.com
Email: Vacation@WillowsSF.com

Restaurants

BOMBAY RESTAURANT, 2200 block of Market.,

CAFE FLORA, Market St, at Noe., California cuisine. ♀♂

CHINA COURT, 19th & Castro Sts., Chinese cuisine.

COVE CAFE, 434 Castro St, near Market, (415) 626-0462. Home-style diner. ♀♂

HOT 'N HUNKY, 4039 18th St, (415) 621-6365. Gourmet hamburgers.

LATICIA'S, 2200 block of Market St, (415) 621-0441. Mexican cuisine, Sun brunch.

LUNA DOLCE, 564 Castro, Lite meals, fine coffees & pastry.

LUNA PIENA, 558 Castro St, (415) 621-2566. Lunch & dinner, Italian cuisine, patio.

★ **LUPIN'S,** 18th St, across from Midnight Sun bar., French cuisine, gay-friendly.

MA TANTE SUMI, 18th St, near Diamond., French with a Japanese flair, gay-friendly.

METRO, 3600 16th St, at the Metro men's bar, (415) 703-9750. Chinese cuisine. ♀♂

★ **NO NAME RESTAURANT,** 2223 Market., Italian cuisine.

ORPHAN ANDY'S, 3991 17th St, near Castro, (415) 864-9795, 24hr burgers. ♀♂

PATIO CAFE, 531 Castro St, (415) 621-4640. Patio. ♀♂

PAZOLI'S, Market, between Castro & Noe., Designer Mexican food with hunky waiters. Gay-friendly.

SAUSAGE FACTORY, Castro St, near 18th St., Italian, gay-friendly.

SOUTH CHINA CAFE, 18th St, near Castro., Chinese cuisine.

WELCOME HOME, 464 Castro St, near 18th, (415) 626-3600. Breakfast thru dinner. ♀♂

Retail & Bookstores

A DIFFERENT LIGHT, 489 Castro St, San Francisco, (415) 431-0891. Gay & lesbian bookstore, music, cards, videos, magazines. Open 10am-11pm & Fri & Sat till 12:00.

HEADLINES FOR WOMEN, 549 Castro St, (415) 252-1280. Fashions, accessories, cards for women.

WILD CARD, 3979-B 18th St, (415) 626-4449. Gay & lesbian erotica, cards, gifts, jewelry.

SF SOUTH OF MARKET
(Includes Folsom area)

Dance Bar/Disco

BOX, THE, 715 Harrison, at 3rd, (415) 647-8258. Thurs dance night, 60% men. ♀♂

★ **ENDUP,** 401 6th St, at Harrison, (415) 357-0827. Hi-energy club with many special dance club parties each with separate appeal. Sun T-dance. Fri "Fag Fridays" special event, call (415) 263-4850.

G-SPOT AT THE ENDUP, at the Endup, 401 6th St., Largest women's dance club in San Francisco, Sat. ♀

STUD, THE, 399 9th St, near Harrison, (415) 863-6623. Younger crowd, scheduled special nights. Tues: Trannyshack transvestite dance bar with live entertainment. Wed hot night with fun 80s music & dance.

Restaurants

CHAT HOUSE, 139 8th St, above CoCo Club, (415) 255-8783.

Leathers/Piercing

LEATHER ETC, 1201 Folsom, at 8th St, (415) 864-7558. Leatherwear, boots, accessories.

STORMY LEATHER, 1158 Howard St, between 7th & 8th St, (415) 626-1672. Erotic boutique with leather, latex, PVC & toys. Mon-Thur 12-6pm, Fri, Sat 12-7pm, Sun 2pm-6pm.

SF DOWNTOWN
(Includes Polk St. & Tenderloin areas)

Accommodations

ALLISON HOTEL, 417 Stockton St, San Francisco, CA, 94108, (415) 986-8737, Fax: (415) 392-0850. Gay-friendly budget hotel, near Union Square.

ATHERTON HOTEL, 685 Ellis St, San Francisco, CA, 94109, (415) 474-5720, (800) 474-5720, Fax: (415) 474-8256. Gay-friendly hotel with restaurant & bar, near Polk St, Union Square, Civic Centre & Castro. Intimate, charming rooms, color TV, phones & private baths.

CARTWRIGHT HOTEL, THE, 524 Sutter St, San Francisco, CA, 94102, (415) 421-2865, (800) 227-3844, Fax: (415) 983-6244. Gay-friendly hotel with private baths, expanded continental breakfast, afternoon tea, evening wine hour, color cable TV, AC, 3 blocks to gay bars.

CLARION BEDFORD HOTEL, 761 Post St, San Francisco, CA, 94109, (415) 673-6040, (800) 227-5642, Fax: (415) 563-6739. Boutique hotel with restaurant & bar, mid-range prices, city views, private baths, gay & lesbian following.

ESSEX HOTEL, THE, 684 Ellis St, San Francisco, CA, 94109, (415) 474-4664, (800) 453-7739, Fax: (415) 441-1800. In CA (800) 443-7739. Hotel, mainly straight clientele. 100 double rooms, walk to Union Square, Polk St, cable cars, Chinatown, theaters, restaurants.

GROSVENOR HOUSE, 899 Pine St, San Francisco, CA, 94108, (415) 421-1899, (800) 999-9189, Fax: 982-1946. Suites with private baths.

HOTEL TRITON, 342 Grant Avenue, San Francisco, CA, 94108, (415) 394-0500, (800) 433-6611, Fax: (415) 394-0555. Rooms & suites with handpainted wall finishes, comforters, fully-stocked honor bars & other amenities. Blocks from the financial district, ideal for business travelers.

KING GEORGE HOTEL, 334 Mason St, San Francisco, CA, 94102, (800) 288-6005, (415) 781-5050, Fax: (415) 391-6976. Gay-friendly hotel 1 block from Union Square. Color TV, telephone, private baths. 10%-15% gay & lesbian clientele.

LOMBARD CENTRAL, A SUPER 8 HOTEL, THE, 1015 Geary Blvd, San Francisco, CA, 94109, (415) 673-5232, (800) 777-3210, Fax: (415) 885-2802. Gay-friendly hotel with breakfast cafe, private baths, color TV, ceiling fans, complimentary wine hour weekdays 5:30-6:30 pm, 2 blocks to gay bars.

RENOIR HOTEL, 45 McAllister St, San Francisco, CA, 94102, (415) 626-5200, (800) 576-3388, Fax: (415) 626-0916 Web: www.renoirhotel.com, Gay-friendly, elegant historical landmark hotel with restaurant, bar, espresso bar & gift shop. Color TV, telephone, private bath & room service.

ROGER'S PLACE, 962 Jones St Suite 1, San Francisco, CA, 94109, (415) 441-5191. Room with king bed, full breakfast. Mostly male clientele. ♂

SAVOY HOTEL, 580 Geary St, San Francisco, CA, 94102, (415) 441-2700. Boutique hotel, 2-1/2 blocks from Union Square, in the Theatre District. Renovated in 1990 in a French Provençal style with feather beds, goose-down pillows, mini-bars, color TVs. 50% gay & lesbian clientele.

YORK HOTEL, 940 Sutter St, San Francisco, CA, 94109, (415) 885-6800, Fax: (415) 885-2115. Reservations only (800) 808-YORK (9675). Gay-friendly hotel, private baths.

■ Bars

GINGER'S TOO!!, 43 6th St, near Market, (415) 543-3622. 99% men, opens 10am. 🐾 🍴 📺 ♂

THREE-O-ONE CLUB, 301 Turk St., 🐾 ♂

WHITE SWALLOW, 1750 Polk St, (415) 775-4152. Piano bar nightly, 9pm-1am. ♂

■ Dance Bar/Disco

CLUB Q, 177 Townsend St, at Club Townsend, (415) 647-8258. Women's dance party 1st Fri of the month. 🍴 ♀

■ Restaurants

GRUBSTAKE, THE, 1525 Pine St, near Polk, (415) 673-8268. Food from 5pm till 4am, weekends from 10am. 🍷

QUETZAL, 1234 Polk St, (415) 673-4181. Indoor/outdoor cafe & restaurant, 6am-11pm 7 days. 🌀

SF MISSION
(Includes S. Van Ness area)

■ Information

WOMEN'S BLDG, 3543 18th St, at Lapidge, (415) 431-1180. Resource center, meetings, events. Women's organizations meet here. Events bulletin board, closed Sun.

■ Accommodations

ANDORA INN, 2434 Mission St, San Francisco, CA, 94110, (415) 282-0337,

(800) 967-9219, Fax: (415) 282-2608. B&B with restaurant & bar, private & shared baths, expanded continental breakfast, some straight clientele. ♀♂

INN SAN FRANCISCO, THE, 943 S Van Ness Ave, San Francisco, CA, 94110, (415) 641-0188, (800) 359-0913, Fax: (415) 641-1701. Feel the years slip away, as you step through the massive, wooden doors of the Inn San Francisco. Each guest room is individually decorated with antiques, fresh flowers, marble sinks, polished brass fixtures and exquisite finishing touches. In the garden, under the shade of an old fig tree, a gazebo shelters the inviting hot tub. Mixed clientele with a very strong gay & lesbian following.

■ Bars

EL RIO, 3158 Mission St, at Precita, (415) 282-3325. 50% gay & lesbian, patio Sun, DJ Fri, rock & roll Sat, salsa tea dance Sun afternoon."

ESPERANZA'S, 80 29th St, (415) 206-1405. Frequented by numerous gay & lesbian friends of Esperanza.

LEXINGTON CLUB, Lexington at 19th., Young crowd. ♀

MUFFDIVE, 527 Valencia St, at The Cassanova., (415) 487-6634. Sun women-only from 9pm. ♀

WILD SIDE WEST, 424 Cortland Ave, (415) 647-3099. Gay women & straight people from the neighborhood. Patio, BBQ." ♀

■ Saunas/Health Clubs

OSENTO, 955 Valencia St, near 20th St, (415) 282-6333. Women's bath, jacuzzi, massage. ♀

■ Restaurants

BARKING BASSET CAFE, 803 Courtland, (415) 649-2146. Small, intimate, great brunch, gay-owned & -operated.

BEARDED LADY, 485 14th St, at Guerrero, (415) 626-2805. Vegetarian restaurant & coffeehouse. Mon-Fri 7am-7pm, entertainment mostly Sat. ♀

CAFE COMMONS, 3161 Mission St, (415) 282-2928. Women's cafe, breakfast, lite meals, 7am-7pm daily. ♀

EL NUEVO FRUTILANDIA, 3077 24th St, near Folsom, (415) 648-2958. Puerto Rican & Cuban cuisine, closed Mon. ♀♂

FIRECRACKER, Valencia & 21st., Chinese cuisine.

ROOSTER, Valencia at 22nd., European cuisine with Chinese accent.

■ Retail & Bookstores

BERNAL BOOKS, 401 Cortland Ave, (415) 550-0293. Very women-friendly general bookstore, also cards, comics, women's magazines. Closed Mon.

MODERN TIMES BOOKSTORE, 888 Valencia St., (415) 282-9246. Large gay, lesbian & feminist selections (books, mags & records), 7 days.

■ Erotica

GOOD VIBRATIONS, 1210 Valencia, (415) 974-8980. Women's erotica, videos.

SAN JOSE

■ Information

BILLY DE FRANK GAY & LESBIAN COMMUNITY CENTER, 175 Stockton Ave, (408) 293-4525. Gay Switchboard: (408) 293-2429. Mon-Fri 3pm-9pm, Sat noon-9pm, Sun 10am-9pm.

■ Bars

BUCK'S, 301 Stockton Ave, at Julian, (408) 286-1176. 75% men, 25% women, CD jukebox. DJ Fri-Sun, small dance floor, 24hrs weekends. ♂

The Inn San Francisco

943 Van Ness Avenue
San Francisco,
California 94110
Fax: (415) 641-1701

(415) 641-0188
(800) 359-0913

Dance Bar/Disco

★ **A TINKER'S DAMN (TD'S),** 46 N Saratoga Ave, near Stevens Creek, Santa Clara, (408) 243-4595. DJ nightly, summer BBQ Sun, 90% men, women welcome.

★ **MARY'S,** 170 W St John Street, (408) 947-1667. Dance bar, video bar, restaurant with dinner & brunch, 75% men, women welcome. DJ nightly, patio. May change in '98.

SAVOY, 3546 Flora Vista Ave, near El Camino Real, Santa Clara, (408) 247-7109. DJ Fri-Sat, men welcome, non-smoking, micro brews, karaoke & comedy."

Cafe

CAFE LIVITICUS, The Alameda, near Julian.,

Restaurants

HAMBURGER MARY'S, 170 W St John St, (408) 947-1667. Patio, Sun brunch, 50% men, 50% women with some straight clientele. May change in '98.

Retail & Bookstores

GIFT SHOP, THE, at the Savoy women's bar, 3546 Flora Vista Ave, (650) 962-9338. Variety of sportswear, t-shirts, caps. Brands like D.Y.K.E., Equipment Clothing Co. & Girl Sport Int'l. Also cards, mugs, pride items, jewelry, cigars, books & magazines.

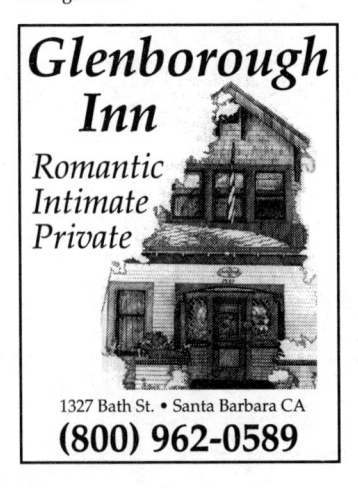

Glenborough Inn
Romantic
Intimate
Private

1327 Bath St. • Santa Barbara CA
(800) 962-0589

SISTERSPIRIT, 175 Stockton Ave, at Billy de Frank Center, (408) 293-9372. Women's bookstore and coffeehouse.

Leathers/Piercing

LEATHER MASTERS, 969 Park Ave, (408) 293-7660, (800) 417-2636. Leathers, cards, videos & erotic toys for men & women.

SAN LUIS OBISPO

SEE MORRO BAY/SAN LUIS OBISPO,

SANTA BARBARA

Information

AIDS LINE, (805) 965-2925. Answering service connects you.

GAY & LESBIAN RESOURCE CENTER, 126 E Haley St, Ste A17, (805) 963-3636.

Accommodations

GLENBOROUGH INN, 1327 Bath St, Santa Barbara, CA, 93101, (805) 966-0589, (800) 962-0589, Fax: (805) 564-8610. Email: glenboro@silcom.com, Step into the past, where life was quieter and the pace relaxed. Sleep in an immaculate, old-fashioned room with fresh flowers and antiques. Enjoy hors d'oeuvres by the fireplace or indulge in the enclosed garden hot tub for private use. Gourmet breakfast delivered to your room. Take the 25-cent shuttle to the beach. Gay-owned and gay-friendly.

IVANHOE INN, 1406 Castillo St, Santa Barbara, CA, 93101, (805) 963-8832, (800) 428-1787, Fax: (805) 966-5523. Gay-friendly B&B & cottage. Variety of units, TV lounge, continental breakfast in picnic basket, welcoming wine & cheese. Nearby ocean beach.

Bars

GOLD COAST, 30 W Cota, near State, (805) 965-6701. 70% men, 30% women, small dance floor.

Restaurants

CHAMELEON, 421 E Cota, (805) 965-9536. Upscale restaurant & bar.

SOJOURNER CAFE, 134 E Canon Perdido St, (805) 965-7922. Natural foods, desserts, espresso.

Retail & Bookstores

EARTHLING BOOKSHOP, 1137 State

St, (805) 965-0926. General bookstore with a small section of women's, gay & lesbian titles.

SANTA CRUZ

■ Information
LESBIAN & GAY COMMUNITY CENTER, 1328 Commerce Lane, (408) 425-5422. Mon 12-2, Tues 2-8, Wed 6-8, Thurs & Sat 12-8, Fri 4-8, Sun 12-6.

■ Women's Accommodations
GROVE, THE: A WOMEN'S COUNTRY RETREAT BY THE SEA, 40 Lily Way, La Selva Beach, CA, 95076, (408) 724-3459. Women-only country retreat. Secluded artist's mini-farm (peacocks, chickens, cats) near spectacular, uncrowded beach south of Santa Cruz. Two separate cottages with kitchen, fireplace. Shared hot tub and sun deck. ♀

■ Bars
DAKOTA, Pacific Ave, near Lincoln. ♀♂

■ Dance Bar/Disco
BLUE LAGOON, 923 Pacific Ave, (408) 423-7117. Alternative dance club, many students..

■ Retail & Bookstores
BOOK LOFT, 1207 Soquel Ave, (408) 429-1812. A used book store with separate room for women's titles.

HERLAND BOOK CAFE, 902 Center St, (408) 429-6636. Women's bookstore & cafe. Quarterly dances.

SANTA MONICA

■ Retail & Bookstores
CALIFORNIA MAP & TRAVEL CENTER, 3312 Pica Blvd, (310) 396-6277.

SANTA ROSA

■ Dance Bar/Disco
SANTA ROSA INN, 4302 Santa Rosa Ave, (707) 584-0345. 50% men, 50% women, patio." ♀♂

■ Cafe
A'ROMA ROASTERS, 95 5th St, in historic Railroad Square, (707) 576-7765. Lesbian owned coffee shop.

■ Retail & Bookstores
COPPERFIELD'S, two shopping center locations: 2402 Magowan, (707) 578-8938, Raley's Town Center, 584-4240., General bookstore with gay section.

NORTH LIGHT BOOKS, 530 E Cotati Ave, Cotati, (707) 792-9755. Lesbian owned bookstore with gay & lesbian books.

SEBASTOPOL

■ Retail & Bookstores
COPPERFIELD'S BOOKS, 138 N Main St, (707) 823-2618. General bookstore with gay & lesbian section.

MILK & HONEY, 137 N Main, (707) 824-1155. Feminist bookstore, gifts.

SEQUOIA NATIONAL PARK

■ Accommodations
ORGANIC GARDENS B & B, 44095 Dinely Dr, Three Rivers, CA, 93271, (209) 561-0916, Fax: (209) 561-1017. Email: eggplant@theworks.com, Web: http://www.theworks.com/~eggplant, Lesbian-owned, gay-friendly B&B with photo & art gallery.

SOLANO BEACH

■ Bars
ENCORE, 207 N Coast Hwy, (619) 793-7784. Bar & rest., DJ some nites. ♀♂

SONOMA

■ Accommodations
GAIGE HOUSE INN, 13540 Arnold Dr, Glen Ellen, CA, (707) 935-0237, (800) 935-0237, Fax: (707) 935-6411. Web: www.gaige.com, Gay-friendly 9-room inn bordered by creek & woodlands, 7 miles from Sonoma & near dozens of wineries. Two-course breakfasts, pool on premises, rooms with king & queen beds, AC, oversized towels, direct-dial phones, English toiletries.

SONOMA CHALET B & B, 18935 Fifth St West, Sonoma, CA, 95476, (707) 938-3129, (800) 938-3129. Gay-friendly B&B & cottages in country setting. Fireplaces or wood-burning stoves, private & shared baths. Expanded continental breakfast, Jacuzzi & free bicycle use.

STARWAE INN, 21490 Broadway (Hwy 12), Sonoma, CA, (707) 938-1374, (800)

793-4792, Fax: (707) 935-1159. Gay-friendly B&B cottages 1 hr from San Francisco & 1 hr from Russian River. Rent entire cottage or separate suites. AC, kitchen, refrigerator, private baths, expanded continental breakfast.

SONOMA COUNTY

■ Accommodations
WHISPERING PINES B & B, 5950 Erland Rd, Santa Rosa, CA, 95404, (707) 539-0198 (Tel/Fax). B&B Sonoma/Napa wine country, private baths, full breakfast, Jacuzzi, 50% gay & lesbian clientele.

■ Women's Accommodations
ASTI RANCH, 25750 River Rd, Cloverdale, CA, 95425, (707) 894-5960, Fax: (707) 894-5658. Women-only cottage near Russian River, 1-1/2 hr north of San Francisco. Kitchen, refrigerator, coffee/tea-making facilities, ceiling fan, private bath & continental breakfast. Non-smoking. ♀

STOCKTON

■ Dance Bar/Disco
CLUB PARADISE, 10100 N Lower Sacramento Rd, (209) 477-4724. 50% men & women, 7 days, 6pm-2am , Fri, Sat 5pm-2am, Sun 3am-2am.

TARZANA

■ Erotica
LOVE BOUTIQUE, 18637 Ventura Blvd, (818) 342-2400. Women-owned & -operated elegant erotic store, intimate lesbian & gay videos & lingerie. We do home parties for women .

UPLAND
SEE POMONA.,

VACAVILLE - FAIRFIELD

■ Information
GAY & LESBIAN LINE (SOLANO COUNTY), (707) 448-1010. leave a message. Call here for Women Preferring Women group.

■ Retail & Bookstores
VACAVILLE BOOK COMPANY, 315 Main Street, (707) 449-0550. General bookstore, gay & lesbian sections. Men's meetings 2nd & 4th Tues, occasional women's meetings.

VALLEJO

■ Dance Bar/Disco
NOBODY'S PLACE, 437 Virginia St, (707) 645-7298. Dance bar in a Victorian building, karaoke, DJ Fri & Sat, 60% men, 40% women.

VENTURA

■ Information
GAY & LESBIAN COMMUNITY CENTER, 1995 E Main St, (805) 653-1979. 1-9 weekdays, 12-4 Sat.

■ Dance Bar/Disco
PADDY MCDERMOTT'S, 2 W Main St, (805) 652-1071. Dance bar, DJ Fri-Sun, BBQ Sun on patio.
STEPHEN J'S, Main at Ventura Ave, (805) 653-6511. Dance bar, DJ Wed, Fri & Sat, 60% men, 40% women.

VICTORVILLE

■ Bars
WESTSIDE 15, THE, 16868 Stoddard Wells Rd, (760) 243-9600. Karaoke, leather & Latino nites, DJ Fri & Sat, 2pm-2am 7 days, 50% men, 50% women, full liquor.

WALNUT CREEK

■ Bars
DJ'S PIANO BAR, 1535 Olympic Blvd, (510) 930-0300. Piano bar, comedy nite Sun, somewhat younger crowd, 60% men, 40% women.
TWELVE TWENTY, 1220 Pine St, (510) 938-4550. Pool tables, live DJ weekends, 60% men, 40% women.

■ Dance Bar/Disco
★ **JUST REWARDS (JR'S),** 2520 Camino Diablo, (510) 256-1200. Huge dance bar & lounge, 80% women (except Fri 95% men for 18 & over).

WHITTIER

■ Accommodations
COLEEN'S CALIFORNIA CASA, Whittier, CA, (562) 699-8427. Gay-friendly B&B 8 miles from downtown LA (20 minutes from Civic Center). Private & shared baths, AC, color cable TV, phone, gay & lesbian following.

■ Dance Bar/Disco
METAMORPHOSIS, 13002 E Philadelphia, (562) 663-7155. Wed only, Latino gay dance nite.

YUCCA VALLEY

■ Accommodations
YUCCA INN RESORT, THE, 7500 Camino Del Cielo, Yucca Valley, CA, 92284, (619) 365-3311. Resort inn hotel & restaurant. Gay following, private baths.

COLORADO STATEWIDE

■ Accommodations
CARITAS BED & BREAKFAST NETWORK, (800) CARITAS, (312) 857-0801, Fax: (312) 857-0805. B&B, home-stay accommodations service. Member: IGLTA

ASPEN

■ Information
ASPEN GAY LESBIAN COMMUNITY, (970) 925-9249. Local gay info, mostly eves 8pm-midnight.

■ Accommodations
HOTEL ASPEN, 110 W Main St, Aspen, CO, 81611, (970) 925-3441, (800) 527-7369, Fax: (970) 920-1379. Email: aspengroup@rof.net, Web: http://www.aspen.com/ha/, This striking, contemporary 45-room hotel offers a variety of rooms & penthouse suites, 4 with private Jacuzzi, most opening onto terraces or balconies. Relax year-round under beautiful mountain skies on the patio courtyard with its heated swimming pool. A fireplace graces the common area. Complimentary mountain breakfast is served. Gym & outdoor Jacuzzi. Gay-friendly.

MOLLY GIBSON'S, 101 W Main St, Aspen, CO, 81611, (970) 925-3434. Lodge with 50 rooms, some with fireplaces, Jacuzzi's. Gay-friendly.

SNOW QUEEN VICTORIAN B & B LODGE, COOPER ST LOFT STUDIO APTS, 124 E Cooper St, Aspen, CO, (970) 925-8455, Fax: (970) 925-7391. Gay-friendly accommodations. Quaint Victorian lodge with a variety of rooms, private baths, 2 kitchen units & TV parlour with fireplace, plus tastefully furnished studio apartments with full kitchen, fireplaces & modern amenities. Continental breakfast.

■ Cafe
HOWLING WOLF, E Hopkins, (970) 920-7771. Popular after-hours cafe, gay-friendly especially Mon & Wed.

■ Retail & Bookstores
EXPLORE BOOKSELLERS & COFFEEHOUSE, 221 E Main, (970) 925-5336, (800) 562-READ (7323). General bookstore with small gay & lesbian section. Gourmet vegetarian cafe upstairs.

BOULDER

■ Information
AIDS INFO, (303) 444-6121. Mon-Fri 8am-8pm, Sat 10am-6pm.

■ Women's Accommodations
BOULDER GUEST HOUSE, (303) 938-8908. Guest room with private bath. ♀

Visit Colorado
(800) CARITAS
Caritas B&B Network

HOTEL ASPEN
The Best Way to Stay in Aspen
(800) 527-7369
(970) 925-3441

270   COLORADO

Dance Bar/Disco
YARD, THE, 2690 28th St Unit C (enter from Bluff St), (303) 443-1987. High energy dance bar, 50% men, 50% women (more women Sat), smoking & non-smoking sections.

Cafe
WALNUT CAFE, THE, 3073 Walnut, (303) 447-2315. Espresso, small food menu, gay friendly.

Retail & Bookstores
ARIA, 2047 Broadway, (303) 442-5694. Gift shop with cards & T-shirts.
BOULDER BOOK SHOP, 1107 Pearl St, (303) 447-2074. General bookstore with gay & lesbian section.
WORD IS OUT, 1731 15th St, (303) 449-1415. Women's bookstore with gay items, gifts, music, etc. Lesbian titles, some gay men's titles. Mon-Sat 10am-6pm, Sun noon-5pm.

CARBONDALE

Women's Accommodations
STARBUCK'S RANCH, 3390 County Rd 113, Carbondale, CO, 81623, (970) 945-5208, E-mail: wordwest@rof.net. Women-only B&B cabin & rooms with mountain views. Color TV, phone, refrigerator, private & shared baths. Hot tub, deck, gazebo, stocked fishing holes, horseback riding & hiking. Breakfast in the sunroom.

COLORADO SPRINGS

Information
LESBIAN & GAY COMMUNITY CENTER & HELP LINE, (719) 471-4429.

Accommodations
PIKES PEAK PARADISE B & B, PO Box 5760, Woodland Park, CO, 80866, (719) 687-7112, (800) 354-0989, Fax: (719) 687-9008. Email: ppp@cyber-bbs.com, We're so happy, you might even say we're...gay! A Southern mansion with views of Pikes Peak, fireplace, queen bed, gourmet breakfast and friendly hosts eager to make you feel at home. Attractions include: US Air Force Academy, Pikes Peak Drive, Cog Railway, hiking, picnics, four-wheeling, fishing, boating, bicycling, hot air balloon rides and more. 50% gay & lesbian clientele.

Bars
HOUR GLASS LOUNGE, 2748 Airport, (719) 471-2104.

Dance Bar/Disco
BACKSTREETS, 2125 E Fountain, (719) 633-2125. Dance bar & dinner theater, restaurant & cocktail lounge, 10am-2am, 7 days.
★ **HIDE & SEEK COMPLEX,** 512 W Colorado Ave, near Walnut (rear), (719) 634-9303. Complex with Hide & Seek dance bar, Branding Iron country & western dance bar, Man Stop game room, Colorado Grill restaurant.

CONIFER

Accommodations
HOUSE AT PEREGRINE'S PERSPECTIVE, THE, PO Box 1018, Conifer, CO, 80433-1018, (303) 697-0558. Email: editor@whitecranejournal.com, Web: http://www.whitecranejournal.com, Gay-owned & -operated B&B 45 min from Denver, log cabin with shared baths, expanded continental breakfast, Jacuzzi. Women welcome.

CREEDE

Accommodations
OLD FIREHOUSE NO. 1, INC., THE,

Pikes Peak Paradise B & B

Secluded Mountain Hideaway
Fireplaces • Hot Tubs
(800) 354-0989
(719) 687-7112
Colorado Springs

Main Street (PO Box 603), Creede, CO, 81130, (719) 658-0212. Gay-friendly Victorian B&B with restaurant & Victorian Ice Cream Parlor. Private baths, full breakfast & library lounge.

DENVER

Information

AIDS LINE, (303) 837-0166, 830-2437, (800) 333-2437, TTD. Mon-Fri 9am-5pm, or tape.

Accommodations

TWIN MAPLES BED & BREAKFAST, 1401 Madison St., Denver, CO, 80206, (303) 393-1832, toll free: (888) 835-5738, Fax: (303) 394-4776. Email: twinmaples@boytoy.com, B&B with spacious rooms, expanded continental breakfast, private or shared baths. We're in the Congress Park neighborhood, near restaurants & shopping. Some straight clientele. ♀♂

VICTORIA OAKS INN, 1575 Race St, Denver, CO, 80206, (303) 355-1818, (800) 662-OAKS (6257), Fax: (303) 331-1095. Email: vicoaksinn@aol.com, **Enjoy warmth, hospitality, and personalized services in surroundings designed for your personal comforts — a home you'd love to come home to.** We have guest rooms furnished with antiques, panoramic views, private & shared baths. Our continental breakfast is inspiring. Walk to the zoo, museum, downtown, gay clubs, and Imax Theatre. ♀♂

Bars

BRIG, 117 Broadway, (303) 777-9378.

CENTERFIELD SPORTS BAR, 2970 Fox St, (303) 298-7378. ♂

COLFAX MINING CO, 3014 E Colfax, (303) 321-6627. ♀♂

DEN, THE, 5110 W Colfax Ave, near Sheridan, (303) 534-9526. Bar & restaurant (dinner only), Sun brunch, 60% men, 40% women. ♀♂

DENVER DETOUR, 551 E Colfax, (303) 861-1497. Bar with lunch & dinner menu, after hours Fri & Sat. ♀♂

GRAND, THE, 538 E 17th Ave, at Pearl, (303) 839-5390. Piano bar. ♂

HIGHLAND BAR, 2532 15th St, (303) 455-9978. DJ on weekends, 80% women.

MIKE'S, 60 S Broadway, (303) 777-0193. Dancing, showbar. ♀♂

SKYLARK LOUNGE, 58 Broadway, (303) 722-7844. Martini bar, mixed alternative bar, 25% gay clientele.

Dance Bar/Disco

★ **C'S,** 7900 East Colfax, (303) 322-4436. Patio. ♀♂

★ **CLUB PROTEUS,** 1669 Clarkson, (303) 869-GODS. Hi-energy dance bar. ♀♂

★ **ELLE,** 716 W Colfax.,

MAXIMILLIAN'S, 2151 Lawrence, (303) 297-0015. Dance to salsa & merengue. ♂

NINTH AVE WEST, 99 W 9th Ave, (303) 572-8006. A swing dancing supper club, 30% gay & lesbian.

RAVEN, 2217 Welton St, Sat many women ♀♂

★ **SNAKE PIT,** 608 E 13 Ave, (303) 831-1234. Sexual dance club, theme nights. ♀♂

TRACKS 2000, 2975 Fox St, (303) 292-6600. Hi engergy dance bar. ♀♂

YE'O MATCHMAKER, 1480 Humboldt, at Colfax, (303) 839-9388. dance bar, eclectic crowd. Popular drag shows, holds pageants frequently, scheduled latino nights. ♀♂

Victoria Oaks Inn

Warmth and Hospitality
Denver
(800) 662-OAKS

COLORADO

■ Cafe

ART OF COFFEE, THE, 1836 Blake St, (303) 294-0200. Coffee house.

CAFE COMMUNIQUÉ, 99 W 9th Ave, (303) 534-1199.

CITY SPIRIT CAFE, 1420 Market, (303) 575-0022.

DAD'S COFFEE HOUSE, Alameda & Pennsylvania, (303) 744-1258. Cafe with "mocktails" & lite menu.

DADS, 282 S Penn, (303) 744-1258. Bar atmosphere with coffeehouse fare, lite menu.

■ Restaurants

AUBERGINE, 225 E 7th Ave, (303) 832-4778. Country French cuisine.

BACKSTAGE, 1380 S Broadway, at BJ's Carousel, (303) 777-9880. Casual dining in an upscale atmosphere. Daily 5pm-10pm, Sun brunch from 9am, closed Mon.

BAROLO GRILL, 3030 E 6th Ave, (303) 393-1040. Northern Italian cuisine.

CAFE BERLIN, 2005 E 17th Ave, (303) 377-5896. German cuisine.

DEN, THE, 5110 W Colfax Ave, at The Den bar., American comfort food.

DENVER SANDWICH, 1217 E 9th Ave, (303) 861-9762.

JAN LEONE, 1509 Marion, (303) 863-8433. Restaurant & bar.

LAS MARGARITAS, 1066 Olde S Gaylord St, (303) 777-0194. Lunch, dinner, Mexican cuisine. 2nd location: 17th Ave at Downing St, (303) 830-2199.

MIKE BERADI'S, 2115 E 17th Ave, (303) 399-8800. Fresh pasta & live opera singers.

THREE SONS, 2915 W 44th Ave, (303) 455-4366. Italian cuisine.

WHITE SPOT RESTAURANT, 800 Broadway, (303) 837-1308, coffeeshop chain.

■ Retail & Bookstores

BOOK GARDEN, 2625 E 12th Ave, (303) 399-2004, (800) 279-2426, Fax: (303) 399-6167. Colorado's complete lesbian bookstore. Large selection of books, jewelry, music, t-shirts, posters and specialty items. Phone and mail order available. A great place to visit for local information!

THOMAS FLORAL & ADULT GIFTS, 1 Broadway #108, near Ellsworth, (303) 744-6400. Gay & lesbian T-shirts & adult gifts.

■ Leathers/Piercing

CRYPT, THE, 131 Broadway, between 1st & 2nd, (303) 733-3112. Denver's number one leather store for men & women.

■ Erotica

HEAVEN SENT ME, 482 S Broadway, (303) 331-8000. Leather, rubber, pride items.

KITTY'S EAST, 735 E Colfax, (303) 832-5140.

---

the Book Garden
a woman's store

Colorado's Complete Lesbian Store

personalized shopping designed for you
special orders welcome

2625 E. 12th Ave. • Denver, CO 80206
(303) 399-2004 • (800) 279-2426
fax (303) 399-6167

Hours
7 days a week
10 a.m.-6 p.m.
Open Thursdays
until 8 p.m.

*3 miles east of downtown
Denver at 12th and Elizabeth*

DURANGO

■ *Information*
GAY & LESBIAN ASSN, (970) 247-7778, 7-10pm, local info.

■ *Accommodations*
RIVER HOUSE BED & BREAKFAST, 495 Animas View Dr, Durango, CO, 81301, (970) 247-4775, (800) 254-4775, Fax: (970) 259-1465.

FLORISSANT

■ *Tours, Charters & Excursions*
MCNAMARA RANCH, 4620 County Rd 100, Florissant, CO, (719) 748-3466. Ride wilderness trails or climb above the timberline. We can plan overnight camping trips or return to the ranch for good food & company. Rides tailored to your stamina. You can also help move sheep from pasture to pasture, bottle-feed lambs or sheer sheep, depending on season. Lodging & horseback riding included in rate. ♀

FT COLLINS

■ *Dance Bar/Disco*
CHOICE CITY SHOTS, 124 Laporte Ave, (970) 221-4333. pub atmosphere in a dance bar, dance music, retro, classic rock, etc, country nites, 7 days 11am-2am, sometimes later (Tues closes at midnite). 📶♀♂
TORNADO CLUB, 1437 E Mulberry, (970) 493-0251. Hi energy dance bar, quiet bar, game room, 50% men, 50% women. 📶♀♂

GEORGETOWN

■ *Women's Accommodations*
FITZPATRICK HOUSE, 3124 Scranton St, Aurora, CO, 80011, (303) 754-7737." Email: docrthouse@aol.com, Lesbian retreat, trade your work in restoring this old Victorian for free stays. ♀

GRAND JUNCTION

■ *Bars*
QUINCY'S, 609 Main St, (970) 242-9633. Gay eves only, straight before 8pm, jukebox & dance floor. ♀♂

PUEBLO

■ *Information*
PUEBLO AFTER 2, PO Box 1602, Pueblo, (719) 564-4004. Community outreach & networking with other statewide organizations. Organizes dances, picnics & group outings. Travelers welcome.

■ *Dance Bar/Disco*
AQUA SPLASH, 806 Santa Fe Dr., (719) 543-3913. Dance bar & lounge, pool table, 4pm-2am Tues-Sat, 90% women. 📶♀
PIRATE'S COVE, 105 Central Plaza, (719) 542-9624. 50/50 men & women, 2am-2pm (closed Mon). ♀♂

STEAMBOAT SPRINGS

■ *Accommodations*
ELK RIVER ESTATES, Box 5032, Steamboat Springs, CO, 80477-5032, (970) 879-7556. B&B, women welcome, some straight clientele. ♂

VAIL

■ *Accommodations*
ASTER FLAT, THE, 5020 Main Gore Place, Unit L1, Vail, CO, 81657, (970) 476-6533. Email: zig@colorado.net, Lesbian concierge, 4-bed/4-bath home in the Gore Creek Meadows of East Vail. The unit is on the 3rd & 4th levels and features a wood-burning fireplace, steam shower, Jacuzzi tub, washer and dryer, fully stocked kitchen, complex pool. All linens are provided. It is short walking distance of a free shuttle stop.
PARK HOUSE, THE, 5020 Main Gore Place, Unit L1, Vail, CO, 81657, (970) 476-6533. Email: zig@colorado.net, Lesbian concierge, 5-bed/5-bath, 5000 sq. ft. home in a quiet residential East Vail neighborhood. The conveniences of home with the luxury services of a 5-star hotel, featuring a wood-burning fireplace, hot tub, sauna, game room with billiards table, large-screen TV, washer & dryer, gourmet kitchen. Beautiful view, all linens provided. Walking distance of a free shuttle stop.

CONNECTICUT

BRIDGEPORT

Dance Bar/Disco
CAUGHT IN THE ACT, 1246 Main St, (203) 333-1258. Unverifiable spring '98.

Restaurants
BLOODROOT RESTAURANT, 85 Ferris St, (203) 576-9168. Vegetarian restaurant, terrace. Closed Mon.

Retail & Bookstores
BLOODROOT BOOKSTORE, in Bloodroot Restaurant bldg, 85 Ferris St., Women's bookstore, closed Mon. Hours the same as Bloodroot Restaurant.

COLLINSVILLE

Retail & Bookstores
GERTRUDE & ALICE'S, 2 Front St, (860) 693-3816. Coffeehouse & general bookstore with gay & lesbian section, Wed & Thurs 10am-9pm, Fri & Sat 10am-11pm, Sun 10am-5pm.

DANBURY

Information
WOMEN'S CENTER, 2 West St, (203) 731-5200. Info & referral, travelers call first. Lesbian support group Wed 7:30pm.

Dance Bar/Disco
TRIANGLES CAFE, 66 Sugar Hollow Rd, 3 miles south of Danbury Mall on Rte 7, (203) 798-6996. 5pm-1am (Fri, Sat till 2am), Sun piano, male strippers Mon, Thurs, Fri, female dancers 1st Fri.

FAIRFIELD

Information
WOMEN'S MUSIC ARCHIVES, (203) 255-1348 for appointment.

HARTFORD

Information
AIDS LINE, (860) 247-2437, 24hrs."
HARTFORD GAY & LESBIAN COMMUNITY CTR, 1841 Broad St, (860) 724-5542. 10am-10pm Mon-Fri, gay group meetings, library. AIDS line: 278-4163.

Accommodations
BUTTERNUT FARM, 1654 Main St, Glastonbury, CT, 06033, (860) 633-7197, Fax: (860) 659-1758. Gay-friendly B&B 10 minutes outside Hartford, on 2 wooded & landscaped acres. With private & shared baths, full breakfast, color TV, VCR, AC & phone.

Bars
BAR WITH NO NAME, 115 Asylum St., Gay-friendly weekdays, futuristic decor, entertainment or drag shows Sun.

Dance Bar/Disco
AVALON, 2 North Rd, East Windsor, (860) 292-8902.
★ CHEZ EST, 458 Wethersfield Ave, (860) 525-3243. Disco.
NICK'S CAFE & CABARET, 1943 Broad St, (860) 956-1573. Dance bar, 60% men, 40% women.
POLO CLUB, 678 Maple Ave, (860) 278-3333. Gay-owned & -operated, Sat & Sun from 3pm.

Restaurants
READER'S FEAST CAFE, 529 Farmington Ave, at Reader's Feast bookstore, (860) 232-3710. Bookstore cafe. Coffeehouse Sats, Sun brunch. Scheduled feminist meetings.

Retail & Bookstores
HILLIARD'S PRIDE, 495 Farmington Ave, (860) 523-7280. Custom gay jewelry.
METROSTORE, 495 Farmington Ave, (860) 231-8845. Videos, books, magazines, leathers, games and more. Mon, Thur, Fri 8am-8pm. Tue, Wed & Sat 8am-5:30pm. Closed Sun.
READER'S FEAST BOOKSTORE & CAFE, 529 Farmington Ave, near Kenyon, (860) 232-3710. General bookstore with gay men's & lesbian sections.

MANCHESTER

Information
WOMEN'S CENTER, (860) 647-6056. Hours irregular, best 8am-4:30pm or write MTC, PO Box 1046, Manchester, 06045-1046."

MIDDLETOWN

Information
WESLEYAN WOMEN'S RESOURCE

CENTER, 287 High St, (860) 347-9411 (ext 2669). Hours vary, library, resource files.

MYSTIC

■ Accommodations
ADAMS HOUSE, THE, 382 Cow Hill Rd, Mystic, CT, 06355, (860) 572-9551. Gay-friendly colonial-style B&B with rooms & self-contained Carriage House. Private baths, TV lounge & expanded continental breakfast. Carriage House has color cable TV, VCR & sauna.

NEW HAVEN

■ Information
YALE WOMEN'S CENTER, 198 Elm St, near College, (203) 432-0388. Mon-Fri 9am-5pm & 7-9pm.

■ Bars
ONE SIXTY-EIGHT YORK ST CAFE, 168 York St, near Chapel, (203) 789-1915. Bar & restaurant, summer patio, women welcome." ♂

■ Dance Bar/Disco
GOTHAM CITY, Crown St, near Church., 🎵 ♂

NEW LONDON

■ Information
WOMEN'S CENTER, 16 Jay St, (860) 447-0366. Lesbian group meetings.

■ Bars
HEROES CAFE, 33 Golden St, (860) 442-4376. ♀♂

■ Dance Bar/Disco
FRANK'S PLACE, 9 Tilley St, next to fire station, (860) 443-8883. Dance & show bar with courtyards, 75% men, 25% women. 🎵 🎤 🎵 ♂

■ Restaurants
KEEP, THE, 194 Bank St, (860) 443-8728. Coffeeshop, poet's corner, changing regional menu daily. 🍴

■ Retail & Bookstores
GREEN'S BOOKS & BEANS, 140 Bank St, (860) 443-3312. Mainstream bookstore with lost of gay & lesbian gifts, jewelry, books, rainbow items. 50% gay/lesbian clientele.

NORFOLK

■ Accommodations
MOUNTAIN VIEW INN & RESTAURANT, Rt 272 South, Norfolk, CT, 06058, (860) 542-6991. Gay-friendly inn & restaurant, private & shared baths.

STAMFORD

■ Dance Bar/Disco
ART BAR, 84 W Park Place, (203) 973-0300. Thurs & Sat alternative nights. Unverifiable spring '98. 🎵 ♂

WATERBURY

■ Bars
★ BROWNSTONE CAFE, 29 Leavenworth, (203) 597-1838. Large, upscale New York-style pub, 5pm-1am Tues-Sun, Fri & Sat 5pm-2am, 50% men, 50% women. ♀♂

■ Dance Bar/Disco
MAXIE'S CAFE, 2627 Waterbury Rd, (203) 574-1629. Dance club, DJ weekends, sand volleyball court. 🎵 ♀♂

WESTPORT

■ Dance Bar/Disco
BROOK CAFE, THE, 919 Post Rd East, (203) 222-2233. Piano, cabaret upstairs. Patio, Sun brunch, women welcome. 🎵 🎤 ♂

WILLIMANTIC

■ Retail & Bookstores
EVERYDAY BOOKS & CAFE, 713 Main St, (203) 423-3474. Alternative bookstore with a gay & lesbian selection. 🍴

DELAWARE

DOVER

■ Dance Bar/Disco
RUMOURS RESTAURANT & NIGHT CLUB, 2206 N DuPont Hwy, (302) 678-8805. Bar & restaurant, closed Mon, male & female strippers, 60% men, 40% women. 🎵 🎤 🎵 🎵 ♿ ♀♂

MILTON

■ Women's Accommodations
HONEYSUCKLE, 330 Union St, Milton, DE, 19968, (302) 684-3284. Women-only

DELAWARE

inn & guesthouses near Rehoboth. Inn has double rooms, outdoor hot tub, massage, women's library & full breakfast. Pool on premises."

REHOBOTH BEACH

Information

CAMP REHOBOTH, 39 Baltimore Ave, (302) 227-5620, www.camprehoboth.com. Gay service organization & local gay information.

Accommodations

BEACH HOUSE, 15 Hickman, (302) 227-7074, (800) 283-4667. B&B, moderate to superior rooms, TV lounge, continental breakfast.

CABANA GARDENS BED & BREAKFAST, 20 Lake Avenue, Rehoboth Beach, DE, 19971, (302) 227-5429, Fax: (302) 227-5380. Email: cabanagardens@ce.net, Gay-owned & -operated B&B with private baths, continental breakfast, private decks with great views.

CHESAPEAKE LANDING, 101 Chesapeake St, Rehoboth Beach, DE, 19971, (302) 227-2973, Fax: (302) 227-0301. Email: chesland4@aol.com, Web: www.atbeach.com/lodging/de/bnb/chesland, In the forest on the lake, by the sea, is Chesapeake Landing. Enjoy the hospitality of our Frank Lloyd Wright-inspired home, the area's only waterfront bed and breakfast resort. Spend lazy afternoons on the beach, half a block away, or soak up the sun beside our sparkling pool. Go fishing or explore the lake in our rowboats and paddleboats. Full gourmet breakfast, private baths, AC, cocktails poolside, on dock or by the fire. Popular with gay women, some straight clientele.

GUEST ROOMS AT REHOBOTH, 45 Baltimore Ave, Rehoboth Beach, DE, 19971, (302) 226-2400 (Tel/Fax). Victorian house with private & shared baths, expanded continental breakfast, color cable TV, AC, hot tub.

MALLARD GUEST HOUSES, THE, 60 Baltimore Ave, Rehoboth Beach, DE, 19971, (302) 226-3448. Guesthouses, private baths.

REHOBOTH GUEST HOUSE, 40 Maryland Ave, Rehoboth, DE, 19971, (302) 227-4117, (800) 564-0493. B&B, variety of accommodations. Shared baths, continental breakfast & nearby ocean beach. Some straight clientele."

RENEGADE RESORT, 4274 Highway One, Rehoboth Beach, DE, 19971, (302) 227-4713, (302) 227-1222." Email: renegade@ce.net, Web: www.therenegade.com, Resort with modern guest accommodations. Gay bars, dance club, restaurant, pool with bar on premises.

SAND IN MY SHOES, Sixth & Canal, Rehoboth Beach, DE, 19971, (302) 226-2006 or (800) 231-5856. B&B, private baths."

SILVER LAKE, 133 Silver Lake Dr, Rehoboth Beach, DE, 19971, (302) 226-2115, (800) 842-2115. B&B guesthouse with lake and ocean view. Luxurious rooms and apartments with modern conveniences, including color cable TV, AC & private baths. Sun room, lounge, expanded continental breakfast."

SUMMER PLACE, THE, 30 Olive Ave, Rehoboth Beach, DE, 19971, (302) 226-0766, (800) 815-3925, Fax: (302) 226-3350. Newly built hotel with 5 apartments & 23 rooms on the ocean block, contemporary furnishings, mostly gay & lesbian clientele.

Bars

★ **BLUE MOON**, 35 Baltimore Ave, (302) 227-6515. Upscale restaurant & bar.

CULTURED PEARL, 19 Wilmington Ave, (302) 227-8493. Sushi bar.

DOS LOCOS, 42 1/2 Baltimore Ave, (302) 226-LOCO. Mexican bar & restaurant.

FROG POND TAVERN, 1st & Rehoboth Ave, (302) 227-2234.

Dance Bar/Disco

CLOUD 9, 234 Rehoboth Ave, (302) 226-1999.

★ **RENEGADE**, at Renegade Resort, 4274 Hwy 1, (302) 227-4713. Disco, bar, restaurant, summer T-dance, patio. Open 7 days in summer, off-season open Fri-Sun

Restaurants

★ **BLUE MOON**, 35 Baltimore Ave, same building as Blue Moon bar, (302) 227-6515. Restaurant & bar, upscale gourmet American cuisine.

CAFE TERIA, 12 Wilmington Ave, (302) 226-2011.
CELSIUS, 50 Wilmington Ave, (302) 227-5767.
FUSION, 50 Wilmington Ave.,
MANO'S, 10 Wilmington Ave, (302) 227-6707.
PLANET X, 33 Wilmington Ave, (302) 226-1928. Vegetarian cuisine.
SAVANNAH'S, 37 Wilmington Ave, (302) 227-1994.
TIJUANA TAXI, 207 Rehoboth Ave, (302) 227-1986. Mexican food."

Retail & Bookstores
LAMBDA RISING, 39 Baltimore Ave, (302) 227-6969. Gay & lesbian bookstore.

WILMINGTON

Bars
EIGHT FOURTEEN, THE, 814 Shipley St, (302) 657-5730. Bar & restaurant. Small dance floor, Thurs Latin night, Fri ladies night, DJ Fri-Sun.

Dance Bar/Disco
EXCHANGE, 914 N Orange St & 6th, (302) 777-7080, dance bar.
ROAM, 913 Shipley St near 10th St, above the Shipley Grill, (302) 658-ROAM (7626). Disco 7 nights, 6pm-1am, Fri 5pm-1am, 70% men, 30% women. Women welcome.

Restaurants
SHIPLEY GRILL, 913 Shipley St, near 10th St, (302) 652-7797. American cuisine, lunch & dinner. Popular, large gay following. "Gay Monday" half price entrees with coupon from Roam disco.

DISTRICT OF COLUMBIA
WASHINGTON

Information
GAY & LESBIAN SWITCHBOARD, (202) 628-4667. 7:30pm-10:30pm 7 days. Irregularly staffed.
LESBIAN LINE, (202) 628-4666, 7:30pm-10:30pm 7 days.
LESBIAN SERVICES OF WHITMAN WALKER CLINIC, 1407 South St NW, (202) 939-7875, 9am-6pm Mon-Fri.

Accommodations
BRENTON, THE, 1708 16th St NW, Washington, DC, 20009, (202) 332-5550, (800) 673-9042, Fax: (202) 462-5872. Guesthouse, women welcome. Spacious rooms furnished in antiques, art, oriental or period carpets. TV lounge & expanded continental breakfast."
CAPITOL HILL GUEST HOUSE, 101 Fifth St NE, Washington, DC, 20002, (202) 547-1050 (Tel/Fax), (800) 261-2768. B&B, 50% gay & lesbian. Comfortable rooms with Victorian-era decor, refrigerator in hall, continental breakfast.

·1836 CALIFORNIA·
A Victorian Bed & Breakfast
(202) 462-6502
Washington, DC

THE EMBASSY INN
1627 16th Street, N.W. (202) 234-7800

THE WINDSOR INN
1842 16th Street, N.W. (202) 667-0300

Washington, D.C. 20009 • (800) 423-9111

DISTRICT OF COLUMBIA

EIGHTEEN THIRTY-SIX CALIFORNIA ST, 1836 California St NW, Washington, DC, 20009, (202) 462-6502, Fax: (202) 265-0342. Centrally-located small, elegant B&B in a 1900 Victorian townhouse. Amenities include telephone, AC, clock radios and private and shared baths. Some rooms have cable TV. Breakfasts are served family-style in the dining room. Minutes from all the capital's attractions. ♀♂ See ad on page 277.

EMBASSY INN, 1627 16th St, Washington, DC, (202) 234-7800 or (800) 423-9111, Fax: (202) 234-3309. Gay-friendly B&B on historical 16th St near restaurants and night life. Rooms with Federalist-style decor, private baths, telephone, color cable TV with free HBO and maid service. Continental breakfast and complimentary coffee, tea and evening sherry. **Enjoy a relaxed atmosphere and personalized service.** See ad on page 277

KALORAMA GUEST HOUSE AT KALORAMA PARK, THE, 1854 Mintwood Pl NW, Washington, DC, 20009, (202) 667-6369, Fax: (202) 319-1262. B&B, mixed straight/gay/lesbian clientele. Private and shared baths. Charming Victorian home in tree-lined downtown residential area. Walk to night spots in Dupont Circle and Adams Morgan, and the Metro. Complimentary continental plus breakfast and evening aperitif.

William Lewis House

Close to Nightlife & Restaurants of Dupont Circle
(800) 465-7574
WASHINGTON, DC

KALORAMA GUEST HOUSE AT WOODLEY PARK, 2700 Cathedral Ave NW, Washington, DC, 20008, (202) 328-0860. B&B, mixed straight/gay/lesbian clientele. Private and shared baths. Lovely Victorian home in tree-lined downtown residential area. Walk to the Metro and night spots in Adams Morgan and Dupont Circle. Complimentary continental plus breakfast and evening aperitif. Ten minutes to most tourist spots.

MORRISON HOUSE, 116 South Alfred Street, Alexandria, VA, (703) 838-8000, (800) 367-0800, Fax: (703) 548-2489. Gay-friendly Federal Period hotel inn with bar & 2 restaurants, minutes from Washington, DC & National Airport. Elegantly decorated, private baths, continental breakfast, English Tea, valet parking. Gay male following.

TAFT BRIDGE INN, 2007 Wyoming Ave NW, Washington, DC, 20009, (202) 387-2007, Fax: (202) 387-5019. Gay-friendly inn in a turn-of-the-century Georgian mansion, priv./shared baths, cont. break.

WILLIAM LEWIS HOUSE, THE, 1309 R St NW, Washington, DC, (202) 462-7574, (800) 465-7574, Fax: (202) 462-1608. Email: wlewishous@aol.com, Web: //www.wlewishous.com, This completely restored house features antique luxuries and many modern conveniences, such as direct-dial phones with answering machines and ceiling fans in each guest room and a hot tub in the garden. We're conveniently located in the heart of the gay community very near 17th St., Dupont Circle, Adams Morgan and The Mall. Three subway lines & many of Washington's best restaurants are within walking distance. You're always welcome at Washington's finest B&B. ♂

WINDSOR INN, 1842 16th St NW, Washington, DC, 20009, (202) 667-0300, (800) 423-9111, Fax: (202) 667-4503. Gay-friendly B&B on historical 16th St. Variety of comfortable, tastefully decorated rooms and suites with modern conveniences. Continental breakfast, complimentary coffee, tea and evening sherry, color cable TV with free HBO. **Enjoy a relaxed atmosphere and personalized service.**

■ Bars

BANANA CAFE, 500 8th St SE, (202) 543-5906. Piano bar & restaurant with dancing. 🍽 ♀♂

CIRCLE TAVERN, 1629 Connecticut Ave NW, (202) 462-5575. 3 levels: video dance bar, restaurant & tavern with terrace. Drag shows Sun. 🎵♪♂

LARRY'S LOUNGE, 1836 18th St NW, (202) 483-0097. Bar & restaurant. 🍴♀♂

NOB HILL, 1101 Kenyon NW, at 11th NW, (202) 797-1101. Bar & restaurant, disco. Cabaret upstairs Sat. Gospel singers Sun. 🎵🍴♪♀♂

PHASE I, 525 8th St SE, (202) 544-6831. Jukebox, 30's +. 🎵♪♀

Q CLUB & RESTAURANT, 1603 17th St NW, at Q St, (202) 232-4141. Martini/piano bar & rest. with video. Wed ladies nite. ♀♂

WAVE BAR & LOUNGE, 1731 New Hampshire Ave, (202) 518-5011. Loungy, sofas. ♂

■ Dance Bar/Disco

BACHELOR'S MILL, 1104 8th St SE, (202) 544-1931. Drag shows Sun, Wed ladies night, closed Mon. 🎵♪🍴♀♂

CIRCLE, TERRACE, UNDERGROUND, PLAYROOM, 1629 Connecticut Ave NW, at The Circle., (202) 462-5575. Dance/video bar & rest. 🎵♪♂

ELAN, 1129 Pennsylvania Ave SE, upstairs, above the Cafe Italiano, (202) 544-6404. Intimate & classy dance bar. ♀

ESCANDALO & BREADBASKET CAFE, 2122 P St NW, 1/2 blk from 21st St, (202) 822-8909. Video dance bar & restaurant. Lots of Latin music, salsa & merengue lessons Mon. Drag shows after hours. 🎵♪📺♀♂

HUNG JURY, 1819 H St NW, near 19th St, (202) 785-8181. Open Fri & Sat, younger crowd." 🎵♀

REMINGTON'S, 639 Pennsylvania Ave, Nr SE 6th, (202) 543-3113. Video C&W dance bar, brunches, 80% men. 🎵♪∪♂

★ **TRACKS,** 1111 1st St SE, (202) 488-3320. Giant hi-energy dance bar, patio, video, after hours, sand volleyball court. Ladies nights, black & white Sun restaurant. 🎵♪♀♂

★ **ZIEGFELD'S & SECRETS COMPLEX,** 1345 Half St SE, at O St, (202) 554-5141. Show bar with dancing. Secrets has male dancers. Drag shows late Thur & on Sun. 🎵♪📺♀♂

■ Cafe

CAFE BERLIN, 322 Massachusetts Ave NE, (202) 543-7656. German cuisine. 📺

CUSANO'S MEET MARKET, 1613 17th St NW, (202) 319-8757.

FRANKLIN'S, 2000 18th St NW, (202) 319-1800. 📺

POP STOP, 1513 17th St NW, (202) 328-0880. Pastries & desserts, light fare. 📺

■ Restaurants

★ **ANNIE'S,** 1609 17th St NW, near Q, (202) 232-0395. Sat, Sun brunch. 🍷 ♀♂

CAFE LUNA, 1633 P St NW, downstairs, (202) 387-4005. 🍷 ♀♂

GRILLFISH, 1200 New Hampshire Ave NW, (202) 331-7310.

HERB'S, 1615 Rhode Island Ave, (202) 333-4372. Restaurant at Holiday Inn, popular for Sun brunch. 📺

JOLT 'N BOLT, 1918 18th St NW, (202) 232-0077. 📺

MEDITERRANEAN BLUE, 1910 18th St NW, (202) 483-2583. Rest. & bar. ♀♂

MR HENRY'S, 601 Penn Ave SE, (202) 546-8412. Restaurant and bar, American cuisine. 🍴✕♀♂

★ **Q CLUB & RESTARUANT,** 1603 17th St NW, (202) 232-4141. Martini & piano bar & rest. with video. Wed ladies nite. ♀♂

RANDOLPH'S GRILL, 1731 New Hampshire Ave NW, at the Carlyle Hotel, (202) 518-5011. 📺

RANDY'S CAFE, 1517 17th St NW, (202) 287-5399.

TWO QUAIL, 320 Massachusetts Ave NE, (202) 543-8030. 📺 🍷

ZUKI MOON, 824 New Hampshire, (202) 333-3312. Noodle house. 📺

■ Women's Groups, Services

BON VIVANT, (301) 907-7920, fax: (301) 907-9118, e-mail: BonVivDC@aol.com. Social club for lesbian professionals.

■ Retail & Bookstores

LAMBDA RISING BOOKS, 1625 Connecticut Ave NW, near R St, (202) 462-6969, Fax: (202) 462-7257. E-mail: lamdarising@his.com. Gay & lesbian books & magazines.

LAMMAS WOMEN'S BOOKS & MORE, 1607 17th St NW, (202) 775-8218, (800) 955-2662, fax: (202) 775-0588. Lammas is DC's one-stop shop for lesbians.

PRIDE EMPORIUM, 2147 P St NW, 2nd floor, above Mr P's Bar, (202) 822-3984. Rainbow, pride items.

FLORIDA STATEWIDE

■ *Accommodations*
CARITAS BED & BREAKFAST NETWORK, (800) CARITAS, (312) 857-0801, Fax: (312) 857-0805. B&B, home-stay accommodations service. Member: IGLTA

AMELIA ISLAND

■ *Accommodations*
AMELIA ISLAND WILLIAMS HOUSE, 103 S 9th St, Amelia Island, FL, 32034, (904) 277-2328, Fax: (904) 321-1325. Reservations only: (800) 414-9257. Email: topinn@aol.com, Web: www.williamshouse.com, Gay-friendly B&B in Antebellum mansion. Color cable TV, VCR, video tape library, AC, ceiling fan, private baths, full breakfast."

BOCA GRANDE

■ *Tours, Charters & Excursions*
WHELK WOMEN, PO Box 1006T, Boca Grande, FL, (941) 964-2027. Go day sailing and dolphin watching in beautiful Charlotte Harbor or Gulf of Mexico with us. Picnic on white sandy beaches of uninhabited barrier islands. Visit Calusa shell mounds, learn sailing techniques (chart reading and taking control at the helm), and swim, sun and relax under sail in the privacy of the open uncrowded harbor. ♀

CEDAR KEY

■ *Restaurants*
BLUE DESERT CAFE, Hwy 24, (904) 543-9111.

COCOA

■ *Bars*
CLUB CHANCES, 610 Forest Ave, (407) 639-0103. Ladies nite Tues, men's nite Mon.

COCOA BEACH

■ *Dance Bar/Disco*
WANNA BE'S, 231 Minutemen Causeway, (407) 868-1898. 2 blocks from beach, Mon-Fri 5pm-2am, Sat-Sun 12pm-12am, 70% men, 30% women, lite menu.

DAYTONA BEACH

■ *Information*
AIDS LINE OUTREACH, (904) 322-4738. Mon-Fri 8am-5pm.
LAMBDA CENTER & HOTLINE, 320 Harvey Ave, (904) 255-0280.

■ *Accommodations*
BUCCANEER MOTEL, 2301 N Atlantic Ave, Daytona Beach, FL, 32118, (904) 253-9678, (800) 972-6056, Fax: (904) 255-3946. Small motel, walking distance to beach & amenities, some straight clientele. Rooms with modern conveniences & complimentary morning coffee or tea in lobby."
COQUINA INN BED & BREAKFAST, 544 South Palmetto Ave, Daytona Beach, FL, 32114, (904) 254-4969 (Tel/Fax), (800) 805-7533. B&B inn 7 rooms & 1 suite in Daytona's historic district. Private baths, gourmet buffet breakfast, locally-made chocolates, color cable TV, AC, ocean & pool nearby, some straight clientele.
VILLA, THE, 801 N Peninsula Dr, Daytona Beach, FL, 32118, (904) 248-2020 (Tel/Fax). Email: thevillabb@aol.com, B&B, some straight clientele. Rooms & apts, variety of modern conveniences, library with TV lounge, continental breakfast, pool & nearby ocean beach."

■ *Dance Bar/Disco*
BARRACKS & OFFICERS CLUB COMPLEX, 952 Orange Ave, (904) 254-3464. Complex has 4 venues. Officers Lounge: bar & lounge. NCO Club: game bar with pool table, darts, etc. Flight Deck: outdoor bar with Sun BBQ. Bar-

FLORIDA 281

racks Dance Club: 70% men, Mon-Sat 5pm-3am, Sun 3pm-3am, shows Wed, Fri-Sun, male dancers Wed, Fri, Sat.

HOLLYWOOD/BARN DOOR COMPLEX, 615 Main St, (904) 252-3776. Show bar, cruise bar, piano lounge, restaurant. Ladies night Tues.

MIKE & HANK'S, small dance bar, check information for new address.

SEVEN SIXTY-NINE CLUB, 769 Alabama St, (904) 253-4361. Bar & restaurant, pool tables, darts, men welcome.

Restaurants

CAFE FRAPPES, 174 N Beach St., Upscale American gourmet cuisine.

FT LAUDERDALE

Information

GAY & LESBIAN COMMUNITY CENTER, 1164 E Oakland Park Blvd, 3rd fl, (954) 563-9500.

Tours, Charters & Excursions

JOURNEYS BY SEA, 1402 E Las Olas Blvd #122, Ft Lauderdale, FL, 33301, (954) 522-5865, (800) 825-3632, Fax: (954) 522-5836. Email: journeys@safari.net, Web: www.safari.net/~journeys, Choose a latitude to match your attitude, then select from our over 400 yachts. Rates are a lot lower than you think! From $195 per person per day, all inclusive. With yacht vacations, YOU decide the ports of call. Most yachts offer snorkeling, scuba diving, windsurfing, kayaking and water skiing. We customize and tailor yacht vacations to every individual desire. All vacations include all meals and the bar.

Accommodations

ADMIRAL'S COURT, 21 Hendricks Isle, Ft Lauderdale, FL, 33301, (954) 462-5072, (800) 248-6669, Fax: (954) 763-8863. Motel near beach & Las Olas Blvd, usually 50% gay & lesbian clientele. Comfortable rooms of various sizes, private baths. Tropical gardens & private dock."

BAHAMA HOTEL, THE, 401 N Atlantic Blvd (A1A), Fort Lauderdale, FL, 33304, (954) 467-7315, (800) 622-9995, Fax: (954) 467-7319. Email: bahama@bahamahotel.com, Web: http://www.bahamahotel.com, Gay-friendly beachfront hotel with 43 rooms, 1 suite and 23 efficiency cottages. Swim in the large, heated, freshwater pool or stretch out for tanning on the sun-drenched patio. Guests enjoy 2 bars and "The Deck" restaurant overlooking the Atlantic. Friendly staff provides outstanding service. Reasonable rates.

KING HENRY ARMS, 543 Breakers Ave, Ft. Lauderdale, FL, 33304-4129, (954) 561-0039 or (800) 205-KING (5464). Clean, quiet & congenial motel with home-like, ultra-clean rooms & private baths. Continental breakfast, tropical patio, BBQ, shuffleboard, pool on premises, beach nearby, walk to strip. Women welcome."

PALM PLAZA, 2801 Rio Mar St, Ft Lauderdale, FL, 33304, (954) 254-1985, (888) 954-7300, Fax: (954) 565-1105. Rooms & apartments on beautiful grounds. Pool, large sunning area, BBQ, continental breakfast, steps to the beach. Gay-friendly with a gay male following.

VILLA VENICE, 2900 Terramar St, (954) 564-7855. Walk to beach.

Women's Accommodations

INN, THE, (800) 881-4814, (954) 568-5770. Women-only B&B. Continental breakfast, pool on premises, Sun tea dance with Louise.

RAINBOW VENTURES "THE INN", 1520 NE 26 Ave, Ft Lauderdale, FL, (954) 568-5770, (800) 881-4814, Fax: (954) 564-8103. Inn, continental breakfast, women only.

Bars

CHARDEE'S, 2209 Wilton Dr, (954) 563-1800. Bar & restaurant, 60% men, 40% women, mature crowd.

TROPICS, 2000 Wilton Dr, Upscale bar.

★ **TWO FIVE O NINE WEST**, 2509 W Broward Blvd, (954) 791-2509.

★ **WHALE & PORPOISE**, 2750 E Oakland Park Blvd, (954) 565-2750. Hi NRG dance bar.

Dance Bar/Disco

★ **COPA**, 2800 S Federal Hwy, near Fed Hwy, (954) 463-1507. Dance bar & 4 other bars, patio. Open late, name entertainment.

282 FLORIDA

END UP, 3521 W Broward Blvd, (954) 584-9301. midnite til 4am, popular late night dance bar, latest bar in town. 🕴 ♀♂

★ **OTHERGLADES,** 2234 Wilton Dr, (954) 566-4100. Lounge & dance bar, famous Sun tea dance. 🕴 ♂

Restaurants

CHARDEE'S, 2209 Wilton Dr, at Chardee's bar., (954) 563-1800. 🍸 🎵 ♀♂

COSTELLO'S RESTAURANT, 2345 Wilton Dr, (954) 563-7752.

COURTYARD CAFE, 2211 Wilton Dr, Wilton Manors, (954) 564-9365. Breakfast & lunch.

DECK RESTAURANT, THE, 401 N Atlantic Blvd, at Bayshore in the Bahama Hotel, (954) 467-7315. Gay-friendly, breakfast, lunch & dinner.

FLORIDIAN, THE, 1410 Las Olas, (954) 463-4041.

HERBAN KITCHEN, 2823 E Oakland Park Blvd, (954) 566-1110. ♀♂

HI-LIFE CAFE, 3000 N Federal Hwy, (954) 563-1395.

LEGENDS CAFE, 1560 NE 4th Ave, (954) 467-2233. Innovative cuisine. ♀♂

TROPICS, 2000 Wilton Dr, (954) 537-6000. Supper club, piano music, steaks, seafood, 80% men, 20% women. ♂

Retail & Bookstores

CATALOG X, 850 NE 13th St, (954) 524-5050. Gay items, clothing, etc.

LAMBDA PASSAGES, (305) 754-6900 (Miami phone #). Gay bookstore (see listing under retail in Miami, FL).

NEWS, BOOKS & CARDS, 7126 N University Dr, Tamarac, (954) 726-5544. Outrageous greeting cards, magazines, novelties.

PRIDE FACTORY, 600 N Federal Hwy, (954) 463-6600. Gay & lesbian bookstore.

FT MYERS

Information

AIDS HOTLINE, Ft Myers: (941) 337-AIDS, Naples: (941) 263-CARE.

THE RESORT
on Carefree Boulevard

Ft. Myers, Florida

(800) 326-0364

FLORIDA 283

■ *Women's Accommodations*
RESORT ON CAREFREE BOULEVARD, THE, 3000 Carefree Blvd, Fort Myers, FL, 33917-7135, (941) 731-3000, (800) 326-0364, Fax: (941) 731-3519. Web: http://www.resortoncb.com. For women like you, who dream of a comfortable, fun community. At The Resort on Carefree Boulevard in Fort Myers, Florida, you'll find affordable luxury. Imagine tennis, swimming, fishing, spa and exercise facilities, dancing, nearby golf. Buy or rent a home that suits your lifestyle. All within easy driving distance of Sanibel and Captiva Islands. **Reserve your place in the sun.** ♀

■ *Bars*
OFFICE PUB, 3704 Cleveland Ave (US Hwy 41), (941) 936-3212. CD jukebox, women welcome.

■ *Dance Bar/Disco*
APEX, 4226 Fowler St, (941) 418-0878. CD jukebox.
★ **BOTTOM LINE,** 3090 Evans Ave, (941) 337-7292. Video, cruise & dance bars, 75% men, 25% women. Ladies nights, women very welcome, many straights."

■ *Cafe*
OASIS, 2222 McGregor Blvd, in Boulevard Plaza, (941) 334-1566. Women-owned, breakfast & lunch menus, some vegetarian meals. May change in 1997.

FT WALTON BEACH

■ *Dance Bar/Disco*
FRANKLY SCARLET'S & CHOO CHOO'S PUB, 217 SE Miracle Strip Pkwy, (850) 664-2966. Dance & lounge bars.

GAINESVILLE

■ *Information*
GAY SWITCHBOARD, (352) 332-0700, 6pm-11pm most evenings or voice mail system listings.

■ *Accommodations*
RUSTIC INN, 3105 S. Main St, High Springs, FL, 32643, (904) 454-1223, Fax: (904) 454-1225. Gay-friendly B&B inn 15 miles out of Gainesville, private baths,

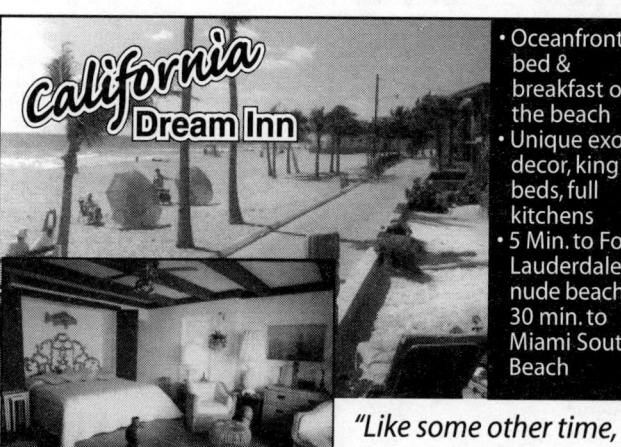

California Dream Inn

- Oceanfront bed & breakfast on the beach
- Unique exotic decor, king beds, full kitchens
- 5 Min. to Fort Lauderdale/ nude beaches; 30 min. to Miami South Beach

(954) 923-2100
Email: dreaminn@gate.net
Hollywood, Florida

"Like some other time, some other place, somewhere redolent of our dreams."
South Florida Magazine

expanded continental or full breakfast, vegetarian cuisine, AC, b&w TV, ceiling fans, pool on premises, gay female following.

■ Bars
WILD ANGELS, 4128 NW 6th St.,

■ Dance Bar/Disco
CLUB DIVERSITY, Hwy 441, just outside town, 1mi S of blinking, light, in town of Micanopy 5-10 mi S of, Gainesville, rainbow flags outside building. Dance & show bar, more popular after hours, large straight following.

UNIVERSITY CLUB, 18 E University Ave, entrance in rear NE 1st Ave, (352) 378-6814. Disco, 60% men, 40% women, male strippers Wed. Fri many women. Younger crowd, large straight following for the drag shows.

■ Retail & Bookstores
WILD IRIS BOOKS, 802 W University Ave, (352) 375-7477. Feminist bookstore with a gay & lesbian section.

HOLLYWOOD

■ Accommodations
CALIFORNIA DREAM INN, 300-315 Walnut St, Hollywood, FL, 33019, (954) 923-2100, Fax: (954) 923-3222. Email: dreaminn@gate.net, Web: http://www.gate.net/~dreaminn, Surrounded by tropical palms and just 50 feet from the ocean, this gay-friendly hotel features oceanfront rooms furnished with a unique and exotic decor, reflecting the tropics with a dash of European charm. Amenities include full kitchens, phone, cable TV, AC, ceiling fans & expanded continental breakfast. 50% gay/lesbian clientele. In-house travel agency: Past Lives Travel, (954) 927-6770, fax: (954) 923-3222, e-mail: atl33019@aol. See ad on page 283.

■ Bars
PARTNERS, 625 E Dania Beach Blvd, Dania, (954) 921-9893. Near the beach, DJ weekends, karaoke nites, Sun buffet, 75% women. Open mike Tues.

ZACHARY'S, 2217 North Federal Hwy, Hollywood, (954) 920-5479. Sports bar, occasional DJ, 75% gay women with 25% straight clientele.

JACKSONVILLE

■ Bars
BOURBON STREET, 10957 Atlantic Blvd, (904) 642-7506. Ladies & men's nights, male dancers.

JUNCTION, 1261 King St, at Lydia, (904) 388-3434. Bar, patio, BBQ Sun, live entertainment weekends, 50% men, 50% women.

PARK PLACE LOUNGE, 2712 Park St, (904) 389-6616. 50% men, 50% women, full liquor."

■ Dance Bar/Disco
BO'S CORAL REEF, 201 5th Ave N, at 2nd St, Jacksonville Beach, (904) 246-9874. Dance & show bar.

★ **METRO,** 2929 Plum St, (904) 388-7192. Dance bar with Rainbow room piano bar, Boiler Room leather area with flicks, best Sat, game room.

MY LITTLE DUDE (JO'S PLACE), 2952 Roosevelt Blvd, at Willow Branch, (904) 388-9503. Dance & show bar, male & female impersonator shows, men welcome.

★ **THIRD DIMENSION,** 711 Edison, (904) 353-6316. Dance, show & patio bars, drag shows Tues, Thurs-Sat, Sun buffet & beer bust 5pm-9pm, 90% men, 10% women.

■ Leathers/Piercing
OLD KENTUCKY LEATHERWORKS, THE, 822 Lomax St, (904) 353-3770. Bondage & fetish accessories. Mon-Fri 10am-6pm, Sat 10am-5pm.

JASPER

■ Accommodations
J&J FARMS, PO Box 1623, Jasper, FL, 32052, (904) 792-2771. B&B on 78.6 acres of private wooded land 15 miles south of Georgia. Many breeds of swans, waterfowl & other animals. Shared baths, TV lounge, full breakfast, pool & Jacuzzi. Women welcome.

FLORIDA 285

KEY WEST

■ Information

KEY WEST BUSINESS GUILD, (800) 535-7797. Local gay business organization.

■ Accommodations

A TROPICAL INN, 812 Duval St, Key West, FL, 33040, (305) 294-9977. Gay-friendly guesthouse in historic Old Key West. Color TV, AC, private baths. Suites with private garden & spa. Continental breakfast in winter season.

ALEXANDER'S GUESTHOUSE, 1118 Fleming St, Key West, FL, 33040, (305) 294-9919 or (800) 654-9919. Email: alexghouse@aol.com, Tasteful gay & lesbian accommodations, an unsurpassed level of convenience & comfort with every amenity, a short walk to entertainment & attractions. Secluded & private grounds... heated pool... rooms & suites uniquely decorated in Key West "casual" style, many with private verandahs or decks. Daily complimentary continental breakfast, poolside... assistance with dining & watersport reservations. Gay-owned & -operated. Out & About Editor's Choice Award, two consecutive years.

ATLANTIC SHORES RESORT, 510 South St, Key West, FL, 33040, (305) 296-2491, (800) 526-3559, Fax: (305) 294-2753. Email: AtlShores@aol.com, Ocean-front Art Deco hotel with restaurant, pool bar & grill in the heart of Old Town, color cable TV, private baths, pool on premises, some straight clientele.

BANANA'S FOSTER BED & BREAKFAST, 537 Caroline St, Key West, FL, 33040, (305) 294-9061, (800) 653-4888. B&B in ideal location. Beach club privileges, everyone welcome.

BIG RUBY'S GUESTHOUSE, 409 Applerouth Lane, Key West, FL, 33040-6534, (305) 296-2323 or (800) 477-7829. Email: BigRubys@aol.com, Guesthouse 1/2 block from Duval St restaurants, shops, bars. Thirteen immaculate rooms with sumptuous beds. Full breakfast. Dinner served major holidays. Ocean beach nearby.

BLUE PARROT INN, 916 Elizabeth St, Key West, FL, 33040, (305) 296-0033, (800) 231-BIRD (2473). Web: http://www.blueparrotinn.com, Tropical retreat 2 blocks from Duval Street. Our pool is heated during the cooler months and is usable year 'round. Beaches, clubs, restaurants and shops are a short walk away.

BRASS KEY GUESTHOUSE, THE, 412 Frances St, Key West, FL, 33040, (305) 296-4719, (800) 932-9119, Fax: (305) 296-1994. Key West's finest 5-star guesthouse offers attentive service and luxury accommodations in a traditional setting of wide verandahs, plantation shutters and ceiling fans. Enjoy expansive sun decks, a sparkling heated pool and a whirlpool spa set among lush, tropical gardens.

Tasteful gay & lesbian accommodations
ALEXANDER'S
G U E S T H O U S E
1-800-654-9919
1118 Fleming St., Key West, FL 33040

FLORIDA

CHELSEA HOUSE, 707 Truman Ave, Key West, FL, 33040, (305) 296-2211, USA & Canada: (800) 845-8859, Fax: (305) 296-4822. Email: chelseahse@aol.com, "All welcome." This 1870 renovation (18 rooms), two blocks from Duval, has off-street parking, pool and tropical gardens on an acre of land. Complimentary continental breakfast is served from 8:30-10:30am by the pool. All rooms have refrigerators, AC, color cable television, ceiling fans, telephone coffeemaker, hairdryer and private bath. Gay-owned and -operated.

DÉJÀ VU, 611 Truman Ave, Key West, FL, 33040, (305) 292-1424, Fax: (305) 292-2258. Bed & breakfast, 10% gay & lesbian clientele, continental breakfast, sauna, Jacuzzi.

DUVAL HOUSE, 815 Duval St, Key West, FL, 33040, (305) 294-1666 or (800) 22-DUVAL (38825). Inn in center of Old Town, 50% gay & lesbian clientele. Double rooms individually decorated with wicker & antiques. Expanded continental breakfast & nearby ocean beach.

DUVAL SUITES, 724 Duval St, Key West, FL, 33040, (305) 293-6600, (800) 648-3780, Fax: 294-9298. Email: pilothous@aol.com, Rooms, suites & cottages, all private baths, AC, 50% gay/lesbian.

EATON LODGE, 511 Eaton St, Key West, FL, 33040, (305) 292-2170, (800) 294-2170. Gay-friendly guesthouse. Color cable TV, VCR, AC, private baths, expanded continental breakfast. Jacuzzi & pool on premises.

GARDEN HOUSE KEY WEST, 329 Elizabeth St, (305) 296-5368, Fax: 292-1160, (800) 695-6453. Guesthouse 2 blocks from Duval St, 50% gay & lesbian clientele. Variety of modestly furnished rooms, expanded continental breakfast buffet.

HERON HOUSE, 512 Simonton St, Key West, FL, 33040, (305) 294-9227, (888) 676-8654, Fax: (305) 294-5692. Email: heronKW@aol.com, Web: http://www.heronhouse.com, Amidst orchids, bougainvillaea, jasmine and palms, a secluded tropical garden fantasy awaits you. This warm, friendly place invites you to relax and dream on spacious sun decks surrounding a sparkling pool. Light, airy and spacious rooms are a careful mix of old and new and have a tropical flare with wicker, casual and comfortable furnishings. Gay-friendly.

ISLAND KEY COURTS OF KEY WEST, THE, 910 Simonton St (office) & 817 Catherine St, Key West, FL, 33040, (305) 296-1148, (800) 296-1148, Fax: (305) 292-7924. Email: rayebv@aol.com, Web: http://www.q-net/islandkeycourts, The only Key West guesthouse offering a special Welcome Package for Women with free gifts & a unique Key West for Women Insider's Guide. Charming guestrooms & apartment suites, very private, "Key West Casual" ambiance, in walk-to-everything Old Town. Fully equipped, private kitchens, baths, garden/patio studios, 1 & 2 bedrooms, sleeping 1-9, AC, cable color TV. Free membership to nearby beach club with pool, gym, spa, 2 restaurants, 3 bars. All-welcome policy.

KEY LODGE MOTEL, 1004 Duval St, Key West, FL, 33040, (305) 296-9915, (800) 458-1296. Centrally located gay-friendly motel. Private baths, color TV, AC, ceiling fans, phones, refrigerator & pool.

KNOWLES HOUSE, THE, 1004 Eaton St, Key West, FL, 33040, (305) 296-8132, (800) 352-4414, Fax: (305) 296-2093. Email: knowles@conch.net, B&B guesthouse, private & shared baths, continental breakfast, pool on premises, some straight clientele.

LA TE DA HOTEL, 1125 Duval St, Key West, FL, 33040, (305) 296-6706, (800) 528-3320, Fax: (305) 296-0438. Hotel with restaurant & show bar, private baths, AC, phone, pool & clothing-optional sun deck. Some straight clientele.

LAVADIA, Mail to: Southernmost Hospitality, 524 Eaton St, #150, Key West, FL, 33040, (305) 294-3800, (888) 294-3800, Fax: (305) 294-9298." Email: keywestlodging@sprynet, Apartments, cottages & luxury homes, all private baths, AC, phone, color cable TV, pool on premises.

MERLINN GUEST HOUSE, 811 Simonton St, Key West, FL, 33040, (305) 296-3336 or Fax: 296-3524. Guesthouse,

FLORIDA 287

private baths, mainly straight clientele."

MERMAID & THE ALLIGATOR, THE, 729 Truman Ave, Key West, FL, 33040, (305) 294-1894, (800) 773-1894, Fax: (305) 295-9925. Email: mermaid@joy.net, Gay-friendly guesthouse, private baths.

ORTON TERRACE, 606 Orton Ave, Ft. Lauderdale, FL, 33304, (954) 566-5068, Fax: (954) 564-8646. Toll-free in USA, Canada & Caribbean: (800) 323-1142. Motel with apartments & guestrooms with full-sized kitchens, TV, phones, AC, color cable TV, pool on premises, steps from the beach.

PILOT HOUSE, 414 Simonton St, Key West, FL, 33040, (800) 648-3780, (305) 293-6600, Fax: (305) 294-9298. Email: pilothousekeywest@sprynet, Guesthouse with private baths, Jacuzzi, pool on premises, 50% gay & lesbian clientele.

RED ROOSTER, 709 Truman Ave, Key West, FL, 33040, (305) 296-6558, Fax: (305) 296-4822. Budget B&B accommodations, 50% gay/lesbian clientele, expanded continental breakfast, private baths.

SEASCAPE, 420 Olivia St, Key West, FL, 33040, (305) 296-7776 (phone & fax). Gay-friendly guesthouse. Double rooms with modern conveniences, spa, nearby ocean beach, continental breakfast, 10% gay & lesbian clientele.

Feel Free...Feel Relaxed...
Feel Welcomed...

HERON HOUSE
512 Simonton Street
Key West, FL
(888) 676-8654

Chelsea HOUSE

CIRCA 1870

All Adult Compound

Clothes Optional Sundeck

Luxury Accommodations

(305) 296-2211
Fax: (305) 296-4822
USA & CANADA
(800) 845-8859

707 Truman Avenue
Key West, FL 33040

SHERATON KEY WEST ALL SUITE RESORT, 2001 S Roosevelt Blvd, Key West, FL, 33040, (305) 292-9800, Fax: (305) 294-6009. An all-suites resort, spacious luxury suites with extensive amenities for comfort & convenience, pool on premises, beach nearby.

SIMONTON COURT HISTORIC INN & COTTAGES, 320 Simonton St, Key West, FL, 33040, (800) 944-2687, (305) 294-6386, Fax: (305) 293-8446. Inn with rooms & cottages, 50% gay & lesbian. VCR's in all units, color cable TV, private baths, expanded continental breakfast. 3 pools on premises, hot tub, nearby ocean beach."

WILLIAM ANTHONY HOUSE, 613 Caroline St, Key West, FL, 33040, (305) 294-2887, (800) 613-2276. Luxury suites & guest rooms in a quiet location. Private baths, AC, spa, 30% gay & lesbian.

■ Women's Accommodations

RAINBOW HOUSE, 525 Simonton St, Key West, FL, 33040, (305) 292-1450, (800) 74-WOMYN (800 749-6696). Web: www.rainbowhousekeywest.com, *Key West's Only Exclusively Women's Guest House* We've expanded! Our lovely accommodations include 38 rooms, suites and kitchenettes, and feature bedrooms with queen bed, private bath, color TV, air conditioning and Bahama fans. Deluxe continental breakfast is served in our air conditioned pavilion. Massage is available. Other amenities include 2 heated swimming pools, 2 hot tubs, extensive decking for sunbathing, a shaded tropical pavilion for lazy-day lounging. Restaurants and night life are within walking distance. The shopping district is a half-block away. It's one block to the Atlantic Ocean and the southernmost point in the continental USA. Call for our color brochure. **See the outside back cover for a color photo of our pool.**

■ Bars

BOURBON STREET PUB, 724 Duval St, (305) 296-1992. DJ.

CLUB INTERNATIONAL, 900 Simonton St, (305) 296-9230. Noon-4am.

DONNIE'S CLUB 422, 422 Applerouth Ln, (305) 294-2655. Conversation bar, new garden bar in rear.

■ Dance Bar/Disco

DIVAS, 700 block of Duval.,

EPOCH, 623 Duval St, (305) 296-8522.

LA TE DA TEA DANCE & TREETOP BAR, 1125 Duval St, at La Te Da Marti, (305) 296-6706. La Te Da tea dance Sun 5pm-9pm around the pool. Treetop has nitely drag shows.

★ **TEA BY THE SEA,** 510 South St, at the Atlantic Shores Hotel pier, (305) 296-2491. T-dance Sun, also sunset dance Fri-Sat.

■ Restaurants

ANTONIA'S, 615 Duval St, (305) 294-6565. Northern Italian cuisine.

CAFE DES ARTISTES, 1007 Simonton, (305) 294-7100. French cuisine, patio.

CAFE MARQUESA, 600 Fleming St, at the Marquesa Hotel, (305) 292-1244. New world cuisine.

CAMILLE'S, 703 1/2 Duval St, (305) 296-4811. Friendly & informal breakfast, lunch, dinner.

CRAB SHACK, 908 Caroline St, (305) 294-9658.

DIM SUM RESTAURANT, 613-1/2 Duval (in rear), (305) 294-6230. Indian, Chinese, Thai & Burmese cuisine. Closed Mon & Tues.

DUFFY'S STEAK & LOBSTER HOUSE, Simonton St, at Truman, (305) 296-4900.

EL SIBONEY, 900 Catherine St, (305) 2964184. Cuban/Spanish food in an unpretentious setting.

GATO GORDO, 404 Southard, between Whitehead & Duval,, (305) 294-0888. Mexican cuisine.

GODFREY'S AT LA TE DA, daily brunch 9am-3pm, dinner 6pm-11pm, except Sun.

LA TRATTORIA VENEZIA, 522 Duval St, (305) 296-1075. Italian & French cuisine.

LIGHTHOUSE CAFE, 917 Duval St, (305) 296-7837. Southern Italian cuisine.

LOUIE'S BACKYARD, 700 Waddell Ave, (305) 294-1061. International & Caribbean cuisine, Sun brunch.

Discover A True Women's Paradise

The Rainbow House®

Key West's Only Exclusively Women's Guest House

has *Expanded*!

2 Swimming Pools!
2 Hot Tubs!
38 Rooms & Suites!

Our Lovely Accommodations Include:
- *Bedroom with Queen or King Bed*
- *Private Bath • Color TV*
- *Air Conditioning & Bahama Fan*
- *Deluxe Continental Breakfast in our Air Conditioned Pavilion*

Other Amenities for your Vacationing Pleasure Include: *2 Swimming Pools • 2 Hot Tubs • Massage Available • Extensive Decks for Sunbathing • Shaded Tropical Pavilion for Lazy Day Lounging • Restaurants & Nightlife within walking distance • 1/2 block to shopping district • 1 block to Atlantic Ocean & Southernmost Point in Continental United States*

Call for a free color brochure.

1-800-74-WOMYN • 1-800-749-6696
(305) 292-1450 • www.rainbowhousekeywest.com
525 United Street, Key West, FL 33040 USA

MANGIA! MANGIA!, 900 Southard St, (305) 294-2469. Italian cuisine.
MANGOS, 700 Duval St, (305) 292-4606. Continental cuisine, vegetarian specialties.
ROOFTOP CAFE, 310 Front St, (305) 294-2042. Famous for key lime pie, continental cuisine.
SQUARE ONE, 1075 Duval St #C12, at Duval Sq, (305) 296-4300. New American cuisine, popular happy hour.

■ Retail & Bookstores
FLAMING MAGGIES, 830 Fleming St, at Margaret, (305) 294-3931. Gay & lesbian bookstore.
KEY WEST ISLAND BOOKSTORE, 513 Fleming Street, (305) 294-2904. General bookstore with a large gay section, opens 10am.

LAKELAND

■ Accommodations
SUNSET MOTEL, 2301 New Tampa Hwy, Lakeland, FL, 33815, (941) 683-6464. Gay-friendly motel with private baths.

■ Dance Bar/Disco
DOCKSIDE, 3770 Hwy 92 E, (941) 665-2590. Full liquor, Mon 6pm-2am, Tues-Sat 4pm-2am, Sun 4pm-12am, DJ Thurs-Sun, drag shows Thurs-Sat.
ROY'S GREEN PARROT, 1030 E Main St, (941) 683-6021. Dance & show bar, male strippers, 90% men, women welcome.

MELBOURNE

■ Dance Bar/Disco
KOLD KEG, 4060 W New Haven Ave, (407) 724-1510. Dance bar, DJ Thurs-Sat, trash nite Thurs, Sat shows, Sun buffet & karaoke.
LOADING ZONE, 4910 Stack Blvd, Palm Bay, (407) 727-3383. High energy dance bar, young crowd, 60% men, 40% women.

MIAMI - SOUTH BEACH

■ Information
AIDS LINE, (305) 576-1111. Health Crisis Network: (305) 751-7775.
WOMEN'S PRESERVATION SOCIETY, 4300 SW 73rd Ave, (305) 266-9480. Lesbian center with activities daily. Friday Night Women's Group meets here. Women's bar alternative.

■ Accommodations
CHELSEA HOTEL, 944 Washington Ave, Miami Beach, FL, 33139, (305) 534-4069, Fax: (305) 672-6712. Gay-friendly hotel 2 blocks from beach. Color TV, AC, phones, fridge & private baths. 24-hour security.
COLOURS AT NEW PENGUIN RESORT & THE MANTELL PLAZA, (800) ARRIVAL (277-4825), (305) 532-9341, Fax: (305) 534-0362. Email: newcolours @aol.com, Web: www.travelbase.com/ colours, Turquoise waters, warm ocean breezes, blue skies, fine dining, and dancing 'til dawn at the hottest clubs_ The New Penguin offers fun, tropical ambiance, Art Deco flair, a new swimming pool, the Front Porch Cafe, and the additional rooms of the original President Hotel on Collins. Directly across Ocean Drive is the hot gay beach scene. The Mantell Plaza, a condo hotel, features kitchenette studios and a large swimming pool.
EUROPEAN GUEST HOUSE, 721 Michigan Ave, Miami Beach, FL, 33139, (305) 673-6665, Fax: (305) 672-7442. Email: sobegay@aol.com, Web: www.europeanguesthouse.com, Enjoy old world charm & beautifully-appointed rooms with modern amenities in South Beach's only gay B&B, 6 blocks from sandy beaches. Rooms have AC, refrigerator, private baths & remote control cable TV. Outside, a hot tub & tropical gardens await you.
FAIRFAX HOTEL, 1776 Collins Ave, Miami Beach, FL, 33139, (305) 538-7082, (888) 676-6100, (800) 832-5736, Fax: (305) 673-9408. Gay-friendly hotel with a 30% gay male following, private baths.
ISLAND HOUSE - ORIGINAL, 715 82nd St, Miami Beach, FL, 33141, (305) 864-2422, (800) 382-2422, Fax: (305) 865-2220. Email: ihsobe@bellsouth.net, Web: www.q-net.com/islandhouse, Island House has two locations. Our original location is well mixed, and women feel perfectly at home here. If you prefer to stay right in South Beach, ask about our

other location. Although it's geared toward men, it's a respectable B&B atmosphere, and women are welcome. ♀♂
JEFFERSON HOUSE, THE, 1018 Jefferson Ave, Miami Beach, FL, 33139, (305) 534-5247, Fax: (305) 534-5953. Email: sobejhouse@aol.com, Web: http://www.sobe.com/jhouse, B&B in the heart of South Beach, some straight clientele. 6 rooms & 1 suite with queen beds, AC & private baths. TV lounge, full breakfast & nearby pool, ocean. ♀♂
LILY GUESTHOUSE, 835 Collins Ave, Miami Beach, FL, (305) 535-9900, (800) 535-9959, Fax: (305) 535-0077. In the Art Deco District, this 1936 historical building was completely remodeled in 1994. The guesthouse consists of two buildings, separated by an interior patio. Amenities include private baths, AC, color cable TV & phone. The rear building has rooms with private entrances, terraces and a common sun deck. We're 1/2-block from the beach and walking distance to nightclubs, restaurants and shopping. Some straight clientele. ♀♂
MIAMI RIVER INN, 118 SW South River Dr, Miami, FL, 33130, (305) 325-0045, (800) HOTEL 89 (468-3589), Fax: (305) 325-9227. Email: miami100@ix.netcom.com, Gay-friendly B&B hotel & apartments. Rooms with private baths, color cable TV, AC, ceiling fans & phones. Meeting rooms, lounge, pool, Jacuzzi & continental breakfast.
RICHMOND HOTEL, 1757 Collins Ave, Miami Beach, FL, 33139, (305) 538-2331, (800) 327-3163, Fax: (305) 531-9021. Email: richmondmb@aol.com, Gay-friendly luxury Art Deco hotel with restaurant, oceanfront location close to Ocean Dr, Lincoln Rd & gay venues. Private baths, continental breakfast, pool & ocean on premises. Gay male following.
SHELBORNE BEACH RESORT — SOUTH BEACH, 1801 Collins Ave, Miami Beach, FL, 33139, (305) 531-1271, (800) 327-8757, Fax: (305) 531-2206. Email: info@shelborne.com, Gay-friendly hotel with 180 rooms, private baths, pool on premises, Jacuzzi.
VILLA PARADISO GUESTHOUSE, 1415 Collins Ave, Miami Beach, FL, 33139, (305) 532-0616, Fax: (305) 673-5874. Email: villap@gate.net, Web: http://www.sobe.com/villaparadiso/, Guesthouse 1/2 block from the beach, 2 blocks from gay beach. Color TV, AC, ceiling fans, telephone, kitchen, all private baths. Some straight clientele. ♀♂
WINTERHAVEN HOTEL, 1400 Ocean Drive, Miami Beach, FL, 33139, (305) 531-5571, Fax: (305) 538-3337, Toll Free: (800) 395-2322. Hotel with restaurant & bar, private baths. 50% gay & lesbian clientele.

■ Camping & RV
SOMETHING SPECIAL, 7762 NW 14th Crt, Miami, FL, 33147, (305) 696-8826, Fax: (305) 864-7023. Women-only camping space & vegetarian restaurant. Shared baths. ♀

■ Bars
EIGHT TWENTY-ONE CLUB, 821 Lincoln Rd, Miami Beach., Women's nite Thurs ♀♂
MARY D'S, at the 821 bar, Thurs women's night. ♀
★ **TWIST,** 1057 Washington Ave, South Beach, (305) 53-TWIST. 2 levels, patio, pool tables. ♂
WESTEND, 942 Lincoln Rd, Miami Beach, (305) 538-WEST. 2 pool tables,

Island House
Miami Beach
An Intimate Hideaway
715 82nd Street
Miami Beach, FL
800-382-2422
fax 305-865-2220
IGLTA

FLORIDA

male strippers, 60% men, 40% women, may change in '97. 🂠 🂠 ♀♂

Dance Bar/Disco

★ **AMNESIA,** 9136 Collins Ave, Miami Beach, (305) 531-5535. Gay Sun only for Atomic Tea Dance, 70% men. Outdoor dance floor 6pm-11pm. 🂠 ♂

GODYVA, at Salvation, women's dance night Fri. 🂠 ♀

LIQUID, 1439 Washington Ave, Miami Beach, (305) 532-9154. Gay Sun only, restaurant in the front. 🂠 ♂

SPLASH, 5922 S Dixie Hwy, S Miami, (305) 662-8779. Dance club, patio, 2 pool tables, shows Mon, 70% men. Fri Bliss women's night. C&W & Latin nites. 🂠 ♪ ♂

SWITCH, at Lucky Cheng's, 600 Lincoln Rd, at Pennsylvania, Miami Beach, Fri women's dance night. 🂠 ♀

★ **WARSAW BALLROOM,** 1450 Collins Ave, S Miami Beach, (305) 531-4499. Large, hi-energy dance bar, strippers, 9pm-5am Wed, Fri & Sun are gay nites. 🂠 🂠 ♪ ♂

Restaurants

CHINA GRILL, 404 Washington Ave, (305) 534-2211. 🂠

DA LEO TRATTORIA, 819 Lincoln Rd, (305) 674-0350. Italian on the beach. 🂠

DABHAUS, 852 Alton Rd, (305) 534-9557. German cuisine, women-owned. 🂠

EL RANCHO GRANDE, 1626 Pennsylvania, (305) 673-0480. Mexican cuisine.

ELEVENTH ST DINER, 11th St, at Collins Ave, Miami Beach, (305) 534-6373. Real diner food, many gays. 🂠

FRONT PORCH CAFE, 1418 Ocean Dr, (305) 531-8300. American cuisine. 🂠

GRILLFISH, 1444 Collins Ave, Miami Beach, (305) 538-9908.

JEFFREY'S, 1629 Michigan Ave, (305) 673-0690. ♀♂

LUCKY CHENG'S, 600 Lincoln Rd, (305) 672-1505.

MEZZALUNA, 834 Ocean Dr, (305) 674-1330. 🂠

PACIFIC TIME, 915 Lincoln Rd, (305) 534-5979. American with Asian influence. Expensive, but good. 🂠

PALACE BAR & GRILL, 1200 Ocean Dr, South Miami Beach, (305) 531-9077. Bar & grill across from a gay beach & 12th St volleyball club. Patio dining. 🂠 🍸

STEPHAN'S, 1430 Washington Ave, (305) 674-1760. Italian cuisine. 🂠

VAN DYKE CAFE, 846 Lincoln Rd, (305) 534-3600. Trendy. 🂠

Retail & Bookstores

GAY MART, 1200 Ocean Dr, (305) 535-1545.

LAMBDA PASSAGES BOOKSTORE, 7545 Biscayne Blvd, near 75th, (305) 754-6900, 759-7141. Gay & lesbian books in English & Spanish. Cards, videos, gifts, etc.

NINTH CHAKRA, THE, 817 Linclon Rd, South Beach, (305) 538-0671. Metaphysical bookstore, Mon-Thur noon-7pm, Fri & Sat noon-8pm, Sun 2pm-6pm.

MICANOPY

Bars

CLUB DIVERSITY, 22822 N Hwy 441, (352) 591-2525. ♀♂

MT DORA

Accommodations

LAKESIDE INN, 100 N Alexander St, Mt Dora, FL, 32757, (352) 383-4101, (800) 556-5016. Historic inn, continental breakfast.

NAPLES

Accommodations

FESTIVE FLAMINGO, (941) 455-8833. Cozy, quiet, gay-friendly accommodation with heated pool. 15 minutes to beach, restaurants, nightlife & more. 🂠

Bars

GALLEY, THE, 509 3rd St, (941) 262-2808. Restaurant & lounge, breakfast to dinner, DJ Fri-Sat, shows Sat, 50/50 Fri & Sat, 80% men other times. ♪ ♀♂

Restaurants

CAFE FLAMINGO, 536 9th St N, (941) 262-8181. Breakfast & lunch, women-owned, Sun brunch 8am-1pm.

OCALA

Bars
CONNECTION, 3331 S Pine Ave, (352) 620-2511. About 70% men, pool table, DJ Fri & Sat, karaoke Sun, possibly drag shows Fri.

ORLANDO

Information
AIDS HOTLINE, (407) 841-2437. 24hrs.
GAY & LESBIAN COMMUNITY SERVICES, HOTLINE & CENTER, 714 E Colonial Drive, (407) 425-4527. 11am-9pm (Fri til 6pm), Sat noon-5pm. Hotline (407) 843-4297.
WOMEN'S RESOURCE CENTER, (407) 426-7960.

Accommodations
A VERANDA B & B, 115 N Summerlin Ave, Orlando, FL, 32801, (407) 849-0321 (Tel/Fax), (800) 420-6822. B&B, 50% gay & lesbian clientele. Color cable TV, AC, telephone, private baths. Expanded continental breakfast, wedding courtyard & fax service.
PARLIAMENT HOUSE HOTEL, 410 N Orange Blossom Trail, Orlando, FL, 32805, (407) 425-7571, Fax: (407) 425-5881. Spacious rooms, pool & private white sand beach on Rock Lake. 5 bars and the Orlando Eagle, Orlando's premier leather/levi bar.
THINGS WORTH REMEMBERING, 7338 Cabor Ct, Orlando, FL, 32818, (407) 291-2127 (Tel/Fax, call before faxing), (800) 484-3585 (code 6908). B&B with memorabilia & autographs from TV, movies, Broadway & sports. One room with queen bed, private bath, continental breakfast.

Women's Accommodations
LEORA B'S BED & BREAKFAST, PO Box 6094, Orlando, FL, 32853, (407) 649-0009. Women-only B&B homestay in downtown historic district. Rooms range from doubles to an apartment, amenities vary, expanded continental breakfast.

Bars
CACTUS CLUB, 1300 N Mills Ave, (407) 894-3041. Conversation bar with outside patio, 70% men, 50% men, 50% women Fri.

LI'L ORPHAN ANDY'S, 5700 N Orange Blossom Trail.,
SADIE'S TAVERN, 415 S Orlando Ave, Winter Park, (407) 628-4562. Popular with gay women, especially Fri (mostly women), DJ Thurs. Friendly mixture of gay women, men & straights.
WYLDE'S, 3400 S Orange Blossom Tr, (407) 843-6334. Male dancers.

Dance Bar/Disco
★ **CLUB AT FIRESTONE**, 578 N Orange Ave, (407) 426-0005. Huge hi-energy dance bar, gay Wed & Sat, enhanced sound & light system.
★ **FACES**, 4910 Edgewater Dr, at Lee, (407) 291-7571.

Lambda Express
Magazine
&
Lambda Express
*Magazine_***Online**

Florida's Best Gay/Lesbian Information Source

http://
www.lambdaexpress.com
P.O.B. 6878
Ocala, Florida 34478-6878
Voice/fax (352) 236-3285
E-mail:
lambda@praxis.net

PHOENIX /CLUB Z, 7124 Aloma Ave, Winter Park, (407) 678-9220. Phoenix: jukebox neighborhood bar, Club Z: industrial Gothic dance bar. 🕸 U 🗺 ♀♂

ROMANS, 3400 S Orange Blossom Trail, (407) 422-6826. Dance & cruise bar, male strippers. 🕸 🗺 🗺 ♂

★ **SOUTHERN NIGHTS,** 375 S Bumby Ave, (407) 898-0424. Dance & show bar, 65% men, 35% women. Piano, patio, Fri buffet & Sun BBQ. Lesbo-A-Go Go women's night Sat." 🕸 🗺 ♪ ♀♂

■ Restaurants

UNION CITY TAVERN, 337 N Shine Ave, (407) 894-5778. California cuisine. ♀♂

WHITE WOLF CAFE, 1829 N Orange Ave, (407) 895-5590. Coffee shop food. 🗺

■ Retail & Bookstores

OUT & ABOUT BOOKS, 930 N Mills, (407) 896-0204. Gay & lesbian books, T-shirts, gifts, jewelry, cards, buttons & art gallery. Mon-Sat 11am-8pm."

RAINBOW CITY, 934 N Mills Ave, (407) 898-6096. Cards, rainbow and pride items. ♀♂

■ Leathers/Piercing

LEATHER CLOSET, 498 N Orange Blossom Trail, (407) 649-2011, Fax: (407) 649-4116. Custom leathers for men & women. Cards & gifts.

PALM BEACH AREA

■ Information

COMPASS COMMUNITY CENTER, 1700 N Dixie Hwy, W Palm Beach, FL, (561) 833-3638, Fax: (561) 833-4941. 10am-10pm (Fri 9am-5pm, Sun 4pm-9pm), Sun closed. Support & social group meetings, teen line, 24hr switchboard.

■ Accommodations

HIBISCUS HOUSE B & B, 501 30th St, West Palm Beach, FL, 33407, (561) 863-5633 (Tel/Fax), (800) 203-4927. Web: http://www.hibiscushouse.com, B&B, some straight clientele. Variety of rooms with modern conveniences, private baths, kitchen privileges & full breakfast." 🗺 ♀♂

HUMMINGBIRD HOTEL BED & BREAKFAST, 631 Lucerne Ave, Lake Worth, FL, 33460, (561) 582-3224, Fax: (561) 540-8817. Gay-friendly B&B hotel, continental breakfast, private & shared baths, AC, color cable TV, VCR, ceiling fans, nearby pool, ocean & lake.

TROPICAL GARDENS BED & BREAKFAST, 419 32nd St, Old Northwood Historic District, West Palm Beach, FL, 33407-4809, (561) 848-4064, (800) 736-4064, Fax: (561) 848-2422. B&B, some straight clientele. Rooms with Caribbean decor, common areas, beach, expanded continental breakfast. 🗺 ♀♂

■ Bars

K & E, 29 S Dixie Hwy, Lake Worth, (561) 533-6020. Bar & restaurant. ♀

■ Dance Bar/Disco

CLUB 502, 502 Lucerne, Lake Worth, (561) 540-8881. Restaurant with Sun T dance, 70% men, 30% women. 🕸 ♀♂

★ **HEART BREAKER,** 2677 Forest Hill Blvd, Lake Shore Plaza, West Palm Beach, (561) 966-1590. Hi-energy laser dance bar, Wed-Sun, 70% men, women welcome. Male dancers, youngish crowd. 🕸 🗺 ♂

HOT SPOTS, 1665 Old Dixie Hwy, Jupiter., 🕸 ♀♂

SIN, Forest Hill & Congress., 🕸 ♀♂

■ Cafe

UNDERGROUND COFFEE WORKS, 105 S Narcissus Ave, West Palm Beach, (561) 835-4792. Coffees & limited menu, mostly vegetarian. Always gay-friendly, most popular with gays Thurs, live bands, large college crowd. 🗺

■ Retail & Bookstores

AMOROSO BOOKS & GIFTS, 205 N Federal Hwy, Lake Worth, (561) 533-5272. Gay pride store, Tues-Sat 10am-6pm, Sun noon-6pm. 2nd location inside Enigma bar.

GAY BOOKS & GIFTS, 2nd at Federal., Gay & lesbian shop.

MAIN STREET NEWS, 255 Royal Poinciana Way, Palm Beach, (561) 833-4027. Gay magazines.

PANAMA CITY

■ Bars

LA ROYALE, 100 Harrison Ave, (850) 784-9311. Pool tables, darts, video games, Sun T-dance, patio, 60% men, 40% women. ♀♂

FLORIDA

■ Dance Bar/Disco
FIESTA ROOM, 110 Harrison Ave, (850) 784-9285. Disco & show bar, patio, 60% men, 40% women. Beer bust Wed. 🎵 ♀♂

PASCO COUNTY

■ Bars
LOVEY'S PUB, 3338 US 19, Holiday, (813) 849-2960. Woman-owned, special events. 🎵 ♀♂

■ Dance Bar/Disco
BT'S, 7737 Grand Blvd, Port Richey, (813) 841-7900. Dance & show bar, DJ, Tues ladies night with female dancers, Thurs men's night with male dancers. Fri & Sat shows, Sun tea dances & buffet Mon. 🎵 ♀♂

■ Restaurants
GRANDE CAFE, Grand near Main, New Port Richey, Bistro atmosphere, fine dining.

PENSACOLA

■ Accommodations
MILL HOUSE INN, 9603 Lillian Highway, Pensacola, FL, 32506, (850) 455-3400, toll-free: (888) 999-4575, Fax: (850) 458-6397. Email: TMHBB@aol.com, Restored 1870's Victorian millhouse on scenic Perdido Bay, all rooms have magnificent bay views. Upper-level secluded back porch, 1st- & 2nd-story verandas, private & shared baths, expanded continental breakfast (full breakfast wknds), 10-min drive to white sand beaches. Women welcome. ♂

■ Beaches
GAY BEACH, Follow Via DeLuna Dr to parking lot #2.

■ Dance Bar/Disco
BEDLAM, 15 E Intendencia, (850) 434-8779. After hours dance club, 18 & up. 🎵 ♀♂

EMERALD CITY, 1406 E. Wright St, near Alcaniz, (850) 433-9491. 🎵 ♀♂

EMMA JONES PRANCE & DANCE, 120 E Main St, (upstairs, above Riviera), After hours. 🎵 ♀♂

RED CARPET, 937 New Warrington Rd, (850) 453-9918. 85% women. 🎵 ♀

★ **RED GARTER,** Main St at Palafox, (850) 433-9292. Dance & show bar, occasional male dancers. 🎵 ♀♂

★ **RIVIERA,** 120 E Main St, near Tarragona, (850) 432-1234. Nice patio, occasional live music. 🎵 ♀♂

■ Cafe
CUP & SAUCER, 7 E Gregory St, (850) 435-9228. Cafe & lite menu. ♀♂

VAN GOGH'S HAUS OF COFFEE & ART, 610 E Wright St, (850) 429-0336.

■ Restaurants
DHARMA BLUE, 300 S Alcaniz, (850) 433-1275. Women-owned, eclectic food & sushi bar.

HALL'S SEAFOOD, 920 E Gregory, (850) 438-9019.

MADISON'S DINER, 1010 N 12th Ave, Sandwiches, seafood, steaks.

SCREAMING COYOTE, 196 N Palafox, Southwestern cuisine.

■ Retail & Bookstores
LUNAR LIBRARY, 5044 N Palafox St, (850) 470-0174. Spiritual shop, some gay & lesbian books.

PENSACOLA PRIDE & CAFE, 9 E Gregory, near Palafox, (850) 435-7272. Gay & lesbian superstore with pride items, books, clothing, beach wear & supplies, gifts. Cafe is nextdoor with coffees & lite menu.

POMPANO BEACH

■ Dance Bar/Disco
★ **ADVENTURES,** 303 SW 6th St, (954) 782-9577. C&W dance club, daily except Mon 4pm-2am, dancing, lessons, wedding chapel. Adventures in Dining restaurant, buffet with prime rib to seafood Tues, Thurs-Sat. 50% men/women. 🎵 ♀♂

■ Erotica
PLEASURE ZONE, 480 S Cypress Rd (unit A), (954) 786-9060. Erotic boutique.

ST AUGUSTINE

■ Women's Accommodations
PAGODA, 2854 Coastal Hwy, St Augustine, FL, 32095-2308, (904) 824-2970. Guesthouse in lesbian cottage community, private & shared baths. ♀

■ Retail & Bookstores
DREAMSTREET BOOKSTORE, 64

ST PETERSBURG - CLEARWATER

■ Information
GAY HOTLINE, (813) 586-4297, 7-11pm or tape.

■ Accommodations
SEA OATS BY THE GULF, 12625 Sunshine Lane, Treasure Island, FL, 33706, (813) 367-7568. Motel, 50% gay & lesbian clientele. Apartments with color cable TV, AC, kitchen & private baths. Ocean & Jacuzzi on premises.

■ Women's Accommodations
BARGE HOUSE, THE, PO Box 46526, Pass-A-Grille Beach, St. Petersburg Beach, FL, 33741, (813) 360-0729. Private cabana or beach cottage, women only.

BOCA CIEGA BED & BREAKFAST, 3526 Boca Ciega Dr. N, St. Petersburg, FL, 33710, (813) 381-2755. Women-only B&B, private bath, continental breakfast, central AC, ceiling fans, maid service, pool on premises, minutes from beaches

■ Bars
HAYMARKET, 8308 4th St, (813) 577-7774. Quiet & intimate, coffees, wines, cocktails, lite menu.

HIDEAWAY, 8302 4th St N., Men welcome.

LOST & FOUND, 5858 Roosevelt Blvd, Clearwater, (813) 539-8903. Show bar.

SPORTS PAGE PUB, 13344 66th St N, Largo, (813) 538-2430, pool table, darts, sandwiches.

■ Dance Bar/Disco
★ **FOURTEEN SEVENTY WEST**, 325 Main St, Dunedin, (813) 736-5483. Dance & show bar, male strippers, 50% men, 50% women.

★ **LOST & FOUND**, 5858 Roosevelt Blvd, Clearwater, (813) 539-8903. Piano bar.

■ Restaurants
A TASTE FOR WINE, 241 Central Ave, (813) 895-1623. Wine tasting, light lunches, cheese & fruit, etc.

ANNA'S PASTA, 4th St N, near 52nd Ave, (813) 522-6627.

KELLY'S FOR JUST ABOUT ANYTHING, 319 Main St, Dunedin, (813) 736-5284. Fine dining.

MAGNOLIA'S R&B CAFE, 5853 Haines Rd.,

PEPPER TREE, 109 8th Ave, Passagrille Beach, (813) 360-1367. Restaurant & bar.

■ Retail & Bookstores
AFFINITY BOOKS, 2435 9th St, (813) 823-3662. Gay & lesbian bookstore, Mon-Tues 10am-6pm, Wed-Fri 10am-8pm, Sat 10am-5pm, Sun noon-5pm.

BRIGIT BOOKS, 3434 4th St North #5, (813) 522-5775. Lesbian & feminist books, cards, jewelry, local info, 7 days.

SARASOTA

■ Accommodations
DRAGON'S DEN, THE, Sarasota, FL, (941) 923-2646. Private guest suite, located in a lovely home in a park-like setting. The suite includes a bedroom, full bath and a sitting room with its own private entrance. Women welcome.

SIESTA HOLIDAY HOUSE, 1011-1015 Crescent St, (Mail: 86 Inlets Blvd, Nokomis FL 34275), Siesta Key, FL, (941) 488-6809, (800) 720-6885. Mail: 86 Inlets Blvd, Nokomis, FL 34275. Gay-owned with mainly straight clientele, 1- & 2-bedroom apartments, steps from Crescent Beach.

■ Bars
CLUB CHADA, 2941 N Tamiami Trail, (941) 355-7210.

HG ROOSTER'S, 1256 Old Stickney Pt Rd, (941) 346-3000. Small, quiet bar with games, DJ Fri-Sun. Women welcome.

■ Dance Bar/Disco
★ **BUMPERS NIGHTCLUB 1927**, Ringling Blvd, near Main, (941) 951-0335. Huge dance bar, Club X at Bumpers Thur & Sat gay nights. Midnight drag or strip shows, drag night 3rd Thurs.

ROWDY'S, 1330 Dr ML King Jr Way (27th St), (941) 953-5945.

■ Cafe
CAFE KALDI, 1568 Main St, (941) 366-BEAN.

SEAGROVE BEACH

■ Accommodations
MAGNOLIA MANOR & SEAVIEW, c/o 26 Chance St, Santa Rosa Beach, FL, 32459, (850) 231-0254 (tel/fax), (800) 854-9266. Beach cottages with cable TV, VCR, central heat/AC, near beach, restaurants, galleries & shops close by. ♀♂

SEBASTIAN

■ Women's Accommodations
PINK LADY INN, THE, 1309 Louisiana Ave, Sebastian, FL, 32958, (561) 589-1345. Women-only inn, 7 miles from ocean & near train tracks (formerly boarding house for railroad). Color TV, 2 rooms with microwave & refrigerator, pool on premises. Smoking outside only, pets permitted with prior permission, no credit cards. ♀

TALLAHASSEE

■ Information
AIDS HOTLINE & INFO, (850) 656-2437.
WOMEN'S CENTER, 112 N Woodward Ave, near Park, (850) 644-4007, 644-6453. Mon-Fri 1-5pm.

■ Bars
BROTHERS, 926-7 Tharpe St, (850) 386-2399. Video bar, Tues-Sun. 18 & over, shows, mostly men from 10pm. ♀♂

■ Dance Bar/Disco
CLUB PARK AVE (CPA), 115 E Park Ave, (850) 599-9143. Gay Sat, shooter boys: male servers of shots, Sun urban gay night with house music. ♂

TAMPA

■ Accommodations
GRAM'S PLACE BED/BREAKFAST & MUSIC, 3109 N Ola Ave, Tampa, FL, 33603, Reservations: (813) 221-0596 (Tel/Fax, call before faxing). Email: GramsPl@aol.com, Web: http://members.aol.com/gramspl/index.html, B&B for those interested in music & the arts. Music played on request. Private & shared baths, eclectic decor, 80% gay/lesbian. ♀♂

■ Camping & RV
SAWMILL CAMPGROUND, 21710 US Hwy 98, Dade City, FL, 33523, (352) 583-0664, Fax: (352) 583-0661. Email: flsawmill@aol.com, Gay-owned & -operated campground 38 miles north of Tampa, with 174 RV & campsites & convenience store, group campsites, bathouse for men & women. ♀♂

■ Bars
JUNGLE, 3703 Henderson Blvd, (813) 877-3290.
SAHARA, 4603 W Kennedy Blvd, (813) 282-0183. DJ Fri, Sat. ♀

■ Dance Bar/Disco
CASTLE/MECCA, at Castle bar, 16th & 9th,, Ybor City (old Labor Temple Bldg)., Thurs-Sun. ♂
CHEROKEE CLUB, 1320 E 9th Ave, Ybor City, (813) 247-9966. Thur-Sat from 9pm, DJ Thurs-Sat. May open Fri for happy hour in '97. ♀
PLEASURE DOME, 1430 E 7th Ave., Gay Tues ♂
RASCALS, 105 W Martin Luther King Blvd, (813) 237-8883. Dance bar & restaurant. ♀♂

■ Restaurants
RASCALS, 105 W Martin Luther King Blvd, (813) 237-8883. Restaurant & gay bar, award-winning cuisine.

■ Retail & Bookstores
TOMES & TREASURES, 202-1/2 S Howard, (813) 251-9368. Gay & lesbian bookstore, 12pm-9pm.

GEORGIA
ATHENS

Dance Bar/Disco
BONESHAKERS, 433 E Hancock, (706) 543-1555. Dance club, variety of music, retro to hi energy, drag shows Mon, 60% men, 40% women.

ATLANTA

Information
AIDS LINE, (404) 876-9944 or (800) 551-2728. 9am-9pm (Sat, Sun noon-5pm).

FOURTH TUESDAY, (770) 662-4353, 662-6868 (events hotline). Networking organization for lesbians.

GAY HELP LINE & GAY CENTER, 71 12th St NE, (404) 892-0661. Staffed 6pm-11pm, 24hr tape.

Accommodations
BONAVENTURE, THE, 650 Bonaventure Ave, Atlanta, GA, 30306, (404) 817-7024, Fax: (404) 249-9988. Email: bonaventure@mindspring.com, Web: http://www.mindspring.com/~friedato, Victorian B&B guesthouse with private & shared baths, expanded continental breakfast, lovely private gardens & fish pond. 50% gay & lesbian clientele.

BOXWOOD HEIGHTS, 511 Toombs St, Palmetto, GA, 30268, (770) 463-9966, (888) 463-0101, Fax: (770) 463-0701. B&B 25 minutes from downtown Atlanta, MARTA pulic transport 1 block. Large guest rooms, private & shared baths, antique furnishings, rocking chair porch, 9 fireplaces. 50% gay & lesbian clientele.

CARITAS BED & BREAKFAST NETWORK, (800) CARITAS, (312) 857-0801, Fax: (312) 857-0805. B&B, home-stay accommodations service. Member: IGLTA

GASLIGHT INN BED & BREAKFAST, 1001 Saint Charles Avenue, Atlanta, GA, 30306, (404) 875-1001, Fax: (404) 876-1001. Email: gaslight n@aol.com, Web: http://www.gaslightinn.com, Extravagantly decorated craftsman-style B&B inn close to downtown Atlanta & walking distance to restaurants, shops, theaters & galleries. All private baths, expanded continental breakfast. Gay-friendly.

MIDTOWN MANOR, 811 Piedmont Ave NE, Atlanta, GA, 30308, (404) 872-5846, (800) 724-4381, Fax: (404) 875-3018. Email: MidtownMoe@aol.com, A Victorian guesthouse in midtown Atlanta, 50% gay & lesbian clientele. Both elabo-

Above The Clouds

We'd like to share our 50-mile view of the Blue Ridge Mountains with women

Tel: (706) 864-5211

rately furnished and budget rooms, breakfast and dinner restaurants 5 blocks. Walk to many gay bars and restaurants. Stay a night or two or a week or two.

Women's Accommodations

ABOVE THE CLOUDS B & B, 206 Cedar Mountain Rd, Dahlonega, GA, 30533, (706) 864-5211. Enjoy the quiet and privacy of a mountain getaway 70 miles north of Atlanta. Our guests occupy a large suite with its own private entrance, kitchen, deck and spa, and private bath. You can visit a local winery and a restored gold mine, shop for native crafts, hike the Appalachain Trail, canoe, ride horses, play golf, or picnic beside a waterfall in the woods. Sound Inviting? Women-only B&B. ♀

SWIFTWATERS, 830 Swiftwaters Rd, Dahlonega, GA, (706) 864-3229 (Tel/Fax), call before faxing. Email: swifth20s@peachnet.campus.mci.net, Women-only B&B, cabins & camping. Private bath & outhouses. ♀

Bars

★ **BLAKE'S ON THE PARK,** 227 10th St, (404) 892-5786. Cheers-type bar with upstairs sports bar, women welcome. Videos & patio. ♀♂

CHAMBER, THE, 2115 Faulkner Rd, (404) 248-1612. gay & straight S&M/fetish club.

CIRCLES, 710 Peachtree St NE, at Ponce de Leon, (404) 815-6687. Open 7 days, karaoke, occasional drag shows, dancing Fri & Sat, 90% women. ♀

CLUB LE BUZZ, 585 Franklin Rd, Marietta, northern suburb 10 min, from downtown, close to exit #112 on I-75, (770) 424-1337. Only gay bar in Cobb county, bar with espresso coffee, DJ music. ♀♂

GUYS & DOLLS, 2788 E Ponce de Leon, (404) 377-2956. Mixed gay & straight crowd, nude dancers, male & female strippers. Mostly gay crowd on Tue & Sun.

MORELAND TAVERN, 1196 Moreland Ave SE, (404) 622-4650. 80% gay & lesbian. ♀♂

★ **MY SISTER'S ROOM,** (404) 875-6699. Cozy, intimate. ♀

OPUS ONE, 1086 Alco Street NE, (404) 634-6478. Juke box, 65% men, 35% women. ♂

SCANDALS, Ansley Square, (404) 875-5957. Open very early, drink till late. ♂

TOWER II, 735 Ralph McGill, (404) 523-1535. Mature lesbians. ♀

Dance Bar/Disco

★ **BACKSTREET,** 845 Peachtree St NE, near 6th (rear), (404) 873-1986. 80% men, women welcome, younger crowd. Patio, cabaret showe, 24hrs daily. Private club, non-members welcome. ♂

★ **FUSION,** 550-C Amsterdam Ave, (404) 872-6411. ♀♂

HOEDOWNS, 931 Monroe Dr, (Midtown Promenade), (404) 876-0001. Open daily, women welcome, patio. ∪♂

★ **OTHERSIDE,** 1924 Piedmont Rd, (404) 875-5238. Theme nights, shows, variety of music, open late weekends. ♀♂

Restaurants

AGNES & MURIEL'S, 1514 Monroe Dr, near Piedmont., (404) 885-1000.

BEE HIVE, 1090 Alpharetta St, Roswell, (770) 594-8765. ♀♂

CAMILLE'S, 1186 N Highland Ave, (404) 872-7203. Italian neighborhood restaurant, 7 nites.

COWTIPPERS, 1600 Piedmont Rd, (404)

Your Visitor's Center in Atlanta

ATLANTA'S GAY & LESBIAN

OUTWRITE
BOOKSTORE & COFFEEHOUSE

■ BOOKS ■ COFFEE ■ GOOD FOOD

The South's Source For Information on Our Lives

991 PIEDMONT AVE AT TENTH STREET
MIDTOWN ATLANTA

(404) 607-0082

GEORGIA

874-3751. Gay-friendly steak & rib restaurant. 🟊

CRESCENT MOON, 254 W Ponce de Leon, Decatur, (404) 377-5623. Breakfast till 3am, vegetarian, sandwiches, etc.

★ **EINSTEIN'S,** 1077 Juniper, (404) 876-7925. Large outdoor patio, continental cuisine, gay-friendly. 🟊

FLYING BISQUIT CAFE, 1655 McClendan Ave, (404) 687-8888. Hearty, healthy breakfast-dinner. 🟊

IMPERIAL FEZ, 2285 Peachtree Rd #102, (404) 351-0870. Authentic Morrocan cuisine. 🟊

PRINCE GEORGE INN, 2625 Piedmont, (at the Armory), (404) 685-8793. Pastas, seafood. ♀♂

RESTAURANT PIROZKI'S, 1447 Peachtree St, (404) 607-0809. Russian restaurant, piano bar, caviar. 🟊

TERRA COTTA, 1044 Greenwood Ave, at N Highland, (404) 853-7888. Tues-Sun, walk ins welcome. 🟊

THAI CHILI, 2169 Briarcliff Rd, (404) 315-6750. 🟊

■ Retail & Bookstores

BRUSHSTROKES, 1510-J Piedmont Ave NE, (404) 876-6567. Gay variety store, with books, magazines, videos, T-shirts, music, cards, jewelry, rainbow items.

CHARIS BOOKS & MORE, 1189 Euclid Ave, (404) 524-0304. Feminist bookstore. Program every Thurs at 7:30pm.

ONE STOP GIFT SHOP, Ansley Mall #310, 1544 Piedmont Ave, (404) 874-6575. Gay & lesbian gift shop.

OUTWRITE BOOKSTORE & COFFEEHOUSE, 991 Piedmont, at Tenth, (404) 607-0082. Gay & lesbian bookstore & coffeehouse. Outwrite has Atlanta's complete selection of books & magazines by, for, and about gay men & lesbians. Come in and browse in a very comfortable bookstore and have a snack in the coffeehouse. Knowledgeable, friendly staff has a great knowledge of the literature and can tell you anything you need to know about what to do and where to go in Atlanta. The new location is located right on Piedmont Park. See ad on page 299.

POSTER HUT, 2175 Cheshire Bridge Rd NE, (404) 633-7491. Leather supplies, cards, books, gifts & lubes.

AUGUSTA

■ Accommodations

PARLIAMENT HOUSE OF AUGUSTA, 1250 Gordon Hwy, Augusta, GA, 30901, (706) 722-1155. Email: gaymotel@aol.com, Totally private complex with 95-room motel, pool, hot tub. Separate men's & women's motel wings. Day passes for pool & locker, Sun Tea Dance 2pm-7pm. Cruise bar to open in '98. 🛏 ♀♂

■ Dance Bar/Disco

B&D'S WEST SPOT, 2823 Dean's Bridge Rd, (706) 793-5111. Show bar on Fri, male & female strippers. 🎵 🍸 ♀♂

WAY STATION, 1632 Walton Way, (706) 733-2603. Mon-Fri 9pm-3am, Sat 8:30pm-2:30am. 🍸 🎵 🟊 ♀♂

CLARKESVILLE

■ Accommodations

OUTSIDER INN & GALLERY, 690 Chitwood Rd, Clarkesville, GA, (706) 754-9260. B&B & art gallery in a handhewn log home in northeast Georgia, private baths, full breakfast, 50% gay & lesbian clientele.

COLUMBUS

■ Bars

MAYFAIR, Brennerman Rd, Unverifiable spring '98.

■ Dance Bar/Disco

CLUB SENSATION, Cocita Rd., Unverifiable spring '98. 🍸 ♂

PILLOW TALK, 1st & Broadway., Unverifiable spring '98. 🍸 ♂

HIAWASSEE

■ Accommodations

MISTY MOUNTAIN INN, A BED & BREAKFAST, 548 Nicholson Trail, Hiawassee, GA, 30546, (706) 896-5619. B&B with local artists' work for sale, private & shared baths, expanded continental, continental or full breakfast, women welcome, some straight clientele. ♂

MACON

■ Information

GAY & LESBIAN LINE, AIDS INFO,

GEORGIA

(912) 750-8080. Rainbow Center, 24 hrs, 7 days.

Dance Bar/Disco
★ **CHERRY ST PUB,** 425 Cherry St, (912) 755-1400. Big dance bar, drag shows Sat, videos, restaurant & lounge bar, large straight following.

Retail & Bookstores
COLORS ON CHERRY, 415 Cherry St, (912) 745-7474. Gay gift shop, gay & rainbow items.

MOUNTAIN CITY

Accommodations
YORK HOUSE BED & BREAKFAST INN, THE, PO Box 126, Mountain City, GA, 30562, (706) 746-2068, (800) 231-YORK (9675), Fax: (706) 746-5641. B&B inn, silver-tray breakfast, private baths, color cable TV, AC, TV lounge, hiking & jogging trails on premises, nearby river, lake & waterfalls, 50% gay/lesbian clientele.

ST. SIMONS ISLAND

Accommodations
LITTLE ST. SIMONS ISLAND, PO Box 21078, St Simons Island, GA, 31522, (912) 638-7472, Fax (912) 634-1811. 10,000-acre private island resort with 7 miles of beach, unspoiled wilderness, various accommodations & family-style meals. Available to private groups, maximum 24 guests. Gay-friendly.

SAVANNAH

Information
LESBIAN & GAY INFO LINE, (912) 236-CITY (2489).

Accommodations
NINE TWELVE BARNARD BED & BREAKFAST, 912 Barnard St, Savannah, GA, 31401, (912) 234-9121. B&B shared baths, expanded continental breakfast, walking distance to Savanna's shops, restaurants & historic Forsyth Park, 15 minutes from beaches.

PARADISE INN, 512 Tattnall St, Savannah, GA, 31401, (912) 443-0200, (888) 846-5093, Fax: (912) 443-9295. Email: info@link2paradise.com, Web: www.link2paradise.com, Newly restored 1866 townhouse with 5 comfortable guestrooms, private baths, expanded continental or buffet breakfast, hot tub. Located in Savannah's Historic District, walking distance to shops, restaurants & bars. 50% gay/lesbian clientele.

PARK AVENUE MANOR B & B, 107-109 West Park Avenue, Savannah, GA, (912) 233-0352. Email: pkavemanor@aol.com, Web: www.bbonline.com/ga/parkavenue, Gay-owned & -operated Victorian B&B, private baths, some with claw-foot tubs, antiques, silk carpets, AC, some straight clientele.

Bars
BROUGHTON BAR & CAFE, 121 E Broughton St, (912) 234-0199. Bar & cafe, pool table, 80% men.

FACES, 17 Lincoln, (912) 233-3520. Noon-3am 7 days, Sun till 2am, 90% men.

Dance Bar/Disco
★ **CLUB ONE,** 1 Jefferson St, at Bay, (912) 232-0200. Alternative dance & show bar, 60% gay. Private club, guests welcome. Mon-Sat 5pm-3am, Sun 5pm-2am.

★ **FELICIA'S,** 416 W Liberty St, (912) 238-4788. Male & female strippers, drag shows Fri-Sun, restaurant.

LOADING DOCK, 641 Indian St, (912) 232-0130. Bar with small dance floor, to open big dance bar in '98.

Restaurants
FANNY'S ON THE BEACH, 1613 Strand, Tybee Island, (912) 786-6109. Bar & restaurant on the beach, frozen drinks, awesome food.

Retail & Bookstores
DREAMWEAVER, 306 W St. Julian St, (912) 236-9003. New Age bookstore.

HOME RUN VIDEO & BOOKS, 4 E Liberty, (912) 236-5192. General bookstore with a gay & lesbian section.

READING EDGE BOOKSTORE, 202 E Broughton St, (912) 236-1006, fax: (912) 236-3245, e-mail: thereadingedge@worldnet.att.net. Burned, may reopen.

Erotica
CAPTAIN VIDEO, 7 W York St, at Bull, (912) 232-2951. Large selection of gay & lesbian videos, cards, 7 days.

GEORGIA

SENOIA

■ Accommodations
CULPEPPER HOUSE B & B, 35 Broad St, Senoia, GA, (770) 599-8182 (Tel/Fax). Gay-friendly B&B 30 miles from Atlanta. AC, shared baths, TV lounge, fax & full breakfast. Gay female following.

STATESBORO

■ Accommodations
STATESBORO INN, 106 S Main St, Statesboro, GA, 30458, (912) 489-8628, Fax: (912) 489-4785. Gay-friendly inn with restaurant in a 15-room Victorian.

VALDOSTA

■ Bars
JESSE'S, Ashley St, at E Central Ave.,

■ Dance Bar/Disco
CLUB PARADISE, 2100 W Hill Ave, near I-75 off-ramp, exit 4, (912) 242-9609. Mon-Sat 3pm til...

HAWAII STATEWIDE

PACIFIC OCEAN HOLIDAYS, PO Box 88245-F, Honolulu, HI, (808) 923-2400, (800) 735-6600, Fax: (808) 923-2499, E-mail: poh@hi.net.net. http://www.tnight.com/poh. Specializing exclusively in Hawaii vacation packages for gay travelers, widest selection of gay & gay-friendly Hawaii hotels, B&Bs, condos. Packages can be customized for length of stay, islands visited, and are offered year-round. Tours are not escorted, so sightseeing & relaxation are at one's leisure.

HAWAII - BIG ISLAND

■ Accommodations
HALE ALOHA GUEST RANCH, 84-4780 Mamalahoa Hwy, Captain Cook, HI, 96704, (808) 328-8955 (Tel/Fax), (800) 897-3188. Email: halealoha@aol.com, Web: http://members.aol.com/halealoha, Discover the "house of welcome and love" with spacious lanais and spectacular ocean views. At 1500 ft in the lush South Kona hillside, guests will enjoy our 5-acre citrus and macadamia nut plantation bordering a state forest preserve. Take a stroll, get a massage or relax in the Jacuzzi.

HALE KIPA 'O PELE, PO Box 5252, Kailua-Kona, HI, 96745, (800) LAVAGLO, (808) 329-8676. Email: halekipa@gte.net., Web: http://home1.gte.net/halekipa/, B&B with bungalow. Ceiling fans, private baths. TV lounge with theatre sound, video tape library, Jacuzzi. Bungalow has mini-kitchen, cable TV & VCR.

HALE OHIA COTTAGES, PO Box 758, Volcano, HI, 96785, (800) 455-3803 or (808) 967-7986, Fax: (808) 967-8610.

Kalani Oceanside Retreat

Comfortable
Delicious
Soulful
Sensual
Natural
Hawaii

(800) 800-6886

Hawaii Big Island

Our Place
PAPAIKOU'S B&B

(800) 245-5250

HAWAII

Email: haleohia@bigisland.com, B&B & cottages, 50% gay & lesbian clientele. Private baths, continental breakfast & heated Japanese Furo.

HULIAULE'A, PO Box 1030, Pahoa, HI, 96778, (808) 965-9175. B&B, some straight clientele. Spacious rooms with private & shared baths. Common areas, refrigerator, garden & full breakfast.

KA HALE NA PUA, PO Box 385210, Kohala Coast, HI, (808) 329-2960, (800) 595-3458. Gay-friendly guesthouse on the slopes of Hualakii, on the Kona Coast. Private baths, continental breakfast.

KALANI OCEANSIDE RETREAT, Box 4500-IP, Pahoa, HI, 96778-9724, (800) 800-6886, (808) 965-7828, Fax: (808) 965-9613. Email: kalani@kalani.com, Web: http://www.kalani.com, Experience Hawaii's real aloha comfort, traditional culture, healthful cuisine & extraordinary adventures: thermal springs, a naturist dolphin beach, snorkel pools, kayaking, etc. Our gay-friendly retreat offers several annual week-long events. Restaurant & native gift shops, private & shared baths, pool. Continental breakfast with rooms.

KEALAKEKUA BAY B & B, PO Box 1412, Kealakekua, HI, 96750, (808) 328-8150, (800) 328-8150. Web: www.keala.com, B&B and guesthouse with private baths, expanded continetal breakfast, ceiling fans, maid service, ocean nearby, 50% gay/lesbian clientele.

OUR PLACE PAPAIKOU'S B & B, PO Box 469, Papaikou, HI, 96781, (808) 964-5250, (800) 245-5250. Email: rplace@aloha.net, Web: http://www.best.com/~ourplace, Four miles north of Hilo, in the village of Papaikou, is our lovely cedar home. It overlooks Ka'ie'ie Stream and is set amid a tropical garden with fragrant flowers and tropical fruit trees (all ORGANICALLY grown). Guestrooms share a common lanai overlooking the stream. Private and shared baths, expanded continental breakfast with organic tropical fruit from the garden and orchard. 50% gay/lesbian clientele.

Tropical Tune-Ups

HAWAIIAN RETREAT FOR WOMEN

Kripalu Yoga & Meditation
Snorkeling & Swimming
Hiking Excursions
Workshops
Kayaking
Massage

Call for dates or inquire about our Custom Retreat packages. Arranged for 2-10 people.

800.587.0405

Email: info@tropicaltuneups.com
Web: http://tropicaltuneups.com

R B R FARMS
Bed & Breakfast

Experience the Splendor of a Real Hawaiian Plantation

BIG ISLAND, HAWAII
800-328-9212

HAWAII

PAMALU, RR 2, Box 4023, Pahoa, HI, (808) 965-0830, Fax: (808) 965-6198. B&B country retreat, private baths, expanded continental breakfast, TV lounge, video tape library, pool on premises, nearby lagoon, some straight clientele.

PLUMERIA HOUSE, 77-6546 Naniloa Dr, Kona, HI, 96740, (808) 322-8164. B&B, some straight clientele. Private & shared baths.

R. B. R. FARMS, PO Box 930, Captain Cook, HI, 96704, (800) 328-9212, Tel/Fax: (808) 328-9212. Email: rbrfarms@gte.net, B&B, women welcome. Double rooms & cottage, private & shared baths, color TV, massage, nearby ocean beach. Full breakfast. A working macadamia nut and coffee plantation adds charm to this renovated plantation home. **Being privately owned, it retains the personal touch and attention to detail that sets us apart among outstanding B&Bs in the world.** Some straight clientele. See ad on Page 303.

RAINBOW DREAMS COTTAGE, 13-6412 Beach Rd, Pahoa, HI, 96778, (808) 936-9883. Oceanfront 2-BR turnkey cottage, furnished in rattan tropical comfort. Sunbathe nude on a black sand beach, snorkel among coral castles, or float in a warm springs pond splashed by cool ocean surf. Some straight clientele

RAINBOW'S INN, PO Box 983, Pahoa, HI, 96778, (808) 965-9011 (Tel/Fax). Email: rainbowadv@aol.com, B&B with private bath, continental breakfast, color TV, VCR, ceiling fans, phone. Some straight clientele.

RAINFOREST RETREAT, HCRI Box 5655, Keaau, HI, 96749, (808) 982-9601, Cell (808) 936-3050, Nursery (808) 966-7712, Fax: (808) 966-6898. Email: orchids@hilo.net, Web: rainforest retreat.com, Gay-friendly guest ranch. Private cottage with kitchen, full bath, color TV & hot tub on lanai, or suite with private entrance, kitchenette, color TV & full bath. Full breakfast, ocean nearby.

SAMURAI, THE, 82-5929 Mamalahoa Hwy, Captain Cook, HI, 96704, (808) 328-9210, Fax: (808) 328-8615. Email: shibui@aloha.net, Inn, some straight clientele. Traditional Japanese and western-style rooms with a variety of conveniences. TV lounge, hot tub, continental breakfast. Nearby ocean beach.

Women's Accommodations

BUTTERFLY INN, THE, PO Box 6010, Kurtistown, HI, 96760, (808) 966-7936, (800) 54-MAGIC. Email: the.butterfly.inn@prodigy.com, Women-only B&B, shared bath, breakfast goodies.

TROPICAL TUNE-UPS, PO Box 4488, Waikoloa, HI, 96738, (808) 882-7355 (Tel/Fax), (800) 587-0405. Email: info@tropicaltuneups.com, Web: http://tropicaltuneups.com, Designed for 2-10 women, deluxe retreat packages include your own private home in a 5-star resort area, rental car, massage, guided excursions, private yoga sessions, airport lei greeting & welcome basket. Our Romantic Tropical Escape package also includes couples massage and a catered dinner with optional commitment ceremony. Customized retreats available. Our Kona Coast homes are oceanfront, or have ocean views and are a short walk to the beach. Attractively furnished, including linens, kitchen, TV, VCR, washer/dryer, microwave. See ad on Page 303.

WOOD VALLEY B & B INN, PO Box 37, Pahala, HI, 96777, (808) 928-8212, (800) 854-6754, Fax: (808) 928-9400. Email: jessie@aloha.net, Web: http://civic.net/webmarket/hawaii/jessie, B&B, men welcome. Cozy double rooms, shared bath, kitchen privileges, steam bath, massage, full vegetarian breakfast. Tent sites with shower/toilet facilities.

Bars

MASK BAR & GRILL, 75-5660 Kopiko St, Kailua-Kona, (808) 329-8558. Karaoke, drag shows & dancing.

Restaurants

GODMOTHER, THE, 15-2969 Main St, Pahoa, (808) 965-0555. Gay-friendly restaurant with bar. New York Italian style, 7 days, breakfast-dinner.

HUGGO'S, 75-5828 Kahakai Rd, Kailua-Kona, (808) 329-1493. Fresh seafood & beef.

ORCHID VILLAGE RESTAURANT, at Waiakea Villas, 400 Hualani St, Hilo, (808) 933-7600.

HAWAII

KAUAI

■ *Information*

AIDS HOTLINE, (808) 822-0878, 9am-5pm Mon-Fri.

■ *Accommodations*

ALOHA KAUAI BED & BREAKFAST, 156 Lihau St, Kapaa, HI, 96746, (808) 822-6966, (800) 262-4652. B&B minutes from town, gay beach & many outdoor attractions. Features private & shared baths, full breakfast, sunset refreshments, pool on premises.

ANAHOLA BEACH CLUB, PO Box 562, Anahola, (808) 822-6966, (800) ANAHOLA. B&B on coconut coast. Delightful rooms with private entrances & ocean views, bunk house, TV lounge, full breakfast, complimentary cocktails.

ANUENUE PLANTATION B & B, PO Box 226, Kapaa, HI, (808) 821-0390, Fax: (808) 821-0693. Email: BnB@anuenue.com. Gay-owned & -operated B&B & cottage, full tropical breakfast, private baths, ceiling fans, women welcome.

HALE KAHAWAI, 185 Kahawai Place, Kapaa, HI, 96746, (808) 822-1031, Fax: (808) 823-8220. Email: BandBKauai@aol.com, Conveniently located in Wailua, Kauai, Hale Kahawai has three guest rooms and one studio apartment. All guest rooms have romantic ceiling fans, queen or king mattresses and tropical furnishings. Island breakfast of local fruits, juices, cereals, breads, coffees and teas. Enjoy spectacular views of Kawaikini Peak and Mount Waialeale. End the day relaxing in the hot tub.

KALIHIWAI JUNGLE HOME, PO Box 717, Kilauea, HI, 96754, (808) 828-1626, Fax: (808) 828-2014. Email: thomasw@aloha.net, Web: http://www.hshawaii.com/kvp/jungle/, Fully-furnished, 2-bedroom vacation rental, 50% gay & lesbian. Modern amenities, glassed-in panoramic views from each room. Nearby beach, olympic-sized pool, gym, snorkeling & windsurfing.

KU'OKO'A AT PLUMERIA MOON, PO Box 385, Kilauea, HI, (808) 828-0228 (Tel/Fax), (888) 8-KUOKOA (586562). Email: kuokoa@gte.net, Experience freedom in a place where dreams really do come true. Imagine your own Hawaiian hideaway, nestled on a bluff overlooking the Pacific Ocean. This meticulously maintained, comfortable, one-bedroom cottage, comes completely furnished and amenities include exercise equipment, satellite TV, VCR, stereo, security system and entry gate. There is an outdoor Jacuzzi and shower overlooking the ocean, and a private path leads you to one of the most secluded beaches on the island. 50% gay/lesbian clientele.

MAHINA KAI, PO Box 699, Anahola, Kauai, HI, 96703, (808) 822-9451(Tel/Fax), (800) 337-1134. Email: trudy@aloha.net, B&B, some straight clientele. Color TV, ceiling fans, private baths, meeting rooms & expanded continental breakfast. Lagoon pool & hot tub on premises.

MOHALA KE OLA B & B RETREAT, 5663 Ohelo Rd, Kapaa, Kauai, HI, 96746, (808) 823-6398 (Tel/Fax), toll-free (888) GO-KAUAI (465-2824). Email: kauaibb@aloha.net, Web: www.waterfallbnb.com, Escape to paradise. Wake to the sound of breeze and birdsongs. Breakfast on fresh island fruit on a private terrace. Because

HALE KAHAWAI
A Serene Haven

Kauai
Hawaii

(808) 822-1031

HAWAII

of the privacy provided for each of our 4 guest rooms, you'll think of Mohala Ke Ola as your own personal retreat. This gay-friendly B&B has magnificent mountain & waterfall views, private baths, TV lounge, continental breakfast, pool & hot tub. Lomi-lomi massage, shiatsu, acupuncture & Reiki are available to guests.

PALI KAI, PO Box 450, Kilauea, Kauai, HI, 96754, (808) 828-6691, toll-free: (888) 828-6691. Email: palikai@aloha.net, B&B, 3 rooms with queen beds. Private baths, 1 outdoor private shower, island-style breakfast & nearby ocean beach." ♀♂

ROYAL DRIVE COTTAGES, 147 Royal Drive, Wailua, Kauai, HI, 96746, (808) 822-2321 (Tel/Fax). Quiet, secluded cottages, some straight clientele. Cozy & comfortable with well-equipped kitchenettes, garden, tropical fruit trees available for guests, nearby ocean beach. ♀♂

Women's Accommodations

MAHINA'S GUEST HOUSE, 4433 Panihi Rd, Kapaa, HI, (808) 823-9364. Women-only guesthouse & hostel with 50% lesbian & bi & 50% straight women. Shared baths, shared kitchen, shamanic healing & tarot readings.

Bars

SIDE OUT, 4-1330 Kuhio Hwy, near the 1st Hawaiian Bank in Kapaa, (808) 822-7330. Gay-friendly bar & restaurant.

MAUI

Information

AIDS INFO, (808) 242-4900. 8:30am-4:30pm Mon-Fri.

MAUI GAY & LESBIAN INFO CENTER, 624 Front St, Lahaina., Booking center for Maui excursions & general gay Maui info. Operated by gay owner of Maui Surfing School & Royal Hawaiian Weddings.

WOMEN'S EVENT HOTLINE, (808) 573-3077.

Tours, Charters & Excursions

MAUI SURFING SCHOOL, INC, PO Box 424, Puunene, Maui, (808) 875-0625, (800) 851-0543, Fax: (808) 875-0623. Gay-owned & -operated company. Specializing in beginners, cowards and non-swimmers! Using the world-famous "learn to surf in one lesson" technique developed by Andrea Thomas, anyone can stand up and actually catch a wave their first time out. Choose from group or private 1, 3 or 5 day sessions. Inquire about our surf camp package.

ROYAL HAWAIIAN WEDDINGS, (808) 875-8569, (800) 659-1866, Fax: (808) 875-0623. Email: jrenner@maui.net, Web: www.hawaiigaywed.com, The first company on the planet to offer gay weddings! Loving, caring services with the

---

Express your love on Maui, the most romantic place in the world.

Royal Hawaiian Weddings

The first in gay and lesbian weddings.

Call us on Maui toll free
1-800-659-1866
www.hawaiigaywed.com

Need a great deal on AIRFARE?
Call Lucy at 1-888-280-7233

A Lesbian-owned Company • Member IGLTA

Andrea & Janet's Maui Condos

- 1 & 2 bedroom spacious ocean/beach front suites
- Pool, tennis, golf, more!

Call Andrea on Maui for reservations:

1-800-289-1522
www.mauicondos.com

Need cheap AIRFARE?
Call Lucy at 1-888-280-7233

Member IGLTA • A Lesbian-owned Company

best photographers, florists, musicians, caterers, etc., to make your ceremony a truly unforgettable experience. Choose one of our plans or customize your own experience. Romantic, secluded beach or tropical garden or private beachfront home settings. We make all travel arrangements from airfare to snorkel trips. ♀♂

Accommodations

ANDREA & JANET'S MAUI CONDOS, (800) 289-1522, (310) 399-1223, Fax: (310) 399-0407. Email: andrea@maui.net, Web: www.mauicondos.com, Two Maui lesbians lovigly offering oceanfront 1- and 2-BR condo accommodations at very affordable rates. Immaculate, spacious, supplied with everything you need for a perfect Maui vacation, such as snorkel gear, boogie boards, tennis racquets and tennis courts, beach chairs, fluffy towels, CD, VCR, pool, spa, sandy beach. Nearby golf, shopping, dining and all the best Maui has to offer.

ANFORA'S DREAMS, Attn: Dale Jones, PO Box 74030, Los Angeles, CA, 90004, (213) 737-0731, Reservations: (800) 788-5046, Fax: (818) 224-4312. Fully-furnished condos, 50% gay & lesbian clientele. Deluxe accommodations include color cable TV, private baths, Jacuzzi, pool & laundry facilities. Ocean & park across the road."

BLAIR'S ORIGINAL HANA PLANTATION HOUSES, Hana, Maui, Mail: 2957 Kalakaua Ave, Honolulu, HI, 96815, (808) 923-0772, (800) 228-HANA, Fax: (808) 922-6068. Email: hana@kestrok.com, Fourteen private homes in a large compound, 50% gay & lesbian. Hot tub, weights, massage, horses & nearby ocean beach.

CAMP KULA MAUI B & B, PO Box 111, Kula, Maui, HI, 96790, (808) 876-0000 (Tel/Fax). Email: camper@maui.net, B&B near ocean beach & waterfalls. Comfortable rooms, common room, TV lounge, kitchen privileges, continental breakfast, tea, coffee. ♀♂

GOLDEN BAMBOO RANCH, 422 Kaupakalua Rd, Haiku, Maui, HI, 96708, (808) 572-7824 (Tel/Fax), (800) 344-1238. Email: golden@maui.net, Web: www.maui.net/~golden, Gay-friendly

---

Underwater Vision Quests

You're swimming along, weightless in a blue world, when a large sea turtle comes into view, flapping his feet lazily in the sunlit water. Without gesture or warning, he flicks his feet a time or two and swims right up to you. For a long moment he pauses, as you regard each other silently, peacefully eye to eye, just inches apart.

Experiences like this, which can be mystical, spiritually expanding and life-changing, are the goal of underwater vision quests conducted by women-owned Octopus Reef Divers & Tours. Owners Renee and Lynn are certified scuba instructors and veterans of over 8,000 dives. They offer instruction for beginners through certification, plus diving adventures in a variety of locations around Maui.

Contact Octopus at (808) 875-0183 or Email aquasong@sprynet.com.

HAWAII

plantation house suites & cottage. Color TV, VCR, phone, ceiling fans & private baths. Expanded continental breakfast. Nearby ocean & natural swimming pools.

HALE HUELO, PO Box 1237, Haiku, HI, 96708, (808) 572-8669, Fax: (808) 573-8403. Email: halehuel@maui.net, Gay-owned & -operated B&B in a jungle paradise, private baths, expanded continental breakfast, pool & Jacuzzi on premises. 50% gay/lesbian clientele.

HALFWAY TO HANA HOUSE, PO Box 675, Haiku, Maui, HI, 96708, (808) 572-1176, Fax: (808) 572-3609. Email: gail@maui.net, Web: www.maui.net/~gailp, B&B, 50% gay & lesbian clientele.

One room with private entrance & bath, close to fresh water pools & beach, tropical breakfast.

HUELO POINT FLOWER FARM B & B, PO Box 1195, Paia, Maui, HI, 96779, (808) 572-1850. Email: huelopt@maui.net, Web: http://www.maui.net/~huelopt, B&B & rental homes with kitchen, refrigerator & private bath. Color TV, Jacuzzi, & exercise equipment. Expanded continental breakfast. 50% gay & lesbian clientele.

JACK & TOM'S MAUI CONDOS, Write: Margaret Norrie Realty, PO Box 365, Kihei, HI, 96753, (800) 800-8608, (808) 874-1048, Fax: (808) 879-6932. Email: mauijack@aol.com, Choose between ocean and garden views for your private Maui condominium. You'll get the feeling that you're settled in and living in paradise. Each 1- or 2-bedroom condominium is within a larger complex. Color cable TV, AC, telephone, ceiling fans, kitchen & laundry facilities. Pool on premises, ocean nearby. 5-day minimum stay.

KAILUA MAUI GARDENS, SR Box 9 (Hana Hwy), Haiku, Maui, HI, 96708, (800) 258-8588, (808) 572-9726, Fax: (808) 572-5934. Email: kmg@maui.net, Web: www.maui.net/~kmg/, Cottage & house rental, 50% gay & lesbian. Quaint to deluxe, BBQ, spas, nearby waterfall. Continental breakfast in cottages, fresh fruit.

KEIKI ANANDA, Makawao, HI, (808) 573-2225 or (808) 572-8496. B&B retreat center, shared baths, vegetarian communal kitchen, yoga & meditation room & instruction, clothing-optional pool on premises, ocean nearby. 50% gay & lesbian clientele.

MAUI ISANA RENTAL CONDO, 515 S. Kihei Rd, Kihei, Maui, HI, 96573-9010, (800) 414-3573, (360) 321-1069. Two-bedroom, 2-bath rental condo, color TV, phone, pool on premises, ocean across street. Condo unit is straight, Maui Isana owners rent to 50% gay/lesbian, 50% straight clientele.

NAPUALANI O' HANA, c/o PO Box 118, Hana, Maui, HI, 96713, (808) 248-8935 or 248-0792, (800) 628-7092. Gay-friendly suites, private baths.

NEW ON MAUI

Alohalani's Guest House
for Women Only

▲ private   ▲ quiet
▲ spacious   ▲ pool
▲ wedding packages

Renew romance
and revitalize your soul

800-511-3121
808-249-0395
remotepo@maui.net

TRIPLE LEI / HUELO POINT LOOKOUT COTTAGES, PO Box 117, Paia, HI, 96779, (808) 573-0914, (800) 871-8645, Fax: (808) 573-0227. Email: dreamers@maui.net, Web: wwte.com/lookout.htm, Two acre estate with 3 self-contained cottages & 1 suite with private entrance & kitchenette. Private baths, color TV, telephone, coffee & tea-making facilities, expanded continental breakfast, hot tub. 50% gay & lesbian clientele.

WAIPIO BAY LOOKOUT LODGING, PO Box 856, Haiku, HI, 96708, (808) 572-4530 (Tel/Fax). Web: http://www.maui.net/~regal/wb.html, Secluded 2-acre estate at the edge of a 300-ft cliff on Maui's North Shore. Oceanfront rooms with private baths, lanais & kitchenettes, continental breakfast. Pool & Jacuzzi on premises.

■ Women's Accommodations

ALOHALANI'S GUEST HOUSE, 193 Lower Waiehu Beach Rd, Wailuku, Maui, HI, 96793, (808) 249-0395, (800) 511-3121, Fax: (808) 249-0396. Email: remotepo@maui.net, Web: www.remotepo.com/cottage.html, New on Maui — a private, lesbian-owned compound for women only. Enjoy private accommodations across from Waiehu Beach Park, with a 180 degree ocean view from your breakfast porch and living room. Our quiet, local community is far from the tourist crowds but convenient to stores and good eats (and we boast a well-stocked kitchen). Two spacious one-bedroom units sleep two to four. Accommodation, air, car packages available.

HALE MAKALEKA, Kihei, HI, 96753, (808) 879-2971. Women-only B&B in garden setting. Spacious room with color TV, private bath & private entrance. Tropical breakfast.

■ Beaches

LITTLE BEACH., This gay beach is part of Makena Beach. It is not legal to go nude in Hawaii. You can be cited.

■ Bars

LAVA BAR & GRILL, 61 S Kihei Rd, (808) 874-5660. Beer bust & BBQ Sun, live music.

■ Erotica

SKIN DEEP, 626 Front St, Lahaina, (808) 661-8531, 661-8288. Tattoos, piercing, leather, adult gifts, jewelry, Harley T-shirts & apparel.

OAHU - HONOLULU

■ Information

AIDS HOTLINE, (808) 922-1313.

GAY & LESBIAN COMMUNITY CENTER, 1566 Wilder Ave, (808) 951-7000, Mon-Fri 10am-2pm.

GAY INFO, (808) 951-7000. 24hr tape.

■ Accommodations

A TROPIC PARADISE, 43 Laiki Place, Kailua, HI, (808) 261-2299, (888) 362-4488, Fax: (808) 263-0795. Email: darreld@gte.net, B&B & vacation home steps from the beach. Private & shared baths, expanded continental breakfast, pool on premises. 50% gay/lesbian clientele.

ALI'I BLUFFS WINDWARD B & B, 46-251 Ikiiki St, Kaneohe, HI, 96744, (808) 235-1124 or (800) 235-1151. B&B, some straight clientele, private baths.

HOTEL HONOLULU, 376 Kaiolu St, Honolulu, HI, 96815, (808) 926-2766, (800) 426-2766 (US/CAN), Fax: (808) 922-3326. Email: hotelhnl@lava.net, Web: http://www.lava.net/~hotelhnl, Hotel 2 blocks from the beach. Theme studios & suites. Next door to gay clubs, restaurants, shops.

PACIFIC OCEAN HOLIDAYS, PO Box 88245, Dept IP, Honolulu, HI, 96830-8245, (808) 923-2400, (800) 735-6600, Fax: (808) 923-2499. Email: poh@hi.net, Web: http://gayhawaii.com, Hawaii accommodations in gay & gay-friendly B&B homes, resort hotels & condos.

WAIKIKI A A STUDIOS (BED & BREAKFAST HONOLULU & STATEWIDE), 3242 Kaohinani, Honolulu, HI, 96817, (808) 595-7533, (800) 288-4666, Fax: (808) 595-2030. Email: BnBsHI@Aloha.net, Web: http://planet-hawaii.com/bnb-honolulu, Studios, hosted rentals & Statewide bed & breakfast reservation service. Gay-friendly, variety of guest quarters with a variety of conveniences.

WAIKIKI JOY HOTEL, 320 Lewers St, Honolulu, HI, 96815, (808) 923-2300, (800) 733-5569, Fax: (808) 924-4010.

HAWAII

Gay-friendly boutique hotel with restaurant & bar, 1-6 blocks to gay bars, 2 blocks to ocean beach, pool on premises, continental breakfast, private baths with Jacuzzi tub.

Transportation
CITY TAXI, (800) 524-2121. Gay-friendly.

Beaches
GAY & STRAIGHT BEACHES, for Queen Surf Beach, go to Kapiolani Park before the Waikiki Aquarium (gay beach is on the right side). Royal Hawaiian Hotel beach is mostly straight, but frequented by many gays. Diamond Head Beach has gay & straight areas. Follow Kalakaua Ave to Diamond Head Rd. After getting to the lighthouse, walk up footpath to beach & look for men in bikinis.

Bars
CLUB MICHELANGELO, 444 Hobron Ln, Waikiki, (808) 951-0008. Karaoke.

DIS & DAT, 1315 Kalakaua Ave, Honolulu, (808) 946-0000. Live Hawaiian music.

IN-BETWEEN, 2155 Lauula St, (808) 926-7060. 2pm-2am daily, Sat & Sun 10-2.

Dance Bar/Disco
DISCOTHEQUE NIGHTCLUB, 478 Ena Rd, at Kalakaua Ave, (808) 946-6499. 70% men, 30% women.

★ HULA'S BAR & LEI STAND, 2103 Kuhio Ave, (808) 923-0669. Video dance bar & tropical patio bar, 11am-2am. May move in '98, call for location.

TRIXX, FRONT BAR, 2109 Kuhio Ave, Waikiki, (808) 923-0669. After beach cruising, Sun backyard BBQ.

VENUS, 1349 Kapiolani Ave, (808) 955-2640. Good DJs, spacious, cushy couches, 8pm-4am daily, valet park.

Restaurants
CAFE SISTINA, 1314 S. King St, (808) 596-0061. Northern Italian cuisine.

KEO'S IN WAIKIKI, 2040 Kuhio Ave, (808) 951-9355. Gourmet Thai cuisine in a casual, elegant setting.

Erotica
SUZIES ADULT VIDEOS, 98-115 Kamehameha Hwy, (808) 487-6969. Gay & all-female videos, novelties, 10am-2am.

IDAHO

ASHTON

Accommodations
FISH CREEK LODGING, See Jackson, Wyoming.,

BOISE

Bars
EIGHTH STREET BALCONY PUB, Capitol Terrace Bldg, 150 N 8th St #224, (208) 336-1313. Pub popular with gays, especially Sun afternoon & evenings.

PARTNERS, 2210 Main St, (208) 331-3551. Open 7 days. Full liquor bar available, dance floor, bands on weekends, 60% women, 40% men.

Dance Bar/Disco
EMERALD CITY CLUB, 415 S 9th, (208) 342-5446. Progressive dance & show bar, 10am-2am, 7 days. DJ nightly, C&W Sun & Wed. Large straight following.

PAPA'S CLUB LEATHERS & FEATHERS, 1108 Front St, (208) 333-0074. Patio, drag shows Fri, full liquor, 60% women, 40% men.

Restaurants
RICK'S CAFE AMERICAIN AT THE FLICKS, 646 Fulton St, at 6th, (208) 342-4288. Gay-friendly restaurant, 4 movie theaters, video store. Gay & lesbian groups meet here weekly.

COEUR D'ALENE

Accommodations
CLARK HOUSE ON HAYDEN LAKE, E. 4550 S. Hayden Lake Rd, Hayden Lake, ID, 83835, (208) 772-3470, (800) 765-4593, Fax: (208) 772-6899. Gay-owned inn with limited restaurant, private baths, full breakfast, Jacuzzi, gay & lesbian following.

LAVA HOT SPRINGS

Accommodations
AURA SOMA LAVA, 97 N 2nd East, Lava Hot Springs, ID, 83246, (208) 776-5800, (800) 776-7237, Fax: (208) 776-5550. Email: asl@micron.net, Guesthouse & small convention center with bookstore, dedicated to mind/body healing, private & shared baths.

ILLINOIS

MOSCOW

■ Information
WOMEN'S CENTER, U of Idaho, Line St, at Idaho St (Old Journalism Bldg), (208) 885-6616, 885-6111 (switchboard). Mon-Fri 8am-5pm, library, programs and events.

■ Retail & Bookstores
BOOKPEOPLE, 512 S Main St, (208) 882-7957. General bookstore with a gay & lesbian section.

ILLINOIS STATEWIDE

■ Information
AIDS HOTLINE, (800) AID-AIDS. Daily 10am-10pm except holidays.

ALTON

■ Bars
MABEL'S, 602 Belle, (618) 465-8687. Show bar, male dancers Fri, 50% men, 50% women.

ATWOOD

■ Accommodations
AT THE WOODS BED & BREAKFAST, 250 N 1500 E, Atwood, IL, 61913, (217) 578-3784. Web: www.atthewoods.com, Gay-friendly B&B 1-1/2 miles north of Atwood, a unique little town 30 miles east of Decatur, IL. This Italianate Victorian brick home, surrounded by prairie lands, is set on 5.8 wooded acres. The home's 14 rooms are exquisitely furnished with antiques and have private and shared baths. A delicious full breakfast is served in the formal dining room.

BLOOMINGTON

■ Information
CONNECTIONS COMMUNITY CENTER, 313 N Main, (309) 827-2437.

■ Bars
BISTRO, 316 N Main, (309) 829-2278. 4pm-1am (Fri till 2am, Sat 8pm-2am, Sun 6pm-1am).

■ Retail & Bookstores
ONCE UPON A TIME ALTERNATIVE BOOKS & GIFTS, 311 N Main St, (309) 828-3998, Fax: (309) 828-8879. E-mail: outbooks@outbooks.com, http://www.outbooks.com. Gay & lesbian bookstore & Out Cafe cybercafe with gourmet coffee, video rentals.

CALUMET CITY

■ Bars
JOHN L'S PLACE, 335 154th Pl, (708) 862-2386. Gay & straight clientele.
MR B'S, 606 Stateline Ave, (708) 862-1221. More women later on weekends, pool table. Twice monthly entertainment.
PATCH, THE, 201 155th St, (708) 891-9854. Jukebox dancing, closed Mon.

■ Dance Bar/Disco
DICK'S RU CRAZEE, 48 154th Pl, (708) 862-4605.
POUR HOUSE, 103 155th Place, (708) 891-3980.

CARBONDALE

■ Information
PRIDE LINE, (618) 453-5151, Mon-Fri 5pm-9pm.
WOMEN'S CENTER, 408 W Freeman, (618) 529-2324, 24hrs.
WOMEN'S SERVICES, at Southern Illinois U, (618) 453-3655.

■ Dance Bar/Disco
CLUB TRAZ, 213 E Main, (618) 549-4270, Tues or Wed-Sun.

CENTRAL ILLINOIS

■ Accommodations
LITTLE HOUSE ON THE PRAIRIE, THE, PO Box 525, Sullivan, IL, 61951, (217) 728-4727. Gay-friendly bed & breakfast. AC, private baths, TV lounge, video tape library, full breakfast. Jacuzzi & pool on premises.

CHAMPAIGN - URBANA

■ Dance Bar/Disco
CHESTER STREET, 65 Chester St, (217) 356-5607. DJ nightly, both gay & straight clientele. Becoming an alternative club, lots of college students.

■ Retail & Bookstores
HORIZON BOOKSTORE, 1115-1/2 W Oregon, Urbana, (217) 328-2988. Progres-

ILLINOIS

Visit Chicago (800) CARITAS — Caritas B&B Network

...sive bookstore with a gay & lesbian selection. Closed Sun.

JANE ADDAMS BOOKSHOP, 208 N Neil, Champaign, (217) 356-2555. Women's bookstore and used books.

CHICAGO INTRO

Information
AIDS FOUNDATION, (312) 922-2322.
HORIZONS HELPLINES, (773) 929-HELP (4357), AIDS/HIV (312) 472-6469. 6pm-10pm daily.
IN TOUCH HOTLINE, (312) 996-5535, 6pm-3am.
KINDREDHEARTS WOMEN'S CENTER, 2214 Ridge Ave, Evanston, (847) 604-0913.

Accommodations
CARITAS BED & BREAKFAST NETWORK, (800) CARITAS, (312) 857-0801, Fax: (312) 857-0805. B&B, home-stay accommodations service. Member: IGLTA

Women's Accommodations
A SISTER'S PLACE — GUESTROOMS FOR WOMEN, (773) 275-1319. A Sister's Place welcomes you to stay in the big city at a confidential location in the home of an artist entrepreneur. This artistically decorated city flat offers comfortable guestrooms, is on bus lines, the Red Line train stop, and is walking distance to Big Chicks, Little Chinatown, theatres and international restaurants. Secure parking lot. Call to set up arrival time at least two weeks in advance. ♀

Beaches
BELMONT ROCKS, gay beach between Diversey Harbor & Belmont Harbor. ♀♂

Retail & Bookstores
BOOKSTORES (GAY & LESBIAN), see Chicago N Halsted & Environs.
WOMEN'S BOOKSTORES, see Chicago N Halsted & Environs.

CHICAGO NORTHALSTED

Accommodations
VILLA TOSCANA GUEST HOUSE, 3447 N Halsted, Chicago, IL, 60657-2414, (800) 684-5755, (773) 404-2643. European-style guesthouse in the heart of gay Chicago. Private & shared baths, color TV, AC, expanded continental breakfast. Two blocks from Lake Michigan, some straight clientele. ♀♂

Bars
CLOSET, THE, 3325 N Broadway, (773) 477-8533. Small bar, popular happy hour, videos. ♀♂

A Sister's Place
B&B For Women Travellers

- Confidential Location In Uptown Chicago
- Easy Access to Public Transportation

Check-in by appointment only
773-275-1319

$45 TO $55 DAILY ROOM RATE

- Pay in Advance by Check or Money Order
- Call 2 Weeks Ahead
- Arrange Arrival Time in Advance

ILLINOIS 313

COCKTAIL, 3359 N Halsted, (773) 477-1420. Upscale cocktail bar, large straight following. ♂

GENTRY ON HALSTED, 3320 N Halsted, (773) 348-1053. Videos. 🕭 ♀♂

★ SIDETRACK, 3349 N Halsted St, (773) 477-9189. Video bar, always crowded. 🍴 ♂

■ Dance Bar/Disco

FUSION, 3631 N Halsted, Hotline: (773) 975-0660, after 9pm (773) 975-6622. Video dance bar." 🕭 🍴 ♂

★ ROSCOE'S, 3354-56 N Halsted St, (773) 281-3355. Video dance bar, 2 other bars, restaurant, patio." 🍴 ♂

■ Restaurants

LAS MAÑANITAS, 3523 N Halsted, (773) 528-2109. Mexican cuisine. 🍴

RHUMBA, 3631 N Halsted St, (773) 975-2345. Brazilian cuisine. 🍴

WILD ONION, 3500 N Lincoln, (773) 871-5555. Pastas, Southwestern & vegetarian cuisine. 🍴

■ Retail & Bookstores

GAY MART, 3457 N Halsted, (773) 929-4272. Cards & gifts geared to the gay & lesbian community, daily from 11am.

RAGIN' RAEJEAN'S, 3450 N Halsted St, (773) 871-1376. Gift shop with gay & lesbian cards, calendars, hi-camp jewelry boxes, rainbow items, etc.

SHIRTS ILLUSTRATED, 3315 N Broadway, (773) 871-4785. Custom-imprint & embroidery on t-shirts, hats, satin baseball jackets, bags or polo shirts.

■ Erotica

CUPID'S TREASURES, 3519 N Halsted St, (773) 348-3884. Fantasy wear for men & women. A love boutique."

CHICAGO NORTHALSTED ENVIRONS

■ Accommodations

BEST WESTERN HAWTHORNE TERRACE, 3434 N Broadway, Chicago, IL, 60657, (773) 244-3434, (888) 675-BEST (2378), Fax: (773) 244-3435. Gay-friendly hotel set in period architecture, all modern conveniences, exercise facility, close to gay nightlife, shopping, theatre, lakefront beaches.

CITY SUITES HOTEL — NEIGHBORHOOD INNS OF CHICAGO, 933 West Belmont, Chicago, IL, 60657, (773) 404-3400, Fax: (773) 404-3405. Reservations: (800) CITY-108. Gay-friendly hotel. Comfortable, affordable, European-style singles thru suites. Lake Michigan nearby.

PARK BROMPTON INN — NEIGHBORHOOD INNS OF CHICAGO, 528 W Brompton, Chicago, IL, 60657, (773) 404-3499, Fax: (773) 404-3495. Reservations: (800) PARK-108. Gay-friendly hotel. Rooms & suites with color cable TV, AC, phone & private baths.

SURF HOTEL — NEIGHBORHOOD INNS OF CHICAGO, 555 W Surf, Chicago, IL, 60657, (773) 528-8400, Fax: (773) 528-8483. Reservations: (800) SURF-108. Gay-friendly hotel near Lake Michigan. Variety of tastefully-appointed rooms, private baths & modern conveniences.

■ Bars

BERLIN, 954 W Belmont Ave, (773) 348-4975. Hi-energy video bar, patio." 🍴 ♀♂

BUDDIES, 3301 N Clark, (773) 477-4066. Bar & restaurant. 30 & over crowd. Male & female bartenders." ♥ 🕭 U ✘ ♂

■ Dance Bar/Disco

GIRLBAR, 2625 N Halsted St, (773) 871-4210. Tues-Thurs 6pm-2am, Fri 3pm-2am, Sat 6pm-3am, Sun 5pm-2am. 🍴 ♀

■ Restaurants

BUDDIES, 3301 N Clark, at Buddies bar, (773) 477-4066. 🍸 ♀♂

■ Retail & Bookstores

UNABRIDGED BOOKS, 3251 N Broadway, near Melrose, (773) 883-9119. General bookstore with large selection of gay & lesbian books.

■ Leathers/Piercing

MALE HIDE LEATHERS, 2816 N Lincoln Ave, near Diversey, (773) 929-0069. Email: MALEHIDELEATHER@webtv/net, Leathers and accessories for men & women. Tue-Sat noon-8pm, Sun 1-5pm, closed Mon.

■ Erotica

PLEASURE CHEST, 3155 N Broadway, (773) 525-7151, 525-7152.

TABOO TABOO, 855 W Belmont, (773)

314 ILLINOIS

723-3739. Leather, latex, fetish store, women welcome.

CHICAGO LOOP

■ Bars
GENTRY, 440 N State., (312) 664-1033. 60% men, 40% women.
STAR DUST REVUE, 440 N Halsted St, (773) 363-7827.

■ Dance Bar/Disco
GENERATOR, 306 N Halsted St., Wed-Sun from 9pm.

CHICAGO NORTH

■ Bars
ANVIL, 1137 W Granville Ave, near Broadway, (773) 973-0006. CD juke box, videos, patio.
BIG CHICKS, 5024 N Sheridan Rd, (773) 728-5511. Eclectic art bar, many straights.
CAFE ASHIE, 5419 N Clark, gay-friendly restaurant & bar with patio.
CHARMER'S, 1502 W Jarvis Ave, near Greenview, (773) 465-2811. 60% men, 40% women.
FRIENDS PUB, 3432 W Irving Park, (773) 539-5229. Videos, small dance floor.
LOST & FOUND, 3058 W Irving Park Rd, at Albany, (773) 463-9617. Buzz to get in, closed Mon.
MADRIGAL'S BAR & CAFE, 5316 N Clark St, (773) 334-3033. Cabaret bar with piano, singers. Cafe has light meals, patio in summer.
SCOT'S, 1829 W Montrose, (773) 528-3253. Videos.

■ Dance Bar/Disco
LEGACY '21, 3042 W Irving Park, (773) 588-9405. Small dance bar.
RAINBOW ROOM BAR & GRILLE, 4530 N Lincoln, (773) 271-4378. Sports bar with DJ & dancing Fri & Sat, grille with sandwiches.

■ Restaurants
ANN SATHER, 5207 N Clark St, (773) 271-6677. Diner with Swedish home cooking. Also at: 929 W Belmont, 1329 E 57th.
JULIE MAI'S LE BISTRO, 5025 N Clark, (773) 784-6000. French & Vietnamese cuisine, steaks.
PEPPER LOUNGE, 3441 N Sheffield, (773) 665-7377. Late-night supper club, gourmet dining till 1:30am.
TOMBOY, 5402 N Clark St, (773) 907-0636. Woman-owned restaurant, eclectic American cuisine.

■ Retail & Bookstores
WOMANWILD, 5237 N Clark St, (773) 878-0300. Extraordinary art/gift gallery offering treasures by 150 women artists!
WOMEN & CHILDREN FIRST, 5233 N Clark St, (773) 769-9299. Feminist & children's bookstore with complete selection of lesbian titles and women's music. Weekly programs, large recovery, psychology & women's spirituality sections. More space & bigger gay section in '98.

CHICAGO NEAR NORTH

■ Accommodations
HOUSE OF TWO URNS, THE, 1239 N Greenview Ave, Chicago, IL, 60622-3318, (773) 235-1408. Reservations: (312) 810-2466, (800) 835-9303. Gay-friendly B&B. Eclectically furnished rooms with shared bath, TV lounge, sitting rooms, refrigerator, continental breakfast & nearby pool.
OLD TOWN BED & BREAKFAST, 1451 N North Park Ave, Chicago, IL, 60610-1226, (312) 440-9268. This modern house is splendidly furnished and decorated with pictures and art objects from three centuries. A walled garden, a library with easy chairs, a marble bath with an oversized tub, and cherrywood sleighbeds invite rest, reflection and renewal. Lake Michigan, Lincoln Park and an urban village surround. Parking is ample. North Michigan Avenue shopping, Gold Coast mansions and fine restaurants are a short walk.

■ Bars
VINYL, 1615 N Clybourn, (312) 587-8469. Wed-Sun, Wed salsa & merengue, Thurs int'l dance party, Fri South Beach dance party & latin music.

■ Restaurants
FIREPLACE INN, 1448 N Wells, near North Ave, (312) 664-5264. Steaks, seafood.

ILLINOIS

CHICAGO SOUTH

Dance Bar/Disco
JEFFREY PUB, 7041 S Jeffrey Ave, near 71st, (773) 363-8555. Dance & video bar, women welcome.

CHICAGO WEST

Information
OAK PARK LESBIAN & GAY ASSN., (708) 848-0273.

Dance Bar/Disco
HUNTER'S, 1932 E Higgins Rd, Elk Grove, (847) 439-8840. Video dance bar, patio.

INNEXILE, 5758 W 65th Street, (773) 582-3510. Video dance bar, patio, women welcome.

NUTBUSH, 7201 Franklin, Forest Park, (708) 366-5117. Disco, videos, male strippers, women welcome.

TEMPTATIONS, 10235 W Grand Ave, Franklin Park, (847) 455-0008. Wed-Sat from 9pm.

Retail & Bookstores
PRIDE AGENDA BOOKSTORE, 1109 Westgate, Oak Park, (708) 524-8429. Gay & lesbian bookstore, gifts.

DEKALB

Information
GAY & LESBIAN BISEXUAL COALITION, (815) 753-0584. Dances, picnics, galas, films, speakers & local info.

EAST ST LOUIS
SEE ST. LOUIS, MO,

GRANITE CITY

Dance Bar/Disco
CLUB ZIPS, 3145 W Chain of Rocks Rd, (618) 797-0700. Dance bar, patio with volleyball.

PEORIA

Bars
DAVID'S, 805 or 807 SW Adams, (309) 676-3987.

QUENCH ROOM, 631 W Main St, near Sheridan, (309) 676-1079. Conversation bar, 50% men, 50% women.

Dance Bar/Disco
DJ'S TIME OUT, 703 SW Adams, (309) 674-5902. Dance & sports bar, 1pm-1am (Thurs-Sat till 2am), Thurs drag shows, 50% men, 50% women.

RED FOX DEN, 800 N Knoxville Ave, (309) 674-8013. 70% men.

QUINCY

Dance Bar/Disco
IRENE'S CABARET, 124 N 5th St, (217) 222-6292. Dance & show bar, 50% men, 50% women.

ROCK ISLAND
SEE DAVENPORT, IA,

ROCKFORD

Information
WOMEN'S SPACE CENTER, 3333 Maria Linden Dr, (815) 877-0118. Women's art gallery.

Dance Bar/Disco
OFFICE & HOT SHOTS, 513 E State St, (815) 965-0344. Mon-Sat 5pm-2am, Sun noon-midnite, DJ Wed-Sat, 60% men, 40% women. Hot Shots is a quieter basement bar with juke box, pool table, darts, 2nd floor lounge open Fri & Sat.

Retail & Bookstores
SOURCE CAFE & BOOKSTORE, THE, 610 E 8th St, (815) 987-0181. General bookstore with a small gay & lesbian section, gifts, etc. Young crowd in cafe.

SPRINGFIELD

Bars
STATION HOUSE, 306 E Washington, (217) 525-0438. Bar & dance bar, DJ nightly except Tues, 50% men, 50% women.

Dance Bar/Disco
OUT NORTH, 3036 Peoria Rd, near Taintor, (217) 753-9268. closed Mon.

SMOKEY'S DEN, 411 E Washington St, near 4th, (217) 522-0301. Disco, DJ wknds, 50% men, 50% women.

Retail & Bookstores
SUNDANCE BOOKSTORE, 1428 E Sangamon Ave, (217) 788-5243. Gifts, music, books, gay & lesbian jewelry,

INDIANA

BLOOMINGTON

Information
GAY & LESBIAN SWITCHBOARD, (812) 855-5688. 7pm-11pm or tape.

Bars
OTHER BAR, 414 S Walnut, (812) 332-0033. Closed Sun.
UNCLE ELIZABETH'S, 9th & Morton, (812) 331-0060. Pool table, patio.

Dance Bar/Disco
BULLWINKLE'S, 201 S College, (812) 334-3232. Dance & show bar, 7pm-3am, closed Sun

ELKHART

Information
SWITCHBOARD CONCERN, (219) 293-8671, 24hrs. Not a gay service, but will put you in touch with local gay organizations. No bar referrals.

EVANSVILLE

Information
TRI-STATE ALLIANCE, (812) 474-4853. Gay and lesbian group providing local information.

Bars
SCOTTIE'S BAR, 2207 S Kentucky Ave, (812) 425-3270. Piano bar, beer garden, male strippers.
UPTOWN BAR, 201 W Illinois St, (812) 423-4861. DJ Fri & Sat.

Dance Bar/Disco
SOME PLACE ELSE, 910 Main at Sycamore, (812) 424-3202. Dance & show bar with Down Under Gay Pride shop, 20% straights.

FT WAYNE

Information
AIDS INFO, (219) 744-1144. Support services, educational programs, 24hrs.
GAY OUTREACH LINE, (219) 456-6570.
HELP LINE & COMMUNITY CENTER, (219) 744-1199 7pm-10pm or tape.

Bars
HENRY'S, 536 W Main St, at Fulton, (219) 426-0531. Not a gay bar, but frequented by some gays, lesbians.

Dance Bar/Disco
★ AFTER DARK, 231 Pearl St, (219) 424-6130. Male dancers Tues, drag shows Thurs & Fri, 70% men, 30% women.

DOWNTOWN ON THE LANDING, 110 W Columbia St, (219) 420-1615. Open Thurs-Sat, mostly straight.
UP THE STREET, 2322 S Calhoun, (219) 456-7166. Small dance bar, 70% women, 30% men.

INDIANAPOLIS

Information
DIVERSITY CENTER & G/L SWITCHBOARD, 1112 Southeastern Ave, S of Washington St, (317) 630-4297. Gay & lesbian community center, library, archives, organized events & meetings. 7-11pm nitely.

Bars
BROTHER'S BAR & GRILLE, 822 N Illinois, (317) 636-1020. Bar & restaurant, American-style, daily from 4pm."
CLUB CABARET, 151 W 14th St, at Capitol., (317) 767-1707. Showbar.
ILLUSIONS, 1446 E Washington St, at Oriental, (317) 266-0535. Showbar, DJ Wed-Sat.
TOMORROW'S, 2301 N Meridian, at 23rd, (317) 925-1710. Pool, video games, shows Sun.
UNICORN CLUB, 122 W 13th St, at Illinois, (317) 262-9195. Members-only club, male strippers.
UTOPIA, 924 N Pennsylvania, near 10th, (317) 638-0215. Open 7 days, DJ Thurs-Sun, full Mediterranean menu.

Dance Bar/Disco
★ METRO, 707 Massachusetts Ave, (317) 639-6022. Video dance bar, bars, gift shop, restaurant, patio, 80% men, 20% women. Gift shop upstairs.

★ TEN, THE, 1218 N Pennsylvania St, near 12th, (317) 638-5802. Dance & show bar, 30% men, 70% women. Closed Sun, men welcome."

VOGUE, THE, 6259 N College Ave, Broad Ripple, (317) 255-2828. Sun night is gay night, "Boing Night."

■ Cafe

ABBEY, THE, 771 Massachusetts Ave, (317) 269-8426. Mon-Thur 7am-1am, Fri-Sat 7am-4am, Sun 10am-10pm. Gay-Friendly.

■ Restaurants

AESOP'S TABLES, 600 N Massachusetts Ave, (317) 631-0055. Mon-Thus 11am-9pm, Fri & Sat 11am-10pm. Mediterranean cuisine, gay-friendly.

BROTHER'S BAR & GRILLE, 822 N Illinois.

RESTAURANT AT METRO, 707 Massachusetts Ave, (317) 639-6077. Italian menu, from 6pm on.

RUTH ELLEN'S, 825 N Pennsylvania., Varied menu.

TOMORROW'S NEAR NORTH CAFE, 2301 N Meridian, at Tomorrow's bar., (317) 925-1710. Lunch & dinner, gay after 5pm, Sun brunch 12pm-3pm."

VARSITY RESTAURANT, 1517 N Pennsylvania, at Varsity bar.

■ Retail & Bookstores

JUST CARDS, 145 E Ohio St, at Delaware, (317) 638-1170. Gifts & cards.

LAFAYETTE

■ Bars

SPORTSMAN BAR, 644 Main St, (765) 742-6321. Pool table, games, DJ Fri & Sat night. 60% men, 40% women.

LAKE STATION

■ Bars

STATION HOUSE, Ripley at Central, (219) 962-1017. DJ Tues, Fri-Sat,

MICHIGAN CITY

■ Bars

TOTAL ECLIPSE, 4960 W US Rte 20, (219) 874-1100. Bar & restaurant, DJ Thurs-Sat, open 7pm-3am, Sun 6pm-midnite.

MUNCIE

■ Dance Bar/Disco

MARK III, 107 E Main St, (shopping plaza), (765) 282-8273. Hi-energy dance bar, 11am-2am (Wed, Fri-Sat till 3am), 50% men, 50% women.

■ Restaurants

CARRIAGE HOUSE, 247 Kilgore Ave, (765) 282-7411. Restaurant & bar, discreetly frequented by gay men & women.

RICHMOND

■ Dance Bar/Disco

COACHMAN LOUNGE, 911 E Main St, (765) 966-2835. C&W & rock music, 7pm-3am Mon-Sat, DJ Fri & Sat, closed Sun.

SOUTH BEND

■ Information

AIDS LINE, (219) 287-8888. In northern IN: (800) 388-AIDS, 9am-5pm or tape."

COMMUNITY RESOURCE CENTER, (219) 232-2522, 9am-5pm Mon-Fri."

WOMEN'S CENTER, Northside 459, Indiana U at SB, (219) 237-4494. Resources, 8am-5pm weekdays."

■ Accommodations

KAMM'S ISLAND INN, KAMM'S ISLAND, 700 Lincolnway W, Mishawaka, IN, 46544, (219) 256-1501, (800) 955-KAMM, Fax: (219) 256-1504. Inn with bar, disco, movie theatre, bistro & shops, some straight clientele. Many modern conveniences including color cable TV, AC & private baths. Continental breakfast, 30% gay clientele.

■ Dance Bar/Disco

SEAHORSE II CABARET, 1902 Western Ave, at Brookfield, (219) 237-9139. Dance & show bar, 80% women, 20% men, closed Sun.

TRUMAN'S, 100 N Center, in the 100 Center, Mishawaka, (219) 259-2282. Dance bar with drag shows Wed.

INDIANA

TERRE HAUTE

Dance Bar/Disco
R PLACE, 684 Lafayette Ave, (812) 232-9119.

IOWA

STATEWIDE

Information
ACCESS OF NE IOWA, (319) 232-6805. Gay & lesbian information line.

AMES

Information
LESBIAN, GAY & BISEXUAL ALLIANCE, at ISU, (515) 294-2104 or 294-1020.

MARAGARET SLOSS WOMEN'S CENTER, at ISU, in the Sloss House, (515) 294-4154. 8am-5pm Mon-Fri, scheduled activities.

CEDAR RAPIDS

Dance Bar/Disco
CLUB BASIX, 1st Ave, between 39th & 40th St.,

COUNCIL BLUFFS
SEE OMAHA, NE,

DAVENPORT
ALSO INCLUDES ROCK ISLAND, IL (309).,

Bars
AUGIE'S, 313 20th St, near 3rd Ave, Rock Island, (309) 788-7389. 6am-3am, 7 days.

CLUB MARQUETTE, 3923 Marquette St, near Kimberley across from K's Merchandise Store., (309) 386-0700. Bar & grill, sandwiches, steaks, shrimp. DJ Fri & Sat, open stage Wed, shows & male strippers, 70% men, 30% women.

Dance Bar/Disco
JR'S, 325 20th St, Rock Island, IL, (309) 786-9411. Disco Mon-Sat 3pm-3am, Sun noon-3am. Drag shows Wed & Fri-Sun, male dancers Fri, female dancers alternate months. Restaurant with sandwiches, steaks, appetizers,Mon-Thurs 5pm-10pm, Fri & Sat 5pm-2am, Sun 5pm-10pm.

Cafe
ALL KINDS OF PEOPLE, 1806 2nd Ave, Rock Island, IL, (309) 788-2567. Coffeeshop, books, t-shirts. Gay-friendly.

Retail & Bookstores
CRYSTAL RAINBOW, 1615 Washington St, (319) 323-1050. Lesbian bookstore with women's spirituality section, aromatherapy, jewelry, some gay men's titles. Coming: juice bar, cafe with soups, salads, sandwiches.

DES MOINES

Information
GAY & LESBIAN RESOURCES CENTER, 414 E 5th, (515) 281-0634.

IOWA AIDS PROJECT, 412 12th St, (515) 284-0254.

YOUNG WOMEN'S RESOURCE CENTER, 554 28th St, (515) 244-4901. 8:30am-5pm Mon-Fri. Closed 12-1pm for lunch.

Accommodations
KINGMAN HOUSE B & B, Des Moines, (515) 279-7312." Tudor B&B with full breakfast, shared baths, RV parking, 5 min from downtown gay bars.

RACCOON RIVER RESORT, 2678 324th Way, Adel, IA, (515) 996-2829. B&B & campground with lodge, tipi & 3 tree houses, RV parking, solar outdoor showers, full breakfast, phone, Jacuzzi.

Bars
DALLY'S PUB & EMPORIUM, 430 E Locust St, (515) 243-9760. Noon-2am, small dance floor.

Dance Bar/Disco
FACES LTD, 416 E Walnut, (515) 280-5463. Downstairs dance bar, upstairs bar, 70% men.

★ GARDEN, THE, 112 SE 4th, near Vine, (515) 243-3965. Big dance bar with techno & house music, videos, patio bar, lounge with drag shows. Wed-Sun 8pm-2am, 70% men.

Cafe
CHAT NOIR, 644 18th, (515) 244-1353. Haute cuisine menu plus coffee & desserts in an old house.

IOWA 319

JAVA JOE'S, 214 4th St, (515) 288-5282. Coffees, espresso. Frequented by gays.

ZANZIBAR'S COFFEE, 2723 Ingersoll, (515) 244-7694. Non-smoking coffeeshop, frequented by gays.

Retail & Bookstores

CONNECTIONS BOOKSTORE, 413 Maple Valley Junction W, (515) 277-5949. New age books, tapes, cards, crystals. Closed Mon.

IOWA CITY

Information

GAYLINE, (319) 335-3251.

WOMEN'S CENTER, 130 N Madison, at Market, (319) 335-1486. 10am-5pm Mon-Fri (Mon & Thurs till 7pm).

Bars

BREAKROOM, 1578 S 1st Ave, (319) 354-9271. NOT a gay bar, popular with gay women. Owner says it's just a "huge mix."

DEADWOOD, 6 S Dubuque, (319) 351-9417. Sun, Mon, Tue, Wed, mixed gay & straight crowd, 25-30% gay.

Dance Bar/Disco

SIX TWENTY, 620 S Madison, near Prentiss, (319) 354-2494. Thurs-Sat 9pm-2am, 70% men.

Cafe

NEW PIONEER CO-OP BAKEHOUSE, 1st Ave at 5th St, Coralville, (319) 358-5513. 7am-7pm, 7 days, toast & sandwich bar.

Retail & Bookstores

ALTERNATIVES, 323 E Market St, Tel/Fax: (319) 337-4124. Lesbian owned/operated store with G&L mugs, cards, jewelery. Mon-Sat 10am-6pm, Sun noon-4pm.

MOON MYSTIQUE, 114-1/2 E College, (319) 338-5752. General bookstore with astrology books, gay, lesbian & feminist books, magazines.

PRAIRIE LIGHT BOOKSTORE, 15 S Dubuque St, (319) 337-2681. General bookstore with a gay & lesbian section.

UNIVERSITY BOOKSTORE, Memorial Union at IU, (319) 335-3179. General bookstore with a gay & lesbian section.

VORTEX, 211 E Washington St, (319) 337-3434. Giftshop with cards, pride jewelry, books, magazines.

NEWTON

Accommodations

LA CORSETTE MAISON INN & THE SISTER INN, 629 1st Ave E, Newton, IA, 50208, (515) 792-6833, Fax: (515) 792-6597. Two gay-friendly, elegant B&B inns, one with restaurant. Variety of rooms with French country decor & modern conveniences, private baths, full breakfast. A 25-min drive from Des Moines.

SIOUX CITY

Information

COMMUNITY ALLIANCE, (712) 258-4704. Email: alliance@pionet.net,

Bars

THREE CHEERS, 414 20th St, (712) 255-8005. 70% men, 30% women, DJ Wed, Fri & Sat.

WATERLOO - CEDAR FALLS

Dance Bar/Disco

BAR, THE, 903 Sycamore, (319) 232-0543. Dance & show bar, DJ weekends, male dancers.

Cafe

CUP OF JOE, 1st & Main St, Cedar Falls.,

GALLERY BUILDING, THE, 320 E 4th St, (319) 274-8889. Cafe & gallery with wine bar in cellar & live entertainment weekends.

Retail & Bookstores

GATEWAYS ALTERNATIVE BOOKS, 109 E 2nd, (319) 277-3973. General bookstore wtih New Age & alternative sections.

KANSAS

KANSAS CITY

SEE KANSAS CITY, MO,

LAWRENCE

■ Information
QUEERS & ALLIES (Q&A) GAY INFO, (785) 864-3091. 9am-5pm, or tape.

■ Cafe
THREE GALS COFFEEHOUSE, 946 New Jersey, (785) 842-2147. Call for schedule, live music, coffee, usually 2nd Sat 8pm at Ecumenical Christian Ministries, 1204 Oread.

■ Restaurants
TELLERS RESTAURANT & BAR, 746 Massachusetts Ave, (785) 843-4111. Tues or Thurs night "Family Night" gay night.

■ Retail & Bookstores
LARRY'S IN LAWRENCE, 1601 W 23rd St, (785) 749-4757. Gay & lesbian bookstore. Music, cards, t-shirts, magazines, etc.

MATFIELD GREEN

■ Women's Accommodations
PRAIRIE WOMEN ADVENTURES & RETREAT, Rural Rte Mail, Matfield Green, KS, 66862, (316) 753-3465, Fax: (316) 753-3466. Be a cowhand on a working cattle ranch & perform actual chores, such as branding, vaccinating & castrating cattle. ♀

TOPEKA

■ Dance Bar/Disco
CLASSICS, 110 SE 8th St, (785) 233-5153. Dance & show bar, 60% men, 40% women.

LYZ, 1009 S Kansas, (785) 234-0482. DJ Fri & Sat, small dance floor, 70% men. Beer garden in summer.

WICHITA

■ Bars
RALPH'S, 3210 E Osie, (316) 682-4461.

T ROOM, 1507 E Pawnee, near Ellis, (316) 262-9327. Pool tabble, darts, small dance floor, 80% men, women welcome.

■ Dance Bar/Disco
DREAMERS II, 2835 S. George Washington Blvd, (316) 682-4490. Occasional lesbian bands, kitchen on weekends, Mon-Thurs 4pm-2am, Fri-Sat 10pm-4am, Sat-Sun 3pm-2am.

METRO, Central & Waco., Male dancers.

OUR FANTASY COMPLEX, 3201 S Hillside, at 31st, (316) 682-5494. Complex with Fantasy dance bar, South 40 C&W bar, drag shows Wed & Sun, BBQ in patio bar, swimming pool, volleyball court, 50% men, 50% women.

■ Cafe
KINDRED KAFE, 3108 E 31 South, (316) 682-3444.

RIVERSIDE PERK, 1144 Bitting, (316) 264-6464. Coffee, sandwiches.

■ Restaurants
LOVERS FAMILY RESTAURANT, at Our Fantasy Complex, (316) 683-2587. ♀♂

UPPER CRUST, 7038 E Lincoln, (316) 683-8088. Restaurant & catering.

■ Retail & Bookstores
MOTHER'S, 3100 E 31st St S, (316) 686-8116. Pride store.

KENTUCKY

BOWLING GREEN

■ Accommodations
MAPLE GROVE FARM, 2841 Hwy 185, Bowling Green, KY, (502) 843-7433. Gay-friendly, 1916 bungalow, minutes from downtown. Private baths, full breakfast & AC.

COVINGTON

SEE CINCINNATI, OH,

FORT KNOX

■ Accommodations
KENTUCKY HOLLER HOUSE, Rt 1 Box 51BB, Harned, KY, (502) 547-4507 Lesbian-owned guesthouse 30 miles from Ft. Knox in a country setting, 2

suites, private baths, expanded continental breakfast, some straight clientele. ♀♂

LEXINGTON

■ Accommodations

BED & BREAKFAST AT SILLS INN, 270 Montgomery Ave, Versailles, KY, 40383, (606) 873-4478, (800) 526-9801, Fax: (606) 873-7099. Email: sillsinn@aol.com, Gay-owned B&B in Kentucky hourse country, 10 min from Lexington, with all private baths, made-to-order breakfast.

■ Bars

WATERING HOLE, Limestone between Short & Church., Very small, karaoke nitely Mon-Sat. 🏠 ♀♂

■ Dance Bar/Disco

★ **BAR COMPLEX, THE**, 224 E Main St, at Esplanade, (606) 255-1551. Dance bar, lounge & show bar, younger crowd, 60% men, 40% women. After-hours Sat, closed Sun. 🎵 ♪ ♀♂

CLUB 141, 141 W Vine St, (606) 233-4262. Dance bar, after hours Sat, closed Sun. 🎵 ♪ ♀♂

LOUISVILLE

■ Accommodations

THREE FORTY-THREE BEHARRELL, 343 Beharrell Ave, New Albany, IN, 47150, (812) 944-0289, (800) 728-3262. Gay & lesbian B&B with comfortable rooms, private & shared baths, private deck, extensive gay & lesbian book collection on premises. Minutes to downtown Louisville & gay, lesbian & cultural attractions. ♀♂

■ Bars

★ **MURPHY'S PLACE**, 306-308 E Main St, (502) 587-8717. Piano bar, 70% men upstairs. ♪ 📺 ♂

TINKERS TOO!, Market St, near Floyd., Women's bar in front, Club Rage mixed dance bar in rear. ♀

TOWN CAFE, 414 W Oak St, (502) 637-7730. Small bar with shows Wed, Fri, Sat. ♪ ♂

■ Dance Bar/Disco

CLUB RAGE, Market St, near Floyd, behind Tinkers II bar., Dance bar. 🎵 ♀♂

★ **CONNECTION, THE**, 120 S Floyd, (502) 585-5752, 583-1166. Hi energy dance bar & restaurant, piano, patio, show theatre. Some nites 40% straight. ♪ 🎵 ♪ ♀♂

■ Restaurants

PICASSO'S, 120 S Floyd, at the Connection bar, (502) 585-5752. Dinner, piano, theater, separate entrance. Opens 6pm nightly. 🍸 ♪ ♀♂

■ Retail & Bookstores

CARMICHAEL'S, 1295 Bardstown Rd, at Longest, (502) 456-6950. General bookstore with gay & women's sections.

HAWLEY COOKE BOOKS, 27 Shelbysville Rd Plaza, (502) 893-0133. Also, 3024 Bardstown Rd in Gardiner Ln Plaza, 456-6660. General bookstores with gay & lesbian sections.

MT CLOSET, 310 E Main St, (800) 606-4524, (502) 587-1060. Gay & lesbian rainbow & gift shop with clothing, cards, jewelry, t-shirts, etc.

LOUISIANA

ALEXANDRIA

■ Dance Bar/Disco

UNIQUE BAR & LOUNGE, 1919 N MacArthur, (318) 448-0555. Hi-energy dance bar. 🎵 ♪ ♀♂

BATON ROUGE

■ Bars

★ **BLUE PARROT**, 450 Oklahoma St, (504) 334-9131. 60% men, 40% women, 2 pool tables, large patio piano bar with BBQs. Leather nite Fri, karaoke Thurs & Fri. Lots of women Tues, Thurs, Fri. 🎵 ♀♂

MIRROR LOUNGE, 111 3rd St, near North, (504) 387-9797. Shows Sat. 📺 ♪ ♂

■ Dance Bar/Disco

★ **EVOLUTION**, 2183 Highland Rd, (504) 344-9291. Alternative hi energy 2-level dance bar, young crowd, 75% gay/lesbian. 🎵 ♀♂

HIDEAWAY CLUB, 7367 Exchange Place, off Woodale Blvd near Tom Dr, (504) 923-3632. Wed-Sat 8pm-2am, men welcome. 🎵 ♀

LOUISIANA

Visit New Orleans
(800) CARITAS
Caritas B&B Network

■ Restaurants
ARZI'S, Government, near Foster., Lebanese & Greek cuisine. 🚭
SUPERIOR GRILL, Government, near Foster., Mexican cuisine. 🚭

■ Retail & Bookstores
HIBISCUS BOOKSTORE, 635 Main Street, (504) 387-4264. New & used gay bookstore, rainbow items.

HAMMOND

■ Dance Bar/Disco
CHANCES, 42357 Veterans, off I-12, exit 40, (504) 542-9350. Large dance & show bar, live bands. 🎵🎶🍸♀♂

HOUMA

■ Bars
KIXX, 112 N Hollywood, (504) 876-9587. ♂

LAFAYETTE

■ Bars
MOJO MONKEYS, 116 Spring St, (318) 261-9020.

■ Dance Bar/Disco
JULES TAVERN, 533 Jefferson, (318) 264-8000. 🍸♂
SOUND FACTORY, THE, 209 Jefferson St, (318) 269-6011. ♂

LAKE CHARLES

■ Dance Bar/Disco
CRYSTAL'S, 112 W Broad St, Hi-energy dance bar & lounge, 70% gay/lesbian. Lounge Mon-Sat 6pm-2am. Dance bar Fri-Sun only from 9pm. 🍸

MONROE

■ Dance Bar/Disco
HOTT SHOTZ, 110 Catalpa St, (318) 388-3262. Male strippers, shows Tues & Fri, 50% men, 50% women, 9pm-2am Tues, Fri & Sat. 🍸🎵♀♂

NEW ORLEANS

■ Information
AIDS HOTLINE, (504) 944-AIDS (2437), (800) 99AIDS9, noon-10pm, 7days.
LESBIAN & GAY CENTER, 816 N Rampart St, (504) 522-1103. Info line Mon-Fri noon-6pm. Programs & weekly movies.

■ Accommodations
BIG D'S BED & BREAKFAST, 704 Franklin Ave, New Orleans, LA, 70117, (504) 945-8049. B&B above Big Daddy's bar, private & shared baths, continental breakfast. ♀♂

BIG EASY GUESTHOUSE, 2633 Dauphine St, New Orleans, LA, 70117, (504) 943-3717.

BON MAISON GUESTHOUSE, 835 Bourbon St, New Orleans, LA, 70116, (504) 561-8498 (Tel/Fax). Email: bmgh@acadiacom.net, Gay-friendly guesthouse apartments & suites, private baths.

BOURGOYNE GUEST HOUSE, 839 rue Bourbon, New Orleans, LA, 70116, (504) 524-3621 or (504) 525-5983. Guesthouse in heart of French Quarter, some straight clientele. Cozy studios, completely furnished suites, courtyard. ♀♂

BYWATER BED & BREAKFAST, 1026 Clouet St, New Orleans, LA, 70117, (504) 944-8438. Staying in the Big Easy? Just a bit down river from the French Quarter is a Victorian cottage in the Bywater neighborhood, near music, clubs, restaurants of French Quarter and Fauberg Marigny. Tastefully decorated with contemporary and antique furniture, and southern folk art. Shared baths, 1 private available. Continental breakfast, use of kitchen, parlors, library, TV, VCR. VISA & MC accepted. Some straight clientele. ♀♂

CARITAS BED & BREAKFAST NETWORK, (800) CARITAS, (312) 857-0801, Fax: (312) 857-0805. B&B, home-stay accommodations service. Member: IGLTA

CRESCENT CITY GUEST HOUSE, 612 Marigny St, New Orleans, LA, 70116, (504) 944-8722. Email: matlyn@bellsouth.net, In the Faubourg Marigny,

3 blocks from the French Quarter & 1/2 block to gay bars. Walking distance to many popular restaurants & nightclubs. Private bath, phone, TV, continental breakfast. Some straight clientele. ♀♂

FOURTEEN TWELVE THALIA, A BED AND BREAKFAST, 1412 Thalia, New Orleans, LA, 70130, (504) 522-0453. Email: grisgris@ix.netcom.com, Self-contained apartment convenient to downtown & Convention Center. Sleeps 2-4 people. Modern conveniences, breakfast supplies provided. ♀♂

FRENCH QUARTER B & B, 1132 Ursulines St, New Orleans, LA, 70116, (504) 525-3390. B&B private apartment. Large rooms, fully furnished kitchen, sleeps 6, massage available. 1/2 blk from French Quarter, 1 blk from Armstrong Pk, walk to everything. Food left in fridge, cook-it-yourself. ♀♂

FRENCHMEN HOTEL, 417 Frenchmen St, New Orleans, LA, 70116, (504) 948-2166, (800) 831-1781. Hotel with restaurant & bar. Double rooms & suites.

GLIMMER INN, 1631 7th St, New Orleans, LA, 70115, (504) 897-1895. Victorian B&B and inn with a New Orleans theme, private & shared baths, expanded continental breakfast, AC. 50% gay/lesbian clientele.

GREEN HOUSE INN, THE, 1212 Magazine St, New Orleans, LA, 70130, (504) 525-1333, (800) 966-1303, Fax: (504) 525-1306. Email: greeninn@aol.com, Welcoming gay and lesbian visitors to enjoy our Southern hospitality. This New Orleans Tropical Guesthouse was built in 1840 and is conveniently located in the historic Lower Garden District. It is close to the French Quarter and the Convention Center. Amenities include king-sized beds, private baths, swimming pool & spa, daily cleaning and continental breakfast, limited shuttle service, and free off-street parking. Some straight clientele. ♀♂

INGRAM HAUS, 1012 Elysian Fields, New Orleans, LA, (504) 949-3110 (Tel/Fax). Web: www.andrewjaegers.com/Ingram, Gay-owned & -operated guesthouse, private baths, 1/2 block to gay bars, minutes from French Quarter, some straight clientele. ♀♂

LA DAUPHINE, RESIDENCE DES ARTISTES, 2316 Rue Dauphine, New Orleans, LA, 70117, (504) 948-2217, Fax: (504) 948-3420. Email: LaDauphine@aol.com, Web: http://www.ladauphine.com, Gay-owned & -operated guesthouse in Faubourg Marigny area, private baths, continental breakfast, non-smoking environment, some straight clientele. ♀♂

The Green House Inn
A New Orleans Tropical Guest House
(800) 966-1303

NEW ORLEANS

HEATED POOL • CABLE TV
PHONE • PRIVATE BATHS
GYM • BREAKFAST

MACARTY PARK GUEST HOUSE
800-521-2790
www.macartypark.com

LAFITTE GUEST HOUSE, 1003 Bourbon St, New Orleans, LA, 70116, (504) 581-2678, (800) 331-7971, Fax: (504) 581-2677. Web: www.lafitteguesthouse.com, Guesthouse on Bourbon St, 50% gay & lesbian. Modern conveniences, Victorian parlor, continental breakfast, wine, hors d'oeuvres.

MACARTY PARK GUEST HOUSE, 3820 Burgundy St, New Orleans, LA, 70117-5708, (504) 943-4994, (800) 521-2790, Fax: (504) 943-4999. Email: faxmehard@aol.com, Web: www.macartypark.com, Relax, swim, party and play in a tropical paradise. Step out of your room and go for a splash in our refreshing heated pool. Enjoy beautiful rooms and cottages in a restored New Orleans Victorian mansion furnished in antiques, reproductions, and some contemporary rooms. Private baths, cable TV, phone, breakfast, complete gym with free weights & universal. A 5-minute getaway from the French Quarter. We also have a variety of accommodations throughout the city. Reasonable rates, free parking. Some straight clientele." ♀♂ See ad on page 323.

MAISON BURGUNDY B & B, 1860 Burgundy, New Orleans, LA, 70116-1923, (504) 948-2355, (800) 863-8813, Fax: (504) 944-8578. B&B 2 blocks from the French Quarter, walk to gay bars & restaurants. All private entrances, private parking, continental breakfast. ♀♂

MENTONE BED & BREAKFAST, 1437 Pauger St, New Orleans, LA, 70116, (504) 943-3019. Private suite with private entrance within walking distance of major attractions. Some straight clientele. Expanded continental breakfast." ♀♂

NEW ORLEANS GUEST HOUSE, 1118 Ursulines St, New Orleans, LA, 70116, (504) 566-1177, reservations only: (800) 562-1177. Guesthouse, private baths, 50% gay & lesbian clientele.

NINE TWELVE PAULINE STREET, 912 Pauline St, New Orleans, LA, (504) 948-6827. Email: bareskin@ix.netcom.com, B&B apartment in Bywater neighborhood, private baths, continental breakfast, self-catering kitchen, private entrance. Some straight clientele. ♀♂

PARKVIEW MARIGNY BED & BREAKFAST, 726 Frenchmen St, New Orleans, LA, 70116, (504) 945-7875. Reservations: (800) 729-4640. Guesthouse, 50% gay & lesbian clientele, private baths.

PAUGER HOUSE GUEST SUITES, New Orleans, LA, (504) 944-2601, (800) 484-8334 (access code: 9834). Gay-owned & -operated rooms, suites or fully furnished apartments in Faubourg Marigny, with phone, AC, private baths, some straight clientele. ♀♂

REINBOWE HOUSE, 2311-15 N Rampart St, New Orleans, LA, 70117, (504) 949-5815, Fax: (504) 949-5917. Email: travres@linknet.net, Guesthouse with private & shared baths, some straight clientele. ♀♂

ROBER HOUSE, 820 Ursulines St, New Orleans, LA, 70116-2422, (504) 529-4663 or 523-1246, (800) 523-9091. Fully-furnished condos in the French Quarter, minutes from attractions. Courtyard & pool, some straight clientele." ♀♂

ROYAL BARRACKS GUEST HOUSE, 717 Barracks St, New Orleans, LA, 70116, (504) 529-7269, (888) 255-7269, Fax: (504) 529-7298. Victorian guesthouse with mostly gay clientele, private baths, rooms with modern conveniences & private entrances. Jacuzzi on premises." ♂

RUE ROYAL INN, 1006 Rue Royal, New Orleans, LA, 70116, (504) 524-3900, Fax: (504) 558-0566. From economical courtyard units to large balcony suites with Jacuzzi & wet bar. 50% gay/lesbian clientele.

URSULINE GUESTHOUSE, 708 rue des Ursulines, New Orleans, LA, 70116, (504) 525-8509, reservations: (800) 654-2351, Fax: (504) 525-8408. In the French Quarter between Bourbon and Royal Streets, some straight clientele. Private courtyard, rooms with private baths and amenities, continental breakfast, complimentary wine, whirlpool. Welcoming both gay women and men. ♀♂

VIEUX CARRE RENTALS, 841 Bourbon St, New Orleans, LA, 70116, (504) 525-3983, Fax: (504) 283-7777. Gay-friendly luxury condos.

LOUISIANA

■ Women's Accommodations

OVER C'S, 940 Elysian Fields Ave, New Orleans, LA, 70117, (504) 943-7166 or after 2pm: (504) 945-9328. Invite friends for coffee on your own verandah. New Orleans comfort is yours in these bright, airy & comfortable 1-bedroom apartments with private baths, cable TV, private phones, microwave & fridge. **Conveniently located above Charlene's world-famous women's club.** Walk to French Quarter attractions, the aquarium and one of the world's largest gambling casinos. Call for reservations. ♀

■ Bars

BIG DADDY'S, 2513 Royal, (504) 948-6288. 50% men, 50% women, congenial family neighborhood crowd. ♀♂

BILLY'S, 2600 Hwy 190 W, Slidell, (504) 847-1921. Small dance floor. ♀♂

BUFFAS, 1001 Esplanade Ave, (504) 945-9373. Bar & restaurant, home cooking, 70% men. ♂

CAFE 19, 625 St Phillip St, (504) 568-1631. Bar & restaurant, breakfast through dinner. ♀♂

CHARLENE'S, 940 Elysian Fields Ave, at Rampart, (504) 945-9328. World-famous women's nightclub plus Over C's apartments for women." ♀

CHEERS, 1711 Hancock, Gretna, (504) 367-0149. 60% gay & lesbian. ♀♂

COUNTRY CLUB, 634 Louisa St, near Royal, (504) 945-0742. Two bars, hot tub, swimming & sunning. ♀♂

FREEDOMS, 1030 Westbank Expy, Gretna, (504) 368-2100. Open from 7pm. ♀

FRIENDLY BAR, 2301 Chartres St, (504) 943-8929. 50% men & 50% women." ♀♂

FULL MOON, 424 Destrehan, in Harvey, (504) 341-4396. Wed-Sun from 7pm, small dance floor. ♀♂

HI HO LOUNGE, 2239 St Claude, (504) 947-9344.

MINT, 504 Esplanade, (504) 525-2000. Show bar, 50% men, 50% women." ♀♂

PHOENIX, THE, 941 Elysian Fields Ave, at Rampart, (504) 945-9264, 24hrs. ♂

PLACE, THE, 2112 St Claude, (504) 943-5059. Pool tables, small dance floor. ♀

RK'S RAINBOW, 626 St Philip St, (504) 598-3900. ♀♂

■ Dance Bar/Disco

ANGLES, 2301 N Causeway, Metairie, (504) 834-7979. Dance bar & lounge. ♀

COPPER TOP, 706 Franklin, (504) 948-2300. Gay & straight crowd, microwavable food. ♀♂

★ **PARADE,** 801 Bourbon St, at Bourbon Pub, upstairs, (504) 529-2107. Dance & video bar, Sun tea dance 5pm till..., women welcome. ♂

New Orleans

CHARLENE'S

The Bar (504) 945-9328

OVER C'S

The Inn (504) 943-7166

World-Famous Women's Night Club & Women's Inn

940 Elysian Fields

Visit Linda & Charlene's
"ON THE COAST"
on Mississippi's Gulf Coast
(228) 467-7298

326 LOUISIANA

PIER 11, 4809 Pontchartrain Dr, Slidell, (504) 645-0603.

RUBYFRUIT JUNGLE, 640 Frenchmen, (504) 947-4000. DJ, live entertainment, many women. The Boy Bar Fri, Hi energy dance & drag show Sat & Sun.

WOLFENDALE'S, 834 N Rampart St, near Dumaine, (504) 596-2236. Drag show Sun.

X'IS LOUNGE, 1302 Allo St, in Marrero, (504) 430-0049. Patio, 60% men, 40% women.

■ Cafe

CAFE MARIGNY, 1913 Royale, (504) 945-4472. Coffees, pastries, bagels & bagel sandwiches, from 7am 7 days.

■ Restaurants

ALBERTO'S, 611 Frenchmen, (504) 949-5952. Italian Creole, gay-friendly.

BUFFAS, 1001 Esplanade Ave, at Buffas bar.,

CAFE SBISA, 1011 Decatur St, (504) 522-5565. Gay-friendly, nouvelle American cuisine.

CLOVER GRILL, 900 Bourbon St, (504) 523-0904. 50's-style diner.

COSIMO'S, 1201 Burgundy St, (504) 586-0444.

KRYSTAL, 116 Bourbon, at Canal, (504) 523-4030.

LUCKY CHENG'S, 720 St Louis, (504) 529-2045.

MAMA ROSA'S SLICE OF ITALY, 616 N Rampart, (504) 523-5546. Italian cuisine, pizza specialties.

MONA LISA, 1212 Royal St, (504) 522-6746. Pizza restaurant.

★ **PETUNIA'S,** 817 St Louis St, (504) 522-6440. Cajun, Creole atmosphere, large gay & lesbian following."

QUARTER MASTER DELI, 1100 Bourbon St, (504) 529-1416. The nellie deli, late-night specialties.

QUARTER SCENE, 900 Dumaine, at Dauphine, (504) 522-6533, 24hrs, closed Tues night.

SEBASTIAN'S LITTLE GARDEN, 538 St Philip, (504) 524-2041.

■ Retail & Bookstores

FAUBOURG MARIGNY BOOKS, 600 Frenchmen St, at Chartres, (504) 943-9875. Gay & lesbian books, music, buttons, jewelry, gay newspapers, men's magazines, etc, 7 days.

RAINBOW FRAMING & GIFTS, 3127 Metairie Rd at Causeway, Metairie, (504) 834-3064. Rainbow items for gays & lesbians.

OPELOUSAS

■ Accommodations

ESTORGE HOUSE, THE, 427 North Market Street, Opelousas, LA, (318) 942-8151. Experience French Louisiana & Southern Hospitality in this B&B, 20 min from Lafayette. Full breakfast, private baths, outdoor hot tub, 50% gay/lesbian clientele.

SHREVEPORT - BOSSIER

■ Information

HOMOSEXUAL INFO CENTER, 115 Monroe St, Bossier City, (318) 742-4709. Gay & lesbian archive, referral service, 8am-5pm Mon-Fri.

■ Dance Bar/Disco

★ **CENTRAL STATION,** 1025 Marshall St, Shreveport, (318) 222-2216. C&W, disco & separate cigar bar, male & female dancers, name entertainers, patio, 50% men, 50% women.

MAINE
STATEWIDE

■ Information

AIDS LINE, (800) 851-AIDS. Tue, Thur-Sat 9am-5pm, Mon & Wed 9am-7:30pm.

GAY & LESBIAN COMMUNITY CENTER, 398 N Main St, Caribou, (207) 498-2088. Answers Mon, Wed, Fri. Open house Wed 7pm-9pm. Newsletter, lending library, events and speakers bureau.

AUGUSTA

■ Accommodations

MAPLE HILL FARM B & B INN, Outlet Rd, RR1 Box 1145, Hallowell, ME, 04347, (207) 622-2708, (800) 622-2708, Fax: (207) 622-0655. Email: maple@mint.net, Web: www.mint.net/maple, Gay-friendly B&B in a Victorian farmhouse on 62 acres 5 minutes from downtown Augusta. Private & shared baths, TV lounge, full breakfast, nearby skiing, hiking & antiquing. 1 rustic campsite."

Dance Bar/Disco
PJ'S, 80 Water St, near Bridge, (207) 623-4041. Tues-Sat 7pm-1am. C&W dance Wed & piano bar nights Thurs & Fri, 50% men, 50% women.

BANGOR

Dance Bar/Disco
CLUB VISIONS, 198 Exchange St, (207) 990-4772. Video & dance bars, occasional drag shows, live entertainment Sun, after hours Fri & Sat. Sun-Thurs 4pm-1:30am, Fri & Sat 4pm-3am.

BAR HARBOR

Accommodations
DEVILSTONE OCEANFRONT INN, PO Box 801, Bar Harbor, ME, 04609, (207) 288-2933, Fax: (207) 288-4388. Email: devilrock@aol.com, On the Shore Path overlooking Frenchman's Bay, antique decor, private baths, continental breakfast, some straight clientele.

HOUSE OF THE MOUNTAIN SUNSETS, RR1, Box 4095, Bar Harbor, ME, 04609-9747, Oct-May: (207) 288-5279; Jun-Sept (pager/voice mail): (207) 759-9059; Fax: (207) 288-0488. Email: bje@acadia.net, Web: www.acadia.net/mountainsunsets, This lovely, contemporary 3-bedroom, 2-bath home comfortably sleeps six. Nestled on three-plus acres of Maine woodlands, guests will enjoy spectacular sunsets over mountain views. Unwind in the luxurious whirlpool tub, dine al fresco on the deck. Our central location is perfect — near Acadia National Park, the golf course & the heart of Bar Harbor. Available for weekly or monthly rental June thru September. Gay-friendly.

LINDENWOOD INN, Box 1328, Clark Point Rd, Southwest Harbor, ME, 04679, (207) 244-5335. Gay-friendly B&B with harbor views & private access to the water. Recently remodeled rooms, private baths, sitting rooms with fireplaces, full breakfast.

MANOR HOUSE INN, 106 West St, Bar Harbor, ME, 04609, (207) 288-3759, (800) 437-0088, Fax: (207) 288-2974. Gay-friendly B&B. Variety of Victorian guest quarters, TV lounge, veranda, gardens, full breakfast. Nearby pools, beaches.

BATH

Cafe
TRUFFLES, 21 Elm St, (207) 442-8474. Gay-friendly, cozy cafe, Wed-Sat breakfast & lunch, Sun breakfast only. Freshly prepared food, vegetarian offerings.

CAMP CAMP

A Summer Camp in Maine for Gay & Lesbian Adults

August 23-August 29 and August 31-September 6

Toll Free: 1-888-924-0380
www.campcamp.com

BAR HARBOR, MAINE

Vacation Rental June-Sept.

House of the Mountain Sunsets

Oct. - May (207) 288-5279
June - Sept. (207) 759-9059
www.acadia.net/mountainsunsets

BELFAST

Accommodations
ALDEN HOUSE BED & BREAKFAST, 63 Church St, Belfast, ME, 04915, (207) 338-2151. Email: alden@agate.net, Web: www.bbonline.com/me/alden, Gay-owned & -operated B&B with full breakfast, 7 doubles with single, full & queen beds, private & shared baths. 50% gay & lesbian clientele.

BETHEL

Accommodations
SPECKLED MOUNTAIN RANCH, RR 2, Box 717, Bethel, ME, 04217, (207) 836-2908. B&B with guided horseback riding, full breakfast, shared baths, living room, kitchen for guests, lake & river nearby, 50% gay/lesbian clientele.

BRUNSWICK

Retail & Bookstores
GULF OF MAINE BOOKS, 134 Maine St, (207) 729-5083. General bookstore with gay & lesbian section.

COREA - ACADIA AREA

Accommodations
BLACK DUCK INN ON COREA HARBOR, THE, PO Box 39, Crowley Island Rd, Corea, ME, 04624, (207) 963-2689, Fax: (207) 963-7495. Email: bduck@acadia.net, Web: www.blackduck.com, Gay-friendly B&B in a tranquil fishing village. Private & shared baths, full breakfast, TV lounge, meeting rooms, maid service. Gay & lesbian following.

DAMARISCOTTA MILLS

Accommodations
MILL POND INN, 50 Main St, Nobleboro, ME, 04555, (207) 563-8014. Gay-friendly inn, private baths.

HALLOWELL

Restaurants
SLATE'S RESTAURANT, 167 Water St, (207) 622-9575. Upscale restaurant with Sun brunch. Sun brunch is popular with local gays.

KENNEBUNK

Accommodations
ARUNDEL MEADOWS INN, PO Box 1129, Kennebunk, ME, 04043-1129, (207) 985-3770. Web: http://www.biddeford.com/arundel_meadows_inn, Gay-friendly B&B near beaches, antique shops, restaurants. Cozy rooms with comfortable sitting areas. Full breakfast with afternoon tea.

KENNEBUNKPORT

Restaurants
BARTLEY'S DOCKSIDE DINING, by the bridge, (207) 967-5050. Open May-Dec, lunch & dinner.

Ewe Hike • Ewe Bike • Ewe Ski • Ewe Zzzz

Small country inn nestled in the heart of Maine's western lakes and mountains.

Lamb's Mill Inn

Box 676 Lamb's Mill Rd.
NAPLES ME. 04055
207-693-6253

- Hot Tub
- Full Country Breakfast
- Private Baths

Innkeepers
Laurie Tinkham • Sandy Long
RESERVATIONS SUGGESTED

LEWISTON

■ Dance Bar/Disco
CONNECTION, Park St, near Main, Fri & Sat only. 🕺 ♀♂
SPORTSMAN'S ATHLETIC CLUB, 2 Bates St, (207) 784-2251. 8pm-1am, 7 days. 🎵🕺 ♀♂

NAPLES

■ Accommodations
LAMB'S MILL INN, Box 676, Lamb's Mill Rd, Naples, ME, 04055, (207) 693-6253. Gay-owned B&B in a 19th-century farmhouse with romantic atmosphere & country charm. All private baths, full breakfast, catered dinner available. MC, VISA."

OCEAN PARK

■ Women's Accommodations
SEAFOREST WOMEN'S RETREAT, (207) 282-1352. Women-only B&B, shared bath. ♀

OGUNQUIT

■ Accommodations
ADMIRAL'S INN & GUESTHOUSE, #70 US Rt. 1, PO Box 2241, Ogunquit, ME, 03907, (207) 646-7093. Located 65 miles north of Boston, we're within walking distance of the beach and village. We are unique in that we offer not only traditional guesthouse accommodations, but also efficiency and motel rooms with refrigerators and private baths. All rooms are air-conditioned and have electic heat and television. Our backyard pool is perfect for enjoying a morning or late-night swim, or a quiet afternoon retreat. 🏊 ♀♂

BEAUPORT INN AND CAFE, PO Box 1793, 102 Shore Rd, Ogunquit, ME, 03907, (800) 646-8681, (207) 646-8680. Email: lobster@cybertours.com, Web: www.ogun-online.com\beauport, Centrally-located B&B with gourmet cafe, 50% gay & lesbian. AC, private baths, TV lounge, expanded continental breakfast.

HERITAGE OF OGUNQUIT, PO Box 1295, Ogunquit, ME, 03907, (207) 646-7787. Email: heritageo@cybertours.com, Web: www.one-on-onepc.com/heritage, Ogunquit is the quicker, more beautiful alternative to P-Town! Located on a quiet street near the end of the famous Marginal Way, (fabulous floral footpath on the oceans edge) this Victorian Reproduction features a hot tub, giant cedar deck, common room with refrigerator, microwave, VCR & TV, movies & wooded privacy. All this in a hypoallergenic, *smoke free* environment only a five-minute walk to beach, town and cove. Private & shared bath, expanded continental breakfast, ample parking. 99% women, and the only lesbian-owned place in town. Off season rates & specials. Year-round!! ♀

Admiral's Inn & Guesthouse

Unique in Ogunquit

(207) 646 7093

THE HERITAGE OF OGUNQUIT

"Beautiful-Place-by-the-Sea"

- 5 min. Walk to Beach
- Non-Smoking

(207) 646-7787

email: heritageo@cybertours.com
www.one-on-onepc.com/heritage

330 MAINE

INN AT TWO VILLAGE SQUARE, THE, 135 US Rte 1, PO Box 864, Ogunquit, ME, 03907, (207) 646-5779, Fax: (207) 646-6797. Email: theinntvs@aol.com, Web: http://www.q-net/theinntvs, A spacious Victorian summer home perched on a hillside. Panoramic ocean views from rooms and sun deck. The Inn is only a five-minute walk to beaches, shops and restaurants. Refreshing heated pool and hot tub.

LEISURE INN, 6 School St, PO Box 2113, Ogunquit, ME, 03907, (207) 646-2737, Fax: (207) 646-2471. Email: ReySaint@aol.com, Web: http://members.aol.com/reysaint, B&B, cottages, apts, 50% straight clientele. Rooms uniquely decorated to reflect old New England charm. Walk to ocean beach, restaurants, shops. Continental breakfast.

MOON OVER MAINE, PO Box 1478, 6 Berwick Rd, Ogunquit, ME, 03907, (207) 646-MOON (6666), (800) 851-6837. Email: MoonMaine@aol.com, B&B with private baths, expanded continental breakfast, Jacuzzi, color cable TV, AC, near gay bars, some straight clientele. ♀♂

OGUNQUIT BEACH INN, 8 School St, Box 1803, Ogunquit, ME, 03907, (207) 646-1112, (888) 97-MAINE (62463), Fax: (207) 646-4724. Gay-owned &-operated B&B guesthouse, inn & cottage 5 min from beach & close to bars, dining & theater. Private & shared baths, expanded continental breakfast. ♀♂

OGUNQUIT HOUSE, 3 Glen Ave, Box 1883, Ogunquit, ME, 03907, (207) 646-2967. Email: OgunquitHs@aol.com, B&B & cottages, 50% gay & lesbian. Variety of comfortable, spacious rooms, some kitchens, refrigerators, TV lounge. Continental breakfast & nearby ocean beach.

TALL CHIMNEYS, 94 Main St, PO Box 2286, Ogunquit, ME, 03907, (207) 646-8974. B&B. Rooms & apt with private & shared baths. ♀♂

YELLOW MONKEY GUEST HOUSE, 168 Main St, Ogunquit, ME, 03907, (207) 646-9056. Seasonal. ♀♂

■ *Bars*

FRONT PORCH, Ogunquit Square, at Main and Shore, (207) 646-3976. Piano bar & restaurant. ♀♂

■ *Dance Bar/Disco*

CLUB, THE, 13 Main St, (207) 646-6655. Dance bar with upstairs cruise bar, Sun T-dance 4pm. Male dancers, preppie crowd, patio. Open April-Oct from 9pm.

■ *Cafe*

CAFE AMORE, 5 Perkins Cove, (207) 646-6661. Coffee & lite fare & breakfast. Woman-owned, location of many women's gatherings, popular with local women.

■ *Restaurants*

ARROWS, Berwick Rd, (207) 361-1100. Restaurant & bar, American cuisine.

SHORE CAFE, 22 Shore Rd, (207) 646-6365. Mediterranean & California cuisine, open May-Oct.

PEMBROKE

■ *Accommodations*

YELLOW BIRCH FARM, Young's Cove Road, Pembroke, ME, 04666, (207) 726-5807. Email: yellowbirchfarm@nemaine.com, B&B or weekly cottage rental on a woman-owned working farm. Fully-furnished two-room cottage, kitchen, outdoor hot shower, private outhouse, expanded continental breakfast. ♀

PORTLAND

■ *Accommodations*

ANDREWS LODGING BED & BREAKFAST, 417 Auburn St, Portland, ME, 04103, (207) 797-9157, Fax: (207) 797-9040. Email: 74232.116@compuserve.com, Colonial house, baths (1 with whirlpool), continental breakfast, 5 min to downtown. Gay-friendly.

PARKSIDE PARROT INN, 273 State Street, Portland, ME, 04101, (207) 775-0224. Email: parpar1@maine.rr.com, Web: http://home.maine.rr.com/pparrot, B&B 4 blocks from the edge of downtown, near restaurants, bars & shops. Private & shared baths, expanded continental breakfast. Some straight clientele. ♀♂

VICARAGE BY THE SEA, THE, PO Box 368B, Harpswell, ME, 04079, (207) 833-5480 (Tel/Fax). Email: jmoulton@biddeford.com, Traditional B&B on

Curtis Cove, a 30 min drive from Portland, with private & shared baths, full breakfast. 50% gay & lesbian clientele.

■ Bars

BLACKSTONES, 6 Pine Street, (207) 775-2885. Fri buffet, 85% men. The CHEERS of the north. 🏠 ♂

SISTERS, 45 Danforth St, (207) 774-1505. Game room, outdoor patio, Wed-Sun from 4pm. 🎵 ♀

■ Dance Bar/Disco

UNDERGROUND, 3 Spring St, (207) 773-3315. Hi-energy dance bar, DJ Wed-Sat, male & female strippers. 🎵 🎭 ♀♂

■ Restaurants

KATAHDIN, 106 High St, (207) 774-1740. Meat & potato menu, blue plate specials. 5pm-10pm (Fri & Sat till 11pm), closed Sun. Large gay following. 🍴

WALTERS CAFÉ, 15 Exchange St, (207) 871-9258. Regional American cuisine, open grill, exhibition-style kitchen. 🍴 ♿ ☕

WESTSIDE, 58 Pine St, (207) 773-8223. Specializing in fresh fish, from 5:30pm, closed Sun. 🍴 🍷

■ Retail & Bookstores

BOOKS ETC, 38 Exchange St, (207) 774-0626. General bookstore with a gay & lesbian selection.

SEBAGO LAKE REGION

■ Accommodations

MAINE-LY FOR YOU, RR2 Box 745, Waterford, ME, 04088, (207) 583-6980. Cottages and campsites along 1800 feet of waterfront with dock and swimming float and women-only section. Climbing, ice caves, canoeing, hiking, water sports. Gay & lesbian clientele, some straights. Maine-ly for You Spring Fling and Autumn Fest women's events are for women only. ♀♂

STONINGTON

■ Women's Accommodations

SEA GNOMES HOME, PO Box 33, Stonington, ME, 04681, (207) 367-5076. Women-only guesthouse. Shared bath, common room, nearby ocean beach." ♀

TENANTS HARBOR

■ Accommodations

EAST WIND INN, PO Box 149, Tenants Harbor, ME, 04860, (207) 372-6366, (800) 241-VIEW. Gay-friendly B&B with restaurant & bar, private & shared baths, full breakfast, AC, TV lounge, mostly straight clientele.

WISCASSET

■ Accommodations

WISCASSET PLACE, Ten Middle Street, Box 33, Wiscasset, ME, 04578-0033, (207) 882-7981. Email: wiscassetplace@clinic.net, Web: http://www.wiscassetplace.com (after Jan 15, '98), Gay-owned & -operated 1927 Colonial Revival B&B, private baths, AC, continental breakfast, 2 rooms with expansive water views. 30 minutes from Freeport, ME outlet shopping, 3 hrs from Boston. 50% gay/lesbian clientele.

MARYLAND

ANNAPOLIS

■ Accommodations

TWO-O-ONE, 201 Prince George St, Annapolis, MD, 21401, (410) 268-8053, Fax: (410) 263-3007. Email: twooonebb@aol.com, Gay-friendly B&B, private & shared baths, full breakfast.

WILLIAM PAGE INN, 8 Martin St, Annapolis, MD, 21401, (410) 626-1506 ext. 7, (800) 364-4160 ext. 7, Fax: (410) 263-4841. Email: wmpageinn@aol.com, Gay-friendly Victorian B&B. Double rooms, 1 suite with color TV & Jacuzzi, private & shared baths.

BALTIMORE

■ Information

AIDS INFO, (410) 837-2050.

GAY & LESBIAN CENTER OF BALTIMORE, 241 W Chase, (410) 837-5445.

GAY & LESBIAN SWITCHBOARD, (410) 837-8888. 7-10pm, 24hr tape.

■ Accommodations

ABACROMBIE BADGER BED & BREAKFAST, 58 W Biddle St, Baltimore, MD, 21201, (410) 244-7227, Fax: (410) 244-8415. B&B, 50% gay & 50% straight

332 MARYLAND

clientele. Rooms with private baths, expanded continental breakfast, AC, color cable TV, phone.

BILTMORE SUITES HOTEL, THE, 205 W Madison St, Baltimore, MD, 21201, (410) 728-6550, (800) 686-5064, Fax: (410) 728-5829. Urban inn, 50% gay & lesbian clientele. Private baths, expanded continental breakfast."

CHEZ CLAIRE, 17 W Chase St, Baltimore, MD, 21201, (410) 685-4666 or 837-0996. B&B with card shop, continental breakfast, some straight clientele. ♀♂

MR. MOLE BED & BREAKFAST, 1601 Bolton St, Baltimore, MD, 21217, (410) 728-1179 or Fax: (410) 728-3379. 1870 Baltimore row house, 2 suites, Dutch breakfast. Mostly straight clientele with a gay & lesbian following.

■ Bars

★ **CENTRAL STATION,** 1001 N Charles St, (410) 752-7133. Upscale bar & restaurant, karaoke Mon, pool tables, continental cuisine, 75% men, 25% women. 🇲 ♂

CLUB BUNS, 606 W Lexington, (410) 234-2866. 🎭 ♂

COCONUTS, 331 W Madison, near Howard., ♀

EAGER STREET SALOON, at Hippo bar location, 1 W Eager St, (410) 547-0069. Bar adjacent to Hippo video dance bar, 80% men, 20% women. Fri women's night. ♂

HEPBURN'S, 504 S Haven St, (410) 276-9310. 🎵 ♀

■ Dance Bar/Disco

★ **ALLEGRO,** 1101 Cathedral St, (410) 837-3906. High-energy dance bar. Tues men's night, Thurs ladies' night." 🎭 ♂

★ **HIPPO,** 1 W Eager St, at Charles, (410) 547-0069. Hi-energy dance & video bar, 80% men, 20% women. 🎭 ♂

PORT IN A STORM, 4330 E Lombard, at Kresson, (410) 732-5608. 🎭 ♀

★ **STAGECOACH,** 1003 N Charles St, (410) 547-0107. C&W dance bar. 🎭 U ♀♂

■ Cafe

CITY CAFE, 1001 Cathedral St, across from Hippo dance bar., Cafe with extensive menu, coffee, sandwiches, soups, desserts. 🇲

■ Restaurants

CENTRAL STATION RESTAURANT, at Central Station bar., ♀♂

CITY DINER, 911 N Charles St., Restaurant & bar, 24hrs 7 days. 🇲

GAMPY'S, 904 N Charles, at Read, (410) 837-9797. Variety menu, lunch, dinner, late evening." 🇲 ♈

MT VERNON STABLE, 909 Charles St., Varied menu, specialty is ribs. 🇲

STAGECOACH RESTAURANT, at Stagecoach bar., ♀♂

★ **STUDIO, THE,** 1735 Maryland Ave, at Gallery bar, (410) 539-6965. Steaks & seafood, dinner only. Closed Sun. ♈ ♀♂

■ Retail & Bookstores

LAMBDA RISING BOOKS, 241 W Chase (at Gay Center), (410) 234-0069. Gay & lesbian bookstore, 10am-10pm 7 days.

CUMBERLAND

■ Accommodations

RED LAMP POST, 849 Braddock Rd, Cumberland, MD, 21502, (301) 777-3262. B&B, some straight clientele. Double rooms with shared baths, TV lounge with fireplaces, weights, nearby lake. Full breakfast, dinner for extra charge." ♀♂

DEALE

■ Women's Accommodations

CREEKSIDE B & B, 6036 Parkers Creek Dr, Deale, MD, 20751, (301) 261-9438, Fax: (410) 867-1253, E-mail: mburt@ui.urban.org. Located on the Chesapeake near Annapolis and Washington, DC, we offer 2 rooms with private bath, pool, deck, pier, canoe, porch swing, hot tub, library and fireplace, old & new oak decor, and a large folk art collection. Full breakfast. "A sumptuous art-lover's, book-lover's, cat-lover's feast, 40 minutes from DC." 🛏 ♀

HAGERSTOWN

■ Dance Bar/Disco

HEADQUARTERS, 41 North Potomac, (301) 797-1553. Daily, dancing Wed-Sun, 5pm-2am, Sun till midnight. 🇲 🎭 ✗ ♀♂

MASSACHUSETTS STATEWIDE

Information
AIDS HOTLINE, (800) 235-2331. Youth hotline, Mass only: (800) 788-1234.

AMHERST

Information
EVERYWOMAN'S CENTER, U of Mass, Wilder Hall, (413) 545-0883. Mon, Tues, Thurs, Fri 9am-4pm. Wed noon-4pm.

U-MASS AREA WOMEN'S CENTERS, call Everywomen's Center, (413) 545-0883, for Mt Holyoke, Smith, Amherst, Hampshire.

Accommodations
IVY HOUSE B & B, 1 Sunset Court, Amherst, MA, 01002, (413) 549-7554 (Tel/Fax). B&B, 50% gay & lesbian clientele. Shared baths, full breakfast.

Retail & Bookstores
FOOD FOR THOUGHT, 106 N Pleasant St, (413) 253-5432. Progressive bookstore with feminist books & music & gay men's section.

BARRE

Accommodations
JENKINS INN AND RESTAURANT, THE, 7 West Street, Route 122, Barre, MA, 01005, (978) 355-6444, (800) 378-7373. Email: jenkinsinn@juno.com, Gay-friendly B&B inn (30% gay/lesbian following), private & shared baths.

BOSTON

Information
AIDS HOTLINE, (617) 536-7733, (800) 235-2331, Youth line (800) 788-1234, TTY (617) 437-1672.

DAUGHTERS OF BILITIS, 1151 Massachusetts Ave, Harvard, Cambridge, at the Old Cambridge Baptist Church, (617) 661-3633. Discussion groups weekly.

GAY & LESBIAN INFO, (617) 267-9001 (TTY & voice), (888) 340-GLBT. Mon-Fri 4-11pm, Sat 5-7:30pm, Sun 5-10pm (irregularly staffed).

WOMEN'S CENTER, 46 Pleasant St, in Cambridge, (617) 354-8807. 10am-10pm Mon-Thurs, till 8pm Fri, 11am-4pm Sat.

Visit Boston (800) CARITAS
Caritas B&B Network

Accommodations
AMSTERDAMMERTJE, PO Box 1731, Boston, MA, 02205, (617) 471-8454 (Tel/Fax). Tel only (800) 484-6401 (* 1676). Web: www.usagaynet.com/whoami/massachusetts/wma69.htm, B&B, approx. 20-min. drive from downtown Boston, private & shared baths, color cable TV, VCR in living room, full breakfast, some straight clientele. ♀♂

CARITAS BED & BREAKFAST NETWORK, (800) CARITAS, (312) 857-0801, Fax: (312) 857-0805. B&B, home-stay accommodations service. Member: IGLTA

CHANDLER INN, 26 Chandler St, Boston, MA, 02116, (617) 482-3450, (800) 842-3450, Fax: (617) 542-3428. Email: inn3450@ix.netcom.com, Web: www.chandlerinn-fritz.com, Gay-friendly intown B&B hotel with a large gay & lesbian following. Walking distance to shopping, restaurants, transportation &

Four Sixty Three Beacon Street

Boston's Best Kept Secret

(617) 536-1302

MASSACHUSETTS

major attractions. Private baths, continental breakfast. 50% gay/lesbian.

CLARENDON SQUARE BED & BREAKFAST, THE, 81 Warren Ave, Boston, MA, 02116, (617) 536-2229. Gay-owned B&B with 3 rooms, private baths, continental breakfast, 50% gay & lesbian clientele.

FOUR-SIXTY-THREE BEACON STREET GUEST HOUSE, 463 Beacon St, Boston, MA, 02115, (617) 536-1302, Fax: (617) 247-8876. Guesthouse offering **gracious lodging in an elegant, renovated, turn-of-the century Back Bay** brownstone near Prudential/Hynes Convention Center, colleges, shopping, restaurants & nightlife. Fully-equipped kitchenettes, private baths, cable TV, AC, direct-dial telephone, electronic voice messaging service. 50% gay & lesbian clientele. See ad on page 333.

GREATER BOSTON HOSPITALITY, PO Box 1142, Brookline, MA, 02146, (617) 277-5430. Web: www.channel1.com/BnB, Accommodations in the Boston area in private homes & inns, all carefully screened for comfort, cleanliness & congeniality of hosts.

OASIS GUEST HOUSE, 22 Edgerly Rd, Boston, MA, 02115, (617) 267-2262, Fax: (617) 267-1920. Email: oasisgh@tiac.net, Web: www.oasisgh.com, Guesthouse with excellent Back Bay location, some straight clientele. We offer the opportunity to stay in the heart of the city and still feel at home. Our lobby, living room, outdoor decks, and accommodations are handsomely appointed with comfortable furnishings which blend with modern conveniences such as color TV, AC, and a computerized phone system. In addition to a continental breakfast, we provide evening cocktail set-ups and hors d'oeuvres in the main living room. Come experience the rewards of staying in an atmosphere that caters to your lifestyle and your budget. ♀♂

■ Women's Accommodations

VICTORIAN BED & BREAKFAST, (617) 536-3285. Women-only B&B. El-

---

O·A·S·I·S GUEST HOUSE B·O·S·T·O·N

- Excellent Back Bay Location
- Walk to Historic Sites, Night Life, Restaurants, & Museums
- AC, TV, Tel., Continental Breakfast

22 Edgerly Rd., Boston, MA 02115

(617) 267-2262
Fax: (617) 267-1920
WWW.OASISGH.COM • EMAIL: OASISGH@TIAC.NET

The Wildwood Inn B & B

121 Church St. • Ware, MA 01082
(See Our Listing in Sturbridge/Ware)

Comfortable, home-like. Beautiful in any season. Romantic.
Centrally located 1 1/2 hrs. from Boston in scenic Central Mass.
Full Breakfast • Private baths. • 8 mi. from I-90 exit 8.

413-967-7798 • 800-860-8098

egant & comfortable guest quarters, TV, full breakfast, soft drinks. ♀

■ Bars

★ **CLUB CAFE**, 209 Columbus Ave, above Metropolitan Health Club, (617) 536-0972. Three bars: Club Cafe bar in front with live piano, Moonshine is a video bar, Satellite Lounge has videos; Club Cafe restaurant lunch & dinner & Sun brunch 11am-3pm. 🎵 ♀♂

UPSTAIRS AT THE HIDEAWAY, 20 Concord Ln, Cambridge, (617) 661-8828. Thurs & Sun women's nite, pool & darts. ♀

■ Dance Bar/Disco

CAMPUS/LIQUID/MANRAY, 21 Brookline Ave, Cambridge, (617) 864-0400. Gay dance nites Thurs (Campus) & Sat (Liquid). ♀♂

H20, 148 Northern Ave, (617) 542-2215. Waterfront dance bar & lounge, lite food, roof deck. ♂

PARADISE, 180 Massachusetts Ave, Cambridge, (617) 864-4130. DJ nightly, upstairs pub, downstairs dance bar. Mon Latino night, Wed male strippers, other nights house music. ♂

SOME PLACE ELSE, 212 Hampshire St, Inman Square, Cambridge, (617) 876-9330. ♀

■ Restaurants

CLUB CAFE, 209 Columbus Ave, (617) 536-0966. Dinner with live piano & Sun brunch. Three bars feature cabaret, videos, movies. ♀♂

GRILLFISH, 162 Columbus Ave, (617) 357-1620.

ICARUS, 3 Appleton St, South End, (617) 426-1790. Restaurant and bar, contemporary American cuisine. Jazz Fri.

MARIO'S, 69 Church St, below the Luxor bar at Luxor complex, (413) 542-3776. Italian restaurant & lounge. ♀♂

TWO TWENTY-FOUR BOSTON STREET, 224 Boston St, Dorchester, (617) 265-1217. New American cuisine, live jazz Fri, Sat.

■ Retail & Bookstores

ARSENIC & OLD LACE, 318 Harvard St #10, Brookline, (617) 734-2455. Occult store, Mon-Wed 11am-7pm, Thurs-Fri 11am-9pm, Sun noon-6pm.

GLAD DAY BOOK SHOP, 673 Boylston Street (2nd floor), near Copley Square, (617) 267-3010. Gay & lesbian bookstore.

NEW WORDS BOOKSTORE, 186 Hampshire St, Cambridge, (617) 876-5310. Email: newwords@world.std.com, One of the country's oldest & largest women's bookstores, offers a full, exciting selection of books by & about women, from the latest feminist bestsellers to hard-to-find small press lesbian titles. We also carry journals, music, cards, bumperstickers & jewelry, & offer community space for readings, info & browsing. Mail order services available.

DON'T LEAVE BOSTON WITHOUT VISITING...

New Words
A Women's Bookstore

- **Complete Selection of Lesbian and Women's Titles**
- **Journals and Cards**
- **CDs and Tapes**
- **Jewelry and Other Gift Items**

186 Hampshire Street
Cambridge, MA 02139
(617) 876-5310
E-mail: newwords@world.std.com

Mon–Fri: 10am–8pm
Sat: 10am–6pm
Sun: Noon–6pm

Full Mail Order Services Available

WE THINK THE WORLD OF YOU, 540 Tremont St, (617) 423-1968, Fax: (617) 350-0083. Gay & lesbian bookstore.

■ Erotica
GRAND OPENING, 318 Harvard St #32, Arcade Bldg, Coolidge Corner, Brookline, (617) 731-2626. Sexuality boutique especially for women.

HAVERHILL

■ Dance Bar/Disco
FRIENDS LANDING AT WATER'S EDGE, 85 Water St, (978) 374-9400. Many rooms, dance bar, karaoke bar, shows, free buffet nitely. Boatslip with space for 35 boats on Merrimac River.

■ Retail & Bookstores
RADZUKINA'S, 714 N Broadway, (978) 521-1333. Women's gifts, cards, books, music, jewelry, crystals & stones. By appt. only.

HYANNIS

■ Dance Bar/Disco
DUVAL STREET STATION, 477 Yarmouth Rd, (508) 775-9835, 771-7511. Bar & Mallory Dock restaurant, lounge. Disco Thu-Sun, oldies Sun.

LENOX

■ Accommodations
GATEWAYS INN, 51 Walker St, Lenox, MA, 01240, (413) 637-2532, (888) 492-9466, Fax: (413) 637-1432. Email: gateways@berkshire.net, Web: www.gatewaysinn.com, Gay-friendly inn with restaurant, bar & gift shop.

SUMMER HILL FARM, 950 East St, Lenox, MA, 01240, (413) 442-2057, (800) 442-2059. B&B in 200-year-old farmhouse on a 20-acre horse farm, private baths, full breakfast, gay-friendly.

WALKER HOUSE, 64 Walker St, Lenox, MA, 01240, (413) 637-1271, (800) 235-3098, Fax: (413) 637-2387. Gay-friendly B&B in 1804 historic building. Guest rooms with antique furnishings, private baths.

LYNN

■ Bars
JOSEPH'S, 191 Oxford St, (781) 599-9483. Viedo bar, DJ nitely, 70% men, 30% women.

■ Dance Bar/Disco
FRAN'S, 776 Washington Street, (781) 598-5618. Disco, Tues karaoke.

MARTHA'S VINEYARD

■ Accommodations
CAPTAIN DEXTER HOUSE OF EDGARTOWN, 35 Pease Point Way, PO Box 2798, Edgartown, MA, 02539, (508) 627-7289, Fax: (508) 627-3328. Seasonal B&B near the harbor, ocean beach, shops & restaurants. Mainly straight clientele. Double rooms furnished with antiques, expanded continental breakfast.

MARTHA'S PLACE, 114 Main St, PO Box 1182, Vineyard Haven, MA, 02658, (508) 693-0253. This stately Greek Revival overlooks Vineyard Haven Harbor, 2 blocks from village shops, restaurants and the beach. Rooms boast harbor views and are decorated with antiques, oriental carpets and crystal chandeliers. Amenities include private baths, bathrobes, Egyptian cotton linens, fireplaces and Jacuzzi. Breakfast in bed is available. Gay-owned & -operated with 50% gay/lesbian clientele and is working toward exclusively gay/lesbian clientele.

MARTHA'S PLACE
Come pamper yourself in Style!
(508) 693-0253
MARTHA'S VINEYARD

NEW BEDFORD

■ Bars
PUZZLES LOUNGE, 428 N Front St, (508) 991-2306. DJ Wed-Sun, karaoke Wed, male dancers Mon & Fri, 50% men, 50% women.

■ Dance Bar/Disco
LE PLACE, 20 Kenyon St, (508) 992-8156. DJ Fri-Sun, male dancers Sun.

NORTHAMPTON

■ Information
LESBIAN & GAY BUSINESS GUILD, (413) 585-8839. They will mail you a gay & lesbian brochure for the area.

NEW ALEXANDRIA LESBIAN LIBRARY, (413) 584-7616. National archives of lesbian herstory, appointment only.

■ Accommodations
BRANDT HOUSE, THE, 29 Highland Ave, Greenfield, MA, (800) 235-3329, (413) 774-3329, Fax: (413) 772-2908. Email: brandt@crocker.com, Web: http://www.brandt-house.com, Gay-friendly, elegant Revival mansion B&B at the foot of the Berkshires, a 20-min drive to Northampton & a 30-min drive to Brattleboro, VT. Enjoy the pleasures of cozy fireplaces, breezy porches, patios and whirlpool baths. Relax in the comfort of spacious, light-filled guest bedrooms with featherbeds, private bath, remote cable TV, phone (upon request), and AC. We're 5 min from historic Deerfield & ideally situated to the north of Northampton and south of Brattleboro, Vermont.

■ Women's Accommodations
APPLE VALLEY B & B, 1180 Hawley Rd, Ashfield, MA, (413) 625-6758. A women-owned, near Northampton, rooms have a cozy sitting area, antique oak furniture. Local activities include hiking, golf, skiing, restaurants, shopping. Shared bath, full breakfast, men welcome. ♀

LITTLE RIVER FARM, 967 Huntington Rd, Worthington, MA, 01098, (413) 238-4261. Women-only B&B in a 150-year-old farmhouse on 41 acres, country setting, farm animals. 2 rooms with private baths, full breakfast. 1/2 hour from Northampton, Jacob's Pillow, Tanglewood, Stockbridge. ♀

OLD RED SCHOOLHOUSE & LESBIAN TOWERS, (413) 584-1228. Women-only apartment with country & art deco decor. 2-bedroom, equipped kitchen, linens, etc. ♀

TIN ROOF BED & BREAKFAST, PO Box 296, Hadley, MA, 01035, (413) 586-8665. Women's space B&B, lesbian-friendly men welcome. Comfortable double rooms with shared bath, expanded continental breakfast. ♀

Brandt House
Country Inn
Women Love the Elegance & Luxury of Brandt House

- Fireplaced bedrooms
- Exquisite decor
- Museum-quality art
- Six private baths
- Alternative nightclubs nearby

Greenfield, MA

(800) 235-3329
(413) 774-3329

Bars

PEARL STEET DISCOTHEQUE, 10 Pearl St, a very short street in downtown, Northampton, (413) 584-7771. 🎵 ♀♂

Dance Bar/Disco

CLUB METRO, 492 Pleasant St, (413) 582-9898. Tues gay night.

GROTTO, 25 West St, at Rt 66 & Green St, (413) 586-6900. Bar, dance club nitely. 🎵 🎶 ♀♂

Retail & Bookstores

PRIDE & JOY, 20 Crafts Ave, (413) 585-0683, 584-4848. Gay & lesbian gift store with cards, original art, books, posters and more.

THIRD WAVE FEMINIST BOOKSTORE, 90 King St, (413) 586-7851, TTY/TDD. Feminist & lesbian books, music, cards, gifts. Local info, closed Mon in winter. May move or change, call for information, new location.

Erotica

INTIMACIES, 28 Center St, (413) 582-0709, Fax: (413) 582-0725. A safe, comfortable, fun atmosphere where women & men can play with the toys & ask questions. Massage oile, lubes, condoms, vibrators, silicone & non-silicone dildos, harnesses, etc.

NORTON

Accommodations

DOWN BY THE BLACKSMITH SHOP BED & BREAKFAST, 102 Crane St, Norton, MA, 02766, (508) 285-9849. B&B, 50% gay/lesbian clientele.

PITTSFIELD

Information

WOMEN'S SERVICES CENTER, (413) 499-2425. Mon-Fri 9am-4pm.

PROVINCETOWN

Information

HELPING OUR WOMEN, 336 Commercial St, Unit 9, (508) 487-HELP (4357). Women's well-being resource center, Mon-Fri 11am-5pm. Free medical referrals.

Tours, Charters & Excursions

SAND FACES, Provincetown dune hikes for women, Apr 1-Oct 31. A service of The Little Inn, 31 Pearl St, (508) 487-2407."

Women's Accommodations

BAYVIEW WHARF APARTMENTS, 421 Commercial St, Provincetown, MA, 02657, (508) 487-1600. 15 apartments in 4 locations around P'town, all but 2 are on the beach. Private baths, color cable TV, full kitchens, some have AC. Men welcome. ♀

BRADFORD GARDENS, 178 Bradford St, Provincetown, MA, 02657, (508) 487-1616, (800) 432-2334, Fax; (508) 487-5596. Year-round B&B & cottages, 80% gay & lesbian. Beautiful oversized rooms with fireplaces & antiques, full gourmet breakfast. Ocean beach & town center nearby. ♀♂ See ad on page 341.

CHECK'ER INN RESORT, 25 Winthrop St, Provincetown, MA, 02657, (508) 487-9029, (800) 894-9029. Email: lilith@ptownlib.com, Web: www.ptownlib.com/checker.html, A friendly, relaxing guest house, conveniently located on a quiet side street, yet close to all the hot spots and beaches. Our expanded continental breakfast is served in a spacious common room, featuring a fireplace, piano, library and cable TV with VCR. Enjoy our private Jacuzzi in a plant filled sun room. Relax on the decks or wander in the gardens. Cozy apartments provide all the comforts of home PLUS daily maid service! All units include free on-premises parking. Mostly women. ♀

DUSTY MILLER INN, 82 Bradford St, Provincetown, MA, 02657, (508) 487-2213. Guesthouse with porch for people-watching, where friendships are struck on our rocking chairs. Private & shared baths, morning coffee & tea. Making guests feel at home is our specialty. Ex-

MASSACHUSETTS 339

The Sweetness of Life
CHECK'ER INN

25 Winthrop Street • Provincetown
(800) 894-9029 (508) 487-9029

Discover Freedom.
Discover Provincetown.

Bradford Gardens Inn 800 432-2334 ▼ **Check'er Inn 800 894-9029**

Dusty Miller 508 487-2213 ▼ Fairbanks Inn 800 324-7265

Gabriels' 800 9MY ANGEL ▼ Gull Walk Inn 800 309-4725

Halle's 508 487-6310 ▼ Heritage House 508 487-3692

Lady Jane's Inn 800 523-9526 ▼ Lavender Rose 508 487-6648

Painted Lady 508 487-1943 ▼ Plums B&B 508 487-2283

Ravenwood 508 487-3203 ▼ Rose Acre 508 487-2347

Windamar House 508 487-0599

The Women Innkeepers
(888) 933-2339
P.O.Box 573, Provincetown, MA 02657
www.provincetown.com/wip

MASSACHUSETTS

pect to feel at ease and in the perfect mood to enjoy the fun of Provincetown. Our rooms are well-appointed and comfortable. ♀

GABRIEL'S, 104 Bradford St, Provincetown, MA, 02657, (800) 9MY-ANGEL, (508) 487-3232, Fax: (508) 487-1605. Email: gabriels@ provincetown.com, Web: www.provincetown.com/gabriels. Centrally located B&B, men welcome. Doubles thru apartments with antique decorations & modern conveniences, TV lounge, library, kitchen privileges, outdoor Jacuzzi, breakfast & beverages. Nearby ocean beach. See ad on page 343.

GULL WALK INN, 300A Commercial St, Provincetown, MA, 02657, (508) 487-9027 (Tel/Fax), (800) 309-4725. We are the oldest women's guesthouse in Provincetown. On quiet lane in center of town, our location ensures that you'll be near everything and yet be sheltered from hustle & bustle of town life. The inn offers five simple and clean guest rooms, two large shared baths, and continental breakfast. With its two porches (one with a distant water view), common room and large private garden, you can relax and feel at home.

HALLE'S, 14 West Vine St, Provincetown, MA, 02657, (508) 487-6310. Comfortable cape-style accommodations in the West End, one block from the beach and a five-minute walk from restaurants, shops and entertainment. Each unit has an outside entrance, soft linens, cozy comforters, deck and garden. Mostly women with men welcome. ♀

HARBOR HILL, 4 Harbor Hill Rd, Provincetown, MA, 02657, (508) 487-0541, Fax: (508) 487-9804. Perched high atop dunes on quiet West End, this women's resort offers unprecedented comfort and convenience. Nearest resort to ocean beach, yet easy walk to heart of town. One and two bedroom villas are furnished from kitchens to fireplaces. Tours of the resort are available. We want to be *Your* **Lifestyle Resort.** ♀ See ad on Page 342.

LADY JANE'S INN, 7 Central St, Provincetown, MA, 02657, (508) 487-3387, (800) LADY JANE (523-9526). Email: ladyjanes@wn.net, Web: http://

Dusty Miller Inn
82 Bradford St.
Provincetown, MA 02657
(508) 487-2213

Gay / Lesbian ♀

The Dusty Miller Inn

Type: Guest house.
Clientele: Mostly women with men welcome.
To Gay Bars: Nearby.
Rooms: 12 rooms, 1 apartment with kitchen, all doubles.
Bath: 10 private, others share.
Meals: Morning coffee or tea.
Dates Open: Year-round.
Rates: In-season $69-$120, off-season $48-$90.
Credit cards: MC, VISA.
Reserve Through: Call direct.
In-Room: Maid service, color TV, fans, Coffee Pots.
Swimming: Ocean beach nearby.
Sunbathing: On ocean beach or in front yard.
Smoking: Permitted with restrictions.
Parking: On premises.
Pets: Permitted in designated rooms.
Handicap Accessibility: No

The *Dusty Miller* is open year-round, and offers accommodations for lesbians & gay men. Brochures available upon request.

MASSACHUSETTS 341

Bradford Gardens Inn

Woman-owned and featured in most national and international B&B guides, Bradford Gardens offers charming, spacious rooms with fireplaces, private baths, cable TV, refrigerators and ceiling fans. Or choose a fireplaced cottage, two-bedroom townhome in our beautiful gardens, or our luxurious penthouse overlooking Cape Cod Bay. Shirred eggs with tarragon mornay sauce, Portuguese flippers and homemade cinnamon-walnut pancakes with blueberry maple syrup are typical breakfast fare. Just park your car in our lot, and it's 5 minutes to the town center for fine dining, nightclubs, whalewatching, beaches, galleries and shopping. This historic 1820 inn offers New England charm and natural informality. Rates: $69-$185. One block from the beach.

(800) 432-2334
(508) 487-1616

178 Bradford St.
Provincetown
MA 02657

MASSACHUSETTS

Where the spirit is free and the view is forever!

Experience unprecedented comfort and convenience at our women oriented resort located in Provincetown's quiet west end.

Each luxury condominium will invite and nurture you each time you return from the wilds that are Provincetown.

Call for weekly rate information or for a tour of the resort. Open year round.

HARBOR HILL at Provincetown

Your lifestyle resort!

Reservations, Sales and Information:

508/487-0541

Harbor Hill
4 Harbor Hill Rd
Provincetown, MA
02657

---

www.ladyjanesinn.com, Located just steps from bay beaches and the center of town, this ideally located inn offers spacious rooms appointed with fine furnishings, private baths, remote color TV's, ceiling fans, air conditioning and outside entrances. On site parking, and complimentary continental breakfast. The inn has a large common room with a refrigerator and VCR. Open all year. ♀ See ad on page 344.

PILGRIM HOUSE INN, 336 Commercial St, Provincetown, MA, 02657, (508) 487-6424, Fax: (508) 487-6296. Everything you require for a perfect Provincetown vacation — from bright, inviting rooms, to Vixen, the on-premises nightclub and lounge. Our unique off-street location is a short stroll down a brick walkway, directly onto Commercial St. Rooms feature queen- or full-sized beds, private baths, AC, color TV and phones. At night, play at Vixen, with dancing, nightly live shows, jazz and blues. Men welcome. ♿ ♀

PLUMS BED & BREAKFAST INN, 160 Bradford St, Provincetown, MA, 02657, (508) 487-2283. Your key unlocks the quiet elegance of this 1860 Victorian whaling captain's house for women. Large, romantic rooms with antiques, lace and flowers. Innkeepers to pamper you. AC, parking, smoke-free and pri-
See ad on page 345

Pilgrim House Inn

Where The Girls Are
In Provincetown

(508) 487-6424

GABRIEL'S
Come Close to Heaven

Fine Accommodations Since 1979

Apartments & Guest Rooms
One Block from the Beach
In the Center of Provincetown
Breakfast • Hot Tubs • Steam Room
Sauna • Excercise Equipment • Massage
Bicycles • Fireplaces • Cable TV • Sun Decks
In Room Phones • Gardens • Barbeque • Parking

800 9MY ANGEL

phone: 508·487·3232
e-mail: gabriels@provincetown.com

www.provincetown.com/gabriels

Lady Jane's Inn

- Color remote televisions
- Continental breakfast
- Hospitality room
- Full private baths
- On site parking
- Individually heated and air conditioned
- Open all year

Lady Jane's Inn is a woman owned and operated guest house in the heart of Provincetown, on a quiet side street, just steps away from shops, restaurants and beaches. The Inn has been carefully and tastefully designed to meet the vacationers' need for comfort and privacy. Each spacious room is scrupulously clean and beautifully appointed with turn-of-century furnishings and ceiling fans. Whatever the season, guests will delight in a lovingly prepared continental breakfast served in the cozy common room or in the sunny, flower filled patio. Provincetown, and Lady Jane's Inn, have much to offer the vacationer.

Your Innkeepers,
Jane Antolini & Sharlene Marchette

7 Central Street, Provincetown, MA 02657

(800) LADY JANE (523-9526) or (508) 487-3387
E-mail: ladyjanes@wn.net http://www.ladyjanesinn.com

MASSACHUSETTS 345

Plums
Bed & Breakfast Inn

Drive past the tumble of Cape Cod houses to Plums Bed & Breakfast, an 1860s Dutch Gambrel. Inside the white picket fence, a garden of lilies, irises and dahlias beckon you across the wisteria-draped porch. Your key unlocks the quiet elegance of the Victorian whaling captain's house.

Inside, wide pine floors shine beneath Eastlake and Renaissance Revival antiques that grace Plums' large rooms. Fresh flowers add to the romance! And white lace curtains adorn windows that reach to high ceilings. Sit at a table of women for breakfast amid sterling silver, brass and period curios. Under a crystal chandelier, enjoy conversation, fresh fruit, baked goods, and gourmet entrees like cheese souffle or French toast stuffed with cream cheese and strawberries. Innkeepers to pamper you, parking and private baths for your comfort.

Come, experience the magic of Plums!
160 Bradford Street • Provincetown, MA 02657
(508) 487-2283 • Brochure available

346 MASSACHUSETTS

vate baths for your comfort. Gourmet breakfast served daily. Experience the magic of Plums, winner of Out & About's Best in Provincetown Editor's Choice Award! ♀

RAVENWOOD GUESTROOMS & APARTMENTS, 462 Commercial St, Provincetown, MA, 02657, (508) 487-3203 (Tel/Fax). Guestroom, year-round apartments & cottage, across from harbor. Men permitted if accompanied by their women friends. Modern conveniences, patio, BBQ, nearby ocean beach, gym & Jacuzzi. Catering arranged. ♀

ROSE ACRE, 5 Center St, Provincetown, MA, 02657, (508) 487-2347. A rambling 1840 Cape House, tucked down a private drive in the center of town. This

---

Rose Acre

A "Provincetown Classic" and women's house offering rooms, apartments and a cottage called "Rosebud." Enjoy the unhurried atmosphere of a rambling 1840 Cape House, tucked down a private drive, with decks, gardens, parking and a yard.

Brochure available.

(508) 487-2347
5 Center St
Provincetown, MA 02657

Circa 1830 Greek Revival style house located on historically famous Commercial Street... in the quiet Gallery District... a five minute stroll to the center of town...

Ravenwood
462

462 Commercial Street
Provincetown, MA 02657
Phone/Fax: (508) 487-3203
Valerie Carrano, Innkeeper

guestroom, apartments & cottage, waterviews & private decks, parking open yearround

"Provincetown Classic" and woman's house was once the domain of a Portuguese fishing family. We are close enough to the bay for some water views, the sound of the fog horn and the sweet smell of fresh salt air. Designed for comfort and the artist in all of us, units are adorned with wicker, art and flowers. A spacious private yard and garden invite you to relax, sun and picnic. ♀

WINDAMAR HOUSE, 568 Commercial St, Provincetown, MA, 02657, (508) 487-0599, Fax: (508) 487-7505. Email: windamar@tiac.net, Web: www.provincetown.com/windamar/, B&B in an elegant, historical, seaside home & apts, men welcome, some straight clientele. Antique decorations, bay views, TV lounge, common room & continental breakfast. Beautiful grounds & flower gardens, nearby ocean beach. ♀

Accommodations

A TALL SHIP, 452 Commercial St, Provincetown, MA, 02657, (508) 487-2247, winter: (508) 877-5442. Apartment rental with kitchen, nightly & weekly, some straight clientele. ♀♂

ADMIRAL'S LANDING GUEST HOUSE, 158 Bradford St, Provincetown, MA, 02657, (800) 934-0925, (508) 487-9665, Fax: (508) 487-4437. Email: admiral@capecod.net, Web: www.capecod.net/admiralslanding, Guesthouse, studio efficiencies. Nearby gym & ocean beach. Simple, elegant rooms, continental breakfast. ♀♂

AMPERSAND GUESTHOUSE, 6 Cottage St, PO Box 832, Provincetown, MA, 02657, (508) 487-0959, (800) 574-9645, Fax: (508) 487-4365. Email: ampersan@capecod.net, Guesthouse near town center, women welcome. Uniquely decorated doubles, suites, studio apartment. TV lounge with gaming table, continental breakfast, nearby ocean beaches. ♂

ANCHOR INN, 175 Commercial St, Provincetown, MA, 02657, (508) 487-0432, (800) 858-2657. Inn with private bath. ♀♂

BAYBERRY, THE, 16 Winthrop, Provincetown, MA, 02657, (508) 487-4605 (Tel/Fax), (800) 422-4605. Email: sixteen@capecod.net, Web: http://www.capecod.net/bayberry, Gay-owned & -operated B&B, private baths, expanded continental breakfast, some straight clientele. ♂

BEACONLIGHT GUEST HOUSE, THE, 12 Winthrop St, Provincetown, MA, 02657, (508) 487-9603 (Tel/Fax), (800) 696-9603. Email: beaconlite@capecod.net, Web: www.capecod.net/beaconlight/, Awaken to the aroma of freshly brewed coffee and home-baked cakes and breads. Relax in the English country house charm of elegant bedrooms and spacious drawing rooms, complete with open fire, grand piano, and antique furnishings. Multi-level sun decks provide panoramic views of Provincetown. Our exceptional reputa-

"Outstanding"
5 Palm Award
Out & About 1997

BENCHMARK
INN & ANNEX
6 DYER • 8 DYER

Top-notch comfort and style. Wet bars, fireplaces, whirlpool baths, dip pool, stunning harborviews and a long list of deluxe amenities.

BENCHMARK INN
THE BEST IS FOR YOU

6 DYER STREET, PROVINCETOWN • www.CapeCodAccess.com/benchmark/

TOLL FREE 888 487 7440

348 MASSACHUSETTS

tion for pampered comfort and caring service has grown by the word of mouth of our many returning guests. ♀♂

BENCHMARK INN & ANNEX, 6-8 Dyer Street, Provincetown, MA, 02657, (508) 487-7440, (888) 487-7440, Fax: (508) 487-3446. Email: inncorp@aol.com, Web: www.CapeCodAccess.com/benchmark/, Luxurious bedrooms and penthouse suite feature fireplace, marble bathroom and private balconied entrance. Many also offer wetbar, whirlpool tub and spectacular harborview. Numerous amenities include robes, phones, fresh flowers, down comforters, turn-down service and breakfast in bed. $140-$260 high season; $75-$195 low & mid. ♀♂ See ad on page 347.

BOATSLIP BEACH CLUB, 161 Commercial St Box 393, Provincetown, MA, 02657, (800) 451-SLIP (7547), (508) 487-1669, Fax: (508) 487-6021. Email: boatslip@provincetown.com, Web: www.provincetown.com/boatslip, Hotel with restaurant, bar & disco. Rooms have contemporary decor & color TV. Massage available. Aerobics, sun cots & morning coffee. ♀♂

BRADFORD CARVER HOUSE, THE, 70 Bradford St, Provincetown, MA, 02657, (508) 487-4966, (800) 826-9083, Fax: (508) 487-7213. Guest Tel: (508) 487-5699. Guesthouse with private & shared baths, expanded continental breakfast, color cable TV, AC, nearby pool, ocean & bar. Mostly men with women welcome. ♂

BRASS KEY GUESTHOUSE, THE, 67 Bradford St, Provincetown, MA, 02657, (508) 487-9005, (800) 842-9858, Fax: (508) 487-9020. Handsomely restored sea captain's house in heart of town. Women welcome. Luxury accommodations feature private bath, AC, color TV/VCR, telephone, refrigerator; some offer fireplace, king bed, whirlpool bath. Heated dip pool, enclosed sun decks, wood-burning fireplace. Open year-round. ♿♂

BUOY, THE, 97 Bradford St, Provincetown, MA, 02657, (508) 487-3082, (800) 648-0364, Fax: (508) 487-4887. Centrally-located guesthouse, private & shared baths, continental breakfast." ♀♂

BURCH HOUSE, 116 Bradford St, Provincetown, MA, 02657, (508) 487-9170. Inn, private & shared baths, continental breakfast. ♀♂

CAPE VIEW MOTEL, Rte 6, PO Box 114, North Truro, MA, 02652, (508) 487-0363, (800) 224-3232. Hotel with fantastic views, 50% gay & lesbian clientele. Rooms & efficiencies, private baths, color cable TV, AC & pool.

---

the BEACONLIGHT GUEST HOUSE

The Kind of House We Wished We Lived In

PROVINCETOWN

(800) 696-9603

(508) 487-9603

DEXTER'S INN

Open Year Round

A Traditional Cape Cod Guest House

6 Conwell Street
Provincetown, MA 02657

508-487-1911
Toll-free: 888-521-1999

Under New Ownership

MASSACHUSETTS 349

CAPTAIN AND HIS SHIP, THE, 164 Commercial St, Provincetown, MA, 02657, (508) 487-1850, (800) 400-CAPT. Guesthouse, private & shared baths. ♀♂

CAPTAIN LYSANDER INN, 96 Commercial St, Provincetown, MA, 02657, (508) 487-2253, Fax: (508) 487-7579. Inn, some straight clientele. ♀♂

CAPTAIN'S HOUSE, 350-A Commercial St, Provincetown, MA, 02657, (508) 487-9353, Reservations: (800) 457-8885. Guesthouse, women welcome, continental breakfast. ♂

CARPE DIEM, 8 Johnson St, Provincetown, MA, (888) 847-7926 or (508) 487-4242. Centrally-located guesthouse. Private & shared baths, TV lounge, continental breakfast & nearby ocean beach. ♀♂

CHICAGO HOUSE, THE, 6 Winslow St, Provincetown, MA, 02657, (508) 487-0537, (800) SEE-PTOWN (733-7869), Fax: (508) 487-6212. Email: chihse@aol.com, Web: http://members.aol.com/ChiHse, Guesthouse with rooms & apartments, continental breakfast, private & shared baths. ♀♂

COMMONS, THE, 386 Commercial St, PO Box 1037, Provincetown, MA, 02657, (508) 487-7800, (800) 487-0784. Spacious light-filled rooms, a private garden, a gourmet Bistro, and a friendly bar are just some of the features. The inn received the 1995 Best Restoration Award from the Provincetown Historical Commission. Conveniently located between downtown and the Gallery District. Our breathtaking view of Provincetown Harbor and Cape Cod Bay will make you fall in love with us. Some straight clientele. ♀♂

CROWN & ANCHOR, 247 Commercial St, Provincetown, MA, 02657, (508) 487-1430. Hotel with restaurant & 3 mostly-male bars, private baths. 🛏 ♀♂

DEXTER'S INN, 6 Conwell St, Provincetown, MA, 02657, (508) 487-1911 (Tel/Fax), toll-free: (888) 521-1999. Steeped in history, we're in the heart of downtown just a short walk to Commercial St, shops, restaurants, galleries and clubs. Our unique cluster of Cape Cod-style rooms (12 private & 3 with shared bath) allows for private entrance from deck or patio. Mornings enjoy breakfast on the garden patio or in our cozy keeping room. Relax and meet new friends on our spacious sun deck and patio. UNDER NEW OWNERSHIP. ♀♂

ELEPHANT WALK INN, 156 Bradford St, Provincetown, MA, 02657, (508) 487-2543 or (800) 889-WALK (9255). Guest phone: (508) 487-2195. Email: elephant@capecod.net, Web: http://

HERITAGE HOUSE

7 Center Street
Provincetown, MA 02657
508-487-3692
heritageh@capecod.net

★ Relax on our veranda ★
★ Enjoy a delicious homemade breakfast ★
★ Affordable rates ★

Give us a call!

REVERE GUEST HOUSE

"HOME SWEET HOME"

14 Court Street • Provincetown

(800) 487-2292

MASSACHUSETTS

www.capecod.net/elephantwalk, Large, mission-style B&B near ocean beach & center of town. Private baths, continental breakfast. ♀♂

ELM HOUSE, 9 Johnson St, Provincetown, MA, 02657, (508) 487-0793, Fax: (508) 487-7549. Guesthouse. Private & shared baths. ♀♂

FAIRBANKS INN, THE, 90 Bradford St, Provincetown, MA, 02657, (508) 487-0386, (800) FAIRBNK, Fax: (508) 487-3540. Email: fairbank@capecod.net, Web: www.capecod.net, 18th century sea captain's house with elegant architecture & wide plank floors from the ship of the captain who built it. ♀♂

GIFFORD HOUSE INN, 9-11 Carver St, Provincetown, MA, 02657, (508) 487-0688, (800) 434-0130. Hotel with 6 bars, women welcome. ♀♂

GRANDVIEW INN, THE, No. 4 Conant St, Provincetown, MA, 02657, (508) 487-9193. Email: vanbelle@capecod.net, Guesthouse with double rooms, private & shared baths, TV lounge, sitting room, beverages in season. 70% men, 30% women. ♂

HARGOOD HOUSE & CHANDLER HOUSE, 493 Commercial St, Provincetown, MA, 02657, (508) 487-9133, Fax: (508) 487-9133. 20 luxuriously-furnished condos with equipped kitchens, private beach. Some condos directly on water. Some straight clientele. ♀♂

HERITAGE HOUSE, 7 Center St, Provincetown, MA, 02657, (508) 487-3692. Email: heritageh@capecod.net, Charming 19th-century sea captain's house with bay views from veranda and many rooms. Centrally-located, but in a quiet residential area. Delicious buffet breakfast with homemade muffins, yogurt, fresh fruit, granola and cold cereal. Parking and airport pick up. Good mix of gay men and women, some straight clientele, shared baths. ♀♂ See ad pg 349

HOLIDAY INN, Rte 6A & Snail Rd, Provincetown, MA, 02657, (508) 487-1711, Reservations direct (800) 422-4224. Gay-friendly hotel with restaurant, bar & disco.

HOTEL PIAF, 3 Prince St, Provincetown, MA, 02657, (508) 487-7458, (800) 340-PIAF, Fax: (508) 487-8646. Email: reserve@piaf.com, Web: http://www.piaf.com, This 1820's restored guesthouse in the heart of Provincetown has three rooms and one suite each with its own private full bath, telephone, and cable TV. Down comforters, terry cloth robes, European bath products, and fresh flowers are just a few of the comforts we've included. Our historic, charming facilities are not lavish and grand, but our attention to detail and our commitment to your comfort is unparalleled. Some straight clientele. ♀♂

JOHN RANDALL HOUSE, 140 Bradford St, Provincetown, MA, 02657, (508) 487-3533 (Tel/Fax), (800) 573-6700. Guesthouse, private & shared baths. ♀♂

LAMPLIGHTER INN & COTTAGE, 26 Bradford St, Provincetown, MA, 02657, (508) 487-2529, (800) 263-6574, Fax: (508) 487-0079. Email: lamplite@lamplite.com, Web: http://www.CapeCodAccess.com/Lamplighter, B&B guesthouse, rooms thru cottage with modern conveniences, lovely gardens, expanded continental breakfast, women very welcome. Nearby gym & ocean beach. ♿ ♂

LAND'S END INN, 22 Commercial St, Provincetown, MA, 02657, (508) 487-0706, (800) 276-7088. B&B, 50% gay & lesbian clientele. Private baths, continental breakfast.

LAVENDER ROSE GUEST HOUSE, 186 Commercial St, Provincetown, MA, 02657, (508) 487-6648, (888) 514-ROSE, Fax: (508) 487-6634. B&B with bar & Mexican/Southwestern restaurant, private & shared baths, AC, ceiling fans, color cable TV, continental breakfast, some straight clientele. ♀♂

LOTUS GUEST HOUSE, 296 Commercial St, Provincetown, MA, 02657, (508) 487-4644. Centrally-located guesthouse, spacious rooms with private & shared baths, deck, garden. One block from ocean beach. Mostly gay & lesbian clientele. ♀♂

NORMANDY HOUSE, 184 Bradford St, Provincetown, MA, 02657, (508) 487-1197 or (800) 487-1197. Guesthouse on the hill, 3 min from Commercial St. Comfortable, immaculate rooms with modern conveniences, common room, sun porch, Jacuzzi, continental breakfast. Nearby ocean beach. 80% gay & lesbian & 20% straight clientele. 🛌 ♀♂

PAINTED LADY, THE, 135 Commercial St, Provincetown, MA, 02657, (508) 487-3608, Fax: (508) 487-1729. Email: rgill@tiac.net, Web: www.gaygetaways.com, San Francisco-style Victorian Painted Lady with 3 rental apartments, minutes from beaches, bars, restaurants & entertainment. Private baths, phones, cable TV, 1 parking space per unit. Some straight clientele. ♀♂

PRINCE ALBERT GUEST HOUSE, THE, 166 Commercial St, Provincetown, MA, 02657, (508) 487-0859, (800) 992-0859, Fax: (508) 487-1533. Email: ohart@capecod.net, Gay-owned & -operated guesthouse, private & shared baths, AC, color cable TV, some straight clientele. ♀♂

REVERE HOUSE, 14 Court St, Provincetown, MA, 02657, (508) 487-2292, (800) 487-2292. Email: reveregh@tiac.net, Web: www.provincetown.com/revere, A restored captain's home circa 1820-1840. The charm and ambiance of this era prevails throughout the 10 antique-filled rooms, which include a comfortable studio with a kitchenette and a private bath. In season, coffee, tea, juice and homemade muffins and breads are served in the common room, which overlooks the garden. It's a short walk to shops, galleries, restaurants and nightclubs. ♀♂See ad pg 349

ROOMERS, 8 Carver St, Provincetown, MA, 02657, (508) 487-3532. Centrally-located guesthouse, women welcome. Double rooms decorated with antiques, common rooms, cont. breakfast. ♂

SANDPIPER BEACH HOUSE, 165 Commercial St, PO Box 646, Provincetown, MA, 02657, (508) 487-1928 or (800) 354-8628. Email: sandpiper@provincetown.com, Web: www.provincetown.com/sandpiper, Turreted Victorian guesthouse near ocean beach. Continental breakfast, variety of rooms, many with bay views. 🏖 ♀♂

SHAMROCK, THE, 49 Bradford St, Provincetown, MA, 02657, (508) 487-1133, (888) 55-IRISH, Fax: (617) 963-2727. Motel, cottages & apartments, 50% gay/lesbian.

SHIREMAX INN, 5 Tremont St, Provincetown, MA, 02657, (508) 487-1233, Toll-free: (888) SHIREMAX (744-7362). Inn, women welcome. Variety of guest quarters, TV lounge, kitchen privileges, expanded continental breakfast. Nearby ocean beach. 🛌 ♂

SIX WEBSTER PLACE, 6 Webster Place, Provincetown, MA, 02657, (508) 487-2266, (800) 6 WEBSTER. Email: sixwebster@aol.com, Web: http://ptown.com/ptown/lodging/sixwebster, Centrally located guesthouse, some straight clientele. Rooms with period furnishings, modern conveniences, private & shared baths, TV lounge, weights, continental breakfast & nearby beaches. ♀♂

SOUTH HOLLOW VINEYARDS, Rte 6A, PO Box 165, North Truro, MA, 02652, (508) 487-6200, Fax: (508) 487-4248. Nestled on five picturesque acres of rolling hills and vineyards, this historic 1836 inn features private tiled baths, four-poster beds, and Jacuzzi suites. Complimentary continental breakfast. Women-owned inn and winegrape vineyard.

SUNSET INN, 142 Bradford St, Provincetown, MA, 02657, (508) 487-9810, (800) 965-1801. Email: sunset1@capecod.net, Web: www.ptown.com/ptown/sunsetinn, Guesthouse with garden patio & sun decks, private & shared baths, continental breakfast, 1 block from beach & 3 blocks from gay nightlife. Some straight clientele. ♀♂

THREE PEAKS, 210 Bradford St, Provincetown, MA, 02657, (508) 487-1717, (800) 286-1715. Email: threepks@capecod.net, Web: www.cape cod.net/threepeaks, East-end B&B near town beaches & shopping. Rooms & apartment with double beds, color cable TV, private baths & continental breakfast. ♀♂

TRADEWINDS INN, THE, 12 Johnson St, Provincetown, MA, 02657, (508) 487-0138, (800) 487-0132, Fax: (508) 487-9484. Web: tradewindsinn.com, Gay-owned & -operated guesthouse with a variety of rooms & conveniences, private & shared baths, TV lounge & continental breakfast. Nearby ocean beach. ♀♂

MASSACHUSETTS

TUCKER INN AT TWELVE CENTER, THE, 12 Center St, Provincetown, MA, 02657, (508) 487-0381, Fax: (508) 487-6236. Web: http://www.provincetown.com/tucker, Something new in Provincetown! Now women-owned, the former Twelve Center Guest House has been renamed and refurbished as a romantic country inn offering a fully equipped cottage and spacious antique-filled rooms with private and shared baths, parking, cable TV and continental breakfast served on a tree-shaded patio. The inn is located on a quiet, peaceful side street, and yet is only a minute's walk from all that Provincetown has to offer. Enhance your vacation with a stay at The Tucker Inn. Some straight clientele. ♀♂

WATERMARK INN, 603 Commercial St, Provincetown, MA, 02657, (508) 487-0165, Fax: (508) 487-2383. Beachfront inn, 50% gay & lesbian clientele. Private baths, color TV, tele., refrigerator.

WATERSHIP INN, 7 Winthrop St, Provincetown, MA, 02657, (508) 487-0094, (800) 330-9413. Web: www.cimarron.net/usa/ma/watership, Centrally located B&B, women welcome. Variety of comfortable rooms, expanded continental breakfast. Nearby pool & ocean beach. ♂

WEST END INN, 44 Commercial St, Provincetown, MA, 02657, (508) 487-9555, (800) 559-1220, Fax: (508) 487-8779. B&B & apartments, private & shared baths, some straight clientele. TV lounge, TV/VCR in apartments. Expanded continental breakfast, beaches nearby." ♀♂

WINDSOR COURT, 15 Cottage St, Provincetown, MA, 01657, (508) 487-2620. Guesthouse with rooms, studios & suites. Bay views, full breakfast, cable TV, optional AC. All rooms have private baths. In-ground pool & year round hot tub.

■ Bars

PORCH BAR, at Gifford House., Conversation bar. ♀♂

■ Dance Bar/Disco

★ **BOATSLIP BEACH CLUB,** 161 Commercial St, at Central, (508) 487-1669, (800) 451-7547. Tea dance daily 3:30pm, C&W dances, ballroom dancing. ♀♂

CLUB ANTRO, Commercial St, next to town hall, Dance club. ♂

★ **PIED PIPER,** 193 Commercial (alley), near Carver, (508) 487-1527. Bar with grill on waterfront deck. After tea gay & lesbian tea-dance 6:30pm till ?" ♀

★ **VIXEN,** at Pilgrim House Inn., Dance bar & lounge at Pilgrim House Hotel. ♀

■ Restaurants

BOATSLIP BEACH CLUB, 161 Commercial St., at Boatslip Hotel, (508) 487-1669. ♀♂

COMMONS BISTRO, 386 Commercial St, at Ocean's Inn, (508) 487-7800. Bistro cuisine, brick oven pizza, outside dining. ♀♂

FRONT STREET, 230 Commercial St, (508) 487-9715. Continental cuisine. ♀♂

■ Retail & Bookstores

DON'T PANIC, 192 Commercial St #4, (508) 487-1280. Gay & lesbian gift shop, T-shirts, buttons.

NOW VOYAGER BOOKSTORE & CAPE & DAGGER, 357 Commercial St, (508) 487-0848. Adjoining stores: Now Voyager is gay & lesbian bookstore, Cape & Dagger is a mystery bookstore.

OUTPOST, 191 Commercial St, (508) 487-6777. Gay & lesbian gift shop & bookstore.

PRIDE'S OF PROVINCETOWN, 182 Commercial Street, (508) 487-1127. Gay & lesbian gift store with cards, original art, books, posters and more.

RECOVERING HEARTS BOOKSTORE, 4 Standish St, (508) 487-4875 (TTY). Women's bookstore & gift gallery. Fiction thru metaphysical, healing, recovery. Open year-round. ♿

WOMENCRAFTS, 376 Commercial St, (508) 487-2501. CELEBRATING OUR 23RD YEAR!! A women's store with jewelry, books, music, pottery, glassware & much more, plus 5% lesbian discount! We're open year-round.

MASSACHUSETTS 353

- 14K GOLD AND STERLING SILVER JEWELRY -

W♀MENCRAFTS

Jewelry, Gift Gallery & Bookstore

CARDS - BABY CLOTHES - T-SHIRTS - BOOKS - MUSIC

POTTERY - GLASSWARE - SWEATSHIRTS - SOX

...where there's 23 years of Lesbian Pride behind everything we sell...

376 Commercial Street
Provincetown, MA 02657
(508) 487-2501

MAIL ORDER & LAY-AWAYS

RANDOLPH

■ Dance Bar/Disco
★ **RANDOLPH COUNTRY CLUB,** 44 Mazzeo Dr, (617) 961-2414. 20 min from Boston, 2 discos. Restaurant open Mon eve only. Swimming pool, sand volleyball court, Sun brunch. Many women Sat.

SPRINGFIELD

■ Bars
PUB, THE, 382 Dwight St, near Taylor, (413) 734-8123. Upstairs, women welcome.

■ Dance Bar/Disco
DAVID'S NIGHTCLUB, 397 Dwight St, (413) 734-0566. NY-style nightclub, Wed-Sun. Shows, T-dance Thur.
FRIENDS, 23 Hampden St, (413) 781-5878. Video dance bar, cabaret, cruise bar, 60% men, 40% women."
OUR HIDEAWAY, 16 Bolduc Ln, Chicopee, (413) 534-6426. 5 min by car from downtown Springfield, 1/2 hr from Hartford. DJ dancing Fri & Sat. Sun tea dance 4pm-2am. Open fall, winter 7 days, summer closed Mon. Sand volleyball spring & summer, patio bar.

■ Restaurants
SILVIO'S RESTAURANT, 382 Dwight St, at The Pub men's bar., Italian food.

STURBRIDGE - WARE

■ Accommodations
WILDWOOD INN B & B, THE, 121 Church St, Ware, MA, 01082, (413) 967-7798, (800) 860-8098. Gay-friendly B&B with lesbian following. Cozy rooms with American primitive furnishings, full breakfast, private & shared baths. Nearby ponds, pools, maps to book & antique shops, hot tubs, nature trails, restaurants. Near Northampton, 8 miles from Mass Pike (I-90). **See our ad in Boston.**

WAREHAM

■ Accommodations
LITTLE HARBOR GUEST HOUSE, 20 Stockton Shortcut, Wareham, MA, 02571, (508) 295-6329, (800) 515-6329. Gay-friendly guesthouse 1 hour from Boston & Provincetown, private & shared baths, continental breakfast.

WORCESTER

■ Dance Bar/Disco
AMEN, 23 Foster St, (508) 754-7742. Gothic with gargoyles, dark paint.

YARMOUTH PORT

■ Accommodations
GULL COTTAGE, 10 Old Church St, Yarmouth Port, MA, (508) 362-8747. Gay-friendly B&B with 3 rooms, shared baths, 50% gay & lesbian clientele.

MICHIGAN
ANN ARBOR

■ Information
AIDS INFO, (734) 572-9355.
GAY, LESBIAN & BISEXUALS PROGRAMS OFFICE, 3116 Michigan Union, 3rd fl, 530 S State St, (734) 763-4186. 8am-5pm weekdays."

■ Bars
AUT BAR, 315 Braun Ct, (734) 994-3677. 7 days 4pm-2am, pool table, dinner daily, Sun Brunch 10am-3pm, upstairs bar.

■ Dance Bar/Disco
NECTARINE, THE, 516 E Liberty, (734) 994-5835. From 9pm, Tues & Fri gay nights.

■ Retail & Bookstores
COMMON LANGUAGE, 214 S 4th Ave, (734) 663-0036. Lesbian, feminist & gay bookstore with tapes, cards, jewelry, posters, non-sexist children's books. Closed Mon."
CRAZY WISDOM BOOKS, 206 N 4th Ave, (734) 665-2757. Holistic, metaphysical bookstore with a large women's spiritual section.
SHAMAN DRUM BOOKSHOP, 315 S State St, (734) 662-7407. General bookstore with a gay & lesbian section.

BATTLE CREEK

■ Dance Bar/Disco
PARTNERS, 910 North Ave, (616) 964-

7276. Dance & show bar with male & female dancers, Mon-Sat 6pm-2am, DJ Fri & Sat. ♪🚻🍸♀♂

DETROIT

■ Information
AFFIRMATIONS, 195 W Nine Mile Rd, Ferndale, (248) 398-7105, (800) 398-4297. Mon-Fri after 6pm, or tape, gay & lesbian community center.

COMMUNITY PRIDE BUILDING, 409-429 Livernois Ave, Ferndale., Office & meeting space for gay & lesbian organizations.

■ Bars
★ **PRONTO VIDEO BAR,** 608 S. Washington, Royal Oak, (810) 544-7900. ♀♂

STINGERS LOUNGE & GRILL, 19404 Sherwood, side entrance, (313) 892-1765. Open daily 4pm-2am, juke box dancing, 50% men, 50% women. 🍸✕🍔♀♂

★ **SUGARBAKERS,** 3800 E 8 Mile, (313) 892-5203. Women's sports bar, softball teams, pool tables, dart boards, big-screen TV. 🍸✕ ♀

■ Dance Bar/Disco
★ **BACKSTREET,** 15606 Joy Rd, at Greenfield, (313) 272-8959. Wed & Sat, preppy crowd, 90% men. 🍸♂

CLUB INUENDO, corner of I-15 service drive & Nevada, (between 6 mile & 7 mile), (313) 892-1444. Mon-Thurs 4pm-2am, Fri & Sat 4pm-5am, Sun 7pm-2am. Full-service kitchen, after hours Fri & Sat. ♪🚻♀♂

GIGI'S, 16920 W Warren Ave, at Clayburn, (313) 584-6525. Go go boys Mon & Fri, shows Tues & Sat, 80% men, 20% women. 🍸👠🚻♂

ONE X WAREHOUSE DANCE CLUB, 2575 Michigan Ave, Detroit, (313) 964-7040. Huge club, open Thurs-Sun, ladies nite Thurs. 🍸♀♂

★ **RAINBOW ROOM, THE,** 6640 E Eight Mile, (313) 891-1020. Lipstick lesbians, shows Fri & Sun, 70% women, 30% men. 🍸♪♀

SILENT LEGACY, 1641 Middlebelt Rd, Inkster, (734) 729-8980. Shows Wed & Fri, female strippers. 🍸♀

ZIPPERS, 6221 E Davison, (313) 892-8120. Opens at 9pm, more women Fri & Sat than other days. 🍴♀♂

■ Restaurants
COMO'S RESTAURANT, 22812 Woodward., Italian cuisine.

LA DOLCE VITA, 17546 Woodward, (313) 865-0331. Italian cuisine. 🚻

PRONTO RESTAURANT, 608 S Washington, Royal Oak, (810) 544-7900. Gay bar & restaurant, patio. ♀♂

■ Retail & Bookstores
A WOMAN'S PREROGATIVE, 175 W 9 Mile Rd, near Woodward & 9 Mile, Ferndale, (248) 545-5703. Lesbian bookstore with music, cards, jewelry & sex toys.

CHOSEN BOOKS, 120 4th Street, Royal Oak, (248) 543-5758. Gay bookstore, mostly male-oriented items.

JUST 4 US, 211 W 9 Mile Rd, Ferndale, (248) 547-5878, fax: (248) 547-4405. Gay gift shop with coffee bar, mostly male-oriented items.

ESCANABA

■ Dance Bar/Disco
CLUB XPRESS, 904 Ludington St, (906) 789-0140. Big party 1 weekend a month, occasional drag shows. 75% men, 25% women. 🍸♂

FLINT

■ Bars
CLUB MI, 2402 Franklin, (810) 234-9481. 80% women, small dance floor. 🍔🍸♀

■ Dance Bar/Disco
CLUB TRIANGLE, 2101 S Dort Hwy, (810) 767-7550. 7 days, male dancers Sun, 50% men/women. 🚻♪♀♂

STATE BAR, 2512 S Dort Hwy, near Lippincott, (810) 767-7050. 50% men, 50% women, male dancers. 🍸♪♀♂

GLEN ARBOR

■ Women's Accommodations
DUNESWOOD & MARGE & JOANNE'S, PO Box 457, Glen Arbor, MI, 49636, (616) 334-3346. A woman's resort on 7 acres in the Sleeping Bear Dunes Nat'l Lakeshore. Private baths, a variety of cooking options. Also available is Marge & Joanne's B&B, also for women only, with shared baths. We're near Traverse City, MI. ♀

MICHIGAN

GRAND RAPIDS

Information
LESBIAN & GAY COMMUNITY NETWORK, (616) 458-3511. Mon-Fri 6pm-10pm.

Dance Bar/Disco
CITY LIMITS, 67 S Division Ave, near Weston, (616) 454-8003. Dance & show bar, male dancers.

DIVERSIONS, 10 Fountain NW, (616) 451-3800. Complex with dance bar, video bar & quiet atrium.

Cafe
SONS & DAUGHTERS COFFEEHOUSE, 962 Cherry St SE, at Sons & Daughters Bookstore., Desserts, cappuccino, espresso. Till midnight weekdays. Three am weekends. No smoking.

Restaurants
DIVERSIONS GRILL, 10 Fountain NW, at Diversions bar, (616) 451-3800. Lunch, dinner.

Retail & Bookstores
SONS & DAUGHTERS BOOKSTORE & COFFEEHOUSE, 962 Cherry St SE, (616) 459-8877. Gay & lesbian bookstore, non-smoking gallery & coffeehouse with desserts, cappuccino, espresso. Open till midnight weekdays, Fri-Sat till 3am."

HONOR

Women's Accommodations
LABRYS WILDERNESS RESORT, 4115 Scenic Hwy, Honor, MI, 49640, (616) 882-5994. Enjoy one of our four housekeeping cabins in the Michigan woods. Lake Michigan & beaches are nearby, lesbian store, sauna & hot tub on premises.

Retail & Bookstores
SEEDS, Rte 1, Box 257, Honor, (616) 882-5994. Lesbian store at Labrys Wilderness Resort, featuring crafts, jewelry, artwork, cards and herbal remedies made by women on the land.

KALAMAZOO

Information
AIDS SERVICES, (616) 381-2437, for emergencies 381-4357.

LESBIAN & GAY LINE, 629 Pioneer St, (616) 345-7878, 7-10 pm Mon-Fri or tape.

Dance Bar/Disco
BROTHERS, 209 Stockbridge, (616) 345-1960. DJ Thurs-Sat, private club, open 7 days, male & female strippers, 50% men, 50% women.

ZOO, 906 Portage St, (616) 342-8888. Patio, 70% men, 30% women.

Retail & Bookstores
PANDORA BOOKS FOR OPEN MINDS, 226 W Lovell St, (616) 388-5656. Women's & gay & lesbian books. Tues-

---

Your own cabin in the woods...

- miles of deserted beaches • pristine waters • guided canoe trips
- 4 housekeeping cabins • sauna • hot tub • 1-mile hike to Lake Michigan

Labrys Wilderness Resort
4115 Scenic Hwy., Honor, MI 49640 (616) 882-5994 women only

Thurs 11-7pm, Fri-Sat 11-6pm, closed Sun-Mon.
RAINBOW A-GO-GO, 1506 S Burdick, (616) 383-1569. Pride items, etc
TRIANGLE WORLD, 551 Portage St, (616) 373-4005. Bookstore with videos, gay & lesbian cards, gifts. Noon-10pm, closed Mon.

LANSING

■ *Information*
LESBIAN & GAY HOTLINE, (517) 332-3200, 7pm-10pm Mon-Fri, 2-5pm Sun, or tape.
LESBIAN CONNECTION, (517) 371-5257. 11am-6pm, local women's info.

■ *Bars*
ESQUIRE CLUB, 1250 Turner St, Old Town Lansing, (517) 487-5338. Pool table, 70% men. ♂

■ *Dance Bar/Disco*
CLUB 505, 505 E Shiawasee, (517) 374-6312. Big screen TV, pool table, 80% women.
CLUB PARADISE, 224 S Washington Square, (517) 484-2399. Hi-energy dance bar, 60% men, 40% women, young crowd, closed Mon.

■ *Retail & Bookstores*
REAL WORLD BOOKS EMPORIUM, 1214-16 Turner St, Old Town Library, (517) 485-2665, Fax: (517) 485-0052. E-mail: RealWorlde@aol.com. Women's, lesbian & gay titles & performance space, noon-8pm Tues-Sun.

MACKINAC ISLAND

■ *Tours, Charters & Excursions*
PROFESSIONAL MARINE SERVICES, 16293 Orchard Creek Hwy, Ocqueoc, MI, 49759, (517) 733-8569 (winter), (906) 847-6580 (summer), (888) 847 6580. Email: dehartec@svr1.pace.k12.mi.us, Lesbian weddings on board a power boat off Mackinac Island, sightseeing trips, dinner cruises. Although lesbian weddings are not yet legal in Michigan, we can still "tie the knot" for you and your life partner, and will issue a certificate. ♀

MARQUETTE

■ *Retail & Bookstores*
SWEET VIOLETS, 413 N 3rd St, (906) 228-3307. Women's bookstore & gift shop, feminist & spirituality books, music, pride items, cards, some gay magazines. Mon-Fri 10am-6pm, Sat 10am-5pm.

MIDLAND

■ *Accommodations*
JAY'S BED & BREAKFAST, 4429 Bay City Rd, Midland, MI, 48642, (517) 496-2498. B&B with shared bath, full breakfast, 25% straight clientele." ♀♂

Marry Her on a Yacht on Lake Huron...

Honeymoon in the old-world Victorian atmosphere of Mackinac Island
PROFESSIONAL MARINE SERVICES
(888) 847-6580

MT CLEMENS

Dance Bar/Disco
MIRAGE, 27 N Walnut, (810) 954-1919. 7 days, male dancers Tues.

MUSKEGON

Dance Bar/Disco
R'S CLUB & DISCOTHEQUE, 3236 Hoyt St, Muskegon Hts., Unverifiable spring '97.

PONTIAC

Dance Bar/Disco
CLUB FLAMINGO, 352 Oakland Ave, (248) 253-0430. Area's largest club, drag shows Thurs, 60% men, 40% women.

PORT HURON

Dance Bar/Disco
SEEKERS, 3301 24th St, (810) 985-9349. Male & female strippers, patio & gazebo, shows Sat.

SAGINAW

Dance Bar/Disco
BAMBI'S, 1742 E Genesee, (517) 752-9179. Dance & show bar, 60% men, 40% women. Unverifiable spring '98.

Ahh!
★ Deluxe Rooms or Cottage Suites
★ Fine Dining at Magnolia Grill
★ Disco Cabaret

Douglas Dunes
— Resort —
(616) 857-1401
Blue Star Highway Douglas, MI 49406

SAUGATUCK - DOUGLAS

Accommodations
DOUGLAS DUNES RESORT, 333 Blue Star Highway, Douglas, MI, 49406, (616) 857-1401, Fax: (616) 857-4052. **Saugatuck/Douglas is the Key West of the north.** Enjoy our wonderful beaches, boutiques, art galleries, and the beautiful people at Douglas Dunes Resort, a deluxe motel with pool, patio bar, disco, cabaret, and award-winning dining at Magnolia Grill.

KIRBY HOUSE, THE, PO Box 1174, Saugatuck, MI, 49453, (616) 857-2904 (Tel/Fax), (800) 521-6473. Email: kirbyhse@aol.com, Web: http://www.bbonline.com/mi/kirby, Inn, some straight clientele. Comfortable rooms with antique furnishings, kitchen privileges, BBQ, Jacuzzi, bicycles, full breakfast buffet.

MOORE'S CREEK INN, 820 Holland St, Saugatuck, MI, 49453, (616) 857-2411, (800) 838-5864. B&B, some straight clientele. Theme rooms with private & shared baths, TV lounge, common rooms, full breakfast. Nearby lake.

NEWNHAM SUNCATCHER INN, 131 Griffith, Box 1106, Saugatuck, MI, 49453, (616) 857-4249. Web: http://wwwbbonline.com/mi/suncatcher/index.html, B&B & separate 2-cottage suite, some straight clientele. Period furniture, shared baths, common room, TV lounge, Jacuzzi, full breakfast.

Camping & RV
CAMPIT, 6635 118th Ave, Fennville, MI, 49408, (616) 543-4335. Campground with mini-store, modern bath & shower facilities, game room, TV lounge, laundry facilities, 37 electric hookups, 30 tent sites & 30 RV spaces. Mostly men, women welcome.

Women's Accommodations
DEERPATH LODGE, PO Box 849, Saugatuck, MI, 49453, (616) 857-DEER (3337), toll-free (888) DEERPATH. Contemporary redwood lodge on 45 acres overlooking the Kalamazoo River, private baths, breakfast, 5 min drive from Saugatuck.

DRIFT WOODS, 2731 Lakeshore Dr, Fennville, MI, 49408, (616) 857-2586. Cottages with private baths. ♀

Beaches
GAY BEACH, follow signs to Oval Beach, then park, walk north.

Dance Bar/Disco
DOUGLAS DISCO & THE CABARET & BISTRO, 333 Blue Star Hwy, Douglas, at Douglas Dunes, (616) 857-1401. Teadance, Sun 4pm in summer. Open 7 days in winter. Cabaret has live singers & piano, bistro quiet bar. Also patio & pool bars. ♀♂

Restaurants
MAGNOLIA'S, at Douglas Dunes Resort, 333 Blue Star Hwy, Douglas, (616) 857-1401. Fine dining, open daily in summer, weekends in winter. ♀♂

SAULT SAINTE MARIE

Retail & Bookstores
OPEN MIND BOOKS, 223 Ashmun, (906) 635-9008. General bookstore with gay section.

SOUTHWEST MICHIGAN

Accommodations
COZY COTTAGES, Envoy Resort Properties, 740 N Rush St #609, Chicago, IL, 60611, (312) 787-2400, Fax: (312) 787-7109, (800) 44-ENVOY (36869). Cozy up for a weekend getaway or crosscountry stopover just 1-1/2 hrs from Chicago & 5 blocks from Lake Michigan. Walk on the beach or explore a pretty little town with fine restaurants, art galleries & jewelry shops...or cross-country ski...or visit the National & State Dunes Parks nearby. Men, women, children, small dogs — everyone is welcome. One cottage is a 2-BR with electric fireplace, the other is a 3-BR with gas fireplace. Both have full kitchens, micros, color TV and VCR, telephones & AC. Towels and linens provided. ♀♂

TRAVERSE CITY

Dance Bar/Disco
SIDE TRAXX, 520 Franklin, (616) 935-1666. Opens 6pm-2am, 7 days, 60% men, 40% women. ♀♂

UNION PIER

Accommodations
WARREN WOODS INN, 15506 Lake Shore Rd, Union Pier, MI, (616) 469-5880, (800) 358 4754. B&B with private baths, full breakfast, near lake & beaches, 1-1/4 hrs from Chicago Loop, gay & lesbian following.

Cozy Cottages

1 1/2 Hours From Chicago In SW Michigan

1-800-44-ENVOY

MINNESOTA

DULUTH

SEE ALSO SUPERIOR, WI,

Information
AURORA: NORTHLAND LESBIAN CENTER, 32 E 1st St #104, (Bldg for women), (218) 722-4903. Mon 9:15-2pm, Wed 10am-6pm, Thurs 1pm-5pm.

Accommodations
STANFORD INN, 1415 E Superior St, Duluth, MN, 55805, (218) 724-3044. Web: http://www.visitduluth.com/stanford, Victorian B&B with private & shared baths, sauna, full gourmet breakfast & room service coffee, some straight clientele. ♀♂

KENYON

Accommodations
DANCING WINDS B & B RETREAT, 6863 Co. #12 Blvd, Kenyon, MN, (507) 789-6606, Fax: (507) 789-5233. Email: dancingwinds@juno.com, B&B & campground with licensed cheesery on farmstead. Full bath, kitchen, living room, TV lounge, full breakfast, fresh goat's milk & cheese. Nearby pool. 50% gay/lesbian.

MINNEAPOLIS - ST PAUL

Information
AIDS LINE, (612) 373-2437. Mon-Thurs 9am-9pm. Fri 9am-6pm.

CHRYSALIS, A CENTER FOR WOMEN, 2650 Nicollet, (612) 871-0118.

GAY & LESBIAN COMMUNITY ACTION COUNCIL, 310 E 38th St #204, (612) 822-0127.

GAY HELP LINE, (612) 822-8661. Mon-Fri 2pm-10pm, Sat 4pm-10pm.

QUATREFOIL LIBRARY, 1619 Dayton Ave, (612) 641-0969. Gay & lesbian library & archives.

Accommodations
CARITAS BED & BREAKFAST NETWORK, (800) CARITAS, (312) 857-0801, Fax: (312) 857-0805. B&B, home-stay accommodations service. Member: IGLTA

EAGLE COVE BED AND BREAKFAST, Box 65, W 4387 120th Ave, Maiden Rock, WI, 54750, (800) 467-0279, (715) 448-4302. Rustic ridgetop B&B retreat 65 miles from Minneapolis, some straight clientele. Color TV, shared baths, fireplace lounge & expanded continental breakfast. ♿ ♀♂

HOTEL AMSTERDAM, 828 Hennipen Ave, Minneapolis, MN, 55429, (612) 288-0459, (800) 649-9500. Renovated hotel with restaurant & bar. Modest accommodations, Sun brunch. ♀♂

Women's Accommodations
COUNTRY GUEST HOUSE, THE, 1673 38th St, Somerset, WI, 54025, (715) 247-3520. Two-bedroom guesthouse cottage on hobby farm along MN/WI border, men welcome. Kitchen, telephone, stereo, walking trails, row boat. ♀

Bars
★ **GAY 90'S, HAPPY HOUR,** 408 Hennepin Ave, near 4th St, Mpls, (612) 333-7755. Complex with hi energy & funk dance bars, cruise bar & very large show bar, leather bar & restaurant.

LOUNGE, THE, 411 N 2nd Ave N, (612) 333-8800. A pleasing mixture of straight & gay clientele (20-50% gay), jazz weekdays, DJ weekends.

MINNESOTA BAR & GRILL, 1501 S 6th St, (612) 317-9800. Bar & restaurant. ♀♂

NINETEEN BAR, 19 W 15th St, near Nicollet, Mpls, (612) 871-5553. 60% men, 40% women. ♀♂

OVER THE RAINBOW, 249 W 7th St, St Paul, (612) 228-7180. Small dance floor. ♀♂

Dance Bar/Disco
★ **CLUB METRO,** 733 Pierce Butler Route, St. Paul, (612) 489-0002. Women's dance bar above Underground men's bar. ♀

MINNESOTA

FIRST AVENUE AND SEVENTH STREET ENTRY, 701 1st Ave N, (612) 332-1775. Alternative dance club, 50% gay & lesbian.

★ **GAY 90'S, HAPPY HOUR,** 408 Hennepin Ave, near 4th St, Mpls, (612) 333-7755. Complex with dance bar, cruise bar, piano bar, show bar, leather bar & restaurant."

GROUND ZERO, 15 NE 4th St, Mpls, (612) 378-5115. Very alternative dance bar, call for schedule.

TOWN HOUSE COUNTRY, 1415 University Ave, near Albert, St Paul, (612) 646-7087. Some nites piano music, Fri nites swing music.

TRIXX, 490 N Robert St, St Paul, (612) 224-0703. Complex with video dance bar and piano bar, 70% men, 30% women.

TROPIX, 400 3rd Ave N, (612) 333-1006. Gay Thurs only.

UNDERGROUND, 733 Pierce Butler Route, lower level of Club Metro women's bar., Hi energy dance club, open Wed-Sat, Thurs leather nite, Fri theme parties (mostly men), Sat mixed men & women.

Cafe

BLUE MOON, 3822 East Lake St, (612) 721-9230.

CAFE WYRD, 1600 W Lake, Mpls, (612) 827-5710. Coffee shop, mostly gay clientele.

CAFE ZEZ, 1362 La Salle Ave, Minneapolis, (612) 874-8477. Popular gay-friendly cafe.

METRO CAFE, 733 Pierce Butler Rd, in the Club Metro, (612) 487-5909. Dinner Wed-Sun.

UNCOMMON GROUNDS, 2809 Hennepin Ave, (612) 872-4811. Open 7 days til 1am.

Restaurants

CAFE BRENDA, 300 1st Ave N, (612) 342-9230.

MINNESOTA BAR & GRILL, 1501 S 6th St, (612) 317-9800. Bar & restaurant.

★ **RUBY'S CAFE,** 1614 Harmon Pl, (612) 338-2089. Mon-Sat 7am-2pm, Sun 8am-2pm.

TIMES BAR & CAFE, THE, 1036 Nicollet Ave, (612) 333-2762. Bar & restaurant.

Retail & Bookstores

A BROTHER'S TOUCH, 2327 Hennepin Ave, Mpls 55405, (612) 377-6279. Gay & lesbian bookstore, records, music, cards, T-shirts, magazines. Mon, Tue 11am-7pm. Wed-Fri 11am-9pm. Sat 11am-6pm. Sun noon-5pm.

AMAZON BOOKSTORE, 1612 Harmon Pl, (612) 338-6560. Founded in 1970, Amazon Bookstore is the oldest feminist bookstore in the country. Open seven days, Amazon carries over 15,000 titles by women, women's periodicals, music, T-shirts, posters, cards & crafts.

RAINBOW ROAD, 109 W Grant, (612) 872-8448. Videos, gifts, cards. 10am-10pm.

MOORHEAD

SEE FARGO, ND,

NORTH-CENTRAL MINNESOTA

Accommodations

MEADOW GROVE B & B, 13661 Powerdam Rd NE, Bemidji, MN, 56601, (218) 751-9654. Gay-owned B&B with mostly straight clientele, near Concordia Language Village. In summer: lakes, fishing & outdoor recreation nearby. Isolated location appeals to artists & writers.

NORTHWOODS RETREAT, 5749 Mt Ash Dr, Hill City, MN, 55748, (218) 697-8119, (800) 767-3020. We're the only resort on this lake.Two cabins, private baths, total privacy & no public access. Private lake with fishing, swimming, paddle boats. All meals included, Free use of outdoor equipment, men welcome.

ROCHESTER

Information

GAY & LESBIAN COMMUNITY SERVICES, (507) 281-3265. Office hours Mon & Wed 5pm-7pm. Call for socials, occasional dances, potlucks, contact service.

MISSISSIPPI

BAY ST LOUIS

■ Bars
CHARLENE & LINDA'S ON THE COAST, 1205 Blue Meadow Rd, (228) 467-7298. Bar & restaurant, 50 miles from New Orleans, close to Casino Magic & 1/2 mile from Gulf Coast beaches. There's volleyball, basketball, tetherball, darts, a beer garden, canoeing & a catfish pond you can fish in. The clubhouse has a juke box, pool table & card table. Open Sat & Sun only, 2pm till ?. ♀♂

BILOXI - GULFPORT

■ Bars
SANCTUARY, on Veterans Blvd, first building on the left north of the RR tracks., Small dance floor, Fri karaoke, patio. ♀♂

■ Dance Bar/Disco
JOEYS ON THE BEACH, 1708 Beach Blvd (Hwy 90), Biloxi, (601) 435-5639. Dance club, 70% men, 30% women. Open Tues-Sun from 4pm till late. ♂

COLUMBUS

■ Bars
COLUMBUS CONNECTION, 851 Island Rd, (601) 329-3926. 75% men, 25% women, male dancers. ♂

HATTIESBURG

■ Dance Bar/Disco
COURTYARD, 107 E Front St, (601) 545-2714. Dance bar & lounge, 50% men & 50% women. Unverifiable spring '98. ♀♂

JACKSON

■ Information
MISSISSIPPI GAY & LESBIAN ALLIANCE, (601) 371-3019.

■ Bars
JT'S, 425 North Mart Plaza, (601) 362-3108, 7 days, 5pm-2am. ♀♂
VILLAGE, THE, 208 W Capitol St, (601) 948-3366. Early crowd. ♂

■ Dance Bar/Disco
CLUB CITY LIGHTS, 220 W Amite, at Mill, (601) 353-0059. Dance & show bar open late. ♀♂
JACK'S & JILL'S, 2000 block of Capitol St, across from Mayflower Cafe, Separate men's & women's bars. ♀♂
POLLY ESTHER'S, 3911 Northview Dr, (601) 366-3247. Gay bar popular with straights, Wed-Thurs 8pm-2am, Fri-Sat 8pm-4am, shows Sun 8pm-2am, 50% gay, 50% straight. ♀♂

MERIDIAN

■ Dance Bar/Disco
CROSSROADS, Hwy 59 South, Savoy exit, (601) 655-8415. Complex with video dance bar, cruise bar, C&W bar, deli, 50% men, 50% women, patio. Unverifiable spring '98. ♀♂

OVETT

■ Information
SISTERSPIRIT, INC, 203 Eastside Dr, PO Box 12, Ovett, MS, (601) 344-1411 (tel/fax), sisterspir@aol.com. Women's cultural organization, camping OK, RV hookups, kitchen, meeting space, library. Women & men welcome to help us build. Looking for social justice, seeking people.

TUPELO

■ Dance Bar/Disco
RUMORS, 637 Hwy 145, in nearby town of Shannon, (601) 767-9500. Dance & show bar, women most welcome, Thurs-Sat 7pm-1am. ♂

MISSOURI

CAPE GIRARDEAU

■ Bars
INDEPENDENCE PLACE, 5 S Henderson, (573) 334-2939. DJ nitely, 50% men, 50% women, Mon-Thurs 8:30-1:30, Fri & Sat 7pm-1:30, closed Sun. ♀♂

COLUMBIA

■ Dance Bar/Disco
STYX, 3111 Old Hwy 63 S, (573) 499-1828. Mon-Sat 1pm-1am, live entertainment of all kinds, 50% men, 50% women. ♀♂

MISSOURI

■ Restaurants
ERNIE'S CAFE, 1005 E Walnut, (573) 874-7804. Gay-friendly restaurant popular with Columbia gay community. Breakfast anytime. American fare includes burgers, steaks, chops, chicken, & wide vegetarian selection. 6am-8pm.

■ Retail & Bookstores
PEACE NOOK, 804-C E. Broadway, (573) 875-0539. Has some gay merchandise.

JOPLIN

■ Dance Bar/Disco
PARTNERS DANCE BAR, 722 Main St (rear), near 8th, (417) 623-9313. 50% men, 50% women. Closed Sun.
PARTNERS WESTERN LOUNGE, 720 Main St (rear), (417) 781-6453. C&W dance bar, 50% men, 50% women. Closed Sun.

KANSAS CITY

ALSO INCLUDES KANSAS CITY, KS (913).,

■ Information
GAY TALK LINE, (816) 931-4470, 6pm-midnight 7 days.

■ Accommodations
DOANLEIGH INN, THE, 217 East 37th St, Kansas City, MO, 64111, (816) 753-2667, Fax: (816) 531-5185. B&B between Crown Center & Country Club Plaza, mainly straight clientele. Eclectic decor, full gourmet breakfast.
INN THE PARK BED & BREAKFAST, 3610 Gillham Rd, Kansas City, MO, 64111, (816) 931-0797, (800) 708-6748. B&B, 50% gay & lesbian clientele. Suites, private baths, full breakfast."

■ Women's Accommodations
B&B IN KC, 9215 Slater, Overland Park, MO, 66212, (913) 648-5457. B&B, men welcome. Color TV, private & shared baths, breakfast."

■ Bars
BLANCA'S, Grand near 11th, 50% men/women.
JAMIE'S, 528 Walnut St, at 6th, (816) 471-2080. Fun bar, men welcome, DJ Wed, Fri & Sat."
MARI'S, 1809 Grand, (816) 283-0511. Bar & restaurant, burgers to steaks & seafood.
MISSIE B'S, 805 W 39th St, (816) 561-0625. Karoake, drag show Mon, Wed, Fri, Sat. 80% men, 20% women.
OTHER SIDE, 3611 Broadway, (816) 931-0501. Video bar, closed Sun, 70% men, 30% women.
UBU, Grand near 14th, 60% women, 40% men, small dance floor, DJ Fri & Sat.
VIEW ON THE HILL, 204 Orchard St, in Kansas, (913) 371-9370. From 4pm, women welcome."

■ Dance Bar/Disco
ATLANTIS, 3954 Central, 753-0112. Gay Thurs only, 70% men, 30% women. Gay-friendly other times.
★ **CABARET,** 5024 Main St, near 50th St, (816) 753-6504. Dance & show bar, after hours till 3am Wed-Sun. 80% men, young preppie crowd.
SOAKIE'S, 1308 Main, (816) 221-6060. R&B, rap, etc., 50% men, 50% women.
TOOTSIES NEW PLACE, 1818-1822 Main St, (816) 471-7704. Dance bar with drag shows, dinner restaurant, noon-midnight, Fri & Sat till 3am.

■ Restaurants
CORNER, THE, Broadway & Westport Rd., Very popular gay-friendly Sat brunch.
LATE NIGHT CAFE, at the Cabaret bar, 5024 Main St, (816) 753-6504. Lite grill menu, dinner only.
MARI'S, 1809 Grand, at Mari's Bar, (816) 283-0511. Downstairs gay bar, upstairs restaurant.
SHARP'S 63RD ST GRILL, 128 W 63rd St, Brookside, (816) 333-4355.
TOOTSIE'S NEW PLACE, 1822 Main St, at Tootsie's bar, (816) 471-7704. Sandwiches days, dinner plates.

■ Retail & Bookstores
LARRY'S GIFTS & CARDS, 205 Westport Rd, (816) 753-4757. Gay & lesbian bookstore. Music, cards, t-shirts, magazines, etc.

■ Erotica
VIDEO MANIA, 208 Westport Rd, (816) 561-6397.

MISSOURI

Visit St. Louis (800) CARITAS
Caritas B&B Network

ST LOUIS

ALSO INCLUDES EAST ST LOUIS, IL (618).,

Information

GAY & LESBIAN ACTION LINE & HOTLINE, (314) 367-0084. 6pm-10pm Mon-Sat.

Accommodations

A ST. LOUIS GUESTHOUSE IN HISTORIC SOULARD, 1032-38 Allen Ave, St Louis, MO, 63104, (314) 773-1016. Of our 8 apartments, 3 are available as guest suites. Each has 2 large rooms, phone, private bath, AC, wet bar with refrigerator and a private entrance opening onto a pleasant courtyard with hot tub. If your visit to St. Louis is for business or pleasure, please consider us your home away from home. A gay bar and restaurant are next door. Women welcome. Cancellation policy: 48 hours in advance. ♂

A ST. LOUIS GUESTHOUSE
In Historic Soulard
St. Louis MO.
(314) 773-1016

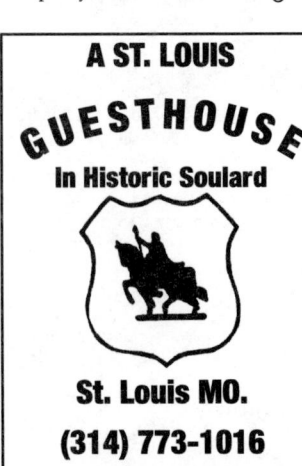

BREWERS HOUSE BED & BREAKFAST, 1829 Lami Street, St. Louis, MO, 63104, (314) 771-1542. B&B, minutes to downtown, the Arch & river. Rooms with unusual decor, some fireplaces. Jacuzzi, continental breakfast, coffee. ♀♂

CARITAS BED & BREAKFAST NETWORK, (800) CARITAS, (312) 857-0801, Fax: (312) 857-0805. B&B, home-stay accommodations service. Member: IGLTA

LAFAYETTE HOUSE BED & BREAKFAST, 2156 Lafayette Ave, St Louis, MO, (314) 772-4429, (800) 641-8965, Fax: (314) 664-2156. Web: http://www.bbonline.com/mo/lafayette/, Gay-friendly B&B with a gay & lesbian following, minutes from downtown, private & shared baths, full breakfast, phone, AC, Jacuzzi.

NAPOLEON'S RETREAT BED & BREAKFAST, 1815 Lafayette Ave, St Louis, MO, 63104, (314) 772-6979, (800) 700-9980. B&B, 50% gay & lesbian clientele. Color TV, AC, ceiling fans, double or queen beds, private baths. Full breakfast, no smoking.

Bars

★ **ALIBI'S,** 3016 Arsenal, (314) 772-8989. Bar & restaurant, shows Fri & sat, patio bar. ♀♂

CHAR-PEI LOUNGE, 400 Mascoutah Ave near E Main, Belleville, IL, (618) 236-0810. Tues-Sun, 6pm-2am, 70% men, 30% women.

CLUB 747, 1624 Delmar, (314) 621-9030. Show bar. ♀♂

DRAKE'S, 3502 Papin, near Grand & Chouteau, (314) 865-1400. Piano bar. ♀♂

GREY FOX PUB, 3503 S Spring, near Grand, (314) 772-2150. Bar & restaurant, patio bar in summer, shows Fri & Sat. ♀♂

LIL'S SECOND TIME AROUND, 317 Mascoutah Ave, Belleville, IL, (618) 233-9425. 50% men, 50% women. ♀♂

★ **LOADING ZONE,** 16 S Euclid, (314) 361-4119. Video bar, happy hour big girl cocktails, younger crowd, 50% men, 50% women. From 2pm, closed Sun. ♀♂

MISSOURI 365

★ **MAGNOLIA'S,** 5 S Vandeventer, (314) 652-6500. Complex with large dance bar, restaurant, cruise bar, leather bar & quiet bar. Women welcome. 🏨 💛 🗐 📺 ✖ ♂

MUSTANG SALLY'S, 408 N Euclid, (314) 367-8887. 🎰 ♀♂

NOVAK'S, 4146 Manchester Rd, (314) 531-3699. Bar & grill. ♀

RAINBOW'S END, 4060 Chouteau, (314) 652-8790. 🎰 ♂

VELVET LOUNGE, 1301 Washington St, (314) 241-2997. 🗐 🎵 🏨 ♂

VICTORIAN, THE, 1449 S Vandeventer, (314) 535-6969. Preppie cocktail lounge. 🎵 ♀♂

■ *Dance Bar/Disco*

★ **ATTITUDES,** 4100 Manchester, (314) 534-3858. Large dance bar, many men Fri for C&W night. 🏨 ✖ ♀

CLUB NERO'S, Sarah Ave., 🍴 🏨 ♀♂

ERNIE'S CLASS ACT, 3576 S Broadway, (314) 664-6221. Informal restaurant & cabaret, live bands, comedy, etc. Closed Sun." 🏨 🎵 ✖ ♀

FACES, 130 4th St (entrance), E St Louis, IL, in E. St Louis, MO, (618) 271-7410. Complex with dance & video bar, cruise bar, show bar. More popular 3am-7am weekends, very popular Sun. Down & Under leather bar downstairs. Women welcome. 🏨 🎵 💛 📺 ♂

★ **MAGNOLIA'S,** 5 S Vandeventer, (314) 652-6500. Complex with large dance bar, restaurant, leather cruise bar & cabaret. Women welcome." 🏨 💛 🗐 📺 ✖ 🎵 ♂

■ *Restaurants*

ANGLES, 3511 Chouteau, at The Complex., American cuisine. Dinner, Sun brunch." 🍷 ♀♂

BALABAN'S, 405 N Euclid, (314) 361-8085. Lunch, dinner, Sun brunch. 🖼

MAJESTIC, 49 W Laclede at Euclid, (314) 361-2011. Very popular diner. 🖼

NINER DINER, 5 S Vandeventer, at Magnolia's, (314) 652-0171. Restaurant & domino parlour. Mostly gay & lesbian crowd. 🖼

ONCE UPON A TIME, Grand at Arsenal.,

SOUTH CITY DINER, 3141 S Grand, (314) 772-6100. Popular diner open 24hrs, very gay-friendly. 🖼

SUNSHINE INN, 8-1/2 S Euclid Ave, (314) 367-1413. Lunch, dinner, Sun brunch, vegetarian menu." 🖼 🏠

■ *Retail & Bookstores*

CHEAP TRX, 3211 S Grand, (314) 644-4011. Good selection of gay & lesbian cards, gifts, boutique items.

FRIENDS & LOVERS, 3550 Gravois Ave, at Grand, (314) 771-9405. Gay & lesbian novelty store.

LEFT BANK BOOKS & LEFT BANK COFFEE, 399 N Euclid Ave, at McPherson, (314) 367-6731. General bookstore & coffeeshop, extensive lesbian & gay section, 10am-10pm (Sun till 5pm). Coffeeshop: from 7am (Sun from 9am).

OUR WORLD TOO, 11 S Vandeventer, (314) 533-5322, (888) 806-5968. Not just a gay and lesbian bookstore anymore! Now, we have a great selection of gifts, music, safer-sex supplies, rainbow items, calendars, tee shirts, pink or black triangle items, awareness pins and pendants, a large AIDS selection, video rentals, magazines, travel guides, women's and feminist titles. Ask for our extensive catalog.

PAGES, VIDEO & MORE, 10 N Euclid Ave, near Laclede, (314) 361-3420. Book & video rental store with large section of gay magazines, cards, books.

Our World Too
Community Book & Gift Shop
Your Gay & Lesbian Pride Shop
EXTENSIVE CATALOG

Call or write for catalog. Also ask for our FREE St Louis Map-Directory if you are planning a visit

11 S. Vandeventer Ave.
St. Louis, MO 63108-3221
(314) 533-5322
FAX: (314) 772-7834
Orders: 888-806-5968
eMail: ourwrldtoo@aol.com

366 MISSOURI

WHIZ BAM!, 3206 S Grand, (314) 664-3663. Gay & lesbian movies, videos, magazines. Mon-Thur noon-9pm, Fri & Sat noon-10pm, Sun noon-7pm.

SPRINGFIELD

■ Dance Bar/Disco

EDGE, 424 N Boonville, (417) 831-4700. Dance floor & video bar with patio. 🕸 ♀♂

MARTHA'S VINEYARD, 219 W Olive St, near Campbell, (417) 864-4572. DJ Fri, Sat, summer patio with outdoor dance floor. Open 7 days, 5pm-1:30am, Sun till midnite. Shows Tues & Sun.
🕸 ♀♂

XANADU, 1107 Commercial, (417) 866-8105. Dance & show bar. 🎵 🕸 ♀♂

MONTANA
BILLINGS

■ Retail & Bookstores

BARJON'S, 2718 3rd Ave North, (406) 252-4398. Alternative bookstore, carries gay guides.

BOZEMAN

■ Information

WOMEN'S RESOURCE CENTER, Rm 15 Hamilton Hall, Montana St Univ, (406) 994-3836. Referrals to local lesbian community, Mon-Fri 9am-4pm."

■ Accommodations

FISH CREEK LODGING, See Jackson, Wyoming.,

LEHRKIND MANSION BED & BREAKFAST, 719 North Wallace Ave, Bozeman, MT, 59715, (406) 585-6932 (Tel/Fax) call before faxing, (800) 992-6932." Email: lehrkindmansion@imt.net, Web: http://www.imt.net/~lehrkindmansion/index.htm, Gay-friendly 1897 Queen Anne mansion with private baths, gourmet breakfast, down comforters, antiques, therapeutic hot tub. Gay & lesbian following.

BUTTE

■ Accommodations

SKOOKUM MOTEL, 3541 Harrison Ave, Butte, MT, 59701, (406) 494-2153, Fax: (406) 723-4601. Email: larryr@buttenet.com, Motel with restaurant, bar & casino, private baths. ♀♂

■ Bars

SILVER DOLLAR, Main at Mercury, (406) 782-7367. NOT A GAY BAR! Discreetly frequented by some gays & lesbians. 🕸

SNOOKUMS AT THE SKOOKUM, 3541 Harrison Ave, at the Skookum Motel, where I-15 meets I-95, (406) 494-5353. Butte's "gayest" bar, casino & restaurant, 80% gay in evenings. Restaurant is a nice little place to eat, coffee shop & dinner items. In summer there's outside dining on a deck.

MISSOULA

■ Information

AIDS HOTLINE, (406) 523-4775."
LAMBDA ASSOC, (406) 523-5567. Group meets at University of Montana.
WOMEN'S RESOURCE CENTER, UC 210, U of M, (406) 243-4153. Mon-Fri 10am-3pm, except summer.

■ Accommodations

FOXGLOVE COTTAGE, 2331 Gilbert Ave, Missoula, MT, 59802, (406) 543-2927. Gay-owned & -operated B&B with, private & shared bath, continental breakfast, near downtown. Some straight clientele. 🛏 ♀♂

■ Dance Bar/Disco

AM-VETS CLUB, 225 Ryman, (406) 543-9174. Open noon-2am, 7 days, gay disco Thurs-Sat, friendly crowd.
🕸 🎵 ✖ ♀♂

■ Cafe

CATALYST ESPRESSO, 111 N Higgins, (406) 542-1337. Mon-Fri 7am-6pm, Sat 8am-6pm, Sun 10am-5pm. Games, magazines, progressive crowd, more gays later. Some extended hours during special gay/lesbian events. 🕸

■ Retail & Bookstores

FREDDY'S FEED AND READ, 1221 Helen Ave, (406) 549-2127. Deli with organic food & bookstore with small, good selection of gay & lesbian titles. 🕸

UNIVERSITY CENTER BOOKSTORE, Campus Dr, University of Montana, (406) 243-4921. Good selection of gay & lesbian books.

RONAN

Accommodations
NORTH CROW RANCH, 2360 North Crow Rd, Ronan, MT, 59864, (406) 676-5169. Guesthouse & campground, shared showers & toilets. ♀♂

YELLOWSTONE NATIONAL PARK AREA

Accommodations
BAR N RANCH, PO Box 127, West Yellowstone, MT, 59758, (406) 646-7229 (Tel/Fax), (800) BIG-SKYS (244-7597). Guest ranch with some gay-only weeks, private baths, Jacuzzi, meals included. Mostly straight with a gay & lesbian following.

YELLOWSTONE RIVERVIEW LODGE B & B, 186 East River Road, Emigrant, MT, 59027, (406) 848-2156, (888) 848-2550. Email: riverview@imt.net, Web: http://www.wtp.net/go/riverview, Gay-owned B&B in a hand-hwen log home, minutes from Yellowstone Nat'l Park. Private & shared baths, full breakfast, camping in 1 teepee on premises.

NEBRASKA

KEARNEY

Information
GLAGN (GAY & LESBIAN ASSOC.), rdevel@itec.net. Dances, socials.

LINCOLN

Information
AIDS INFO, (402) 484-8100. '
GAY & LESBIAN RESOURCE CENTER & LINE, (402) 472-5644.
WOMEN'S CENTER, UNL Union Room 340, 14th & R Sts, (402) 472-2597.

Dance Bar/Disco
PANIC, 200 S 18th St, at N St, (402) 435-8764. Dance bar with patio, live bands, male & femal strippers. 4pm-1am, Sat & Sun 1pm-1am. ♀♂

Q, 226 S 9th St, (402) 475-2269. Large, progressive, late-nite dance club, patio. Shows some Sun, occasional bands, male strippers, game area with pool table & darts, good mix of men & women. Opens 8pm. ♀♂

OMAHA

ALSO INCLUDES COUNCIL BLUFFS, IA (712).,

Information
AIDS INFO, (402) 342-4233.
GAY & LESBIAN INFORMATION LINE, (402) 341-0330.

Bars
DIAMOND BAR, 712 S 16th St, near Leavenworth, (402) 342-9595, 7 days. ♂

GILLIGAN'S PUB, 1407 Harney, (402) 449-9147. Bowling leagues. ♀♂

Dance Bar/Disco
★ **CHESTERFIELD,** 1901 Leavenworth, (402) 345-6889. Juke box dance bar, DJ Thurs-Sat. ♀♂

★ **CLUB JAMES DEAN,** 1507 Farnham, (402) 341-2500. Large club with 3 rooms, large dance floor. ♀

DC'S, 610 S 14th, near Pacific, (402) 344-3103. C&W dance bar. ♀♂

★ **MAX & STOSH'S SALOON, THE,** 1417 Jackson, at 15th, (402) 346-4110. Hi-energy video dance bar, game room, patio bar, male dancers, Stosh's leather cruise bar is inside, 60% men, 40% women. ♀♂

Cafe
DOWNTOWN GROUND, 1117 Jackson St, in Old Market, Omaha, (402) 342-1654. Coffeehouse, juice bar, food & entertainment.

Retail & Bookstores
NEW REALITIES, 1026 Howard St, near 11th, (402) 342-1863. General bookstore with gay & lesbian section, gifts. Music, new age, recovery & self-help.

SCOTTSBLUFF

Information
PANHANDLE GAY & LESBIAN SUPPORT & SERVICES, Box 1046, Scottsbluff, NE, (308) 635-8488.

NEVADA

LAKE TAHOE

SEE LAKE TAHOE AREA, CA,

LAS VEGAS

■ Information

AIDS HOTLINE, (702) 474-2437 OR (800) 842-AIDS, in Spanish (800) 344-7432.

GAY & LESBIAN COMMUNITY CENTER, 912 E Sahara, (702) 733-9800, 10am-8:30pm, Sat 12pm-8pm, Sun 12pm-6pm.

■ Accommodations

LAS VEGAS PRIVATE BED & BREAKFAST, Las Vegas, NV, (702) 384-1129 (Tel/Fax). My home features a unique European decor with lots of amenities. Tropical plants and trees surround the pool area. Futher back are aviaries, with tropical birds and parrots. Las Vegas has 24-hr entertainment. Other activities: desert sightseeing, water sports on Lake Mead, Grand Canyon tours, Laughlin excursions, winter skiing, and hiking to hot springs along the Colorado River.

■ Bars

★ **ANGLES 'N LACE,** 4633 Paradise Rd, at Naples, (702) 791-0100. Video & dance bar, ladies nite Thurs, 24hrs.

CHOICES, 1729 E Charleston, (702) 382-4791. Game room, slots, women welcome, 24hrs.

KEYS, 1000 E Sahara, (702) 731-2200. Piano bar.

SPOTLIGHT LOUNGE, 957 E Sahara, enter from Commercial Center, (702) 696-0202. 24hrs, slots, pool table.

TROPICAL ISLAND, 3430 E Tropicana, (702) 456-5525.

■ Dance Bar/Disco

★ **BACKSTREET BAR,** 5012 S Arville, (702) 876-1844. C&W dance bar, 50% men, 50% women, beer bust 2 days a week, dance lessons.

FLEX, 4371 W Charleston Blvd, (702) 385-FLEX. Bar, disco, strippers, drag shows, 24hrs. Tues women's nite.

FREE ZONE, 610 E Naples, (702) 794-2300. Dance bar & restaurant, DJ nitely.

★ **GIPSY,** 4605 Paradise Rd, at Naples, (702) 731-1919. Dance & show bar, strip shows, slots, 10pm, 50% men, 50% women.

■ Cafe

MARIPOSA CAFE, 4643 S Paradise, (702) 650-9009.

■ Restaurants

FREE ZONE, 610 E Naples, (702) 794-2300. Elegant restaurant & dance bar.

■ Retail & Bookstores

GET BOOKED, 4640 Paradise Rd, (702) 737-7780. Gay, lesbian & feminist bookstore with music, video rentals, cards & t-shirts, rainbow items.

RENO

■ Bars

CLUB 1099, 1099 S Virginia St, at Caliente, (702) 329-1099. videos, 24hrs, patio, pool table, slots, darts.

FIVE STAR SALOON, 132 West St, near 1st, (702) 329-2878. DJ weekends. Slots, 24hrs.

NEW BAR (NO NAME AT PRESS TIME), 600 W 5th, (702) 323-6565. Outdoor deck, darts, pool table, 60% women, 40% men.

LAS VEGAS PRIVATE Bed & Breakfast

LUCKY YOU!

(702) 384-1129

QUEST, THE, 210 W Commercial Row, (702) 333-2808. DJ Fri & Sat, slots.

Dance Bar/Disco
BAD DOLLY'S, 535 E 4th St, near Valley, (702) 348-1983. Slots, top 40's, darts, pool table, Thurs C&W, Wed Bra nite, 80% women.

Retail & Bookstores
SILVER SAGE, 1557 S Virginia St, (702) 348-0022. Metaphysical bookstore with small women's section.

Erotica
FANTASY FAIRE, 1298 S Virginia St, (702) 323-6969. A boutique for lovers. Leather, toys, cards, gifts, lotions & potions.

STATELINE
SEE LAKE TAHOE AREA, CA,

NEW HAMPSHIRE
STATEWIDE
Information
AIDS INFO LINE, (800) 752-AIDS.

ASHLAND
Accommodations
COUNTRY OPTIONS, 27-29 N Main St, Ashland, NH, 03217, (603) 968-7958. B&B in a warm country style, furnished with antiques. Shared baths, mountain views, full breakfast. 50% gay & lesbian clientele.

BETHLEHEM
Women's Accommodations
HIGHLANDS INN, THE, Box 118, Valley View Lane, Bethlehem, NH, 03574, (603) 869-3978. **The North Country's only lesbian-owned and -operated inn.** B&B inn on 100 acres. **A Lesbian paradise** with 20 comfortable rooms wtih excellent views, antique furnishings, private & shared baths, TV lounge, kitchen privileges, library, heated pool, BBQ grills, hot tub, hiking, skiing and full breakfast, spectacular sunsets. Rates $55-$110, weeklong & midweek discounts. Winner 1995, '96, '97 Out & About Editor's Choice Awards. Our sign always says "no vacancy" so please ignore it. Non-smoking rooms.

CENTRE HARBOR
Accommodations
RED HILL INN, RFD #1, Box 99M, Centre Harbor, NH, 03226, (603) 279-7001. Email: info@redhill.com, Web: www.redhill.com, Gay-friendly inn with bar and restaurant. Variety of guest quarters with comfortable antique furniture, some Jacuzzis, some fireplaces. TV lounge, full breakfast, nearby lake.

CONCORD
Accommodations
WHITE RABBIT INN & CATERING, 62 Main St, Allenstown, NH, 03275, (603) 485-9494, (888) 216-9485, Fax: (603) 485-

---

a Lesbian Paradise

The Highlands Inn

100 Secluded Acres
Pool • Hot Tub • Trails

P.O. Box 118-I
Valley View Lane
Bethlehem, NH 03574

(603) 869-3978

Winner Out & About Editor's Choice
Award 1995,96&97

9522. Email: scott@whtrabbit.com, Web: www.whtrabbit.com, B&B inn in a brick Georgian mansion, 20 min. south of Concord. Private & shared baths, expanded or full continental breakfast, banquet & catering facilities. 50% gay/lesbian clientele.

FRANCONIA

■ Accommodations
BLANCHE'S B & B, Easton Valley Rd, Franconia, NH, 03580, (603) 823-7061. Email: shannon@ncia.net, Gay-friendly B&B, shared baths, home-cooked breakfasts."

BUNGAY JAR, PO Box 15, Easton Valley Rd, Franconia, NH, 03580, (603) 823-7775, (800) 421-0701, Fax: (603) 444-0100. Email: info@bungayjar.com, Web: www.bungayjar.com, Not a neighbor is visible from our private balconies. We're off the beaten path, yet near all major White Mountain attractions. Walk through the woods to a hidden stream. Meditate by the water lily pond. Relax in the library, the sauna or by the fireplace. Breakfast specialties. New Garden Suite: king bed, fireplace, 2-person Jacuzzi, kitchen/dining area, porch & mountain view. Non-smoking environment. Gay-friendly.

HORSE & HOUND INN, THE, 205 Wells Rd, Franconia, NH, 03580, (603) 823-5501, (800) 450-5501. Gay-friendly B&B inn with restaurant & lounge. Private & shared baths, TV lounge, full breakfast & nearby lake. Gay male following."

HART'S LOCATION

■ Accommodations
NOTCHLAND INN, THE, Hart's Location, NH, 03812-9999, Reservations: (800) 866-6131 or (603) 374-6131, Fax: (603) 374-6168. Email: notchland@aol.com, Gay-friendly inn with restaurant. Private baths, full breakfast, dinner, spa, river on premisis. No smoking environment."

KEENE

■ Accommodations
POST AND BEAM BED & BREAKFAST, HCR 33, Box 380, Centre St, Sullivan, NH, 03445, (603) 847-3330, (888) 3 ROMANCE, Fax: (603) 847-3306. Email: postandbeam@top.monad.net, Web: http://www.nhweb.com/postandbeam/, Gay-owned B&B with gay & straight clientele, 12 min from Keene, 30 min from Brattleboro. Private & shared baths, full or continental breakfast.

MANCHESTER

■ Dance Bar/Disco
CLUB MERRIMAC, 201 Merrimac, near Pine, (603) 623-9362. Private club."

FRONT RUNNER, 1st St, near Elm behind Northend Supererete, (603) 623-6477. Huge dance bar.

THE 313, 313 Lincoln St, Live bands.

NASHUA

■ Information
GAY INFO LINE, (603) 224-1686.

NEWFOUND LAKE

■ Accommodations
CLIFF LODGE COTTAGES, Route 3A HC60, Box 199, Bristol, NH, 03222, (603) 744-8660. Old-style rustic cottages next to main house, bar & restaurant, gay & lesbian following.

INN ON NEWFOUND LAKE, THE, Rt 3A, Bridgewater, NH, 03222, (603) 744-9111, (800) 745-7990, Fax: (603) 744-3894. Email: inonlk@cyberportal.net, Victorian inn on the lake, restaurant & tavern on premises. Private beach, boat dock, exercise room & Jacuzzi. Mostly straight clientele with a gay male following, 2 hrs from Boston.

PORTSMOUTH

■ Accommodations
PAYNE'S HILL B & B, 141 Henry Law Ave, Dover, NH, (603) 740-9441 (Tel/Fax). B&B in a restored New Englander, walking distance to downtown Dover, 12-min drive from central Portsmouth, 3 rooms share baths, expanded continental breakfast. 50% gay/lesbian clientele.

■ Dance Bar/Disco
CLUB ONE NORTH, 948 Rte 1 Bypass in Portsmouth, 3/4 mile outside Portsmouth, (603) 431-5400. Disco, Wed-Sun

NEW JERSEY

8pm-1am. Wed men's nite, Thurs karaoke.

RANDOLPH

Accommodations
INN AT BOWMAN A B & B, THE, Rte 2, Randolph, NH, 03570, (603) 466-5006." Gay-owned B&B guesthouse inn with 5 rooms & suites, private & shared baths, color TV, AC, expanded continental or buffet breakfast, Jacuzzi.

NEW JERSEY STATEWIDE

Information
AIDS HOTLINE, (800) 281-2437. NJ State Dept of Health, Aids Education.

Dance Bar/Disco
LADIES 2000, (609) 784-8341. Scheduled women's dance parties throughout NJ and nearby PA.

ASBURY PARK

Information
GAY & LESBIAN COMMUNITY CENTER OF NJ, 626 Bangs Ave, (732) 774-1809. 7pm-10pm Mon-Fri.

Bars
BOND ST BAR, 208 Bond St, near Cookman, (732) 776-9766. Men welcome.

Dance Bar/Disco
DOWN THE STREET, 230 Cookman Ave, (732) 988-2163. Dance & show bar, male dancers Wed, women welcome. Outdoor deck in summer."
WOMEN'S BAR, at Down the Street, A separate back bar for women inside the dance bar. Dance floor is shared.

ATLANTIC CITY

Accommodations
ROSE'S COTTAGE, 161 Westminster Ave, Atlantic City, NJ, 08401, (609) 345-8196. Guesthouse. Doubles or singles with shared baths, TV lounge & nearby ocean beach."
SURFSIDE RESORT HOTEL, 10-18 S. Mt. Vernon Avenue, Atlantic City, NJ, 08401, (609) 347-SURF (7873), (888) 277-SURF (7873). Web: www.studiosix.com, Resort complex with restaurant, grill, bars, cabaret, dance club & sun deck. Heated pool, private & shared baths, women welcome.

Bars
REFLECTIONS LOUNGE, South Carolina, at Boardwalk, (609) 348-1115. Pool tables & video machines.

Dance Bar/Disco
★ **STUDIO SIX DANCE CLUB,** 12 S Mount Vernon, above the Brass Rail bar, (609) 348-3310. Progressive, hi-energy video dance bar, 70% men, 30% women. Top entertainment, frequent stars, balcony bar, custom sound, 10pm-8am.

Restaurants
BRASS RAIL KITCHEN, at Brass Rail, 12 South Mt Vernon, (609) 348-3310. Dinner only.

HOBOKEN

Dance Bar/Disco
EXCALIBUR 2001, 1000 Jefferson St, at 10th St, (201) 795-1023. NY-style dance bar 3 min from Manhattan, Tiki Bar is outdoor patio bar. Open Thurs-Sun 9pm-2am, Fri & Sat 9pm-3am, Fri Noche Latina, drag show 1am, Sat Pulse Latin & house music.

JEFFERSON

Dance Bar/Disco
YACHT CLUB, 5190 Berkshire Valley Rd, (973) 697-9780. Large bar, male & female dancers Wed & Sat, 60% men, 40% women.

LONG BRANCH

Dance Bar/Disco
PHARAOHS, 115 Ocean Ave, Long Branch, (732) 870-6336. Open Fri-Sun.

LYNDHURST

Bars
LA CAFE & PIANO LOUNGE, 198 Stuyvesant Ave, (201) 933-2151. Piano Fri & Sat.

NEW JERSEY

MAYS LANDING

Dance Bar/Disco
INTERLUDE LOUNGE, 5045 Black Horse Pike, near Hamilton Mall, (609) 625-9487. From 8pm. Unverifiable spring '97.

MORRISTOWN

Information
GAY ACTIVIST ALLIANCE, (973) 285-1595. Helpline nightly 7:30pm-10:30pm or tape.

NEW BRUNSWICK - SOMERSET

Information
PRIDE CENTER OF NEW JERSEY, 211 Livingston Ave, (908) 846-CCDC (2232), 7pm-10pm, Tues 11am-1pm.

Dance Bar/Disco
DEN, 700 Hamilton St, Somerset, (908) 545-7329. Huge dance floor, beer bar & cafe, billiard room.

Restaurants
FROG & THE PEACH, 29 Dennis St, (908) 846-3216. Restaurant & bar, late-night menu.

STAGE LEFT BAR & RESTAURANT, 5 Livingston Ave, (908) 828-4444. Gay-friendly bar. Many gays & lesbians late Fri & Sat (after midnight) after gay bars close.

NEWARK - ORANGE

ALSO INCLUDES EAST ORANGE.,

Dance Bar/Disco
MURPHY'S, 59 Edison Pl, near Mulberry, (973) 622-9176. Lunch service, gay eves only. 60% men, 40% women."

PENSAUKEN

Retail & Bookstores
GENERAL STORE, THE, Rts 130 & 73, Gay pride merchandise.

PERTH AMBOY

Bars
OTHER HALF, corner of Convery Blvd (Rte 35) & Kennedy St, (908) 826-8877. DJ Fri & Sat, 85% men, women welcome.

PLAINFIELD

Accommodations
PILLARS OF PLAINFIELD BED & BREAKFAST, THE, 922 Central Ave, Plainfield, NJ, 07060-2311, (908) 753-0922 (Tel/Fax), (888) PILLARS (745-5277). Email: Pillars2@juno.com, Web: http://bestinns.net/usa/nj/rdpillars.html, B&B with RV hookup, 50% gay & lesbian clientele. AC, private baths, TV lounge, expanded continental breakfast & kitchen privileges."

RED BANK

Retail & Bookstores
EARTH SPIRIT, 16 W Front St, (908) 842-3855. New Age center & bookstore. Feminist literature, gay & lesbian studies.

RIVER EDGE

Dance Bar/Disco
★ FEATHERS, 77 Kinderkamack Rd, (201) 342-6410. Two floors, different music each night. Male dancers Fri, drag shows Tues, Wed oldies, Thurs shows & Latin nite, Sun show. Women welcome.

SAYREVILLE

Dance Bar/Disco
COLISEUM, Rt 9 N at 35 N, (732) 316-0670.
SAUVAGE - PLAYERS, Rte 35 - 1 Bridge Plaza, (732) 727-6619. Bands & singers, comedians, female dancers.

SOMERDALE

Dance Bar/Disco
GALAXY, 5 E Somerdale (White Horse Pike), (609) 435-0888. 8pm-3am Tues-Sun, Sun drag shows, Tues ladies nite, Wed oldies & karaoke, Fri & Sat hi energy techno dance.

SOMERSET

SEE NEW BRUNSWICK/SOMERSET,

TRENTON

Dance Bar/Disco
BUDDIES' PUB, 677 S Broad St, (609) 989-8566. DJ Fri & Sat, 50% men, 50% women. Moving Oct '98 to cnr of S Broadway & Hudson, will become a cafe. ⚧♪♀♂

WOODBURY

Information
RAINBOW PLACE OF SOUTH JERSEY, 1103 N Broad St, (609) 848-2455. Let phone ring.

NEW MEXICO
ALBUQUERQUE

Information
COMMON BOND G&L COMMUNITY CTR, (505) 891-3647. Helpline usually answers 6pm-9pm or tape.

WOMEN'S CENTER, 1160 Mesa Vista Hall, at the U of NM, (505) 277-3716. 8am-5pm, closed Sat, Sun.

Accommodations
BRITTANIA AND W. E. MAUGER ESTATE B & B, 701 Roma Ave NW, Albuquerque, NM, 87102, (505) 242-8755, (800) 719-9189, Fax: (505) 842-8835. Web: http://www.thuntek.net/tc_arts/mauger, B&B inn, 50% gay & lesbian. Variety of Victorian-style rooms with modern conveniences, TV lounge & full breakfast. Catering available, nearby river.

CASITAS AT OLD TOWN, THE, 1604 Old Town Rd NW, Albuquerque, NM, (505) 843-7479. Suites with private entrances. Private baths, AC, kitchen, refrigerator, coffee/tea-making facilities & fireplace. Minutes from Old Town." ♀♂

GOLDEN GUESTHOUSES, 2645 Decker NW, Albuquerque, NM, 87107, (888) 513-GOLD (513-4653), (505) 344-9205, Fax: (505) 344-3434. Email: GoldenGH@aol.com, Web: http://www.highfiber.com/~goldengh/, Two casitas with private bath, continental breakfast, minutes from Old Town Plaza, 1 block from Rio Grande Nature Preserve. Some straight clientele. ♀♂

HACIENDA ANTIGUA BED AND BREAKFAST, 6708 Tierra Dr NW, Albuquerque, NM, 87107, (505) 345-5399, (800) 201-2986. Web: www.haciendantigua.com/bnb/, Gay-friendly B&B in a 200-year-old adobe hacienda in the north valley residential area of Albuquerque. Fireplace & private bath in every room.

HATEFUL MISSY & GRANNY BUTCH'S BOUDOIR & MANURE EMPORIUM, PO Box 556, Veguita, NM, 87062, (800) 397-2482, (505) 861-3328. B&B with Granny Butch's Genital Store & Art Gallery, men very welcome. Color cable TV, VCR, video tape library, ceiling fans, private baths, full breakfast. ⚧ ♀

El Peñasco
PLACITAS, NM

**Historic adobe house nestled in the mountains between Albuquerque and Santa Fe.
Enjoy quiet charm and privacy. Women-owned.**

- kiva fireplace in bedroom, kitchen stocked with breakfast foods, private patio
- sleeps 1-4, $75-95, weekly rates available

Call (888) 576-2726
or (505) 771-8909

e mail: stormie p@aol.com

NEW MEXICO

RAINBOW LODGE BED & BREAKFAST, THE, 115 Frost Rd, Sandia Park, NM, 87047, (505) 281-7100. Email: rainbowbed@aol.com, B&B located between Albuquerque & Santa Fe, private & shared baths, expanded continental breakfast, color cable TV, VCR, ceiling fans, outdoor hot tub, 50% gay/lesbian clientele.

RIO GRANDE HOUSE, 3100 Rio Grande Blvd NW, Albuquerque, NM, 87107, (505) 345-0120 or (505) 344-9463. Email: nmypinon@aol.com, Gay-friendly B&B 3 miles from Old Town. Single & double rooms with southwestern flavor & exotic collectibles, modern conveniences, full breakfast.

TARA COTTA, 3118 Rio Grande Blvd NW, Albuquerque, NM, 87107, (505) 344-9443 (Tel/Fax). B&B guesthouse, private bath, continental breakfast, color cable TV, VCR, swamp cooler, ceiling fans, hot tub, 50% gay/lesbian clientele.

W. J. MARSH HOUSE VICTORIAN B & B, THE, 301 Edith SE, Albuquerque, NM, 87102-3532, (505) 247-1001, Toll-free: (888) WJ MARSH (956-2774). Gay-friendly B&B inn with separate Victorian cottage & 2 in-house ghosts. Private & shared baths, AC, full gourmet breakfast in house. Cottage has full kitchen, color cable TV & ceiling fans. 50% gay & lesbian clientele.

■ Women's Accommodations

EL PEÑASCO, PO Box 846, Placitas, NM, 87043, (505) 771-8909, (888) 576-2726. Email: stormie p@aol.com, Enjoy the history & charm of New Mexico in this 1-bedroom casita nestled in the mountains, midway between Albuquerque & Santa Fe. The adobe house features a kiva fireplace in the bedroom, bath with shower & tub, cable TV & a fully equipped kitchen which we stock with breakfast foods. Shopping, casinos, hiking & biking are 10 minutes away. Prefer women only, but men welcome. ♀ See ad on page 373.

■ Bars

ALBUQUERQUE SOCIAL CLUB, 4021 Central Ave NE, (505) 255-0887. Private club, 80% men. The Cheers of Albuquerque."

MARTINI GRILLE, 4100 Central Ave SE, (505) 255-4111. Gay- & cigar-friendly martini & piano bar & restaurant, 4pm-2am, pasta, gourmet chicken dishes, steaks, very gay-frienly.

■ Dance Bar/Disco

★ **ALBUQUERQUE MINING CO (AMC),** 7209 Central Ave NE, at Chama, (505) 255-0925. Four bars, including The Pit, a levi/leather bar, a patio bar, open all year. We have something for everyone. All bars open at 3pm 7 days a week. 70% men, 30% women.

LEGENDS WEST, 6132 4th St NW, (505) 343-9793.

★ **PULSE,** 4100 Central Ave SE, (505) 255-3334. Alternative club, young crowd, go go boys, DJs, Tues-Sun 8pm-2am, 50% gay/lesbian.

■ Cafe

DOUBLE RAINBOW, 3415 Central SE, (505) 255-6633. Gay-friendly coffeeshop/lunch cafe.

■ Retail & Bookstores

FULL CIRCLE BOOKS, 2205 Silver Ave SE, near Yale, (505) 266-0022. Women's, gay men's & lesbian books, jewelry, music, t-shirts. Lesbian meetings.

SISTERS' & BROTHERS' BOOKSTORE, 4011 Silver Ave SE, (505) 266-7317. Lesbian, gay and bisexual bookstore.

■ Leathers/Piercing

LEATHER SHOPPE, THE, 4217 Central NE, (505) 266-6690. Largest selection of erotic leather for men & women in the Southwest. Sun-Thu noon-10pm. Fri-Sat noon-2am.

■ Erotica

CASTLE SUPERSTORE, 5110 Central Ave SE, (505) 262-2266, (800) 344-9076. Large selection of gay books, magazines, videos, and much, much more. Open 365 days a year.

CHIMAYO

■ Accommodations

CASA ESCONDIDA, PO Box 142, Chimayo, NM, 87522, (505) 351-4805, (800) 643-7201, Fax: (505) 351-2575. B&B on 6 acres, 8 rooms with all private baths, full breakfast, hot tub, American Mission-style furniture. Town of Chimayo is famous for weaving. 50%

CASTLE SUPERSTORES®

(800) 344-9076

Visit Our New Website:
www.castlesuperstores.com

America's Safer Sex Superstores® Because We Care®

- Video Sales • Video Rentals • Playful Greeting & Post Cards • Leather Goods & Apparel • Restraints • Latex Garments • Rubber Goods • Wildest Selection of Adult Toys • Gag Gifts • Novelties • Games • Condoms • Lubes • Books & Magazines • T-Shirts • Whips & Chains • Wrapping Papers • Calendars • Novels • Sensual Oils • Sexy Lingerie & more & more ...

OPEN 365 DAYS
Rediscover America's Favorite Pastime

(505) 262-2266
5110 Central Ave. S.E.
Albuquerque, NM 87108

ESPAÑOLA

Accommodations

INN OF LA MESILLA, THE, Rt 1, Box 368A, Española, NM, 87532, (505) 753-5368. Gay-friendly B&B with private baths, full breakfast. Lesbian following with gay men welcome."

RANCHITO SAN PEDRO DE CÓCONO, PO Box 1849, Española, NM, 87532, (505) 753-0583. Email: j-hart@roadrunner.com, Web: http://www.bookgrrls.com/jan/, B&B, 2 private rooms, kitchen (continental breakfast included), outdoor patio with kiva fireplace. Just off the Santa Fe-Taos Hwy 84, 18 mi. north of Santa Fe at the southern edge of Española. 50% gay & lesbian clientele.

GILA WILDERNESS

Accommodations

N BAR RANCH - OUTLAW LAND & CATTLE CO., PO Box 409, Reserve, NM, 87830, (505) 533-6253 (Tel/Fax), (800) 616-0434. A working horse & cattle ranch high in the mountains of western New Mexico, surrounded by the Gila National Forest. Ride on a pack trip down the Gila River or work cattle like a real cowhand.

ARIUS COMPOUND

Experience Adobe Living In Your Own Casita

Santa Fe

(800) 735-8453

PECOS

Women's Accommodations

SALTAMONTES RETREAT — GRASSHOPPER HILL, Old Colonias Rd, 2 Llanitos Ln, E. Pecos, Mail to: PO Box 374, Pecos, NM, 87552, (505) 757-2528." Practical, low-budget lodging, 1/2 hr NE of Santa Fe, near Pecos Nat'l Wilderness, shared baths, communal kitchen, outdoor hot tub. Mostly women, some straight clientle.

RED RIVER

Accommodations

VALLEY LODGE, PO Box 304, Main St, Red River, NM, 87558, (505) 754-2262, Reservations (800) 951-2262. Gay-friendly motel with suites & cabins. Color cable TV, telephone & private baths.

SANTA FE

Information

AIDS INFO, (505) 266-0911 or tape.

Accommodations

ARIUS COMPOUND, PO Box 1111, 1018-1/2 Canyon Rd, Santa Fe, NM, 87504-1111, Out of Town: (800) 735-8453, Local: (505) 982-2621, Fax: (505) 989-8280. Email: len@ariuscompound.com, Gay-friendly Casitas, 40% gay clientele. Color cable TV, telephone, ceiling fans, kitchens, fireplace & private bath. Redwood hot tub.

FOUR KACHINAS INN BED & BREAKFAST, 512 Webber St, Santa Fe, NM, 87501, (505) 982-2550, (800) 397-2564, Fax: (505) 989-1323. Email: 4kachinas@swcp.com, Web: http://www.4kachinas.com/bbinn/, Gay-friendly B&B, private baths, expanded continental breakfast.

HEART SEED B & B AND SPA, PO Box 6019, Santa Fe, NM, 87502-6019, (505) 471-7026. Email: hrtseed@nets.com, Web: http://www.nets.com/heartseed, Gay-friendly accommodations. Four rooms (two with kitchenettes) on 100 beautiful acres. Large deck, full day spa with masseuse on premises. Mountain bikes available, full gourmet breakfast.

NEW MEXICO

INN OF THE TURQUOISE BEAR, 342 E Buena Vista Street, Santa Fe, NM, 87501, (505) 983-0798, (800) 396-4104, Fax: (505) 988-4225. Email: bluebear@roadrunner.com, This Spanish-Pueblo Revival style adobe B&B was built from a core of rooms dating to the mid 1800's. With its signature portico, tall pines, magnificent rock terraces, meandering paths and flower gardens, the inn offers a romantic retreat. As the only gay-oriented B&B in downtown Santa Fe, it's the perfect choice for both couples and individuals traveling alone. Some straight clientele.

OPEN SKY B & B, 134 Turquoise Trail, Santa Fe, NM, 87505, (505) 471-3475, (800) 244-3475. Email: skymiller@aol.com, B&B, 50% gay & lesbian clientele. Double rooms, private baths, color TV, extended continental breakfast, nearby river & lake.

TRIANGLE INN - SANTA FE, THE, PO Box 3235, Santa Fe, NM, 87501, (505) 455-3375 (Tel/Fax). Email: TriangleSF@aol.com, Web: http://www.roadrunner.com/~triangle/, Lesbian-owned Inn, men welcome. Individually decorated adobe casitas with modern conveniences, fully-equipped kitchens, Jacuzzi, common sun deck, expanded continental breakfast. ♀♂

■ Dance Bar/Disco
DRAMA CLUB, 125 N Guadalupe, (505) 988-4374. Live bands Thurs, occasional drag shows, gay comedy. Weekly poetry Tues, Trash Disco Wed, retro 70s.

■ Cafe
GALISTEO CORNER CAFE, 201 Galisteo, (505) 984-1316. Breakfast, lunch, specialty coffees. Coffeehouse till 10pm summer weekends.

■ Restaurants
COYOTE CAFE, 132 W Water St, (505) 983-1615. Nationally acclaimed modern Southwestern cuisine. Gay-friendly.

DANA'S AFTER DARK, 222 N Guadalupe, (505) 982-5225. Open after bars close, sandwiches, soups, coffees, pastries.

DAVE'S NOT HERE, 1115 Hickock St, at Agua Fria, (505) 983-7060. Very popular with the lesbian community.

GERONIMO, 724 Canyon Rd, (505) 982-1500. In an adobe house, nouvelle Southwestern cuisine.

PLAZA CAFE, 54 Lincoln Ave, on The Plaza, (505) 982-1664. Dinner with New Mexican & Greek items.

SANTA CAFE, 231 Washington Ave, (505) 984-1788. Restaurant & bar, popular with gays.

VANESSIE OF SANTA FE, 434 W San Francisco, (505) 982-9966. Piano bar & restaurant, lobster, steaks, etc.

WHISTLING MOON, 402 N Guadalupe, (505) 983-3093. Mediterranean cuisine.

TAOS

■ Accommodations
DON PASCUAL MARTINEZ B & B, PO Box 1205, Ranchos de Taos, NM, (505) 758-7364. Rustic, comfortable adobe B&B with private baths, phone, color cable TV, mostly straight clientele with a gay & lesbian following.

RUBY SLIPPER, THE, PO Box 2069, Taos, NM, 87571, (505) 758-0613. 7 guest rooms with private baths, hot tub, in-room coffee & tea, breakfast. Predominantly lesbian & gay clientele. Rave reviews, come see what everyone is talking about. ♀♂

Stay Gay in Santa Fe

Inn of the Turquoise Bear

an historic bed & breakfast
Santa Fe, New Mexico

(800) 396-4104

NEW YORK

ALBANY

■ Information
GAY & LESBIAN CENTER, 332 Hudson Ave, (518) 462-6138.
WOMEN'S BLDG, 79 Central Ave, (518) 465-1597. Many services, Mon-Fri 10am-4pm.

■ Dance Bar/Disco
★ **POWER COMPANY,** 238 Washington Ave, (518) 465-2556. Dance bar, Fri-Sun, 18+ up.
★ **WATER WORKS PUB,** 76 Central Ave, near Henry Johnson Blvd, (518) 465-9079. Cruise bar downstairs, dance bar upstairs, women welcome. DJ Wed-Sun.

■ Cafe
RAINBOW CAFE, 332 Hudson Ave, in gay center bldg., Coffeehouse & library, 7 nites.

■ Fitness Centers
FEMALE FITNESS, 79 Central Ave, 2nd floor of women's bldg, (518) 465-1597. Women's gym.
FITNESS FOR HER, 333 Delaware Ave, Delmar, (518) 478-0237. Women's gym.

■ Restaurants
EL LOCO MEXICAN CAFE, 465 Madison Ave, (518) 436-1855.

■ Retail & Bookstores
ART & DESIRE, 79 Central Ave, (518) 433-8909, (518) 433-7064. Women-made art & gifts. Books. Cafe.
DEJA VU, 37 Central Ave, (518) 463-4153. Gay & lesbian video sections, 10am-midnite.
PEACE OFFERINGS, 33 Central Ave, (518) 434-4037. T-shirts, hats, cards, jewelry.

BINGHAMTON

■ Information
GAY, LESBIAN & BI RESOURCE LINE, (607) 729-1921, in NY state (800) 287-7557. Mon-Thurs 7:30pm-9:30pm, may expand hours. Ask about gay & lesbian socials & group potlucks.
WOMEN'S CENTER, (607) 724-3462 or 785-3429.

■ Dance Bar/Disco
RISKY BUSINESS, 201 State St, (607) 723-1507. Video dance bar, occasional male dancers.
SQUIGGY'S, 34 Chenango St (rear), (607) 722-2299. Pool table & conversation bar, DJ weekends."

■ Retail & Bookstores
E&R GIFTS & GRAPHICS, 215 Main St, (607) 729-5305. Alternative New Age cards, books, gifts. Closed Sun.
GRACIE'S GIFTS, 201 State St, at Risky Business bar, (607) 723-1507. T-shirts, novelties.

BROOKLYN

■ Bars
★ **CARRY NATION,** 363 5th Ave, between 5th & 6th Sts, (718) 788-0924. Pool table, juke box.
CELEBRITY'S, 8705 3rd Ave, Bay Ridge, (718) 745-9652. Tues-Sun from 6pm, Sun from 4pm, pool table, darts.
FRIENDS, Atlantic at Henry, Brooklyn.,
SANCTUARY, 444 7th Ave, at 15th St, Park Slope, (718) 832-9800. Lounge with bar, pool table, performance space & intimate conversation areas, live DJ Fri & Sat.

■ Dance Bar/Disco
SPECTRUM, 802 64th St, (718) 238-8213. Video dance bar Wed-Sun.

■ Cafe
RISING CAFE, 186 5th Ave, (718) 622-5072. Women-owned gay & lesbian cafe with social events & a pub/coffeehouse feel.

■ Retail & Bookstores
BEYOND WORDS, 186 5th Ave, (718) 857-0010. Gay & lesbian bookstore.

BUFFALO

■ Information
AIDS HOTLINE, 206 S Elmwood Ave, at Chippewa, (716) 847-AIDS (2437), Mon-Fri 9am-5pm or tape.

■ Accommodations
BEAU FLEUVE B & B, 242 Linwood Ave, Buffalo, NY, 14209, (716) 882-6116.
OLD SCHOOLHOUSE GUEST

HOUSE, 1148 Townline Rd, Alden, NY, 14004, (716) 683-6590. Guesthouse, women welcome. Double rooms with shared baths, color TVs, continental breakfast.

Bars
★ **CATHODE RAY,** 26 Allen St, (716) 884-3615. Video bar, 75% men, 25% women."

LAVENDER DOOR, 32 Tonawanda St, (716) 874-1220. Patio, 30's crowd, closed Mon."

Dance Bar/Disco
CLUB 153, 153 Delaware Ave, Fri & Sat only.

★ **CLUB MARCELLA,** 622 Main St, (716) 847-6850. Dance club, 50% gay, more gay Wed, Fri-Sun, straight nite Thurs.

COMPTON'S AFTER DARK, 1239 Niagara St, (716) 885-3275. DJ Fri & Sat, patio in summer.

FUEL, 884 Main St, (716) 882-5009. Dance & cruise bar, Wed-Sun.

★ **UNDERGROUND,** 274 Delaware Ave, (716) 855-1040.

Retail & Bookstores
RAINBOW PRIDE GIFTSHOP, 175 Hodge St, (716) 881-6126. Rainbow items, cards, gifts & t-shirts, videos, jewelry. 2nd location at Buddies Bar.

TALKING LEAVES, 3158 Main St, (716) 837-8554. General bookstore with feminist, lesbian, gay section. Closed Sun.

CATSKILL MOUNTAINS

Accommodations
BRADSTAN COUNTRY HOTEL, Route 17B, PO Box 312, White Lake, NY, 12786, (914) 583-4114 (Tel/Fax). Hotel & cottages. Large gay female following, some gay men. Suites, sun deck, piano lounge, cabaret & expanded continental breakfast.

PALENVILLE HOUSE, Jct Rts 23A & 32A, PO Box 465, Palenville, NY, 12463-0465, (518) 678-5649, Fax: (518) 678-9038. Email: palenville@aol.com, Web: http://members.aol.com/palenville, Gay-owned B&B with private & shared baths, full country breakfast, 10-person hot tub, 50% gay & lesbian clientele.

NEW YORK 379

STONEWALL ACRES, PO Box 556, Rock Hill, NY, 12775, (914) 791-9474, in NYC Metro area: (800) 336-4208. Guesthouse with 2 cottages, some straight clientele. Double rooms in main house, private baths, BBQ area, full breakfast.

CRANBERRY LAKE

Women's Accommodations
AMETHYST B & B, PO Box 522, Cranberry Lake, NY, 12927, (315) 848-3529. In winter: 322 Jodyway, Timonium, MD 21093, Tel: (410) 252-5990. Women-only B&B with breakfast in the Adirondack Mtns of NY state, shared baths, full breakfast, many outdoor activities, lake & docks on premises.

ELMIRA - CORNING

Accommodations
RUFUS TANNER HOUSE, 60 Sagetown Rd, Pine City, NY, 14871-9502, (607) 732-0213, Fax: (607) 735-0620. Email: RufusTan@servtech.com, Gay-friendly B&B, 50% gay & lesbian clientele. Large rooms decorated in Victorian furniture & antiques, 1 with whirlpool tub. Full breakfast.

Bars
DAVID, THE, 511 Railroad Ave, (607) 733-2592. DJ Fri-Sun, 60% men, 40% women.

Dance Bar/Disco
BODY SHOP, on Railroad Ave, a block down from The David, (607) 733-6609.

FIRE ISLAND

Accommodations
CAROUSEL GUEST HOUSE, PO Box 4001, Cherry Grove, Fire Island, NY, 11782-0998, (516) 597-6612. Guesthouse 300 feet from beach, mostly men. Twin & double beds, shared baths, weights & continental breakfast.

CHERRY GROVE BEACH HOTEL, PO Box 537, Sayville, NY, 11782-0537, (516) 597-6600, Fax: (516) 597-6651. Email: grovehotel@aol.com, Web: www.grovehotel.com, Hotel with restaurant, bar & disco, near ocean, private baths.

NEW YORK

DUNE POINT, Box 78, Cherry Grove, Fire Island, NY, 11782, (516) 597-6261, Fax: (516) 597-7048. Guesthouse on the ocean, private & shared baths. 🏖♀♂

PINES PLACE, PO Box 5309, Fire Island Pines, NY, 11782, (516) 597-6162. Email: pinesplace@aol.com, B&B, women welcome. Private & shared baths. ♂

■ Bars

CHERRY PIT, Bayview Walk, Cherry Grove, Video bar & restaurant. ♀♂

CHERRY'S, Bayview Walk, Cherry Grove., (516) 597-6820. Piano bar, shows & cabaret. 🎵🎤♀♂

TOP OF THE BAY, Dock Walk, at Bay Walk, Cherry Grove, (516) 597-6699. Bar & restaurant. ♀♂

■ Dance Bar/Disco

ICE PALACE, Cherry Grove, at the Beach hotel, (516) 597-6600. Disco daily, Sat & Sun tea dance. 🎵♀♂

■ Restaurants

BLUE WHALE, The Pines., 🎵♂

CHERRY PIT, Bayview Walk, Cherry Grove, Restaurant & video bar. ♀♂

EL HOTSPOT, Bayview Walk, Cherry Grove,

MICHAEL'S, Dock Walk at Bay Walk, in Cherry Grove.,

TOP OF THE BAY, Dock Walk, Cherry Grove, at Top of the Bay bar., ♀♂

HIGHLAND

■ Dance Bar/Disco

PRIME TIME, Rte 9W N, (914) 691-8550. Male dancers Fri & Sat. 🎵♀♂

ITHACA

■ Information

WOMEN'S COMMUNITY BUILDING, 100 W Seneca St, (607) 272-1247.

■ Accommodations

PLEASANT GROVE B & B, 1779 Trumansburg Rd (Rte 96), Jacksonville, NY, 14854-0009, (607) 387-5420, (800) 398-3963. Email: jlg4@cornell.edu., Gay-friendly B&B, 60% gay & lesbian clientele. Double rooms with private & shared baths, full breakfast. Nearby lakes & streams.

■ Women's Accommodations

SLEEPING BEAR WOMEN'S B & B, 208 Nelson Rd, Ithaca, NY, 14850, (607) 277-6220. Women-only B&B in log home, quiet setting, full breakfast, hot tub, shared bath. Jun-Dec, lesbian-owned/-run. ♀

■ Dance Bar/Disco

COMMON GROUND, 1230 Danby Rd (Rte 96-B), (607) 273-1505. Bar & restaurant, DJ Thurs-Sat, restaurant Fri-Sun, 50% men, 50% women. 🎵♀♂

■ Restaurants

ABC CAFE, 308 Stewart Ave, (607) 277-4770. Alternative-style cafe & restaurant, vegetarian cuisine. Brunch, dinners & baked goods, brunch weekends, live music. 🍽🎵

■ Retail & Bookstores

BOREALIS BOOKSTORE, 111 N Aurora, (607) 272-7752. General bookstore specializing in gay & lesbian books.

JAMESTOWN

■ Dance Bar/Disco

NITE SPOT, 201 Windsor, (716) 483-2614. Shows Sun, DJ Wed, Fri-Sun, open daily from 7pm except in winter, 60% men, 40% women. 🎵🎤♂

SNEAKERS, 100 Harrison St, (716) 484-8816. DJ Fri & Sat. 🎵🎵♀♂

KINGSTON

■ Restaurants

ARMADILLO BAR & GRILL, 97 Abeel St, (914) 339-1550. Frozen Margaritas a specialty. 🍽

■ Retail & Bookstores

ALTERNATIVE VIDEO SHOP, 932 Rt 28, (914) 334-8105. Large selection of lesbian & gay videos, all denoted by rainbow stickers. 2nd location Ulster Video & Gifts, 584 Ulster Ave, (914) 331-6023.

LAKE GEORGE

■ Accommodations

KING HENDRICK MOTEL, 1602 State Route 9, Lake George, NY, 12845, (518) 792-0418. Gay-friendly motel. Cabins, efficiencies, modern conveniences, continental breakfast. 🏖

LONG ISLAND

Information

AIDS INFO, (516) 385-AIDS (2437).

HUNTINGTON WOMANSPACE, (516) 673-9721. Switchboard, lending library, workshops, discussions, programs, local information. No specific hours but they answer messages.

LONG ISLAND CRISIS CENTER, (516) 679-1111, 24hr straight switchboard with some gay info & peer counselors.

WOMEN'S ALTERNATIVES COMMUNITY CENTER, (516) 483-2050. Women's meetings, events & concerts, lesbian discussions.

Accommodations

COZY CABINS, Box 848, Montauk Hwy, Wainscott, East Hampton, NY, 11975, (516) 537-1160. Cabins, motel/inn near ocean beaches. Some straight clientele. ♀♂

SAG HARBOR BED & BREAKFAST, Sag Harbor, NY, (212) 505-7869 or (516) 725-5945 wknds, Fax: (516) 725-5945. Country home B&B in nature preserve, gay men welcome. Three bedrooms, private baths, bicycles, full breakfast. Nearby ocean beach.

Beaches

FOWLER BEACH, on Flying Pt Rd in South Hampton., One side of the beach is gay & lesbian.

Bars

AUNTI M, 3547 Merrick Rd, Seaford, in Blockbuster Shoppin Center, (516) 679-8820. Pub, most popular on weekends, free pool on Mon. ♀♂

★ **BEDROCK,** 121 Woodfield Rd, W Hempstead, (516) 486-9516. Dancing Fri, entertainment Sat, closed Mon. ♀

CLUB 608, 608 Sunrise Hwy, W Babylon, (516) 661-9580. 75% men, 25% women.

FOREVER GREEN, 841 N Broome Ave, Lindenhurst, (516) 226-9357. Jukebox dancing, DJ weekends." ♀

SIDE TRACKS, 1055 Front St, Uniondale, (516) 486-8589. ♀

Dance Bar/Disco

★ **ST MARKS PLACE,** 6550 Jericho Tpke, Commack, (516) 499-2244. Mainly women, men welcome.

★ **THUNDERS,** 1017 E Jericho Tpke, Huntington, (516) 423-5241. Nightly specials & The Loft piano bar, co-ed Fri." ♂

Erotica

HEAVEN SENT ME, 108 Cain Dr, Hauppauge Industrial Park, (516) 434-4777 or (800) 451-0022. Private club, bar alternative, with adult books & novelties for gay men & women.

NEW PALTZ - HIGHLAND

Accommodations

INN AT APPLEWOOD, THE, 120 North Rd, Highland, NY, (914) 691-2516, Fax: (914) 691-7607. Email: thewould @aol.com, Web: thewould.com, Gay-friendly inn with old-resort atmosphere, The Would restaurant on premises. Rooms have private baths, AC, color TV, full breakfast. 50% gay/lesbian clientele.

Restaurants

LOCUST TREE INN, 215 Huguenot St, (914) 255-7888. Dating from 1759, American continental menu, casual country dining. Lunch, dinner, Sun brunch.

WOULD RESTAURANT, THE, 120 North Rd, Highland, at the Inn at Applewood location., New American cuisine, fine dining, awardwinning chef.

Retail & Bookstores

PAINTED WORD BOOKS & CAFE, 36 Main St, (914) 256-0825. General bookstore with gay & lesbian section, coffee, desserts & snacks.

NEW YORK INTRO

Information

GAY & LESBIAN CENTER & SWITCHBOARD, 208 W 13th St, (212) 777-1800 or 620-7310. AIDS info (800) 734-7104.

IDENTITY HOUSE, 39 W 14th St #205, (212) 243-8181. Events, socials, counseling, workshops.

LESBIAN HERSTORY ARCHIVES, (718) 768-3953. Call for hours.

LESBIAN SWITCHBOARD, (212) 741-2610. Mon-Fri 6pm-10pm.

SOCIAL ACTIVITES FOR WOMEN

Visit New York City (800) CARITAS — Caritas B&B Network. (SAL), (718) 630-9505. 24hr hotline for current lesbian events in the metropolitan NY area.

■ Accommodations

ABODE, LTD, PO Box 20022, New York, NY, 10021, (212) 472-2000, (800) 835-8880. Manhattan apartment rental service with a gay & lesbian following. All accommodations are fully-furnished & meet the highest standards of cleanliness & attractiveness."

CARITAS BED & BREAKFAST NETWORK, (800) CARITAS, (312) 857-0801, Fax: (312) 857-0805. B&B, home-stay accommodations service. Member: IGLTA

■ Dance Bar/Disco

CHOCOLATE DREAMS & IN THE PINK, ("where there's always Pink on the Inside"), (718) 783-6642. Dance parties for women of color. In the Pink is usually last Sat of month, Chocolate Dream is usually on Fri, both from 11pm till... For exact schedule call our hotline. 🏨 ♀

Winner '94 -'95 Out & About Editor's Choice Awards

New York City COLONIAL HOUSE INN

(800) 689-3779
(212) 243-9669

SHESCAPE, (212) 686-5665. Weekly dance parties. Call 24-hour hotline for schedule. 🏨 ♀

■ Retail & Bookstores

GAY & LESBIAN BOOKSTORES, see Greenwich Village, Uptown sections.

NYC LOWER MANHATTAN

INCLUDES SOHO, CHELSEA, EAST & WEST VILLAGE, & the East Side up to 30th St.,

■ Information

LESBIAN & GAY COMMUNITY SERVICES CENTER, 208 W 13th St, (212) 620-7310. Many meetings, groups, social events, women's dances, 9am-11pm, visitor's info package, local info.

SALGA (SOUTH ASIAN LESBIAN & GAY ASSOC)., Meets 3rd Sun 6pm at the Lesbian & Gay Community Center, 208 W 13th.

■ Accommodations

A GREENWICH VILLAGE HABITUÉ, New York's West Village, (212) 243-6495. Private, fully-equipped apartments, 50% gay & lesbian clientele. AC, color TV, telephone.

ABINGDON B & B, 13 8th Ave, New York, NY, 10014, (212) 243-5384, Fax: (212) 807-7473. Quaint West Village guesthouse with distinctively decorated rooms. Color TV, AC, private & shared baths, expanded continental breakfast, non-smoking environment. 50% gay & lesbian clientele.

CHELSEA MEWS GUESTHOUSE, 344 W 15th St, New York, NY, 10011, (212) 255-9174. Guesthouse, women welcome. Color TV, AC, telephone, refrigerator, private & shared baths, continental breakfast. ♂

CHELSEA PINES INN, 317 W 14th St, New York, NY, 10014, (212) 929-1023, Fax: (212) 620-5646. Email: cpiny @aol.com, B&B inn in an 1850's modernized brownstone with an Art Deco look. Women welcome. We offer clean, comfortable rooms with firm beds, private & semi-private baths, color cable TV, free HBO, AC, refrigerator, hair dryer & phone. Our continental breakfast includes homemade bread, house-blend coffee & fresh fruit. We're on the border of Greenwich Village & Chelsea & close to shopping, theatres, sights, restaurants & the nightlife of the famous Sheridan Square/Christopher St. area. Subway & bus stops at our corner make getting around the city easy & economical. ♂

COLONIAL HOUSE INN, 318 W 22nd St, New York, NY, 10011, (212) 243-9669, (800) 689-3779, Fax: (212) 633-1612. Web: www.colonialhouseinn.com, Conveniently-located B&B. Private and shared baths. All rooms have phones, cable TV and AC. Some have refrigerators and fireplaces. From $65. Reservations suggested. ♀♂

INCENTRA VILLAGE HOUSE, 32 Eighth Ave, New York, NY, 10014, (212) 206-0007, Fax: (212) 604-0625. 1841 Greenwich Village guesthouse with rooms & suites, private bath, AC, phone, TV. Shops, bars & restaurants nearby. Some straight clientele. ♀♂

■ Women's Accommodations

EAST VILLAGE BED & BREAKFAST, 244 E 7th St #6, New York, NY, 10009, (212) 260-1865. Women-only B&B, 2-bedroom apartment situated in a tasteful 2nd-floor apartment. Located in an urban, multi-cultural, multi-ethnic neighborhood close to shops, galleries and affordable restaurants. Greenwich Village, SoHo, Chinatown and other areas of interest are within easy reach. The kitchen comes complete with items for preparing your own continental breakfast. You are usually on your own in your own apartment. ♀

■ Bars

BMW BAR, 199 7th Ave, between 21st & 22nd, Chelsea, (212) 229-1807. Open 24 hrs, live acoustic jazz, 7pm-3am. 🎵

BOILER ROOM, 86 E 4th St, near 2nd Ave, East Village, (212) 254-7536. Pool tables, jukebox, popular on weekends. 🏠🎵♂

COMMUNITY BAR & GRILL/ DENDOR LOUNGE, 216 7th Ave (22nd & 23rd), (212) 242-7900, (888) 984-7900.

CUBBYHOLE, 281 W 12th St, (212) 243-9041. 60% women. 🎵♀♂

DUPLEX, 61 Christopher St, near 7th Ave, (212) 255-5438. Piano bars, cabaret, upstairs pool table. Large gay following. 📺🎵

EIGHTY EIGHT, 228 W 10th St, near Bleecker, (212) 924-0088. Piano bar, upstairs cabaret, some straight clientele, Sun brunch, name performers. 🎵♀♂

FLAMINGO EAST, 219 2nd Ave (13th St), (212) 533-2860. Always gay-friendly, but gay on Wed with drag show (gay dance nite last Wed of month), lounge upstairs, restaurant downstairs. ♂

G LOUNGE, 223 W 19th St, Chelsea, (212) 929-1085. Lounge with sofas & banquettes, juice bar, coffees, power drinks, as well as full liquor & full wine list. ♂

EAST VILLAGE BED AND BREAKFAST

A place for women only.

Since 1989

(212) 260-1865

**244 E. 7th St
New York, NY 10009**

NEW YORK

HENRIETTA HUDSON, 448 Hudson St, (212) 924-3347. Cheers for the lesbian set, bar & vegetarian restaurant, summer lite menu, men welcome.

LIQUIDS, 226 E 10th St, East Village, (212) 677-1717. Cocktail bar with sofas.

MARIE'S CRISIS, 59 Grove St, near 7th Ave, (212) 243-9323. Piano bar, sing-a-longs.

MEOW MIX BAR, 269 E Houston St, (212) 254-1434. Dancing Fri & Sun, late-nite crowd, East Village baby dykes.

PIECES, 8 Christopher St, near 6th Ave, (212) 929-9291. Bar & cabaret with DJ, singers, different themes nightly. Young, trendy crowd.

RUBYFRUITS, 531 Hudson St, (212) 929-3343. Bar & dinner restaurant, Sun piano & singer.

STONEWALL, 53 Christopher St, (212) 463-0950. Videos, pool table, popular happy hour, 80% men, 20% women. Tourists & regulars.

WONDER BAR, 505 E 6th St, near Ave A, East Village, (212) 777-9105. Small video cruise bar, 6pm-4am, live DJ nightly.

■ Dance Bar/Disco

★ **CLIT CLUB,** 432 West 14th St, near 10th Ave, (212) 529-3300. Fri women's dance parties, lesbian videos. Mixed nights Tues & Sat.

CRAZY NANNY'S, 21 7th Ave S, at Leroy, (212) 929-8356. DJ & dancing Sun, upstairs dance floor, men welcome.

DRINKLAND, 339 E 10th St, (212) 420-0670. 2 lounges with asylum motif (totally white padded walls), young crowd.

FAT BOY, 409 W 14th St, (212) 388-0360. Scandalo dance nite Thurs, Latino dance nite from 11pm, Latin house & Latin hip hop, Zone dance nite Fri.

HERSHEE BAR, (212) 631-1093. Fri only women's dance club, hot women, great music, sexy dances. Call for current location.

MOTHER, 432 W 14th St, at Washington, (212) 366-5680. Gay on certain nights, call to confirm schedule. Fri Clit Club women's nite.

ROXY, THE, 515 W 18th St, (10th & 11th), (212) 645-5156. Sat night dance parties, women welcome. Tues Power Skate men's rollerskating."

SHESCAPE, (212) 686-5665. Scheduled dance parties for women. Call 24hr hotline for current schedule.

SOUND FACTORY, 618 W 46th St, near 11th Ave, (718) 507-7533. Fri dance club on 3 levels with different sounds.

■ Cafe

A DIFFERENT BITE CAFE, 151 W 19th St, (212) 989-4850. Popular with the early evening before-the-bars crowd.

■ Restaurants

BLACK SHEEP, THE, 344 W 11th St, (212) 242-1010. Old-fashioned country French cuisine, Sat & Sun brunches are very gay.

CHELSEA GRILL, 135 8th Ave, between 16th & 17th, Chelsea, (212) 929-9766. Burgers.

CHELSEA LOBSTER COMPANY, 156 7th Ave (18th St), Chelsea, (212) 242-5732. Seafood.

LA NOUVELLE JUSTINE, 206 w 23rd St, (212) 727-8642. Fetish-themed restaurant with dominant waiters.

LIPS, 2 Bank St, (212) 675-7710. Drag waitresses & drag memorabilia.

LUCKY CHENG'S, 24 1st Ave, (212) 473-0516. Bar & Chinese restaurant, drag queen waitresses, 75% gay.

MANATUS, 240 Bleecker St, (212) 989-7042. Open 24hrs. Sandwiches through dinners. "Manatus" was the Indian name for Manhattan.

MARY'S, 42 Bedford St, (212) 741-3387. Dinner 6pm-midnight 7 days, reservations suggested.

PANGEA RESTAURANT, 178 2nd Ave, (212) 995-0900. Mediterranean & Italian cuisine.

PARIS COMMUNE, 411 Bleecker St, (212) 929-0509. French cuisine.

UNIVERSE GRILL, 44 Bedford St, Chelsea, (212) 989-5621. Lunch, dinner, Sat & Sun brunch.

■ Retail & Bookstores

A DIFFERENT LIGHT, 151 W 19th St, (212) 989-4850, (800) 343-4002 (24hrs).

Julie's

Live DJ (Wed-Sun)

- 2-for-1 Happy Hour Mon-Fri (5-7pm)
- Open Nightly from 5pm
- Never a Cover

- TUESDAY "KARAOKE NIGHT"
- WEDNESDAY "SALSA MERANGUE NIGHT"
- THURSDAY "SINGLES NIGHT"
- FRIDAY "TOP 40"
- SATURDAY "LATIN HOUSE MUSIC"

Julie's
204 East 58th St. New York, New York 10022
212-688-1294

Martino's restaurant

Featuring superb Italian cuisine at affordable prices.

"...an evening here offers cocktails, conversation, fine food, terrific service and prices that everyone can afford."
HX Magazine

Lunch • Dinner • Sunday Brunch

Proudly serving the Gay & Lesbian Community
230 East 58th Street (between 2nd & 3rd Avenues) phone: 212•751•0029

Just a few steps from Julie's and The Townhouse Bar

Gay & lesbian bookstore with coffee bar, reading area. 10am-midnight 7 days.

CREATIVE VISIONS, 548 Hudson St, (212) 645-7573. Gay & lesbian bookstore.

OSCAR WILDE MEMORIAL BOOKS, 15 Christopher St, near Gay St, (212) 255-8097. Lesbian and gay books, 11:30-7:30pm daily. Sat 11:30-8:30.

RAINBOWS & TRIANGLES, 192 8th Ave, (212) 627-2166. Gay cards & gifts.

■ Erotica

GAY PLEASURES, 548 Hudson St, (212) 255-5756. Gay & lesbian erotica.

NYC UPPER MANHATTAN

INCLUDES MIDTOWN FROM 31ST STREET, UPPER EAST SIDE &, Upper West Side.,

■ Accommodations

ROSE COTTAGE, 1 Block West of Broadway, Midtown Manhattan, NY, (212) 663-0606. Studio apartment, cable color TV, AC, phone, kitchen, private bath, continental breakfast, 50% gay/lesbian clientele.

THREE THIRTY-THREE WEST 88TH ASSOCIATES, 333 West 88th St, New York, NY, 10024, (212) 724-9818, (800) 724-9888, Fax: (212) 769-2686. Email: albertmc@mail.idt.net, Web: http://idt.net/~albertmc, For visits to New York, consider these exceptional one-bedroom apartments, just restored, in an 1890's brownstone on the west side of Manhattan, directly across the park from the Metropolitan Museum of Art. Unhosted B&B apartments & hosted B&B rooms in the middle of Manhattan. Color TV, AC, telephone, kitchen & private baths. Well-behaved pets & children permitted. ♀♀♂

■ Bars

BRANDY'S, 235 E 84th St, near 2nd Ave, (212) 650-1944. Piano bar starts at 9:30pm, sing-a-long cabaret, 50% gay/lesbian crowd. 🎵 ♀♂

DON'T TELL MAMA, 343 W 46th St, near 8th Ave, (212) 757-0788. Piano bar & cabaret with a large gay following. 🎵 ⚧

EIGHT OF CLUBS, 230 W 75th St, near Broadway, (212) 580-7389. Video cruise bar with outdoor patio. 🏠 ♂

JULIE'S, 204 East 58th St, between 2nd & 3rd Aves, (212) 688-1294. An established bar/club on the Upper East Side catering to the Women's Community. Live DJ Wednesday thru Sunday. Tuesday is Karaoke, Wednesday is Salsa Merengue, Thursday is Single's night, Friday is Top 40 and Saturday features Latin House music. Opens at 5pm daily. 2-4-1 Happy Hour Mon-Sat 5-7pm, Sunday 3-5pm. 🎵 🍴 ♀ See ad on page 385.

PEGASUS, 119 E 60th St, between Lexington & Park, (212) 888-4702. Piano & cabaret, martini bar. 🎵 樂 ♀♂

■ Restaurants

MARTINO'S, 230 East 58th St, between 2nd & 3rd Aves, (212) 751-0029. This charming Upper East Side restaurant offers an excellent variety of dishes at an affordable price. A charming place for women to dine with women. Open for Lunch, Dinner & Sunday Brunch. "An evening here offers cocktails, conversation, fine food, terrific service and prices everyone can afford." — *HX* magazine. ⚧ See ad on page 385.

MIKE'S BAR & GRILL, 650 Tenth Ave, (212) 246-4115. Bar & restaurant with eclectic cuisine. 🍸 ⚧

TOWNHOUSE, 206 E 58th St, (212) 826-6241. International cuisine, supper club starting 7pm. 🍸 🎵 ♀♂

Beautifully-Furnished Apartments In Manhattan

333 WEST 88

New York City
(800) 724-9888

NEW YORK

■ Retail & Bookstores
EVE'S GARDEN, 119 W 57th St #420-FR, 5th/6th Aves, (212) 757-8651. Sexuality boutique by women for women & their partners. Mon-Sat noon-7pm." ♀

NIAGARA FALLS

■ Women's Accommodations
OLDE NIAGARA HOUSE, 610 4th St, Niagara Falls, NY, 14301, (716) 285-9408, Fax: (716) 282-0908. B&B, very basic accommodations, full breakfast. Gay women & straight couples.

NYACK - UPPER NYACK

■ Dance Bar/Disco
BARZ, 327 Rte 9W, Upper Nyack, (914) 353-4444. Dance bar, male dancers, 50% men, 50% women. 🍴 🎵 🎯 ♀♂

■ Restaurants
COVEN CAFE, 162 Main St, Upper Nyack, (914) 358-9829. Fine dining, restaurant & bar. Gay owned & operated. All welcome, men's night Wed. 🎯 🍷 🎵

ONEONTA

■ Bars
BLACK OAK TAVERN, 14 Water St, (607) 432-9566. NOT a gay bar but gay-friendly crowd." 🎯 🏠 ✕

OTEGO

■ Accommodations
A WOODCHUCK'S HOLLOW, 463 County Hwy 7, Otego, NY, 13825, (607) 988-2713. 1 bedroom efficiency on 70 acres. AC, kitchen, refrigerator & private bath. Color cable TV, telephone & maid service available upon request. 2-day minimum stay. 65% gay & lesbian clientele. ♀♂

PLATTSBURGH

■ Dance Bar/Disco
BLAIR'S, 30 Marion St, (518) 561-9071. Dancing Fri & Sat, 50% men, 50% women." 🍴 ♀♂

PORT CHESTER

■ Bars
SANDY'S OLD HOMESTEAD, 325 N Main St, (914) 939-0758. Bar & restaurant, 50% gay clientele, 50% gay women, men welcome. Private party with DJ last Sat of month is women's dance party" 🏠 🎯

POUGHKEEPSIE

■ Bars
CONGRESS, THE, 411 Main Mall E, (914) 486-9068 or 486-9531. Jukebox dancing, pool tables, 49th year." 🏠 🍴 ♀♂

QUEENS

■ Bars
EL BAR, 63-14 Roosevelt, Woodside, (718) 651-4145. Drag shows Fri, DJ nightly. 🏠 🎯 🎵 🎯 ♀♂

■ Dance Bar/Disco
AMNESIA, 32-03 Broadway, Astoria, (718) 204-7010. Alternative dance club, noon-4am 7 days, always gay-friendly, Insomnia gay dance party Tues. 🍴 🎯
KRASH, 34-48 Steinway, Astoria, (718) 937-2400. Large dance club, open Mon & Thurs-Sat, 60% men, 40% women. 🍴 🏠 ♀♂

RHEINBECK

■ Retail & Bookstores
HABITU, 11 Mill St, (914) 876-6652. Gay-related cards, books, gift items, Mon, Wed-Sat 11am-6pm, Sun 11am-5pm.

ROCHESTER

■ Information
AIDS HOTLINE, (716) 442-2200. 9am-5pm Mon-Fri.
GAY ALLIANCE & GAY SOURCE INFO LINE, 179 Atlantic Ave, (716) 244-8640 or tape. Community center Mon-Thurs 1pm-9:30pm, Fri 1pm-6pm, lending library, annual Pride parade & picnic, weekly youth group meetings, publishes Empty Closet. Women's coffeehouse 3rd Fri.

■ Bars
ANTHONY'S 522, 522 E Main, (716) 325-1350 or 325-2060. 50% men, 50% women. 🏠 ♀♂
AVENUE PUB, 522 Monroe Ave, at Goodman, (716) 244-4960. DJ Thurs-Sun. More women Wed, Sat. 🏠 ♂
MUTHERS, 45 S Union St, (716) 325-

6216. Bar serving burgers & wings, women's nite Thurs, Tea dance Sun, DJ Fri-Sun. 🍴🎵✖🏠♂

TARA LOUNGE, 153 Liberty Pole Way, near Andrews, (716) 232-4719. CD jukebox & games downstairs. Piano bar, cabaret upstairs. Patio, women welcome. 🎵🏠♂

■ Restaurants

EDIBLES, 704 University Ave, (716) 271-4910. 🌱

SLICE OF LIFE, 742 South Ave, (716) 271-8010. Feminist vegetarian cafe.

■ Retail & Bookstores

PRIDE CONNECTION, 728 South Ave, (716) 242-7840. All lesbian & gay clothing, gifts, cards, books, jewelry, videos, magazines, etc. Mon-Sat 10am-9pm, Sun noon-6.

SCHENECTADY

■ Accommodations

WIDOW KENDALL, THE, 10 N Ferry St, Schenectady, NY, 12305-1609, (518) 370-5511, (800) 244-0925, Fax: (518) 382-2640. Gay-friendly B&B, shared bath, 4-course breakfast.

■ Bars

BLYTHWOOD, THE, 50 N Jay St, (518) 382-9755, 9pm-4:30am 365 days, women welcome. 50th year. 🏠♂

SENECA FALLS

■ Information

WOMEN'S HISTORICAL SITES, National Women's Hall of Fame, 76 Fall St, 568-8060, Elizabeth Cady Stanton Home (restored), 32 Washington St, located in Women's Rights National Park (write: c/o Nat'l Park Service, US Dept. of Interior, Seneca Falls, NY 13148, 568-2991.

■ Accommodations

GUION HOUSE, 32 Cayuga St, Seneca Falls, NY, 13148, (315) 568-8129, (800) 631-8919. Web: www.flare.net/guion house, Gay-friendly B&B. Private & shared baths, expanded continental breakfast.

STATEN ISLAND

■ Information

LAMBDA ASSOCIATES, (718) 876-8786. Active local gay & lesbian group, annual picnic, potlucks, monthly trips, get togethers, theatrical productions. Mtgs. wkly. Annual gay pride dinner dance.

■ Dance Bar/Disco

VISIONS, 492 Bay St, (718) 273-7354. Wed-Sat 9pm-4am, male dancers Fri, drag shows Sat. 🍴🎵♀♂

SYRACUSE

■ Information

AIDS HOTLINE, (315) 475-AIDS (2437), 475-2430.

GAY PHONE, (315) 443-3599, 24hrs, very irregularly staffed.

WOMEN'S INFO CENTER, 601 Allen St, at Harvard, (315) 478-4636 or tape. Irregularly staffed.

■ Bars

MY BAR, 205 N West St, (315) 471-9279. DJ Sat, 70% women. 🏠✖♀

TU TU VENUE, 731 James St, (315) 475-8888. Bar & restaurant. ♀♂

■ Dance Bar/Disco

MR T'S, 218 N Franklin St, at Herald Place, (315) 471-9736. DJ Wed-Sun, 80% men, 20% women. 🍴♂

PLATEAU, 1203 Wilton Ave, (315) 468-9830. W-Su from 7pm, DJ wnds. 🍴♀

■ Retail & Bookstores

MY SISTERS' WORDS, 304 N McBride Street, (315) 428-0227. Fem. bookstore.

TARRYTOWN

■ Retail & Bookstores

RAZZMATAZZ FINE GIFTS, 35 N Broadway, (914) 631-4646.

UTICA

■ Information

AIDS LINE, (315) 724-3921. Tape Mon-Wed-Fri 11am-2pm.

■ Dance Bar/Disco

THAT PLACE, 216 Bleecker Street, (315) 724-1446. 7 days, patio, DJ Thurs-Sat, levi leather night 1st Sat of month, Upstate NY leather contest in Oct. 🍴♀♂

WHITE PLAINS

Information
LESBIAN LINE, (914) 949-3203.

Dance Bar/Disco
CLUB 202, 202 Westchester Ave, (914) 761-3100. Male strippers Wed-Sun, patio, summer BBQ's. 70% men, 30% women.

WINDHAM

Accommodations
POINT LOOKOUT MOUNTAIN INN, Mohican Trail, East Windham, NY, 12439, (518) 734-3381, Fax: (518) 734-6526. Gay-friendly inn with restaurant, bar, fireplace lounge, gourmet food shop, gifts. Rooms with spectacular views, color TVs, fireplace lounge, expanded continental breakfast, nearby river & lake.

WOODSTOCK AREA

Accommodations
RIVER RUN BED & BREAKFAST INN, Main St, Fleischmanns, NY, 12430, (914) 254-4884. Gay-owned & operated, gay-friendly B&B in an 1887 country village Victorian 35 minutes from Woodstock & 2-1/2 hours from NYC. Mostly private baths.

YOUR RAINBOW MTN REALTY CONNECTION
Teri Sferlazza
(828) 254-7266

NORTH CAROLINA
ASHEVILLE & ENVIRONS

Realtors/Relocation
TERI SFERLAZZA, YOUR RAINBOW MTN. REALTY CONNECTION, (828) 254-7266, (800) 357-4206. Asheville is called The Land of the Sky for its magnificent mountain views! It offers architectural tours, Biltmore House, galleries, antique shopping, hiking, white water rafting, skiing & more! We have a strong political & social lesbian, gay & transsexual community & welcome inquiries. Known as an artists community, Asheville will lift your spirit! Call for a Welcome to Asheville info package. **Let me assist you in finding your mountain home.**

Accommodations
ANOTHER POINT OF VIEW, 108 Weeping Cherry Forest Rd, Fairview,

Bird's Nest Bed & Kitchen
Country Living in the City
- A short walk to downtown Asheville
- Magnificent Views
- Seclusion & Quiet
- Boating, Hiking, Skiing

Asheville, NC
(704) 252-2381

NC, (704) 628-0005. Guest apartment, private bath, AC, color Cable TV, VCR, fruit & wine basket on arrival, some straight clientele. ♀♂

BIRD'S NEST BED & KITCHEN, THE, 41 Oak Park Rd, Asheville, NC, 28801, (704) 252-2381. Looking for the perfect guest place with beautiful views of the Smokey Mtns and lots of privacy? This recently remodeled turn-of-the-century home is it! **Very spacious and comfortable.** Located within walking distance of downtown Asheville. Private entrance, private bath, AC, master bedroom, kitchen and sun porch. No smoking, no pets. Mostly women with men welcome. ♀ See ad on page 389.

CABIN AT WOLF LAUREL, 25 Mineral Springs Rd, (704) 254-0024. Two-story hand-hewn cabin with decks, ♀♂

CORNER OAK MANOR, 53 Saint Dunstans Rd, Asheville, NC, 28803, (704) 253-3525. Elegantly-decorated, gay-friendly B&B with lesbian following. Rooms & cottages with private baths, AC & ceiling fans. Full breakfast.

INN ON MONTFORD, THE, 296 Montford Ave, Asheville, NC, 28801, (704) 254-9569, (800) 254-9569, Fax: (704) 254-9518. Gay-friendly B&B. Private baths, gym & full breakfast.

MADRIGAL, 2465 Buck Creek Rd, Marion, NC, 28752, (704) 724-4310" For recovering people who are gay & lesbian, no drugs or alcohol. ♀♂

MARSHALL HOUSE B & B, PO Box 865, Marshall, NC, 28753, (704) 649-9205, Fax: (704) 649-2999. Gay-friendly B&B with private & shared baths, expanded continental breakfast, 18 miles northwest of Asheville.

■ Women's Accommodations

CAMP PLEIADES, Route 2, Box 250, Hughes Gap Rd, Bakersville, NC, 28705, summer (704) 688-9201, Fax: (704) 688-3449. Winter call (904) 241-3050, Fax: (904) 241-3628. Toll-free: (888) 324-3110. Email: starcamp@aol.com, Winter mail: 390 Garden Lane, Atlantic Beach, FL 32233. A mountain resort for women, 60 miles north of Asheville. Explore 67 acres of private, heavily wooded property, clear-running streams, swimming pond, campfire circle, hiking trails. Enjoy sports, arts & crafts, mountain biking, horseback riding, whitewater rafting. Sleep in cozy private and group cabins. Relish wholesome family-style meals. Memorial Day to Labor Day, plus Fall Foliage Weekends. Men welcome certain times of year. ♀

EMY'S NOOK, 6 Edwin Place, Asheville, NC, 28801, (704) 281-4122 (Tel/Fax). A women-only guesthouse in the Grove Park area, just north of downtown Asheville. Our guest space is for women wanting the convenience of a quiet, tranquil place in the city combined with easy access to mountain fun. We are only 5 minutes from Asheville's

Camp Pleiades
A Mountain Retreat

Walk a wooded trail through mountain forest, cool off in a stream-fed pond, create artwork in a crafts studio, share meals with old friends and new ... a mountain resort just one hour north of Asheville.

April - October
Rt. 2, Box 250, Hughes Gap Rd.
Bakersville, NC 28705
704/688-9201

(1-888) 324-3110
e-mail Starcamp@aol.com

November - March
390 Garden Lane
Atlantic Beach, FL 32233
904/241-3050

NORTH CAROLINA

wide variety of shops, restaurants & nightlife. Amenities include shared bath, light continental breakfast, BW or color TV and ceiling fans. ♀

MOUNTAIN LAUREL B & B, 139 Lee Dotson Rd, Fairview, NC, 28730, (704) 628-9903. 25 min. from Asheville, NC, in the heart of the Blue Ridge Mountains. Brand new home nestled in the Western NC Mts. with panoramic views. We are creating a getaway with romantic charm and gourmet hospitality, catering to lesbians and gay men. Huge rooms, king and queen beds, private baths, Jacuzzi, breakfast and dinner menus with gastronomic delights, wraparound deck. Distinctive "classy" comfort in secluded, private mountain setting. ♀♂

SOPHIE'S COMFORT, (803) 787-5777 (Reservations). Women-only B&B with private bath, vegetarian continental breakfast, 20-min drive to Asheville, 10-min village of Black Mountain. ♀

TWENTY-SEVEN BLAKE STREET, (704) 252-7390. Suite with private entrance, cable TV & off-street parking. ♀

■ Bars

O'HENRY'S, 59 Haywood St (downtown), (704) 254-1891. Private club, 70% men, 30% women, twice monthly shows. ♂

■ Dance Bar/Disco

HAIRSPRAY, METROPOLIS, BARBERSHOP, 38 N French Broad Ave, (704) 258-2027. Entertainment complex, 3 atmospheres in 1 location. Dance bar, indoor-outdoor patio, quiet bar. ♀♂

SCANDALS, 12 Grove St, (704) 252-2838. Wed-Sat, younger crowd. ♀♂

■ Restaurants

GROVE STREET CAFE, 12 Grove St, adjacent to Scandals bar, (704) 252-2838. ♀♂

■ Retail & Bookstores

CRYSTAL VISIONS, Hwy 25 at I-26 (exit 13), Naples (16 mi south of central Asheville), (704) 687-1193. Jewelry, crystals, metaphysical books, lifestyle resource center, 10-6 Mon-Fri, 10-5 Sat.

MALAPROP'S BOOKSTORE & CAFE, 55 Haywood St, (704) 254-6734. General bookstore with emphasis on women's issues on most subjects. Large lesbian and gay selection. Open every day.

RAINBOW'S END, 10 N Spruce St, (704) 285-0005. Bookstore with rainbow & pride items.

BAT CAVE

■ Accommodations

OLD MILL B & B, Hwy 64/74-A/9, Lake Lure Hwy, Box 252, Bat Cave, NC, 28710, (704) 625-4256. B&B with gift shop. Some straight clientele. Variety of rooms with modern conveniences, TV lounge, full breakfast & nearby river. ♀♂

Mountain Laurel B&B

- Getaway with Romantic Charm
- Gourmet Hospitality
- Panoramic Views
- In the Western NC Mnts
- Distinctive "Classy" Comfort
- A Secluded Mountain Setting

139 Lee Dotson Rd., Fairview
(704) 628-9903

NORTH CAROLINA

BLOWING ROCK

Accommodations
STONE PILLAR B & B, PO Box 1881, 144 Pine St, Blowing Rock, NC, 28605, (704) 295-4141, (800) 962-9955. Email: stonepillar@blowingrock.com, Web: http:www.blowingrock.com/northcarolina/stonepillar, Gay-friendly B&B, double rooms with various conveniences, private baths, common areas with fireplaces, full breakfast. Nearby town pool.

CHAPEL HILL

Women's Accommodations
JOAN'S PLACE, c/o M. Joan Stiven, 1443 Poinsett Dr, Chapel Hill, NC, 27514, (919) 942-5621. B&B for women in my home. Rustic setting, secluded among trees. Share one full bath and my living room and large deck. Continental breakfast. ♀

Restaurants
WEATHERVANE, THE, Eastgate Shopping Center, (919) 929-9466. American, Southern, Int'l cuisine, lunch, brunch, dinner. Mon-Thurs 10am-10pm, Fri-Sat 10am-11pm, Sun 12pm-6pm.

Retail & Bookstores
INTERNATIONALIST BOOKS, 405 W Franklin St, (919) 942-1740. Progressive bookstore with gay & lesbian section.

CHARLOTTE

Information
AIDS HOTLINE, (704) 333-AIDS (2437). 8:30am-5pm Mon-Fri or tape.
GAY & LESBIAN SWITCHBOARD, (704) 535-6277, 6:30pm-10:30pm nightly.

Bars
★ **LIAISONS,** 316 Rensselaer, (704) 376-1617. Upscale cocktail bar, daily 5pm-1am. Moving in '98, call for address. ♀♂

Dance Bar/Disco
AMBUSH, 4701 N Tryon St, (704) 596-8303. Sports bar & dance club. ♀
CLUB MYXX, 3110 s Tryon St, (704) 525-5001. Primarily African-American, but everyone is welcome, 3rd Fri Sistahs Night Out for women. Open Fri & Sat only hip hop & underground dance club. ♀♂
MYTHOS, 300 N College, (704) 375-8765. Gay Sun & Wed, drag shows Thurs. Check for changes in gay nights schedule. ♂
★ **OLEEN'S,** 1831 South Blvd, at Worthington, (704) 373-9604. Shows Fri-Sun, 50% men, 50% women. ♀♂
SCORPIO, 2301 Freedom Dr, near Camp Green, (704) 373-9124. Huge complex with dance & show bar, C&W bar, patio, Tues-Sun form 9pm. One bar overlooks the dance bar. Popular Sun. ♀♂

Joan's Place
Bed & Breakfast for Women

A rustic house in a quiet, country setting 2 miles south of Chapel Hill, NC. Open year-round. Reservations encouraged.

(919) 942-5621

M. Joan Stiven
1443 Poinsett Dr.
Chapel Hill, NC 27514

NORTH CAROLINA 393

★ **THREE HUNDRED (300) STONEWALL**, 300 E Stonewall St, (704) 347-4200. Huge, well-ventilated dance bar complex, 2-level dance floor, outdoor bar & patio.

■ *Cafe*
SEVEN SEEDS, 1213-B W Morehead St, (704) 358-0106 or 532-9995.

■ *Restaurants*
FAT CITY, 3127 N Davidson St, (704) 343-0240. Deli, bar.

THREE HUNDRED EAST, 300 East Boulevard, (704) 332-6507. Popular Sun brunch.

■ *Retail & Bookstores*
WHITE RABBIT BOOKS, 834 Central Ave, (704) 377-4067. Gay & lesbian bookstore with erotica, leather.

CRYSTAL COAST

■ *Accommodations*
WILLIAM & GARLAND MOTEL, PO Box 204, Hwy #58, Salter Path, NC, 28575, (919) 247-3733. Gay-friendly motel at Salter Path Dunes Nat'l Park, beach access, private baths, color cable TV, AC, kitchen, refrigerator.

DURHAM

■ *Accommodations*
MINERAL SPRINGS INN, 718 South Mineral Springs Rd, Durham, NC, 27703, (919) 596-2162 (Tel/Fax), (888) 833-6900. Email: boucvalt@ix.netcom.com, Web: http://pw2.netcom.com/~boucvalt/main.html, Inn with private & shared baths, full breakfast, Jacuzzi & weights, women welcome.

■ *Bars*
BOXER'S, 5504 Chapel Hill Blvd, at Straw Valley (15-501 & I-40), (919) 489-7678. 75% men, 25% women. Pool tables, big-screen TV.

■ *Dance Bar/Disco*
ALL ABOUT EVE, 711 Rigsbee Ave, (919) 688-3002. Big dance bar with deck bar. DJ Fri & Sat, men very welcome. Non-smoking.

BOXER'S RINGSIDE, 308 W Main St, downtown Durham, To open in late summer-fall '98, the largest gay bar in the Triangle area. 4 levels, roof deck & patio, dance bar.

■ *Cafe*
FRANCESCA'S, 706-B 9th St, (919) 286-4177. Italian cuisine.

■ *Retail & Bookstores*
REGULATOR BOOKSHOP, 720 Ninth Street, (919) 286-2700. General bookstore with strong men's and women's sections.

FAYETTEVILLE

■ *Dance Bar/Disco*
SPEKTRUM, 107 Swain St, (910) 868-4279. Hi-energy, house, techno & rave music, 7 days 5pm-3am. Drag shows Sat & Sun, Fri male & female strippers. Patio with summer BBQ.

FRANKLIN

■ *Accommodations*
PHOENIX NEST, 1228 Lowery Lane, Franklin, NC, 32734, (850) 421-1984." Email: tippy@nettally.com, Lesbian-owned & -operated mountain cabin in the woods on top of a mountain, kitchen utensils & linens provided, phone & AC. Some straight clientele.

■ *Women's Accommodations*
MOUNTAIN MAGIC, (850) 231-0254, (800) 854-9266. Mountain chalet with stone fireplace, deck with a view. Modern conveniences, men welcome.

RAINBOW ACRES (HONEY'S), Mail: PO Box 1367, Franklin, NC, 28734, (704) 369-5162. For weekly rentals: (800) 442-6400 (ask for Caren). Women-only guesthouse with kitchen privileges, private & shared baths."

GREENSBORO

■ *Accommodations*
BILTMORE GREENSBORO HOTEL, THE, 111 W Washington St, Greensboro, NC, 27401, (800) 332-0303 or (910) 272-3474, Fax: (910) 275-2523. Urban inn, private baths, 50% gay & lesbian clientele.

■ *Dance Bar/Disco*
BABYLON, 221 S Elm St, (910) 275-1006. Private club, from 9pm. Younger crowd with special events for young people, Tues country nite, Thurs pool tournament.

NORTH CAROLINA

PALMS, THE, 413 N Eugene St, near Lindsay, (910) 272-6307. DJ Mon-Wed, Fri & Sat, 60% men, 40% women. Private club, male strippers Mon, Fri, Sat.

WAREHOUSE 29, 1011 Arnold St, (910) 333-9333. Entertainment Sun, male strippers & drag shows, 70% men, 30% women.

Retail & Bookstores

WHITE RABBIT BOOKS, 1833 Spring Garden, (910) 272-7604. Gay & lesbian bookstore with cards, gifts, jewelry, rainbow items, T-shirts, magazines, music, videos for sale & rent.

GREENVILLE

Dance Bar/Disco

PADDOCK CLUB, 1008-B Dickinson Ave, (919) 758-0990. Dance & show bar, closed Mon, Tue. Fri good night for women.

HICKORY

Information

AIDS LINE, (704) 322-1447. 9am-5pm.

Dance Bar/Disco

CLUB CABARET, 101 N Center St, (704) 322-8103. Dance & show bar Wed-Sun 9pm-2am, male strippers Wed.

HOT SPRINGS

Accommodations

DUCKETT HOUSE INN, on Hwy 209, PO Box 441, Hot Springs, NC, 28743, (704) 622-7621. B&B farmhouse in heart of Unaka Mountains on Appalachian Trail, 50% gay & lesbian clientele, shared baths. Creek, nearby river, access to hot springs.

MOREHEAD CITY

Dance Bar/Disco

SH'BOOM'S, 415 Morehead Ave, Atlantic Beach, (919) 726-7000.

RALEIGH

Information

GAY & LESBIAN HOTLINE, (919) 821-0055, 7-10pm or tape.

Dance Bar/Disco

★ **LEGENDS,** 330 W Hargett St, (919) 831-8888. Mon industrial alternative, Wed, Fri & Sat dance nites, Sun & Tues drag shows, Thurs lesbian nite.

Restaurants

BLACK DOG CAFE, 208 E Martin, (919) 828-1994. Lunch, dinner. Near galleries, gay-friendly.

FIVE EIGHTEEN WEST, 518 W Jones., Northern Italian cuisine.

IRREGARDLESS CAFE, 901 W Morgan Street, (919) 833-8898. Open for lunch, dinner and Sun brunch.

VERTIGO, 426 S McDowell St, (919) 832-4477. Late-night menu on weekends.

Retail & Bookstores

WHITE RABBIT BOOKS, 309 W Martin St, (919) 856-1429. Gay & lesbian bookstore.

SPRUCE PINE

Women's Accommodations

SHEPHERD'S RIDGE, (704) 765-7809. Women-only guesthouse, private bath.

WILMINGTON

Accommodations

ROSEHILL INN BED & BREAKFAST, 114 South 3rd St, Wilmington, NC, (910) 815-0250, (800) 815-0250, Fax: (910) 815-0350. In Wilmington's Victorian Historic District, full breakfast, private baths, near dining & shopping.

Beaches

GAY BEACH, north end of Wrightsville Beach, 7 miles east of Wilmington.

Dance Bar/Disco

MICKEY RATZ, 115 S Front St, (910) 251-1289. Private club, huge patio, BBQ's. Male strippers Wed & Sat, drag shows Fri & Sun. Closed Mon & Tues.

WINSTON-SALEM

Dance Bar/Disco

BOURBON STREET, 916 Burke St, (910) 724-4644. Dance & show bar, male dancers.

CLUB ODYSSEY, 4019-A Country Club Rd, (910) 774-7071. Big dance club, drag shows Fri & Sun, large straight following.

NORTH DAKOTA
FARGO

Information
PRAIRIE GAY & LESBIAN COMMUNITY, (701) 235-7335. A straight hotline will answer and put you in touch with the gay group.

Dance Bar/Disco
DECA DANCE, gay & lesbian dances. Winter-May: 1st & 3rd Fri, 9:30pm-1:30am in the banquet facility at the north end of the bowling alley, 2630 S University. In summer locations change.

OHIO
STATEWIDE

Information
AIDS HOTLINE, (800) 332-2437, Spanish (800) 344-7432.

AKRON

Information
AIDS HOTLINE, (330) 375-2437, 24hrs.

Bars
TEETER TOTTER TAVERN, 1009 S Main, (330) 253-0458.

Dance Bar/Disco
INTERBELT, 70 N Howard Street, (330) 253-5700. Big dance bar, patio.
ROSETO CLUB, 627 S Arlington, (330) 724-4228. Dance club, volleyball court. Membership charge.

Restaurants
CAFE 115, 115 E Market St.,
CONNIE'S DIAMOND DELI, 378 S Main St.,
SANDWICH BOARD, THE, 1667 W Market St, Sandwiches, soups, vegetarian dishes, desserts. Mon-Sat 11am-8pm.

ASHTABULA

Bars
LEEWARD LOUNGE, THE, 1026 Bridge St (Ohio 531), (216) 964-9935. Open daily 7pm-2:30am. Food 'til 1:30am.

ATHENS

Accommodations
SUSAN B. ANTHONY MEMORIAL WOMEN'S LAND TRUST, SBAMUH, PO Box 5853, Athens, OH, 45701, Women-only campground & cabin on 150 woodland acres in southeastern Ohio. No electric, solar shower, outhouse. Reservation only, groups welcome.

BOWLING GREEN

Information
WOMEN'S CENTER, (419) 372-2281. Student group, Women For Women."

CANTON

Bars
LA CASA LOUNGE, 508 Cleveland Ave, NW Canton, (330) 453-7432. DJ.
SIDESTREET CAFE, 2360 Mahoning, at Superior, (330) 453-8055. Pool room, game room, DJ Sat, dance floor.

Dance Bar/Disco
BOARDWALK, 1227 W Tuscarawas, (330) 453-8000.

CINCINNATI

ALSO INCLUDES COVINGTON, KY (606).,

Information
COMMUNITY CENTER, THE, 214 E 9th St, (513) 651-0040, switchboard (513) 651-0070.
WOMEN HELPING WOMEN, (513) 381-5610. Info and referral, 24hrs.

Accommodations
PROSPECT HILL B & B, 408 Boal St, Cincinnati, OH, 45210, (513) 421-4408. B&B on wooded hillside, 50% gay & lesbian clientele. Rooms with antique furnishings, deck, fireplace & buffet breakfast."

Bars
COLORS, 4042 Hamilton Ave, (513) 681-6969. Mon martinis, 75% gay, 25% straight.

Dance Bar/Disco
BULLFISHES, 4023 Hamilton Ave, (513) 541-9220.

OHIO

CHASERS, 2640 Glendora, (513) 861-3966. Dance & show bar."

★ SHIRLEY'S, 2401 Vine St, (513) 721-8483.

Cafe
TASTE OF WORLD CAFE, 4037 Hamilton Ave, (513) 542-CAFE. Live music on the patio 8:30pm-11pm.

Restaurants
BOCA, 4034 Hamilton, (513) 542-2022. Restaurant & bar.

DINER ON SYCAMORE, 1203 Sycamore.,

MULLANE'S PARKSIDE CAFE, 723 Race St, (513) 381-1331.

PETERSON'S, 1111 St Gregory St, (513) 651-4777. Downtown location on 7th St.

Retail & Bookstores
CRAZY LADIES BOOKSTORE, 4041 Hamilton Ave, (513) 541-4198. Women's bookstore. Lesbian support group meets here. Crazy Ladies Lesbian & Feminist Center 4039 Hamilton.

LEFTHANDED MOON, 48 E Court St, (513) 784-1166. Men's clothing & gifts, accessories, pride items, cards, books.

PINK PYRAMID, 36A W Court St, near Race, (513) 621-7465. Gay & lesbian bookstore with cards & gifts.

CLEVELAND

Information
GAY & LESBIAN CENTER, 1418 W 29th St, hotline: (216) 781-6736, 24hrs. Center: (216) 522-1999.

WOMEN'S CENTER, (216) 651-1450.

Women's Accommodations
BUNGALOW B & B, 720 E 254th St, Euclid (Cleveland), OH, 44132, (216) 289-7078, Fax: (216) 289-7079.
Email: haha@multiverse.com, Women-only B&B with rooms & suite, private & shared baths, continental breakfast. Hosts are active in the women's community & culture. We're 5 blocks from the lake & near city parks & trails. Moms with children welcome.

Bars
FIVE-CENT DECISION, 4365 State Road, (216) 661-1314. Jukebox dancing, DJ Fri, country nites 1st & 3rd Fri.

HAWK, 11217 Detroit Ave, near 112th, (216) 521-5443. Pool table, juke box, 50% men/women.

HI & DRY, 2207 W 11th St, (216) 621-6166. Bar & eatery with live jazz Fri & Sat, variety of music other nights. Burgers, vegetarian items, pastas, steaks, gyros. Popular with gays.

MJ'S PLACE, 11633 Lorain Ave, (216) 476-1970.

MUGGS AT WESTIES PUB, 3194 W 25th St, (216) 661-5365. Cocktail lounge, mellow.

OHIO CITY OASIS, 2909 Detroit Ave, (216) 574-2203. C&W night Sun, mostly men weekdays, 50/50 men & women weekends.

PARADISE INN, 4488 State Rd, at Behrwald, (216) 741-9819. Small bar, good music. Since 1954.

REC ROOM, THE, 15320 Brookpark Rd, (216) 433-1669. Big screen TV, juke box, 2 pool tables, bowling.

Dance Bar/Disco
AUNT CHARLIE'S THE CAGE, 9506 Detroit, (216) 651-0727. Shows Mon, strippers Wed, Fri & Sun.

CODE BLUE, 1946 St. Clair Ave, (216) 241-4663. Wed-Sun, open cocktail hour Wed & Thurs

GRID, THE, 1281 W 9th St, (216) 623-0113. High energy dance bar and lounge, videos. Male strippers Wed, Sat & Sun. 10% women.

★ U4IA, 10630 Berea Rd, (216) 631-7111. Dance & show bar, 80% men, 20% women. Open Fri-Sun only. After hours weekends.

Cafe
PHOENIX CAFE, 3750 Pearl Rd, at Archwood, (216) 741-6010. Gay-friendly.

RED STAR CAFE, 11604 Detroit Ave, (216) 521-7827. Gay-friendly.

SPANIEL'S COFFEE CAFE, 2710 Lorain Ave, (216) 651-4060.

TRUFFLES, 11118 Clifton, (216) 961-7439. Pastries.

Restaurants
BILLY'S NORTHCOAST CAFE, 11110 Clifton, (216) 281-7722.

OHIO

CIELO'S TRATTORIA, 6504 Detroit Rd, (216) 939-1190. Italian cuisine.

HARMONY BAR & GRILL, 3359 Fulton Ave, (216) 398-5052. Vegetarian, Eastern European, American & Italian cuisines.

SNICKERS, 1261 W 76th Ave, (216) 631-7555.

Retail & Bookstores

BOOKSTORE ON W 25TH, 1921 W 25th St, (216) 566-8897. General bookstore strong gay & lesbian sections (new & used books).

Erotica

★ BODY LANGUAGE, NE crn of W 115th St & Lorain, mail to: 3291 W 115th St, (216) 251-3330. Erotic hardware and romantic software for men & women. Also cards, gifts and videos.

BROOKPARK NEWS AND BOOKS, 16700 Brookpark Rd, (216) 267-9019. Full line of gay & lesbian videos, magazines, novelties & erotica.

ROCKY'S ENTERTAINMENT EMPORIUM, 13330 Brookpark Rd, (216) 267-4936.

COLUMBUS

Information

STONEWALL GAY & LESBIAN CENTER, 1160 N High St, (614) 299-7764. Mon-Thurs 10-7, Fri 9-5, or tape.

Accommodations

GARDENER'S HOUSE, THE, 556 Frebis Ave, Columbus, OH, 43206, (614) 444-5445, (800) 54-ROSES (76737). B&B, continental breakfast, shared baths, outdoor spa.

Women's Accommodations

SPRINGWOOD HOCKING HILLS CABINS, 28560 Blackjack Rd, Logan, OH, 43138, (614) 385-2042. Lesbian-owned & -operated cabins, private baths, phone, AC, kitchen, Jacuzzi, men welcome.

Bars

BLAZER'S PUB, 1205 N High St, (614) 299-1800. Pool tables, electronic darts, jukebox, Sun cookouts.

CLUB 20, 20 E Duncan St., (614) 261-9111.

CLUBHOUSE CAFE, 124 E Main St, (614) 228-5090. Coffee, desserts, pool table, movies, also drinks.

FAR SIDE, 1662 W. Mound St, (614) 276-5817. Couches, a fireplace, patio.

HAVANA, 862 N High St, (614) 421-9697. Upscale video bar with live DJ, cigar smoking room, piano happy hour, Tues-Fri & Sun. Lots of fun parties.

ROCKHOUSE TAVERN & GRILL, 80 South 4th St, (614) 228-7625. Upscale tavern, 2 bars on 2 levels.

★ SLAMMERS, 202 E Long St, (614) 221-8880. Bar & restaurant with patio, pool table, Sun cookouts.

SUMMIT STATION, 2210 Summit St, near Alden, (614) 261-9634. DJ Thurs-Sat, occasional live bands

★ UNION STATION VIDEO CAFE, 630 N High St, (614) 228-3740. Upscale video bar, pool tables, darts, preppy young crowd, 70% men. Mon-Fri 4pm-2:30am, Sat 3pm-2:30am, Sun show tunes 2pm-2:30am. Good food, full-service kitchen 4pm-9pm.

Dance Bar/Disco

CLUB ALIVE, 203 King Ave, (614) 297-8990. Chemical-free social Sat. 1st Fri under 21, 2nd Sat ballroom dancing 8:30pm-10pm.

★ TRENDS/GARAGE, 40 E Long St, near High, (614) 461-0076. Dance & quiet bars, patio bar, college crowd, 80% men, 20% women.

★ WALL STREET, 144 N Wall Street, (614) 464-2800. Mainly women, popular, C&W Thurs. Wed boys nite 70% men.

Cafe

COFFEE TABLE, 731 N High St, (614) 297-1177.

★ COMMON GROUNDS, 2549 Indianola, (614) 263-7646. Mainly women's coffeehouse.

CUP O' JOE, 627 S 3rd St, (614) 221-1563. Coffee, desserts.

Restaurants

GRAPEVINE CAFE, 73 E Gay St, (614) 221-VINE (8463). Nightclub & eatery. Closed Mon.

★ OUT ON MAIN, 122 E Main St, (614) 224-9520, 11am-2:30am, 7 days.

OHIO

■ Retail & Bookstores

AN OPEN BOOK, 761 N High St, (614) 291-0080. Gay & lesbian bookstore.

KUKALA'S TANNING & TEES, 636 N High St, (614) 228-8337. Gay stuff & things. Cards, T-shirts, gifts & books. Tanning. Also Diablo body piercing.

DAYTON

■ Information

AIDS LINE, (937) 223-2437.

GAY & LESBIAN HOTLINE, (937) 274-1776. 7pm-11pm 7days.

■ Bars

LADYHAWK SOCIAL CLUB, 2600 Valley St, (937) 233-5879. Intimate pub for women only, games on tables, ballroom tunes, a little country.

REFLECTIONS, 629 S Main St, (937) 223-1595. Women only.

RIGHT CORNER, 105 E 3rd St, at Jefferson, (937) 228-1285. Pub.

■ Dance Bar/Disco

DOWNUNDER, 131 N Ludlow, (937) 228-1050.

FOURTEEN SEVENTY WEST, 34 N Jefferson, at Dixie, Alternative dance club, 2-level dance complex & showbar, many straights.

KAMIKAZE BEACH SIDE, 5605 Old Troy Pike, Huber Hts, (937) 235-8661. Dance bar, outside swimming pool with waterfall. Open 9pm summers, 8pm winters, Tues straight with karaoke, Wed lesbian nite, Thurs drag shows, Fri men's nite, Sat 30% straight, Mon 30% lesbian.

■ Retail & Bookstores

BOOKS & CO., 350 E Stroop Rd, at Farhills, (937) 298-6540. General bookstore with gay, lesbian and women's sections.

Q GIFT SHOP, 850 N Main, inside Jessie's Celebrity., 2nd location: 1966 N Main St, (937) 274-4400. Rainbow & pride items, cards, jewelry, etc.

GLENFORD

■ Women's Accommodations

SPRINGHILL FARM, 5704 Highpoint Rd, Glenford, OH, 43739, (740) 659-2364. Small resort with fishing pond & trails. Variety of guest quarters with various conveniences, private baths, Jacuzzi, nearby lake. Women only."

LIMA

■ Dance Bar/Disco

SOMEWHERE IN TIME, 804 W North St, (419) 227-7288. Hi-energy dance bar, DJ Fri & Sat, male strippers, 50% men, 50% women.

LORAIN

■ Bars

SERPENT, THE, 2223 Broadway, (440) 246-9002. DJ Fri & Sat. Patio bar & dancing, 60% men, 40% women.

MANSFIELD

■ Dance Bar/Disco

HUNT CLUB, 1400 W 4th St, (419) 529-6262. Alternative nightclub & restaurant.

SANDUSKY

■ Bars

RAINBOW BAY, 306 W Water St, (419) 624-8118.

SPRINGFIELD

■ Dance Bar/Disco

CHANCES, 1912-1914 Edwards Ave, (937) 324-0383. Dance/disco patio, male or female strippers or drag shows twice monthly, Wed-Sun 8:30pm-2:30am.

TOLEDO

■ Information

TALLULAH'S, 6725 W Central, (419) 843-7707. Women's community center, Mon, Fri, Sat 11am-6pm, Tues, Wed, Thurs 11am-8pm.

■ Accommodations

ZELKOVA COUNTRY MANOR, 2348 S. County Rd 19, Tiffin, OH, (419) 447-4043, Fax: (419) 447-6473. Email: zelkova@bpsom.com, Georgian Revival B&B with spa, restaurant & bar on 27 acres, 30 mi south of Toledo & 60 mi north of Columbus. Suites with private

OKLAHOMA 399

baths, full breakfast, AC & pool. 50% gay/lesbian clientele.

Bars
BLU JEANS, 3606 W Sylvania Ave, (in the shopping center), (419) 474-0690. Game room & restaurant with fine dining & extensive menu. Karaoke Tues & Thurs, usually 4pm-2:30am.
R HOUSE, 5534 Secor Rd, (419) 474-2929, 2 floors.

Dance Bar/Disco
★ **BRETZ**, 2012 Adams Street, (419) 243-1900. Video dance bar, younger crowd, 70% men. Fri & Sat after hours 4:30am, closed Mon & Tues.
CAESAR'S, 725 Jefferson, (419) 241-5140. Dance & show bars Fri-Sun, shows Tues-Sun.

WARREN

Bars
ALLEY, THE, 441 East Market St, (enter in rear), (330) 394-9483. DJ Fri, Sat, 25% men, 75% women.
CRAZY DUCK, THE, 121 Pine Ave, (330) 394-3825. DJ Fri & Sat, patio.
QUEEN OF HEARTS, 134-136 Pine Ave, near Market St, (330) 395-1100. Jukebox, DJ Fri & Sat, 80% men, 20% women. Summer patio.

YELLOW SPRINGS

Restaurants
WINDS CAFE, 215 Xenia Ave, (937) 767-1144. Restaurant & bar, patio, bakery. Lunch, dinner Mon-Sat, Sun brunch.

Retail & Bookstores
EPIC BOOKSTORE, Dayton St, near Corry, (937) 767-7997. Gay & lesbian sections.

YOUNGSTOWN

Information
AIDS HOTLINE, (330) 742-8811. Manned 8am-4pm or leave message for return call.

Bars
PHIL'S, 10 E La Clede, (330) 782-6991.

Dance Bar/Disco
SOPHIE'S LOUNGE, 2 E LaClede St, (330) 782-8080. Shows Sun, 50% men, 50% women.
TROUBADOUR, 2618-24 Market St near, Indianola (rear), (330) 788-4379. Shows Thurs, 60% men, 40% women.

OKLAHOMA

NORMAN

Retail & Bookstores
MYSTIC FOREST TREASURES, 323 White St, (405) 447-5111. Gift shop with new age items, gay & lesbian & feminist poster & T-shirts, books, artwork, crafts, jewelry, rainbow items. 11-6 Mon-Sat. Lesbian-owned.

OKLAHOMA CITY

Information
GAY, LESBIAN & AIDS REFERRAL, (405) 525-2437.

Accommodations
HABANA INN, 2200 NW 39th Expwy, Oklahoma City, OK, 73112, (405) 528-2221, (800) 988-2221. Hotel, bar, & restaurant, women welcome, some straight clientele. Private baths.

Bars
HI LO CLUB, 1221 NW 50th St, (405) 843-1722. Quiet piano bar, shows weekends."
KA'S, 2024 NW 11., Beer bar.
LIDO, 2200 NW 39th Expy, inside Habana Inn complex., Quiet piano bar, karaoke Thurs, 70% men.
PARTNERS 4, 2805 NW 36th, (405) 942-2199.

Dance Bar/Disco
★ **COPA**, 2200 NW 39th Expy, at Habana Inn Complex, (405) 525-0730. Hi energy dance & show bar, 60% men, 40% women. Tues-Sun male dancers, Tues live underwear contests.
COYOTE CLUB, 2120 NW 39th, (405) 521-9533. Womens dance club, Thurs-Sun.
★ **FINISH LINE**, 2200 NW 39th Expy, at Habana Inn Complex, (405) 525-0730. DJ, pool table, darts, C&W dance lessons certain nites.
WRECK ROOM, 2127 NW 39th, (405) 525-7610. Weekends only, after-hours

OKLAHOMA

juice bar, very young crowd, large straight following.

Restaurants
GUSHER'S RESTAURANT, 2200 NW 39th Expy, at the Copa bar in Habana Inn, (405) 525-0730. Dinner.

PATIO CAFE, 5100 N Classen, (405) 842-7273. Breakfast & lunch all day.

PIZZA HAVEN, 2124 NW 39th St, (405) 557-1200.

Retail & Bookstores
HERLAND SISTER RESOURCES, INC., 2312 NW 39th St., (405) 521-9696. Feminist bookstore, open Sat 10am-6pm & Sun 1pm-6pm. Scheduled coffee house, workshops & resources, 2 retreats per year.

JUNGLE RED, 2200 NW 39th St, inside the Habana Inn, (405) 524-5733. Cards, T-shirts, leather, rainbow items, magazines, etc.

TULSA

Dance Bar/Disco
★ **CONCESSIONS,** 3340 S Peoria, (918) 744-0896. 9pm-2am Wed-Sun, male strippers Thurs, drag shows Sun, 60% men, 40% women.

★ **SILVER STAR SALOON, THE,** 1565 S Sheridan, (918) 834-4234. C&W dance bar, dance lessons.

Bontemps Motel

- Cable TV HBO
- Double/Queen Beds
- Kitchenette Available
- In-Room Phones
- Weekly Rates

Burns Oregon

(800) 229-1394

TNT, 2114 S Memorial, near 21st, (918) 660-0856.

Cafe
GOLD COAST CAFE, 3509 S Peoria,

Restaurants
WILD FORK, 1820 Utica Sq, (918) 742-0712. Woman-owned elegant restaurant.

Retail & Bookstores
PRIDE STORE, 1307 E 38th St, (918) 743-4297. Rainbow store inside the Pride Center.

OREGON
ASHLAND

Accommodations
WILL'S RESTE, 298 Hargadine St, Ashland, OR, 97520, (541) 482-4394. Web: http://members.aol.com/llinmarin/willsreste/index.htm, B&B guesthouse, some straight clientele. Cozy, comfortable rooms with antique furniture. Self-contained cottage. Hot tub, continental breakfast & nearby pool & lake.

Women's Accommodations
SISTERFIELDS BED & BREAKFAST COUNTRY RESORT, PO Box 1101, Ashland, OR, 97520, (541) 512-0357. B&B with private bath, continental breakfast, men welcome.

Restaurants
WHISTLE STOP CAFE, 258 A St #3-B, (541) 488-3354.

BANDON

Accommodations
LAKECREST VACATION HOME, Rt 1, Box 930, Bradley Lake, Bandon, OR, 97411, (541) 347-4409. Email: psselect@harborside.com, Vacation home on the S Oregon coast, mostly straight with a gay & lesbian following.

BROOKINGS

Accommodations
OCEANCREST HOUSE, 15510 Pedrioli Dr, Brookings, OR, (800) 769-9200, (541) 469-9200, Fax: (541) 469-8864 (shared). Email: innkeep@wave.net, Web: http://bestinns.net/usa/or/ocean.html, Gay-friendly B&B, large detached room, pri-

vate bath, color cable TV, expanded continental breakfast.

SOUTH COAST INN BED & BREAKFAST, 516 Redwood St, Brookings, OR, 97415, (800) 525-9273, (541) 469-5557, Fax: 469-6615. Email: scoastin@wave.net. Craftsman-style home on the coast, gourmet breakfast, ocean views, Jacuzzi, sauna, color TV, private baths. 50% gay & lesbian clientele.

BURNS

Accommodations
BONTEMPS MOTEL, 74 West Monroe, Burns, OR, 97720, (541) 573-2037, (800) 229-1394, Fax: (541) 573-2577. Friendly atmosphere, vintage charm and style. Suites, kitchennettes and studios have cable TV and HBO, in-room phones and double or queen beds. Continental breakfast served. We're about 130 mi. SE of Bend, our natural paradise is perfect for hunters, fishermen and rock hounds. We're south of Malheur Nat'l Forest and just north of Malheur Lake. 50% gay and lesbian clientele. Gambling casino to open 4 blocks away in '98.

CORVALLIS

Restaurants
NEARLY NORMALS, 109 NW 15th St, (541) 753-0791. Gonzo cuisine, vegetarian.

Retail & Bookstores
GRASS ROOTS, 227 SW 2nd St, (541) 754-7668. Alternative lifestyle bookstore with women's & gay men's books, women's music.

EUGENE

Information
AIDS & HIV SERVICES, (541) 342-5088. Mon-Fri 9am-5pm.

Dance Bar/Disco
CLUB ARENA, 959 Pearl, downstairs from Pass the Pepper Restaurant, (541) 683-2360. Dance & show bar from 7pm daily, 60% men, 40% women, large straight clientele.

NEIGHBORS, 1417 Villard St, (541) 338-0334. Dance bar & restaurant, lunch & dinner, serves from 11am to closing. Tues women's nite, DJ Tues, Wed, Fri, Sat, drag show Wed, open 7 days.

Cafe
BEANERY, 152 W 5th St, (541) 342-3378.

Restaurants
EMERALD CITY BISTRO, 525 Willamette, (541) 485-2363. Women's events some evenings.

PASS THE PEPPER, 959 Pearl, (541) 683-2360. Breakfast-dinner, closed Sun.

Retail & Bookstores
MOTHER KALI'S BOOKS, 720 E 13 Ave, (541) 343-4864. Email: kali@efn.org, Women's bookstore. Our lesbian section is the largest in the northwest. Mon-Fri 9am-6pm, Sat 10am-6pm. Free parking in basement via the alley.

Mother Kali's Books
"Celebrating Women's Lives in All Our Diversities"

Books
Music
Cards

(541) 343-4864
Mon-Fri 9-6
Sat 10-6

Mail Order
Used Books

720 E. 13 AVE
Eugene OR 97401

FREE PARKING IN BASEMENT
Email: kali@efn.org

402 OREGON

PERALANDRA, 5th St, by Pearl, (541) 485-4848. Metaphysical bookstore, books & music. Mon-Sat 10am-6pm.

RUBY CHARM, 152 W 5th, (541) 344-4074. New Age, goddess shop, jewelry.

KLAMATH FALLS

■ *Information*
HIV RESOURCE CENTER, (541) 883-2437. Tape."

LINCOLN CITY

■ *Accommodations*
OCEAN GARDENS INN, 2735 NW Inlet, Lincoln City, OR, 97367, (541) 994-5007, (800) 866-9925. Guest line (541) 994-3069. Oceanfront inn. Rooms & suites with kitchenettes, all private baths. 50% gay & lesbian clientele.

MEDFORD

■ *Restaurants*
CADILLAC CLUB, 207 W 8th St, (541) 857-9411.

NEWPORT

■ *Women's Accommodations*
GREEN GABLES BED & BREAKFAST, 156 SW Coast St, Newport, OR, 97365, (541) 265-9141. B&B, shared bath, men welcome. ♀

■ *Restaurants*
COSMOS CAFE & GALLERY, 740 W Olive St, (541) 265-7511. Continental breakfast thru dinner. Specialty, vegetarian cuisine. Gay friendly.

■ *Retail & Bookstores*
GREEN GABLES BOOKSTORE, 156 SW Coast St, (541) 265-9141. Women's books & music and children's books.

PORTLAND

■ *Information*
AIDS HOTLINE, (503) 223-AIDS or (800) 777-AIDS. Mon-Fri 10am-9pm. Sat & Sun noon-6pm.

■ *Accommodations*
A TUDOR HOUSE BED & BREAKFAST, 2321 NE 28th Ave, Portland, OR, 97212, (503) 287-9476, Fax: (503) 288-8363. Gay-friendly B&B, private & shared baths, full breakfast.

BRIGHTRIDGE FARM B & B, 18575 Brightridge Rd, Sheridan, OR, (503) 843-5230." B&B with private baths, full breakfast, mostly straight clientele with a gay & lesbian following.

HOLLADAY HOUSE, 1735 NE Wasco, Portland, OR, 97232, (503) 282-3172. The hospitality of two grandmothers makes you feel welcome. We're close to a large shopping mall, congenial markets and coffee bars, and only 15 minutes from downtown via light rail. Mary Rose will help you locate places of women's musical interest. When visiting Portland, enjoy our breakfast and clean, comfortable rooms. We hope you find our neighborhood as special as we do.

MACMASTER HOUSE CIRCA 1895, 1041 SW Vista Ave, Portland, OR, 97205, (503) 223-7362, reservations: (800) 774-9523. Web: www.macmaster.com, Gay-friendly B&B with antique shop. Color TV, AC, private & shared baths, full breakfast, pool nearby.

SULLIVAN'S GULCH BED & BREAKFAST, 1744 NE Clackamas Street, Portland, OR, 97232, (503) 331-1104, Fax: (503) 331-1575. Email: thegulch@teleport.com, Web: www.teleport.com/~thegulch/, B&B in quiet area close to everything. Private baths, ceiling fans, expanded continental breakfast. No smoking inside. ♀♂

■ *Bars*
EMBERS AVENUE, 110 NW Broadway., ♪ ♫ ♀♂

HOBO'S, 120 NW 3rd, (503) 224-3285. Piano bar, yuppie crowd, Fri & Sat jazz, pool room in rear, lounge food, full dinners. ♀♂

JOQ'S, 2512 NE Broadway, near 14th, (503) 287-4210. Tavern. ♀♂

■ *Dance Bar/Disco*
★ EGYPTIAN CLUB, THE, 3701 SE Division, (503) 236-8689. 7pm-2am, younger crowd. ♀

PANORAMA, 341 SW 10th Ave, in same complex with Boxxes, Brig & Fish Grotto, Dance bar, Fri & Sat only with after hours till 4am. ♀♂

RAGE NIGHTCLUB & CAFE, 333 SW Park, near Stark, (503) 286-1764. Mainly under 21yrs, mixed crowd, Thurs 10pm-

OREGON

2am, Fri & Sat 10pm-4am (after-hours till 4am Fri-Sat), alternative music disco upstairs.

■ Cafe

ADOBE ROSE, 1634 SE Bybee Blvd, (503) 235-9114. New Mexico cuisine.

CHEZ WHAT?, 22nd & Alberta, (503) 281-1717.

ESPRESS IT, 1026 SW Stark, next door to Scandals, (503) 227-2551. Espresso bar, light meals, conversation, art.

JOHN ST CAFE, 8338 N Lombard, (503) 247-1066.

■ Restaurants

BASTA TRATTORIA, 410 NW 21st St, (503) 274-1572.

BIJOU CAFÉ, 132 SW 3rd, (503) 222-3187. Breakfast & lunch, gay-friendly.

BIMA, 1338 NW Hoyt, (503) 241-3465.

CADILLAC CAFE, 914 NE Broadway, near Ninth, (503) 287-4750. Breakfast, lunch, 7 days.

CASWELL RESTAURANT, 533 SE Grand Ave, (503) 232-6512.

CHAMELEON, 2000 NE 40th, Hollywood District, (503) 460-2682. Restaurant & bar, eclectic menu from Italian to Thai cuisine.

CUP AND SAUCER, 3566 SE Hawthorne Blvd, (503) 236-6001. Gay-friendly restaurant.

FISH GROTTO, 1035 SW Stark, (503) 226-4171. Seafood, lunch, dinner.

FOX & HOUNDS, 217 NW 2nd., Restaurant & lounge, karaoke.

HAMBURGER MARY'S, 239 SW Broadway, (503) 223-0900.

HOBO'S, 120 NW 3rd, at Hobo's bar, (503) 224-3285. From 4pm.

LA CATALANA, 2821 SE Stark, (503) 232-0948. Catalan cuisine.

LAURELTHIRST PUBLIC HOUSE, 2958 NE Glisan, (503) 232-1504. Pub & restaurant.

OLD WIVES' TALES, 1300 E Burnside St, at 13th Ave, (503) 238-0470. Vegetarian & special diet menu, breakfast thru dinner. Sat & Sun brunch, children's play area.

STARKY'S, 2913 SE Stark, at 29th, (503) 230-7980. Lounge & restaurant, 65% men, 35% women. Fine dining, lunch & dinner."

WILD ABANDON, 2411 SE Belmont, (503) 232-4458. Nouvelle American cuisine.

■ Retail & Bookstores

CRIMSON PHOENIX, THE, 1876 SW 5th Ave, (503) 228-0129. Gifts, cards, incense. We honor sexual diversity.

IN OTHER WORDS — WOMEN'S BOOKS & RESOURCES, 3734 SE Hawthorne Blvd, (503) 232-6003. Women's books, videos, gifts.

IT'S MY PLEASURE, 3106 NE 64th, (503) 280-8080. Women's cards, music, crafts, safe sex items, videos, feminist novelties & erotic toys.

POWELL'S BOOKS, 1005 W Burnside, (503) 228-4651. General bookstore with an extensive gay & lesbian section.

POWELL'S TRAVEL STORE, 701 SW 6th Ave, (503) 228-1108.

TWENTY-THIRD AVE BOOKS, 1015 NW 23rd Ave, near Lovejoy, (503) 224-5097. General bookstore with gay & lesbian sections.

■ Leathers/Piercing

SPARTACUS LEATHERS, 300 SW 12th Ave, (503) 224-2604. 10am-11pm Mon-Sat, 12-6 Sun.

Holladay House
Bed and Breakfast

Preferred by many Women Travelers

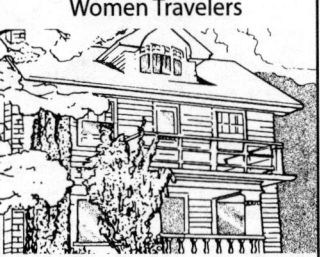

(503) 282-3172

Smoking Restricted

OREGON

ROGUE RIVER

Accommodations

WHISPERING PINES BED & BREAKFAST RETREAT, 9188 W. Evans Creek Rd, Rogue River, OR, 97537, (541) 582-1757, (800) 788-1757. Email: whispering_pines@hotmail.com, B&B retreat, some straight clientele. Variety of guest quarters with shared bath, TV lounge, Jacuzzi. Expanded continental breakfast & nearby river.

ROSEBURG

Information

GAY & LESBIAN SWITCHBOARD, (541) 672-4126, 24hrs. Answering service will patch call.

OWL (OREGON WOMEN'S LAND TRUST), (541) 679-4655. A working women's farm. Work trade or camping & visitor fees. Write first to PO Box 1692, Roseburg, OR 97470.

SALEM

Accommodations

MIDDLE CREEK RUN BED & BREAKFAST, 25400 Harmony Rd, Sheridan, OR, (503) 843-7606, (800) 843-7606." Gay-owned & -operated, 1902 Queen Anne B&B with shared baths, full breakfast, 50% gay/lesbian clientele.

Dance Bar/Disco

THREE HUNDRED CLUB, 300 Liberty St SE, in Pringle Park Plaza, (503) 363-0549. Dance bar with restaurant, 50% gay/lesbian, 50% straight.

Restaurants

A CHANGE OF SEASONS, 300 Liberty St SE, adjacent to 300 Club Bar, (503) 365-9722. Continental cuisine, dinner theater in same bldg, 50% gay/lesbian clientele.

OFF CENTER CAFE, 1741 Center St, NE, (503) 363-9245. A congenial gathering place for people of all persuasions, serving breakfast through dinner. Schedule varies.

Retail & Bookstores

ROSEBUD & FISH, 524 State St, (503) 399-9960. Alternative bookstore with gay & lesbian section, 7 days."

YACHATS

Accommodations

MORNING STAR B & B, 95668 Hwy 101, Yachats, OR, (541) 547-4412, Fax: (541) 547-4335. Email: artgal@teleport.com, Web: www.teleport.com/~artgal, Lesbian-owned & -run B&B & art gallery, ocean views, private baths, Jacuzzi, some straight clientele.

OCEAN ODYSSEY VACATION RENTALS, PO Box 491, Yachats, OR, 97498, (541) 547-3637, reservations (800) 800-1915. Gay-friendly, women-owned vacation rentals in Yachats & Waldport, OR. Tri-levels to family beach cottages, some with awesome views, some on the beach.

OREGON HOUSE, THE, 94288 Hwy 101, Yachats, OR, 97498, (541) 547-3329. Email: orehouse@aol.com, Gay-friendly oceanfront inn with small gift shop. Accommodations vary in size (rooms thru cottages), furnishings & amenities. Some with kitchens, fireplaces, Jacuzzi, most have ocean views.

SEE VUE, 95590 Hwy 101, Yachats, OR, 97498, (541) 547-3227. Gay-friendly motel. Variety of rooms with various motifs, modern conveniences, private baths & nearby ocean beach.

YACHATS INN, PO Box 307, Yachats, OR, 97498, (541) 547-3456. Gay-friendly ocean-view motel units with private baths, some with fireplaces, kitchens, indoor pool.

PENNSYLVANIA

ALLENTOWN

■ Bars
CANDIDA, 247 N 12th St, (610) 434-3071. Lite menu.

■ Dance Bar/Disco
STONEWALL, 28-30 N 10th St, (610) 432-0706 or 432-0215. Video dance bar, DJ Wed-Sun, drag shows Wed, 90% men. Second floor Moose Lounge & restaurant, lite menu."

ALTOONA

■ Dance Bar/Disco
ESCAPADE, 2523 Union Ave, (814) 946-8195. 60% men, 40% women. DJ Fri & Sat. Open 7 days, 8pm-2am.

BETHLEHEM

■ Dance Bar/Disco
★ **DIAMONZ,** 1913 W Broad St, (610) 865-1028. Dance club & dinner lounge, live entertainment, separate game room, 60% women, 40% men.

BOYERS

■ Accommodations
CAMP DAVIS, 311 Redbrush Rd, Boyers, PA, 16020, (412) 637-2402. Gay & lesbian campground with cabins, tent sites, RV parking sites, creek & swimming hole.

BRIDGEPORT

■ Dance Bar/Disco
LARK, THE, 302 DeKalb St, (610) 275-8136. DJ Fri & Sat, 75% men, 25% women. Sun dinner."

ERIE

■ Information
ERIE GAY & LESBIAN INFO, mail: 1115 W 7th St, Erie, PA, 16502-1105, (814) 456-9833 or (814) 453-2785. Email: egcn@ncinter.net, Web: www.eriegaynews.com, Leave message. Aids info call (800) 400-AIDS.

■ Bars
EMBERS, 1711 State St, (814) 454-9171. DJ Wed-Sat.

■ Dance Bar/Disco
VILLAGE, THE, 133 W 18th St, (814) 452-0125. Big dance bar, serves food, Mon, Tues 8-2, Wed-Sun 4-2., closed Sun, 50/50 men & women.

■ Cafe
AROMA'S COFFEE HOUSE, 2164 W 8th St, (814) 456-5282. Smoke-free coffees, lite menu, desserts.

CUP-A-CINO, 18 North Park Row, (814) 456-1151. Live music Sat. Poetry readings & storey nights scheduled Thur.

■ Restaurants
COQUI'S GOURMET DELI, 3443 W Lake Rd, (814) 835-2272.

TAPAS BODEGA, 17 West 9th St, (814) 454-8797, light, unusual & ethnic cuisines.

■ Retail & Bookstores
SCAPERS LTD, 2508 Peach St, (814) 456-7002. Gallery of gay & lesbian art, rainbow items, gifts.

GREENSBURG

■ Bars
RK'S, 108 W Pittsburgh St, (724) 837-6614. Shows weekends.

HARFORD

■ Accommodations
NINE PARTNERS INN B & B, 1 N Harmony Rd, PO Box 300, Harford, PA, 18823, (717) 434-2233.

HARRISBURG

■ Information
GAY & LESBIAN SWITCHBOARD, (717) 234-0328. Mon-Fri 6pm-10pm. Unverifiable spring '98.

■ Bars
NEPTUNE LOUNGE, 268 North St, near 3rd, (717) 233-0581. Video bar & restaurant, DJ Fri-Sun, 75% men, 25% women.

STRAWBERRY CAFE, 704 N 3rd St, near Briggs, (717) 234-4228. Video bar, 80% men, 20% women (more on wknds). Closed Sun.

■ Dance Bar/Disco
B-TELS, 891 Eisenhower Blvd, (717) 939-1123. DJ Fri & Sat, pool tables, games,

406 PENNSYLVANIA

7:30pm-1am Thurs, 7pm-2am Fri & Sat.
STALLION, 706 N 3rd St (rear), (717) 232-3060. Complex with multiple bars.

Restaurants
PAPER MOON, 268 North St, at Neptune Lounge men's bar, (717) 233-0581. Continental cuisine.

INDIANA

Retail & Bookstores
JOSEPHINE'S BOOKS, 1176 Grant St #2180, (412) 465-4469. Feminist bookstore specializing in books written by women. Large selection of lesbian titles. Also, women's crafts. Mon-Fri 11am-8pm, Sat 10am-4pm.

JOHNSTOWN

Accommodations
ROLLING STONE ACRES B & B, 1740 Frankstown Rd, Johnstown, PA, 15902, (814) 539-0842. B&B with full or continental breakfast, shared bath, 50% gay/lesbian clientele.

Dance Bar/Disco
LUCILLE'S, 520 Washington St, (814) 539-4448. 70% men, 30% women, game room. From 8pm, closed Sun, Mon.

KUTZTOWN

Accommodations
GRIM'S MANOR, 10 Kern Road, Kutztown, PA, 19530, (610) 683-7089. B&B, some straight clientele. Variety of rooms, private baths, TV lounge, kitchen, full homestyle breakfast."

LANCASTER

Information
GAY HELP LINE, (717) 397-0691. Wed, Thur, Sun 7pm-10pm.

Bars
SUNDOWN LOUNGE, 429 N Mulberry St, near Lemon, (717) 392-2737. Quiet neighborhood bar from 8pm, Fri & Sat from 3pm, closed Sun."

Dance Bar/Disco
TALLY-HO, 201 W Orange St, at Water, (717) 299-0661. 75% men, 25% women.

Restaurants
LOFT, THE, 201 W Orange St, above Tally-Ho bar, (717) 299-0661. Closed Sun.

MANHEIM

Bars
CELLAR BAR, 168 S Main St, (717) 665-1960. Dance bar, DJ Fri & Sat.

NEW HOPE

Accommodations
FOX & HOUND B&B OF NEW HOPE, 246 W Bridge St, New Hope, PA, 18938, (215) 862-5082 or (800) 862-5082 (outside of PA). Web: http://www.visitbucks.com/foxandhound, B&B, 50% gay/lesbian clientele. Large rooms with antique furnishings, private baths. Near pool, river, walking distance to town center. Continental breakfast Mon-Fri, full breakfast Sun.
LEXINGTON HOUSE, THE, 6171 Upper York Rd, New Hope, PA, 18938, (215) 794-0811. B&B, private baths, some straight clientele."
RAVEN, THE, 385 W Bridge St, New Hope, PA, 18938, (215) 862-2081. Motel with restaurant & bar, private & shared baths."
YORK STREET HOUSE B & B, THE, 42 York Street, Lambertville, NJ, 08530, (609) 397-3007, Fax: (609) 397-9677. Email: nferg@msn.com, Elegant 1909 Manor House with private baths, full breakfast, 2 blocks to shops, a short walk to New Hope, PA. 50% gay & lesbian clientle.

Bars
★ **RAVEN, THE,** 385 W Bridge St, at The Raven Hotel, (215) 862-2081. Indoor & poolside bars, patio, & restaurant. Popular Sun afternoon.

Dance Bar/Disco
★ **CARTWHEEL CLUB,** 437 York Rd, at junction Hwy 202, (215) 862-0880. Large club with piano bar, video dance bar, restaurant, outdoor deck, drag shows Mon, male strippers Wed.

PENNSYLVANIA

■ Restaurants
CARTWHEEL, 437 York Rd, at Cartwheel bar., Dinner. ♀♂

■ Retail & Bookstores
BOOK GALLERY, 19 W Mechanic St, (215) 862-5110. Alternative bookstore with emphasis on feminist, lesbian & gay books. Some Pride items.

EMBER GLOW, 27 W Mechanic St, (215) 862-2929. Gift shop with large selection of pride items.

■ Erotica
GROWNUPS, 2 E Mechanic St, (215) 862-9304. Erotic store with pride items.

JOY'S BOOKS, 103 Springbrook Arms, Rt 29, Lambertville, NJ, (609) 397-2907. Adult bookstore with gay & lesbian section, 10am-10pm. Across the bridge from New Hope.

NEW MILFORD

■ Camping & RV
ONEIDA CAMPGROUND AND LODGE, PO Box 537, New Milford, PA, 18834, (717) 465-7011 or (717) 853-3503. Guesthouse, campground & lodge with clubhouse & sauna, women welcome. Variety of guest quarters with modern conveniences, RV & tent sites, shared baths, TV lounge, library, fitness center. ♀♂

PHILADELPHIA

■ Information
AIDS LINE, (215) 985-AIDS (2437).
GAY SWITCHBOARD, (888) 843-4564. 7-10pm, or tape.

■ Accommodations
ANTIQUE ROW BED & BREAKFAST, 341 South 12th St, Philadelphia, PA, 19107, (215) 592-7802, Fax: (215) 592-9692. B&B & fully furnished flat, 50% gay & lesbian clientele. Private & shared baths, color cable TV, AC & full breakfast.

CARITAS BED & BREAKFAST NETWORK, (800) CARITAS, (312) 857-0801, Fax: (312) 857-0805. B&B, home-stay accommodations service. Member: IGLTA

GASKILL HOUSE, 312 Gaskill St, Philadelphia, PA, 19147, (215) 413- 2887 or (215) 413-0669. Email: erosphilly@aol.com, B & B guesthouse in the Society Hill District, full breakfast buffet, private baths, some straight clientele. ♀♂

Visit Philadelphia
(800) CARITAS
Caritas B&B Network

GLEN ISLE FARM COUNTRY INN, Downingtown, PA, 19335-2239, (610) 269-9100, Reservations/Info: (800) 269-1730, Fax: (610) 269-9191. Bed & breakfast inn opening spring 1994. Private & shared baths, full breakfast.

UNCLES UPSTAIRS INN, 1220 Locust St, Philadelphia, PA, 19107, (215) 546-6660, Fax: (215) 546-1653. B&B with gay/lesbian bar on premises, private baths, continental breakfast, color TV, AC, phone, women welcome. ♂

■ Bars
BACKSTAGE, 614 S 4th St, near Kater, (215) 627-9887. Restaurant & bar, continental cuisine. ♀♂

EIGHTH ST LOUNGE, 8th at Callowhill, (215) 925-1900. Cocktail lounge & restaurant, DJ Wed-Sun, club circuit crowd.

PORT BLUE, 2552 E Allegheny Ave, (215) 425-4699. ♀♂

TAVERN ON CAMAC, 243 S Camac St, near Locust, (215) 545-6969. Piano bar, restaurant downstairs." ♂

★ **VENTURE INN,** 255 S Camac St, near Spruce, (215) 545-8731. Bar and restaurant. ♂

■ Dance Bar/Disco
FLUID, 613 S 4th St, (215) 629-3686. Gay Sun, younger crowd. ♂

★ **PALMER SOCIAL CLUB,** 601 Spring Garden St, (215) 925-5000. Private club, after hours with NYC flavor, liquor till 3am, 3 floors with different DJs, 7 nites, 20% gay. ♂

★ **SISTERS,** 1320 Chancellor St, at Juniper, (215) 735-0735. ♀

TYZ, 1418 Rodman St, at Rodz bar, (215) 546-4195. Priv. after-hours club, 90% men, 10% women. Guests welcome. ♂

PENNSYLVANIA

★ **WOODY'S,** 202 S 13th St, at Chancellor, (215) 545-1893. Pub and separate hi-energy video dance bar, C&W nites, internet bar, swing music Thurs. Pub has lunch, Sun brunch, late-nite food. Most popular bar in Philadelphia.

■ Cafe

FIFTH ST CAFE, 517 S 5th St, (215) 925-3500.

MILLENIUM, 212 S 12th St, (215) 731-9798. Popular with gays.

■ Restaurants

ASTRAL PLANE, 1708 Lombard St, near 17th, (215) 546-6230. New American cuisine, Sun brunch."

BONAPARTE'S, Broad & Spruce.,

CAFE ON QUINCE, at Bike Stop bar., Theater crowd.

CHEAP ART CAFE, 260 S 12th St.,

★ **JUDY'S CAFE,** 627 South 3rd St, (215) 928-1968. Ecclectic menu, vegetarian available.

TAVERN ON CAMAC, 243 S Camac St, at Raffles bar, (215) 545-6969. Continental menu, moderate prices.

★ **VENTURE INN,** 255 S Camac St, at Venture Inn men's bar.,

★ **WALDORF CAFE,** 20th & Lombard, (215) 985-1836.

■ Retail & Bookstores

AFTERWORDS, 218 South 12th St, (215) 735-2393. General bookstore with gay titles.

GIOVANNI'S ROOM, 345 S 12th Street, at Pine, (215) 923-2960. Gay, lesbian, feminist bookstore, 11:30am-9pm (Wed till 7pm, Fri till 10pm), Sat 10am-10pm. Sun, 1-7pm."

HOUSE OF OUR OWN, 3920 Spruce St, (215) 222-1576. Women's studies, new & used.

PITTSBURGH

■ Information

GAY CENTER, 5808 Forward Ave, Squirrel Hill, (412) 422-0114. Answers Mon-Fri 6:30pm-9:30pm, Sat 3pm-6pm.

■ Accommodations

INN ON THE MEXICAN WAR STREETS, THE, 1606 Buena Vista St, Pittsburgh, PA, 15212, (412) 231-6544. Inn in a Victorian-era row house, close to downtown, private & shared baths, expanded continental breakfast, women welcome.

VICTORIAN HOUSE, 939 Western Ave, Pittsburgh, PA, 15233, (412) 231-4948. Five min from downtown, spacious rooms, full breakfast, gay-friendly B&B.

■ Bars

BREWERY TAVERN, 3315 Liberty Ave, at Herron, (412) 681-7991.

★ **IMAGES,** 965 Liberty Ave, near 10th St, (412) 391-9990. Video bar, male strippers, karaoke, 50% men, 50% women.

LIBERTY AVE SALOON, ask locally for address, Restaurant by day, gay/lesbian bar by nite, pool tables.

★ **NEW YORK, NEW YORK,** 5801 Ellsworth, at Maryland Shadyside, (412) 661-5600. Piano bar & restaurant, outdoor deck, Sun brunch, 50/50 men & women.

RUSTY RAIL SALOON, 704 Thompson Ave, McKees Rocks, (412) 331-9011.

■ Dance Bar/Disco

CJ DEIGHAN'S, 2506 W Liberty Ave, Dormont, (412) 561-4044.

DONNIE'S PLACE, 1226 Herron Ave, at Ruthven, (412) 682-9869. 3 floors with bar downstairs, upstairs dance bar, basement leather bar, 2 patios, pool tables.

HOUSE OF TILDEN, 941 Liberty Ave (2nd floor), (412) 391-0804. Private club, dance bar upstairs, lounge downstairs, after hours till 3am. 80% men, 20% women.

REAL LUCK CAFE, 1519 Penn Ave, (412) 566-8988. Bar, upstairs disco, 50% men, 50% women."

■ Cafe

COMMON GROUND, 5888 Ellsworth Ave, Shadyside, (412) 362-1190. Coffeehouse popular with women.

■ Restaurants

LIBERTY AVE SALOON, 941 Liberty Ave, downstairs., Lunch & dinner.

NEW YORK, NEW YORK, 5801 Ellsworth Ave, at NY NY bar., (412) 661-5600. Sun brunch 11am.

PENNSYLVANIA

Retail & Bookstores
A PLEASANT PRESENT, 2218 Murray Ave, (412) 421-7104, Fax: (412) 421-7105. Large selection of gay & lesbian gift items.
SAINT ELMO'S OUTWORDS, 2208 E Carson Street, (412) 431-9100. Gay & lesbian bookstore within general bookstore.

POCONOS MTN AREA

Accommodations
RAINBOW MOUNTAIN RESORT, 210 Mt. Nebo Rd., East Stroudsburg, PA, 18301, (717) 223-8484. Email: mountain@ptdprolog.net, Web: http://www.rainbowmountain.com, Resort with bar, disco, restaurant. Variety of guest quarters with private & shared baths, spectacular views, color TV, outdoor activities areas, full breakfast & dinner. Outdoor Olympic-sized pool.

Women's Accommodations
BLUEBERRY RIDGE, Mail to: McCarrick/Moran, RR 1 Box 67, Scotrun, PA, 18355, (717) 629-5036 or (516) 473-6701. Women-only B&B near Camelback ski area & Delaware Water Gap. Modern rooms, outdoor hot tub & full country breakfast.
STONEY RIDGE, mail to: P. McCarrick, RR 1 Box 67, Scotrun, PA, 18355, (717) 629-5036 or (516) 473-6701. Two-bedroom cedar log home, stone fireplace, beautifully furnished with antiques. Women only, nearby river & lake.

READING

Bars
NOSTALGIA, 1101 N 9th St, at Robeson, (610) 372-5557. Mostly women in evenings, especially Fri, Sat.
RAINBOW, S 10th St, (610) 373-1058. Small dance floor, DJ Fri & Sat.

Dance Bar/Disco
SCARAB, THE, 724 Franklin St, (610) 375-7878. Nightly, 50% men, 50% women. Closed Sun.

Retail & Bookstores
LAVENDER HEARTS, 13 North 9th St, (610) 372-1828. Alternative bookstore with crystals, new age items, gay & lesbian videos.

SCRANTON

Accommodations
WINTER PINES, RD 2, Box 2099, Hallstead, PA, 18822, (717) 879-2130. B&B in a restored farmhouse with 17 acres, a pond, volleyball, horseshoes & farm animals.

Dance Bar/Disco
BUZZ, 131 N Washington Ave, (717) 969-2899. Dance club, male dancers twice a month, open 7 days till 2am.

STATE COLLEGE

Information
GAY & LESBIAN SWITCHBOARD, (814) 237-1950. 6pm-9pm daily or tape.

STONEY RIDGE

For a warm, country feeling

Secluded, cedar log home
with all modern
conveniences, near skiing,
canoeing, hiking, antiquing

(717) 629-5036

Mail to: P. McCarrick, RR1 Box 67
Scotrun, PA 18355

410 PENNSYLVANIA

Bars
CHUMLEY'S, 108 W College Ave, (814) 238-4446. 50% men, 50% women. Popular with women for Sun evening happy hour.

Dance Bar/Disco
PLAYERS, 112 W College Ave, inside the Hotel State College, (814) 237-4350. Gay night Sun, but never all gay.

SUNBURY

Bars
RAINBOW INN, Klinger Rd, (717) 988-4688. Open weekends.

VALLEY FORGE

Accommodations
MANOR HOUSE, THE, 210 Virginia Ave, Phoenixville, PA, 19460, (610) 983-9867. Gay-friendly B&B, 10% gay clientele. Private or shared baths, full breakfast, AC, TV lounge, laundry facilities, kitchen for guests' use, nearby lake.

WILKES-BARRE

Dance Bar/Disco
RUMORS, between Wilkes-Barre & Plains on Rte 315, (717) 825-7300. About 1/2 mile out of Wilkes-Barre & 3/4 miles past junction of Hwys 315 & 115. Dance bar & rest., dinner W-Su, open 7 days, 4pm-2am. 50% men, 50% women.
SELECTIONS, 45 Public Square, (717) 829-4444. DJ Fri & Sat, C&W music Thurs.
VAUDEVILLA, 465 Main St, Kingston, (717) 287-9250. From 7pm, DJ Fri, closed Sun."

WILLIAMSPORT

Bars
PEACHIE'S COURT, 320 Court St, (717) 326-3611. 3pm-2am Mon-Sat, small dance floor.

Dance Bar/Disco
RAINBOW ROOM, 761 W 4th St, near Camel St, Open Mon-Fri.

YORK

Information
HELP LINE, (717) 755-1000, ask for York Support. Gay and lesbian community group providing social activities, networking, monthly meetings, newsletter.

Bars
FOURTEEN KARAT, 659 W Market St., Juke box & CDs, 80% men, 20% women. Closed Sun.

Dance Bar/Disco
ALTLAND'S RANCH, RR 6, Box 6543, Spring Grove, about 15 miles west of York off Rte 30 W, (717) 225-4479. Large dance bar, Fri & Sat only. Fri C&W, 50/50 men & women Sat.

Retail & Bookstores
HER STORY BOOKSTORE, 2 W Market St, Hallam, (717) 757-4270. Women's books.

RHODE ISLAND
NEWPORT

Accommodations
BRINLEY VICTORIAN INN, 23 Brinley St, Newport, RI, 02840, (401) 849-7645, (800) 999-8523, Fax: (401) 845-9634. Gay-friendly B&B inn.

CAPTAIN JAMES PRESTON HOUSE, 378 Spring St, Newport, RI, 02840, (401) 847-4386, Fax: (401) 847-1093. Email: EEXK82A@prodigy.com, Web: http://pages.prodigy.com/EEXK82A, Gay-friendly Victorian B&B with private & shared baths, expanded continental breakfast. An easy walk to Newport attractions, beaches & shopping. Gay & lesbian following.

HYDRANGEA HOUSE INN, 16 Bellevue Ave, Newport, RI, 02840, (401) 846-4435, (800) 945-4667, Fax: (401) 846-6602. Email: bandbinn@ids.net, Gay-friendly bed & breakfast in excellent location. Rooms elegantly decorated with antiques & plush carpeting. Full breakfast. Nearby ocean beach & gym. 50 % gay & lesbian clientele.

MELVILLE HOUSE INN, 39 Clarke St, Newport, RI, 02840, (401) 847-0640, (800) 711-7184, Fax: (404) 847-0956. Email: innkeeper@ids.net, Conveniently located B&B, mostly straight clientele. Colonial decor, private & shared baths & expanded continental breakfast. Ocean nearby.

PROSPECT HILL GUEST HOUSE, 32 Prospect Hill St, Newport, RI, (401) 847-

7405 or (401) 847-7383. Guesthouse with art gallery, private baths, continental breakfast, some straight clientele. David's bar & disco next door. ♀♂

Bars
DAVID'S, 28 Prospect Hill, near Spring, (401) 847-9698. DJ Fri & Sat, patio, 60% men, 40% women.

PROVIDENCE

Information
AIDS LINE, (800) 726-3010.

GAY & LESBIAN HELPLINE, (401) 751-3322, 7-11pm Mon-Fri or tape.

SARAH DOYLE WOMEN'S CENTER, 185 Meeting St, near Brown at Brown University, (401) 863-2189. Women's resources, gallery, library, programs & info.

Bars
CLUB INTOWN, 95 Eddy St, (401) 751-0020. 80% men, 30% women, male strippers Sun.

SKIPPERS, 70 Washington St, (401) 751-4241. 60% men, 40% women.

WHEELS, 125 Washington, (401) 272-6950. 70% men.

Dance Bar/Disco
★ **DEVILLE'S CAFE,** 10 Davol Square, Historic Simmons Bldg, (401) 751-7166. Nightclub with cafe, 5pm-1am Tues-Thurs, 5pm-2am Fri, 6pm-2am Sat, 6pm-midnight Sun.

LOFT, THE, 325 Farnham Pike, Smithfield, (401) 231-3320. Disco with huge swimming pool. Winter: 4pm-1 or 2am. Summer: Dance parties start by the pool & end by the disco, May-Oct noon-1am.

MIRROR BAR, 35 Richmond, (401) 331-6761. Large dance bar, 70% men, 30% women.

UNION STREET STATION, 69 Union St, (401) 331-2291. 60% men, 40% women.

Restaurants
LUCY'S, 441 Atwels Ave, (401) 273-1189.

Retail & Bookstores
DORRWAR BOOKS, 312 Wickenden St, (401) 521-3230. General bookstore with a gay & lesbian selection, closed Sun.

WESTERLY

Accommodations
VILLA, THE, 190 Shore Road, Westerly, RI, 02891, (401) 596-1054, (800) 722-9240, Fax: (401) 596-6268. Web: www.thevilla atwesterly.com, Gay-friendly B&B with lush gardens, Italian fountains and majestic porticos and verandas. After sunning, splash and frolic in our sparkling sapphire pool and unwind in the outdoor hot tub. In winter, escape to your own fireplace or the hot waters of your private Jacuzzi. Just five minutes from beaches, we're at the crossroads of historic Westerly and the quaint seaside village of Watch Hill, close to Mystic and the Foxwoods Resort & Casino.

The Villa
An Oasis of Privacy and Luxury

- Fireplace & Jacuzzi Suites
- Outdoor Hot Tub & Mediterranean Pool
- Adjacent to Golf Course
- Ocean Beaches Nearby

Westerly, Rhode Island

(800) 722-9240
www.thevillaatwesterly.com

RHODE ISLAND

WOONSOCKET

Dance Bar/Disco
KINGS & QUEENS, 285 Front St, (401) 762-9538. Dance & show bar, 50% men, 50% women.

SOUTH CAROLINA

ANDERSON

Dance Bar/Disco
EUROPA, 116 E Benson St., Open 7 days.

BEAUFORT

Accommodations
TWOSUNS INN BED & BREAKFAST, 1705 Bay Street, Beaufort, SC, 29902, (803) 522-1122 (Tel/Fax), (800) 532-4244. Area code changing to (843) in March, 1998. Email: twosuns@islc.net, Web: twosunsinn.com, Gay-friendly B&B on the bay in a charming coastal town, 45 mi from Savannah, GA & 65 mi from Charleston, SC, with private baths, full breafkast. Small gay male following.

CHARLESTON

Accommodations
CALHOUN HOUSE, 273 Calhoun St, Charleston, SC, 29401, (803) 722-7341. Email: CHS65@AOL.COM, Guesthouse. Color cable TV, AC, ceiling fans, private & shared baths, TV lounge & continental breakfast.

CHARLESTON BEACH B & B, PO Box 41, Folly Beach, SC, 29439, (803) 588-9443. A destination for all seasons! The only gay and lesbian accommodations at the ocean between Fort Lauderdale and North Carolina. Ten miles to historic district of Charleston, America's premier walking city! Fine restaurants, cultural events and plantations. Eight rooms, affordable prices, expanded continental breakfast, social hour, spa and pool and AC.

EIGHTEEN FIFTY-FOUR BED & BREAKFAST, 34 Montagu Street, Charleston, SC, 29401, (803) 723-4789. B&B, some straight clientele. Suites with private baths, kitchens, color TV, private garden area & continental breakfast.

Bars
DUDLEY'S, 346 King St, near Burns Alley, (803) 723-2784. Private club, 70% men, 30% women. Cd jukebox, call ahead for guest membership.

Dance Bar/Disco
ARCADE, 5 Liberty St, near King, (803) 722-5656. 2 bars: country bar & hi-energy disco.

DEJA VU 2, 445 Savannah Hwy, (803) 556-5588. Shows, exotic dancers, bands, Wed-Sun from 7pm, in winter from 5pm.

Restaurants
RIVER CAFE, 88 Sandbar Lane, Folly Beach, (803) 588-2255. Fresh seafood, sandwiches, full liquor.

Retail & Bookstores
HEALING RAYS, 57 Broad St, (803) 853-4499. Feminist books & gifts, closed Mon.

COLUMBIA

Information
AIDS HOTLINE, (803) 779-7257, (800) 723-7257. 9am-5:30pm Mon-Fri.

GAY & LESBIAN PRIDE MOVEMENT INFO LINE, 1108 Woodrow St, (803) 771-7713. Answers irregularly.

Bars
CAPITOL CLUB, 1002 Gervais, (803) 256-6464. Private club, conversation

---

Charleston Beach B&B

P.O. Box 41
Folly Beach
South Carolina
29439

(803) 588-9443

SOUTH CAROLINA

lounge, some straight clientele. Travelers call first.

Dance Bar/Disco
DOWNTOWN, 1109 Assembly, (803) 771-0121. Male strippers, cruise bar.

★ **METROPOLIS**, 1800 Blanding, (803) 799-8727. Thurs-Sun 10pm-3 or 4am, male strippers Fri, drag shows Thurs-Sun, 50% men, 50% women.

TRAXX, 416 Lincoln St, at the railroad tracks, (803) 256-1084.

Restaurants
ALLEY CAFE, 911 Lady St, (803) 771-2778. Woman-owned.

FOLLY BEACH

, See Charleston.,

GREENVILLE

Information
GAY & LESBIAN SWITCHBOARD, (864) 271-4207.

Bars
CLUB 621, 621 Airport Rd, (864) 234-6767. Private club, travelers call for arrangements, drag shows Fri 3am. Mon-Tues 7pm-4am, Wed 7pm-5am, Thurs 7pm-4am, Sun 3pm-midnite.

SPANKY'S, 1607 Laurens Rd, (864) 233-0105.

Dance Bar/Disco
CASTLE, THE, 8 LeGrand Blvd, at Greenacre, (864) 235-9949. Dance & show bar. Private club, travelers call for arrangements, Thurs-Sat 9:30pm-4am, Sun 9:30pm-3am.

HILTON HEAD

Bars
MOONJAMMERS (MJ'S), 11 Heritage Plaza, (803) 842-9195. 8pm-2am 7 days, 60% men, 40% women, live entertainment twice a month.

MYRTLE BEACH

Bars
RAINBOW HOUSE BISTRO, Chester St near 10th Ave, (803) 626-7298. 60% women, 40% men, finger food.

TIME OUT, 520 8th Ave N, (803) 448-1180. Private club, daily from 5pm, 75% men, 25% women.

Dance Bar/Disco
ILLUSIONS, 1017 S Kings Hwy, (803) 448-0421. Alternative club.

METROPOLIS MYRTLE BEACH, 904 N Chester St, (803) 626-3151.

ROCK HILL

Bars
HIDE-A-WAY, 405 Baskins Rd, (803) 328-6630. Private club, live bands, Thurs-Sat 8pm-close, 70% women.

SPARTANBURG

Bars
CAVE, THE, Hwy 29 near Westgate, (864) 576-2683. From Spartanburg, Hwy 29 toward Greere. About midway on right side, behind Value Furniture. Cruise bar, 75% men, 25% women.

CHEYENNE CATTLEMEN'S CLUB (TRIPLE C), 995 Asheville Hwy, (864) 573-7304. 8pm-2am Tues-Sat, Sun 3pm-2am, occasional male strippers & drag shows, 90% men.

SOUTH DAKOTA
RAPID CITY - BLACK HILLS

■ Information
BLACK HILLS GAY & LESBIAN PHONE LINE, (605) 394-8080. Mon-Sat 6pm-10pm or tape.

FACES OF SOUTH DAKOTA, 2218 Jackson Blvd #8, (605) 343-5577, fax: (605) 394-8962. Gay organization, office & library, Mon-Fri usually 9am-5pm, Tues 7pm-10pm, Sat 1:30pm-5pm.

■ Accommodations
CAMP MICHAEL B & B, 13051 Bogus Jim Rd, Rapid City, SD, 57702, (605) 342-5590. Email: campmike@rapidnet.com, Web: www.campmike.com, B&B on 3 acres, 12 miles outside Rapid City, 15 minutes from Mt. Rushmore & Deadwood gambling. Three rooms share 2nd floor with living & dining room & baths. Video & book libraries. ♀♂

■ Camping & RV
DUSTER'S PLAYGROUND RV PARK, 702 Box Elder Rd, east of Rapid City, (605) 923-9701. 18 complete RV hookups, bar & restaurant, sand volleyball court, golf driving range, horseshoes, near a golf course. ♀♂

■ Bars
DUSTER'S PLAYGROUND, 702 Box Elder Rd, east of Rapid City at exit 63, off I-90, (605) 923-9701. DJ & live bands, 18 complete RV hookups, bar & restaurant, sand volleyball court, golf driving range, horseshoes, near a golf course. ♀♂

SIOUX FALLS

■ Information
GAY & LESBIAN COALITION, Suite 217, 8th & Railroad Pl, (605) 333-0603. Meets 3rd Sat 7:30pm.

■ Dance Bar/Disco
TOUCHÉ'Z, 323 S Phillips Ave (rear), near 12th St, (605) 335-9874. Dance bar & quiet bar areas, patio. 8pm-2am nightly, 60% men, 40% women.

TENNESSEE
BRISTOL

■ Accommodations
BELVEDERE HEIGHTS B & B, 100 Belvedere Heights, Bristol, TN, (423) 764-3860 (Tel/Fax). Gay-friendly B&B in a 1930s mansion, private baths, full breakfast, AC, phone, color TV.

CHATTANOOGA

■ Bars
MS TWISTERS, 1815 23rd St, (423) 622-2555. ♀

■ Dance Bar/Disco
ALAN GOLD'S, 1100 McCallie, at National, (423) 629-8080. Dance & show bar, DJ nightly, 20% gay/lesbian. ♀♂

CHUCK'S II, 27 W Main St, (423) 265-5405. C&W dance bar, 60% men, 40% women. ♀♂

MIRAGE, 115B Honest St, (423) 855-8210. Dance & show bar. ♀♂

GATLINBURG

■ Accommodations
CHRISTOPHER PLACE, 1500 Pinnacles Way, Newport, TN, 37821, (423) 623-6555, (800) 595-9441 (for brochure), Fax: (423) 613-4771. Email: thebestinn@aol.com, Inn with restaurant, 50% gay & lesbian clientele. Color cable TV, VCR, video tapes, AC, private baths, some hot tubs & fireplaces. TV lounge, game

---

camp michael

Good Food,
Good Friends,
A Comfortable
Bed
Rapid City
(605) 342-5590

TENNESSEE

room, tanning bed, sauna & pool. Full breakfast.
LAUGHING OTTER, 1321 Nobel St G, Alcoa, TN, (423) 983-9150. Fully-furnished, secluded cabin on wildlife sanctuary, 50% gay & lesbian clientele.

JOHNSON CITY

Dance Bar/Disco
NEW BEGINNINGS, 2910 N Bristol Hwy, (423) 282-4446. Dance bar, show bar, restaurant, Tues-Thurs, Sun from 9pm, Fri & Sat from 8pm, 50% men, 50% women. Closed Mon.

KNOXVILLE

Information
GAY & LESBIAN HELPLINE, (423) 531-2539, 7pm-11pm daily, staff permitting.

Dance Bar/Disco
CAROUSEL II, 1501 White Ave SW, near 15th, (423) 522-6966. Dance & show bars, 24 hr restaurant, 50% men, 50% women.

★ **ELECTRIC BARROOM,** 1213 Western Ave, (423) 525-6724. Huge gay & alternative dance bar, restaurant & giftshop in a warehouse, Wed-Sun 9pm-3am.

NETWORK, 4541 Kingston Pike, Disco internet bar, 5pm-2am daily.

Retail & Bookstores
DAVIS-KIDD BOOKSELLERS, 113 N Peters Rd, (423) 690-0136. General bookstore with gay & lesbian sections.
ZEPHYR WINDS OF CHANGE BOOKSTORE, 4921 Homberg Dr #B1 & B2, (423) 588-8061, Fax: (423) 588-3228. Mainly metaphysical bookstore with gay & lesbian sections.

MEMPHIS

Information
FRIENDS FOR LIFE HIV RESOURCES, 24hr Hotline: (901) 278-AIDS (2437). Office, 9am-5pm, (901) 272-0855.
GAY & LESBIAN SWITCHBOARD, 1486 Madison Ave, (901) 324-4297.

Bars
AUTUMN STREET PUB, 1349 Autumn, (901) 274-8010. Dance & show bar, full liquor.

CROSSROADS, THE, Jefferson at Claybrook., 75% men, 25% women, opens 11am.
ONE MORE, Peabody & Cooper, (901) 272-1700. 80% women.

Dance Bar/Disco
★ **AMNESIA,** 2866 Poplar Ave., Show, dance and conversation bars, 50% men/women, young crowd.
BACKSTREET, 2018 Court., After hours, 50% men, 50% women.
LORENZ, 1530 Madison, (901) 274-8272. Dance & cruise bar.
★ **MADISON FLAME, THE,** 1588 Madison Ave, (901) 278-9839. We're the hottest women's bar in Tennessee! Disco on weekends, country dancing Thurs, men welcome.

THE MADISON FLAME

Memphis'
Hottest
Night
Spot

1588 Madison Ave
Memphis, TN 38104

(901) 278-9839

Sharon Wray, prop.

416 TENNESSEE

N'COGNITO, 338 S Front, at Vance.,

Retail & Bookstores
MERISTEM, 930 S Cooper St, (901) 276-0282. Feminist & lesbian books, music, crafts, local info.

Erotica
GETWELL BOOKMART, 1275 Getwell, near airport, (901) 454-7765, 24hrs.

NASHVILLE

Accommodations
SAVAGE HOUSE INN B&B & TOWNHOUSE TEAROOM, 165 8th Ave North, Nashville, TN, 37203, (615) 254-1277. Hotel with restaurant & bar, 50% gay & lesbian clientele.

Bars
YNONAH'S SALOON, 1700 4th Ave S, (615) 251-0080. Popular for after hours, patio, bar, volleyball.
YOUR WAY CAFE & WOMEN'S CHOICE BAR, 512 2nd Ave, (615) 256-9682. Sun brunch. ♀

Dance Bar/Disco
★ CONNECTION, THE, 901 Cowan St, (615) 742-1166. Very large gay bar, dance bar, show bar, restaurant, patio, 70% men, 30% women, 30% straight.

Restaurants
MAGNOLIA'S, 2535 Franklin Rd, at Chute Complex men's bar, (615) 297-4571. Different menu daily. ♂
TOWNE HOUSE, 165 8th Ave N, at Gaslight bar, (615) 254-1277. Steaks, seafood.
WORLD'S END, 1713 Church St., Restaurant with bar, frequented by gays.

Retail & Bookstores
OUT LOUD BOOKS & GIFTS, 1805-C Church St, (615) 340-0034. Gay & lesbian bookstore, rainbow items, jewelry, cards, videos, etc.
TEN PERCENT GIFTS & ACCESSORIES, 901 Cowan St, at Connection nightclub., Gay novelties, magazines, guides, etc. Open Tue-Sun 10pm-3am.

OAK RIDGE

Retail & Bookstores
BOOKSTORE, THE, 113 Tyrone Rd, (423) 482-5286. General bookstore with a feminist section. We will special order women's or gay books."

SEWANEE

Accommodations
WILD HEART RANCH, PO Box 130, 1070 Old Sewanee Rd, Sewanee, TN, 37375, (423) 837-0849. A-frame cabins, lodge, campsites near 7000 acres of horse trails. Set-ups for 50-ft-long horse trailers, unlimited camping, spaces for 24 trailers, cabins & lodge sleep up to 20. Gay-friendly.

TEXAS
ABILENE

Dance Bar/Disco
JUST FRIENDS, 201 S 14th, (915) 672-9318. Dance bar with second bar in rear. ♀♂

AMARILLO

Bars
WHISKERS, 1219 W 10th St., ♂

Dance Bar/Disco
★ CLASSIFIEDS, 519 E 10th Ave, (806) 374-2435. Large alternative dance bar, DJ nightly, mostly gay weeknites, open Tues-Sat 4-2am. ♀♂
RITZ, 323 W 10th St, at Van Buren, (806) 372-9382. Small dance bar, patio. ♀♂
SASSY'S, 309 W 6th St, between Van Buren & Harrison, (806) 374-3029. 75% women. ♀

ARLINGTON
SEE FT. WORTH/ARLINGTON,

AUSTIN

Information
AIDS SERVICES, (512) 451-2273.
CORNERSTONE COMMUNITY CENTER, 1117 Red River, (512) 708-1515.

Accommodations
BELLO VISTA, 2121 Hilltop, Wimberley, TX, (512) 847-6425. Gay-owned & -operated B&B in an artsy village 30 mi from Austin & 4- mi from San Antonio, private baths, continental breakfast. Some straight clientele. ♀♂

TEXAS 417

CARITAS BED & BREAKFAST NETWORK, (800) CARITAS, (312) 857-0801, Fax: (312) 857-0805. B&B, home-stay accommodations service. Member: IGLTA
PARK LANE GUESTHOUSE, 221 Park Lane, Austin, TX, 78704, (512) 447-7460, (800) 492-8827. Cottage & guesthouse, private bath, expanded continental breakfast, AC, ceiling fans, nearby pool & lake. Cottage has color TV, VCR, kitchen. ♀♂
SUMMIT HOUSE, 1204 Summit St, Austin, TX, 78741-1158, (512) 445-5304. Email: summit@texas.net, Web: http://summit.home.texas.net, room with queen bed, private bath, full breakfast, mostly gay & lesbian, some straight clientele. ♀♂
ZILLER HOUSE, 800 Edgecliff Terrace, Austin, TX, 78704, (512) 462-0100, (800) 949-5446, Fax: (512) 462-9166." Gay-owned & -operated B&B with 5 luxurious rooms, private baths, expanded or full breakfast, pool on premises, 50% gay/lesbian.

Bars
BOUT TIME, 9601 N I-35, on access road, just N of Rundberg St, (512) 832-5339. Only bar in town that opens 7am. 2 pool tables, Wed oldies, DJ Thurs-Sat, drag shows some Sats, volleyball Sun. ♀♂

Dance Bar/Disco
DICK'S DEJA DISCO, 113 San Jacinto, (512) 457-8010. Some oldies nites. ♂
★ **OILCAN HARRY'S**, 211 W 4, (512) 320-8823. Upscale crowd, male dancers, 95% men. ♂
★ **RAINBOW CATTLE CO.**, 305 W 5th St, (512) 472-5288. Large C&W dance bar, 60% men, 40% women. ♀♂

Restaurants
KATZ'S DELI, 618 W 6th, (512) 472-2037. NY-style deli, 24hrs.
RYTHM HOUSE, 624 W 34th St, (512) 458-4411. Women-owned restaurant with bar & nitely live music. Mon women musicians.

Retail & Bookstores
BOOK WOMAN, 918 W 12th St, (512) 472-2785. Women's bookstore, cards, gifts, jewelry.
CELEBRATION!, 108 W 43rd St, near Speedway, (512) 453-6207. Women's book- & giftstore, cards, gifts, ritual supplies, jewelry, beads."

Visit Austin (800) CARITAS — Caritas B&B Network

BEAUMONT

Information
TRIANGLE AIDS NETWORK, (409) 832-8338.

Dance Bar/Disco
COPA, 304 Orleans St., Drag shows Sun, male strippers, usually 60/40 men & women. ♂
CROCKETT ST STATION, 497 Crockett St, (409) 833-3989. Dance & showbar, male strippers Sat, 50/50 men & women. ♀♂

BRYAN

Dance Bar/Disco
CLUB, THE, 308 N Bryan, (409) 823-6767. Dance bar, variety of music, shows Fri, 7 days 9pm-2am. ♀♂

CORPUS CHRISTI - ROCKPORT

Information
AIDS INFO, (512) 814-2001.

Accommodations
ANTHONY'S BY THE SEA, 732 S Pearl, Rockport, TX, 78382, (512) 729-6100, (800) 460-2557. B&B near ocean beach. Private & shared baths & modern conveniences. Full gourmet breakfast, weights & Jacuzzi." ♀♂

Bars
★ **HIDDEN DOOR**, 802 S Staples, (512) 882-5002. Cruise bar, women welcome. ♂

Dance Bar/Disco
MINGLES, 512 S Staples, (512) 884-8022. Tejano, dance & country music. ♀
PALADIUM, Corona near Everhart., 18 & over. ♂

418 TEXAS

YOUR COMMUNITY REALTOR
Deb Elder
(972) 623-5122

UBU CLUB, 511 Star St, (512) 882-9693. Alternative dance club, 18 yrs & over. Male & female strippers, 50% gay & lesbian.

ZODIAC, 4125 Gollihar, (512) 853-4077. 50% men, 50% women, DJ Wed, Fri & Sat, shows & male strippers Fri.

DALLAS

Information

AIDS INFO, (214) 559-AIDS (2437), 9am-9pm daily.

FOUNDATION FOR HUMAN UNDERSTANDING, 2701 Reagan St, (214) 521-5342.

Realtors/Relocation

MASTER REALTORS, DEB ELDER, (972) 623-5122, (800) 303-0071. Relocating? Let me tour you through Dallas' many interesting neighborhoods. I can assist with **leasing (no fees to you), buying, selling,** or I can help you find a realtor wherever you relocate. Give me a call with your mailing address and I'll send an informative Welcome Wagon packet on Dallas' gay and lesbian community.

Accommodations

COURTYARD ON THE TRAIL, 8045 Forest Trail, Dallas, TX, 75238, (214) 553-9700 (Tel/Fax), (800) 484-6260 pin #0465. Email: akrubs4u@aol.com, B&B close to downtown, yet in a country setting. Guestrooms have king-sized beds, marble baths, direct pool & courtyard access. Full breakfast, dinner by prearrangement, some straight clientele.

INN ON FAIRMOUNT, 3701 Fairmount, Dallas, TX, 75219, (214) 522-2800 or Fax: (214) 522-2898. Web: innonfairmount-dallas.com, B&B inn close to gay bars & restaurants. Color TV, AC, private baths, continental breakfast, Jacuzzi.

SYMPHONY HOUSE, 6327 Symphony Lane, Dallas, TX, 75227-1737, (214) 388-9134. Email: SymphonyHouse @webtv.net, Gay vacation & party rental home, 4 rooms, 2 shared baths, some straight clientele.

Bars

HIDEAWAY CLUB, 4144 Buena Vista, near Fitzhugh, (214) 559-2966. More upscale, quieter crowd, piano bar in front, video bar in rear, large patio with fountains, waterfall, 75% men, 25% women. Cookouts Sun in summer.

KOLORS, 2525 Wycliff, (214) 520-2525. Neighborhood cruise bar on one side, disco on other, Mon amateur strip, Tues & Sat drag show.

SIDE II BAR, 4006 Cedar Springs Rd, (214) 528-2026. Jukebox, pool table.

Dance Bar/Disco

BUDDIES II, 4025 Maple Ave, (215) 526-0887. Mostly women.

JUG'S, 3810 Congress, (214) 521-3474.

ROSE ROOM, THE, 3911 Cedar Springs, upstairs of Village Station, (214) 380-3808. Showbar.

★ **SUE ELLEN'S,** 3903 Cedar Springs, (214) 380-3808. Video dance bar, patio, volleyball. Fri & Sat after-hours, men welcome.

★ **VILLAGE STATION,** 3911 Cedar Springs, near Throckmorton, (214) 380-3808. Video dance bar and Rose Room, Las Vegas-style show bar upstairs. Many straights.

Restaurants

BRONX, THE, 3835 Cedar Springs, (214) 521-5821. New American, Southwest & traditional cuisine, dinner only. Sun brunch.

HUNKY'S, 4000 Cedar Springs, (214) 522-1212. Lunch and dinner.

PANDA'S, next to JR's, 3923 Cedar Springs., (214) 528-3818. Oriental cuisine.

SPASSO'S PIZZA, 4000 Cedar Springs #E, (214) 521-1141. Pasta, etc.

Retail & Bookstores

CROSSROADS MARKET, 3930 Cedar

TEXAS

Springs, at Throckmorton, (214) 521-8919. Gay & lesbian bookstore.
OFF THE STREET, 4001-B Cedar Springs, (214) 521-9051. Cards, gifts & t-shirts.

DENISON

■ Dance Bar/Disco
GOOD TIME LOUNGE, 2520 N Hwy 91N, (903) 463-9944. Juke box disco, male & female strippers on show nites.

DENTON

■ Dance Bar/Disco
MABLE PEABODY'S BEAUTY PARLOR & CHAINSAW REPAIR, 1215 E University Dr, (940) 566-9910. Private club, 50% men, 50% women. Closed Mon.

EL PASO

■ Information
AIDS INFO, (915) 543-3574, Spanish 543-3575.
LAMBDA LINE & GAY CENTER, 910 N Mesa, (915) 562-4297. Gay info line 24hrs, unverifiable spring '98.

■ Bars
BRIAR PATCH, 204 E Rio Grande, (915) 577-9555. 25% women.
HAWAIIAN BAR, 919 E Paisano, (915) 541-7009. Drag shows Fri & Sat, Sun Mexican food, 70% men.
WHATEVER LOUNGE, 701 E Paisano, (915) 533-0215. 60% men, 40% women, Latin.

■ Dance Bar/Disco
OLD PLANTATION, 219 S Ochoa St, at 1st, (915) 533-6055. Dance bar, male strippers Thurs & Fri, drag shows Sun, 70% men. Open Thurs-Sun, after-hours Fri & Sat.
★ **SAN ANTONIO MINING CO,** 800 E San Antonio St, at Ochoa, (915) 533-9516. Summer patio, male strippers Sun, drag shows Wed, many women for Fri cocktail hour.
U-GOT-IT, 216 S Ochoa, (915) 533-9310. Open Fri only 9pm-2am, Latin & country music.

■ Cafe
DOLCE VITA, Cincinnati, at Mesa.,
SOJOURNS, San Francisco, at Mills, above the San Francisco Bar & Grill., Popular with women.

FT WORTH - ARLINGTON

■ Accommodations
TWO PEARLS BED & BREAKFAST, 804 South Alamo St, Weatherford, TX, 76086-5309, (817) 596-9316. B&B 25 miles west of Ft Worth, private & shared baths, full breakfast, AC, ceiling fans, TV lounge, video tape library, 50% gay/lesbian clientele.

■ Bars
CORRAL, THE, 621 Hemphill St, at Cannon, (817) 335-0196.
★ **SIX FIFTY-ONE CLUB,** 651 S Jennings Ave, near Cannon, (817) 332-0745. 70% men, 30% women.

■ Dance Bar/Disco
DJ'S, 1308 St Louis St, near Magnolia, (817) 927-7321. Dance & show bar with restaurant, 60% women, 40% men."
LANCASTER BEACH CLUB, 2620 E Lancaster at Beach., Large dance club.

■ Restaurants
DJ'S RESTAURANT & BAR, 1308 St Louis, (817) 927-7321.

GALVESTON

■ Women's Accommodations
RAINBOW REFLECTIONS, (409) 763-2450. Women-only non-smoking B&B on Galveston Island, near beach, 2 rooms, shared bath, delux continental breakfast.

■ Bars
LONGFELLOW'S, 2405 Postoffice, (409) 763-8800. Open 7 days 2pm-2am, 80% men, 20% women.
ROBERT'S LAFITTE, 2501 Ave Q, at 25th, (409) 765-9092. Popular for drag shows.

■ Dance Bar/Disco
EVOLUTION, 2214 Mechanic St, near 22nd St, (409) 763-4212. Video dance bar, many straights.
★ **KON TIKI (KT),** 315 Tremont, (23rd),

420 TEXAS

(409) 763-6264. Dance & show bar, 50% men, 50% women. Male & female strippers."

GUN BARREL CITY

Bars
MIKE'S TWO THIRTY-ONE CLUB, 602 S Gun Barrel Ln, (903) 887-2061. Open 7 days 1pm-1am, Sat till 1am, pool table, patio, jukebox, 75% men, 25% women.

HOUSTON

Information
AIDS HOTLINE, (713) 524-AIDS.
GAY & LESBIAN CHAMBER OF COMMERCE, (713) 523-7576.
GAY & LESBIAN SWITCHBOARD, (713) 529-3211, Mon-Sat 7pm-10pm.

Accommodations
GAR-DEN SUITES, 2702 Crocker St, Houston, TX, 77006, (713) 528-2302, (800) 484-1036 (code 2669)." B&B in a cottage setting in the heart of the Montrose area, close to bars & restaurants. Suites with private baths, continental breakfast. Mostly men with women welcome.
LOVETT INN, THE, 501 Lovett Blvd, Houston, TX, 77006, (713) 522-5224, Fax: 528-6708, (800) 779-5224. Lodging & catering accommodations. Guestrooms have queen sized beds, color TVs, phones, most have private baths. Pool & spa on premises."

Bars
BRICKS II, 617 Fairview, (713) 528-8102.
CHANCES, 1100 Westheimer, (713) 523-7217.
LAZY J, 312 Tuam St, near Bagby, (713) 528-9343. 65% men, 35% women, drag shows Sat, Wed women's pool nite certain times of year.
MELAS, 302 Tuam, (713) 523-0747. Latin Tejano "country bar," Tejano music.
MS B'S, 9208 Buffalo Speedway, at The Ranch, (713) 666-3356. Quiet bar, pool table, darts, men welcome.
★ **RANCH, THE,** 9218 Buffalo Speedway, (713) 666-3464. Three bars, men welcome, connected to Ranch & XTC.

SIX ELEVEN CLUB, 611 Hyde Park Ave, at Stanford, (713) 526-7070. Patio, Irish pub setting, DJ weekends, burger nites most Thurs, 60% men, 40% women.

Dance Bar/Disco
CLUB D-EON'S & GIRLS, 4550 Holmes Rd, (713) 734-2922. Small dance floor, catering to the gay & lesbian black community.
INCOGNITO, 2524 McKinney, at Live Oak, (713) 237-9431. 9pm-2am, male & female dancers Fri & Mon, Fri boys night out, Sun drag shows, 60% men, 40% women. Patio with cookouts most Sun.
INERGY, 5750 Chimney Rock, (713) 666-7310. Latin Tejano crowd, open Wed-Sun. Fri mainly women, Sat mainly men
NEW BARN, 1100 Westheimer B (in rear), (713) 521-9533. C&W dance bar, 7 days noon-2am, 75% men, 25% women.
RASCALS, 1318 Westheimer, (713) 942-CLUB. Dance bar.
XTC, same location as The Ranch bar, 9218 Buffalo Speedway, (713) 666-3464. Hi-energy dance bar, open Fri, Sat. Men welcome.

Cafe
BARNABY'S CAFE, 604 Fairview, (713) 522-0106.

Restaurants
BABBA YAGA'S, 2607 Grant, (713) 522-0042.
CAFE ADOBE, Westheimer, at Sheppard., Mexican cuisine. Mon after 7pm is party night.
CHARLIE'S, 1102 Westheimer, (713) 522-3332. Popular for after hours food.
LA STRADA, 322 Westheimer, (713) 523-1014. Italian, gay-friendly. Fantastic Sun brunch is popular with gays.
MICHELANGELO'S, 307 Westheimer, (713) 524-7836. Upscale Italian cuisine, valet parking.
RUGGLES, 903 Westheimer, (713) 524-3839. Live jazz nightly. They will serve you dinner from the restaurant next door.

■ Retail & Bookstores

CROSSROADS MARKET, 1111 Westheimer, (713) 942-0147. Gay & lesbian bookstore & gifts.

LOBO, 3939-S Montrose, suite S, (713) 522-5156. Gay & lesbian books, videos, leather, etc.

LAREDO

■ Dance Bar/Disco

DISCOVERY, 2019 Farragut, (956) 722-9032. Dance bar, unverifiable spring '98. 🎵♀♂

LONGVIEW

■ Dance Bar/Disco

DECISIONS, 2103 E Marshall, (903) 757-4884. Daily 5pm-2am, disco Fri-Sun & 2nd Wed of month. Quiet bar with CD juke box, pool tables, games, Sun drag shows. 🎵♀♂

LIFESTYLES, 916 S Eastman, (903) 758-8082. 🎵♀♂

LUBBOCK

■ Information

GAY HELP LINE, (806) 766-7184.

■ Dance Bar/Disco

CAPTAIN HOLLYWOOD, 2401 Main St at Avenue X, (806) 744-4222. DJ nightly, variety of music, drag shows Tues, Sun, open from 8pm 7 days. 🎵♀♂

MCALLEN

■ Bars

PBD LOUNGE, 2908 Ware Rd, at Daffodil, (956) 682-8019. Drag shows alternate Sat, male strippers, 70% men, 30% women, patio. 🎵♂

■ Dance Bar/Disco

TENTH AVENUE, 1820 N 10th St, (956) 682-7131. Large dance bar. 🎵♀♂

ODESSA

■ Dance Bar/Disco

FICTIONS, 409 N Hancock, (915) 580-5449. 🎵♀♂

MISS LILLI'S NITESPOT, 8401 Andrews Hwy, near Yukon, (915) 366-6799. Disco, all kinds of music, open Wed-Sun. 🎵♀♂

RIO GRANDE VALLEY

■ Information

GAY ALLIANCE, (210) 428-6800.

SAN ANGELO

■ Dance Bar/Disco

SILENT PARTNERS, 1819 S Harrison St, (915) 949-9041. Moving in '98, call for new address &/or phone. 🎵♀♂

SAN ANTONIO

■ Information

AIDS INFO, (210) 225-4715, 24hrs. Hispanic AIDS Committee: (210) 734-UNITY.

GAY & LESBIAN COMMUNITY CENTER, 3126 N St Mary's, (210) 732-4300, Mon-Sat 1-8, Sun 1-6.

LESBIAN INFO, 1136 Hildebrand, (210) 828-5472.

■ Accommodations

ADELYNNE'S SUMMIT HAUS & SUMMIT HAUS II, 427 W Summit, San Antonio, TX, 78212, (800) 972-7266, (210) 736-6272, (210) 828-3045, Fax: (210) 737-8244. B&B. Rooms, suite & cottage with color TV, AC, ceiling fans, refrigerator, coffee/tea-making facilities, private baths & full breakfast. ♀♂

ARBOR HOUSE INN & SUITES, 540 South St. Mary's St, San Antonio, TX, 78205, (210) 472-2005, Toll-free: (888) 272-6700, Fax: (210) 472-2007. Gay-owned, gay-friendly all-suite hotel in five turn-of-the-century houses connected by a courtyard. All private baths, continental breakfast, 1-1/2 blocks from the Riverwalk.

GARDEN COTTAGE, THE, San Antonio, TX, (210) 828-7815, (800) 235-7215, Fax: (210) 828-4539. Email: juma@texas.net, Cottage, some straight clientele. Fully-furnished, modern conveniences, kitchen. Massage available, public pool nearby. ♀♂

PAINTED LADY INN ON BROADWAY, 620 Broadway, San Antonio, TX, 78215, (210) 220-1092. Gay-friendly guest hotel, continental breakfast, limited room services, theme rooms.

SAN ANTONIO BED & BREAKFAST, 510 E Guenther, San Antonio, TX, 78210-

1133, (210) 222-1828. B&B in King William Historic Neighborhood. Color TV, AC, refrigerators, private & shared baths, meeting rooms. Use of nearby condo pool." ♀♂

Women's Accommodations
DESERT HEARTS COWGIRL CLUB, HC-3 Box 650, Bandera, TX, 78003, (210) 796-7446. Women-only guest ranch. Shared bath, all meals included." ♀

Bars
MICK'S HIDEAWAY, 5307 McCullough, (210) 828-4222. Small cocktail lounge, darts, pool table, 50% men, 50% women. ♀♂

NEW PONDEROSA, THE, 5007 S Flores, (210) 924-6322. More mature crowd. 🍴 🎵 Ⓝ ♀

PEGASUS, 1402 N Main, (210) 299-4222. Upscale crowd, front cruise bar with male strippers. Quiet back bar & patio bar. Sand, pool, sun deck, patio. First smokeless bar in San Antonio. 🍴 🎵 ♂

Dance Bar/Disco
★ **PETTICOAT JUNCTION,** 1818 N Main Ave, (210) 737-2344. Open 7 days, 3 bars: hi NRG, country & Tejano dance bars, patio & volleyball. 🎵 ♀

★ **SILVER DOLLAR SALOON,** 1418 N Main Ave, (210) 227-2623. C&W & Tejano dance bar. 🎵 U Ⓝ ♂

★ **WOODY'S,** 826 San Pedro, at West Laurel, (210) 271-9663. Video bar, younger preppie crowd, 2pm-2am daily, 75% men, 25% women, male strippers. 🎵 🎵 ♂

Retail & Bookstores
ON MAIN, 2514 N Main, near Woodlawn, (210) 737-2323. Cards & gifts. 🎵

TEXTURES, 5309 McCullough, (210) 805-8398. Women's bookstore, Mon-Fri 11am-6pm, Sat 11am-5pm, Sun 1pm-5pm.

ZEBRAZ GIFTS, 1216 Euclid Ave, (210) 472-2800. Alternative gift items, 9am-9pm Mon-Fri, 11am-9pm Sat.

SOUTH PADRE ISLAND

Accommodations
UPPER DECK, A GUESTHOUSE, 120 E Atol, Box 2309, South Padre Island, TX, 78597, (956) 761-5953, Fax: (956) 761-4288. Email: spiup@aol.com, Hotel & bar on beach, private baths, good mix of gay men & women. Daytime rates for pool, hot tub, locker, game room. 🏊 ♀♂

Bars
CREW'S QUARTERS, at Upper Deck, The first alternative bar on the island. Full liquor. ♿ ♀♂

SOUTH PLAINS

Information
AIDS INFO, (806) 796-7068, 9am-5pm Mon-Fri.

TEMPLE

Bars
BILL'S HARD TIMES, 414 S 1st St, (254) 778-9604. Wed-Sun 9pm-2am. 🎵 ♂

TYLER

Dance Bar/Disco
OUTLAW, 4 Miles South Loop 323 on Hwy 110, (903) 509-2248. Gay-friendly dance club. 100% gay Wed nights, partially gay Fri nights. 🎵 🎵

WACO

Dance Bar/Disco
DAVID'S, 507 Jefferson, at North 5th, (254) 753-9189. Upper level country dance bar. Lower level dance music. BBQs, patio in summer. 🎵 🎵 ♀♂

WICHITA FALLS

Dance Bar/Disco
ODDS, Sheppard Access Rd, at Old Iowa Park, (940) 696-4800. 🎵 ♂

RASCALS, 811 Indiana, (940) 723-1629. Daily noon-2am, drag shows Fri, 35% men, 65% women. 🎵 🎵 ♀♂

UTAH
STATEWIDE

Information
AIDS INFO, (800) FON-AIDS.

ESCALANTE

Accommodations
RAINBOW COUNTRY TOURS & B&B, 586 E 300 S, Escalante, UT, 84726,

(801) 826-4567, (800) 252-UTAH (8824). Email: rainbow@color-country.net, Modern home with spa, cable TV, full breakfast. Enjoy hiking, jeep tours, horseback riding & bicycling. Call for brochure.

MEXICAN HAT

■ Accommodations
VALLEY OF THE GODS BED & BREAKFAST, PO Box 310307, Mexican Hat, UT, 84531, (801) 683-2292 (Tel/Fax), cellular: (970) 749-1164. Gay-friendly B&B in the 4-Corners Region. Private baths, full breakfast, large gay/lesbian following.

MOAB

■ Accommodations
MT. PEALE BED & BREAKFAST COUNTRY INN, PO Box 366, LaSal, UT, 84530, (801) 686-2284 (Tel/Fax), (888) 687-3253, mobile: (801) 260-1305. Web: www.moab-canyonlands.com/mtpeale, B&B & cottages with private & shared baths, buffet breakfast, near Canyonlands & Arches Nt'l Parks, 50% gay & lesbian clientele.

MONTICELLO

■ Accommodations
GRIST MILL INN, THE, 64 South 300 East, Monticello, UT, 84535, (435) 587-2597, Fax: (435) 587-2580. Email: gristmill@sisna.com, Web: www.utah.com/lodging/gristmill, Gay-friendly B&B in a restored flour mill with original mill equipment left in place, adding character & charm to the country Victorian decor. Private baths, Jacuzzi, full breakfast. Dinner available by reservation, chef on staff.

OGDEN

■ Dance Bar/Disco
BRASS RAIL, 103 27th St, at Wall, (801) 399-1543. Dance bar, private club, open 7 days, shows Sat. 🍽 ♪ ♀♂

PARK CITY

■ Retail & Bookstores
A WOMAN'S PLACE BOOKSTORE, 1890 Bonanza Dr, (801) 649-2722. General bookstore with special emphasis on women's studies.

ST GEORGE

■ Accommodations
GREENE GATE VILLAGE HISTORIC B & B INN, 76 W Tabernacle St, St. George, UT, 84770, (435) 628-6999, (800) 350-6999, Fax: (435) 628-6989. Email: greene@power-tech.net, Gay-friendly B&B inn with restaurant. Private baths, AC, phone, pool, Jacuzzi, full breakfast. 60 miles to ski resort, golf nearby.

SALT LAKE CITY

■ Information
AIDS FOUNDATION, (801) 487-2323.

■ Accommodations
ANTON BOXRUD B & B, 57 South 600 East, Salt Lake City, UT, 84102, (801) 363-8035, (800) 524-5511, Fax: (801) 596-1316. Centrally-located gay-friendly B&B. Private & shared baths, TV lounge, full breakfast & Jacuzzi.

■ Dance Bar/Disco
BRICKS, 579 W 2nd S, (801) 328-0255. Private liquor club, alternative dance bar, huge patio, 20% gay clientele, ues-Sat from 9:30. Gay Fri only, 60% men, 40% women. T Young gays frequent the 18 & over section. 🍽 ♪ ♀♂
KINGS, 108 S 500 West, (801) 521-5464. Private liquor club, show bar with small dance floor, large stage. 🍽 ♪ ♀♂
PAPER MOON, 3424 S State, (801) 466-8517. Private liquor club, dance bar. 🍽 ♀
★ **SUN**, 200 S 700 W, at 2nd South, (801) 531-0833. Private liquor club, alternative bar, patio, more straight weekdays except Tues, more gay weekends, 50% men, 50% women, busiest Tues & Sat.. ✕ 🍽 ♀♂

■ Restaurants
BACI TRATTORIA, 134 W Pierpont Ave, (801) 328-1500. Italian cuisine, gay friendly.
CAFE PIERPONT, 122 W Pierpont Ave, (801) 364-1222. Mexican cuisine, gay friendly.

DODO, THE, 680 S 900 E, (801) 328-9348. American cuisine, gay friendly.

FRUGGLES, 367 W 2nd South, (801) 363-7000. Great selection of salads, pastas. Gay-friendly.

MARKET STREET BROILER, 260 S 1300 E, (801) 583-8808. Gay-friendly restaurant near U of U. Cocktails available with membership.

MARKET STREET GRILL, 48 Market St, (801) 322-4668. Gay-friendly restaurant. Fresh seafood, daily specials, prime businessman's lunch. Cocktails available with membership.

■ *Retail & Bookstores*

A WOMAN'S PLACE BOOKSTORE, 1400 Foothill Dr, (801) 583-6431. General bookstore with special emphasis on women's studies & a gay & lesbian section.

BLUE MARBLE, 1400 S 1100 East, (801) 466-7417. Pride & rainbow items, etc. 11am-6:30pm Mon-Fri, 11am-5pm Sat.

FERTILE GROUND, 274 E 900 S, (801) 521-8124. Women-oriented new-age store & gallery.

GOLDEN BRAID BOOKS, 1515 S 500 E, (801) 322-0404. New age books, cafe.

GYPSY MOON EMPORIUM, 1011 E 900 South, (801) 521-9100. Mythology & folklore, feminist & women's books.

INKLINGS BOOKSTORE, 247 E 900 S, (801) 355-4991. Gay & lesbian bookstore.

NEW PATHWAYS, 3159 W 5400 S, suburb of Kearns, (801) 966-8352. Unique gifts, New Age music, herbs & supplies.

SOUTH CENTRAL UTAH

■ *Accommodations*

SKYRIDGE, A BED & BREAKFAST INN, near Capitol Reef National Park, Torrey, UT, (435) 425-3222 (Tel/Fax). Email: www.bbiu.org/skyridge, Artist-owner designed inn on 75 acres has unparalleled views of multicolored cliffs, domes & forested mountains. Rooms have queen-sized bed, private bath, TV/VCR & phone. Rooms with patio, deck, Jacuzzi or hot tub available. Elegant full breakfast. Experience this spectacular park — cooler than Arches/Zion in the summer & less crowded than both!

ZION NATIONAL PARK

■ *Accommodations*

RED ROCK INN, 998 Zion Park Blvd, PO Box 273, Springdale, UT, 84767, (801) 772-3139. Email: rrinn@infowest.com, Gay-friendly motel cottages near Zion National Park. Color cable TV, AC, refrigerator, coffee & tea-making facilities & private baths. Nearby pool & river.

VERMONT
ANDOVER

■ *Accommodations*

INN AT HIGHVIEW, THE, RR 1, Box 201A, East Hill Road, Andover, VT, 05143, (802) 875-2724, Fax: (802) 875-4021. Email: hiview@aol.com, The inn's hilltop location offers incredible peace, tranquility and seclusion, yet is convenient to all the activities that bring you to Vermont, such as skiing, golf, tennis and antiquing. Ski cross-country or hike our 72 acres. Swim in our unique rock garden pool. Enjoy our gourmet dinner, relax by a blazing fire, snuggle under a down comforter in a canopy bed, or gaze 50 miles over pristine mountains. Gay-friendly.

The Inn at HighView

Vermont The Way You Dreamed It Would Be

ANDOVER

(802) 875-2724

VERMONT 425

ARLINGTON

Accommodations
CANDLELIGHT MOTEL, Rt 7A, PO Box 97, Arlington, VT, 05250, (802) 375-6647, (800) 348-5294. Mixed clientele, short drive to ski areas, outlet shops, & restaurants. Fireside lounge, continental breakfast.

HILL FARM INN, RR2 Box 2015, Arlington, VT, 05250, (802) 375-2269, (800) 882-2545, Fax: (802) 375-9918. Web: www.hillfarminn.com, Gay-friendly inn. Private & shared baths.

BENNINGTON

Information
BENNINGTON AREA AIDS PROJECT, (802) 442-4481. 7pm-10pm.

BRANDON

Accommodations
LILAC INN, 53 Park St, Brandon, VT, 05733, (802) 247-5463, Fax: (802) 247-5499. Gay-friendly B&B with restaurant & bar. Near skiing.

BRATTLEBORO

Information
AIDS PROJECT, (802) 254-4444, 10:30am-3pm Mon-Fri. Hotline (800) 882-2437.

Restaurants
COMMON GROUND, 20 Elliot St, (802) 257-0855. Natural foods, no smoking.

Retail & Bookstores
EVERYONE'S BOOKS, 23 Elliot St, near Main, (802) 254-8160. Alternative bookstore with lesbian & gay section.

BURLINGTON

Accommodations
BLACK BEAR INN, Bolton Access Rd, mail: H.C. 33, Box 717, Bolton Valley, VT, 05477, (802) 434-2126, (800) 395-6335, Fax: (802) 434-5161. Email: blkbear@wcvt.com, Web: www.blkbearinn.com, In the Green Mountains, 20 minutes from Burlington and Stowe, our cozy, slope-side gay-friendly inn features individually decorated rooms and suites, many with VT firestoves or fireplaces. Warm summer days and cool evenings are perfect for sightseeing, horseback riding, relaxing in one of our hot tubs, or in the heated pool. Skiing, ice skating, etc, are nearby. AAA 3-Diamond Rating.

HOWDEN COTTAGE, 32 N Champlain St, Burlington, VT, 05401-4320, (802) 864-7198, Fax: (802) 658-1556. B&B, mainly straight clientele, continental breakfast. Lake nearby, pool at YMCA. Convenient to Marketplace shopping complex, Lake Champlain & restaurants.

Dance Bar/Disco
ONE THIRTY-FIVE PEARL, 135 Pearl St, at Elmwood, (802) 863-2343. Dance bar with occasional drag shows, open 7:30 Mon-Thurs, from 5pm Fri-Sun. 1st Fri women's nite 6pm-9pm with buffet.

Retail & Bookstores
CHASSMAN & BEM BOOKSELLERS, 81 Church St Market Place, (802) 862-4332. General bookstore with a gay & lesbian selection.

DUMMERSTON

Dance Bar/Disco
RAINBOW CATTLE CO., Rte 5, East Dummerston., (802) 254-9830. Dance bar & quiet bar, occasional drag shows, DJ Fri-Sun, closed Mon & Tues.

Bare It All At the Black Bear Inn

BURLINGTON, VT
(800) 395-6335

EAST HARDWICK

■ Women's Accommodations
GREENHOPE FARM, RFD 1, Box 2260, E Hardwick, VT, 05836, (802) 533-7772. Post-and-beam guesthouse on a mountainside, x-country ski miles of groomed trails. Vegetarian cuisine, no smoking, gay men welcome. ♀

FAIR HAVEN

■ Accommodations
MAPLEWOOD INN, Route 22A South, Fair Haven, VT, 05743, (802) 265-8039, (800) 253-7729, Fax: (802) 265-8210. Email: maplewd@sover.net, Web: http://www.sover.net/~maplewd, Gay-friendly B&B. Rooms & suites with color cable TV, AC, fireplaces & private baths. Expanded continental breakfast, nearby lake.

MONTGOMERY CENTER

■ Accommodations
PHINEAS SWANN B & B, PO Box 43, The Main Street, Montgomery Center, VT, 05471, (802) 326-4306. Country inn central to everything, 50% gay & lesbian clientele. Private & shared baths, ceiling fans, TV lounge, full gourmet breakfast & afternoon tea.

The Highlands Inn
A Lesbian Paradise
- 100 Secluded Acres
- Pool • Hot Tub • Trails

(603) 869-3978

P.O. Box 118-I,
Valley View Lane
Bethlehem, NH 03574

MONTPELIER

■ Information
COALITION OF LESBIANS & GAY MEN, PO Box 1125, (802) 454-8552.

■ Cafe
ABOUT THYME CAFE, on State St.,

■ Restaurants
HORN OF THE MOON CAFE, 8 Langdon St, (802) 223-2895. Vegetarian natural food, 7 days. Good mix of clientele."

■ Retail & Bookstores
BEAR POND BOOKS, 77 Main St, (802) 229-0774. General bookstore with small gay & lesbian section.

ST JOHNSBURY

■ Women's Accommodations
HIGHLANDS INN, THE, Box 118, Valley View Lane, Bethlehem, NH, 03574, (603) 869-3978. B&B inn on 100 acres. **A Lesbian paradise** with 20 comfortable rooms with excellent views, antique furnishings, private & shared baths, TV lounge, kitchen privileges, library, heated pool, BBQ grills, hot tub, hiking, skiing and full breakfast, spectacular sunsets. Rates $55-$110, weeklong & midweek discounts. Winner 1995, '96, '97 Out & About Editor's Choice Awards. Our sign always says "no vacancy" so please ignore it. Non-smoking rooms. ♀

SHAFTSBURY

■ Accommodations
COUNTRY COUSIN, RR 1, Box 212 Old Depot Rd, Shaftsbury, VT, 05262, (802) 375-6985 or (800) 479-6985. B&B, private baths, TV lounge, music room, hot tub, full breakfast." ♀♂

STOWE

■ Accommodations
BUCCANEER COUNTRY LODGE, 3214 Mountain Rd, Stowe, VT, 05672, (802) 253-4772, (800) 543-1293. Lodge with breakfast near lake, village, mountain, nightlife & recreational activities. Full breakfast except in spring, complimentary hot soup & mulled cider dur-

ing ski season. Gay-friendly hosts are avid skiers.

FITCH HILL INN, RR 2 Box 1879, Fitch Hill Rd, Hyde Park, VT, 05655, (802) 888-3834, (800) 639-2903, Fax: (802) 888-7789. Country-English elegance at an affordable 1794 historic inn, in a mountain setting 10 mi. from Stowe. The five rooms share baths and are attractively decorated with antiques. Hearty breakfast included. Mostly straight clientele.

HONEYWOOD COUNTRY LODGE, 4527 Mountain Rd, Stowe, VT, 05672, (802) 253-4124, (800) 659-6289, Fax: (802) 253-7050. Email: honeywd@aol.com, Gay-friendly B&B motel on 4 acres, private baths, continental-plus breakfasts, in winter cross-country ski from front door, nearest AAA 3-Diamond lodging to Stowe Mtn. Resort.

WATERBURY-STOWE AREA

Accommodations

GRÜNBERG HAUS BED & BREAKFAST, RR2, Box 1595 IP, Route 100 South, Waterbury-Stowe, VT, 05676-9621, (802) 244-7726, (800) 800-7760. Email: grunhaus@aol.com, B&B guesthouse, mainly straight clientele. Individually-decorated rms furnished with antiques. Jacuzzi, sauna, tennis court, library, full breakfast, many complimentary items. River & lake nearby.

VIRGINIA
ARLINGTON

Information
GAY ALLIANCE, (703) 522-7660 (tape).

CAPE CHARLES

Accommodations

CAPE CHARLES HOUSE, 645 Tazewell Ave, Cape Charles, VA, 23310, (804) 331-4920. Email: stay@capecharleshouse.com, Gay-friendly B&B on Virginia's Eastern shore, just 40 minutes from Norfolk. Five rooms with private baths & sitting area. Gourmet breakfast included. Swimming, water sports, wildlife preserve all nearby.

PELICAN WATCH COTTAGE, 116 1/2 Tazewell Ave, Cape Charles, VA, (757) 331-2709. Email: pelicanwatch@juno.com, Charming efficiency cottage, two short blocks to lovely beach on Chesapeake Bay. Nestled privately in alleyway of a sleepy Victorian village. Charter a sunset sail, enjoy the storybook tugboats, observe a wide variety of shore birds, stroll historic town, visit our new museum, fish, bike, shop, swim or, better yet, do nothing! Cape Charles, a well-kept secret, presently being discovered. Woman-owned & -operated, 50% gay/lesbian clientele.

INTOUCH

106 acres of Camping and Events

Home of
Virginia Women's Music Festival
May 28 -31, 1998

July 4th Kick-Back
July 3-5, 1998

Wild Western Women's Weekend
Sept. 18-20, 1998

Rt. 2 Box 1096
Kent's Store, Va. 23084
(804) 589-6542

VIRGINIA

WILSON - LEE HOUSE BED & BREAKFAST, 403 Tazewell Ave, Cape Charles, VA, 23310-3217, (757) 331-1954, Fax: (757) 331-8133. Email: WLHBnB @aol.com., Web: www.accomack.com/ WLHBnB, Gay-friendly B&B with private baths (1 with whirlpool), full breakfast, steps to the beach, sunset cruises arranged.

CHARLOTTESVILLE

■ Camping & RV
INTOUCH WOMEN'S CAMPING & EVENT CENTER, Rt 2, Box 1096, Kent's Store, VA, 23084, (804) 589-6542. Email: intouchjg@aol.com, A women's camping and event center near Fernville, VA, INTOUCH is 106 acres of **almost heaven** with a 7-acre lake. 50 campsites and cabins, hiking and mountain bike trails, outdoor showers, sand volleyball court, playing field, stage, and pavilion. Reservations required for non-members. ♀ See ad on page 427.

■ Dance Bar/Disco
CLUB 216, 218 Water St, (804) 296-8783. Private dance club, men's cruise bar. Travelers: call in advance. Women's bar to open in fall '98. 🛎 ♀♂

■ Restaurants
EASTERN STANDARD, 102 Old Preston Ave, (804) 295-8668. ES Cafe: casual cafe & restaurant; Eastern Standard: fine dining upstairs. Discreetly frequented by gays later in the evenings. About 40% gay. 🛎 🚫

CHESAPEAKE

■ Retail & Bookstores
CURIOUS GOODS, 2981 S Military Hwy., New age supplies, wiccan, pagan, druid, etc.

FREDERICKSBURG

■ Bars
MERRIE MAN'S, 715 Caroline, (540) 371-7723. Bar & restaurant. ♀♂

LEXINGTON

■ Accommodations
INN AT UNION RUN, THE, 325 Union Run Rd, Lexington, VA, 24450, (540) 463-9715, (800) 528-6466, Fax: (540) 463-3526. Gay-friendly country inn near Roanoke, full breakfast, private baths, Jacuzzi, AC, nearby lake & river.

LURAY

■ Accommodations
CREEKSIDE: A COUNTRY GUEST COTTAGE, Walnut Glen, 4632 Old Forge Rd, Luray, VA, 22835, (540) 743-5040. Gay-friendly cottage a 90-min drive from Washington, DC. Private bath, color TV, AC, fresh-water stream on premises.

LYNCHBURG

■ Information
GAY INFO LINE, (804) 847-5242.

NELLYSFORD

■ Accommodations
MARK ADDY, THE, 56 Rodes Farm Dr, Nellysford, VA, 22958, (804) 361-1101, (800) 278-2154. Email: markaddy@symweb.com, Web: www.symweb.com/rockfish/ mark.html, Gay-friendly 1884 country inn located between the Blue Ridge Mountains & Charlottescille. Private baths (1 with double whirlpool bath), bountiful breakfast, AC, down comforters.

NEW MARKET

■ Accommodations
A TOUCH OF COUNTRY, 9329 Congress St, New Market, VA, 22844, (540) 740-8030. B&B near caverns & historic points of interest, 50% gay/lesbian clientele. Double rooms decorated with a country flavor. Full breakfast.

NEWPORT NEWS

■ Bars
CORNER POCKET, 3516 Washington Ave, (757) 247-6366. Pool table. 🛎 ♀♂

NORFOLK - VIRGINIA BEACH

■ Information
GAY INFO LINE, (757) 622-5617.

Accommodations

CORAL SAND MOTEL, 2307 Pacific Ave, Virginia Beach, VA, 23451, (757) 425-0872 or (800) 828-0872. Guesthouse & motel, telephones, cable color TV, some kitchens, private & shared baths, continental breakfast, women welcome. ♀♂

Beaches

GAY BEACH, between 21st & 24th Sts & 83rd St. Mostly gay.

Bars

★ **AMBUSH,** 475 S Lynnhaven Rd, Virginia Beach, (757) 498-4301. Bar & restaurant, pool tables, karaoke, 90% men, women welcome.

Dance Bar/Disco

★ **CHARLOTTE'S WEB,** 6425 Tidewater Dr, Norfolk, (757) 853-5021. Men's night Wed with male dancers.

CK PEARLS, 1118 Green Run Square, Virginia Beach, (757) 368-0713. Dance bar & restaurant, 85% women. Generally more mature professional crowd.

HERSHEE BAR, 6117 E Sewell's Pt Rd (rear entrance), Norfolk, (757) 853-9842. Bar & restaurant, younger crowd.

★ **LATE SHOW,** 114 E 11th St, Norfolk, (757) 623-3854. Bar & restaurant. Private after-hours dance bar midnite till 8am. Non-members, ask other bars entrance requirements, or call first. ♀♂

NUTTY BUDDYS, 143 E Little Creek Rd, Wards Corner, Norfolk, (757) 588-6474. Dance bar, lounge, bar & restaurant, 75% men.

★ **RAINBOW CACTUS,** 3472 Holland Rd, Virginia Beach, (757) 368-0441. C&W dance bar & restaurant, 85% men.

Restaurants

CHARLIE'S, 1800 Granby St, Norfolk, (757) 625-0824. 7am-3pm.

Retail & Bookstores

LAMBDA RISING BOOKS, 9229 Granby St, Ocean View, (757) 480-6969. Gay & lesbian books, cards, magazines & gifts.

LEATHER & LACE, 149 E Little Creek Rd, Norflok, (757) 583-4334.

PHOENIX RISING EAST, 619 Colonial Ave, 2nd fl, Norfolk, (757) 622-3701. Gay & lesbian bookstore with cards, magazines & gifts.

PORTSMOUTH

SEE NORFOLK/VIRGINIA BEACH,

RICHMOND

Information

AIDS LINE, (804) 358-6343. Mon-Fri 10am-9pm or tape.

GAY INFO LINE, (804) 967-9311. Recorded information.

Accommodations

BELLMONT MANOR BED & BREAKFAST, 6600 Belmont Rd, Chesterfield, VA, 23832, (804) 745-0106. Email: bellmont@aol.com, Gay-friendly B&B with antique shop, 20 minutes from downtown Richmond. Country gourmet breakfast, air conditioning, private & shared baths, 50% gay & lesbian clientele.

Bars

CASABLANCA, 6 E Grace St, (804) 648-2040. Bar, lite menu, 80% men, 20% women.

CLUB COLORS, 534 N Harrison St, (804) 353-9776. Younger crowd, gay Fri-Sun. Call for schedule of women's nites, drag shows & dance nites.

GODFREY'S BAR & RESTAURANT, ask locally for address., Sun brunch with drag show. ♂

Dance Bar/Disco

BABES OF CARYTOWN, 3166 W Cary St, near Auburn, (804) 355-9330. Bar & restaurant, more gay evenings. Patio, DJ Fri & Sat, many men Sun for Sun brunch. C&W dancing Tues.

BOOM DANCE NIGHT, at Cafine's cafe bar, 401 E Grace St, (804) 775-2233. 10pm-4am Sat only

★ **FIELDEN'S,** 2033 W Broad St, (804) 359-1963. After hours private club, progressive dance club. Travelers welcome.

Cafe

CAFINE'S, 401 E Grace St, (804) 775-2233. Lunch cafe Tues-Fri. Fri nite mainly straight with live bands, Boom Sat dance

VIRGINIA

club 10pm-4am, 70% gay & lesbian, 30% straight.

Restaurants
GODFREY'S, 308 E Grace, (804) 648-3957. Bar & restaurant, more gay in evening. Tues-Fri 11-2am, Sat 3pm-2am, Sun 11am-2am, Sun brunch with drag show.

Retail & Bookstores
CARYTOWN BOOKSTORE, 2930 W Cary St, at Sheppard, (804) 359-4831. General bookstore with women's & gay selections.

PHOENIX RISING, 19 N Belmont Ave, (804) 355-7939. Gay & lesbian bookstore.

ROANOKE

Information
GAY INFO LINE, (540) 982-3733.

Bars
BACKSTREET, 356 Salem Ave, (540) 345-1542. Pool table, dart board, pinball, 7 days, 7pm-2am.

Dance Bar/Disco
PARK, THE, 615 Salem Ave SW, (540) 342-0946. Video dance bar, lounge, 70% men, 30% women. Wed, Fri-Sun. Sun drag shows

Retail & Bookstores
OUT WORD CONNECTION, 114-A Kirk Ave SW, (540) 985-6886. Gay & lesbian bookstore.

MARC-JAMES MANOR
A contemporary interpretation of an English manor house

Commitment ceremonies a specialty

Bellingham WA
(360) 738-4919

WASHINGTON
BELLINGHAM

Information
AIDS SUPPORT, (360) 671-0703, crisis center 734-7271.

Accommodations
MARC-JAMES MANOR, 2925 Vining St, Bellingham, WA, 98226, (360) 738-4919. A contemporary interpretation of an English manor house, situated on two acres in the Highland Heights district of Bellingham. The guest suite has a private entrance off a semi-secluded courtyard, queen-sized bed, private bath, wet bar and wood-burning fireplace. Relax in the hot tub. Located one hour south of Vancouver and 90 minutes north of Seattle. Some straight clientele. Our specialty: gay & lesbian commitment ceremonies, we arrange for catering.

Dance Bar/Disco
RUMORS, 1119 Railroad, (360) 671-1849. DJ Wed-Sat, opens noon-2am 7 days.

Cafe
MATT'S PLACE, 308 W Champion, (360) 671-6268. Espresso bar & cafe, lite menu & desserts.

Retail & Bookstores
RAINBOW BRIDGE, 304 W Champion, (360) 715-3684. Gay & lesbian bookstore with coffee & pastries, video rentals, cards, novelties.

CHELAN

Accommodations
MARY KAY'S ROMANTIC WHALEY MANSION INN, 415 Third St, Chelan, WA, 98816, (509) 682-5735, (800) 729-2408 (USA & Canada), Fax: (509) 682-5385. Email: whaley@televar.com, Web: http://www.lakechelan.com/whaley.htm, Gay-friendly B&B. Elegant Victorian-style rooms with modern conveniences & 5-course candlelight breakfast."

EVERETT

Bars
EVERETT UNDERGROUND, 1212 California St, (425) 339-0807. Unverifiable spring '98.

FORKS

■ Accommodations
MANITOU LODGE, Kilmer St, Forks, WA, 98331, (360) 374-6295." Email: ededed@insync.net, Web: http://www.northolympic.com/manitou/, Gay-friendly B&B on Washington State's Olympic Peninsula, all private baths.

INDEX

■ Accommodations
WILD LILY RANCH, PO Box 313, Index, WA, 98256, (360) 793-2103. B&B with bath house, some straight clientele, women welcome." ♀♂

KENT

■ Bars
SAPPHO'S, 226 1st Ave S, (253) 813-2776. Bar & restaurant. DJ & dancing Fri & Sat. ♀♂

■ Retail & Bookstores
NEW WOMAN BOOKS, 326 W Meeker, (253) 854-3487. Feminist & lesbian books.

LA CONNER

■ Accommodations
HERON IN LA CONNER, THE, 117 Maple Street, PO Box 716, La Conner, WA, 98257, (360) 466-4626. 9 rooms & 3 suites in a Victorian-style home, all private baths, expanded continental breakfast.

WHITE SWAN GUEST HOUSE, 1388 Moore Rd, Mt Vernon, WA, 98273, (360) 445-6805. Web: www.cnw.com/~wswan/, Gay-friendly B&B. Variety of guest quarters including private cottage. Kitchen privileges, lounge, garden, sun deck, expanded country continental breakfast.

LOPEZ ISLAND

■ Accommodations
INN AT SWIFTS BAY, Lopez Island, WA, 98261, (360) 468-3636, Fax: (360) 468-3637. Email: inn@swiftsbay.com, Web: www.swiftsbay.com, **A Small Inn with a National Reputation**...we've gained national recognition as one of the finest accommodations in the beautiful San Juan Islands of Washington State. This elegant country home sits on 3 wooded acres with a private beach nearby. The inn has 5 quiet and romantic guest rooms, 3 with private baths and fireplaces. The hot tub is at the edge of the woods...we provide the robes and slippers. Gay-owned with mix of gay/lesbian and straight clientele.

LUMMI ISLAND

■ Accommodations
RETREAT ON LUMMI ISLAND, (360) 671-6371, ask for Mary Ellen or Marie. Email: okeefe@pacificrim.net, First-floor of home with 2 bedrooms, kitchen, bath, large living & dining spaces & spectacular views. Plenty of hiking, biking & spectacular views. ♀♂

MARYSVILLE

■ Accommodations
EQUINOX INN, 13522 12th Ave NW, Marysville, WA, (360) 652-1198. B&B on 2-1/2 acres in the woods on Tulilap Indian reservation, private baths, full breakfast, many outdoor activities, 15- to 30-min drive to casino. Some straight clientele. ♀♂

INN at SWIFTS BAY

A Small Inn with a National Reputation

LOPEZ ISLAND
(360) 468-3636

MORTON

Accommodations
ST HELENS MANORHOUSE B & B, 7476 Hwy 12, Morton, WA, 98356, (360) 498-5243. Gay-friendly B&B with gift shop, shared baths."

OCEAN PARK

Accommodations
SHAKTI COVE COTTAGES, PO Box 385, Ocean Park, WA, 98640, (360) 665-4000. 10 cottages with private baths, color TV, 5-minute walk to beach, some straight clientele. ♀♂

OLYMPIA

Accommodations
OYSTER BAY, 2830 Bloomfield Rd, Shelton, WA, (360) 427-7643." Gay-owned & -operated waterfront B&B in a log home with shared baths, expanded continental breakfast, executive chef on premises. Arabian horses & riding instruction available, Puget Sound nearby, some straight clientele. ♀♂

Dance Bar/Disco
NIKI'S, 311 E 4th Ave, (360) 956-0825. Wed-Sat 7pm-2am. ♀♂
THEKLA, 116 E 5th St, (360) 352-1855.

ORCAS ISLAND

Accommodations
FOXGLOVE COTTAGE, Rt 1, Box 1238, Eastsound, WA, 98245, (360) 376-5444 (Tel/Fax). Email: shull@fidalgo.net, Fully-furnished 1-bedroom cottage, sleeps 3. Color cable TV, telephone, full kitchen. Pool, ocean & lake nearby. ♀♂

Women's Accommodations
ROSE COTTAGE, Rt 2, Box 951, Eastsound, WA, 98245, (360) 376-2076. Email: lal@fidalgo.net, Web: www.pacificws.com/rosecottage, Fully-furnished efficiency unit, men welcome. Private bath, ocean beach on premises. ♀

PORT ANGELES

Accommodations
MAPLE ROSE INN, 112 Reservoir Rd, Port Angeles, WA, 98363, (360) 457-ROSE (7673), (800) 570-2007." Email: maplerose@tenforward.com, Web: www.northolympic.com/maplerose, Gay-owned & -operated B&B on the Olympic Peninsula, private baths, expanded or full breakfasts, 50% gay/lesbian.

PORT TOWNSEND

Accommodations
GAIA'S GETAWAY, 4343 Haines St, Port Townsend, WA, 98368, (360) 385-1194. Email: quimpers@olympus.net, Large studio apartment with queen bed, private bath, color cable TV & fully-

Ravenscroft Inn
A Bed & Breakfast

"Where they turn short stays into lasting memories."

(360) 385-2784   (800) 782-2691
533 Quincy Street, Port Townsend WA 98368
Fax (360) 385-6724

equipped kitchen. Gay-friendly with a gay & lesbian following.
RAVENSCROFT INN, 533 Quincy St, Port Townsend, WA, 98368, (360) 385-2784, (800) 782-2691, Fax: (360) 385-6724. Welcome to paradise, your room is ready.... Enjoy colonial hospitality in a Victorian seaport. The Ravenscroft Inn, whose photogenic breakfast room was featured on the front cover of Inn Places-1994, looks forward to welcoming you to our special corner of the world: the captivating Olympic Peninsula.

SEATTLE

■ Information
LESBIAN RESOURCE CENTER, 1808 Bellevue Ave E #204, (206) 322-3953, 2pm-7pm Mon-Fri.

■ Accommodations
BACON MANSION, 959 Broadway East, Seattle, WA, 98102, (206) 329-1864, (800) 240-1864, Fax: (206) 860-9025. Web: http://www.site-works.com/bacon, B&B guesthouse, 40% gay and lesbian clientele. This English Tudor house is in the Harvard-Belmont district on Capitol Hill, one of Seattle's most exciting neighborhoods for dining, sightseeing, nightlife and boutiques. Choose from well-appointed moderate rooms, suites and even a carriage house. Eight rooms have private baths. We have immense, beautifully-decorated day rooms and a large, private patio. Don't miss it!"

BED & BREAKFAST ON BROADWAY, 722 Broadway E., Seattle, WA, 98102, (206) 329-8933, Toll-free: (888) 329-8933, Fax: (206) 726-0918. B&B with private baths, private baths, expanded continental breakfast, collection of original paintings & artwork by Northwest artists. 50% gay & lesbian clientele.

CAPITOL HILL INN, 1713 Belmont Ave, Seattle, WA, 98122, (206) 323-1955, Fax: (206) 322-3809. Web: www.capitolhillinn.com, Lavishly furnished 1903 Victorian on Capitol Hill with antiques, fireplaces, brass beds, private baths, full breakfast, non-smoking.

CHAMBERED NAUTILUS BED & BREAKFAST INN, 5005 22nd Ave NE, Seattle, WA, 98105, (800) 545-8459, (206) 522-2536, Fax: (206) 528-0898. Gay-friendly B&B. All private baths, full breakfast, nearby lake.

COUNTRY INN, 685 NW Juniper St, Issaquah, WA, 98027, (425) 392-1010, Fax: (425) 392-9110. B&B in the middle of 5 acres, 50% gay & lesbian. Rooms with private baths, refrigerator, AC & maid service, continental breakfast.

GASLIGHT INN, 1727 15th Ave, Seattle, WA, 98122, (206) 325-3654, Fax: (206) 328-4803. Email: innkeepr@gaslight-inn.com, Web: www.gaslight-inn.com. Guesthouse minutes from downtown, some straight clientele. Comfortable & unique double rooms with modern conveniences. Living room, library, continental breakfast, beverages, fruit. Smoke-free indoors. ⚦ ♀♂

LANDES HOUSE, 712 11th Ave E, Seattle, WA, 98102, (206) 329-8781, (888) 329-8781, Fax: (206) 324-0934. B&B, some straight clientele. Private & shared baths, hot tub, expanded continental breakfast. ⚦ ♀♂

ROBERTA'S BED & BREAKFAST, 1147-16 Avenue East, Seattle, WA, 98112, (206) 329-3326, Fax: (206) 324-2149. Email: robertasbb@aol.com, Gay-friendly B&B with private baths, full "wild-west-sized" breakfast, near Volunteer Park & Broadway.

SCANDIA HOUSE, 2028 34th Ave S, Seattle, WA, 98144, (206) 725-7825, Fax:

Bacon Mansion

Seattle's Finest B & B

(800) 240-1864

WASHINGTON

(206) 721-3348. B&B with lake & mountain views, 50% gay & lesbian clientele. Color TV, phone, king bed & private bath. Expanded continental breakfast.

Transportation

FIRST CLASS LIMOUSINE, (206) 329-5395, (800) 225-6717, www.limo.com. Woman drivers.

Bars

ART BAR, 2nd Ave, off Pine or Pike., Live music weekends.

C.C. ATTLES, 1501 E Madison, bar: (206) 726-0565, grille: (206) 323-4017. Bar & restaurant, intimate veranda bar.

DOUBLE HEADER, 407 2nd Ave, (206) 464-9918. Oldest gay bar in Seattle.

ELITE II, 1658 E Olive Way, (206) 322-7334. Pool table, darts, micro brews, good mix of men & women.

FOXES, 1501 E Olive Way, (206) 720-9963. Show bar, 7 days, 70% men.

★ **HAMBURGER MARY'S,** 1525 E Olive Way, (206) 324-8112. Bar & restaurant, 60% men, 40% women.

SAFARI SPORTS BAR & GRILLE/JUNGLE ROOM DANCE CLUB, 1518 11th Ave, (206) 328-4250. Safari's is a sports bar, Jungle Room Dance Club opens weekends.

SIX-ELEVEN TAVERN, 611 2nd Ave, (206) 340-9795.

THUMPER'S, 1500 E Madison, (206) 328-3800. Video bar and restaurant, upscale clientele.

WILDROSE, 1021 E Pike, at 11th, (206) 324-9210. Beer, wine & espresso, non-alcoholic drinks, desserts, smoke-free area.

Dance Bar/Disco

EASY, THE, 916 E Pike, (206) 323-8343. DJ Thurs-Sat, darts & pool table. Full-service restaurant.

★ **NEIGHBOURS,** 1509 Broadway near Pike, (enter rear alley), (206) 324-5358. High tech dance & cruise bar, younger crowd. Buffet Fri & Sat, 90% men, 10% women.

★ **RE-BAR,** 1114 Howell St, (206) 233-9873. Always gay-friendly. Thurs Queer Night, very popular, Sat Queen's nite out. Gay comedy most weekends. Women's dance last Sat of month.

★ **TIMBERLINE,** 2015 Boren Ave, (206) 622-6220. C&W dance bar, 60% men, 40% women, straight following. Closed Mon.

Cafe

BEYOND THE EDGE CAFE, 703 E Pike, (206) 325-6829. Daily specials, art shows.

ROSEBUD RESTAURANT & BISTRO, 719 E Pike, (206) 323-6636. Espresso/cappuccino cafe with desserts. Lunch, dinner Sat, Sun brunch.

Restaurants

CADILLAC GRILLE, 1501 E Madison, at CC Slaughter's bar, (206) 323-4017. '50's Grandma cooking, take-out bakery, hand-packed ice cream.

HAMBURGER MARY'S, Olive Way, at Denny, (206) 324-8112. Bar & restaurant.

SIMPATICO, 4430 Wallingford Ave N, (206) 632-1000. Italian bistro.

Retail & Bookstores

BAILEY COY BOOKS, 414 Broadway E, near Harrison, (206) 323-8842. General bookstore with gay & lesbian section.

BEYOND THE CLOSET BOOKSTORE, 518 E Pike St, (206) 322-4609. Gay & lesbian bookstore, Sun-Thurs 10am-10pm, Fri & Sat 10am-11pm.

PINK ZONE, 211 Broadway East, (206) 325-0050. Gay & lesbian gift shop. Body piercing.

RED & BLACK BOOKS, 432 15th Ave E, (206) 322-7323. General bookstore with small gay & lesbian section.

Leathers/Piercing

CRYPT, THE, 1310 E Union St, near 14th, (206) 325-3882. Safe-sex toys, video sales & rentals, magazines, lubes, lotions."

TATOO YOU, 1017 E Pike St, (206) 324-6443. Tattoo studio, Tue-Sat 1pm-8pm.

Erotica

TOYS IN BABELAND, 711 E Pike St, (206) 328-2914. Adult toys, etc, for women.

CASTLE® SUPERSTORES

(800) 344-9076

Visit Our New Website:
www.castlesuperstores.com

America's Safer Sex Superstores® Because We Care®

• Video Sales • Video Rentals • Playful Greeting & Post Cards • Leather Goods & Apparel • Restraints • Latex Garments • Rubber Goods • Wildest Selection of Adult Toys • Gag Gifts • Novelties • Games • Condoms • Lubes • Books & Magazines • T-Shirts • Whips & Chains • Wrapping Papers • Calendars • Novels • Sensual Oils • Sexy Lingerie & more & more ...

OPEN 365 DAYS
Rediscover America's Favorite Pastime

(253) 471-0391
6015 Tacoma Mall Blvd.
Tacoma, WA 98409

(360) 308-0779
2789 NW Randall Way
Silverdale, WA 98383

WASHINGTON

SEAVIEW

■ Women's Accommodations
ENCHANTED BLUE WAVE BED & BREAKFAST, PO Box 718, 1004 41st Place, Seaview, WA, 98644, (360) 642-3471, Fax: (360) 533-5371. Email: bluewave@mailexcite.com, Web: www.enchantedbluewave.com, Come, be pampered at The Wave oceanfront mansion. Amenities include an Italian marble fireplace, antique furnishings, a Baldwin concert grand piano, games room, pool table, big-screen TV, VCR and movies, fitness room, outdoor spa with private deck and an English garden sun deck. Scrumptious breakfasts are served, and we offer complimentary champagne or sparkling juice for your celebrations. Lesbian-owned, women only. ♀

SILVERDALE

■ Erotica
CASTLE SUPERSTORE, 2789 NW Randall Way, (360) 308-0779, (800) 344-9076. Large selection of gay books, magazines, videos, and much, much more. Open 365 days a year. See ad on page 435.

SPOKANE

■ Dance Bar/Disco
DEMPSEY'S BRASS RAIL, W 909 1st St, (509) 747-5362. Disco & restaurant, 50% men, 50% women. 🕺 ♀♂

HOUR PLACE, W 415 Sprague, (509) 838-6947. Dance bar & restaurant. 🕺 ♀♂

PUMPS II, W 4 Main, (509) 747-8940. 50% men, 50% women (Fri 60% women). 🕺 ♀♂

■ Retail & Bookstores
AUNTIE'S BOOKSTORE, 313 W Riverside, (509) 838-0206. General bookstore with a gay & lesbian section.

TACOMA

■ Information
RAINBOW CENTER, 1501 Pacific Ave #310-D, (253) 383-2318.

TACOMA LESBIAN CONCERN (TLC), (253) 752-6724. Charitable support group, monthly newsletter, resource list, social group. Travelers welcome.

■ Dance Bar/Disco
GOLD BALL TAVERN, 2708 6th Ave, (253) 527-4820. Full liquor, patio, gambling, 80% women, dancing weekends. 🕺 ♀

SILVERSTONE, Broadway at 9th, Dance bar, lounge & restaurant. ♀♂

TWENTY-FOURTH ST TAVERN, 2409 Pacific Ave, (253) 572-3748. Dance, show & cruise bar, DJ Fri & Sat. 🕺 ♂

■ Restaurants
SPOUT-N-TOAD, THE, 1111 Center St, (253) 272-1412. Gay-friendly restaurant & bar with karaoke nitely, drag shows Sun.

Winter Weekday Special
Three Nights for Two
holidays excluded

The Enchanted Blue Wave

A Magical Oceanfront Retreat
A Bed & Breakfast for Women

360-642-3471

P.O. Pox 718
Seaview, WA 98644

Ocean View Rooms   Outdoor Spa   Game Room
www.enchantedbluewave.com   bluewave@mailexcite.com

WEST VIRGINIA   437

Erotica
CASTLE SUPERSTORE, 6015 Tacoma Mall Blvd, (253) 471-0391, (800) 344-9076. Large selection of gay books, magazines, videos, and much, much more. Open 365 days a year. See ad on page 435.

WHIDBEY ISLAND - LANGLEY

Accommodations
GALITTOIRE, 5444 S Coles Rd, Langley, Whidbey Island, WA, 98260-9508, (360) 221-0548. Email: galittoire@whidby.com, Web: http://www.whidbey.com/galittoire, Gay-owned, gay-friendly guesthouse in the woods. TV lounge, video tape library, full breakfast, 35% gay/lesbian clientele.

GALLERY SUITE, THE, PO Box 458, Langley, WA, 98260, (360) 221-2978. B&B on the waterfront, 50% gay & lesbian clientele. Private apartment with kitchen, continental breakfast, snacks & nearby gym.

WEST VIRGINIA STATEWIDE

SEE ALSO DISTRICT OF COLUMBIA., Some locations close to Washington, DC, are listed there instead of under their WV cities.

CHARLESTON

Bars
TAP ROOM, 1022 Quarry, at Broad, (304) 342-9563. Mostly gay clientele.

Dance Bar/Disco
BROADWAY, THE, 210 Broad Street, (304) 343-2162. Mon-Thurs 4pm-3am, Fri 4pm-4am, Sat 1pm-3am. DJ Wed-Sun, patio, Sun tea dance 4pm-8pm. 75% men, 25% women

GRAND PALACE, 617 Brooks St, near Smith, (304) 345-0377. Disco & show bar. DJ 7 nights, videos, patio, 50% men, 50% women.

TRAX, 504 W Washington St, (304) 345-8931. Huge alternative dance club, open 7 days, 80%-90% gay & lesbian

Restaurants
LEE ST. DELI, Lee St, near Broad St.,

HUNTINGTON

Bars
BEEHIVE, 1121 7th Ave, above the Driftwood bar, (304) 696-9858. Show bar, Beehive dance bar open Fri-Sun, 60% men, 40% women.

Dance Bar/Disco
DRIFTWOOD, 1121 7th Ave, near 12th St, (304) 696-9858. DJ & shows, Fri-Sun, 60% men, 40% women.

POLO CLUB, 733 7th Ave (rear), (304) 522-3146. Drag shows Sat & Sun, DJ Wed, Fri, Sat, Sun (opens early Sun).

STONEWALL, 820 7th Ave, (304) 528-9317.

HUTTONSVILLE

Accommodations
HUTTON HOUSE BED & BREAKFAST, PO Box 88, Huttonsville, WV, 26273, (800) 234-6701. Gay-Friendly B&B, private & shared baths."

RICHARD'S COUNTRY INN, US 219 Route 1 Box 11-A-1, Huttonsville, WV, 26273, (304) 335-6659, (800) 636-7434. Email: rikcountryinn@rocketmail.com, In the Potomac Highlands of rural West Virginia just 4-1/2 hours from Washington, DC. Gay-friendly B&B inn and cottage with restaurant and bar. Private and shared baths, TV lounge, full breakfast.

MARTINSBURG

Accommodations
BOYDVILLE, THE INN AT MARTINSBURG, 601 S Queen St, Martinsburg, WV, 25401, (304) 263-1448. Gay-friendly B&B, private baths."

MORGANTOWN

Information
GAY & LESBIAN HELPLINE, (304) 292-GAY2 (4292). Irregularly staffed eves & weekends or tape.

Dance Bar/Disco
CLASS ACT, 335 High St, (rear), (304) 292-2010. occasional DJ Thurs-Sat, 10%

WEST VIRGINIA

alternative straight crowd, 50% men, 50% women.

VIENNA

Dance Bar/Disco
TRUE COLORS, 102 12th St, 3 blks north of Grand, (304) 295-8783. Alternative night club, DJ Wed-Sun, patio, open from 7pm, closed Tues.

WASHINGTON

Accommodations
GUEST HOUSE, THE, H.C. 83 Box 18, Settlers Valley, Lost River, WV, 26810, (304) 897-5707, Fax: (304) 897-5707. Email: guesthse@cfw.com, B&B, 50% gay & lesbian. Variety of spacious rooms. Private baths, TV lounge, indoor hot tub, outdoor Jacuzzi & full breakfast.

WHEELING

Dance Bar/Disco
DREAM HARBOR, 1107 Main St,

TRICKS, 1429 Market St (rear), behind Market St News, (304) 232-1267. DJ Fri & Sat, open Wed-Sun, shows Sat.

WISCONSIN

APPLETON

Bars
RASCALS BAR & GRILL, 702 E Wisconsin Ave, (414) 954-9262. Cocktail lounge, quiet conversation. Outdoor bar & picnic area, BBQs, pig roasts, lite grill menu.

BELOIT

Retail & Bookstores
A DIFFERENT WORLD, 414 E Grand Ave, (608) 365-1000. Women's & children's books, gifts, boutique items, arts, crafts & mail order. Women's groups meet here. Closed Sun.

DELAVAN

Accommodations
ALLYN MANSION INN, THE, 511 E Walworth Ave, Delavan, WI, 53115, (414) 728-9090, Fax: (414) 728-0201. Email: joeron@allynmansion.com, Web: www.allynmansion.com, Gay-friendly B&B in award-winning restored mansion with authentic Victorian antique furnishings. Shared baths, AC, some working fireplaces, full breakfast. Strictly a no smoking environment.

EAGLE RIVER

Accommodations
EDGEWATER INN MOTEL AND RESORT, THE, 5054 Highway 70 West, Eagle River, WI, 54521, (715) 479-4011, Fax: (715) 479-7894, (888)-EDGEWTR (334-3987). Email: edgewater@edgeinn.com, Gay-friendly motel, inn & resort with cottages, near lakes. Private baths, color cable TV, coffee/tea-making facilities, phones, fax, maid, & laundry service, 50% gay & lesbian clientele.

EAU CLAIRE

Bars
SCOOTERS, 411 Galloway, (715) 835-9959.

WOLFE'S DEN, THE, 302 E Madison St, (715) 832-9237. Strippers & shows weekends, 75% men, 25% women.

FT ATKINSON

Bars
FRIENDS, 10 E Sherman Ave, (920) 563-0040. 60% women, 40% men, juke box, darts.

GREEN BAY

Information
AIDS INFO, (920) 437-7400 or tape. In WI, outside of Green Bay (800) 675-9400. Mon-Thurs 8:30am-4:30pm, Fri till 12:30pm.

AIDS PROJECT, (920) 733-2068.

Bars
BRANDY'S II, 1126 Main Street., 70% men.

JAVA'S, 1106 Main St, (920) 435-5476. Lounge with Za's dance bar.

NAPALESE LOUNGE, 515 S Broadway, near Clinton, (920) 432-9646. Moving in '98, call for information for new address & tel.

SASS, 840 S Broadway, (920) 437-7277.

WISCONSIN

Women's sports bar, videos, pool table, foosball, darts.

■ Dance Bar/Disco
ZA'S, 1106 Main St, near Webster, (920) 435-5476. Video dance & show bar, 50% gay, 50% straight. Java's lounge is inside Za's, serving food Fri-Sun.

HAYWARD

■ Accommodations
LAKE HOUSE B & B, THE, N 5793 Division (on the lake), Stone Lake, WI, 54876, (715) 865-6803. 80% gay & lesbian clientele, private baths.

LA CROSSE

■ Bars
PLAYERS, Main St, between 2nd & 3rd., DJ Fri & Sat, jazz quartets, etc.
RAINBOW'S END, 417 Jay St, (608) 782-9802. Small dance floor, pool tables.

■ Retail & Bookstores
RAINBOW REVOLUTION BOOKSTORE, 122 5th Ave S, (608) 796-0383. Gay & lesbian bookstore. Fiction, non-fiction, metaphysics, alternative spirituality.

LAKE GENEVA

■ Accommodations
ELEVEN GABLES INN ON THE LAKE, 493 Wrigley Dr, Lake Geneva, WI, 53147, (414) 248-8393, (800) 362-0395. Gay-friendly B&B, private baths, expanded continental breakfast (wknd/holiday: full breakfast), color cable TV, ceiling fans, AC, lake on premises.

LAKE MILLS

■ Bars
CROSS ROADS BAR, W 664d Hwy B, (920) 648-8457. Tues-Sun 1pm till late (later Fri & Sat), juke box, darts, 50% men, 50% women.

MADISON

■ Information
APPLE ISLAND, meets at 953 Jennifer St, The Wilmar Center, (608) 258-9777. Women's cultural & events space, dances Sat. Travelers welcome.

CAMPUS WOMEN'S CENTER, at Univ of Wisconsin, 710 University Ave, Rm 202, (608) 262-8093. Lesbian groups meet here.

GAY & LESBIAN PHONE LINE, (608) 255-4297, 255-8582, 255-0743. Mon-Fri 9am-9pm or tape.

WI AIDS HOTLINE, (800) 334-2437 in Wisconsin only.

■ Accommodations
CHASE ON THE HILL BED & BREAKFAST, 11624 State Road 26, Milton, WI, 53563, (608) 868-6646. Email: mchase@jvlnet.com, Farmhouse B&B, 50% gay & lesbian clientele. 3 rooms with double or queen beds, private & shared baths. TV lounge, full breakfast & nearby lake."

PRAIRIE GARDEN B & B, W 13172 Hwy 188, Lodi, WI, 53555, (608) 592-5187, (800) 380-8427. B&B on a farm 1/2 hour north of Madison, near canoeing, fishing & nude beach.

■ Bars
KIRBY'S KLUB, 119 Main St, (608) 251-1030. Pool, darts, dance floor, occasional shows, fireplaces.

RAY'S BAR & GRILL, 3052 E Washington, (608) 241-9335. Dance bar & Men's Room cruise bar, patio with volleyball court, Sun BBQs in summer. Also restaurant with sandwiches & steaks.

■ Dance Bar/Disco
CARDINAL, 418 E Wilson St, at Franklin, (608) 251-0080. Alternative hi-energy dance bar, very gay-friendly.

■ Restaurants
RAY'S GRILL, 3052 E Washington Ave, (608) 241-9335. Serving till 8pm.

■ Retail & Bookstores
A ROOM OF ONE'S OWN, 317 W Johnson St, near State, (608) 257-7888. Women's books and gifts and information center."

MIMOSA COMMUNITY BOOKSTORE, 212 N Henry, (608) 256-5432. General bookstore with gay & lesbian sections.

PIC-A-BOOK, 506 State Street, (608) 256-1125. General bookstore with gay & lesbian selections.

440 WISCONSIN

RAINBOW BOOKSTORE CO-OP, 426 W Gilman, (608) 257-6050. General leftist bookstore with good gay & lesbian section.

Erotica

FOUR STAR VIDEO HEAVEN, 315 N Henry St, (608) 255-1994. Items for gay men & women.

MAUSTON

Camping & RV

OUTBACK, THE, W5627 Clark Rd, Mauston, WI, 53948, (608) 847-5247. Campground on 77-1/2 acres of Womyn-Only land with trails set throughout the property. Campsites set high on a wooded ridge. For winter fun we have x-country ski trails and miles of snowmobile trails. Downhill skiing nearby. Social gatherings and activities available. Boys allowed up to age 10. ♀

MILWAUKEE

Information

AIDS LINE, (414) 273-AIDS (2437). Mon-Thur 9-9, Fri 9-6 or tape.

GAY INFO LINE, (414) 444-7331. Irregularly staffed, but frequently available.

LESBIAN ALLIANCE METRO MILWAUKEE, (414) 264-2600. Tape, calls are returned.

Accommodations

CARITAS BED & BREAKFAST NETWORK, (800) CARITAS, (312) 857-0801, Fax: (312) 857-0805. B&B, home-stay accommodations service. Member: IGLTA

Bars

FANNIE'S, 200 E Washington Ave, at Barclay, (414) 643-9633. DJ on Sat. Patio, men welcome.

IN BETWEEN, 625 S 2nd St, (414) 273-2693.

KATHY'S NUT HUT, 1500 W Scott, (414) 647-2673. Occasional live entertainment.

M&M CLUB, 124 N Water St, at Erie, (414) 347-1962. Piano bar, popular cocktail hour, Sun brunch. 70% men, 30% women.

MAMA ROUX, 1875 N Humboldt, (414) 347-0344. Burgers, soups, Creole items.

RENE'S COZY CORNER, 3500 W Park Hill, (414) 933-7363. DJ weekends, 70% men, 30% women.

STATION 2, 1534 W Grant, (414) 383-5755. Patio in summer, slightly more mature crowd, men welcome. ♀

WOODY'S, 1579 S 2nd St, (414) 672-5580. Neighborhood bar, 50/50 men & women.

Dance Bar/Disco

★ **CLUB 219**, 219 S 2nd St, near Oregon, (414) 271-3732. Upstairs dance bar, 50% men, 50% women. Downstairs cruisy video bar.

DISH, 235 S 2nd, (414) 273-DISH. ♀

JUST US, 807 S 5th St, (414) 383-2233. DJ Fri & Sat. Sat 50% men, 50% women. ♀♂

Cafe

CAFE KNICKERBOCKER, 1030 E Juneau Ave, (414) 272-0011.

SILVER DOLLAR CAFE, 831 S 16th St.,

Restaurants

GRUBB'S PUB, 801 S 2nd St, at La Cage bar, (414) 383-8330. After hours restaurant. ♀♂

LA PERLA, 734 S 5th, (414) 645-9888. Mexican cuisine.

M&M CLUB RESTAURANT, 124 N Water St, at M & M bar., Lunch & dinner, Sun brunch. 80% men. ♂

MAMA ROUX BAR AMERICAIN & GRILL, 1875 N Humboldt.,

WALKER'S POINT CAFE, 1106 S 1st Street, (414) 384-7999. Open 10pm-5am only, popular after-hrs restaurant. ♀♂

Retail & Bookstores

AFTERWORDS, 2710 N Murray Ave, (414) 963-9089. Gay & lesbian bookstore with espresso bar. Mon-Thur 10am-10pm, Fri & Sat 10am-11pm, Sun noon-6pm."

WISCONSIN

DESIGNING MEN, 1200 S 1st St, (414) 389-1200. Exclusive gay & lesbian gift & jewelry store.

NORWALK

■ Women's Accommodations
DOE FARM, c/o WWLC, Rt 2 Box 150, Norwalk, WI, 54648, (608) 269-5301. Women-only lodge & camping. ♀

OGDENSBURG

■ Tours, Charters & Excursions
QUIET TRAILS, PO Box 85, Ogdensburg, WI, (414) 244-7823. Day canoe trips with shuttle, extended canoe camping (3-5 days) & canoes for rent. Mostly women, men welcome." ♀

RACINE - KENOSHA

■ Bars
WHAT ABOUT ME?, 600 6th St, (414) 632-0171. 60% women, 40% men. ♀♂

■ Dance Bar/Disco
CLUB 94, 9001 120th Ave, (Hwy 194 & Hwy C, exit 345), Kenosha, (414) 857-9958. DJ wknds, videos, 60% men, 40% women, closed Sun & Mon. ♀♂

JODEE'S INT'L, 2139 Racine St, at 22nd St, (414) 634-9804. Dance & show bar, DJ wknds, summer BBQs, 60% men, 40% women. From 7pm." ♀♂

SHEBOYGAN

■ Bars
BLUE LITE, 1029 N 8th St, (920) 457-1636. Lounge with upscale atmosphere, 70-80% men, good late-nite crowd 11pm-2:30am. Open 7pm-2am Tues-Thurs, 7pm-2:30am Fri & Sat 3pm-2am Sun. ♂

■ Restaurants
TRATTORIA STEFANO, 522 S 8th St, (920) 452-8455. Italian cuisine.

STURGEON BAY - DOOR COUNTY

■ Accommodations
CHANTICLEER GUESTHOUSE, 4072 Cherry Rd, Sturgeon Bay, WI, 54235, (920) 746-0334. Inn in a turn-of-the-century farmhouse 40 minutes from Green Bay, 50% gay & lesbian clientele. All rooms have private baths & fireplaces. Heated pool, sauna, expanded continental breakfast."

SUPERIOR

■ Bars
MAIN, THE, 1217 Tower Ave, (715) 392-1756. ♀♂

■ Dance Bar/Disco
JT BAR & GRILL, 1506 N 3rd, (715) 394-2580. Dance bar & restaurant with burgers & pizza, DJ Fri & Sat, karaoke Thurs, strippers, beer garden, 50% men, 50% women, ♀♂

WASCOTT

■ Women's Accommodations
WILDERNESS WAY RESORT & CAMPGROUND, PO Box 176, Wascott, WI, 54890, (715) 466-2635. Women-only resort campground on lake. Fully-furnished cabins with private baths, 6 electric hookups, 20 tent sites, showers & restrooms, common room with fireplace. Boat & canoe use with cabin rental." ♀

WATERLOO

■ Information
MODE THEATER, 121 S Monroe St, (920) 478-9632, (800) 280-9632, Fax: (920) 478-9630. Gay & lesbian art shows, theater, concerts. Planning center for commitment ceremonies. Looking for buyers of this non-profit enterprise.

WAUKESHA

■ Retail & Bookstores
BY THE LIGHT OF THE MOON, 880 N Grand Ave, (414) 574-7651. Bookstore specializing in books by women authors & on women's health, Tues & Wed 10am-5pm, Thurs & Fri 10am-6pm, Sat 10am-4pm.

GOOD EARTH, 340 W Main St, (414) 521-0664. New age & spirituality books.

MARTHA MERRELL'S BOOKSTORE, 228 W Main St, (414) 547-1060. General bookstore with women's studies & feminist selections.

WAUSAU

Dance Bar/Disco
OZ, 320 Washington, (715) 842-3225. 70% men, 30% women. DJ Sat.

WYOMING
ETNA

Information
BLUE FOX STUDIO & GALLERY, 107452 Hwy 89, (307) 883-3310., E-mail: bluefox@silverstar.com. 1 hour outside Jackson on the main hwy between Cheyenne & Jackson. Gay-owned jewelry & pottery studio. Ask for Tony or Wayne for gay info on Jackson area when enroute to Jackson Hole from Salt Lake City.

JACKSON

Accommodations
FISH CREEK LODGING, Warm River, PO Box 833, Ashton, ID, 83420-0833, (208) 652-7566. Log cabin & loft with kitchen, library & telephone, near Jackson, Wyoming. Nearby river & lake.

REDMOND GUEST HOUSE, Box 616, Jackson, WY, 83001, (307) 733-4003. Self-contained apartment with private entrance, private bath, color cable TV, fireplace & kitchen. 50% gay & lesbian clientele."

Women's Accommodations
BAR H RANCH, Box 297, Driggs, ID, 83422, (208) 354-2906, (800) 247-1444. One-BR deluxe loft with kitchen, bath & woodstove. Stay in a genuine canvas Sioux teepee in a private pasture surrounded by willows & aspens. Mostly women with men welcome.

Retail & Bookstores
GRAND BASKET, 140 N Cache, (307) 739-1139. Gourmet food gifts & gift baskets. We ship anywhere in the US & specialize in Wyoming-made products.

VALLEY BOOKSTORE, 125 N Cache, (307) 733-4533. General bookstore with a good gay & lesbian section.

RIVERTON

Restaurants
COUNTRY COVE RESTAURANT, (307) 856-9813. Gay-friendly family restaurant, breakfast & lunch & steaks & seafood at dinner, 7:30am-3pm & 5pm-9pm, closed Sun. Candle & giftshop next door.

THERMOPOLIS

Accommodations
OUT WEST BED & BREAKFAST, 1344 Broadway, Thermopolis, WY, 82443, (307) 864-2700. B&B in 1908 Queen Anne home, overlooks Owl Creek Mtns. Shared baths, full breakfast, world's largest mineral hot spring in town's state park, 136 miles to Yellowstone Nat'l Park, 84 miles to Cody, WY. 50% gay/lesbian clientele.

WOMEN'S MAIL ORDER

Herbal Soaps
Oat & Mineral Soaks
Custom Gift Baskets
Massage Oils
Bath Oils

Celebrating our 11th year of making fine herbal body care products. Contact us for a free catalog. Mention this ad and receive a free sample of herbal soap. **Lesbian-owned and operated!**

Environmentally friendly
No animal ingredients
No animal testing

Brookside

Brookside Soap Co.
www.halcyon.com/brookside/
e-mail: BrooksideSoap@msn.com
P.O. Box 55638 Seattle, WA 98155
phone (425) 742-2265 fax (425) 355-6644

BROOKSIDE SOAP COMPANY, PO Box 55638, Seattle, WA, 98155, (425) 742-2265. We are beginning our 11th year of producing high-quality personal bodycare products. The women of Brookside excel at creating all-vegetable, environmentally responsible products with the finest natural ingredients. We are proud to create the highest quality Herbal Bar Soaps, Aromatherapy Bath Oils, Aromatherapy Massage Oils and Oat & Mineral Soaks. Gift baskets are available for shipment. We also produce Best Friend — Shampoo Bar Soap for your pets. Write or email us for a free catalog at BrooksideSoap@msn.com. You can also find us at www.halcyon.com/brookside/

CHARIS VIDEO, PO Box 310797, Dept POI9, Brooklyn, NY 11231. **RENT LESBIAN VIDEOS THROUGH THE MAIL!!** Charis Video makes almost every lesbian title available to rent: independent films (*Watermelon Woman, Everything Relative*), Hollywood-made films (*Bastard Out of Carolina*), erotica (*Teasers*), plus comedy, documentaries and more! Charis has been the lesbian video resource for over ten years, and is dedicated to making lesbian titles available to the community. To join, send $20.00 (includes first rental), or write for more information. Charis is lesbian-owned and -operated.

WOMEN'S MAIL ORDER

From enlightening advice to electrifying erotica, we offer a way to buy sex toys, books and videos that's friendly, feminist and fun. Please visit! ...but if you can't, our catalogs: Toys $2. Books & videos $2.

**1210 Valencia #PI
San Francisco, CA 94110
415-974-8980
Sun-Thurs 11am-7pm
Fri & Sat 11am-8pm
http://www.goodvibes.com**

Good Vibrations

GOOD VIBRATIONS, 1210 Valencia #PI, San Francisco, CA, 94110, (800) BUY-VIBE, (415) 974-8980. 2nd location: 2504 San Pablo Ave, Berkeley, (510) 841-8986. Founded by therapist, Joani Blank, **Good Vibrations** has offered women a friendly, feminist and fun way to buy sex toys since 1977. Our sister business, **The Sexuality Library,** features hundreds of high-quality books and videos with everything from enlightening advice to electrifying erotica, including a selection of videos made by and for women. **Good Vibrations** and **Sexuality Library** catalogs are $2 each, $4 for both, and all products are sold in our world-class **Good Vibrations** retail store. Drop by and check out our antique vibrator museum when you're in town!

WOMEN'S MAIL ORDER

Women Loving Women

For a change in your life, we invite you to try: **THE WISHING WELL**. Features current members' self-descriptions (listed by code), letters, photos, resources, reviews, and more. Introductory copy $5.00 ppd. (discreet first class). A beautiful, tender, loving alternative to "The Well of Loneliness." Confidential, sensitive, supportive, dignified. Very personal. Reliable reputation, established 1974. Free, prompt information. Women are writing and meeting each other EVERYWHERE through:

The Wishing Well

PO Box 178440
San Diego CA 92177-8440
(619) 270-2779

laddiewww@aol.com
http://www.sdcw.org/members/wishingwell

WOMEN'S MAIL ORDER

WOMYN TO WOMYN, mail: WtoW, 110 Cummings Lane, Rison, AR, 71665, (870) 325-7006. WtoW is a lesbian/bi correspondence club magazine with 60+ pages containing over 300 very "diversified" members, a photo section, poetry, articles, recipes, book reviews, directory listings of wimmins resources, shops, merchandise, health, travel, support groups and much more, including our own "Dear WtoW" advice column. Confidential using code numbers and mail forwarding. Send U.S. $4.00 via check or money order, or $4.50 via international money order for a discreetly-mailed 60+- page issue of WtoW Magazine and info.

Womyn to Womyn

LESBIAN/BI Correspondence Club Magazine with 60+ pages containing over 300 very "diversified" Members, photo section, poetry, articles, recipes, book reviews, directory listings of wimmins resources/shops/merchandise/health/travel/support groups & much more including our own "Dear WtoW" advice column. CONFIDENTIAL using CODE numbers & mail forwarding. Send U.S. $4.00 chk/mo OR $4.50 IMO for a "discreetly" mailed 60+ page Issue of WtoW magazine & info. to:

WtoW, 110 Cummings Lane, Rison, AR 71665 (870) 325-7006